Questions and Answers on Real Estate

Questions and Answers on Real Estate

ROBERT W. SEMENOW, B.S. in Econ., Litt. M., J.D., L.L.D.—EXECUTIVE VICE-PRESIDENT, NATIONAL ASSOCIATION OF REAL ESTATE LICENSE LAW OFFICIALS • HONORARY LIFE MEMBER, GREATER PITTSBURGH BOARD OF REALTORS • FORMERLY PROFESSOR OF URBAN LAND STUDIES, UNIVERSITY OF PITTSBURGH, AND DIRECTOR OF PENNSYLVANIA REAL ESTATE BROKER'S LICENSE LAW • AUTHOR, SELECTED CASES IN REAL ESTATE (PRENTICE-HALL, INC.)

Eighth Edition

Englewood Cliffs, N. J.

Published by PRENTICE-HALL, INC.

PRENTICE-HALL INTERNATIONAL, INC., *London*
PRENTICE-HALL OF AUSTRALIA, PTY. LTD., *Sydney*
PRENTICE-HALL OF CANADA, LTD., *Toronto*
PRENTICE-HALL OF INDIA PRIVATE LTD., *New Delhi*
PRENTICE-HALL OF JAPAN, INC., *Tokyo*

EIGHTH EDITION

Library of Congress Cataloging in Publication Data

Semenow, Robert William
Questions and answers on real estate.

Includes bibliographical references.
1. Real property--United States--Examinations, questions; etc. 2. Real estate business--Law and legislation--United States--Examinations, questions, etc. I. Title.
KF570.Z9S4 1975 346'.73'0437 74-17160
ISBN 0-13-749234-0

THIS BOOK is respectfully dedicated to the many license law officials in this country and Canada, who, by their conscientious application to duty in the administration and enforcement of license laws and in the promotion of educational courses, institutes, and clinics, are doing so much to safeguard the interests of the public, protect the legitimate broker, and elevate the standards of real estate.

Preface

SINCE the first edition of *Questions and Answers on Real Estate* was published in 1948, the book has been the main "tool" for applicants taking the state real estate licensing examinations. It has also been the ready reference guide for the every day real estate practitioner. Attorneys find it a quick reference for many real estate problems encountered in the real estate field.

An eloquent testimonial in this connection is the fact that there are one million copies in print to date. In recent years, real estate activities have expanded along many technical lines. Increased real estate activities have witnessed a volume of legislation in recent years, affecting every segment of the business, and much of it is oriented toward consumer protection. Court decisions interpreting and implementing such legislation also have an impact upon real estate practice.

Significantly, most states have increased educational requirements and strengthened examinations for licensure to improve competency of licensees, for the protection of the public.

In this laudable endeavor to elevate standards and improve competency, the new eighth edition of *Questions and Answers On Real Estate* has been revised and enlarged. The new edition has added vital segments in order to keep abreast of the dramatic changes in real estate practice in the 1970's. The more than 4,500 questions and answers, including more than 500 arithmetic problems, with complete answers on every day real estate problems, definitions and almost 500 court decisions, will prove a valuable asset.

The real estate business is rapidly approaching the professional status of the attorney and doctor, and acceptance by the public, as such.

The encouragement, cooperation and advice of the following license law officials are here most gratefully acknowledged.

Mary L. Goodwin, Alabama; Robert T. Diggins, Alaska; M. H. Fisher, Alberta; J. Fred Talley, Arizona; Kenneth H. Graves, Arkansas; P. Dermot Murphy, British Columbia; Robert W. Karpe, California, and John E. Hempel, California; Keith T. Koske, Colorado; James F. Carey, Connecticut; Thelma Lewis, Delaware; William R. Downing, District of Columbia; Frank A. Wilkinson and C. C. Stafford, Florida; E. A. Borgschatz and C. L. Clifton, Georgia; Yukio Higuchi and Mary V. Savio, Hawaii; Marion J. Voorhees, Idaho; Dr. Dean Barringer, Illinois and Melvin M. Landau, Esq., Illinois; Carl J. Nicholson, Indiana; C. R. Galvin, Iowa; John Ball, Kansas; Carl J. Bensinger, Kentucky; Alvin J. Unick, Louisiana; Paul A. Sawyer, Maine; Charles G. Chambers, Maryland; John W. McIsaac, Massachusetts; Beverly J. Clark, Michigan; Joseph G. Bentheimer and Edward J. Driscoll, Minnesota; James D. Hobson, Jr., Mississippi; Thelma D. Peterson, Missouri; Matt H. Brown, Montana; Paul Quinlan, Nebraska; R. E. "Skip" Hansen, Nevada; Alice C. Hallenborg, New Hampshire; Frederick A. Organ, New Jersey; Kenneth R. Miller, New Mexico; Elia J. Malara, New York; Joseph F. Schweidler, North Carolina; Dennis D. Schulz, North Dakota; Robert M. Gippin, Ohio; Charles C. Case, Jr., Oklahoma; J. P. Cox, Ontario; M. J. Holbrook,

Oregon; P. John Donnelly, Pennsylvania; Claude Bourbonnais, Quebec; Reginald D. Whitcomb, Rhode Island; Ralph H. Baer, Jr., South Carolina; Jack C. Burchill, South Dakota; Ted R. Nelson, Tennessee; Andy James, Texas; Stephen J. Francis, Utah; Nelda G. Rossi, Vermont; Ruth J. Herrink, Virginia; Leonard Monsanto, Virgin Islands; George B. Oakes, Washington; Donald E. Portis, West Virginia; Roy E. Hays, Wisconsin; Glenn "Jack" Hertzler, Wyoming. I am grateful to H. Bemis Lawrence, Esq., Louisville, Kentucky, for his generous assistance over the years.

A special debt is owed to my cousin and former law partner, Roger I. Harris, Esq., former Vice-President and Chief Counsel, General Dynamics Corporation, who contributed the chapter on Condominiums, Cooperatives, Syndication and Real Estate Investment Trusts.

R. W. S.

Table of Contents

Table of Cases

Explanation of abbreviations used:

A. .... Atlantic
Cal. App. .... California Appellate
F.(2) .... Federal Reporter (Second Series)
Ill. App. .... Illinois Appellate
N.Y. App. .... New York Appellate
N.Y.S. .... New York Supplement
N.E. .... Northeastern
N.W. .... Northwestern
Pac. or P. .... Pacific
Pa. Sup. .... Pa. Superior
So. .... Southern
S.E. .... Southeastern
S.W. .... Southwestern
U.S. .... United States

Introduction

IT IS of fundamental importance to know that the extent of the right which a man acquires in property can be no greater than that enjoyed by his predecessor in title. This is a principle very frequently met with in connection with deeds and mortgages. Very often an owner will be heard to exclaim: "What do you mean I do not own this property? I have a deed to it." Yet if the previous owner did not own the entire tract or there was some encumbrance against it, it follows that his purchaser received no better title than he had. Therefore, a cautious and prudent purchaser will have the title examined in order to ascertain the extent of the present owner's interest in the property. And so, it is often necessary to trace the title through a long line of previous owners, in order to ascertain the extent of the original owner's interest in the subject property.

From time to time, a state will pass "curative" acts intended to correct defects in the title, such as validating improper acknowledgments or executions. In the few states where registered titles pertain under the Torrens system, a purchaser relies upon the registered title, without further search.

By way of further introduction, it should be noted that the rights a person has in real estate are determined and protected by the law. The purpose of law it may be said, is to define and to assert legal rights and, as collateral thereto, to prevent and punish legal wrongs. Blackstone defines law as "a rule of civil conduct prescribed by the supreme power in the State, commanding what is right and prohibiting what is wrong." In the widest sense of the word, law may be said to be a "rule of action prescribed by a superior which an inferior is bound to obey." The social concept of law is that it consists of rules for the guidance of man in his relations to his fellow man and to organized society as well. There are two types of law: (1) the unwritten law; (2) the written law. By the unwritten law we mean the customs of a community. Custom is not to be confused with usage. Custom has the force of law whereas usage is merely a fact. There may be usage without custom, but there can be no custom without usage. "Usage," it is said, "consists merely of the repetition of acts, while custom is created out of their repetition." The common law is a set of cases establishing principles of law. Written law embraces constitutions, statutes, and court decisions. The Federal Constitution is the fundamental law of the land and is representative of a system of laws and customs. A statute is a law enacted by the legislative body of the state or by the Federal Congress. A court is a body in the government to which is delegated the public administration of justice. Civil courts are created by statutes which define their composition and jurisdiction. Courts of law are not law-making bodies. They have the very important function, which sometimes closely approaches legislation, of interpreting the Constitution of the United States, the laws passed by Congress, the state constitutions, and state statutes. If a constitutional question is involved, for example, the deprivation of property without due process of law, recourse, by appeal, may be had to the United States Supreme Court, the court of last resort. Thus, it can be seen that the decisions of the courts are of the utmost importance as the source of all law. The body of the Federal law applies generally throughout the country, but each state, by reason of its particular development and the peculiar conditions and influences which prevail, has its own laws based upon its own constitution, court decisions, and customs. Court decisions, as well as statutes, may be tempered by the social needs of the society within the confines of the particular state. In most of the states in the eastern part of the country, the common law, as introduced from England, predominates, whereas in the South, codified law, resulting from French and Spanish influence, is the rule. It must be realized that there is no body of real estate law applicable to all of the states or even to a majority, but that the laws relating to deeds, mortgages, landlord and tenant, and other subjects differ materially even from one state to its immediate neighbor. Fundamental concepts and principles, however, are applicable to practically all the states, so that attention and discussion are directed, in the main, to the fundamentals of the law as it applies to each subject discussed. The same approach is true of the problems, questions, and answers included in this work.

Definitions of Real Estate Terms

Abandonment
A conveyance or recorded instrument used to terminate a homestead.

Absolute fee simple title
One that is unqualified; it is the best title one can obtain.

Abstract of title
A condensed history of the title, consisting of a summary of the various links in the chain of title, together with a statement of all liens, charges, or encumbrances affecting a particular property.

Acceleration clause
A clause in a mortgage, land purchase contract or lease stating that, upon default of a payment due, the balance of the obligation should at once become due and payable.

Access right
The right of an owner to have ingress and egress to and from his property.

Accretion
Addition to the land through natural causes—usually by change in water flow.

Acknowledgment
A formal declaration made before a notary public or other person empowered to perform the service, by the signatory to the instrument, as to the genuineness of the signature.

Acre
A measure of land, 160 square rods (4,840 square yards, 43,560 square feet).

Administrator
A person appointed by court to administer the estate of a deceased person who left no will; that is, who died intestate.

Advance fee
A fee paid in advance of any service rendered in the sale of a property or in obtaining a loan.

Ad Valorem
A tax according to a fixed percentage of its value.

Adverse possession
The right of an occupant of land to acquire title against the real owner, where possession has been actual, continuous, hostile, visible, and distinct for the statutory period.

Affiant
A person who has made an affidavit.

Affidavit
A statement of declaration reduced to writing, and sworn or affirmed to before some officer who has authority to administer an oath or affirmation.

Agent
One who represents another from whom he has derived authority.

Agreement of sale
A written agreement whereby the purchaser agrees to buy certain real estate and the seller agrees to sell upon terms and conditions set forth therein.

Air rights
The ownership of the right to use, control or occupy the air space over a designated property.

Alienation
The transfer of real property by one person to another.

Alluvion
Also alluvium. Soil deposited by accretion; increase in land on shore or bank of river due to change in flow of stream.

Amenities
The satisfaction of enjoyable living to be derived from a home; or a beneficial influence arising from the location of the property.

Amortization
The liquidation of a financial obligation on an installment basis.

Annuity
A sum of money or its equivalent that constitutes one of a series of periodic payments.

Appellant
The party who takes an appeal to a higher court.

Appellee
The party against whom the appeal is taken to a higher court.

Appraisal
An estimate of quantity, quality, or value. The process through which conclusions of property value are obtained; also refers to the report setting forth the estimate and conclusion of value.

Appraisal by capitalization
An estimate of value by capitalization of productivity and income.

Appraisal by comparison
Comparability to the sale prices of other similar properties.

Appraisal by summation
Adding together of parts of a property separately appraised to form the whole: for example, value of the land considered as vacant added to the cost of reproduction of the building, less depreciation.

Appurtenance
That which belongs to something else; something which passes as an incident to land, such as a right of way.

Architect
A person whose profession is designing buildings, drawing up plans, and generally supervising construction of the building.

Arpen
French measurement term, being 7/8 of one acre.

Assessed valuation
Assessment of real estate by a unit of government for taxation purposes.

Assessment
A charge against real estate made by a unit of government to cover the proportionate cost of an improvement, such as a street or sewer.

Assignee
The person to whom an agreement or contract is assigned.

Assignment
The method or manner by which a right, a specialty, or contract is transferred from one person to another.

Associate broker
A person who has qualified as a real estate broker, but works for a broker named in the associate broker's license.

Attestation
The witnessing of a signature to an instrument at the request of the person who signed it.

Avulsion
Removal of land from one owner to another when a stream suddenly changes its channel.

Backfill
The replacement of excavated earth into a hole or against a structure.

Balustrade
A small supporting column for a handrail.

Bargain and sale deed
Deed which conveys the property for valuable consideration.

Barge board
A wide trim board placed on the ends of a gable roof.

Base and meridian
Imaginary lines used by surveyors to find and describe the location of lands.

Baseboard
The board skirting the walls of a room at the floor line.

Basement floor
The lowest floor level in a building.

Bench marks
A location indicated on a durable marker by surveyors.

Bilateral contract
Both parties expressly enter into mutual engagements (reciprocal).

Binder
An agreement to cover a down payment for the purchase of real estate as evidence of good faith on the part of the purchaser; in insurance: a temporary agreement given to one having an insurable interest, and who desires insurance subject to the same conditions which will apply if, as, and when a policy is issued.

Blanket mortgage
A single mortgage which covers more than one piece of real estate.

Blight
A reduction in the productivity of real estate due to a variety of causes, which have a harmful effect upon the appearance of the property area affected.

Board foot
Unit of measurement for lumber; one foot long, one foot wide, one inch thick..

Bona fide
In good faith, without fraud.

Bond
Any obligation under seal. A real estate bond is a written obligation, usually issued on security of a mortgage or a trust deed.

Bridging
Small wood or metal pieces used to brace floor joists.

Broker
One employed by another, for a fee, to carry on any of the activities listed in the license law definition of the word.

B.T.U.
British thermal unit. The quantity of heat required to raise the temperature of one pound of water one degree Fahrenheit.

Building code
Regulating the construction of buildings within a municipality by ordinance or law.

Building line
A line fixed at a certain distance from the front and/or sides of a lot, beyond which no building can project.

Bundle of legal rights
Establishes real estate ownership; consists of right to sell, to mortgage, to lease, to will, to regain possession at end of a lease (reversion); to build and remove improvements; to control use within the law. May be compared to a bundle of sticks, each stick representing a separate right or privilege.

Business chance broker
One who negotiates the sale of a mercantile business for another for a fee.

Caveat Emptor
"Let the purchaser beware"; the buyer is duty-bound to examine the property he is purchasing and he assumes conditions which are readily ascertainable upon view.

Certificate of no defense
An instrument, executed by the mortgagor, upon the sale of the mortgage, to the assignee, as to the validity of the full mortgage debt.

Certificate of reasonable value
Written statement issued by the V.A. as to the maximum.

Certiorari
A writ obtained from an appellate court, directing a lower court to send up the record for review and determination or for trial by the lower court.

Cestui Que Trust
The person who has a beneficial interest in an estate, the legal title to which is vested in another person.

Chain
Unit of land measurement—66 feet.

Chain of Title
A history of conveyances and incumbrances affecting the title.

Chattel
Personal property, such as household goods or removable fixtures.

Check
See quadrangle.

Chimney cap
The finishing course at the top of the chimney.

Closing statement
An accounting of funds in a real estate sale made by a broker to the seller and buyer, respectively.

Cloud on the title
An outstanding claim or encumbrance which, if valid, would affect or impair the owner's title; a judgment, or dower interest.

Cognovit note
Note authorizing confession of judgment.

Collateral
Security given for the fulfillment of a debt or obligation.

Color of title
That which appears to be good title, but as a matter of fact, is not good title.

Commingle
To mingle or mix a client's funds in the broker's personal account.

Commission
Sum due a real estate broker for services in that capacity; the administrative and enforcement tribunal of real estate license laws.

Common law
Body of law that grew up from custom and decided cases (English law) rather than from codified law (Roman law).

Community property
Property accumulated through joint efforts of husband and wife living together.

Compound Interest
Interest paid on original principal and also on the accrued and unpaid interest.

Condemnation
Taking private property for public use, with compensation to the owner, under the right of eminent domain.

Condominium
Individual ownership units in a multi-family structure, combined with joint ownership of common areas of the building and ground.

Conduit
A pipe or channel for conveying fluids or wires.

Confession of judgment
An entry of judgment upon the debtor's voluntary authority to any attorney to do so in his behalf.

Construction loan
Provides for progressive payments of the loan proceeds during erection of the building.

Constructive eviction
Breach of a covenant of warranty or quiet enjoyment; for example, the inability of a purchaser or lessee to obtain possession by reason of a paramount outstanding title.

Constructive notice
Notice given by the public records.

Contract for sale
Also familiarly known as Land Sales Contract, Contract to Purchase Real Estate, or a Conditional Sales Contract. (See Land Sales Contract).

Conventional mortgage
One which is not insured by the F.H.A. or guaranteed by the V.A.

Conveyance
The means or medium by which title to real estate is transferred.

Cornice
An ornamental projection at the top of a wall.

Covenant
An agreement between two or more persons, by deed, whereby one of the parties promises the performance or nonperformance of certain acts, or that a given state of things does or does not exist.

Coverture
The status of a married woman.

Cubage
Front or width of building multiplied by depth of building and by the height, figured from basement floor to the outer surfaces of walls and roof.

Cul de sac
A passage way with one outlet; a blind alley.

Curtesy
The right which a husband has in his wife's estate at her death.

Curtilage
Area of land occupied by a building and its yard and outbuildings, actually enclosed or considered enclosed.

Damnum Absque Injuria
A loss which does not give rise to an action for damages against the person causing it.

Dba
Abbreviation for "doing business as."

Declaration of no set-off
See Certificate of no defense.

Decree of Foreclosure
Decree by a court upon the completion of foreclosure of a mortgage, lien or contract.

Dedication
An appropriation of land by an owner to some public use together with acceptance for such use by or on behalf of the public.

Deed
A writing by which lands, tenements, and hereditaments are transferred, which writing is signed, sealed, and delivered by the grantor.

Default
The nonperformance of a duty, whether arising under a contract, or otherwise; failure to meet an obligation when due.

Defeasance
An instrument which nullifies the effect of some other deed or of an estate.

Deficiency judgment
The difference between the indebtedness sued upon and the sale price or market value of the real estate at the foreclosure sale.

Depreciation
Loss in value, brought about by deterioration through ordinary wear and tear, action of the elements, or functional or economic obsolescence.

Depth table
Tabulation of factors representing the rating of value per front between a selected "standard" depth (usually 100 feet) and other lots of greater or lesser depth.

Devise
A gift of real estate by will or last testament.

Discount
A loan placement charge made by the lending institution to the seller, by increas-

ing the yield on the investment (also known in the trade as Points).

Discrimination
In real estate, prejudice or refusal to rent or sell to a person because of race, color, religion or ethnic origin.

Dispossess
To deprive one of the use of real estate.

Domicile
The place where one has his permanent residence and, usually, is a registered voter.

Dower
The right which a wife has in her husband's estate at his death.

Duplex
A single two-story structure designed for two-family occupancy.

Duress
Unlawful constraint exercised upon a person, whereby he is forced to perform some act, or to sign an instrument, against his will.

Earnest money
Down payment made by a purchaser of real estate as evidence of good faith.

Easement
The right, liberty, advantage or privilege which one individual has in lands of another (a right of way).

Economic life
The period over which a property may be profitably utilized.

Egress
The right to return from a tract of land (used with ingress).

Ejectment
A form of action to regain possession of real property, with damages for the unlawful retention.

Emblements
The right of a tenant to harvest and remove, after his tenancy has ended, such annual products of the land (corn, wheat), as have resulted from his own labor and care; also known as "way-growing crop".

Eminent domain
The right of the people or government to take private property for public use upon payment of compensation.

Encroachment
A building, part of building, or obstruction which intrudes upon or invades a highway or sidewalk or trespasses upon property of another.

Encumbrance
A claim, lien, charge, or liability attached to and binding upon real property, such as a judgment, unpaid taxes, or a right of way; defined in law as any right to, or interest in, land which may subsist in another to the diminution of its value, but consistent with the passing of the fee.

Entity
A thing that has individual notice; a corporation is a legal entity.

Equity
The interest or value which an owner has in real estate over and above the mortgage against it; system of legal rules administered by courts of chancery.

Equity of redemption
Right of original owner to reclaim property sold through foreclosure proceedings

on a mortgage, by payment of debt, interest, and costs.

Erosion

The wearing away of land through processes of nature as by streams and winds.

Escheat

Reversion of property to the sovereign state owing to lack of any heirs capable of inheriting.

Escrow

A deed delivered to a third person for the grantee to be held by him until the fulfillment or performance of some act or condition.

Estate

The degree, quantity, nature and extent of interest which a person has in real property.

Estate in reversion

The residue of an estate left in the grantor, to commence in possession after the termination of some particular estate granted by him. In a lease, the lessor has the estate in reversion after the lease is terminated.

Estoppel certificate

See Certificate of no defense.

Et al

An abbreviation for alii, "and others". Also used as an abbreviation for alius, "and another".

Ethics

That branch of moral science, which treats of the duties which a member of a profession or craft owes to the public, to his client, and to the other members of the profession.

Et ux.

Abbreviation for *et uxor,* meaning "and wife".

Eviction

A violation of some covenant in a lease by the landlord, usually the covenant for quiet enjoyment; also refers to process instituted to oust a person from possession of real estate.

Exclusive agency

The appointment of one real estate broker as sole agent for the sale of a property for a designated period of time.

Execution

A writ issued by a court to the sheriff directing him to sell property to satisfy a debt.

Executor

A person named in a will to carry out its provisions.

Ex officio

By virtue of his office. For example, in Iowa and Nebraska, the Secretary of State is ex officio chairman of the Real Estate Commission.

Extender clause

Clause in an exclusive listing contract, which carries the original exclusive period over for an additional period, to protect the broker, if a sale is made to a prospect he obtained during the original listing period.

Extension agreement

Agreement between mortgagee and mortgagor to extend the maturity date of the mortgage after it becomes due.

"Fannie Mae"

The secondary mortgage market. It provides a market for mortgages held by primary lenders, such as banks and savings and loan associations and provides the primary market with a ready market for mortgages, so as to permit a greater turnover of money for loans.

Fee-tail estate
An estate of inheritance given to a person and the heirs of his body. If the grantee dies without leaving issue, the estate terminates and would revert to the grantor.

F.H.A.
Federal Housing Authority; an agency of the Federal Government that insures real estate loans.

Fee simple
The largest estate or ownership in real property; free from all manner of conditions or encumbrances.

Finder's fee
A fee or commission paid to a broker for obtaining a mortgage loan for a client or for referring a mortgage loan to a broker. It may also refer to a commission paid to a broker for locating a property.

Fixture
An article that was once personalty, but has become real estate by reason of its permanent attachment in or to the improvement.

Firm commitment
A commitment by the F.H.A. to insure a mortgage on specified property with a specified mortgagor.

Flashing
Metal strips placed around roof openings to provide water tightness.

Forcible entry and detainer
A legal action to recover possession of premises which are unlawfully held.

Foreclosure
A court process instituted by a mortgagee or lien creditor to defeat any interest or redemption which the debtor-owner may have in the property.

Foreshore
Land between high-water mark and low-water mark.

Foundation
The walls of a building below the first or ground floor.

Fraud
The intentional and successful employment of any cunning, deception, collusion, or artifice, used to circumvent, cheat or deceive another person, whereby that person acts upon it, to his detriment, loss, or disadvantage.

Freehold
An estate in fee simple or for life.

Front foot
A standard of measurement, one foot wide, extending from street line for a depth, generally conceded to be 100 feet.

Gable roof
A pitched roof with sloping sides.

G.I.
A member or veteran of the United States military service.

G.I. loan
Loan guaranteed by the Veterans Administration under Servicemen's Readjustment Act of 1944, as amended; only honorably discharged veterans and their widows are eligible.

General warranty
A covenant in the deed whereby the grantor agrees to protect the grantee against the world.

Gradient
The slope, or rate of increase or decrease in elevation, of a surface, road or pipe, expressed in inches of rise or fall per horizontal linear foot or percent.

Grantee
A person to whom real estate is conveyed; the buyer.

Grantor
A person who conveys real estate by deed; the seller.

G. R. I.
Graduate Realtors Institute; one who successfully completes the three year program given by the state Real Estate Association.

Gross lease
A lease of property whereby lessor is to meet all property charges regularly incurred through ownership.

Ground rent
A rent reserved by a grantor to himself, his heirs and assigns in conveying land in fee.

Habendum clause
The "To Have and To Hold" clause which defines or limits the quantity of the estate granted in the premises of the deed.

Hand money
Same as an earnest money deposit.

Hectare
A metric measure of surface area (2.471 acres).

Hereditaments
The largest classification of property; includes lands, tenements, and incorporeal property, such as rights of way.

Holdover tenant
A tenant who remains in possession of leased property after the expiration of the lease term.

Homestead
Real estate occupied by the owner as a home; the owner enjoys special rights and privileges.

Housing for the Elderly
A project designed specially for older persons (62 years or over) which provides living unit accommodations, and common social and activities space, and facilities for health and nursing services for residents.

H.U.D.
Department of Housing and Urban Development.

Hypothecate
To give a stock as security without giving up possession of it.

Inchoate
Not yet vested or completed. Right to dower is inchoate until the husband dies.

Indenture
A formal written instrument made between two or more persons in different interests; name comes from practice of indenting or cutting the deed on the top or side in a waving line.

Ingress
Access to enter a tract of land; used with egress—to go in and out.

Installment contract
Purchase of real estate upon an installment basis; upon default, payments are forfeited.

Ipso facto
By the fact itself.

Irrigation district
Quasi-political districts created under special laws to provide for water services to property owners in the district.

Jalousie
A kind of blind or shutter made with slats fixed at an angle.

Joint and several liability
A debt incurred by two or more persons "jointly and severally" whereby one action may be brought against all of the parties or an action may be brought against one party for the entire debt.

Joint tenancy
Property held by two or more persons together with the distinct character of survivorship.

Judgment
Decree of court declaring that one individual is indebted to another and fixing the amount of such indebtedness.

Judgment d. s. b.
D. s. b. is the abbreviation for the Latin *debitum sine brevi,* which means "debt without writ." It is a judgment confessed by authority of the language in the instrument.

Junior mortgage
A mortgage second in lien to a previous mortgage.

Laches
Delay or negligence in asserting one's rights.

Land contract
A contract for the purchase of real estate upon an installment basis; upon payment of last installment, deed is delivered to purchaser.

Land economics
Branch of the science of economics which deals with the classification, ownership, and utilization of land and buildings erected thereon.

Landlord
One who rents property to another.

Lands, tenements and hereditaments
A term used in the early English law to express all types of real estate.

Lease
A contract, written or oral, for the possession of lands and tenements on the one hand and a recompense of rent or other income, on the other hand.

Leasehold
An estate in realty held under a lease.

Legal description
A description recognized by law, which is sufficient to locate and identify the property without oral testimony.

Lessee
A person to whom property is rented under a lease.

Lessor
See Landlord.

License
A privilege or right granted by the State to operate as a real estate broker or salesman. An authority to go upon or use another person's land or property, without possessing any estate therein.

License year
Period specified in license law for license; usually different from calendar year.

Lien
A hold or claim which one person has upon property of another as security for a debt or charge; judgments, mortgages, taxes.

Life estate
An estate or interest held during the term of some certain person's life.

Lis Pendens
Suit pending; usually recorded so as to give constructive notice of pending litigation.

Listing
Oral or written employment of broker by owner to sell or lease real estate.

Littoral
Belonging to shore as of sea or Great Lakes; corresponds to riparian rights.

Lot line
A legally defined line dividing one tract of land from another.

Louver
A domed turret with lateral openings in a roof.

Mansard roof
A roof with two slopes on each of the four sides, the lower steeper than the upper.

Market value
The highest price which a buyer, willing but not compelled to buy, would pay, and the lowest a seller, willing but not compelled to sell would accept.

Marketable title
Such a title as a court would compel a purchaser to accept; it is free from any encumbrances or clouds.

Marshalling
Where a creditor has two or more funds out of which to satisfy a debt, he cannot so elect as to deprive another individual, who has but one fund, of his security.

Mechanic's lien
A species of lien created by statute which exists in favor of persons who have performed work or furnished materials in the erection or repair of a building.

Meeting of minds
A mutual intention of two persons to enter into a contract affecting their legal status based on agreed-upon terms.

Merchantable title
(*See* Marketable title).

Messuage
Dwelling house and adjacent land and outbuildings.

Metes and bounds
A description in a deed of the land location, in which the boundaries are defined by directions and distances.

Mill
One-tenth of one cent; the measure used to state the property tax rate. That is,

a tax rate of one mill on the dollar is the same as a rate of one-tenth of one per cent of the assessed value of the property.

Monument
An artificial or natural landmark, e.g. the Revolutionary oak tree, a stone peg.

Moratorium
Emergency act by a legislative body to suspend the legal enforcement of contractual obligations.

Mortgage
A conditional transfer of real property as security for the payment of a debt or the fulfillment of some obligation.

Mortgagee
A person to whom property is conveyed as security for a loan made by such person (the creditor).

Mortgagee in possession
A mortgage creditor who takes over the income from the mortgaged property upon a default on the mortgage by the debtor.

Mortgagor
An owner who conveys his property as security for a loan (the debtor).

Multiple listing
The arrangement among real estate board or exchange members whereby each broker brings his listings to the attention of the other members so that if a sale results, the commission is divided between the broker bringing the listing and the broker making the sale, with a small percentage going to the board or exchange.

NAR
National Association of Realtors.

Net lease
A lease, under which lessor receives a fixed rental and lessee pays taxes, utilities and all other operating expenses.

Net listing
A price, which must be expressly agreed upon, below which the owner will not sell the property and at which price the broker will not receive a commission; the broker receives the excess over and above the net listing as his commission.

N.S.F. check
Not sufficient funds check—(not honored by bank).

Nudum pactum
"naked pact"—no contract.

Nuncupative will
An oral will.

Obsolescence
Impairment of desirability and usefulness brought about by physical, economic, fashion or other changes.

Offset statement
Statement by owner of property or owner of lien against property, setting forth the present status of liens against subject property.

Open listing
An oral or general listing.

Option
The right to purchase or lease a property at a certain price for a certain designated period, for which right a consideration is paid.

Overhang
The part of the roof extending beyond the walls, to shade building and cover walls.

Over-improvement
An improvement which is not the highest and best use for the site on which it is placed by reason of excess in size or cost.

Package mortgage
One which includes personal property within the lien of the mortgage.

Partition
A division made of real property among those who own it in undivided shares.

Party wall
A wall erected on the line between two adjoining properties, belonging to different persons, for use of both properties.

Patent
Conveyance of title to government land.

Percentage lease
A lease of property in which the rental is based upon the volume of sales made upon the leased premises.

Perch
A unit of land measurement; 16½ feet.

Percolation test
A soil test to determine if soil will take sufficient water seepage for use of a septic tank.

Personalty
All articles or property that are not real estate.

Pi
A symbol (π) designating the ratio of the circumference of a circle to its diameter $\pi = 3.1416$.

Plat book
A public record of various recorded plans in the municipality or county.

Plottage
Increment in unity value of a plot of land created by assembling smaller ownerships into one ownership.

Pocket license card
Evidence of licensure, which should be carried by the licensee at all times and presented when requested by any person with whom the licensee is dealing in regard to real estate.

Points
(See Discount).

Police power
The inherent rights of a government to pass such legislation as may be necessary to protect the public health and safety and/or to promote the general welfare.

Postponement of lien
The subordination of a presently prior lien to a subsequent judgment or mortgage.

Prima facie evidence
Evidence considered in law to be sufficient to establish a fact, if not contradicted.

Principal
The employer of an agent; the person who is ordinarily liable primarily.

Principal meridian
A north-south line projected through a prominent landmark established under the Government Survey system.

Principal note
The promissory note which is secured by the mortgage or trust deed.

Property
The right or interest which an individual has in lands and chattels to the exclusion of all others.

Prospectus
A printed advertisement for a new enterprise, such as rural property or subdivision.

Public policy
That principle of the law, which holds that no person can lawfully do that which has a tendency to be injurious to the public or against the public good.

Public trustee
A person appointed or required by law to execute a trust.

Purchase money mortgage
A mortgage given by a grantee to the grantor in part payment of the purchase price of real estate.

Quadrangle
A tract of the land in the U.S. Governmental Survey System measuring 24 miles on each side of the square, sometimes referred to as a "check."

Quasi contract
An obligation for a party to do something, which is imposed by law.

Quiet enjoyment
The right of an owner to the use of property without interference of possession.

Quiet title
A court action brought to establish title and to remove a cloud on the title.

Quit claim deed
A deed given when the grantee already has, or claims, complete or partial title to the premises and the grantor has a possible interest that otherwise would constitute a cloud upon the title.

Quit notice
A notice to a tenant to vacate rented property.

Quotient
The number obtained when one quantity is divided by another.

Range
A strip of land six miles wide determined by government survey, running in a north-south direction.

Ratification
Giving approval by act or conduct of something done by another, without authority.

Realtor
A coined word used to designate an active member of a local real estate board affiliated with the National Association of Realtors.

Redemption
The right of a mortgagor to redeem the property by paying the debt after the expiration date; the right of an owner to reclaim his property after a sale for taxes.

Reduction certificate
A certificate showing the balance due on a mortgage at the time of closing the sale.

Reformation
An action to correct a mistake in a deed or other instrument.

Release
The relinquishment of some right or benefit to a person who already has some interest in the property.

Release of lien
The discharge of certain property from the lien of a judgment, mortgage, or claim.

Remainder estate
An estate in property created at the same time and by the same instrument as another estate and limited to arise immediately upon the termination of the other estate.

Reproduction cost
Normal cost of exact duplication of a property, as of a certain date.

Res gestae
Attendant facts and circumstances to the issue involved.

Res judicata
A matter judicially decided.

Restriction
A device in a deed for controlling the use of land for the benefit of the land.

Restriction covenant
A clause in a deed limiting the use of the property conveyed for a certain period of time.

Reversion
The residue of an estate left to the grantor, to commence after the determination of some particular estate granted out by him.

Right of way
An easement over another's land—also used to describe strip of land used as a roadbed by a railroad or other public utility for a public purpose.

Riparian
Pertaining to the banks of a river, stream, waterway, and so forth.

Riparian owner
One who owns lands bounding upon a river or water course.

Running with the land (Easement)
An easement which inures to the benefit and advantage of subsequent owners of the land, for which it was originally created.

Satisfaction piece
An instrument for recording and acknowledging payment of an indebtedness secured by a mortgage.

Section
A section of land established by government survey and containing 640 acres.

Seizin
Possession of real estate by one entitled thereto.

Separate property
Property owned by a husband or wife which is not community property; acquired by either spouse prior to marriage or by gift or devise after marriage.

Septic tank system
Private sewage disposal section for an individual home.

Setback
The distance from curb or other established line, within which no building may be erected.

Severalty ownership
Real property owned by one person only; sole ownership.

Siding
Finish covering on exterior walls.

Simple listing
Listing property with a broker for sale or rent other than through exclusive agency or an exclusive right-to-sell contract; an open listing, usually verbal.

Simple proportion
Relationship between four quantities in which the quotient of the first, divided by the second, is equal to that of the third, divided by the fourth; also geometrical proportion—a method for finding the fourth quality in such a relationship when 3 are given.

Sinking fund
Fund set aside from property which, with accrued interest, will eventually pay for replacement of the improvements.

Sky lease
Lease for a long period of time of space above a piece of real estate; upper stories of a building to be erected by the tenant; upon the termination of lease, the improvement belongs to the lessor.

Special warranty deed
A deed wherein the grantor limits his liability to the grantee to anyone claiming, by, from, through or under him, the grantor.

Specific performance
A remedy in a court of equity compelling the defendant to carry out the terms of the agreement or contract which was executed.

Squatter's rights
Occupancy of land by virtue of long use against the recorded title owner.

Statute of frauds
Requires certain contracts relating to real estate, such as agreements of sale, to be in writing, in order to be enforceable.

Subdivision
A tract of land divided into lots suitable for home-building purposes.

Subletting
A leasing by a tenant to another, who holds under the tenant.

Subordination clause
A clause in a mortgage or lease, stating that rights of the holder shall be secondary or subordinate to a subsequent encumbrance.

Subpoena
A legal order or writ commanding the named individual to appear and testify in a legal proceedings.

Sump pump
An automatic water pump used in basements to raise water to the sewer level.

Surrender
The cancellation of a lease by mutual consent of lessor and lessee.

Survey
The process by which a parcel of land is measured and its area ascertained.

t/a
Abbreviation for "trading as."

Tax
A charge assessed against persons or property for public purposes.

Tax deed
A deed for property sold at public sale by a political subdivision, such as a city, for

nonpayment of taxes by the owner.

Tenancy at will
A license to use or occupy lands and tenements at the will of the owner.

Tenancy in common
Form of estate held by two or more persons, each of whom is considered as being possessed of the whole of an undivided part.

Tenant
A person who holds real estate under a lease (lessee).

Tenant at sufferance
One who comes into possession of lands by lawful title and keeps it afterwards without any title at all.

Tenement
Everything of a permanent nature which may be holden.

Termites
Ant like insects which destroy woodwork used in the building.

Terre tenant
One who has the actual possession of land.

Tier
A strip of land six miles wide running in an east-west direction, as determined by Government Survey.

Title
Evidence of ownership, which refers to the quality of the estate.

Title by adverse possession
Acquired by occupation and recognized as against the paper title owner.

Title insurance
A policy of insurance which indemnifies the holder for any loss sustained by reason of defects in the title.

Topography
The contour and slope of land, hills, valleys, streams, etc.

Torrens system
A system of title records provided by state law.

Tort
An actionable wrong.

Township
A territorial subdivision, six miles long, six miles wide, and containing 36 sections, each one mile square.

Trust deed
A form of mortgage by which borrower conveys title to a trustee, who holds title for protection of the lender, as security for the loan debt.

Trustee
A person in whom an estate, interest, or power, in or affecting property, is vested or granted for the benefit of another person.

Trustor
One who deeds his property to a trustee.

Ultra vires act
A contract entered in excess of the corporation's express or implied powers of its charter.

Unearned increment
An increase in value of real estate due to no effort on the part of the owner; often due to increase in population.

Unilateral contract
One in which one party makes an express undertaking, without receiving in return any promise of performance from the other.

United States governmental survey system
Also known as the Rectangular Survey System; a method of describing or locating real property by reference to the governmental survey.

Unlawful Detainer
The statutory proceedings by which a landlord removes a tenant who holds over after his lease has expired or after his tenancy is terminated by notice or after default in payment of rent or other obligations.

Usury
Charging more than the legal rate of interest for the use of money.

V.A. loan
(*See* G.I. loan).

Vara
Spanish term of measurement, being 33$\frac{1}{3}$ inches.

Vendee
The purchaser of real estate under an agreement.

Vendor
The seller of real estate, usually referred to as the party of the first part in an agreement of sale.

Waiver
The renunciation, abandonment, or surrender of some claim, right, or privilege.

Warranty deed
One that contains a covenant that the grantor will protect the grantee against any claimant.

Waste
Wilful destruction of any part of the land or improvements, so as to injure or prejudice the estate of a mortgagee, landlord or remainderman.

Water table
Distance from surface of ground to a depth at which natural ground water is found.

Windowsill
The lower or base framing of a window opening.

Without recourse
Words used in endorsing a negotiable instrument to denote that the endorser will not be liable to a future holder, in event of non-payment.

Writ of execution
A writ which authorizes and directs the proper officer of the court (usually the sheriff) to carry into effect the judgment or decree of the court.

Yield
The annual percentage rate of return on an investment in real estate, stocks or bonds.

Zone
The area set off by a governing body for specific use; such as, residential, commercial, industrial use.

Zoning
An area in a municipality restricted by ordinance for a particular use, such as single family, multiple-family, commercial, or industrial.
"Spot zoning" occurs when tract in question is singled out for treatment, differing

unjustifiably from that of similar surrounding land, thereby creating an island having no relevant differences from its neighbors.

Zoning ordinance

Exercise of police power of a municipality in regulating and controlling the character and use of property.

Chapter I

BROKERAGE

THE REAL ESTATE broker, or sales person is a quasi-professional.

In organized real estate circles, the real estate broker or salesperson is considered a professional. If such person is a member of the National Association of Realtors, or the National Association of Real Estate Brokers, Inc., he is required to adhere to a rigid code of ethics in dealings with the public and fellow members. This high standard of conduct is translated into the real estate brokers licensing law.

If a real estate licensee is to discharge creditably the duties which devolved upon him or her, it is essential that such person have full knowledge of the applicable law to real estate practice. Real estate brokerage represents a combination of the principles of the law of principal and agent and the law of contracts. A real estate broker is an agent in the fullest sense of the word, in that he represents another (the owner) from whom he has derived his authority. The interests of three persons are involved in a real estate transaction: the owner, the broker and the purchaser, with whom the broker negotiates, in the interests of the owner.

Two contracts are involved relating to the broker's activities. The first is the contract of employment between the broker and the owner; the second is the contract of sale, between the owner and the buyer (or lessee), which the broker negotiates, as agent for the owner. The contract between the owner and broker is known as the listing contract. It spells out upon what terms a sale, or lease, are to be negotiated by the broker, duration of the contract, and compensation to be paid by the owner to the broker for his services, if he performs his contract. The compensation due the broker is called a commission.

When the broker obtains a qualified buyer upon the seller's terms, as specified in the listing contract, the broker is entitled to the agreed upon commission. This is true, even though the owner has changed his mind about selling, or arbitrarily refuses to sign the contract of sale. The broker may sue the owner, because the broker has fully performed the contract of employment. There are many real estate activities performed by a broker, or sales person, other than negotiating the sale of residences, commercial or industrial properties. Each activity, such as leasing or management is predicated upon a contract of employment between the principal (owner) and the agent (broker), and it must be examined to determine the respective rights, duties and liabilities of the respective parties. It is important that the contract of employment express clearly the intention of the parties.

Since commissions are the heart of the real estate brokerage business, the listing contract should be free of ambiguity as to its meaning and intent. Should a controversy arise between owner and broker and it becomes necessary for the latter to prosecute a claim for commission in a court of law, the affirmative burden of proof is upon the plaintiff broker to prove (1) that he was properly licensed (2) that the broker had a contract of employment from the owner and (3) that he (or she) was the efficient and procuring cause of the sale.

Every state, the District of Columbia, most Canadian provinces, the Virgin Islands and Guam now have license laws. The plaintiff broker must assert and prove licensure as a prerequisite to a recovery. It cannot be assumed. Some state license laws provide that the broker must be licensed at the time the cause of action arose. The phrase "time the cause of action arose" has been interpreted differently.

In the case of *Kemmerer v. Roscher,* 100 N.W. 2d 314 (Wis. 1960), an exclusive listing was given "To Freeman F. Kemmerer and/or Fontana Realty Company, Inc., Broker" for a one year period. At the time the listing was obtained, Kemmerer, the individual, was licensed, but Fontana Realty Company, the Corporation, was not licensed. The property was sold during the one year period through another broker. At the time the Agreements of Sale were signed, the corporation was licensed. In a suit for commission, the court denied a recovery, citing an earlier case, *Payne v. Volkman,* 183 Wis. 412, 198 N.W. 438 (1924), where an action was begun by two associated brokers, one of them licensed, the other unlicensed. The court held that "the contract being invalid as to the unlicensed broker, the contract is invalid *in toto.*"

The case of *Rosenthal et al. v. Art Metals, Inc., et al.,* 101 N.J. Super. 156 (1968) involves the provision in the New Jersey license law similar to the Wisconsin law prohibiting a suit unless the broker was licensed "at the time the alleged cause of action arose." The plaintiff was licensed in New York, but not in New Jersey, at the time the *listing* was obtained. He did obtain a New Jersey license prior to the signing of the agreements of sale. The Appellate Court decided against the broker, since negotiations were carried on in New Jersey before he obtained a New Jersey license. Upon appeal, the Supreme Court affirmed. To the same effect is the case of *Certified Realty Co. v. Reddick,* 456 P. 2d 502 (Oregon 1969).

The New York court, in *Bendell v. Dominicis,* 167 N.E. 452 (1929), construed the same clause and its decision was of a similar tenor. The court stated succinctly:

> Otherwise an unlicensed broker might negotiate sales with impunity up to the point of a complete agreement and then obtain his license for the purpose of recovering his commissions on the execution of a formal contract. The law is not so toothless.

The United States Circuit Court of Appeals took an opposite view involving a similar issue. In the case of *Schreibman v. L.I. Combs and Sons, Inc., et al.,* 377 F. 2d 410 (1964), the plaintiff broker, licensed in New York, obtained a license in Indiana, *after* he secured a listing in Indiana. He was licensed at the time the agreements of sale were signed between the owner and the buyer, procured by him. The Federal Circuit Court of Appeals held that since the plaintiff was licensed *at the time the cause of action arose* (when the agreements were signed), the District Court was in error in dismissing the suit. The case was returned to the District Court for hearing on its merits. The California courts have had occasion to examine their statute which is of identical import. In earlier cases of *Houston v. Williams,* 200 P. 55, *Davis v. Chapman,* 282 P. 992, *Wise v. Radis,* 242 P. 90, citing the California cases as authoritative, the Iowa Supreme Court, in *Pound v. Brown,* 140 N.W. 2d 183 (1966) also decided in favor of the broker.

In this connection, the language of the Illinois license law requires a plaintiff broker to be licensed

> prior to the time of offering to perform any such act or service or procuring any promise or contract for the payment of compensation for any such contemplated act or service.

It is important that a broker or salesman renew his license promptly so as not to prejudice a claim for commission. The law charges the broker with knowledge whether or not his sales person is properly licensed. A broker endangers his right to a commission, where he employs an unlicensed sales person, who embarks upon negotiating a real estate deal before obtaining the necessary license. This is true even though application has been made and the examination taken. It is immaterial that the sales person obtains a license prior to the consummation of the transaction: *Certified Realty Co. v. Reddick,* 156 P. 2d 502 (Or. 1969).

In an Arizona case, *Farragut Baggage and Transfer Co. v. Sharon Realty Inc.,* 501 P. 2d 88 (1972), the Court of Appeals reversed a $3,500 verdict in favor of the broker, where a salesman was licensed by another broker on February 4, 1970. This connection was severed on March 16, 1970 and a salesman's license was issued in the employ of the plaintiff broker on June 15, 1970. Lease negotiations were carried by the salesman, occurring in the latter part of March 1970, or early in April 1970. Negotiations continued until June 29, 1970, when a formal lease was executed. The salesman had made application to the Real Estate Department for transfer of license on March 17, 1970, but the request was not accompanied by the transfer fee of $5.00. The fee was subsequently received on June 15, 1970 and the license was issued. Accordingly, the salesman was not licensed from March 16, 1970 until June 15, 1970 while negotiations were conducted. The court held that a plaintiff cannot recover where his cause of action cannot be established without showing that he had broken the law.

In the California case of *Firpo v. Murphy,* 236 P. 968 (1925), a similar factual situation was presented and the court held that a broker who employed an unlicensed salesman could not recover a commission for securing leases of a building through such salesman.

FEE splitting between brokers

Air travel has brought distant cities together in a matter of hours. It has multiplied the number of real estate transactions negotiated by two brokers, whose offices are miles apart. In associating with a real estate broker from another state, the licensee should make certain that the other broker is properly licensed in his home state and is eligible to cooperate.

The licensee should also examine the license law and the Rules and Regulations in his own state, to ascertain whether he can share his commission legally with the non-resident broker. Apropos of the matter is the case of *Wheaton v. Ramsey,* 436 P. 2d 248 (Idaho) (1968). Ramsey was a licensed broker in Montana; Wheaton was licensed in South Dakota. At the time of the suit for a share in the commission, Ramsey was a resident of Idaho and for that reason, suit was brought in that state. In late 1963, Wheaton, appellant, contacted defendant, Ramsey, concerning her ranch listings in Montana and obtained from her information concerning the Goat Mountain Ranch. The parties discussed the possible joint sale of the property and agreed that in such event, they would split the real estate commission. In October 1963, appellant traveled to Montana with prospective purchasers, Mr. and Mrs. O. W. McPherson, and spent several days showing them the ranch. In December 1963, the McPhersons agreed with the defendant to purchase the ranch for $275,000. Upon completion of the sale in January 1964, the defendant received a five per cent commission of $13,750. Ramsey refused to pay to appellant any share of the commission on the ground that her own Montana real estate license would be jeopardized, since Wheaton was not licensed in Montana. The Court said:

> The principal issue is whether by Montana law the understanding between appellant and respondent Ramsey constituted an illegal agreement, inasmuch as appellant was unlicensed in Montana, so that such agreement cannot now be enforced. Both parties concur that an agreement between real estate brokers to share a commission is not within the statute of frauds and may be made orally. *Reilly v. Maw,* 146 Mont. 145 (1945), *Iusi v. Chase,* 169 Cal. App. 2d 83

(1959). The controlling statute is Montana's Real Estate Licensing Act of 1963. . . . It provides that " . . . it is unlawful for any licensed broker to employ or compensate directly or indirectly any person for performing any of the acts regulated by this Act, who is not a licensed broker or licensed salesman; provided, however, *that a licensed broker may pay a commission to a licensed broker of another state so long as such non-resident broker has not conducted and does not conduct in this state any service for which a fee, compensation or commission is paid . . .* " (emphasis supplied)

The statute is dispositive of appellant's complaint; it would be unlawful for respondent Ramsey to compensate appellant directly or indirectly pursuant to the fee-splitting arrangement. The agreement, therefore, is unenforceable . . .

In the case of *Thorpe v. Ross J. Carte,* 250 A 2d 618 (Md. 1969), a broker was to receive a commission of six per cent. He orally agreed with an unlicensed engineering and surveying firm, which assisted in finding a buyer, to share his commission. There was an agreement that the *seller,* rather than the broker, would pay a part of the commission to the engineering firm. The court held that the contract was illegal and that the broker could not recover anything. The court said:

We see the effect of this contract to be the same as if Carte (the broker) had received the commission and then himself split it. What one does by another he does himself and the intents and purposes of (the law) could not be effectuated if a broker could do by manifestly obvious indirection what he is forbidden to do directly.

The case of *Quickshops of Mississippi, Inc. v. J. Bruce,* 232 So. 2d 351 (1970) presents an everyday question whether an unlicensed broker is entitled to recover commission on a business opportunity property, where real estate, although significant, was not the dominant factor in the transaction. This presents a factual question for determination by a jury. The court sustained the verdict of the jury in favor of the broker.

The opinion of the Mississippi Supreme Court emphasizes the fact that the license law statute is penal in nature and must be strictly construed. The court referred to the New York rule (*Weingast v. Rialto Pastry Shop,* 152 N.E. 693 New York 1926), which holds that a broker may recover a commission in the sale of a going business "despite the fact that real estate forms an incident of the transaction and he does not hold a real estate broker's license."

However, in the California case of *Abrams v. Guston,* 243 P. 2d 109 (1952), where the sale of the realty and the personal property located thereon constituted one complete and entire transaction, it being evident that the mill and machinery located on the leased property were of value to the purchaser only if he obtained the lease upon the property, the court held that the broker making the deal required a license. This case differs from *Marks v. McCarty,* 205 P. 2d 1025 (Cal. 1949), where the real estate and the personal property were each given a separate sales price in the escrow. An unlicensed person was denied a commission in the sale of a restaurant, including stock, fixtures, lease and good will, on the grounds that the sale involved an interest in real estate, as a matter of law: *Cohen v. Scola,* 80 A. 2d 643 (N.J. 1951).

An agreement to divide a commission between two licensed brokers may be verbal: *J. A. Carter & Associates Inc. v. Devore,* 281 So. 2d 245 (Fla. App. 1973).

A "finder's fee"

A finder's fee commonly refers to the payment of a commission to a broker for obtaining a mortgage for a buyer. It may also refer to a person who acts as a go-between an owner and a purchaser and receives a fee from the owner. In the latter capacity, a "finder" plays a very limited role, with minimal duties in a real estate transaction. He is, in a sense, an "originator" in the deal. A "finder" is one who finds, interests, introduces and brings together parties in a deal, even though he has no part in negotiating the terms of the transaction; *Consolidated Oil & Gas, Inc. v. Roberts,* 425 P. 2d 282 (1967); *Shoenfeld v. Silver Springs, U. S. Dist. Ct. Eastern Division* (Wisc. 1971). Each case depends upon its particular facts.

Court decisions are not in harmony in adopting a line of demarcation between what constitutes a person a finder and when the activities fall within the definition of a real estate broker under the license law. Suppose Adams, a good friend of Costello, meets him at their country club and Adams learns that Costello wants to sell his home for $65,000. Adams tells him that he thinks he knows some one who would be interested at that price. Costello replies, "send him over, and if he buys the property, I will *pay* you $5,000." Adams sends Chase to Costello, who buys the property at $65,000. Upon the facts stated, it would appear that Adams could recover the $5,000, as a finder's fee, even though he has no license.

A "finder's fee" was denied by the court to an unlicensed person in the sale of a hotel, since real estate was a dominant feature of the transaction: *Sorice v. DuBois et al,* 167 N.Y.S. 2d 227 (1966); *Cary v. Borden Co.,* 386 P. 2d 585 (Colo. 1963).

In the California case of *Sullivan v. Collins* 435 F2d 1128, where the plaintiff did considerably more, the United States Court of Appeals affirmed a verdict to $55,000 as a "finder's fee" in favor of the plaintiff, an IBM operator and a musician.

> ". . . what plaintiff did in addition to bringing the buyer and seller together was out of a spirit of helpfulness and not with the expectation or purpose of additional reward. These activities, if they affected the transaction at all, were purely incidental."

Referrals/rental listing agency operation

Some firms have been the subject of litigation by real estate licensing commissions, on the grounds of operating as brokers without a license. Apparently, the agency does not enter into any agreement with the owner or with a prospective tenant; it simply makes available to the prospect a list of rental properties. The agency receives only an initial fee, usually in the amount of $20.

In the case of *Real Estate Commission v. Phares (Homefinders)* 268 Md. 344 (1973), the Maryland Court of Appeals decided against the Real Estate Commission. The Maryland Legislature then amended the license law to include in the definition of a real estate broker "any person who aids, attempts, or offers to aid, for a fee, any person in locating or obtaining for purchase or lease any residential real estate."

In a 1974 suit, (Civil 73-701-T) the United States District Court of Maryland dismissed the suit of Ron Phares, t/a Homefinders, against the Real Estate Commission in Maryland, which sought an injunction against the Commission from enforcing the Act against them. The court held that the subject amendment bears a rational relationship to legitimate state objectives and that the law does not deny the plaintiff equal protection or due process.

A salesman's right to a commission

The employment of a sales person by a broker should be in writing signed by both parties. A sample form of a contract appears at the end of this chapter. Some employment contracts provide that if a salesman is discharged or resigns, he shall not engage in real estate activity as a broker for himself, or as a broker or salesman for another broker, within a certain area of the first broker's office or branch office, for a certain period of time. If such restraint of trade is *reasonable,* as to area and time, it will be upheld.

The situation frequently arises where a salesman leaves a broker's employ, after he was working on a deal, and a sale results subsequently to his prospect. Is the salesman entitled to a commission? The question depends upon the particular facts in the case. Pertinent facts would include the extent of the salesman's activities in the transaction, was the deal "alive," and how long after the salesman's departure were the agreements signed: *Clair v. Kall and Kall, Inc.* N.Y. Misc. 2d (1960). Clearly, if the agreements were signed before the salesman left the broker's employ, but consummation occurred subsequent to his severance of employment, the salesman would be entitled to a commission.

Another situation develops where a salesman's employer refuses to sue an owner, and the salesman sues in his own name. In the case of *Turnblazer v. Smith,* 379 S.W. 2d 772 (Tenn. 1964), the court refused a recovery. It said:

> The real estate salesman works merely for and under the control of the real estate broker and he is "engaged by and on behalf of a licensed real estate broker". Therefore, he works for the broker and does his bidding and is under his control. He does not perform services for others for which he may claim commission.

Employment

Employment is an important prerequisite to the recovery of a commission in a court of law. The cases are legion where a broker was unsuccessful in recovering a commission, because he could not prove a contract of employment. It is regrettable that the law in every state does not require a broker's employment to be in writing. At the present time, twenty states do require a broker's employment to be in writing (Arizona, California, Hawaii, Idaho, Indiana, Kentucky, Louisiana, Michigan, Minnesota, Mississippi, Montana, Nebraska, New Jersey, New Mexico, North Dakota, Ohio, Oklahoma, Oregon, Texas, Utah, Washington, and Wisconsin—also the District of Columbia and the province of Ontario). Georgia requires exclusive listing to be in writing. These states also require a definite expiration date in exclusive listing contracts. A number of states require a definite expiration date by rule and regulation of the Commission. A written listing eliminates misunderstanding and curtails litigation. In the long run, it inures to the benefit of the licensee, because it is strong evidence of employment.

Where the law requires the listing to be in writing, it should contain a description of the property, terms of the sale, amount or percentage of commission to be paid, the expiration date and signature by the party to be charged.

In states where an oral listing is valid, many owners are full of curiosity; in an active market, they may be just curious to see what they could get for their property or they entertain a half-hearted idea that they want to sell it. If a buyer is obtained, they have a change of mind. In a suit, there is a complete variance as to the facts; whereas, if there were a written employment, the writing would speak for itself. In the Missouri case of *Windsor v. International Life Ins. Co.,* 29 S.W. 2d 1112 (1930), where a broker, unsolicited, visited defendant and offered to exchange a business building for farm lands, an officer of the defendant said he was not interested, but would be interested in exchanging farm lands for high class apartment properties. The broker said he would see what he could do. Nothing was said about commission. Later, broker sued for commission. Court held that there was no employment, so no recovery.

In the case of *Yurgelin v. Emery,* 282 Mass. 571 (1933), the Court held that a single inquiry by the owner as to the amount of commission a broker would charge, was insufficient to warrant a finding that the owner expressly or impliedly contracted with the broker to find a purchaser.

A writing authorizing an agent to sell "property descibed on the reverse side of this card," was held sufficiently signed where the owner's signature appeared at the end of the face side of card: *Kelley v. J. R. Rice Realty Co.,* 235 Ky. 643 (1930).

In the case of *Svoboda v. De Wald,* 159 Neb. 594 (1955) the court held that the broker's name on the agreement of sale constituted a written listing.

A sign on a property reading "SEE YOUR BROKER" does not create employment. The Pennsylvania Supreme Court so held in the case of Appeal of *Lancaster Farmers National Bank,* 219. A. 2d 647 (1966), reversing an award in favor of a broker by a lower court. The testimony tended to show that appellee (broker) had no specific contract to sell and that he was never contacted by the appellant (seller) and given authority to sell the subject property. The broker contacted the Bank to ascertain whether the particular property was available *after* he learned that the Millers were interested in purchasing it. The Bank had placed a sign on the property indicating that it was for sale and directing interested parties *to contact their brokers.* The plaintiff broker had previously dealt with the Bank, having sold a property for it and having received a commission in the sale. The Court said:

> The fact that a broker has previously made a sale and received a commission does not entitle him to a commission on a subsequent sale made by him for the same vendor, if he has not been employed to effect that sale. Thus, the previous transaction, not being sufficiently probative in itself, to create a subsequent agency, did not entitle appellee to a commission. Neither was the sign directing prospective purchasers to contact their brokers an offer of employment. In *Lanard and Axilbund v. Thomson Printing Co.,* 84 Pa. Super. 199 (1924), defendant notified approximately one hundred real estate brokers by postal card that it had property to rent. The Superior Court there held that: "The postal card amounted to no more than a notice that defendant had a property to rent. It did not authorize plaintiffs to secure a tenant." The sign in the instant case also was nothing more than a notice that the property was available. It created no agency.

A case in the same area of law, in which one broker sued another broker successfully, is the case of *Levit v. Bowers,* 2 Ill. App. 2d 343 (1954). In that case, the defendant, a Realtor, held an exclusive agency for the sale of a large plot of ground in Chicago. In June 1949, he mailed a letter to about one thousand real estate brokers in the Chicago Loop, offering to pay a full commission to a broker who "successfully negotiates a sale" of all or a portion of the property. The plaintiff broker recovered a verdict for $4,200 and the defendant broker appealed.

It was the defendant's contention that the words "successfully negotiating sale" meant that no commission would be paid unless the sale was consummated. In regard to the meaning of the words in controversy, the Court said:

> The letter in question was prepared and signed by a Realtor and sent to one thousand real estate brokers—men who make their living as agents for buyers and sellers of real estate. The final transfer was beyond their control.... If a sale had to be consummated before the broker was entitled to his commission, then the solicitation by the defendant of the services of a thousand Realtors in the Chicago Loop was hardly more than a snare and a delusion.... The property being vacant and the transaction being for cash and was left no matter of substance to be decided.

In the case of *Sackett v. Ford,* 1 Tenn. 506, the court held that where a broker asks an owner the price of his house, and introduces him to a customer who subsequently purchases it, he is not entitled to a commission, unless he was employed by the owner to make the sale, although he may have, to some extent, influenced the sale: *Hunger v. Judy,* 194 Kan. 159 (1965).

In the ordinary situation between owner and broker, where the listing price is given to the broker, the usual interpretation is that the asking terms are intended to merely guide the broker in starting negotiations: *Bonanza Real Estate Co. v. Crouch,* 517 P 2d 1371 (Wash. App. 1974).

No particular form of words is necessary to employ a broker although a mere statement to a broker of the price at which the owner will sell is not, in itself, sufficient to imply a contract of employment. The broker must act with the consent of the principal, whether such consent be given by written instrument, orally, or by implication from the conduct of the parties. *Young v. Zimmer,* 56 (Ill. App. 2d 298 1965).

In Corpus Juris Secundum, 32 Section 12, it is said:

> . . . the mere leaving of a description of the property at the office of a broker, by the owner or his agent, with the request that the broker sell the property at a designated price and upon designated terms, amounts to an employment of the broker; but the mere fact that a broker asks and obtains from the owner the price at which he is willing to sell does not of itself establish the relation of principal and agent between them.

It is important that the broker have a definite understanding with the owner *that he will be paid a commission,* if the broker obtains a buyer upon the seller's terms.

In the Kentucky case of *O. L. Hamilton v. Booth,* 332 S.W. 2d 252 (1960), a broker sued for a $750 commission. The only question involved was whether the contract of sale between the owner and the buyer constituted a *written* contract of employment between the owner and the broker, as required under Kentucky law. The Court said:

> This sales agreement between the defendant and the purchaser of his property has no resemblance of a contractual arrangement between the defendant and plaintiff. It recites that the property was sold through Bud's Hamilton Realty Auction Co., (this is a printed form) but these words standing alone are meaningless. If plaintiff was to recover on the basis of this writing, it should show an agreement with him and the terms of the agreement. It fails to show either. The plaintiff, therefore, had no claim based on this writing as a contract.

In the case of *Tucker v. Green,* 96 Ariz. 371 (1964) the court held that the owner's liability to broker for commission on sale owner made directly with prospective purchaser of broker depended on whether the owner had knowledge, *before consummating the sale,* that purchaser had been produced by broker.

A clear statement of the application of employment by implication rule is found in the annotation to *Reeve v. Shoemaker,* (Iowa) 205 N.W. 742, 43 A.L.R. 839 reading:

> Where a broker approaches an owner of real estate and negotiates for the purchase of certain of his property, no promise to pay for the broker's services voluntarily rendered will be implied if the owner is justified by the circumstances in presuming that the broker is a prospective purchaser or is representing a prospective purchaser in the negotiations.

Similarly, in the case of *Morton v. Barney,* 140 Ill. App. 333 (1908), the court said:

> Nor can a broker by letters of his own and addressed to a possible purchaser or by writing an owner that he has offered the property to such proposed purchaser make a contract of employment for himself, entitling him to commission. *It takes two to make a contract of that kind* and an owner is under no obligation to respond to every letter he may receive from a real estate broker he has not employed. (emphasis supplied).

Where a broker has been discussing with an owner the possibility of a sale of his home, but it is uncertain whether the owner has really made up his mind to go ahead with a sale, the broker, in order to protect himself against a loss of time and money, can protect himself, to some extent, by putting the owner on notice that he is employed. A letter, in following form, might well be used in this connection:

June 15, 1974

Dear Mr. and Mrs. Henry Stone:

In accordance with our conversation today, we are pleased to list your property at 6715 Murray Avenue, Pittsburgh, Pennsylvania, for sale. We will endeavor to obtain a purchaser at your suggested price of $20,500 and, of course, will expect the usual commission of 7%.

If you decide at a future date not to sell and to terminate our employment or if you decide to change the selling price, please notify us immediately.

We hope to be able to obtain a purchaser upon your terms and to your complete satisfaction.

Thanking you for this business, we are,

Sincerely Yours,

MODERN REAL ESTATE COMPANY

By Frank W. Smith

President

Upon receipt of such a notice, the owners, if they do not want to sell, will undoubtedly notify the broker to that effect. If no notice is given and the broker obtains a bonafide buyer and brings suit for a commission, proof of the letter will carry great weight as to employment.

Authority of person listing property

Where the property is listed with the broker by a person who is not the owner, the broker should make careful inquiry as to such person's authority to list the property. Often a son or daughter of foreign parents, or of persons of little business experience, will do the negotiating with the broker. Should he obtain a buyer upon the terms requested, he may find that the old folks have changed their minds and want to continue in the neighborhood where they have lived for many years. A suit for commission is futile unless the broker can prove that the child was the authorized agent of the parents. Agency is often a difficult burden for a claimant to establish, as the affirmative burden of proof rests upon the plaintiff broker. The broker would have a cause of action against the child, but a judgment would probably be uncollectible.

In the case of *Sylvester v. Johnson,* 110 Tenn. 392 (1903) the defendant's daughter, who generally conducted defendant's affairs, gave the broker the sole agency for the sale of a lot. He placed his "For Sale" sign on it. *This was done with defendant's knowledge, and without objections.* The daughter referred a prospective buyer to the broker, with the statement that the matter was entirely out of her hands, and there was no denial of the existence of the agency. The broker was held to be the defendant's sole agent and he could recover.

Where a broker obtains a listing from a husband and knows that the wife, who is also an owner, will not sign a contract of sale, so that the buyer cannot obtain good title, the broker cannot collect a commission, if he obtains a buyer. The marital relationship does not make one spouse the agent for the other, per se. It is important to obtain authority to sell from both parties: *Ginn v. MacAluso,* 310 P. 2d 1034 (N.M.

1957). Where husband and wife own property jointly and they are living separate and apart, a cautious broker will accept a listing signed only by *both* parties.

In the case of *Virginia M. Pepper, appellant, v. J. C. Chatel, appellee,* No. 30561, Municipal Court of Appeals for the District of Columbia (1962), the appellant had inherited certain property prior to her marriage, which she listed with the broker under her maiden name. The broker produced a buyer the next day and a contract was immediately executed by appellant under her maiden name. At settlement, however, appellant's husband refused to join in the conveyance and the sale was not consummated.

Appellant testified that at the time of signing, she was unaware that her husband had to join in the conveyance, and that the broker failed to so advise her, although he knew at the time that she was married. The broker testified that he did not learn of her marriage until after the contract was executed. The Court said:

> In the case before us appellant testified that she was unaware of the necessity of having her husband join in the conveyance. Nevertheless, we are of the opinion that the evidence supports the conclusion that the broker is entitled to his commission. It is clear from the finding that the broker did not learn appellant was married until after the contract was executed, and that he acted in good faith when he procured a purchaser acceptable to appellant.

In the case of *Cohen v. Garlick,* 344 Mass. 654 (1962), an auctioneer firm was hired by an owner of real estate to sell it at auction. The auctioneer announced in effect that "broker participation" would be "allowed" to a broker representing the successful bidder at the time of his purchase if the broker had registered his "client" with "us," and would be "paid by us after settlement." A broker for the successful bidder had duly registered him on a form stating that if "my client" were the successful bidder "I am to receive" such commission, "payable to me upon settlement." The Court held that the facts did not permit an inference that the owner of the property had authorized the auctioneer firm to bind him to pay such commission nor justify a ruling that the owner was liable to the successful bidder's broker therefor.

In dealing with an officer of a corporation owner, it is important that the broker ascertain whether the officer has the necessary authority to list the property with the broker. The affirmative burden of proof rests upon the broker and it may be difficult to discharge this burden: *Barker v. Great Southern Dev. Co., Inc.,* 249 Miss. 662 (1964). In the Florida case of *McCabe v. Howard,* 281 So. 2d 362 (Fla. App. 1973), the broker had shown the property to an officer of the corporation; the corporation president bought it in his own name. The broker had the affirmative burden to prove the president was acting as agent of the corporation, in order to recover.

Broker is a fiduciary—Duty of loyalty

If a real estate broker is to discharge creditably the duties which devolve upon his office, it is necessary that he have a knowledge of certain cardinal and fundamental principles of law which affect the everyday practice of his business. Real estate brokerage represents a combination of the principles of the law of principal and agent and the law of contracts. A real estate broker is an agent in the fullest sense of the word, in that he represents another from whom he has derived his authority. A broker occupies a position of trust and confidence toward his principal, and there are certain important duties that every agent owes to his principal. The first of these is that he must be loyal to his trust. This duty embraces substantially all the others. To be loyal to his trust, an agent cannot so exercise his duties as to garner a profit for himself at the expense of his principal. The courts have decided that in order for a broker to be loyal to his trust he must not sell to himself, purchase for himself, or purchase from himself. Where a property is listed with a broker for sale, it is the duty of the broker to determine a fair market value for that property and list it at that price. A broker will not be permitted to purchase a property which has been listed with him for sale where he feels that the list price is below the normal market price and purchases it either in his own name or in the name of another person in trust for himself, and then resells the property at a profit. The reason for this rule is interestingly given in a New Jersey case in which the Court said as follows:

> Owing to the greed and selfishness of human nature there must, in the great mass of transactions, be a strong antagonism between the interest of the seller and the buyer, and universal experience shows that the average man, when his interests conflict with his employer's, will not look upon his employer's interests as more important and entitled to more consideration than his own.

In the Missouri case of *Blakeley v. Bradley et al.,* 281 S.W. (2d) 835, (1955) the Supreme Court extended the principle that a broker should not purchase a property listed with him unless this fact is made known to his principal in advance, to include also the broker's employees and their near relatives. *Curroto v. Hammack,* 241 S.W. 2d 897 (Mo. 1951).

A vacant lot in Kansas City, Missouri, was listed with the broker and was sold a few days later to a "straw" party, for the real party in interest, a medical clinic. Three days later, the "straw" party deeded the property to the clinic. In a suit for commission, these facts being established, a recovery was denied: *King v. Pruitt,* 288 S.W. 2d 923 (1956).

Where a seller employs a broker to sell his property, he bargains for the disinterested skill, diligence and zeal of the broker for his (the seller) own exclusive benefit; *Yerkie v. Salisbury,* 287 A. 2d 498 (Md. 1972).

In construing loyalty, the courts have held that a real estate broker may not have a secret personal interest in the subject matter of his employment or make a secret profit or become the purchaser of his principal's property, indirectly, unless he discloses to his principal everything within his knowledge which might affect the principal's interests or influence his action in relation to the subject matter of employment: 8 Am. Jur. Secs. 89, 152.

In the case of *Cox v. Bryant,* 347 S.W. 2d 861 (Mo. 1961), a farm was listed with a broker at $40,000. Cox, a salesman, agreed to buy the farm at the listed price and agreements were signed to that effect. The agreements recognized the Jim Morris Sales Co. as the broker in the deal and the Bryants agreed to pay the broker a 5 per cent commission. The owners refused to go through with the deal and the salesman, Cox, brought suit for specific performance. At the trial of the case, it developed that Cox was to receive 60 per cent of the commission to be paid his broker in the transaction. This fact was fatal to Cox's cause of action. The Court said:

> In this case, before Cox could properly become the purchaser, it was his duty to terminate all agency relationships with the Bryants and thus place himself in the character and position of a purchaser.
>
> Among the facts that Cox should have disclosed to the Bryants was the fact that he was to receive a $1,200 commission for the sale to himself...

The case of *Nutter, appellant, v. Becktel,* 433 P. 2d 993 (Ariz. 1967), is of a similar vein.

The courts throughout this country have likewise adhered strictly to the principle of law that a broker is a fiduciary in the strictest sense of the word and owes a high degree of loyalty to his principal. In the case of *Cochrane v. Wittbold,* 102 N.W. 2d

459 (Mich. 1960), a saleswoman employed by a broker caused her parents to purchase for her land listed for sale with her employer. She collected a commission on the sale, without disclosing identity of true purchasers to seller, and almost immediately resold it to another for a profit. Such conduct, the Court held, was violative of the State Corporation and Securities Commissions rules, prohibiting a broker from purchasing property listed with him, without making full disclosure to listing owner. Such action was also contrary to public policy of the state.

It was held in *Simone v. McKee,* 298 P. 2d 667 (Cal. 1956) that a broker retained by owner to sell realty, owed owner affirmative duty to disclose second offer to owner, and failure to disclose was equivalent to affirmative representation that no other offer existed.

A broker is bound to disclose *all* offers, even though he, personally may believe the offer is too low and informs the prospect that it would be an insult to submit such an offer to the owner: *E.A. Strout Agency v. Wooster,* 118 Vt. 66 (1955).

In the case of *Haymes v. Rogers,* 319 P. 2d 339 (Ariz. 1950), the plaintiff, a broker, sued to recover a commission. From a verdict in favor of the broker, the owner appealed. After failing to sell the property at $9,500, the price originally listed with the broker, he stated to the purchaser his belief that the property could be bought for $8,500. After sale of property for $8,500, the broker sued to recover commission. The appellate court held, *as a matter of law,* plaintiff could not recover as there was a breach of fiduciary relationship. Mr. Justice Udall filed a vigorous dissenting opinion, in which he said:

> Will not the court's opinion be construed as holding that if a broker states to a purchaser or even indicates in any manner that property might be acquired for less than the listed price his right to a commission is thereby forfeited? If such be the declared law of this state, it will certainly give a wide avenue of escape to unscrupulous realty owners from paying what is justly owed to agents who have been the immediate and efficient cause of the sale of their property.
>
> It would be a most naive purchaser who would not know or assume that the owner of realty might sell for less than the original asking price.

A Louisiana case is squarely opposed: *Wolf v. Casamento,* 185 So. 537 (1939). Other cases are in harmony with the Arizona decision, although other circumstances entered into the case, as where broker acted in his own interest, or withheld information from his principal.

In the case of *Heard, et al. v. Miles,* 32 Tenn. 410 (1949), two real estate brokers claimed a commission. The owner recognized the efforts of Joyner-Heard Realty Co. as the procuring cause, but paid the money into court, since there were two claims. The unsuccessful broker, Marx & Bensdorf, Inc., had negotiated three leases on the subject property. This broker also had negotiated several forbearance agreements on an existing mortgage. The last lease contained a *new* clause that a commission would be paid "on any subsequent agreement to sell or exchange, made with or through Lessee." The property was sold to the tenant. No one ever called the owner's attention to the added clause. Although the court pointed out that the broker was not guilty of any fraud, intentional bad faith or unfairness, it could not recover because it was the *duty* of the broker here to disclose to its principal the provision in the renewal lease for the benefit of the broker. The principle of disclosure, the court said, "is one of prevention, not remedial justice, which operates however fair the transaction may have been—however free from every taint of moral wrong."

If the suit had been between the owner-lessor and the lessee, the *prime* parties to the lease, the owner would have been bound by the terms of the lease, whether she read it or understood it. But this was an action by an agent against his principal and the law is far more exacting.

A broker, with whom property is listed for sale, must reveal to his owner the fact that he is a part purchaser of such property. In real estate parlance, this is where the broker takes "a piece of the action." His failure, to do so, will defeat his claim for a commission in the sale. In the case of *Thompson v. Hoagland,* 242 A 2d 642 (N.J. 1968), the court said:

> The broker was and is looked upon as a fiduciary and is required to exercise fidelity, good faith, and primary devotion to the interests of his principal . . .
>
> It is a corollary of the principle discussed above that failure of the broker to inform the principal that the purchaser is an *alter ego* of the broker or a relative or partner renders the transaction voidable at the option of the principal.

Where the broker makes full disclosure of his interest, the law does not prevent him from purchasing property listed with him for sale and making a profit. In the case of *Sylvester v. Beck,* 406 Pa. 607 (1962), the plaintiff sued a real estate broker for damages alleging a breach of trust in the purchase and resale of real estate. The plaintiffs won a jury verdict in the amount of $9,000. The lower court entered judgment in favor of the broker, notwithstanding the verdict. (Judgment N.O.V.) The plaintiffs appealed. The defendant was authorized to sell the property for $15,000 and he displayed his broker's "for sale" sign on the property. Later the plaintiffs agreed to sell the property to the broker for $14,000. Within one month, the broker sold the property for $25,000. A few weeks later, both deals were closed on the same day. Subsequently, when the plaintiffs learned that the defendant had realized a huge profit in a quick resale of the property, they entered suit. The Court said:

> The fact that the defendant entered into a contract to resell the property twenty-seven days after he had contracted to purchase it and did not disclose this particular fact to the plaintiffs until after the final settlement does not, in itself, entitle the plaintiffs to damages. The agency having ended when the plaintiffs agreed to sell, the agent was under no obligation to furnish his former principal with the details of events that took place subsequent to the termination of their relationship of principal and agent.

Agent must obey instructions

The second fundamental duty that an agent owes to his principal is that he must obey the instructions that are given him by his principal. If a broker undertakes to judge that he may depart from the instructions of the owner, and that such variation would not be material, he does so at his own peril, and should any loss result by reason of the agent's deviation from his given instructions, he will be personally liable. For example, where a broker is engaged to sell property on a cash basis but instead accepts notes which are later declared invalid, the agent will be held personally responsible for the resulting loss. The owner, however, should be specific in his instructions.

A broker was held liable, in damages, to his principal, where he reduced the price of the property, in effecting an exchange deal without authorization from his owner: *Earle v. Lambert et al.,* 205 Cal. App. 2d 452 (1962).

A real estate broker is a *special* agent with *limited* authority. A broker is employed for the specific purpose of negotiating a sale. When he accomplishes that purpose, his authority as agent ends. He has no authority, once the agreements of sale are signed, to permit the purchaser to take possession of the premises prior to the closing of the deal, or to enter to make repairs or to decorate the premises. If the deal fails to be consummated through no fault of the buyer, the broker could be held personally responsible for the buyer's expense. The Iowa Supreme Court held that a real estate agent who contracted for a new well, and who was not authorized by actual owners to represent them in doing so, was liable for the cost of drilling the new well; *Cryder Well Co. v. Brown, et al.,* 136 N.W. 2d 519 (1965). If a buyer requests some special privilege or consideration, the request should be referred to the owner.

In the absence of a special agreement, it is the principal's judgment and not the agent's, that is to control: *Gallagher v. Jones,* 129 U.S. 195, 9 Ct. 335, 32 L Ed 658, 660; *Quinn v. Phipps,* 113 So. 419.

Where the agent does not exceed his authority, or where his representation to the buyer was only a repetition, in good faith, of a statement authorized by his principal, the agent is not personally liable to the buyer. *Peek v. Meadors,* 500 S.W. 2d 333 (Ark. 1973).

Agent must not be negligent

A broker should apprise the owner of all offers received, even though the offer to the broker may seem unworthy of acceptance: *E. A. Strout Realty Agency, Inc. v. Wooster,* 99 A 2d 689 (Vt. 1955). A regulation of the California Real Estate Commissioner provided, in substance, that "a check being held in an uncashed form must be specifically disclosed to the seller or offeree before he accepts the offer." A salesman received a deposit check of $5,000 on a five acre tract. The check remained in the office safe for four months while negotiations continued. Finally, the salesman began to lose faith in the buyer and discussed his fears with the broker. The buyer was asked to issue a new check or authorize presentation of the original check to the bank. He refused and it was learned that he had closed his account and that at no time did the buyer have funds on deposit to cover the check. The Commissioner ordered a suspension of the broker's license for negligence in the matter.

An attorney failing to disclose an encumbrance of record against a property which his principal is purchasing will be personally responsible to his principal for any damages sustained by the latter.

Where a broker accepts a note from the purchaser for a deposit, in lieu of cash funds, the broker would be liable to his principal, if the transaction was not consummated and the buyer failed to pay the note. Other situations which would be tantamount to negligence could be where the broker held a check for the earnest money for an unduly long period of time, at the request of a buyer, or where he accepted a post dated check, unless, in each of these situations, he advised his principal of the *facts* and the principal approved. It is common real estate practice for a broker to accept a check instead of cash, as an earnest money deposit. Where the broker deposits such check promptly and should the bank upon which it is drawn refuse payment because of insufficient funds, no liability can be visited upon the broker on that account. Likewise, if the buyer dies before the bank honors the check, the broker would not be personally responsible.

Act in person

Fourth, an agent must perform acts in person. He cannot delegate the authority which he has received from his principal to another. An owner employs a broker because of the confidence that he has in the ability and integrity of that particular person, and so a broker has no right to delegate his authority to another without consent or request of his principal, except as to matters which are of a purely ministerial or mechanical character, and where such delegation does not involve discretion, confidence, or skill.

In the California case of *Goodwin v. Glick,* 139 A C A Supp. 958 (1956), the defendant had given an exclusive listing to Petrol Realty Co. of San Pedro, upon a San Pedro Realty Board form, which provides that the listing broker might refer the listing to members of the Board. The property was sold by another member of the Board. The court said, inter alia,

> that the provision therein contained authorizing the agent named to refer the listing to the Realty Board, which, in turn, is authorized to refer it to its members, must be construed as an authorization to Petrol Realty Co. to appoint members of the Realty Board to whom it is referred as its agent (Petrol's) and not as agents of the defendant (owner).

In a Pennsylvania case, *Campbell v. Grange,* 23 D & C 2d 344 (1961), the court denied a recovery to a cooperating broker of a real estate board. The court held the selling broker was a subagent of the listing broker, and could not sue the owner, with whom the selling broker had no privity of contract.

However, circumstances may modify the rule.

In the South Dakota case of *Croughaw v. Gerlach,* 68 S.D. 93 (1941), a broker sued for commission. The defendant was a resident of Minnesota and owned a farm in Moody County, South Dakota. One, Dwight Lloyd, an attorney at Flandreau had authority to find a purchaser for the land and was acting as defendant's agent for that purpose. The plaintiff broker contacted the attorney and contends that Lloyd agreed that if the plaintiff found a purchaser, a commission would be paid to him. Later, the broker obtained a prospect and negotiations were conducted with Lloyd but no sale resulted. Later, the same prospect saw Lloyd and rented the property for one year with an option to purchase. He later bought it. The court held that Lloyd was not authorized to employ a subagent to sell the farm at the expense of the defendant. There was nothing to show that defendant had any knowledge that the plaintiff was the inducing cause of the sale, so that there was no ratification by the seller. A delegation of his authority may, however, be permitted by the usages of the trade. Where a nonresident owner of land employs an agent, also a nonresident, to sell his land, it will be presumed that such agent has authority to appoint a subagent in the locality where the land is located in order to facilitate the sale of such land. Where, however, an owner knows that a broker employed by him to sell land has secured the services of a subagent by promising the subagent half commission from the owner and the owner assents thereto either expressly or by remaining silent when it is his duty to object if he has any objection, the owner is directly liable to the subagent for his share of the commission.

Most larger real estate boards operate a multiple listing service (MLS). Under this system, each member receives all listings of property given to every other member of the multi-service. Under the rules of the multi-list association, the listing broker receives a percentage of the commission, if the listed property is sold by another broker member, and the selling broker receives a higher percentage of the commission. The multi-list association receives an over-riding small percentage of the commission to defray its expenses. A member of a MLS is not prohibited from cooperating on a sale with a non-member. A Pennsylvania case holds that a MLS cannot refuse a licensed broker admission to its multiple listing service. To do so is a violation of the Sherman anti-trust law, and constitutes an unlawful restraint of trade: *Collins v. Main Line Board of Realtors,* 304 A. 2d (1973). If this decision is followed in other states, it would not necessarily follow that real estate boards would lower their high standards of competency and ethics for *admission* to the board, even though a non-member could participate in their multi-list service.

Account for money and property

Lastly, an agent must account for money and property of his principal. Money and property entrusted to his care should, in all cases, be kept separate and apart from his own funds. If a broker carelessly mingles his employer's funds with his own, and the bank in which the funds are on deposit should fail, the broker will be personally responsible for the loss. Most state license laws provide the commingling of trust funds with a broker's personal funds shall constitute grounds for suspension or revocation of license. The account of the employer's funds should be kept as a trustee account, and so long as the agent exercises due care and caution in selecting a safe depository for such funds, he will not be personally responsible for any later loss. This matter is of particular importance because not infrequently a real estate broker, by agreement between the parties, retains the deposit money until such time as the deal is consummated. One trust account is sufficient for all trust funds coming into the broker's hands.

(The handling of deposit money will be discussed in greater detail in the following chapter on Agreements of Sale).

Signed agreement does not guarantee broker's commission

It has been the general rule of law that a broker is entitled to his commission when an agreement of sale is signed by the seller and the buyer, produced by the broker. The criteria are that the broker has procured a purchaser, ready, able and willing to buy.

In the Ohio case of *McGarry Realty Co., et al. v. McCrone, et al.,* 97 Ohio App. 543 (1954), the plaintiff negotiated the sale of certain property and the plaintiff knew that the funds necessary to purchase the property were to be provided by the buyers' relatives. The day following the execution of the agreements of sale, the purchasers called the plaintiff and told him they could not get the money. The Court said:

> We find no Ohio case where this question has been clearly presented, but no principle of law has been more clearly affirmed by the courts of this state than that an agent should not be permitted to benefit by his own failure to perform his full duty in representing his principal . . .

It would appear, then, in these circumstances that a broker should have the agreements of sale signed by the persons who will furnish the funds necessary for the purchase. After the deal is closed, such person (the relative) can transfer the property to the party, for whom the property is desired.

An *able* purchaser means a purchaser of substance, financially; that he was able to command the necessary money to close the transaction: *Sharp v. Long,* 283 So. 2d 567 (Fla. App. 1973); *Gopher State Bus. Opportunities, Inc. v. Stockman,* 121 N.W. 2d 613 (Minn. 1963).

In practically all states, a broker who receives an earnest money deposit is required to deposit such earnest money in a trust or escrow account until the transaction is consummated or terminated. Many brokers desire to hold the deposit money in order to guarantee payment of their commission. Where the broker receives a substantial portion of the consideration price, without authorization, and the seller defalcates, the broker would be liable to the buyer for his resulting loss.

A case of great importance, which rejects the premise that the owner is liable to the broker for a commission where the buyer defaults after signing a sales agreement is the case of *Ellsworth Dobbs, Inc. v. Johnson (owner) and Iarussi (buyer),* 50 N.J. 528 (1967). In joining the buyer as defendant, the broker charged the buyer with breach of an implied agreement to pay the commission if he failed to complete the purchase and thus deprived the broker of commission from the seller. The trial judge held, as a matter of law, that the broker's commission vested upon execution of the contract of sale, and the commission was not dependent upon the closing of title. The jury found for the broker in the amount of $15,000 against the owner. In reversing the lower court, the Supreme Court said:

> The present New Jersey rule as exemplified by the cases cited is deficient as an instrument of justice. It permits a broker to satisfy his obligation to the owner simply by tendering a human being who is physically and mentally capable of agreeing to buy the property on mutually satisfactory terms, so long as the owner enters into a contract with such person. The implication of the rule is that the owner has the burden of satisfying himself as to the prospective purchaser's ability, financial or otherwise, to complete the transaction; he cannot rely at all on the fact that the purchaser was produced in good faith by the broker as a person willing and able to buy the property. . . . If it later appears that the purchaser is financially not able to close the title, or even that he never did have the means to do so, the owner must pay the broker his commission so long as he acted in good faith. Such a rule, considered in the context of the real relationship between broker and owner, empties the word "able" of substantially all of its significant content and imposes an unjust burden on vendors of property. . . . Thus, when the broker produces his customer, it is only reasonable to hold that the owner may accept him without being obliged to make an independent inquiry into his financial capacity. That right ought not to be taken away from him, nor should he be estopped to assert it, simply because he "accepted" the buyer. . . . In a practical world, the true test of a willing buyer is not met when he signs an agreement to purchase; it is demonstrated at the time of closing of title, and if he unjustifiably refuses or is unable financially to perform *then,* the broker has not produced a willing buyer.

It should be noted that when it became clear to the seller that there was no hope of the buyers completing the sale, because they could not finance the purchase, the parties exchanged mutual releases, which the court held, under the facts present, did not, and was not intended to amount to the equivalent of performance of the contract. In holding the buyer responsible to the broker, the court said:

> This court has held that when a prospective buyer solicits a broker to find or to show him property which he might be interested in buying, and the broker finds property satisfactory to him which the owner agrees to sell at the price offered, and the buyer knows the broker will earn commission for the sale from the owner, the law will imply a promise on the part of the buyer to complete the transaction with the owner. If he fails or refuses to do so without valid reason, and thus prevents the broker from earning the commission from the owner, he becomes liable to the broker for breach of the implied promise. The damages chargeable to him will be measured by the amount of commission the broker would have earned from the owner.

This New Jersey case has been cited with approval in *Staab v. Messier,* 264 A. 2d 790 (Vt. 1970) in the east and on the west coast in the case of *Brown v. Grimm,* 481 P. 2d 63 (Or. 1971), where the court said: "The leading case in the United States adopting this view is *Ellsworth Dobbs, Inc. v. Johnson,* 50 N.J. 528 (1967)."

Forfeiture of deposit money—when commission is payable

Many listing contracts in current use provide: "A deposit made if forfeited by the buyer, shall first apply to the broker's commission; the balance, if any, shall belong to the owner."

While a broker is certainly entitled to a return for his efforts good conscience requires that it shall not be at the expense of an innocent principal. Suppose the clause in question is used and the broker obtains a purchaser for a property at $10,000, and collects a deposit of $500. Later, the buyer defaults and forfeits the deposit money. Should the broker be permitted to retain the *entire* deposit as commission on the ground that the owner has a legal right to sue the defaulting buyer, even though litigation may prove futile? It is scarcely ethical that the broker should keep all the money paid on account of the purchase of the owner's property, and the latter required to pursue litigation, entailing additional expense of costs and attorney's fees, for recovery of a judgment which may be uncollectible. In addition, the property may be "tied up" for a considerable period of time from the date when the agreements were signed. Fair dealing requires that the down payment be divided equally between broker and owner, up to an amount where the broker receives full payment of his commission. A *common* provision used in the agreement of sale relative to the earnest money reads:

> Should the buyer fail to make settlement, as herein provided, the sum or sums paid on account of the purchase price, at the option of the seller, may be retained by the seller, either on account of the purchase price, the resale price, or as liquidated damages. In the latter case, the contract shall become null and void. In the latter event, all monies paid on account shall be divided equally between the seller and the broker, but in no event shall the sum paid to the broker be in excess of the amount of commission due him.

Care must be exercised, however, even with respect to the use of the above clause. In *Kulp Real Estate v. Rudolph Favoretto et ux.,* 127 316 A. 2d 71 (N.J. 1974), the Court, following the landmark decision of the Dobbs case cited earlier, found such a clause in a listing agreement unenforceable and void as against public policy. The Court found that there was "... a substantial inequality of bargaining position between the broker and vendors," because the broker was an experienced firm and the vendors, who had no prior real estate experience, signed a printed standardized form of brokerage agreement without benefit of counsel. While this holding may not be followed widely in other jurisdictions, it may be wise when employing such a clause to make sure that the client understands it before he signs the listing agreement.

In *Hersh v. Kelman,* 104 N.E. 2d 35 (1951), plaintiff obtained a purchaser and a $200 deposit on an "open listing." Before the owner would sign the agreement, he had the broker write into the agreement "commission to be paid when deal is consummated." The buyer moved to Detroit and defaulted. The seller sold the property through another broker and paid a commission. The first broker sued for a commission. The lower court decided in favor of the broker. The appellate court reversed. The Court said:

> Failure of the prospective purchasers to consummate the deal, without any fault on the part of the seller, relieved the seller completely under the special terms of the contract from liability for the payment of any commission.

In the case of *Jones v. Palace Realty Co.,* 226 N.C. 303 (1946), the North Carolina Supreme Court held that it was the event of closing the deal and not the date of its expected or contemplated happening that made the promise to pay enforceable. In the case of *Bechtel Properties, Inc. v. Blanken,* 299 F. 2d 928 (D.C. 1962), the agreement provided that "if the purchaser shall fail to make full settlement, the deposit herein provided for may be forfeited at the option of the seller. ... " The agreement further provided that:

> The entire deposit shall be held by Sam Blanken & Co. until settlement hereunder is made or until the deposit is forfeited. ...

The broker had obtained a purchaser, who had shown himself ready, able and willing to perform. Certain matters arose which could not be resolved and the lower court said: "Apparently the transaction was just abandoned by the parties when the property was resold by the defendant." The appellate court said:

> In view of the fact that the contract was not settled, through no fault of the agent, and apparently by mutual agreement of the seller and the purchaser (or, if not by mutual agreement, at least with the acquiescence of the seller), the commission agreement could not be performed in accordance with its terms. This is not to say, however, that the agent is to be deprived by that reason, of his commission, which was in the total amount of $7,000.

In the New Mexico case of *Stewart Realty v. Brock,* 60 N.M. 216 (1955), the broker had a listing of a ranch at $85,000, the broker's commission was to be 5 per cent. The broker obtained a buyer at that price, who paid $8,500, as a deposit. The buyer wanted to withdraw from the deal. The seller agreed, if the buyer would pay an additional $1,500. The buyer paid the $1,500. The broker claimed a commission of $4,250. The owner offered 5 per cent of the $8,500 deposit, or $425. Upon suit, the court allowed the full amount of the commission claimed.

Sometimes, in an instalment purchase contract, the broker receives his commission as the instalments are paid. In the case of *Hussey v. Stephens,* 194 S.E. 2d 243 (S.C. 1973), the broker negotiated the sale of a motel for the sellers, who obtained a purchase money mortgage for $335,000, payable in annual instalments of $25,000, in three payments of $8,333.33 each. The broker's commission was $10,000, with $2,000 paid at the time of the sale and the balance at the rate of $727.27, beginning September 1, 1969, each time a $25,000 payment was made. The buyer made two annual payments, but on April 30, 1971, reconveyed the motel to the sellers for $30,000 and cancellation of the mortgage. The broker then sued for the balance of the commission. The Supreme Court held that the reconveyance of the property to the sellers, did not constitute an acceleration of the commission upon satisfaction of the mortgage and reversed the lower court's award of commission.

A situation could arise where, under such an instalment contract, the contract is rescinded before maturity, and in consideration of the return of the property, the seller foregoes the remaining payments. As a cautionary measure, the listing agreement should anticipate this possibility and the broker should protect himself, accordingly: *Larkins v. Richardson,* 502 P. 2d 1156 (Ore. 1972).

Rate of commission

If, in the contract of employment, nothing is said in regard to the rate of commission, then the broker is entitled to a reasonable rate of compensation, this rate being the one used generally in the business in the particular locality in which the property is situated. It is assumed here, of course, that the broker is licensed. Since an owner entrusts his property for sale to a person whose ordinary business is to sell real estate on a commission basis, the law presumes, in the absence of any agreement to the contrary, that commission or compensation is to be paid for the services rendered. The rate is not fixed by any statute, but is a matter of custom or trade usage. The broker can recover on a "quantum meruit" (what he deserves) basis, or what his services are worth. In order to avoid any controversy or future litigation, it is always desirable that the rate of compensation should be agreed upon in advance, at the time of the employment. There is no provision in any license law regulating or attempting to regulate the rate of commission to be charged. It is one of voluntary agreement between the parties.

The United States Department of Justice instituted suits against a number of metropolitan real estate boards alleging that board rules, fixing or recommending rates of commissions, were violative of the Sherman anti-trust law. Consent degrees have been entered in a number of these suits, whereby the boards agreed to discontinue the practice. Members are free to "negotiate" the amount of commissions with owners. In practice, the prevailing rates of commission in the area have been followed.

An agreement of sale recited that the owner agrees to pay the broker a commission of $9,000, pursuant to a listing agreement. In a suit, where the purchaser failed to consummate the deal, the trial judge instructed the jury that it was their duty "to determine what amount of money was fair and reasonable to recompense her for her services." The jury awarded $1,000. The Supreme Court overruled the verdict and held that the plaintiff was entitled to $9,000. *Gaynor v. Laverdure,* 291 N.E. 2d 617 (Mass. 1973).

In states where a written listing is required by statute, the listing must state the amount of the commission agreed to be paid to the broker. It cannot be supplied later by an oral promise. *Gray v. Kohlhase and Lines,* 502 P. 2d 169 (Ariz. 1973). This is the general rule, followed in Idaho, New Mexico, Oregon and Texas. The minority rule followed in California is to the effect that the amount of commission may be shown by parol where there is a sufficient memorandum to show the *fact* of employment: *Beazell v. Schrader,* 381 P. 2d 390 (Cal. 1963).

Sale of stock in lieu of deed

Sometimes, a broker, employed to sell real estate of a corporation, will procure a purchaser, who agrees to accept a transfer of stock of the corporation, representing the purchase price for the property, instead of a deed. The broker is, nevertheless, entitled to a commission, despite the fact that there is a transfer of personal property, rather than conveyance of real estate. Where a corporation sells corporate stock, representing the value of the real estate sold through a broker, and said stock is transferred to the buyer, the broker is entitled to his commission on the sale of the shares of stock: *Heymann v. Electric Service Mfg. Co., Inc.,* 194 A. 2d 429 (Pa. 1963).

Authorization to sell in management contract

In the case of *Adams and Leonard, Realtors, v. Wheeler,* 493 P. 2d 436 (Okla. 1972), the plaintiffs had Property Management Agreement for a definite period of time. It contained the provision:

> The agent shall have the sole exclusive right to sell and offer for sale the property covered herein, if the property is sold or offered for sale during the terms of this agreement.

The owner sold the property himself while the agreement was in force. The plaintiff did not have anything to do with the sale. The court said:

> The broker performed no services concerning the sale of the property. Until he had performed some of such services the contract was unilateral. The agreement could not be construed as constituting a completed and enforceable 'right to sell' real estate listing contract. . . . We see no reason why a valid and enforceable 'exclusive right to sell' contract could not be incorporated in a property management agreement, if the 'exclusive right to sell' contractual provisions are complete concerning their rights and obligations if the property is offered for sale or sold. However, if the 'exclusive right to sell' provisions are incomplete and unenforceable, an action for damages will not lie for breach of the unenforceable contract.

The Supreme Court affirmed the lower court's denial of a commission.

Minimum net sale price

Where the owner has fixed a minimum net price, below which the agent may not sell the property, the question frequently arises as to whether or not the broker is entitled to any excess realized over and above the net price. In other words, assume that an owner has left property for sale with a broker, with the understanding that the property is not to be sold for less than $10,000, and the broker negotiates a sale at a price of $12,000. The question arises as to the distribution of the $2,000 excess. It must be remembered here that the first duty that an agent owes to his principal is that he must do everything possible to assert and protect his principal's interest; and so the courts have held that under the circumstances which have just been outlined, the $2,000 belongs to the owner. This is so unless it is *expressly* stipulated that the broker is to retain the excess as his commission.[1] While net listings are used frequently, they are not looked upon with favor in good real estate circles. Since the property belongs to the owner, he should receive the highest possible price for it and the broker should look to his compensation upon a basis commensurate with his services. There is a creed that "labor is worthy of its hire." A broker who receives $1,200 commission (6%) upon a $20,000 sale has, usually, earned a fair return for his services. In a number of areas, consonant with inflation, the going rate of commission is 7 per cent.

Where a property is listed with a broker, upon a net listing basis of $30,000 and the broker obtains an offer of $37,500, it seems unconscionable that the broker will earn 25 per cent on the deal. Net listings, further, are conducive to fraud in that a broker is often sorely tempted to employ a straw purchaser and then resell the property at a handsome profit. Alabama, British Columbia, California, Georgia, Maryland, Michigan, Ontario, Tennessee, and Utah prohibit or regulate net listings.

In order for a broker to recover commission under an express contract requiring a net price to the owner, he must procure a purchaser at a price sufficiently in excess of the net price to cover commissions. An owner listed with a broker for sale certain real estate, which consisted of 13 houses. The owner wrote the broker: "I think you might proceed and sell the entire 13 houses separately for $50,000 net cash to me. Your commission is 3% to come out of the last sale made." The houses were sold for the aggregate of $50,000. The owner refused to pay a commission and the broker sued for $1,500. The broker could not collect, because, as the Court stated:[2]

> Where one states to a broker that he will sell land for a certain sum 'net' to him, the broker, on procuring a purchaser, is entitled to no commission unless the sum received exceeds the 'net' price, the word 'net' meaning that which remains after deducting all charges and outlay. We see no weakening of the effect of the word 'net' by the words used in the communication which the prospective vendor sent to the broker, quoted above, that the commission was to come out of the last sale made. The agreement was in writing and there is nothing in the case which would justify a departure from the evident purpose of the agreement that the vendor was to get $50,000 net cash, clear and above any commissions.

In the case of *Quality Home Builders v. Harrick,* 173 S.E. 2d 846 (Va. 1970), an owner listed property for sale with a broker for $455,000 *net,* sale was ultimately consummated for $455,000 but the defendant refused to pay any commission to the plaintiff broker. The court held that there was a special contract between the broker and owner predicated upon the consummation by the broker of a sale at the net price named. Since no sum was received over and above the net price designated, the broker could not recover for his efforts. In the case of *Nelson v. Rosenblum Co.,* 182 N.W. 2d 666 (Minn. 1970), property was listed with a broker at $36,000 *net* and the broker obtained a purchaser who entered into a legally enforceable purchase agree-

---

[1] Nelson et al v. Rosenblum Inc. 182 N.W. 2d 666 (Minn. 1970).

[2] Fink v. Doughtery, 90 Pa. Super. 443 (1927).

ment for the price of $37,500. Earnest money was paid by the purchasers to the defendant. Before date of settlement, the purchasers advised the broker that they had taken employment in Florida and they would default upon the contract and forfeit the earnest money. The owner demanded the entire deposit sum of $2,500. The court noted that the parties did not condition payment of the commission upon actual consummation of the purchase agreement. It held that without any fraud, concealment or other improper practice on the part of the broker, the principal accepts the person presented and enters into a binding and enforceable contract with the purchaser, the commission is fully earned.

Employment of several brokers

The rule of law is that two or more brokers possess concurrent authority to sell, and that the sale of the property by one of them terminates the agencies of the others by removing the subject matter of the contract. It is advisable for an owner listing a property for sale with a number of real estate brokers to inform each broker that the property has been listed for sale with other concerns, and that upon the sale of the property by one, the employment of the others shall automatically cease. In Virginia, the law is that if two or more brokers, knowing of one another's employment, are employed to sell the same land, the owner, if he shows no favoritism, may sell to the purchaser who is first produced and the broker producing such purchaser is the one entitled to commission.[3]

A serious difficulty, where a property has been listed with a number of real estate offices, is that frequently a single purchaser is the prospect of a number of brokers. When a sale results in that purchaser, which broker is entitled to the commission? The test for recovery is determining which broker was the efficient and procuring cause of the sale. It is most important, then, for a broker, in order to protect his rights to a commission, that he acquaint the owner with the identity of every prospect to whom he submits the property. One good-sized commission, as a result of such notice, will adequately compensate a broker for the detail work entailed. It is not to be inferred that a broker may merely submit the name of a prospect and then sit idly by and await the fortuitous circumstance of a sale ultimately occurring. He cannot be guilty of abandonment and then claim compensation because a sale is made to his original prospect. He must activate the sale although the mere introduction of the principals may suffice, and if that sets in motion a series of events which culminate in a sale, a commission is earned. The rule is well stated by the West Virginia Court[4] to be: "If a broker sets in motion machinery by which sale is made, which without break in its continuity, was procuring cause of sale, he is entitled to commission, although he does not conduct *all* negotiations." In the case of *Dobson v. Wolf,* 54 N.W. 2d 469 (South Dakota, 1952) the Court said:

> If a broker does not have the exclusive sale of property, he does not become entitled to a commission merely by showing the property to the person who eventually buys it, but a personal introduction of the purchaser to the owner is not essential and it is sufficient if, through the efforts of the broker, the parties are brought into communication with each other. *It is not enough that a broker's efforts may have contributed to the negotiations resulting in the Sale.* "If this were the rule," says the court in *Carney v. John Hancock Oil Co.,* 187 Minnesota 293, "no owner desiring to sell could safely employ more than one broker, for in the event of each of several being able to convince a jury that he had contributed anything to a sale, the principal

[3] Cannon v. Bates, 115 Va. 711

[4] Averill v. Hart & O'Farrell, 101 W.V. 411 (1926).

might be held for as many commissions as there were brokers employed. The law contemplates no such absurdity."

To the same effect is *Vreeland v. Vetterlein,* 33 New Jersey 247 (1869), in which it is said:

> Where the property is openly put in the hands of more than one broker, each of such agents is aware that he is subject to the arts and chances of competition. If he finds a person who is likely to buy, and quits him without having effected a sale, he is aware that he runs the risk of such persons falling under the influence of his competitor—and in such case, he may lose his labor. This is a part of the inevitable risk of the business he has undertaken.

Where claims for commission have been advanced by several brokers, who claim to have produced the same purchaser for the owner's property, an owner should hesitate in voluntarily paying such commissions. There have been many instances where an owner has voluntarily paid a commission to one broker, and a court and jury have subsequently decided that the sale resulted from the efforts of a second broker, so that the owner was compelled to pay a second commission. Where the owner is in doubt regarding which broker's effort produced the sale, he should pay the amount of commission into court and there have the matter settled by a court of law without any further liability to himself.

In the case of *Julius Heller Realty Co. v. Jefferson Gravoco Bank,* 144 S.W. 2d 174, 176 (Mo. 1940), the Court succinctly quoted the law as follows:

> In other words in these cases where an owner appoints more than one broker to procure a purchaser for his property, the rule is to the effect that he "who sows the seed and tills the crop is entitled to reap the harvest—rather than one who volunteers to assist in tilling a crop, the seed for which he has not sown." The question of whether the plaintiff was procuring cause of the sale was for the jury to determine. Verdict in favor of owner affirmed.

Where a broker fails to acquaint the owner with the identity of his prospect, the owner may not know that the prospect is also the prospect of another broker at the same time. It is wise to keep the owner informed of negotiations as they proceed. Where this is done, and a sale results, the owner, no doubt, will feel that the commission paid, was well earned. It cannot be emphasized too strongly, that a broker should acquaint the owner with the identity of *every* prospect, to whom the property is submitted. One good-sized commission, as a result of such notice, will adequately compensate a broker for the detail work entailed: *Tucker v. Green,* 96 Ariz. 371 (1964). Such a notice may be, as follows:

SLOAN and SLOAN, Realtors
Real Estate and Insurance
1294 State Street
Philadelphia, Pa.

261-3700 Date *July 19, 1974*

Mr. *and Mrs. James L. Stone*
Street *3107 Waldheim Drive, Ambler, Pa.*

Please be advised that we have recently submitted to *Don Cook, Mrs. Ann Bennett, and Lawrence Clifford* your property listed with this office, located at *864 Main Street, Narberth, Pa.*

Price quoted *$18,500.* We will endeavor to interest this prospect further. If they return to examine same, or call by phone, please notify us at once, as your cooperation will greatly assist in the sale of your property.

SLOAN and SLOAN
By *Andrew Sloan* Salesman

NOTE: — If any change has taken place since your property has been listed with this office, we would appreciate word from you at once.

In the case of *Watts v. Barker,* 275 Ky. 411 (1938), the Court said that where a property has been listed for sale with more than one broker, the owner is liable for only one commission, even if more than one broker has dealings with the ultimate purchaser; the broker who succeeds in bringing the seller and buyer together and induces them to enter into the contract is the one who earns the commission, regardless of which broker first introduced seller and purchaser. The Court further stated that the seller would not be liable to brokers with whom she had listed real estate, if trade was closed through another broker with whom she had also listed realty and the owner had not been advised by a first broker that the purchaser was her customer, until after the sale had been completed.

Of course, all parties must act in good faith. A purchaser cannot accept the services of a broker, and when the deal is imminent, arbitrarily or capriciously dismiss the broker and refuse to do business with him. Nor can he circumvent the broker by using a third person as the purchaser for him. In *Orr v. Woolfolk,* 250 Ky. 279 (1933), the Court said, "Where a broker's prospect interests another who becomes the eventual purchaser of property which the owner had listed with broker for sale, the broker is entitled to his commission." This does not mean that where a broker negotiates the sale of a property in a subdivision to a purchaser and the buyer interests a friend in an adjoining house, who buys directly from the owner, that the broker is entitled to a commission on the second sale.

In *Beougher v. Clark,* 81 Kan. 250 (1909), the Court has stated the principle of law as follows:

> The law will not permit one broker who has been entrusted with the sale of land and is working with a customer whom he has found, to be deprived of his commission by another agent stepping in and selling the land to the customer so found by the first broker. The utmost good faith must be exercised between the principal and the broker.

To the same effect is *Greshman v. Lee,* 152 Ga. 829 (1921).

Must be efficient and procuring cause of sale

To determine which of several brokers is entitled to the commission, where each claims to have found the same purchaser, is often a problem of no little difficulty. Where all the brokers are employed independently, at least, it would seem that the ordinary rule applicable to the case of the employment of a single broker would apply; that is, that the broker who was the efficient procuring cause of the sale is entitled to the commission and that this right cannot be affected because the principal in person, or by another agent, takes into his own hands and completes the transaction which the broker has inaugurated.

Where two or more brokers are employed, there is no implied contract to pay more than one commission, and it therefore becomes necessary to lay down a rule for determining which one of different possible claimants is entitled to be paid. Where several brokers have each endeavored to bring about a sale which is finally consummated, it may happen that each has contributed something without which the result would not have been reached. One may have found the customer, who otherwise would not have been found, and yet the customer may refuse to conclude the bargain through his agency; and another broker may succeed where the first has failed. In such a case, in the absence of any express contract, the one only is entitled to a commission who can show that his services were the really effective means of bringing about the sale, or "the predominating efficient cause."

Where several brokers are openly and avowedly employed so that each can be said to have undertaken the employment on that basis, it is held in many cases that the entire duty of the principal is performed by remaining neutral between them and that he has a right to sell to the buyer who is first produced by any of them without being called upon to decide which of the several brokers was the primary cause of the sale.

Other cases state the rule somewhat less broadly, and it is everywhere agreed that in order to be entitled to the benefit of it the principal must in fact have remained neutral, and he certainly must not knowingly permit, much less aid in or connive at, the appropriation by one man of the rewards of what was really the result of another man's effort. However, payment of a commission to one broker by an owner is not admissible as evidence in a suit by a second broker for a commission claimed in the sale to the same prospect.[5]

The general rule of law throughout the country is well stated in the case of *Trent Trust Co. v. Mac Farlane,* 21 Hawaii 435 (1913), where the Court held that a broker is not entitled to a commission on a sale effected through another broker, even though a purchaser was introduced by the first broker or even though the sale may be aided by the first broker's previous efforts, provided the owner acts in good faith.

If one of several brokers gives notice to his principal that he cannot effect a sale, he will not be entitled to commissions because another broker, who is informed by the first that the property is for sale, succeeds in finding a purchaser. So, if two brokers are employed, and one of them enters into negotiations with a purchaser, which fail and are abandoned, he will not be entitled to commissions because another broker subsequently succeeds, wholly through his own efforts, in making a sale to the same person and upon substantially the same terms as those proposed by the first broker. The same result will follow where one broker has not been able within a reasonable time to effect a sale, and another broker afterwards succeeds in selling to a purchaser first approached by the former broker. The principal, acting in good faith, and with no intention of defeating the broker's claim, may revoke his authority, while his efforts are yet unsuccessful, even though the principal in person or through another broker subsequently sells to a purchaser to whom the first broker endeavored to sell. It has been repeatedly said that the broker must be the *efficient and procuring* cause of the sale, in order to be entitled to a commission. "It is the broker who shakes the tree and not the one who runs up and gathers the apples, who is entitled to the commission." *Nichols v. Pendley,* 331 S.W. 2d 675 (Mo. 1960). *Brennan v. Roach,* 47 Mo. App. 290 (1891).

A number of courts have pronounced the rule that sale of the property by one of the brokers *terminates the authority of the brokers* immediately, *although they have no actual notice of the sale: Hunt v. Judd,* 225 Ill. App. 395 (1922); *Kennedy v. Vance,* 201 Okla. 80 (1949). *Dindo v. Cappelleti,* 77 A. 2d 840 (Vt. 1951).

Owner sells below listed price

If a broker or salesman brings to the owner, a purchaser, who is willing and able to buy at a price below the listed price, the commission is earned if the owner actually

[5] Walker v. Randall, 85 Pa. Super. 443 (1925)

sells the property to that prospect, or is willing to sell to that buyer: *Bass Investment Co. v. Banner Realty, Inc.* 436 P. 2d 894 (Ariz. 1968).

The same rule of law applies if the property is sold by the owner at a higher price than the listing price given to the broker, to a prospect procured by the broker.

Abandonment of effort

Clearly, if one broker abandons his efforts, he cannot later claim a commission if a sale is made by the owner, or through another broker, to his original prospect. For example:

Broker "A" had an open listing on a property of $30,000.00. He showed it to a prospect, Mrs. White, who was interested but did not make up her mind to buy it. Broker "B" showed Mrs. White various properties. He did not show the subject property, but mentioned it to her. She said she had already seen it through Broker "A." About two weeks later she called Broker "A" and stated that she wanted to go through the house again with her husband but he told her it was too late—"the house is sold." A few days later she called Broker "B" and when she mentioned that the house she was interested in was sold, he expressed surprise because he had had no notice of cancellation of the listing. He called the owner, who referred him to her attorney. The attorney told Broker "B" that there was a signed agreement from a buyer, but it was subject to the buyer's selling his present home and that he was going to advise his client, the owner, not to accept the deal, whereupon, the owner accepted the deal with Mrs. White. Now, Broker "A" is claiming a commission, as is also Broker "B." Here, "A" is not entitled to any commission as there was an abandonment of negotiations when "A" told Mrs. White, "the house is sold, you are too late," and did nothing more.

In the case of *Mammen v. Snodgrass,* 13 Ill. App. 2d 538 (1957), the court said:

> The law is well settled in this state that the fact that the seller consummates a sale or that it is made upon different terms from those proposed to the broker, does not necessarily deprive the broker of compensation. If he is the efficient procuring cause of the transaction, he is entitled to his commission.
>
> But that a sale is finally brought about by the efforts of the principal with a person with whom the broker had previously negotiated without success, does not furnish a basis for commission, if it appears that the broker has for a long time ceased negotiations with the purchaser and abandoned the property. A time must necessarily arrive after a prospective purchaser has declined to purchase when the owner may treat the negotiation at an end and begin an entirely new and independent solicitation....

In the North Carolina case of *Jackson v. Northwestern Life Insurance Co.,* 133 F.2d 111 (1943), the Court held that a broker was not entitled to a commission where he had failed to effect an agreement and abandoned his efforts, even though he may have introduced to each other parties who otherwise would never have met. The plaintiff broker did nothing for fourteen months and the deal was closed through another broker. Whether there has been an abandonment of effort, so as to deprive a broker of a claimed commission, when a sale takes place to a prospect whom the broker contacted, is a question of fact, rather than of law. Determination is within the purview of the jury.

Introducing purchaser to owner may be sufficient

Mere introduction of the purchaser to the owner by the broker may be sufficient performance of the broker's contract of employment with the owner, depending, of course, upon the facts in the particular case. If negotiations are taken up from the point of introduction by the buyer and seller without the aid or intervention of the broker and a sale results, the broker is entitled to his commission. The question is: "Did the broker set in motion a series of circumstances, which, without interruption, culminated in a sale?" If the introduction did that, the broker is considered the efficient and procuring cause of the sale, and he can recover.

It is not a question of how much work a broker did in a particular transaction, but, rather, how effective his work was. If he did the "spade work," by obtaining a prospective purchaser, the owner cannot then take the purchaser, deal with him directly, and turn the broker out of doors.

Nor can the owner take the matter into his own hands and complete the sale, either above or below the listing price, and then refuse to pay a commission.

The general rule of law is that, where there has been no direct communication between the broker and the purchaser, it must be shown affirmatively that the latter was induced to enter into the negotiations which resulted in the purchase through the means employed by the broker for that purpose. If the broker employed other persons to aid him, whether under pay or not, or if he put up maps, signs, notices, or otherwise advertised the property, and if by means of these measures, a person was induced to open negotiations with the owner which resulted in his buying the property, the sale may be said to have been effected through the broker's instrumentality. But it must be made to appear that what the broker did was the immediate and efficient cause of such negotiations. If the broker merely talked about the property with different persons and one of them, on his own accord and not in behalf of the broker, mentioned to another that the property was for sale and such last mentioned person thereupon looked into the matter and finally became the purchaser, the agency of the broker in inducing the sale was not sufficiently direct to entitle him to a commission: *Reap Realty Co. v. Hadlock,* 181 N.E. 2d 732 (Ohio 1961).

It is not a question of how much a broker did but rather, how effective was what he did, in promoting the sale.

Where a broker posts a "for sale" sign on a property listed with him for sale, and a prospect looks up the identity of the owner in the county offices, and then deals with the owner directly, ignoring the broker, it may be claimed that the broker was the instrumentality by which the sale was made, and that he has a case in court for his commission. Proof may be difficult to establish in such a borderline situation.

In the case of *Essres Realty & Insurance Inc. v. Zeif,* 512 P. 2d 650 (Colo. App. 1973), the court held that where a broker opens negotiations but fails to bring buyer and seller together, and later, the owner sells to the same buyer without any further effort on the part of the broker, there can be no recovery of commission.

A broker must produce a buyer while the premises are still on the market. In terminating employment an owner must act in good faith. Where an owner gives a second broker an exclusive listing agency, while an open listing is still in existence, the open listing given to a broker earlier is not automatically terminated. The owner must give notice of cancellation of employment to the first broker. A broker is not entitled to compensation for merely procuring a customer to take an option which has never been exercised.

To avoid any presumption that the employment of the broker is to continue until a sale is effected, the owner should take some action to notify the broker that his employment is terminated.

Broker should respect another broker's listing

Where one broker has an exclusive right to sell listing, other brokers should respect such listing and refrain from negotiating with the owner or a prospect during the exclusive period. Failure to do so may result in serious consequences. Several license laws provide it ground for suspension or revocation of license if a licensee is found guilty of "having negotiated the sale, exchange, or lease of any real property directly with an owner or lessor knowing that such owner or lessor had a written outstanding contract granting exclusive agency in connection with another real estate broker": *O'Horo v. Ohio Real Estate Commission,* 4 Ohio App. 2d 75 (1964). It follows that if a real estate licensee is to be accepted by the *public* as a professional, it is only reasonable and to be expected that such licensee will maintain a high standard of ethics towards his fellow licensees, as well as the public.

Duration of employment

Where no time is fixed for the duration of a broker's employment, either party, acting in good faith, may terminate the contract at will. Ordinarily, the contract continues for a reasonable time. What is a reasonable time depends upon the circumstances in the particular case.[6] In the matter of the sale of the ordinary dwelling house, a few months might be said to be a reasonable time within which the broker should procure a customer. Where a broker was put in charge of selling 250 lots under an agreement which specified no particular duration, and the broker had sold only two lots in four months, it was held that he had demonstrated his inability to perform even though he was entitled to a reasonable time within which to do so. For that reason the owner was justified in terminating the contract by notice to the broker.

A previous sale of the property revokes the agent's authority, and no notice to the broker of the sale is necessary.

In the case of *Hunt v. Judd* 225 Ill. App. 395, the Court held that where several real estate brokers are employed to sell a property, sale of the property by one of the brokers terminates authority of the others at once, although they have no actual notice of the sale. To the same effect is *Kennedy, et al. v. Vance,* 201 Okla. 80 (1949), in which the Court said:

> Since the plaintiffs were not given an exclusive right to sell, they assumed the risk of knowing that the land might be sold by the owner or another agent before they could find a purchaser, ready, able and willing to buy on the terms specified and that such a sale would ipso facto revoke their agency, *Mecham on Agency* (Second Edition) Page 625.

Owner's right to terminate agency

Where a broker is employed to sell lands for his principal and there is no stipulation in the contract as to the duration of the broker's employment, the courts have held that the principal may terminate the agency at any time and discharge the broker, subject to the rule, however, that the purpose of the revocation cannot be to deprive the broker of an earned commission. In other words, it must be in good faith. It may be in writing, oral, or implied from the circumstances. An agency once terminated is not revived by subsequent acts.

If, however, the purchaser is found within the time limited, it is immaterial that the actual sale was not fully consummated until afterwards. Where no time has been fixed, performance within a reasonable time will be sufficient, unless the offer to the broker has been withdrawn earlier. Where no time is fixed, a sale made within a reasonable time is sufficient. A lapse of one year does not necessarily terminate the broker's authority, but the authority continues until revoked, and the lapse of time

---

[6] Richter v. First National Bank of Cincinnati, 82 Ohio App. 421 (1947); Roudebush Realty Co. v. Toby, 135 N.E. 2d 270 (1955).

is merely one fact to be considered by the jury in determining whether the authority has been revoked.

A broker may recover any expenses incurred in connection with the agency, previous to the revocation of his authority. Barnes employed Adams to sell real estate. In an action in assumpsit by Adams against Barnes to recover damages for a breach of contract, it appeared that Adams had agreed to sell a tract of land belonging to Barnes, which had been laid out in 449 building lots, for which Adams was to receive as compensation $100 for the sale of each lot. Adams erected a temporary office upon the land and incurred expenses amounting to $230. After Adams had sold two of the lots, it was found that Barnes' wife would not join in the deeds, and thereupon Barnes notified Adams that he was unable to carry out the agreement. The Court directed a verdict for Adams for the amount of his expenses.

Where there is an open listing and a broker has a sale imminent, the owner is liable for a commission, even where he sells the property two days later to another party, without the assistance of a broker. In the case of *Romine v. Greene,* 13 N.J. Super. 261 (1951), the Court held that the broker was entitled to a commission, where the defendant accepted an offer to sell two days after the broker procured purchaser at same price. Since the broker had no notification of sale prior to his performance, the owner was liable for commission "unless he could prove a binding agreement for sale made so short a time before plaintiff's performance that reasonable opportunity to notify plaintiff was not afforded under the circumstance." Citing *Mecham on Agency* (Second Edition) Page 625, *Kennedy and Kennedy v. Vance,* 202 P. 2d 214 (Okla. 1949), the Court stated as a general rule of law that the prior sale (by owner) itself acts as a revocation of the power, if insufficient time has elapsed between such sale and performance by the broker to give reasonable opportunity, under all the circumstances of the case, for notification of the prior sale to the broker. However, a broker who obtains a buyer cannot be deprived of his commission merely because the owner is negotiating for the sale on his own account, even though such negotiations materialize into a sale at a later date. Mere preliminary discussion or negotiation is not enough. There must be a binding agreement for the sale: *Hartig v. Schrader,* 190 Ky. 511 (1921); *Hawks v. Moore,* 27 Ga. App. 555 (1921).

Agency coupled with an interest

Where the employment is coupled with an interest of the broker in the subject matter of the employment, the owner cannot arbitrarily terminate the broker's employment. Such an employment is irrevocable even after death. The Arizona Supreme Court so held in the case of *Phoenix Title and Trust Co. v. Grimes,* 416 P. 2d 979 (1966). In this case a broker joined with others in the purchase, subdividing, development and resale of desert land for their mutual benefit. The broker was given the exclusive right to sell the property. He performed all conditions of his contract for three years, prior to his death. The defendants then served notice upon the broker's executor that they refused to permit the executor to carry on, in performing the terms of the agreement. The court held that:

> If the agency or power of the agent is coupled with an interest in the subject matter of the agency, the power so coupled will survive to the personal representative of the agent upon the death. Although contracts to perform personal acts which can only be performed by the particular person contracted with are discharged by death of the person who is to perform such acts, this rule does not apply where the services were such that they could be performed by others acting on behalf of the personal representatives of the decedent: In re Burke's Estate 198 Cal. 163, 244 Pac. 340. We are convinced here that the executor could hire qualified licensed real estate agents to carry on the agency herein, which was coupled with an interest.

In the case of *Rucker & Co. v. Glenman,* 130 Va. 511 (1921) an owner entered into an agreement with a broker whereby the owner agreed to subdivide a plot of land and place it in the hands of the broker for sale. The owner was to receive a minimum of $4,000 from the sale of the lots and the net proceeds over this amount were to be divided equally between owner and broker. The court held that this was not an agency coupled with an interest, but merely a method for providing for broker's commission by division of the net proceeds. In *Barnard v. Gardner Investment Co.,* 129 Va. 346 (1921), the court held that a listing "coupled with an interest" is revocable unless the words used mean an interest in the land itself, as distinguished from an interest in the proceeds of the sale.

Commission dependent upon transfer of title

A broker may, by special agreement with his principal, contract to make his compensation depend upon the actual signing of the contract, or upon the actual passing of title, or other contingencies. Even under these conditions, a broker may recover his commissions at the time fixed in the contract of sale if it develops that the negotiations fall through by reason of some defect in the title of the seller, or upon the arbitrary refusal of the seller to go through with the deal. The owner is not permitted to plead that his failure to consummate the transaction will operate to deprive the broker of his commission.

Where the default or failure is on the part of the seller, the courts generally hold that the broker may recover the commission agreed upon. Where the failure or default is attributable to the purchaser, the rule is different.

In every case the fundamental doctrine, under varying forms of expression, is that the duty assumed by the broker is to bring the minds of the buyer and seller to an agreement on a sale and on the price and terms upon which it is to be made and that, until this is done, his right to commission does not accrue. A broker is not entitled to commissions when the customer through no fault of the seller refuses to complete the contract; but it is different when the customer has entered into a contract binding upon both parties or into an agreement to pay a stipulated sum as damages in case of refusal to complete the contract.

A broker who has fully earned his commission is generally not bound by any subsequent agreement that no commission is to be paid until the deed passes, for such an agreement is without consideration and cannot affect the obligation of the owner to the broker; and the agreement is not more binding when it recites a nominal consideration or good and valuable consideration when in fact, none passed. The fact that the seller refused to make the contract unless the broker agreed to wait for his commission until the deal was closed has been said not to furnish sufficient consideration. If the agreement of sale provides that the broker's commission is to be paid *at settlement,* the contract means exactly what it states, and if the settlement does not materialize, the broker is not entitled to commission, nor is this clause to be interpreted to mean that commission is to be paid when settlement *should have* taken place.

In the case of *Jones v. Palace Realty Co.,* 226 N.C. 303 (1946), the Court held under contract for payment of commission to broker out of sales price of property:

> when the deal is closed up, he could not recover when the deal was never closed due to inability of purchaser to comply. It was the actual event of closing the deal and not the date of its expected or contemplated happening that made the promise to pay enforceable.

To the same effect is the Michigan case of *Kostan v. Glasier,* 60 N.W. 2d 283 (1953), where commission was "payable only when and if deal is finally closed."

It is well settled law that language in an agreement of sale that commission to the broker is "payable when title closes, or upon delivery of deed" does not constitute a condition precedent for payment of a commission, but rather the *time* when the commission is to be paid to the broker. However, the broker and owner may, by express language, make the broker's right to a commission depend upon a future happening, such as the actual passage of title from seller to buyer. If the contingency does not materialize, it is fatal to the broker's claim for a commission: *Amies v. Wosnofsko,* 171 N.E. 136 (N.Y. 1031).

In the case of *Richard v. Falletti,* 13 N.J. Sup. 534 (1951), suit was brought by broker to recover unpaid half of a broker's commission earned on sale of defendant's land. The lower court rendered judgment for defendants on ground that plaintiff's right was contingent on delivery of deed, which had not taken place. The Superior Court, Appellate Division, reversed, holding that obligation to pay full commission was not contingent on delivery of deed, and that broker completed performance, and earned commission, when he induced purchaser to sign sales agreement.

Whether a broker is the efficient and procuring cause of the sale is a question of fact, which falls within the province of a jury to determine. It is not a question as to how much a broker does in a deal, but how *effective* is what he does. The case of *Mehlberg v. Redlin,* 96 N.W. 2d 399 (S.D., 1959), is in point. The Court made the significant observation:

> As background of the events of Friday, April 26, 1957, it should be noted that theretofore plaintiff had devoted time, effort and expense in establishing a market place to which both vendors and purchasers of real estate would be induced to resort. It was this preliminary activity of plaintiff which brought both Redlin and Rev. Schumann to that office. These facts suggest that to conclude plaintiff's only contribution toward bringing Redlin and the synod together, was the answering of a single telephone call, is to ignore an important part of her activities.

The fact that a broker has established "a market place" for buyers and sellers of real estate is significant. Some brokers have had the experience that, occasionally, an easy deal takes place—the property sells itself—and the broker receives a substantial commission. The seller is unhappy in that he feels he has paid the broker a substantial sum of money for "doing nothing." The owner has lost sight of the fact that the broker rendered quick service and that the broker's established place of business as "a real estate market" made this possible.

Exclusive listings

Most brokers prefer a written exclusive listing contract and some real estate offices will not accept a verbal listing, particularly if the office belongs to a multi-list association. In an exclusive listing, the broker is assured that he will have the unrivaled right for a named period of time to negotiate the sale of the property in question. In return for this protection, the broker will usually advertise the property and make an added effort to sell the property. It should be remembered that there is an important distinction between an exclusive agency contract and an exclusive right to sell contract. They are not the same. In an exclusive agency contract, the broker is protected during the period specified against a sale of the same property by another broker.

It has already been indicated that a written exclusive right to sell listing is to the broker's advantage and will inure to his benefit, in the long run. Brokers prefer a written exclusive listing contract, and some offices will not accept a verbal listing.

This is particularly true of Realtors. In an exclusive listing, the broker is given the exclusive privilege to sell the property for a definite period of time. However, this does not prevent the owner from selling his property during the exclusive period, without being liable to the broker for a commission. The exclusive agency protects the broker's right to a commission, in the event that it is sold by another broker, or any person, other than the owner, during the exclusive period.

There is an important difference between an exclusive agency listing and an exclusive right to sell listing. Under the latter form of listing, the broker *is* protected against a sale by the owner during the designated exclusive period. Should a sale occur by the owner, the listing broker would be entitled to a commission on the sale. Such words as: "I hereby give to Ajax Realty Co. the sole and exclusive right to sell; and to pay a commission upon the sale, exchange, or lease with option to purchase by whomsoever the same may be made or effected" or similar words, are necessary: *Flynn v. LaSalle National Bank,* 9 Ill. 2d 129 (1958).

Since most states require a definite expiration date in an exclusive listing contract, a listing which provides for a definite period (90 days) and then states that the listing shall continue in force, unless the owner gives the broker 30 days *written* notice of termination, would be deemed an unethical practice. In practice, brokers generally refer to an exclusive right to sell listing simply as an "exclusive" listing.

Many brokers mistakenly believe that they have an exclusive agency for an indefinite period, where the owner gives no notice to terminate, when they do not have such protection. For example, the following form is sometimes used:

The undersigned hereby employs Stanley Sims as the sole and exclusive agent for the sale of the property described on the reverse hereof for a term of three (3) months and agrees to pay to the said agent a commission of five (5) per cent on the gross consideration upon its sale or exchange, by whomsoever the same may be made or effected.

The agent's authority hereunder may be revoked by the owner at any time after the expiration of the above term when no negotiations are pending for the sale and exchange of the property, but only upon and after 30 days' notice in writing to that effect given to the agent. And if, subsequently to such revocation, the property should be sold or exchanged to anyone with whom the agent had heretofore been negotiating the said commission will be paid to said agent.

Suppose that a few days before the expiration of the three-month period, the broker showed the property to a prospective purchaser, who purchased the property 20 days after the three-month period expired, through another broker and the owner had not given notice to terminate the agency. The case poses two questions: (1) Was the exclusive agency still in effect? (2) Was the sale made to one with whom the broker "had heretofore been negotiating" ? The law is now well established that the contract above does *not* confer an exclusive agency after its original term and until it is revoked by 30 days' written notice from the owner. *The exclusive character prevails only during the original term.* After that, the agency continues only as an open or general listing, until revoked. During the original period the broker can recover commission no matter who makes the sale; in order to recover after the expiration of the original three-month period, the broker must prove that he was the procuring cause of the sale. *Negotiating* means more than introducing or pointing out the property to the prospective purchaser. To negotiate means to discuss and arrange the details. Merely to call attention to the property without further discussing the details which necessarily follow for the consummation of the sale cannot be called a negotiation. On the other hand suppose that an owner, Ashworth, employed a broker, Bonwit, to sell his property under the following agreement:

The undersigned owner hereby employs Bonwit as the sole and exclusive agent for the term of three (3) months from the date hereof, and solely and exclusively thereafter until the expiration of thirty (30) days after written notice has been given to the broker by the owner.

The contract provides for a 5 per cent commission on the selling price, in event of a sale, whether made by another broker or by the owner himself. The contract of employment is dated January 3, 1974. No notice of termination is given by Ashworth to Bonwit, but on May 3, 1974, Ashworth, himself, sells the property to Crane. Bonwit now claims a commission. In this case the broker could recover, because the *exclusive* character of the employment has been continued by express agreement between the parties.

A written exclusive listing for a definite period of time, may be extended *orally* for an additional period of time, by mutual agreement of owner and broker.

Exclusive right to sell

It sometimes happens that the owner has been negotiating with several prospects in the recent past, before giving the listing. He may require that the broker agree that if the property is sold to those named prospects of the owner, he will not demand a commission. The names of the owner's prospects should be submitted in writing, to the broker. It is a fundamental maxim that the parties are bound by the terms of their own contract. If an owner of real estate chooses to make a contract with a broker in which it is stipulated that the broker shall have the exclusive right to sell the property within a specified time and that he shall be entitled to receive a certain commission if the sale be made within the time designated, no matter who makes it, he is bound by its terms and cannot be relieved from a bad bargain because his agreement may have been foolish or improvident. Our cases have gone thus far and no further.

Assume that an owner has signed a prepared listing contract. The contract is signed on February 4, 1974. The exclusive listing is for two months. It may be surprising to know that the contract could be terminated by the owner on February 5, 1974. Certainly, the broker has a cause of action, but what is the measure of damages? It is not the amount of commission which the broker might have earned on the deal, but rather the damages and expenses which he has actually sustained *at the date of the breach.* This amount is usually negligible. The Supreme Court of Arkansas so held in the case of *Nance v. McDougald,* 211 Ark. 800 (1947).

In the case of *Jenkins v. Vaughn,* 197 Tenn. 578 (1955), the court granted a commission on the sale of a drugstore stating "if broker had rendered a substantial performance by spending time and money in an effort to perform, the offer becomes binding and irrevocable."

Where a principal revokes the broker's agency before the expiration of the listing period, he renders himself liable, unless such revocation is for cause, for such damages as are the proximate result of the termination of the employment contract: *Sinden v. Loabs,* 30 Wis. 2d 618 (1966). There were mutual promises, constituting consideration (a bilateral contract). Even where obligations are imposed upon one party (a unilateral contract), the owner may not breach it, where there has been *substantial* performance by the broker, such as advertising and obtaining interested prospects. Clearly, considerations of practical justice warrant and require that if there has been part or substantial performance on the part of the broker, the owner cannot arbitrarily cancel the employment before its expiration date: *Hutchinson v. Dobson-Bainbridge Realty Co.,* 31 Tenn. App. 490 (1946). If a broker has a bona fide purchaser, *before* the revocation was communicated to him, he would be entitled to recover his commission.

In the case of *Covino v. Pfeffer,* 160 Conn. 212, (1970), the plaintiff broker sued the former owners to recover a commission, under the following facts: On April 11, 1968, the owners gave the broker an exclusive right to sell listing, which expired on July 11, 1968. During the last week of June 1968, the ultimate purchaser first saw the property. On or about July 7, 1968, the defendant knew that the broker's prospect would buy the house. On July 9, 1968, the buyer made application for a mortgage loan. Even though the sales agreement was signed subsequent to expiration date of the listing, the court held that the broker was entitled to a commission. The court rejected the contention of the defendants that "the owners shall not be deemed to have sold the property, which is the subject of an exclusive sale contract, unless and until negotiations with the prospective purchaser have been consummated into a binding and enforceable contract for sale. The expiration date of an exclusive listing may be waived, where after the time limit has expired the owner urges and encourages the broker to continue his efforts and the broker does so with the knowledge, approval and encouragement of the principal: *Ferris v. Meeker Fertilizer Co.,* 482 P. 2d 523 (Ore. 1971).

Furnish owner with copy of listing

Good ethics require that a broker voluntarily furnish the owner with a fully completed copy of the listing of the contract at the time it is signed. Some brokers are reluctant to give the owner a copy of the listing because they do not want him to know, perhaps, that it may run on indefinitely, unless written notice of cancellation (usually 30 days) is given to the broker.

To obviate this practice, which is considered unethical in good real estate circles, many Commissions, by statute or Rule and Regulation, require a *definite* expiration date in listing contracts. Since there is often controversy as to whether the broker actually furnished the owner with a copy of the listing, it is a good precaution to have the owner sign his name on the original copy retained by the broker, under a clause: "I hereby acknowledge receipt of a fully completed copy of this Listing Contract." The clause should be in prominent type. Failure to furnish the owner with a copy of the listing may constitute grounds for suspension or revocation of license. However, in the case of *Fleetham v. Schneekloth,* 52 Wash. 2d 176 (1958), the court held that failure to furnish a copy of the listing to the owner was not a fatal bar to a recovery of commission in a law suit against the owner.

A Rule and Regulation of the Pennsylvania Real Estate Commission requires that in the use of an exclusive right to sell contract, that the broker shall carry on the face of the listing the statement, *in bold type,* that, *"The Broker earns his commission on the sale by whomsoever made, including the owner."* In the case of *Williams v. Brittingham,* 38 D & C 342 (Pa. 1965), the broker sued the owner for a commission. The listing contract did not contain the required bold type language. The Court of Common Pleas stated that,

> the act is a penal statute and must be strictly construed . . . the same result must follow in application of regulations promulgated under it by the commission . . . The purpose of the Act is to police real estate brokerage operations, and not to change the substantive law of contracts or agency . . . Had the legislature intended to make such violations a defense to an action to recover commissions, it would and could have done so . . .

Some states, by Rule or Regulation, require that the original period for an exclusive listing shall not exceed one year. In the case of *Schechter v. Voltz,* 179 Pa. Superior Ct. 119 (1955), the appellate court held that a listing for a period "until sold" was not void, but was valid for a *reasonable time.*

There is no statutory limitation on the duration of a listing contract. This is a matter of agreement between an owner and broker.

Termination of exclusive right to sell listing contract

Two questions arise in regard to exclusive listings as follows:

1. Can such a contract be terminated before the expiration date?
2. Is the broker entitled to a commission upon a sale to a prospect procured by him, who signs an agreement of sale subsequent to the expiration date in the listing?

The cases make a distinction in listing contracts as to whether they are unilateral or bilateral. In a unilateral contract, where the broker does not in any way *obligate* himself to advance the sale of the property in the interest of the owner, then what has been previously stated in regard to the owner writing a cancellation of employment applies. A unilateral listing contract imposes a duty only upon the owner to pay a commission if the broker obtains a buyer; it imposes no duty upon the broker to endeavor to get a buyer. However, in a bilateral contract where the broker expressly obligates himself to advance the cause of his principal's property, then, the owner may not captiously or arbitrarily terminate the employment without being liable for the commission as damages to the broker. Such a clause creating a bilateral listing contract may read:

> I acknowledge that the listing of this property, and your endeavor and efforts to procure a purchaser, through advertising, co-brokers, or otherwise, shall constitute a good and sufficient consideration for this agreement.

In the Missouri case of *Chamberlain v. Grisham,* 230 S.W. 2d 721 (1950), the Court held that after brokers listed the property and endeavored to procure a purchaser, contract became a bilateral one and was no longer revocable by owner at will. In other words, if there is substantial performance, the listing cannot be withdrawn. The listing contract must impose some duty or obligation upon the broker, as well as the owner, in order to give it a bilateral character. In some states, brokers use a form which recites, "In consideration of $1, receipt whereof is hereby acknowledged, etc.,"

In the absence of court decisions in this area of subject matter, it would be presumptuous to speculate as to the bi-lateral quality of such a provision, where the broker does *nothing* to effectuate a sale; particularly in the light of court decisions oriented towards consumer and public protection.

A provision in the listing contract requiring the broker to re-list the property promptly with the members of a multi-list association, of which he is a member, would indicate an irrevocable bi-lateral contract, when the property is so listed in the multi-list association.

It is also well to provide a clause in the listing agreement that if the owner rescinds the contract before its expiration, or is guilty of a breach, he agrees to pay to the broker a designated sum, which may well be the amount of the commission as *liquidated damages,* and call it "liquidated damages." The contract of employment should be under seal.

The extender or carry over clause

The extender or "carry over" clause in an exclusive right to sell listing is that clause which provides that the right of a broker to a commission will be protected by the owner, if the property is sold to a prospect, procured by the broker, within a specified period of time, *after* the expiration of the original listing period. The period of protection is usually six months, but it may be longer or shorter. It is only fair and conscionable to include such a clause. Otherwise, an owner and buyer could conspire to postpone the closing until the listing period expired, and then, close the deal,--often at a price, which squeezes out the amount of the broker's commission.

An extender clause, commonly used, reads:

> In the event that, after the expiration of the listing term, the undersigned owner shall sell, transfer, lease or exchange the above property, directly or indirectly, within a period of six months, from the expiration of this listing contract, or any extension or renewal therof, to any person or persons, with whom Ideal Realty Company has been negotiating or dealing for the sale, lease, or exchange of said property, in which event the undersigned owner agrees to pay Ideal Realty Company the above commission, which shall become immediately due and payable.

Many different words are used in an endeavor to make the broker's entitlement to a commission effective, such as, if the property is sold to anyone, to whom said property was "submitted" by the said broker; to whom said property was "shown"; to whom the property had been "introduced"; to any person, with whom the broker had "negotiated"; placed the owner "in touch with"; had "contact with," or the like. Should a sale result during the extender period, under any of the above terms, the broker would have his "foot in the door," so to speak, for a commission claim.

The word "negotiate" is used extensively, and in some areas, the following words are added: "and whose names have been filed with me on or before the expiration date of the original listing." In the case of *Advance Realty Co. v. Spanos,* 348 Mich. 464 (1957), the court held that the broker's use of the words "to *produce*" a purchaser meant "to bring forth" or to be the cause of the sale.

Where the term of the listing has expired, the owner, in the absence of fraud or bad faith, may contract with a prospect "introduced by the broker within the period of performance, either upon the same terms or upon others, more or less favorable than those the broker was authorized, without receiving any liability to compensate the latter for his services": *Everson v. Phelps,* 115 Oregon 523; *Schmidt, Inc. v. Brock,* 97 Ohio App. 469 (1953).

The listing contract involved in *Bonn v. Summers,* 249 N.C. 357 (1950), required names of prospects shown the property to be filed within three days after the listing expired.

In the case of *E. M. Boerke, Inc. v. Williams* 28 Wis. 2d 627 (1966), a property was listed exclusively with a broker, to remain in effect until January 15, 1957. It contained a six month's extender clause. The listing provided that, the broker was to receive a commission if property was sold during the extended period "to anyone with whom you negotiated during the life of this contract, and whose name you have filed with me in writing prior to the termination of this contract." On January 15, 1957, the plaintiff mailed his list of names (including name of the ultimate purchaser) to the defendants in Florida. The letter from the broker did not reach the defendants until after January 15, 1957. The plaintiff contended that the contract expired at midnight on January 15, 1957, so that the mailing was timely. The defendants argued that the contract expired 24 hours earlier.

The court held that any ambiguity should be resolved against the broker, who prepared the listing contract. Also, that the "mailing" on January 15 did not satisfy the (time) requirement that the notice be "filed with me." The court said:

> To construe or define "mailing" as "filing" is to ignore the proper meaning of the word. Mailing merely initiates the process by which an article in the due course of the post will be

delivered. The requirement of the contract in question is that the notice be filed or delivered to the party offering property for sale.

The general rule of law in this connection is stated in the case of *Everson v. Phelps,* 115 Oregon 523, where a broker in Tillamock sued for commission upon a sale made several days after the exclusive agency had expired. The claim was refused. The Court said: "Where there is no fraud or bad faith on the part of the employer and the broker does not perform within the time limit, the employer, after the expiration thereof, may contract with a customer introduced by the broker within the period for performance, either upon the same terms or upon others more or less favorable than those the broker was authorized, without receiving any liability to compensate the latter for his services."

In the case of *Schmidt, Inc. v. Brock,* 97 Ohio App. 469 (1953), the plaintiff alleged that it had a buyer, but defendant waited until exclusive expired and then sold it the next day to the buyer. The Court held that the broker could not recover as the plaintiff showed that no bad faith or any unjustifiable conduct by the defendant prevented the sale by him.

In the case, *McGuire v. Sinnett,* 158 Ore. 390 (1938), a broker had a listing contract which expired on August 23, 1936. A salesman for the broker showed the property to a prospect before the written listing expired. A second broker advertised the property after the listing expired and on September 1, 1936, the same prospect made an offer to purchase the property through the second broker and the deal was closed. The first broker sued the owner for a commission, contending that he was protected for 90 days under a clause in his listing contract which provided that the owner would pay the broker a commission if the broker placed the owner "in touch with a buyer to or through whom, within ninety (90) days after the expiration hereof, I (Seller), may sell, exchange or convey said property." The Supreme Court permitted the broker to recover, stating:

> In the case before us, the broker is entitled to his commission in one of the three following instances: (1) If he found a buyer ready and willing to enter into a contract with the defendant on terms and price agreed to by the defendant; (2) if he placed the defendant in touch with a buyer to whom the defendant sold the property during the life of the contract or within ninety days after the expiration thereof; or (3) if he was procuring cause of the sale.

The broker was entitled to a commission upon proving that he placed a purchaser in touch with the seller during the term of the listing and the buyer consummated the deal within ninety days from the expiration date of the listing. The language of the listing contract is important. "In touch with," or "in contact with" is far different from "with whom the broker has been negotiating." To negotiate means more than merely submitting or showing the property to a prospective purchaser. In the Ohio case of *Kalna v. Fialko,* 125 N.E. 2d 565 (1955), the court held that "to negotiate" means to transact business, to procure, to induce, to treat with another respecting a purchase and sale. In a 1968 case, *King v. Dean,* 238 N.E. 2d 828 (Ohio 1968), the court stated that "negotiation is not a single act, but a process. It involves a dialogue or back-and-forth communication with a purpose; in this case, to sell real estate."

"Negotiation" requires that efforts of the broker to interest a prospect must have proceeded to a point where the prospect is considered a likely purchaser: *Jessup v. La Pin,* 150 N.W. 2d 342 (Wis. 1967).

The case of *Nichols v. Pendley,* 331 S.W. 2d 673 (Mo. 1960), involved a suit for a real estate commission. On March 2, 1958, the parties entered into a written contract whereby, the owners appointed the broker as an exclusive agent for a period of two weeks to sell their residence at a price of $8,750. The contract further provided that "if this property is sold during the time this agreement is in force, or if sold to anyone to whom said property was submitted by Nichols Agency within three months from the termination date hereof, then in that event the undersigned shall pay to said Nichols Agency, broker, 5 per cent of the sales price as his commission due." It is admitted that within the two weeks exclusive period, a salesman of the broker offered the property to Woolevers for sale and took them through the house. They made no offer. The owners were present at the time. A sale was made to the Woolevers during the 90-day period following the expiration of the original term. The case turned on the interpretation of the word "submitted." The Court stated that:

> The defendants contend that the word 'submitted' means that the efforts of the broker must have proceeded to the point where the Woolevers were 'likely purchasers.' Other cases cited referred to 'negotiating.' It has been held generally that 'negotiating' implies a situation where the interest of the buyer has been aroused to the point that the purchaser may be considered a likely purchaser. Negotiation implies a discussion of terms, a bargaining. It is generally used in connection with the *consummation* of business matters. The word 'submitted' means 'to leave or commit to the discretion of another.'

The Court stated:

> It is a close question. The acts of the plaintiff went far enough to fulfill the terms of the contract. But we are of the opinion that under the facts of this case the plaintiff 'submitted' the property to the purchasers within the exclusive period when he offered defendant's property to the Woolevers for sale and took them through the house in the presence of the defendants.

The broker recovered.

Lease with option to purchase in lieu of outright sale

Most exclusive listings relate to a sale or exchange of an owner's property, but are silent as to a broker's right to a commission, if the owner and the broker's prospect sign a lease during the exclusive period of the listing, with an option to purchase. The parties may wait until the broker's listing has expired and then enter into a contract of sale during the term of the lease, circumventing the broker's commission.

In the case of *Cunningham v. Aeschliman,* 296 N.E. 2d 326 (Ill. 1973), a seller and a prospect obtained by a broker entered into an option to purchase the property. This option was executed during the period of the broker's listing. The property was leased to the optionee. During the lease term, the property was sold by the owner to the broker's prospect. The court permitted a commission recovery on the sale.

Ambiguity construed against broker

The listing agreement should be clear and unambiguous as to its terms. Since the broker is the party who prepared the listing contract, ambiguity as to its meaning, or doubt as to its interpretation will be construed most strongly against him.

In the case of *Roy Annett, Inc. v. Kellin,* 112 N.W. 2d 497 (Mich. 1961) a farm was listed for sale with a broker under an exclusive listing. The extender clause provided " . . . (c) if said property is sold by the owner within 6 months thereafter to any person with whom said broker negotiated with respect to a sale during the term," the owner was obligated to pay the broker a commission. The broker had a prospect during the original listing period. A second broker negotiated a sale to this prospect during the "6 months" carry over period. The first broker sued for a commission. The court decided against the broker, holding that the property was not sold "by the owner", but through another broker. The broker could have protected himself by stating in the extender clause "by whomsoever sold" or "if sold by the owner or anyone else."

In the case of *E. M. Boerke, Inc. v. Williams,* 28 Wis. 2d 627 (1965), the broker held an exclusive listing "until January 15, 1957, with a six months extender clause." The listing required the broker "to file with me prior to the termination of this contract", the names of prospects, with whom the broker negotiated during the exclusive period. The broker *mailed* a list of his prospects (one of whom bought the property during the extender period) on January 15, 1957. The Supreme Court stated:

> . . . we conclude that the doubt must be resolved in favor of the defendant's (seller's) position that the contract terminated on the end of the day of January 14, 1957. Hence, the action taken by the plaintiff (broker) on January 15, in mailing the list of names, was not timely. To construe or define *mailing* as *filing* is to ignore the plain meaning of the word. Mailing merely initiates the process by which an article in the due course of the post will be delivered.

However, in the Arkansas case of *Holbert v. Block-Meeks Realty Co.,* 297 S.W. 2d 924 (1957) where the broker had an exclusive listing contract "till 8/15/55" and seller signed agreements of sale on that date, the court held that the broker was protected and could recover.

Broker may buy listed property

There is nothing illegal about a broker or sales person purchasing a property listed with the broker's office, so long as the broker hides nothing from his owner and there is full disclosure of all facts which might influence his principal: *Sylvester v. Beck,* 406 Pa. 607 (1962). But, where the broker already has a purchaser committed at a higher price, ready to purchase the same property, the broker is then derelict in his duties to his principal, and would be held accountable.

Sometimes, the listing contract will specifically provide that the listing broker has the option to purchase the property at the listed price. While not illegal, it raises a question of professional ethics. Should the broker exercise the option and shortly thereafter sell the property at a higher price to a third party, the owner will probably entertain serious reservations as to that broker's integrity and good faith.

Purchaser may be liable for deceit

It sometimes happens that a broker brings a property to the buyer's attention and then the latter deals with the owner direct. Many brokers have had instances where they show the outside of a listed dwelling and the prospect disclaims any interest and will not even make an inspection of the interior. Later on, the broker finds that the prospect has purchased the property. If the broker had previously notified the owner as to the identity of the prospect, he would have a good cause of action for commission. Clearly, if the owner is unaware of the interest of the broker's prospect or identity, the difficulty of recovering a commission is apparent. A *purchaser* may lay himself open to a lawsuit for commission by the broker, after the broker has submitted the property to him, by stating to the owner that there is no broker in the deal. A cautious or prudent seller, who has listed his property with one or more brokers for sale, will include a clause in the agreement of sale to the effect that the purchaser warrants that there is no broker involved in the sale. In the case of *McCue v. Deppert,* 21 N.J. Sup. 591 (1952), a broker, McCue of Rumson, New Jersey, sued a purchaser, Peter C. Deppert, under these very facts. There the property was listed at $30,000, and a McCue salesman showed Deppert the property. He said he would return with his wife. Instead, he went directly to the owner, Kramer, who lived at Lakewood, and bought the property for $25,000, "because there was no broker charge." The broker sued the buyer. The lower court decided against the broker, but upon appeal, the Superior Court held that the buyer could not "rely on his wrongful acts, in preventing the plaintiff from meeting the condition of procuring a ready, able and willing purchaser."

Another similar case was decided by a lower court in Ohio in 1952, in the case of *Schlesinger v. Zeilengold,* where the broker sued the buyer in an action of deceit and recovered a verdict of $2,800.00. The case involved a commercial property in Lyndhurst, Ohio. There the buyer secured from the broker certain pertinent information about the property and then used it on his own. He then professed to be totally uninterested in the property and refused to enter into any discussion with the broker about its purchase. The buyer at the time was in direct negotiation with the owner. The Court's decision holds, in effect, that a prospective purchaser who perpetrates a fraud upon a broker thereby preventing the broker from pursuing his lawful and legitimate rights under his employment contract, commits an actionable wrong in tort.

Acting as broker for buyer and seller

It is a generally accepted rule that a broker cannot act as the agent for both parties in the same transaction. Each is entitled to his undivided efforts and to the unimpaired use of his skill, knowledge, and experience. It is not possible for a broker to fulfill these requirements if he is at the same time giving an equivalent service to the other party to the contract. The interests of buyer and seller are diametrically opposed to each other. The seller is interested in getting as high a price for his property as he possibly can, while the purchaser is naturally interested in obtaining the property at as low a price as possible, and so it is impossible for an agent to represent justly these conflicting interests. The agent must not, in other words, occupy the position of a judge, impartially weighing the merits of both sides. He has been engaged by a principal to present in as convincing a manner as he can the claims of his principal, and it is therefore imperative that the broker do all in his power to secure the most favorable price possible under the circumstances. This is so whether the sale is for cash or whether there is an exchange of property involved. This general rule has been followed strictly in most states.

The case of *Hughes v. Robbins, et al.,* 164 N.E. 2d 469 (1959), involved a suit by a broker for commissions, against both seller and buyer in an exchange deal. The plaintiff claimed that both parties knew of the dual agency and there was no unfairness, double dealing, fraud, or damage to the parties. Hood, a defendant, testified that he knew of the double employment. Robbins, the other defendant, emphatically denied knowledge. The Court denied a recovery. The Court said:

> We find that all of such evidence as was submitted is not sufficient to justify a finding that the defendants, Mr. and Mrs. Robbins, knew of, consented to, or acquiesced in the dual agency. . . . It should be further observed that even if the defendants Hood were aware of this dual agency, and the defendants Robbins were not so aware still the broker cannot recover from either of the defendants, his principals—the rule being that the broker cannot recover from either of his principals unless both with knowledge of, consented to and acquiesced in such double employment . . .

It has been well written that "no servant can serve two masters, for either he will hate the one and love the other or else he will hold to the one and despise the other."

The fact that no actual damage resulted from the conduct of the broker here cannot prevent the application of this general rule, which is intended not as a remedy for the actual wrong, but, preventive of the possibility of it.

In the case of *Investment Exchange Realty v. Hillcrest Bank, Inc. et al,* 513 P. 2d

282 (Wash. 1973), the court said:

> The test can only be met by a clear and express disclosure of the dual agency relationship with consent thereto by both parties (buyer and seller).

To the same effect is the case of *Ornamental and Structural Steel, Inc. v. BBT Inc.,* 500 P. 2d 1053 (Ariz. 1973).

The case of *Sherman v. Bratton,* 497 S.W. 2d (Tex. App. 1973), involved a situation where the plaintiff, licensed as a broker, as an attorney, and as an engineer, sued for a commission in the leasing of a property in Dallas. The broker's contract of employment with the owner was verbal. Since the broker was not employed in the capacity of attorney or engineer, but was employed as a broker, and the other professional services being only incidental to his employment, he could not recover in his suit for commission because the Texas law requires a broker's employment to be in writing.

Under certain circumstances broker may recover

Under certain extenuating circumstances, however, there has been a divergence from this principle of law. Even though the transaction is an exchange, the broker cannot recover commissions if he is entrusted with any discretion and has an agreement to receive any commission from one party without the knowledge of the other party. The rule, however, does not apply to an exchange of property where the broker has no discretion but is simply to bring the parties together. In such case the broker is merely a middleman. It may be said that an owner might reasonably assume that in an exchange of property, a broker receives commissions from both sides.

In summing up the law it may be stated that a broker may only recover commission from both parties to the same transaction when (1) he merely brings the parties together, (2) nothing is left to his discretion, (3) no special confidence reposes in him, (4) the fact that he is acting in a dual capacity is known to both parties, and (5) he is employed by both parties.

Broker's right to commission strengthened where agreement of lease states broker negotiated the sale or lease

It is fairly customary for an agreement of sale to state that the Brookline Realty Co. negotiated the sale and the seller agrees to pay it a commission of 7 per cent on the sales price. There was a question, for a long time, whether a broker could sue an owner, resting his case on this clause, since the agreement of sale is a contract between buyer and seller and the broker is not a party to this agreement. There are supreme court cases in Pennsylvania and Virginia which hold that the clause is meaningful and support a claim for commission. Both cases arose in connection with such a clause in leases. In the case of *Richard B. Herman and Co. v. Stern,* 419 Pa. 272 (1965), the plaintiff broker sued for a commission on the sale of a certain business property, upon a clause in the lease negotiated by the broker that in the event that the property were sold to the tenant, the broker would be entitled to a commission.

The Court said:

> Appellant (Stern) obligates himself in clear and unambiguous language, for a recited consideration from the broker, under seal, to pay specific commissions. That this particular agreement is contained in the lease agreement between the lessor, appellant and lessee, Sailor, is neither unusual nor legally objectionable. Its presence in the document can be only to create a binding agreement between principal, appellant and the agent, appellee, who signed as agent, for those commissions. Otherwise, its existence cannot be rationally explained. There is no legal or logical reason for prohibiting the inclusion of such promise. It is a practical manner of handling an

everyday business matter in an efficient and legally effective manner, avoiding the necessity of other separate contracts.

To the same effect is the case of *W. D. Nelson & Co., Inc., v. Taylor Heights Development Corp.,* 207 Va. 386 (1966).

Care in making representations

If a broker is authorized to sell property for his principal as well as to initiate negotiations, it is very important that the broker be circumspect in the representations which he makes to prospective purchasers concerning the property for sale. Representations include not only actual statements made by the broker, but also any impression or belief that his conduct is calculated to produce in the mind of the other party as to the facts. The law holds the broker responsible for his representations in almost the same manner as if he were acting for himself. Not only will the broker lose his right to commission when he has been guilty of misrepresentation, but, in addition, he may find himself the defendant in an action brought by the disappointed purchaser, such as a fruitless action against the principal in the contract, for any damages or expenses incurred by the disappointed purchaser.

Even more important, the broker may find himself the defendant in an action before the Real Estate Commission for violation of the license law.

The general rule of law is well stated by the Nebraska Supreme Court[7] as follows: "A person is justified in relying on a representation made to him in all cases where the representation is a positive statement of fact and where an investigation would be required to discover the truth."

To answer an inquiry regarding termites by saying, "There are no termites in this house," is a statement of fact. But to say, "I have seen no termites," is not a misrepresentation, although there are termites, but the broker was unaware of that fact. The better practice would be for the broker to advise the prospect to inquire from the owner, or to have a termite inspection made.

In order to protect himself from a possible suit or complaint, the broker, in filling out the data and information to be included in the listing contract, should receive all possible information from the owner. This information should be above the signature of the owner, with the statement:

"I/We represent the information contained in this listing, as part thereof, is true and correct." Unless the broker, as a licensee, held out to the public, qualified in the field of real estate, knows or should know, that a certain item of information is false, he is held blameless, if it later turns out that the item is false. The owner would be responsible. On the other hand, if a broker makes an unauthorized or unwarranted representation, on his own initiative, the broker will be held personally responsible.

Puffing of goods

There is also a doctrine of law to be noted here known as "puffing of goods." Where the broker makes extraordinary and extravagant statements regarding the property for sale, as, "It is the most beautiful spot in the world," and, "The sun shines daily," and where there is no serious intent to include in the contract for sale that the property possesses all the magical powers and charms claimed for it, the deluded victim has only his pains for his trouble and no remedy at law. A principal selling property is presumed to know whether the representations he makes concerning it are true or false, and if he knows them to be false, then he commits a positive fraud.

[7] Martin v. Hutton, 90 Neb. 34 (1912).

If he does not know whether his representations are true or false, then his actions constitute gross negligence, and in contemplation of law, a representation founded on a mistake resulting from such negligence is fraud. The purchaser confides in the information furnished him by the owner upon the assumption that an owner knows his own property, and it is consequently immaterial to the purchaser whether the misrepresentation proceeded from a mistake or fraud. The injury to him in both cases is the same, whatever may have been the motive of the seller.

The law imposes the same obligations upon an agent acting for the owner of the property. He must be just as scrupulous in the statements which he makes concerning it as the principal would be were he conducting the negotiations personally. If the misrepresentations made by the broker were made upon the information supplied by the owner, the broker is entitled to his commission from the owner if he procures a purchaser, and he is not liable to buyer for damages.

Not liable for honest mistakes

A real estate broker is not personally responsible for an error or mistake which he honestly makes, unless he has been careless, grossly negligent, or has gone contrary to his honest convictions and beliefs.

It sometimes happens that a broker acts for an undisclosed principal, and the prospective purchaser deals exclusively with the agent as owner of the property. In such case the agent is as liable as if he were the principal. It is the duty of the agent, if he desires to avoid personal liability on the contract, not only to disclose the fact that he is acting in a representative capacity but also to disclose the identity of his principal. If he fails to do so, it must be taken that he assumes and intends to bind himself.

Broker's liability for earnest money

The retention of deposit money, paid by a buyer on account of the purchase price, will be discussed in connection with agreements of sale. The subject is also pertinent to brokerage. We have already indicated that most state license laws *require* a broker to deposit earnest money in a trust or escrow account until the transaction is consummated or terminated. Failure to do so constitutes grounds for suspension or revocation of license. Where there is a written listing, signed by the owner, it is important that it should contain a clause to the effect that the broker should hold all deposits of earnest money in escrow until the transaction is consummated or terminated. Under such authority, the broker should encounter no difficulty in convincing his owner that the broker should hold the earnest money deposit. Of course, money paid the broker by a purchaser can be recovered by the purchaser where the owner refuses to execute the agreement or is guilty of a breach of the agreement. This is so even though the agreement provides that "It is understood that the broker is acting as agent only and will in no case whatever be held liable to either party for the performance of any term or covenant of this agreement or for damages for nonperformance thereof." This clause is not really necessary where the broker's principal is disclosed, since the action generally will be directed against the owner. But the buyer can sue the broker if the broker retains the deposit money, provided the buyer has a right of action against the owner.

Commission upon cancellation of lease

The question frequently arises as to a broker's right to collect commission upon the unexpired term of a lease negotiated by the broker where the lease is terminated by a sale or where the management of the property is taken out of the broker's hands before the expiration of the lease term. Thus, two different situations are presented. In the first case, assume that a lease has been negotiated by a broker for a three-year term and the lease contains a provision that it can be terminated in event of sale of the property upon the owner giving the tenant 60 days' notice in writing to that effect. Suppose, at the end of one year, the owner makes a bona fide sale and gives the tenant the required 60 days' notice. The broker is obviously not entitled to a commission on the rent for the remaining 22 months since he negotiated the lease and is cognizant of the sales clause and his commission upon the lease term is necessarily contingent upon the tenant remaining in possession during the *entire* three-year period. In the second case, where no sales clause is contained in the lease and the owner sells the property subject to the existing lease, the situation is different. Upon negotiation of the lease by the broker, he becomes entitled to a commission for the full period of the lease. Where the new owner takes the property out of the broker's hands, his rights against the original owner continue unabridged. However, custom, as evidenced by the practice among brokers or under the rules of a real estate board, may permit a reduction of the full amount of commission claimed under these circumstances.

In the case of *Rosenfield v. Cadence Industries Corp.,* 348 N.Y. S. 2d 523 (1973), the landlord *negotiated* the termination of a lease with the tenant, which still had 5 years and 6 months to run. The lease provided that the landlord would pay the broker 5% commission on all rents collected. The lease also provided that no commission would be paid, if the lease were terminated by bankruptcy of the tenant, assignment for benefit of creditors, or destruction of premises by fire or other casualty. The court held that the broker was entitled to commission for the unexpired term of the lease.

Trade-ins

"Trade-ins" are a comparatively recent phase in the development of real estate practice and the broker plays a prominent role in this operation. An explanation may be best illustrated by an example. Jones, a broker, advertises a property at $27,000. Adams contacts the broker and desires to buy the house, but he must first sell his own home in order to raise the necessary finances to make the deal. The broker then enters into an arrangement with Adams, whereby his property is listed for sale with Jones at a price of $17,000 for a 90 day period and the broker agrees that if the house is not sold within that period that he will purchase the property at $15,000. Of course, if Jones sells the Adams house during the 90 day listing period, he will expect the usual rate of commission. Jones has the opportunity of making two commissions, but he also takes the risk that if he does not sell the Adams house, he will have to tie up his own funds and later may have to sell below the $15,000 figure: *Jones v. Howard,* 234 Ill. 404 (1908).

Salesperson—employee or independent contractor?

It is a serious matter whether a sales person affiliated with a broker is an employee or an independent contractor. Under the first classification, the position of the sales person is much the same as a clerk or bookkeeper in the broker's office. This means that the broker must make returns to the Internal Revenue Service of money withheld, carry Workmen's Compensation Insurance, and is responsible for accidents occurring in the course of the sales person's real estate activities. In the classification of the sales person as an independent contractor, the broker is freed from such responsibilities. At times, the distinction between an employee and an independent contractor is a tenuous one, since, in relation to an owner and a buyer, the broker necessarily reserves some direction and supervision, and accordingly, assumes some responsibility to the owner and purchaser. There has been some movement for the single license concept, abolishing the distinction between a broker's license and a sales person's license, or an associate broker's license. So far, the single license concept has not been adopted in any state.

In determining whether a sales person is in fact an employee, or whether the person is an independent contractor, it necessarily depends upon the arrangements in effect in the particular real estate office. A written contract is *essential,* and equally important is whether the conditions stated in such contract are actually carried out. The mere term "independent contractor," does not, per se, establish such relationship. It is not the *form* of the agreement, but the *substance,* which controls. Some of the attributes of an independent contractor relationship would not require the sales person follow any prescribed schedule of office work hours; attend office or sales meetings; assignment of particular listings to such person; no specified time for duration of the relationship; file daily reports; salesperson assumes expenses of automobile; dues to associations and license fees, as well as entertainment, incidental to negotiating a sale. In short, he has no expense account, for which the broker is responsible.

The broker, under the independent contractor arrangement, can provide office space, telephone and stenographic services. The broker is obligated to pay the agreed upon commission, when it is received by the broker. In the case of *Bidwell v. Iowa Employment Security Commission* involving an unpaid contribution, under the Iowa Employment Security Law, the Commission held that the real estate salesman was an independent contractor (1973).

AUTHORIZATION TO SELL CONTRACT
(Listing Contract)

Dated .... April 1, 1974.............
at Glendale, Kentucky

Listing Price: $17,000.
Between .... *LOIS MAE GIRARD, single* ....
Owner

....
AND

REALTY SALES COMPANY, 428 MARKET ST., GLENDALE, KY. for the sale of real estate at *1101 Riverview Ave., Glendale (3) Ky.*...

In consideration of $1.00, receipt whereof is hereby acknowledged, and other valuable consideration, the undersigned Owner hereby employs ...... REALTY SALES COMPANY ...... as the sole and exclusive agent irrevocably for a period of ...... three (3) months ...... from the date hereof, for the sale of premises described on the reverse of this contract, and which data constitutes a material part of the contract of employment, and agrees to pay said ...... REALTY SALES COMPANY .. .... a commission of ...... seven (7) per cent ...... on the gross consideration price or at any other terms and price accepted by the Owner, upon the sale, exchange or transfer, or upon the exercise of an option to purchase clause in a lease, whether made by myself or by any other person during the above mentioned term of employment, or any extension or renewal thereof.

The authority of ...... *REALTY SALES COMPANY* ...... shall terminate at the expiration of the above term, unless renewed, without any further liability on the part of the owner unless the sale, transfer, lease or exchange of the above property is made or effected directly or indirectly by me, the undersigned owner, or through any other person within a period of ...... *six (6) months* ...... from the expiration of this employment contract or any extension or renewal thereof, to any person or persons with whom ...... *REALTY SALES COMPANY* ...... has been negotiating or dealing for the sale, lease, transfer or exchange of said property, in which event, the owner agrees to pay .... .. *REALTY SALES COMPANY* ...... the above commission, which shall become immediately due and payable.

I hereby authorize said ...... *REALTY SALES COMPANY* ...... to place a "For Sale" sign upon said property, which shall be the only such sign displayed thereon during the term of this contract or any extension or renewal therof.

All earnest money deposits paid upon the purchase price shall be held by the agent in an escrow or trust account until consummation of the deal or termination thereof.

In event said deposit money or any part thereof is forfeited as liquidated damages, such sum or sums shall be divided equally between broker and owner. However, broker shall not receive any sum greater than the agreed upon commission.

I HEREBY ACKNOWLEDGE RECEIPT OF A COPY OF THIS AUTHORIZATION TO SELL CONTRACT.

.... Lois Mae Girard......... (SEAL)
Owner

REALTY SALES COMPANY
by .... Marie E Baier......... (SEAL)
Broker

This contract is hereby renewed and extended upon the same exclusive right to sell terms and conditions for a period of .... from .... 197 ... to .... 197 ...

.... (SEAL)
Owner
REALTY SALES COMPANY
by .... (SEAL)
Broker

A-1 (a) SIMPLE LISTING CARD

LISTED BY *Office*

District .... *Edgewater*......... Date Listed .... *April 1, 1974*........
Constr. & Design .... *Brick*...........................
Rooms, 1*st* Floor .... *3* .... 2nd .... *3* ...... 3rd....... *None* ......
Bath.... *tile*..... Shower..... *yes* .... Breakfast Room, Sun Room .... *No*......
Hardwood Floors .... *yes*.... Double .... *yes*.... Water Heater.... *Galv*.......
Insulated... *yes*...
Heating System..... *Hot Air* ..... Coal ..... Coal & Fruit Cellars ..... *yes*......
Plumbing ...... *Galv*.......

CLASS
.... 4
.... 3
.... 2
X 1

Screens .... *yes* Weather Stripped ...... *yes* .... Concrete Porches .... *yes* ..... Roof...... *asb. slat Copper Gutters*...... Spouting ..... *Galv*.......
General Condition..... *good* ..... when Built ..... *1950*...... Builder..... *G.C. Carson*... Garage... *Integral*...
Lot Size ...... *75 × 150*....... Level .... *Slopes rear* ...... Alley .... *yes*
Paved Street... *yes*...
Assessment...... *$6500*...... Taxes: City ..... *$90*..... School...... *$54*......
County... *$36*... Total... *$180*...
Mortgage ..... *$4000*..... Monthly Payment ..... *$100*..... Interest Rate......
7%... Mortgage... *City Bank*...
Rental ...... *Owner occupied*...... Tenant...... Phone ..... Sale Clause .....
Place Sign... *yes*...
Special Features ...... *Possession June 17, 1974*............................
....
Directions...
Price ...... *$17,000* .... Address ...... *1101 Riverview Ave., Glendale, Ky.*

Title in name of ...... *Lois Mae Girard*.................................

I hereby represent and warrant the above information to be true and correct.

Lois Mae Girard
Owner

SALESMAN'S CONTRACT

(Recommended by Oakland, California, Real Estate Board)

RUSH REALTY COMPANY hereinafter referred to as "Company"

and DOROTHY FISHER hereinafter referred to as "Salesman",

hereby agree, subject to termination at the will of either party, to the following conditions and details of their relationship, namely:

(1) FACILITIES:

Company shall provide Salesman with advertising and with necessary office equipment including space, desk, telephone, signs, business cards and stationery, and shall assist and cooperate with Salesman in connection with his work.

(2) GENERAL CONDITIONS:

(a) Salesman shall read and shall govern his conduct by the Code of Ethics of the National Association of Real Estate Boards, the Real Estate Law of the State of California and the By-Laws of the Oakland Real Estate Board and regulations of Multiple Listing Division of the Real Estate Board, and any future modifications or additions thereto.

(b) The schedule of customary commissions of the Oakland Real Estate Board shall be used in every transaction, and any variation therefrom must first be approved by Company; and Salesman hereby admits knowledge of customary schedules of commissions as published by the Real Estate Board.

(c) Salesman shall furnish his own automobile and pay all expenses thereof and shall carry liability and property damage insurance satisfactory to Company.

(d) Salesman must remain continuously licensed by the State of California to sell real estate as a salesman.

(e) Salesman shall not obligate Company for materials or services without the knowledge and first obtaining consent of Company.

(f) Salesman shall use only such real estate forms as have first been approved by Company.

(g) Salesman hereby acknowledges he is an independent contractor, and is not a servant, employee, joint-adventurer or partner of the Broker. (Note) In some offices, Salesmen are employees of the Broker and (g) may be changed accordingly.

(h) Other Clauses:

(3) COMMISSIONS:

All commissions resulting from real estate transactions procured by Salesman shall be divided between Company and Salesman on a basis of 45 per cent of the net commission to Salesman. Any expense incurred in negotiating the sale, including listing and Board Multiple Listing commissions, shall first be deducted from the gross commission before such division. No commission shall be considered earned or payable to Salesman until the transaction has been completed and the commission collected by Company.

(4) LISTING COMMISSIONS — SALES — RENTALS AND LEASES:

Sales:

(1) Upon sale of property by other than listing Salesman, he shall be paid out of the commission received by Company, as follows:

a. 10 per cent on signed non-exclusive listings.

b. 15 per cent on signed exclusive listings.

c. 15 per cent of entire commission on signed exclusive listings sold by another Company.

d. 15 per cent of the gross commission on Board Multiple Listings remaining after payment of the Multiple Listing fee.

(2) Company reserves the right to reject any exclusive listing deemed unsatisfactory and to return said listing to the owner.

(a) Upon termination of Salesman's association by decision of Salesman, Company shall not be liable to Salesman for a commission on any listing procured by Salesman or on any sale of property unless an offer in writing has been obtained from a bona fide purchaser accompanied with a deposit under the listing prior to the termination of association and the same transaction is later completed.

(b) Upon termination of association by decision of Company, Salesman shall receive agreed listing commission on his listings if sold within the life of such listings.

(c) All listings and prospects are the property of the Company.

(5) COMMISSIONS OTHER THAN CASH:

In connection with any type of transaction, if it becomes necessary or desirable to receive all or any part of a commission in property other than cash, then approval of Company must first be obtained.

In such event, Company and Salesman may agree to:

(a) divide such property between Company and Salesman in kind, or

(b) pay Salesman his full share of the commission in cash and retain full ownership in the property so received, or

(c) retain such property in the names of Company and Salesman and thereafter dispose of the same at such time and in such manner as Company and Salesman shall deem advisable. Any profit or loss and any carrying charge or other expense with respect to such property shall be shared between Company and Salesman in the same proportion as their respective interests in the commission involved.

(6) ESCROWS:

Company shall order all title searches and handle all escrows.

(7) ADVERTISING:

All advertising must be first approved by Company before publication; such advertising shall be at Company expense.

(8) TELEPHONE AND TELEGRAMS:

Salesman shall make no long distance telephone calls, nor shall Salesman send any telegrams, without the approval of Company. All messages over $1.00 shall be paid ½ by the Company and ½ by the Salesman for whose benefit the cost was incurred.

(9) LITIGATION

In the event any transaction in which Salesman is involved results in dispute, litigation, or legal expense, Salesman shall cooperate fully with Company and Company and Salesman shall share all expense connected therewith in the same proportion as they would normally share the commission resulting from such transaction without a dispute or litigation. It is the policy to avoid litigation wherever possible, and Company reserves the sole right to determine whether or not any litigation or dispute shall be prosecuted, defended or settled, or whether or not legal expenses shall be incurred.

(10) DIVISION OF COMMISSION:

Any arrangement for division of commission with other brokers must be first approved by Company. In the event that two or more salesmen licensed with Company participate in a commission on the same transaction it shall be divided between the participating Salesmen according to a written agreement or by arbitration.

(11) DEPOSITS, ETC.:

All monies, documents or property received by Salesman in connection with any transaction of Company shall be delivered to Company immediately. All checks must be made payable either to Company, to a title insurance company, or to any other escrow holder.

In the event all or any portion of a deposit is forfeited, disbursement of Company's share shall be the same as though the forfeited amount was a commission received in connection with the transaction.

(12) CORRESPONDENCE:

All letters received and a copy of all letters written by Salesman pertaining to the business or Company shall be turned over to Company for its records. All letters are to be approved by Company before mailing.

(13) OTHER CLAUSES:

Upon termination of salesman's employment, all office material and data, including listings, prospect books and files, office supplies, keys, etc, shall be returned to the company.

The undersigned hereby agrees to abide by all of the foregoing specifications and use his skill, efforts and workmanship in cooperating with Company to carry out the terms of this agreement for the mutual benefit of Company and undersigned Salesman.

Dated this *4th* day of *February*, 19 *72*

By *William A. Rushton*
Wa. Rush Realty Company

Dorothy Fischer
Salesman

Questions on Brokerage

1. Q. Is there any economic justification for a real estate broker?
   A. Yes, services have value as much as productive goods such as food or clothing.
2. Q. What is the relationship between broker and owner?
   A. Principal (owner) and agent (broker) relationship.
3. Q. Is a salesperson's relationship to the broker, one of master and servant (employer—employee), or independent contractor?
   A. The relationship is determined by the *substantial* content of the contract between the broker and sales person. Under the master—servant relationship, the salesperson would usually be required to attend office meetings and file daily reports. Car expense would be assumed by the employing broker, as well as license fees and entertainment, etc. As an independent contractor, the salesperson's time is his own.
4. Q. In order to recover a real estate commission in court, what must a broker first aver in the complaint and prove?
   A. That he was a duly licensed broker.
5. Q. What two other averments must the broker prove?
   A. He was employed by the owner.
   He was the efficient and procuring cause of the sale or lease.
6. Q. What states, at the present time, do not require a license in order to operate as a broker?
   A. None
7. Q. How many provinces in Canada do not require a broker to have a license?
   A. None
8. Q. Daisy Reston, single, lists property for sale on January 2, 1974 with Bennett Realty, at $18,500. She marries Henry Boyd on February 28, 1974. Bennett obtains a cash offer of $18,500 on March 21, 1974. Henry refuses to sign the sales agreement. Can Bennett recover a commission from Daisy?
   A. Yes. The property was owned by Daisy alone when it was listed. The broker performed his part of the contract in full; the marriage, after the listing, has no effect.
9. Q. Can Henry Boyd be sued as a defendant in the preceding case?
   A. No; since he was not a party to the listing contract.
10. Q. Can both Daisy and Henry be jointly named?
    A. Yes, but the suit would be dismissed as to Henry.
11. Q. C.D. Sloan owns a vacant commercial building in a downtown area. He places a large sign reading "For Sale or For Rent, Call 261-1225" or "SEE YOUR BROKER." Randolph, a prospect, contacts a broker, Marlin, who calls Sloan and obtains the terms of sale. Later, a sale is made by Sloan to Randolph at $72,000. Marlin claims the usual commission of 7 per cent in that area. Can he recover?
    A. No. The statement "See Your Broker" does not establish a contract of employment between Sloan and Marlin. In states requiring a listing contract to be in writing, Marlin, of course, could not recover.
12. Q. In how many ways may a broker establish a contract of employment?
    A. 1. by express contract.
    2. by ratification by the owner.
    3. by conduct of the parties.

13. Q. Adams employed the Boston Auction Company to sell his residence at auction. The auctioneer announced that "broker participation" would be allowed if the broker had registered his client with "us," if his party was the successful bidder. A broker, Clark, registered the successful bidder with the auctioneer, who refused to pay any commission. Clark sued Adams. Can he recover?
    A. No. There was no privity of contract between Adams and Clark. The auctioneer had no authority to bind the owner.
14. Q. Broker Jones secures an oral listing from seller, MacDonald, to sell his house for $17,500; agreement to terminate in 30 days, commission to be 6%. Jones secures a buyer for the property at $17,500. The owner refused to permit broker to complete sale and completes it himself. Jones demands his commission. Can broker recover?
    A. In those states which require a listing contract to be in writing, he could not recover. In the other states, he could recover.
15. Q. A broker is employed by a wife to sell her real estate; he secures a buyer on her terms; the husband refuses to sign the contract of sale and the deal falls through. Is the broker entitled to a commission from the wife?
    A. Yes. He has fully performed his contract of employment since he produced a purchaser, ready, able, and willing to buy. However, if he had good reason to believe that the husband would not join in the contract of sale the decision would be different.
16. Q. An owner gives an exclusive listing to broker Abel for a six months period. During the exclusive period, he gives a nonexclusive listing to Kane, who produces a buyer. What is the owner's liability for commission?
    A. He is obligated to pay full commission to both Abel and Kane.
17. Q. A salesman is assisted in a deal by another salesman employed by another broker. The first salesman pays one-half of his commission to the salesman who assisted him. Is this legal?
    A. No; the salesman has no right to recognize anyone other than his employing broker. The latter should deal and recognize the other broker and not the other broker's salesman.
18. Q. Why does an exclusive right to sell listing contract afford the broker more protection than an exclusive listing?
    A. Full commission is assured the broker, regardless of who sells the property during the term of the listing.
19. Q. Assuming you are a broker and discover you have obtained an Exclusive Right to Sell contract from a property owner who is incompetent. What are your rights in enforcing this contract?
    A. None. Contract is void.
20. Q. If you have a property listed for sale and find a prospect who is willing to take an option on the same at the terms offered, are you entitled to your commission?
    A. No. An option does not bind the purchaser to buy, and the broker is entitled to his commission only if the option is exercised.
21. Q. If you listed a house for sale, which had wall to wall carpeting in the living room and hall, would you make reference to the carpeting in your listing?
    A. Yes. A statement in listing may save argument and perhaps loss of sale later.
22. Q. Name five methods by which an agency may be terminated.
    A. 1. By agreement between principal and agent.
       2. By expiration of the term.
       3. By extinction of subject matter.
       4. By death of either principal or agent.
       5. By incapacity of either principal or agent.
23. Q. A broker is employed by the son of A and B, husband and wife, to sell the parents' real property. The mother has authorized the son to list the property but the father has not. The broker secures a buyer on the exact terms of the listing; the father

refused to sign an agreement of sale and the deal falls through. Can the broker recover a commission?

A. The broker can recover from the mother since the son was her authorized agent. Or, the broker could sue the son, who gave the listing, as he represented he was duly authorized to do so. He could not recover from the father.

24. Q. Cook, a salesman employed by Ajax Realty Co., negotiated a sale of real estate. The owner refused to pay the commission and the firm declines to sue. Cook sues the owner. Can he recover?

A. No.

25. Q. A broker claimed a commission for procuring a purchaser for an owner's property. He obtained a buyer. When the deal was closed, title was taken in the name of the father of the purchaser and the property leased to the son. Can the broker recover a commission?

A. Yes, the broker clearly made the deal and the arrangement for taking title would not defeat his earned commission.

26. Q. William Rushton, a broker, had an exclusive listing on Andrew Erbel's home, which expired on August 30, 1974. Before the listing expired Rushton procured Frank Stone as a prospect. On August 16, 1974, Erbel *leased* the property to Stone for six months and on December 6, signed an agreement to sell him the property. Is Rushton entitled to a commission?

A. Yes; it appears that the lease was merely an arrangement to circumvent the commission claim and that the parties to it did not act in good faith.

27. Q. The National Insurance Company owned a farm. Wilson, a broker, offered to trade an apartment house, listed with him for sale, for the farm. He dealt with Alberts, treasurer of the Company. The treasurer stated: "We want high class apartment property." The broker replied "All right, sir, I will see what I can do." An exchange was made through another broker. Can Wilson recover against National Insurance Company?

A. No. There is no express or implied contract of employment. It would appear that plaintiff was representing the apartment building owner, since the Insurance Company had not listed the farm with him.

28. Q. A property was listed with James who was not licensed but who obtained his broker's license before he rendered any services. Two days after he received his license he negotiated a real estate deal. Can he recover a commission?

A. No. Since James did not have a license when he obtained the listing he could not recover a commission.

29. Q. Ahern lists property for sale with Brett, a broker, at $6,000. Brett purchases the property in Cobb's name and sells it to Simmons for $7,500. Brett collects a commission from Ahern of $300. Later Ahern discovers the real facts. What redress does he have?

A. He can recover the $1,500 profit and, in addition, can recover the $300 commission paid to Brett. The broker forfeits his right to a commission because of his duplicity.

30. Q. Aiken lists property for sale with Benson, a broker, at $8,000, the broker to receive a commission of five per cent. Benson procures a buyer who refuses to pay more than $7,500. Two months later the deal is made at $7,500 and Benson claims $375 as commission. Aiken refuses to pay claiming the listing was at $8,000. Can Benson recover?

A. Yes. The courts will not permit an owner to take advantage of a broker's efforts and then turn him "out of doors." The agent here was still the efficient and procuring cause of the sale.

31. Q. Bowles, a broker, was employed by Archer to sell three lots for him. It was not an exclusive agency. Bowles procured Mrs. Crane who was acting for herself and her husband. Each purchased one lot, as did Drake, whom Mrs. Crane had informed that

the lots in question were for sale. Bowles sued Archer for a commission on the sale of all three lots. Can he recover?

A. Bowles can recover commissions only upon the sale of the two lots to the Cranes. The broker was in no way directly connected with the sale of the lot to Drake. The law deals only with proximate and not remote causes.

32. Q. The plaintiff broker, Bender, "worked upon" one Collins and induced him to look at property owned by Allen, listed with Bender for sale. Collins finally decided not to buy himself, but upon Collins' advice, Collins' brother bought directly from the owner, Allen. Is Bender entitled to a commission on the sale?

A. No. In the absence of collusion or fraud, the plaintiff was not the procuring cause of the sale to Collins' brother.

33. Q. Jones gave Peters an exclusive listing upon his property at $9,000. The agreement was for a term of 3 months at 5 per cent commission. The agreement provided for termination after the term upon 30 days' written notice from the owner. "In default of such notice, this exclusive contract shall renew itself from term to term as an exclusive contract . . . until notice herein provided shall be given to terminate." The agreement was dated November 28, 1973. Notice of termination was given on May 16, 1974. The property was sold by the owner, Jones, on July 26, 1974. Is the broker entitled to his commission?

A. Yes. The written notice of termination given May 16, 1974 was too late to terminate the contract during the term in which it was given. It operated to terminate the listing as of August 28, 1974. Inasmuch as the property was sold on July 26, 1974, Peters was entitled to his commission.

34. Q. Smith, a minor, employs Black to sell a piece of real estate which he owns. Black, dubious as to Smith's age, makes inquiry. Smith misrepresents his age to be 25 years. After Black sells the property, Smith disaffirms the contract of employment and refuses to pay Black any commission. Can Black recover?

A. No. Black's suit in assumpsit (upon a contract) is against an infant upon a *voidable* contract. Smith cannot make himself of age by misrepresenting his age. He is still an infant in fact and the law permits him to plead infancy as a defense. An infant is liable for deceit, which is a tort (an actionable wrong) action. Black could sue Smith in a trespass action upon the tort.

35. Q. Andrews, an owner, wrote Burns, a broker, "You might proceed and sell the entire 13 houses separately for $50,000 net cash to me. Your commission of 3% to come out of the last sale made." The houses were sold by Burns for an aggregate amount of $50,000. Andrews refuses to pay any commission. Can Burns recover?

A. No. The broker is not entitled to any commission unless the sum received exceeds the specified "net" price, the word "net" meaning that which remains after deducting all charges such as commission.

36. Q. Flynn, a broker, asks Dubbs, an owner, the price of his house, and introduces him to a client, who subsequently purchases it. Can he recover a commission?

A. No. Even though he may have, to some extent, influenced the sale, he cannot recover, because he cannot prove an employment. "How much do you want for it ?" does not constitute employment.

37. Q. Arthur listed property for sale with Blaine at $12,000. Blaine negotiated a sale to Clancy, who paid $1,000 down. After the agreement of sale is signed, Arthur obtains a memorandum from Blaine that "commission is to be paid at the time of settlement." Settlement is never made due to mutual releases by seller and buyer. Can Blaine recover from Arthur for commission?

A. Yes. There was no legal consideration for the promise to wait for his commission until the date of settlement. The mutual releases do not absolve the seller from payment of a commission.

38. Q. Woods mails a description of his property to Talley, a broker, with a request that he sell it at $18,500 cash. Nothing is said about commission. The broker obtains a buyer

at $18,500 cash. There is an argument about paying a commission. Can Talley recover?

A. Yes. There is an implied promise to pay the usual commission, since the broker obtained a satisfactory buyer upon the seller's terms. He could recover on a "quantum meruit" basis, what he deserves, which would be the usual commission.

39. Q. Young is a tenant of Fox for certain premises used as a variety store. Young lists the business for sale with Boone, a real estate broker. Boone advertises the business for sale and interests Dunn, a prospective purchaser. Dunn and Young call upon Fox for the purpose of transferring the lease, but Fox refuses, and as a result Dunn purchases the building from Fox. Can the broker, Boone, recover a commission from Fox?

A. No. In the first place Boone cannot establish a contract of employment with Fox, and, in the second place, Boone was not the direct proximate cause of the real estate sale.

40. Q. Benson, a broker, obtained an inquiry from Mann for certain industrial real estate, at a purchase price of $20,000. Benson had the same property listed with him by Ambers, the owner, at $14,000. Benson informed Ambers that he himself would purchase the property at Ambers' price. Agreements were signed and Benson assigned the agreements to Mann. Ambers sues Benson for $6,000. Can Ambers recover? Is Benson entitled to a commission on the $20,000 deal?

A. Ambers can recover. Benson is not entitled to any commission. An agent is a fiduciary. He owes a high degree of loyalty to his principal. He cannot make a secret profit at the expense of his principal. Since Benson offered to buy the property *after* he had a purchaser at a higher price, he forfeits his rights to a commission.

41. Q. The real estate broker's license of Adams expired on December 31, 1971. On January 6, 1972, he negotiated a sale of property listed in his office at a price of $40,000. He did not renew his license until January 28, 1972. The owner refused to pay a commission and Adams sued. Can he recover?

A. No. The broker is not entitled to compensation on a transaction negotiated after his license has expired and before renewal license was issued.

42. Q. Peters gave Brent an exclusive agency to sell his real estate for $8,500. The contract is dated February 28, 1974. It runs for 6 months and then indefinitely as an *exclusive agency* unless terminated by 30 days' written notice from the owner. After procuring a few prospects in March 1974, nothing is done by Brent upon the listing. Peters sells the property in July 1974 through another broker, Kane, to whom he pays the usual commission. Can Brent collect a commission?

A. Yes. Although his right would appear unconscionable, the exclusive listing "ran on" until Peters took the necessary steps to cancel it, by giving Brent written notice to that effect. If the license law, or Rule of the Commission, requires a *definite* expiration date for the listing, Brent could not recover.

43. Q. Jones lists his property for sale verbally with three real estate offices. Brown, a broker, shows the property to Neil. Later Neil calls at the office of a second broker, Clark, who shows him several properties, including Jones's property. Neil tells Clark that he has already seen the property but Clark insists that he make another inspection. Clark calls Neil's attention to the construction, fixtures, and appointments. Neil is impressed and several days later calls at the house alone and gives Jones a check for $500 on the purchase. The deal is closed. Jones pays Brown a one-half commission and pays Clark a one-half commission. Both Brown and Clark sue Jones. Who will win?

A. Clark appears to be the broker who actually effected the sale. But the question of which broker is the efficient and procuring cause of the sale is a question of fact for a jury to decide. In claims from more than one broker, an owner should pay the money into court, so as to confine his liability to the payment of a single commission.

44. Q. A broker holds a license expiring on June 28, 1974. On July 2, 1974, he has not

renewed his license. On that date, he negotiates the sale of property of an owner. Indicate by check-mark, which of the following will apply.

A. He is still registered ________.
The sale is illegal ________.
The broker forfeits his commission ✓________.
The registration of the broker may be revoked ________.

45. Q. Name two persons to whom a broker may lawfully pay compensation for services in a real estate transaction.
A. His licensed real estate salesman.
A licensed real estate broker.

46. Q. In obtaining a listing of a residence for sale, name at least ten factors in regard to the property, which a broker should include on his listing card data.
A. Construction and design; layout of rooms and sizes; types of floors; baths; heating system; age of building; roof construction and spouting; size of lot; garage; taxes and mortgage data; amount of assessment; screens; weather-stripping; type of plumbing; special features.

47. Q. What is the legal terminology of the relationship between a broker and his client?
A. Agency.

48. Q. Are these three reasons why a broker should obtain an exclusive listing?
A. (a) Guarantees a broker he will earn a commission—Yes ________. No X.
(b) Protects against other brokers stealing his prospects—Yes X. No ________
(c) Causes the broker to feel more secure—Yes X. No ________.

49. Q. If a listing does not state a definite expiration date, it may nevertheless be terminated in several ways. Name them.
A. Performance, lapse of time, revocation, abandonment, renunciation. (In some states, listing is void.)

50. Q. Broker Smith gives you information concerning one of his listings and you sell the property. Should you negotiate through Smith or directly with the owner? Why?
A. With Smith, because he has the only legally enforceable contract of agency employment.

51. Q. What is the difference between a "Realtor" and a "Real Estate Broker"?
A. A "Realtor" is a member of the local, state, and national real estate association. A "Real Estate Broker" is any licensed broker.

52. Q. Ash lists a property for sale with Burns on Jan. 16, 1974. Ash leaves for a 2-month vacation but dies while he is away. Burns, unaware of Ash's death, obtained a signed agreement for the property from Johnson upon Ash's terms. Ash's heirs refuse to honor it or to pay Burns a claimed commission. Can Burns recover?
A. No. Ash's death automatically cancelled Burns's employment. The fact that Burns was unaware of Ash's death is immaterial.

53. Q. Ahern lists his property for sale with Brown by telephone. Brown calls Foster's attention to the property by phone. Ahern and Foster are friends, and Foster has visited Ahern's home a number of times. When Brown calls Ahern's attention to Foster as a prospect, Ahern replies, "Oh, I talked to him about buying my property years ago." Later Ahern sells to Foster. Is Brown entitled to a commission?
A. Yes. He has brought the parties to an agreement. Although his services, measured in time, may not have amounted to much, yet he was responsible in bringing the parties together, which resulted in the agreement.

54. Q. Broker Jones had a property listed with his office in December 1973. He showed it to Hensel and introduced Hensel to Dixon, the owner, on January 28, 1974, but did nothing more. The listing expired on February 15, 1974. Dixon sold the property to Hensel on March 25, 1974. Is Jones entitled to a commission?
A. No. Opening negotiations but failing to bring owner and prospect to an agreement,

is insufficient. Since the listing had expired when the agreement was made, the broker could not recover.

55. Q. Weston employs Richter to sell his property. The listing makes no mention as to who shall hold the deposit money. Richter obtains a purchaser on Weston's terms. Weston refuses to sign the contract of sale unless the deposit money is paid to him. Is his contention sound?

A. Yes. The listing should authorize the broker to hold the deposit money in his escrow account.

56. Q. Does the license law require a seller to permit the broker to hold any earnest money deposit in the broker's escrow account ?

A. No. But the law requires deposit money *paid* to the broker to be deposited in an escrow account.

57. Q. What different types of listing are used in real estate practice?

A. Open listings (non-exclusive), exclusive, exclusive right to sell and multiple listings, net listings.

58. Q. Which type of above listing would give the owner the greatest opportunity to sell his property?

A. Under the multiple listing, since all members of the multi-list association would have the right to sell the property.

59. Q. Is it legal for a broker to purchase a property listed with his office for sale?

A. Yes, if the broker discloses all information to the owner, which might influence the owner's decision to sell.

60. Q. Does the law *require* a broker to obtain an earnest money deposit, in order to have a binding agreement of sale?

A. No, but the broker would be rendering a disservice to the owner, if he did not *request* a deposit commensurate with the sales price.

61. Q. A broker has been authorized by all parties involved to negotiate an exchange of certain properties. Would he be entitled to commission on all the properties in the transaction?

A. Yes. His dual employment is known and recognized by the parties involved.

62. Q. Jane Thomas, who generally conducted her father's (Tom Thomas's) affairs, gave Fair the sole agency for the sale of a lot. He placed his sign on it. This was done with the father's knowledge, and without objection. Jane referred a prospect to the broker, stating that the matter was entirely out of her hands. Can Fair recover from Thomas upon a sale to the prospect?

A. Yes. Under the doctrine of estoppel, the father is prevented from denying the authority of the daughter to list the property with the broker.

63. Q. Allen employed Black, a broker, to sell some investment property for him. Black obtained Clay as a purchaser. At the time of closing the deal it developed that the property did not have the rental income claimed by Allen, whereupon Clay refused to go through with the deal. Is Black entitled to a commission?

A. Yes. He complied with his contract of employment with Allen.

64. Q. A minor, Young, employed Bell to sell his property. Bell obtained a purchaser, Cooper, upon Young's terms, and Cooper made a substantial down payment. Young refused to accept the offer, stating that he had changed his mind. Can the broker collect a commission?

A. No. Who deals with an infant does so at his peril. The contract is voidable and may be disaffirmed by the minor.

65. Q. Miss Agatha Vebler listed property, which she had inherited, with Smith-Jones Realty Company. The next day, the firm produced a purchaser and Miss Vebler signed the contract of sale. Prior thereto, Miss Vebler married Anthony Taylor. At the closing, the husband refused to join in the deed and the deal fell through. Can the plaintiff broker recover a commission?

A. Yes. The broker acted in good faith, without any knowledge that the owner was married when she signed the contract of sale.

66. Q. A principal directs a broker to sell his property for $50,000. The broker might have obtained $50,000, but by collusion with the purchaser he sells it to him for $40,000, with the consent of the owner, who knows nothing of the collusive agreement and is anxious to sell at any price. The owner, later learning of the broker's infidelity, refuses to pay him any commission. What are the rights of the parties?

A. The broker cannot collect any commission and the owner can recover from the broker any secret profit, which the broker may have made in the transaction. The broker has violated his duty of loyalty to his principal and forfeits his rights to any compensation.

67. Q. Baker, a licensed broker, negotiated a real estate transaction to a purchaser referred to him by Calhoun, a registered engineer. The agreement of sale executed by the parties provided that $2/3$ of the commission was to be paid to Baker and $1/3$ to Calhoun. Suit was filed jointly by Baker and Calhoun but at the time of trial, Calhoun withdrew his suit. Can Baker recover?

A. No. Since the suit was a joint action and Calhoun was not licensed, this fact is fatal to Baker's action. It is obvious that both Baker and Calhoun were acting jointly in negotiating the sale. The fact that the owner was to pay $1/3$ of the commission directly to Calhoun, is a mere subterfuge.

68. Q. Axford employs Bird, a licensed broker, to sell property for which he is to receive a specified sum as his commission. Without informing Axford, Bird also acts for the buyer, who also promises him a commission. When Axford discovers that Bird is acting for both parties, he goes through with the deal but refuses to pay the broker's commission. Bird sues. Can he recover?

A. No. A broker cannot represent both parties in the same transaction. The law does not permit a servant to serve two masters. The broker's employment by the seller is incompatible with his similar employment by the buyer.

69. Q. Under what circumstances, if any, may a seller impose the condition on a broker that he is to receive commission only in the event that the sale is consummated by the execution and the delivery of the deed?

A. Only if the condition is agreed upon before the broker has procured a bona fide purchaser for the property and a properly executed agreement of sale.

70. Q. Barnes, a broker employed by Arthur, procures an agreement of sale signed by Clark and upon the owner's terms of sale. However, the agreement provides for closing the deal six months hence. Arthur has another purchaser for the property at the same price with the closing fixed for thirty days. Arthur refuses to sign Barnes' agreement. Is Barnes entitled to a commission?

A. No. Six months is an unreasonable length of time for the closing, and Arthur is within his rights in objecting to the delay.

71. Q. Brett, a licensed real estate broker, obtained from Ash, an owner, the terms upon which Ash would be willing to sell his property. Brett submitted these terms to Connor, a prospective purchaser. Brett did nothing more. Ash and Connor thereafter and without Brett's knowledge, entered into an agreement of sale for the property upon the original terms. Brett sued for commission. The Court held that Brett was not entitled to the commission. What were the reasons for the Court's finding?

A. Brett was not the efficient and procuring cause of the sale. There is no evidence in the facts stated that Brett brought the parties together, or that Brett disclosed Connor's identity to Ash.

72. Q. A real estate broker is forced to sue to collect a commission that is due him. In addition to the facts setting forth his cause of action, what fact does the License Law require him to allege in his complaint and prove on the trial of his case?

A. That he was properly *licensed* as a real estate broker at the time the cause of action arose.

73. Q. In dealing with an officer of the corporate owner of property listed for sale, what

precaution should the broker take?

A. The broker should ascertain whether the officer of the corporation has been authorized by a resolution of the board of directors to list the property for sale.

74. Q. Can a broker's claim for commission be found upon an implied contract of employment?

A. Only in those states, which do not require a listing contract to be in writing.

75. Q. Jones, broker, obtains an oral listing from Smith, to sell Smith's residence. Jones obtains a signed offer to purchase from Greene and before presenting the offer to Smith, goes to Smith and obtains a written listing from him. Two days later, agreements are signed by Smith and Greene. The sales agreement states that Smith owes Jones a 6 percent commission. Can Jones recover a commission?

A. Yes. The post listing agreement, supported by the obligation of Smith to pay Jones a commission would constitute ratification of Jones' employment.

76. Q. A broker negotiated an option to purchase real estate, which expired on May 15, 1974. On July 1, 1974, the optionee exercised the option and purchased the property. The broker claims a commission. Can he recover?

A. No. Since the optionee did not exercise his option prior to the expiration date, the option expired and the broker's rights terminated at the same time.

77. Q. A contract for the sale of real estate provides as follows: "The seller agrees that John Doe brought about this sale and agrees to pay him the broker's commission of five hundred dollars." Subsequent to the execution of the contract, John Doe, in a conversation with the seller, states that he will not claim his commission unless title is actually closed. Thereafter, and prior to the date set for the closing of the title, John Doe demands his commission from the seller who refuses to pay, claiming that John Doe was not entitled to a commission until the actual closing of title. Who will win?

A. John Doe, the broker, will win as his commission was earned when he produced a purchaser ready, able, and willing to buy upon the seller's terms upon the execution of the sales agreement. There was *no* consideration for Doe's promise to wait until the closing for his commission.

78. Q. What protection does a written listing give an owner?

A. The terms of the contract, such as expiration date and commission, are clearly defined so that controversy and litigation can be avoided.

79. Q. May a real estate broker or salesman pay a portion of his commission to an unlicensed person for his assistance in a sale?

A. No. It is unlawful.

80. Q. Broker Carroll has an exclusive listing on certain property from an owner and receives an unsolicited bona fide offer from Broker Woodruff. He refuses to submit the offer to the owner on the grounds that his exclusive agency does not obligate him to deal with or through any other broker, and that the prospect must deal with him directly and not through any other broker. Is he correct?

A. No. The broker is obligated to submit any offer or information which he may have regarding the subject of the agency. While Carroll may refuse to split a commission, his duty to his principal requires him to divulge the offer through Woodruff. The owner may decide to pay each broker a full commission.

81. Q. Abel listed his property with broker Berm at $15,500. Berm receives an offer of $10,500 from a prospect. Should he ignore the offer or obtain a deposit from the prospect and communicate it to Abel?

A. He should accept the deposit and advise Abel of *all* information which has come to his knowledge. It is up to the owner to accept or reject the offer.

82. Q. If the broker or salesman selling a property is the owner thereof or has an ownership interest therein, should that fact be disclosed to the purchaser before the latter obligates himself to buy?

A. Yes. A broker or salesman is not permitted to act as an undisclosed principal in a real estate transaction, whether it be as purchaser or seller.

83. Q. Smith is employed as a real estate salesman by Brown, a broker. While so employed, he attempts to sell Albert's property to Cox. A few days later, Smith and Brown "fall out" and Smith resigns from Brown's employ. Smith's license is returned to the Real Estate Commission for cancellation. He then makes a connection with the real estate office of Edwards. After applying for a transfer of license to Edwards, but before the new license has been issued, Smith negotiates and concludes the sale of Albert's property to Cox. Is Brown, Smith or Edwards entitled to a commission?

A. No one is entitled to a commission under the law. Since Smith's contract with Brown was terminated, he had no license in force when the deal with Cox was made. Smith had no assurance that the transfer of license to Edwards would be made. The salesman must be licensed whenever negotiations for the sale of real estate are carried on.

84. Q. A salesman in the employ of a real estate broker put through a sale. He demanded commission on behalf of his firm and the seller refused to pay it. His employing broker refused to be involved in litigation regardless of the merits of his claim. Thereupon the salesman sued the seller in his own name. Can he recover?

A. No. A salesman usually has no standing in a court of law; an action for commission must be instituted in the name of the broker employed by owner.

85. Q. Adams employed Bell, a broker, to sell his property. Parker employed Cross, a second broker, to buy property in the neighborhood. Parker contacted Bell and persuaded Bell to help him buy Adams' property, Bell to "put the pressure" on Adams. Bell was to receive a commission from Parker and to split the commission which Parker paid Cross. Adams signed the agreement of sale. When Adams discovered these facts, he refused to perform the contract. Will he succeed?

A. Yes. The collusion between the purchaser and Bell to take an unfair advantage of Adams will defeat any rights that Bell might otherwise have against Adams. The broker, Bell, forefeits any claim to commission.

86. Q. Jones gives you an exclusive listing on a home; you procure a buyer, ready, willing, and able. You now discover that Jones does not own the house but that his brother does. May you recover your commission from Jones?

A. Yes. You have fulfilled the terms of your contract with Jones. By holding himself out as the owner, Jones is liable.

87. Q. Blake, a broker, sells a parcel of real estate for Young, an infant, aged 17 years and 10 months. When Young becomes of age, he disaffirms the contract of sale. The broker demands that Young pay him the commission and upon Young's refusal institutes suit for payment. Can Blake recover?

A. No. The contract was voidable at Young's option, and he was, therefore, within his legal rights in disaffirming it.

88. Q. Harris, broker, obtained a purchaser, and a $500 deposit, on an "open" listing. The listing was for $12,000 and the buyer agreed to pay $11,200. Before the owner, Grant, would sign the agreement, he had Harris write in, "Commission to be paid when deal is consummated." The buyer moved to Detroit and defaulted. Grant sold the property through another broker. Can Harris recover?

A. No. Failure of the buyer to close the deal, without any fault of the seller, relieved the seller under the special terms of the contract from liability for the commission.

89. Q. Enumerate five duties which an agent owes to his principal.

A. 1. Loyalty to his trust.
2. Must obey instructions.
3. Must account for money and property.
4. Must not be negligent.
5. Must act in person.

90. Q. Under what circumstances, if any, may a broker recover a commission from both buyer and seller?

A. A broker can recover a commission from both parties when:

1. He is employed by both parties.
2. He merely brings the parties together.
3. Nothing is left to his discretion.
4. No special confidence is reposed in him.
5. The fact that he is acting in a dual capacity is known to both parties.

91. Q. The listing contract provided for a six months' "carry over" clause—if property was sold for $65,000 to a buyer procured by the broker, he was entitled to a commission. During the six-month period, the property was sold for $45,000 through another broker. It was established that the plaintiff broker presented no offer to the owner, but he had submitted the property to the ultimate purchaser during the original term of the listing; but, he did not offer $65,000. Can the broker recover?

A. No. The broker did not *procure* an acceptable buyer. He cannot recover a commission for an independent sale at a later date to the prospect for a substantially lower amount than that quoted by the owner.

92. Q. Fordham desires to list his property for sale with you at $38,000. Before accepting the listing, you make a careful appraisal of the property and it amounts to $29,500. You offer to list it at $30,000. The owner insists on listing it and advertising it at $38,000, and agrees to pay the advertising costs. Should you accept the listing?

A. No. An unrealistic listing will not sell and the broker will save time and effort by not accepting the listing.

93. Q. Should a broker keep his commissions in his trust account at all times?

A. No; only until the particular deal is closed.

94. Q. What points should an exclusive listing cover?

A. Description of property, price, terms, encumbrances, definite period for which listing is binding, agreement to pay a commission in case of sale, exchange or lease.

95. Q. David A. Stone lists his property for sale with the Rogers & Co. at $14,500. The only offer Rogers receives is $7,700, cash, from Adams. Rogers states, "It would be an insult to even submit such a ridiculous offer." Two months later, Stone sells directly to Adams at $7,700. When Rogers finds out, he sues for a commission. Can he recover?

A. No, he was not the efficient and procuring cause of the sale. He was duty bound to submit the offer to Stone.

96. Q. Hill is looking for a commercial property in the retail district of Phoenix. He contacts the A. L. Weaver Co., and promises Weaver that he will pay him $5,000 if he can locate a satisfactory site. Six suitable properties are listed for sale with the Weaver Agency. Shortly thereafter, a sale is made by the Wilson Heirs, owners, to Hill. Weaver demands the $5,000 from Hill, which is refused. Can he recover?

A. No. The broker's employment by the Wilson Heirs precludes any recovery from Hill.

97. Q. In the above case, can he recover from the Wilson Heirs?

A. No. The broker's attempt to collect a commission from both parties in the same transaction impinges upon his duty of loyalty to either party.

98. Q. An orange grove was listed by the owner, Margaret O'Neill, with the Citrus Realty Co., at $125,000. Citrus obtained a signed offer to purchase at that price, with a $2,500 earnest money payment, from Home Fruit Co., a Florida corporation. The agreements were signed on February 15, 1974 and the deal was to be closed on March 15, 1974. Home Fruit Co. was unable to obtain financing, because of a bad credit rating and a bankruptcy proceedings in 1973. Is the broker entitled to a commission?

A. No. The broker must produce a purchaser of *substance,* or one able to command the necessary money to close the transaction.

99. Q. Henry Colt was licensed in Texas as a real estate broker, as an attorney, and as an engineer. A Dallas property was listed with his office for sale. He negotiated the sale between the seller and buyer. The seller refused to pay any commission since the

listing was not in writing as required by Texas law. Can he recover?

A. No. Since he was acting exclusively as a real estate broker, the listing had to be in writing.

100. Q. How, if at all, should a broker go about negotiating a sale of property listed exclusively by another broker?

A. Contact the listing broker and operate through him as a co-broker.

101. Q. A broker holding a listing on a property secures a deposit from a prospect. The buyer signs four copies of the Agreement and one copy is left with the buyer. What two steps should he take next?

A. 1. Deliver three copies to seller for signature.
2. If accepted, leave one signed copy with the seller, deliver one signed copy to buyer, and retain one for himself.

102. Q. What is the difference, if any, between a "client" and a "customer"?

A. A customer transacts business with a real estate broker in one transaction.
A client is one who retains services of broker to represent his interests in real estate.

103. Q. A broker fails to renew his license by July 1, 1974. Then he continues to operate and does not renew his license until July 15, 1974. On July 5 he completes a transaction and retains his commission. The owner of the property demands that he receive the full amount including that portion retained by the broker for his commission. Can a broker collect a commission under these circumstances?

A. No. He was not licensed and not legally operating as a licensed broker at the date the sale was made.

104. Q. Tucker, a broker, sees a "For Sale" sign on Boyer's home and brings Davis, a prospective purchaser, to the property and introduces him to Boyer. Davis buys the property and Tucker claims a commission. Will he recover?

A. No. Tucker is a "volunteer" and cannot show a contract of employment with the owner. Boyer may well believe that Tucker was the agent of Davis.

105. Q. Smith, a broker, has a customer for a warehouse. He contacts an official of a manufacturing building and inquires if the company will consider the sale of one of its buildings. The officer replies in the affirmative and states a price of $30,000. Smith introduces his customer to the official and later a sale is made. Is the broker entitled to commission from the company?

A. No. The broker is unable to establish that he was employed by the seller, which is a prerequisite to recovery; or, that the official was authorized to act for the corporation.

106. Q. In the general function of an appointed property manager are a number of specific duties. List briefly the specific duties which you consider the most important.

A. 1. Determine proper schedule of rents.
2. Secure desirable tenants.
3. Collect rentals.
4. Render service; provide for building maintenance and repairs.
5. Keep adequate accounts.
6. Study to increase efficiency.
7. Assist in planning space, etc.

107. Q. A broker obtained a written contract of employment from an owner on January 3, 1974, which provided: "This agency shall continue 30 days from date hereof and thereafter until three days have elapsed after receipt of written notice from the Owner, terminating this agency, sent by registered mail, or delivered in person to said agent." On June 6, 1974, the legislature passed an act which provided that the practice of demanding or receiving a fee under agreements which contain no definite termination date is ground for revocation of a license. The question arose whether the act was retroactive so as to invalidate the agency employment. Decide.

A. The act is operative. The general rule is that the legislature cannot pass a law which impairs the obligation of a contract. The California appellate court held that it is equally well settled that the legislature, in the exercise of its police power, may regulate the conduct of business, and every contract is made in subordination to that authority and must yield to its control.

108. Q. What is a listing?
A. A detailed record of property listed with a broker for sale or rent; the contract of employment between owner and broker.

109. Q. A prospect desires to purchase property listed with a broker at $26,000 and proposes two offers, one at $23,000 and the second for the full price of $26,000. The second offer is to be submitted, however, only in the event that the owner rejects the first offer. Should the broker take two offers in this matter?
A. No. He must be loyal to his principal and should inform the prospective purchaser that he can only submit the offer at $26,000.

110. Q. Why should a broker purchasing a property from an owner disclose his personal purchase?
A. Acting as a principal is incompatible with a broker's employment as an agent in a fiduciary capacity.

111. Q. A broker has a 30-day exclusive listing. He advertises the property extensively at his own expense, but is unable to produce a buyer within 30 days. Two days after the exclusive expires, the seller negotiates a deal direct. The broker sues for a commission on the grounds that the deal had been made as a result of his advertising. Can he recover?
A. No. This is a risk which the broker assumes when he advertises and is unable to obtain a buyer during the period of his exclusive agency.

112. Q. Adams gives Bair a written exclusive listing for 60 days. Adams dies during the 60-day period. Is the agency cancelled?
A. Yes. Death automatically cancels the agency, unless it is coupled with an interest.

113. Q. Adam Blake is licensed as an individual broker. He obtains a listing from Joe P. Brown on January 4, 1974. He then decides to incorporate. A charter is granted on February 18, 1974 and all of the assets of Blake (including listings) are transferred to the corporation, Enterprise Realty Co. A sale of the subject property is made on March 15, 1974 and a license is issued to the corporation on March 18, 1974. Brown refuses to pay any commission. Can Blake, individually, or the corporation recover?
A. No; the corporation, not Blake, made the sale. The corporation was not licensed when the sale was made.

114. Q. Is it good practice to include the "carry over" clause in a listing contract that "if the property is sold within 6 months to any person to whom the broker showed the property," the broker is entitled to a commission?
A. No. The broker might be the procuring cause of the sale without ever actually showing the property to a prospect.

115. Q. If the listing contract is ambiguous, how will the courts construe it?
A. Most strongly against the broker, because he prepared it.

116. Q. In the "carry over" clause in a listing, various terms are used such as "any person with whom you had negotiations," "submitted the property to," "had contact with," "showed the property to," "on information given, received, or obtained through this agency," "to any prospect secured by you," or "to any person with whom you have been dealing." Which of the above terms are acceptable from the standpoint of fair practice?
A. "With whom you had negotiations."

117. Q. Kentucky requires a listing contract to be in writing. Plaintiff broker sued for a $750 commission and relied on a *sales* agreement signed by the seller and buyer, which contained a printed clause that the property was sold "through Bud Hamilton Realty Auction Co." Could the plaintiff recover on this writing as a contract?
A. In the case of *Hamilton v. Booth,* 332 S.W. 2d 252 (Ky. 1960), the Court held that broker could not recover on this writing between seller and buyer.

118. Q. Nebraska requires a listing contract to be in writing. A contract of sale contained a clause "I further agree to pay the above named agent the cash commission agreed upon in the amount of $3,500." At the bottom left-hand side, underneath Witness, broker signed "Bill B. Svoboda." Does the broker have a written contract of employment?

A. Lower court held against broker. The Supreme Court reversed: *Svoboda v. DeWald,* 159 Neb. 594 (1955). The appellate court found that the writing complied with the requirements of the Statute, in that 1. it was in writing; 2. contained a description of the property; 3. commission to be paid; and 4. it was signed by the parties.

119. Q. A property is listed with a broker at $12,000. He feels it is a bargain and after one week, he has an agreement of sale signed by his wife's mother. The broker has no buyer in mind at that time. Six months after the deal is closed, the broker sells the property for $14,000. Is the broker guilty of misconduct?

A. Yes; in failing to disclose his true interest in the transaction. There is nothing wrong in a broker buying property listed with him for sale, if he feels it is a good buy, so long as he acts "above board" and lets the owner know his true position in the situation.

120. Q. Steiner owned a property upon which there was a mortgage, delinquent in a large amount. He gave an exclusive right to sell on the property to Stoner for 90 days, hoping to salvage something from a sale. During the 90-day period, the owner and the mortgagee resolved their differences by having the owner give the mortgagee a voluntary deed in return for a cash payment of $500. The broker claimed a commission on the value of the property (listing price). Could he recover?

A. Yes; the Court held that it was a voluntary sale based upon a valuable consideration, so that the broker was entitled to his commission.

121. Q. Woodruff gave a six months' exclusive listing on his property to Woodring. During the exclusive period, the state instituted condemnation proceedings against the property and made an award of $40,000. Is the broker entitled to a commission?

A. No; it was an involuntary sale, for which the owner was in no way responsible.

122. Q. Hoyle lists his property for sale with Doyle, a good friend who is a member of a multi-list association. It is sold by Boyle, a fellow member. Upon Hoyle's refusal to pay the commission, Boyle sues him. Can he recover?

A. No. There is no privity of contract (employment) between Hoyle and Boyle.

123. Q. What is meant by the "carry over" or "extender" clause in an exclusive contract?

A. It is the clause which reads, in effect, that if a sale or exchange is made within six (6) months after the exclusive period has expired, to any person with whom the broker had been negotiating, he is entitled to his commission.

124. Q. Would it be proper for a real estate salesman to negotiate for the sale of property with the parents of minors who are lawful owners?

A. No. The proper party with whom to negotiate would be the guardian of the minors.

125. Q. On or about April 26, 1974, the owner listed his property for sale exclusively until "on or about the 15th day of June" on which date defendant anticipated removing with his family to Miami, Florida. Plaintiff advertised the property and showed the property. On May 20th, it was sold through another broker. Is the plaintiff entitled to recover a commission?

A. Yes. (*Werder v. Browne,* 78 GA. App. 587.) The Court held that the alleged date on which the contract was to come to an end was not so vague and indefinite as to render the contract void and unenforceable. The date of removing to Miami was a definite time capable of being sustained by proof.

126. Q. Plaintiff broker sued for $2625 commission in connection with the sale of a motor court on U. S. Highway, south of Savannah. The broker failed to plead that he was a licensed broker. Was this fatal to his claim?

A. Yes. (*Lynes Realty Co. v. Mays,* 80 Ga. App. 4.)

127. Q. Should a listing contract authorize a broker to sign a binding contract of sale for the

owner?

A. No.

128. Q. An exclusive listing of a house is obtained by Adam Boyer and/or Fairplay Realty Company, a corporation, on April 2, 1974 for 3 months. Boyer is licensed at the time but the corporation (Boyer, president) is not licensed until May 13, 1974. The property was sold on May 10, 1974. Boyer sued for commission on the sale. Can he recover? Reasons.

A. No; the listing is *several* and since the corporation was not licensed when the deal started, neither the corporation nor Boyer can recover.

129. Q. A licensed broker sued an owner for a commission upon an employment contract that the seller was to obtain " $125,000 cash or better, or $125,000 with *reasonable* financing." The broker obtained a responsible buyer who was willing to pay $55,000 cash and execute a $70,000 mortgage, payable within 15 years, with interest at 5%. The seller refused to accept the deal. Is the broker entitled to his commission? Discuss.

A. Yes; broker's deal would constitute "reasonable financing."

130. Q. An owner gave an exclusive listing to a licensed broker to sell his property for $100,000, with a cash payment of $29,000 and "terms to suit." The broker produced a buyer who agreed to pay $5,000 down, $24,000 in cash at the closing; purchase money mortgage for the balance. The owner refused to sign the agreement and the broker sued for commission. Can broker recover commission?

A. No; terms are "to suit" seller. He need not be satisfied with any deal broker negotiates. The contract is too indefinite.

131. Q. Fred Lane signs an exclusive right to sell listing with the Rucker Agency on April 9, 1974 for a period of three months. During the exclusive period, Lane sells the property himself. Rucker sues for a commission. Lane defends on the grounds that it was verbally agreed between him and Rucker that if he sold the property himself during the exclusive period, no commission would be due Rucker. Is this a good defense?

A. No. Under the Parol Evidence Rule, oral testimony cannot be introduced to vary or contradict a written instrument, except for fraud, accident or mistake. Lane would have to allege and prove that the oral understanding was fraudulently omitted from the written listing.

132. Q. Stone, a broker, sues both the seller, Adams, and the buyer, Baker, for commissions in an exchange deal. Baker admitted that he knew of the dual employment. Adams emphatically denied knowledge. The broker claimed that both parties knew of the dual agency and there was no unfairness, double dealing, fraud or damages to the parties. Can the broker recover from Adams; can he recover from Baker?

A. He cannot recover from either. The rule of law is that a broker cannot recover from either of his principals unless *both* had knowledge of, consented to and acquiesced in such employment.

133. Q. Broker Hayes negotiated a deal between Stevens, seller, and Todd, buyer. After the agreements were signed, Hayes gave Todd permission to fill in some of the subject property, which was to be used for parking. The deal fell through and Todd now sues Hayes for $725, cost of fill in and paving. Can he recover?

A. Yes. Hayes is a special agent, with only limited authority to obtain a buyer. He exceeded his authority when he authorized the buyer to fill in and pave the lot. He is personally liable for the buyer's expense.

134. Q. Eaton lists his property for sale with Foster for $15,000. After some efforts, Foster is unable to sell the property and he then offers to buy the property at $14,000. Eaton agrees to sell at that price. Within three weeks, and before the deal is closed, Foster sells the property for $24,000. After both deals are closed, Eaton learns of the $24,000 sale, and sues Foster for the profit. He claims that the broker made an

unconscionable profit, was guilty of bad faith and breached his duty of loyalty to his principal. Can he recover?

A. No. The parties acted as principals. So long as the agent did not conceal anything from his principal while he was acting as an agent, he owes no duty to the former owner after he acquires ownership in good faith.

135. Q. Alberts owned a vacant tract of land. He arranged with Bates, a broker, that the latter would have the engineering work done to lay out the land into a 40 lot subdivision. Bates was to have the exclusive sale of the lots for a three year period. At the end of the first year, few lots have been sold and Alberts desires to terminate the agency. Can he do so?

A. No. The agency is coupled with an interest and cannot be revoked; even if Alberts died during the three year period, the agency would still continue.

136. Q. What is the function of the real estate broker or salesperson?

A. To bring about an agreement of sale between his principal, the owner, and a third party, the purchaser.

137. Q. What is the difference between a "finder" and a broker?

A. A "finder" merely brings a buyer to the attention of an owner while a broker *negotiates* a sale to a buyer for the owner.

138. Q. Is it necessary for "a finder" to have a state license?

A. No; if he "remains pure" in abstaining from any negotiations between owner and purchaser.

139. Q. Must such an arrangement between owner and "finder" be in writing in order to be enforceable?

A. No.

140. Q. Must there be an express contract, oral or written, between owner and the "finder"?

A. Yes; since any suit for a "fee" would have to be based upon a contract.

141. Q. Is there any difference between a "volunteer" and a "finder"?

A. Yes; a volunteer negotiates between owner and prospect, but he cannot recover any commission, because he cannot prove he was employed. A "finder" locates a prospect for the owner, and does nothing more, but a sale is made. However, there must be an understanding (contract) between owner and "finder" for payment of a "fee."

True and False

1. There is economic justification for a real estate broker. T F
2. In relation to a broker, the owner is the principal. T F
3. A salesperson is the agent of the owner. T F
4. Preparation of a listing contract constitutes the unauthorized practice of law. T F
5. A salesperson is the "alter ego" of the owner. T F
6. A broker's suit for a commission is brought in a court of equity. T F
7. A suit for a commission is a suit in assumpsit. T F
8. A broker's contract of employment with a salesperson must be in writing. T F
9. A listing contract given by a husband to a broker for sale of property owned by himself and wife will be binding upon the wife. T F
10. A listing contract for a farm is not the same as the listing contract for a dwelling. T F
11. Where a prospect answers a broker's advertisement and inspects the subject property, he is the broker's client. T F
12. A broker can maintain an office in his living room if the neighbors in the same block have no objection. T F
13. Where a property is listed for sale with several brokers, under an open listing, and the property is sold by one broker, the owner must immediately notify the other brokers that the property has been sold. T F
14. If a written listing contract does not state the commission in dollars or a percentage of the sales price, the broker cannot recover. T F

15. An exclusive right to sell listing for 30 days is preferable to an open listing for 90 days. T F
16. A broker's commissions stem mainly from residential sales. T F
17. A selling broker is a sub-agent of the listing broker. T F
18. The statute of frauds governs the relationship between broker and salesman. T F
19. The first essential in a suit for real estate commission is a state license. T F
20. A licensed broker may divide his commission with an unlicensed attorney, who cooperated in making the sale. T F
21. An exclusive listing contract for more than one year is void. T F
22. The broker generally pays for advertising a property for sale. T F
23. If a broker has an exclusive agency listing, he can recover a commission if the owner sells the property himself during the term of the listing. T F
24. A broker managing real estate is entitled to any secret rebates, so long as he does not pay more than the market price for any item. T F
25. The contract giving employment to the broker is known as the listing contract. T F
26. A salesman, who leaves his broker, may take all of his listings to his new broker. T F
27. A licensed salesman may divide his commission with another licensed salesman with his broker's consent. T F
28. He could, with the *other* broker's consent. T F
29. A listing contract which authorizes the broker to sign a contract of sale for the seller is unusual. T F
30. A broker employing 10 or more salesmen must have a sales manager. T F
31. The principal in a listing contract is the seller. T F
32. The State Real Estate Board or Commission has authority to fix 6 per cent as the rate of commission on real estate. T F
33. A broker is obligated to advise a seller of his responsibility to pay such loan discount (points) as is imposed when the sales contract calls for F.H.A. or G.I. financing. T F
34. A listing contract without a definite expiration date is not valid in all states. T F
35. The duration of a listing contract, in the absence of a specified period, is determined by the Statute of Frauds. T F
36. "Earnest money" is the commission which the broker receives in the deal. T F
37. "Realtor" is the term used by a broker after he successfully negotiates a deal. T F
38. A contract between two brokers to cooperate on a real estate deal need not be in writing. T F
39. A broker may pay compensation only to his salesmen and to licensed brokers. T F
40. A straight salary may be paid by a broker to an unlicensed person who only solicits listings. T F
41. All listing contracts should be made in triplicate so that there are copies for the buyer, seller and broker. T F
42. The broker generally pays the fee for recording a deed. T F
43. The Real Estate Commission determines the rate of commission to be charged for selling real property. T F
44. A listing contract is ended if the salesman who obtained the listing dies. T F
45. An open listing is a listing in which the sales price is not set. T F
46. An "exclusive" listing is preferable to an "open listing." T F
47. A broker should close the deals negotiated by his salesmen. T F
48. An exclusive listing contract on real property would not be valid for a period longer than six months. T F
49. A seller can refuse to pay a broker an earned commission when he discovers that the buyer is also paying the broker a commission. T F
50. A salesman should understand the law of principal and agent. T F
51. A salesman, who solicits listings, but does not sell, is not required to have a real estate license. T F

52. There is no statutory lien for a broker's unpaid commission. T F
53. The usual "open listing" provides for the payment of a commission to the broker who lists the property first and an additional compensation to the broker who sells it. T F
54. A broker should deliver voluntarily a copy of the authorization-to-sell contract to the owner who signed. T F
55. A broker who has not been employed by the owner can recover a commission, if he obtains a buyer whom the owner accepts. T F
56. A salesman may not divide his commissions with the salesman of another broker. T F
57. A listing contract might be renewed after its expiration date. T F
58. A broker may not represent more than one party to a transaction unless he so advises both of them and has their consent. T F
59. A broker who asks for a listing "until sold" offends good real estate ethics. T F
60. A listing contract is terminated by the death of the owner. T F
61. If a real estate broker has no written listing, he may collect a commission if he can produce two witnesses to the transaction. T F
62. The fact that the person who signed the listing did not own the property is no defense in an action for a real estate commission. T F
63. It is not important to specify the amount of commission to be charged for the sale of property because that is fixed by law. T F
64. It is unlawful to charge a commission for the sale of improved real estate in excess of 7 per cent of the sale price. T F
65. Commission for sale of real estate is determined by agreement between the parties. T F
66. Procuring listings by house to house solicitation is beneath the dignity of a broker. T F
67. It is unlawful for a real estate salesman to receive compensation for the sale of property from anyone except the broker with whom he is licensed. T F
68. A salesman should advertise the sale of real estate in his own name. T F
69. Placing "Sold" signs on property sold by a broker is one of the best ways of securing new listings. T F
70. It is best that a broker accept nothing but exclusive listings. T F
71. An exclusive agency is preferable to an exclusive right-to-sell contract. T F
72. A salesperson leaving a broker's employ can recover from the broker commissions due, upon signed agreements, but not yet closed. T F
73. A broker has the last word to decide upon commission controversies between two of his salespersons. T F
74. The law obligates every agent to act in and for the best interest of his employer. T F
75. A salesman selling his own property or that of the broker by whom he is employed should inform the prospective buyer of that fact. T F
76. A person who answers the broker's ad and looks at the real estate with idea of purchasing same is the broker's client. T F
77. Employment of a broker to find a tenant for real estate need not be in writing to be enforceable. T F
78. An agreement employing a real estate broker is terminated by the death of the owner prior to procuring a purchaser, ready, able, and willing to buy on owner's terms. T F
79. A real estate broker is required to use ordinary diligence to keep his employer advised of his actions in the course of his agency. T F
80. It is lawful for a broker to agree with the tenant of a house, which the broker has for sale, to pay the tenant a part of the commission if the tenant will show the property to any prospect of the broker who later buys the property. T F
81. An exclusive listing and a net listing are the same and the terms may be used interchangeably. T F
82. If an oral listing agreed upon has no expiration date, it remains in effect a

reasonable time. T F
83. If a broker has an exclusive agent agreement, he may recover a commission from the owner if the owner sells the property himself during the term of the listing. T F
84. An "exclusive listing" means one confined to a single piece of real estate. T F
85. An owner cannot refuse to sign a sales agreement when the broker employed by him obtains a buyer upon the seller's terms. T F
86. A salesman cannot collect a commission in his own name and divide it with his broker. T F
87. A real estate broker and a real estate salesman may not enter into a partnership. T F
88. A principal is the employer of a broker. T F
89. A broker's client and a broker's prospect are one and the same. T F
90. A defrauded client has no right of court action against a broker but must sue the surety company, if the broker is bonded. T F
91. Commission rates to be charged on real property sales are limited to a certain scale by the legislature. T F
92. If a broker has real estate for sale and finds a prospect willing to take an option to purchase the property at the price stated, the broker is entitled to a commission. T F
93. Commission rates are usually recommended by the local real estate board. T F
94. A salesman licensed under one broker may deal directly with another broker and obtain a commission from the second broker. T F
95. Under no circumstances can a broker collect a commission from the buyer. T F
96. In a disputed commission claim with an owner, the broker can insist that the matter be heard by the local real estate board. T F
97. The Real Estate Commission is the proper forum to decide real estate commission disputes. T F
98. Obtaining a listing by telephone may be hard to prove. T F
99. An exclusive listing refers to a single tract of land. T F
100. From the owner's standpoint, an exclusive agency contract is preferable to an exclusive right to sell listing. T F
101. It is unlawful for a broker to give part of his commission to the buyer for the purchase of a new electric range. T F
102. A real estate broker under an agency acts in a fiduciary relationship to his principal. T F
103. In real estate a broker usually acts for and on behalf of the owner or seller. T F
104. If you have real estate listed for sale and find a prospect ready, willing, and able to take an option to purchase the property on the terms at which the property is offered, you have earned and are entitled to a commission. T F
105. The use of a listing form which also contains an option agreement between owner (seller) and broker is not considered good practice. T F
106. A net listing or an exclusive contract to sell a parcel of real estate at a net price to the owner makes the broker an optionee. T F
107. A broker accepting a net listing to sell a piece of real property should not accept any compensation from the purchaser unless he reveals this fact to the seller. T F
108. An exclusive listing contract on real property would not be valid for a period longer than 90 days. T F
109. An agent is the "alter ego" of his principal. T F
110. It is proper for a broker to buy an interest in a property listed with him without making the fact known to the listing owner. T F
111. It is unlawful for a broker to purchase property listed with him in the name of a "straw" man. T F
112. An owner should always be given a copy of the exclusive contract he signs. T F
113. An agreement between brokers to split a commission need not be in writing. T F
114. A broker usually acts for and in behalf of the purchaser. T F

115. When no rate of commission is stated in a listing, and the property is sold, the usual or customary rate which is charged in that locality is used. T F
116. A listing obtained exclusively by one firm only for a limited period of time is called an exclusive listing. T F
117. If a salesman's name is used in advertising property for sale, the ad should also contain the name and address of the broker. T F
118. A real estate broker holding a 60-day exclusive agency to sell a parcel of real estate, may continue his efforts to sell such property even though the owner died during the 60-day period. T F
119. A real estate salesman, having consummated a sale of real property, has the choice of demanding his share of the commissions earned, either from the broker employing him or the seller, who for some personal reason refuses to pay the broker. T F
120. A real estate broker holding a 60-day exclusive agency to sell a parcel of real property may, without disclosing the relationships, sell the property to his wife and receive a commission for such sale. T F
121. A real estate broker is entitled to a commission for the consummation of a sale of real property upon the asking price set by the seller even though he was in a position to obtain another purchaser willing to pay more than the asking price. T F
122. An owner is under no obligation to pay a commission to the broker when it is ascertained, after the execution of the contract of purchase, that the purchaser was induced to enter into the contract of purchase because of some misrepresentations made by the broker. T F
123. Where a broker introduces a purchaser to an owner, whose property is listed with the broker, the broker is entitled to a commission if a sale follows through direct negotiations between the principals. T F
124. Where the property is listed at a price of $25,000 or higher, the broker's employment must be in writing. T F
125. A broker cannot collect a commission unless he obtains a contract signed by the owner. T F
126. The broker who first calls the buyer's attention to the property is the one entitled to the commission. T F
127. When deposit money is received by the broker, he may use such money for his personal account up to the amount of his commission as soon as agreements of sale are signed. T F
128. Brokers employing salesmen are relieved of all responsibility for the acts of the salesmen if the salesmen are bonded. T F
129. The real estate salesman should not be concerned with the restrictions attaching to a property while attempting to negotiate its sale. T F
130. A salesman transferring to another broker is entitled to take with him the listings which he obtained personally while working for the first broker. T F
131. All brokers are members of the National Association of Real Estate Brokers. T F
132. A real estate salesman must be at least 21 years of age. T F
133. A broker can recover upon a quantum meruit basis where he effects a sale and no agreement exists as to his commission. T F
134. In an integrated association, every licensed broker would be a member of the state real estate association. T F
135. In an estate by the entireties, either husband or wife may give a valid listing of the property to a broker. T F
136. One who takes and passes a real estate course given by a real estate Board is entitled to use Graduate Realtors' Institute. T F
137. A broker, under an exclusive listing, should not disclose the identity of his prospect until agreements are signed. T F
138. Compensation to a broker must be in the form of money. T F

139. In order to prosecute a person for acting as a broker, without a license, it is essential to prove that he received compensation or expected compensation. T F
140. A person, employed by a licensed broker, to auction real estate, requires a license. T F
141. A real estate listing may be taken in the name of a salesman so long as the transaction is closed in the name of the broker. T F
142. A broker employed "to sell" a property can sign an agreement of sale for the owner, which would be enforceable. T F
143. A broker is entitled to a commission under an "exclusive right-to-sell listing," if the owner sells the property himself during the term of the listing. T F
144. If owner and broker have not expressly agreed upon the rate of commission, the broker is entitled to recover on a "quantum meruit" basis, if he makes the deal. T F
145. The principal in a listing agreement is the seller. T F
146. Earnest money is the commission which the broker receives when the deal is closed. T F
147. A property is listed at $20,000. The broker tells a prospect that he knows the owner will accept $18,000. The prospect offers $18,000, which is accepted by the owner. The broker has violated his duty to the owner. T F
148. A salesman may deduct his share of the commission from a down payment before turning it over to the broker. T F
149. The commission rate for selling real property is usually at the same rate as for leasing. T F
150. Where an owner lists a property for sale with a broker "at a sale for not less than $5,000," the broker is entitled to $1,000 commission if he sells the property for $6,000. T F
151. If an owner lists a property for sale with one broker, he cannot employ another broker to sell the same property unless the first broker withdraws. T F
152. An agency to sell real estate usually comes under the Statute of Frauds. T F
153. Where a property is listed for sale with the broker at $7,000, and a sale is made to the broker's prospect at $5,000, the broker is entitled to a commission. T F
154. Every real estate contract negotiated by a broker should contain a clause recognizing the broker as the procuring cause of the sale. T F
155. A broker who initiates a deal is entitled to a commission if, a year later, a sale is made by the parties direct without the assistance of the broker. T F
156. A broker is the "efficient and procuring" cause of a sale when he procures a buyer, ready, able, and willing to buy. T F
157. A broker can compel the payment of his commission out of the proceeds of the deal at the time it is closed. T F
158. A broker may file a lien against the owner's real estate for an unpaid commission. T F
159. A listing contract containing a confession of judgment clause for the broker's commission is considered bad practice. T F
160. A commission agreed upon by broker and buyer will prevent the broker from collecting a commission from the seller. T F
161. Whether a broker is the efficient cause of a sale is a question of law and not of fact. T F
162. An exclusive agency contract permits the owner to sell without liability for a commission to the broker. T F
163. An unlicensed broker may collect a commission in the sale of real estate, by court action, if he has a signed exclusive listing from the seller. T F
164. A "post dated check" given for a deposit has the same effect as a N.S.F. check. T F
165. The broker who obtains the buyer's signature on the "dotted line" is the one entitled to a commission. T F
166. A broker has the legal right to render an opinion on the validity of title to real estate. T F
167. The commission to be charged for the sale of real estate is determined by the

license law. T F

168. If you, a licensed real estate salesman, obtained a real estate listing, and subsequently located a buyer for your listing, you would be within your rights under the real estate license law to close the transaction, so long as your broker received his rightful share of the commission. T F
169. A broker may collect a commission from both parties in an exchange deal with their knowledge and consent. T F
170. Where two brokers claim a commission in the sale of a house, the owner should pay the broker who makes the first claim. T F
171. Where two or more brokers claim a commission for the sale of the same property, the owner should pay the money into court. T F
172. A contract accompanied by deposit money is not always *conclusive* evidence that the broker is entitled to the commission. T F
173. Where a broker obtains a signed agreement of sale and has an exclusive right to sell contract, the owner must sign the agreement of sale. T F
174. Most prospects are alert to observe misrepresentations of salesmen and brokers. T F
175. A satisfied customer for a home represents economic justification for a broker. T F
176. In order to protect his commission, it is advisable for a broker to draw up a contract of sale. T F
177. A broker's contract of employment which cannot be completed in one year must be in writing. T F
178. A broker may be held responsible for representing property as "the most quiet spot in the world." T F
179. Placing a "For Sale" sign upon vacant property without the owner's authority constitutes unethical conduct. T F
180. In order to secure a listing of property to sell, it would be permissible to give a friend a ten dollar bill to assist you in securing the listing. T F
181. A broker is entitled to his commission if he produces a buyer ready, willing, and able to meet the terms proposed by the seller in his listing, even if the owner refuses to go through with the deal. T F
182. A broker usually does not require the signatures of both husband and wife on an "authorization to sell" their community property. T F
183. A "key lot" is the most desirable lot on which to build a residence in any subdivision. T F
184. Quantum Meruit means the reasonable value of a broker's services. T F
185. An owner is never liable for more than one commission in the sale of a single property. T F
186. In a suit upon a "quantum meruit" basis, the broker seeks to recover the usual or prevailing rate of commission. T F
187. An escrow company may be fined for paying commissions to any unlicensed person. T F
188. The data on the reverse side of a listing contract constitutes a part of the employment contract. T F
189. Failure to give an owner a copy of the listing contract prevents the broker from recovering his commission. T F
190. A broker may purchase property listed with him for sale if he informs the seller he is acting as a principal. T F
191. A broker who has been refused a commission can block a sale if he notifies the title company or escrow company, in writing, of his commission claim. T F
192. A broker has a right to file a Mechanic's Lien for his unpaid commission. T F
193. A salesman cannot sue an owner direct for his share of the commission. T F
194. A bilateral listing contract is preferable to a unilateral contract from the broker's standpoint. T F
195. A broker who has failed to show the buyer the property listed with him, cannot

recover a commission. T **F**

196. A broker is a nonproductive element of goods in our society. T **F**
197. Inquiry of a seller as to price and availability for sale does not constitute a contract of employment. **T** F
198. Three different actions may be brought against a broker who makes a secret profit at the expense of his principal. **T** F
199. Where two real estate closings occur at the same time, the broker may close one deal and his salesman the other. T **F**
200. A broker is a special agent and not a general agent of his principal. **T** F
201. A real estate broker's commission is deemed to have been earned by him at the closing of title. T **F**
202. Open listing means the price is not set. T **F**
203. Experts agree that an advertising budget should not exceed 10% of gross commission. **T** F
204. A real estate broker holding a sixty-day exclusive agency to sell a parcel of real property should discontinue his efforts to sell such property if the owner dies during the sixty-day period. **T** F
205. When the sales contract calls for FHA or GI financing, the broker is required to advise the seller that he is obligated to pay discount points on the loan. **T** F
206. A broker must first air a commission dispute before the local real estate board's grievance committee before suing in court. T **F**
207. A corporation officer, who is licensed as a broker, has authority to list a corporate property for sale with another licensed broker. T **F**
208. A "For Sale—See your broker" automatically gives any broker authority to sell the property. T **F**
209. A listing contract may contain a clause authorizing the listing broker to execute a binding contract of sale for the owner. **T** F
210. A "policy book" containing rules and regulations of the real estate office, signed by a salesperson, but not by the owner, is a valid contract. **T** F
211. A principal and agent relationship; a master and servant relationship and a broker—independent contractor relationship are one and the same. T **F**
212. All full time brokers are Realtors. T **F**
213. Whenever a broker is authorized to negotiate for the sale of property, he is also authorized to accept a deposit. **T** F
214. If a real estate broker failed to disclose the identity of his prospective customer, and if the negotiations failed, and the purchaser sought out the owner and consummated the deal direct, the broker would not be entitled to his commission. **T** F
215. A real estate broker should never act as an escrow holder in transactions covering property in which he personally owns an interest. **T** F
216. A real estate broker is entitled to a commission for the consummation of a sale of real property for the asking price set by the seller, even though he was in a position to obtain another purchaser willing to pay more than the asking price. T **F**
217. It is unethical for a licensee to advise that the asking price of the seller is too high or too low. T **F**
218. A broker should not bother an owner by submitting an offer which the broker considers ridiculously low. T **F**
219. The listing employment contract should be signed by the salesman who obtained the listing. T **F**
220. A Real Estate Commission may sell real estate without a license. T **F**
221. "Puffing of goods" as applied to real estate means extravagant statements regarding the desirability of the property. **T** F
222. A gives B, a broker, an exclusive listing on March 21, 1974 for 90 days. B dies on April 24, 1974. The listing is cancelled. **T** F
223. A listing by a minor is voidable by him. **T** F

224. A listing which provides for a 15 per cent commission is void. T F
225. The National Association of Realtors regulates the rate of commission to be charged. T F
226. In a multi-list association, the listing broker and the selling broker usually receive an equal amount of the commission. T F
227. "Caveat emptor" relieves an owner or broker from any misrepresentation. T F
228. In a multi-list association, the selling broker generally has no right to sue the owner for a commission. T F
229. A selling broker is a subagent of the listing broker. T F
230. A broker's suit for commission is based on privity of contract with the owner. T F
231. Brokerage is the most profitable segment of the ordinary licensee's business. T F
232. The usual listing contract, employing the broker "to sell" the property, authorizes the broker to sign the contract of sale. T F
233. An owner-builder of more than 20 houses requires a broker's license. T F
234. The penalty for selling real estate without a license is the same as paying a commission to an unlicensed person. T F
235. The law does not require a person to obtain a license for negotiating a sale until the contract is signed by the parties. T F
236. A person may call himself a Realtor once he passes the state licensing examination. T F
237. Where a property, subject to a mortgage, is listed for sale by the owner, the mortgagee must agree to the listing. T F
238. Where a property is leased, the broker must receive consent of the tenant, to a listing given to him by the owner. T F
239. Once a salesman is licensed, he should concentrate on selling and discontinue further study in real estate courses. T F
240. By-laws of a real estate board do not take precedence over the Rules and Regulations of a Real Estate Commission. T F
241. The North Carolina Real Estate Board and the North Carolina Real Estate Association are the same. T F
242. A broker is a quasi-professional. T F
243. A broker may rely on the seller's statement as to zoning of the listed property. T F
244. It is the broker's duty to notify the owner at what time the buyer has defaulted and forfeited his deposit money. T F
245. If a listing is void under the Statute of Frauds, oral testimony by disinterested witnesses, would render the listing valid. T F
246. A broker may advertise State appproved Broker or Realtor when he receives his license. T F
247. The state may waive the initial examination if the applicant has passed the 3 year Graduate Realtors Institute program. T F
248. The Graduate Realtors Institute is a major step forward in attaining professional acceptance by the public. T F
249. A salesman owes a prospect the duty to disclose the lowest price the seller will take, if it is considerably less than the listing price. T F
250. A property is listed at $15,000. The broker tells the buyer that he knows the owner will accept $13,000. The prospect offers $13,000, which is accepted. The broker has violated his duty to the owner. T F
251. A salesman negotiates a deal and witnesses the signatures of buyer and seller. The seller's prime duty is to pay the salesman the commission. T F
252. The salesman should close the deal negotiated by him, since he has dealt with both buyer and seller. T F
253. A person who has passed the state's broker examination, may advertise real estate for sale. T F
254. A salesman is duty bound to disclose the lowest price an owner will take, even

though it is much lower than the listing price. T F

255. The fixing of a commission rate by a real estate Board for the members thereof, is considered illegal by the U.S. Department of Justice. T F
256. If a listing is void under the Statute of Frauds, broker cannot recover advances made by him on behalf of the owner. T F
257. A broker should know the zone of a listed property. T F
258. Cities and villages may add their own licensing requirements to those established by the Legislature. T F
259. Where a broker sues for a commission on a "quantum meruit" basis, and obtains a verdict, his commission will always be the prevailing rate in the community. T F
260. The National Association of Realtors was formerly the National Association of Real Estate Boards. T F
261. The National Association of Real Estate Brokers, Inc., is the same as the National Association of Realtors. T F
262. Most states now have educational and/or apprenticeship prerequisites for a broker's license. T F
263. An able buyer is one, produced by a broker, who is financially substantial. T F
264. A broker can advance a salesperson's commission from his escrow account, only in a hardship case. T F
265. The term of a written exclusive listing can be extended orally. T F
266. A sales person can file a lien against an owner for an unpaid commission. T F

Multiple Choice

1. The average real estate broker finds commissions are earned mainly from sales of
   (a) commercial properties.
   (b) dwellings.
   (c) industrial properties.
   (d) investment properties.
2. A salesman receiving a deposit should
   (a) place it in his "Special Account."
   (b) place it in the broker's general account.
   (c) turn it over to his broker.
   (d) place it in the sales person's trust account.
3. In an exchange deal, a salesman employed by a broker "a" may receive a share of commission from
   (a) broker "B," who represented one of the principals.
   (b) from salesman "c," employed by "b."
   (c) from salesman "d," employed by "a."
   (d) none of these persons.
4. Upon the death of a broker, his listings may be taken over by
   (a) his widow.
   (b) his son, who is of lawful age.
   (c) by a trust company.
   (d) none of these.
5. An oral agreement between two licensed brokers to divide a commission is
   (a) void.
   (b) valid.
   (c) voidable.
   (d) must be approved by seller.
6. If a property consisting of 10 dwellings is listed at not less than $65,000 to the owner, and after one year, the dwellings are sold separately, but in the aggregate, the sum realized is $65,000, the broker can recover, as his commission
   (a) the amount of deposit money held in his escrow account at that time.
   (b) 7%, which is the going commission rate in that area.
   (c) on a quantum meruit basis.

(d) nothing.

7. In a multi-list association, the selling broker, as between him and the listing broker, usually receives
   (a) one-half of the net commission paid.
   (b) less than one-half.
   (c) more than one-half.
   (d) the amount determined by the executive board.
8. A contract of employment between Davis Realty Co. and Helen Miller, sales person, provided, in part, "No commission shall be considered earned, or payable to sales person until the transaction has been completed and the commission collected by the company." Helen procured a buyer and agreements were signed. Before the deal was closed, she changed employers
   (a) she can recover her commission.
   (b) she cannot recover a commission.
   (c) she would first have to terminate her new employment.
   (d) she can sue the owner.
9. Two rival brokers claim the commission in a real estate deal. Broker "A" sues the owner. The owner should
   (a) pay the broker with whom the property was listed.
   (b) pay the money into court (interpleader).
   (c) pay each broker one half.
10. An open listing is one which allows the broker
   (a) a reasonable period of time to obtain a buyer.
   (b) a definite period of time within which to obtain a buyer.
   (c) 90 days within which to obtain a buyer.
   (d) the customary period of time to procure a buyer.
11. In a multi-list association, a salesman, who negotiates a sale, is directly responsible to
   (a) the listing broker.
   (b) his employing broker.
   (c) the buyer.
   (d) the seller.
12. Real estate practice dictates use of
   (a) an open listing.
   (b) a net listing.
   (c) exclusive listing.
   (d) an exclusive right to sell listing.
13. A proper recital of the commission to be paid in a written listing should read at
   (a) the rate usually charged in the area.
   (b) fixed percentage on the sales price.
   (c) on a quantum meruit basis.
   (d) the rate prescribed by the law.
14. Real Estate brokerage is governed by the law of
   (a) statute of frauds.
   (b) agency.
   (c) the commercial code.
   (d) conveyancing.
15. Where a broker obtains a buyer, how many contracts are essential in order for the broker to establish a valid commission claim?
   (a) one.
   (b) two.
   (c) three.
   (d) four.
16. In listing property for sale, which item is *not* necessary for a valid exclusive listing agreement?
   (a) Date of listing.

(b) Address of property.
(c) Legal description.
(d) Listing period.

17. Another broker has a listing on a property you desire to show a prospect. Which one of the following should you do?
(a) Call the local Real Estate Board.
(b) Wait until the other broker's listing expires.
(c) Get in touch with the other broker and ask his permission to show the property.
(d) Show your prospect the property and then call the owner for a listing.

18. A real estate listing is
(a) a list of all property held by one owner.
(b) employment of a broker by owner to sell or lease real property.
(c) a written list of improvements on the land.
(d) a rendition of property for taxation.

19. An agent is one employed by a
(a) salesman.
(b) principal.
(c) master.
(d) broker.

20. All real estate listed for sale by a broker should be advertised in the name of the
(a) seller.
(b) salesman who obtains listing.
(c) salesman on the premises.
(d) principal licensed broker.

21. What is the maximum commission rate that a broker may charge on the sale of improved property?
(a) 6%.
(b) 5%.
(c) 7%.
(d) Any rate agreed upon by agent and principal.

22. An agency coupled with an interest is one
(a) that cannot be terminated before its expiration date.
(b) where broker makes a secret profit at the expense of his principal.
(c) where broker receives interest-bearing note in payment of his commission.
(d) where a suit is filed for commission, which constitutes a lien on the real estate.

23. Alberts negotiated a sale between his owner, Burrows and a buyer, Champ. Later, owner and buyer agree to call the deal off. The broker, Alberts, can
(a) recover a commission from Burrows.
(b) recover a commission from Champ.
(c) recover from Burrows and Champ.
(d) recover from neither Burrows nor Champ.

24. A real estate transaction may be closed by the salesman, if
(a) the salesman obtained the listing.
(b) the listing was obtained by another salesman in the same office.
(c) the listing was obtained by a salesman employed by another broker.
(d) none of these.

25. It is possible for an owner to have more than one agent endeavoring to sell his property. It is:
(a) an open listing contract.
(b) multiple listing.
(c) a non-exclusive listing.
(d) a general listing.

26. The first step necessary for a licensed broker to recover a commission is to
(a) find a buyer.
(b) find a seller.

(c) have a contract of employment.
(d) advertise the property for sale.

27. In the real estate business another term for principal is
(a) customer.
(b) prospect.
(c) client.
(d) alter ego.

28. The relationship of a licensed real estate broker to his principal is that of a
(a) trustee.
(b) salesman.
(c) fiduciary.
(d) beneficiary.

29. A contract authorizing the sale of real property which is signed by a minor is
(a) voidable.
(b) terminated.
(c) void.
(d) valid.

30. A valid listing on community property must be given by
(a) husband.
(b) husband and wife.
(c) seller and mortgagee.
(d) broker and salesman.

31. A prospect, to whom a broker shows the property, ordinarily has a right to rely upon the broker's representations as to
(a) title.
(b) future prospects.
(c) all statements made by the broker regarding the property.
(d) past rentals of the property.

32. Hilton Co. listed a manufacturing plant with Commercial Realty, Inc. at $150,000. Higgins, a sales person, obtained a prospect, Harrison Mfg. Co., at $140,000, but informed Hilton he had an offer of $100,000. Commercial Realty prepared agreements at $100,000 with Triangle Inc., a "straw" party, as the buyer. Because of dire financial straits, Hilton accepted the $100,000 offer. Under these circumstances, Hilton Co. can:
I. sue Commercial Realty, Inc. for compensatory and punitive damages.
II. sue Higgins for compensatory and punitive damages.
(a) I only.
(b) II only.
(c) both I and II.
(d) neither I nor II.

33. Henry gives a listing to Fairvue Realty on May 3, 1974 for 90 days. It provides for a commission to be paid "upon the sale or exchange" of the property. The broker obtains a prospect, Crawford, on July 31, 1974. On August 1, Crawford enters into a lease for one year, at $200 per month, with an option to purchase; any rent paid to apply to the purchase price. Under these circumstances:
I. Fairvue can recover commission on the sale.
II. Fairvue can recover a commission on the rent paid.
(a) I only.
(b) II only.
(c) both I and II.
(d) neither I nor II.

34. Miller, a broker, receives $1,000 from Gray, upon the sale of Lee's home. Miller's commission is $725. The sale is not consummated because of a defect in Lee's title. Under these circumstances:
I. Gray can recover the $1,000 from Miller.
II. Gray can recover the $1,000 from Lee.

(a) I only.
(b) II only.
(c) both I and II.
(d) neither I nor II.

35. Michael Martin, negotiates a sale of a dwelling, for Allen, a builder, at $45,000 and receives an earnest money deposit of $2,000. At the closing, the buyer, Phelps, claims that the builder has used second grade facing brick, contrary to specifications, and refuses to close the deal. Under these circumstances, the broker should:
    I. Refund the money to Phelps.
    II. report the matter to the Real Estate Commission.
    (a) I only.
    (b) II only.
    (c) both I and II.
    (d) neither I nor II.
36. Aiken orally agrees to sell his residence to a friend, Barton, at $40,000, in the presence of Hays and Oakes. Aiken and Barton shake hands "on the deal." Later, Aiken refuses to go through with the deal, although Barton has, in the interim, signed a written agreement to sell the property to Cook at $42,750. Under these circumstances:
    I. Barton can compel Aiken to consummate the deal in action for specific performance.
    II. Barton can recover damages from Aiken.
    (a) I only.
    (b) II only.
    (c) both I and II.
    (d) neither I nor II.
37. A broker told a buyer that the house was connected to a township sewer, when it was serviced by a septic tank system. It cost the buyer $700 to change to the township system. The buyer seeks to recover this amount. Buyer
    (a) can recover from the owner.
    (b) can recover from the township.
    (c) can recover from the broker.
    (d) can recover from no one.
38. A property was listed at $18,500. A prospect told the broker that he wanted the property and would pay that price, but asked the broker to submit a signed offer of $16,600 and see if the owner would accept that price. The owner accepted. Later, the broker sued him for commission.
    (a) he can recover.
    (b) he cannot recover.
    (c) he can recover from buyer.
    (d) he can file a suit for "unjust enrichment" against the buyer.
39. A broker obtained an exclusive listing on a property for 30 days at $20,000. On the last day of the listing, the broker brought an offer to purchase the property signed by E. Gilligan. When asked who E. Gilligan was, the broker replied "A client of our firm." The deal was closed. Actually, the buyer was the mother-in-law of the broker and was a member of his household. Later the seller brought action to rescind the transaction.
    (a) the transaction will be rescinded.
    (b) it will not be rescinded since the property was sold at the listing price.
    (c) the transaction will not be rescinded, but the broker will have to forfeit his commission.
    (d) the buyer will own the property as trustee for the seller.
40. A purchaser paid the consideration price of $13,200. The broker mistakenly paid $13,500 to the owner who returned the excess $300 to the buyer. The broker sued the buyer for the $300.
    (a) he cannot recover, because there is no privity of contract between broker and

buyer.
(b) he can recover on the doctrine of quasi-contract.
(c) he must sue in seller's name.
(d) he could bring a criminal action against the buyer for obtaining money falsely.

41. The state of Arizona requires listings to be in writing. Wayne obtains a listing from King, but no mention is made of the commissions to be charged. Later Wayne tells King his commission will be 6 per cent. Wayne obtains a buyer, whom King accepts. Under these circumstances:
I. Wayne is entitled to 6 per cent commission.
II. Wayne can recover on a quantum meruit basis.
(a) I only.
(b) II only.
(c) both I and II.
(d) neither I nor II.

42. Flynn and Filson are co-owners of a property. Flynn lists it for sale with Boulevard Realty, Inc. for $60,000, with commission at 6 per cent. Boulevard obtains a bona fide purchaser at that price. Filson refuses to sign the agreement of sale. Boulevard Realty sues for commission:
I. Boulevard Realty can recover from Flynn.
II. Boulevard Realty can recover from Filson.
(a) I only.
(b) II only.
(c) both I and II.
(d) neither I nor II.

43. Caldwells listed their home for sale with A. W. Moon Realty for $23,000 on July 16, 1973. On September 15, 1973, Hewitt, a salesperson, brought the owners a signed offer to purchase at $22,500 and recited a $2,000 earnest money deposit. In fact, it was a note in that amount. Moon did not learn about the note, in lieu of cash deposit, until 10 days later. Hewitt was instructed to obtain cash, but was unsuccessful. The deal was to be closed on December 15, 1973. It was not until April 2, 1974, that the Caldwells learned about the note, and also that the buyers would not go through with the deal. Under these circumstances:
I. the broker cannot collect a commission.
II. the broker's license can be suspended or revoked.
(a) I only.
(b) II only.
(c) both I and II.
(d) neither I nor II.

44. Lee has given open listings to Aber & Co. and to Sweeney & Co. on March 18, 1974. Aber shows the property to a prospect, Clark, on March 27, 1974. Sweeney negotiates a sale to Clark on May 31, 1974. Lee pays Sweeney the Commission:
I. Aber can sue for conspiracy against Lee and Sweeney.
II. Aber is entitled to one-half of the commission from Sweeney.
Under these facts which of the following would apply?
(a) I only.
(b) II only.
(c) both I and II.
(d) neither I nor II.

45. Which one of the following funds should not be placed in the real estate trustee account?
(a) Earnest monies.
(b) Rental collections.
(c) Installment land contract collections.
(d) Insurance premiums.

46. A broker, Adams, listed Bigbee's property for sale at $12,500. He obtains a prospective purchaser, Clark, at $14,250. Adams can
(a) report the sale to Bigbee at $12,500 and keep the $1,750 excess as his commission.

(b) obtain a "straw" party, Davis, at $12,500 and then resell to Clark at $14,250.
(c) report the sale to Bigbee at $14,250 and collect commission on the sale.
(d) Adams can buy, in his own name, at $12,500 and resell at $14,250.

47. A broker is holding an earnest money deposit, equal to the amount of his commission. The seller, at the closing, not only refuses to pay the broker a commission but demands that the broker pay him the entire deposit money. The broker should
(a) refuse to permit the closing of the deal.
(b) retain the earnest money as his commission.
(c) file a complaint with the Real Estate Commission.
(d) pay the earnest money to the seller and then sue for his commission.

48. In the absence of a prior agreement as to when the broker's commission is earned, such commission is earned at
(a) consummation of the deal.
(b) meeting of the minds of buyer and seller.
(c) time broker introduced buyer to seller.
(d) when deed is delivered.

49. A licensed broker may share his commission with
(a) a licensed salesman employed by another broker.
(b) any licensed broker in another state, who shows the property.
(c) neither (a) nor (b).
(d) both (a) and (b).

50. "In consideration of your efforts to obtain a purchaser, I hereby list with you for sale," etc., is a
(a) bilateral contract.
(b) unilateral contract.
(c) mutual contract.
(d) none of these.

51. An owner lists a property for sale with a broker at $10,000, who finds a purchaser who is willing to pay $11,500 for the property. The broker should
(a) report the sale to the owner on the basis of the $10,000 listing and keep the $1,500 as his commission.
(b) report the sales price to the owner and take commission on the $11,500.
(c) figure his commission on $10,000 and divide the $1,500 excess equally between owner and himself.
(d) buy the property himself at $10,000 and resell it to his buyer at $11,500.

52. A broker receiving a deposit from a purchaser should
(a) Give it to the owner.
(b) Deposit it immediately in his general office checking account.
(c) Deposit it in his personal account.
(d) Deposit it in a trust account at a bank.

53. Real estate listed for sale with a broker should be advertised in the name of
(a) the owner.
(b) the licensed broker.
(c) the salesman to whom the listing has been assigned.
(d) the broker and the salesman to whom assigned.

54. The amount of commission to be paid to a broker is fixed by
(a) law.
(b) State Real Estate Department.
(c) agreement of the parties.
(d) the local real estate board.

55. A real estate broker must bring an action in the courts to recover real estate commission within
(a) one year.
(b) four years.
(c) time fixed by law for suits on simple contracts (Pa. 6 yrs.)

(d) ten years.

56. Adams listed his property for sale with Boyer at $40,000. The listing does not state that Boyer is to hold the earnest money in his escrow account. Boyer negotiates a deal at $40,000 to Clifton and receives an earnest money deposit of $2,500. Adams refuses to sign the agreement unless the $2,500 is paid to him. The agreement of sale recites "receipt of a deposit of $2,500 is hereby acknowledged on account of the consideration price." The deposit money should be
    (a) paid to the seller.
    (b) retained by Boyer in his escrow account.
    (c) an escrow account for the $2,500 should be opened in the joint name of Adams and Boyer.
    (d) an escrow account should be opened in the joint names of Adams, Boyer and Clifton.
57. Which one of the following will not terminate a principal-agent relationship
    (a) insanity of either principal or agent.
    (b) death of principal.
    (c) death of agent.
    (d) change of business location of agent.
58. A contract which provides for the payment of a commission to a broker even though the owner makes a sale without the aid of the broker is called an
    (a) exclusive listing.
    (b) open listing.
    (c) option.
    (d) exclusive right to sell.
59. If an owner refuses to pay the broker a commission, the broker may
    (a) file a complaint with the Real Estate Commission.
    (b) file a lien against the real estate sold.
    (c) bring court action.
    (d) take out a bond.
60. When broker and salesman have a dispute over the commission upon a deal, they should
    (a) complain to the owner.
    (b) bring action in court.
    (c) file a joint complaint to the Commission.
    (d) compel arbitration.
61. An owner employs a broker to sell his real estate and promises to pay a commission; the broker brings about a sale on terms orally accepted by the owner so that the sale is fully consummated. Under such circumstances the broker's employment is
    (a) valid.
    (b) void.
    (c) voidable.
62. If a broker receives more than one worthy, bona fide offer for the same property at approximately the same time, he should
    (a) submit only the highest offer.
    (b) submit all offers to the owner.
    (c) submit only the one he considers for the seller's best interest.
63. Michael Flynn employs Dan Greene, a broker, to negotiate the purchase of a store building and agrees to pay him a commission of $500. Greene contacts the owner, Adam Steele, and obtains a listing of $9,000, with a 6% commission to Greene, if a sale is made. Agreements of sale are signed at $9,000. Buyer and seller later refused to pay Greene. The broker
    (a) can recover only from Flynn.
    (b) can recover only from Steele.
    (c) can recover from both Flynn and Steele.
    (d) can recover from neither.
64. Adam Smith is 17 years of age, married, and owns a vacant lot in his own name. He

employs the Ajax Realty Co. to sell the lot for $6,000. Mary Richards, a licensed salesman, procures a buyer at the listed price and the deal is closed. Smith refuses to pay a commission on the grounds of infancy. Which of the following can recover a commission?
(a) Ajax Realty Co.
(b) Mary Richards.
(c) Ajax Realty Co. and Mary Richards in a joint action.
(d) no one.

65. A broker is entitled to his commission when
(a) he lists the property.
(b) he has shown the property to several prospects.
(c) he brings together a willing buyer upon the seller's terms.

66. To be enforceable a listing must be signed by
(a) broker.
(b) seller.
(c) buyer.
(d) tenant.

67. The broker's fiduciary relationship with the client requires that
(a) he act as a reasonable and prudent person.
(b) he discuss all angles of each deal with his salesmen.
(c) act in the highest and best interests of his client.
(d) he act commensurate with his compensation.

68. A broker receives an offer to purchase upon a form, which states: "This offer shall remain open irrevocably for a period of five days." On the third day, the prospective buyer notifies the broker he does not want the property and requests the return of his $500 deposit. The broker should:
(a) return the deposit to the buyer.
(b) inform the buyer he must wait the full five days to see if the seller accepts.
(c) notify buyer he must go through with the deal.

69. "Ethics" most nearly means
(a) observing usual closing hours of other businesses.
(b) belonging to the proper civic clubs and community projects.
(c) observing duties to clients, colleagues and public.

70. An exclusive listing is
(a) a listing given to several brokers.
(b) an implied listing.
(c) a listing on an exclusive or elegant property.
(d) a net listing.
(e) a listing given to one broker only for a limited period of time.

71. There are two ways of determining the amount of compensation a broker is to receive. One of these is
(a) by overage.
(b) by time and effort.
(c) by provisions of the real estate license law.
(d) by diligence.
(e) by agreement.

72. The second way is:
(a) upon a quantum meruit basis.
(b) arbitration.
(c) decision of local Real Estate Board.

73. Adams obtains a listing from Bell, which expires March 27, 1974. He obtains Chase, a prospective buyer, on March 21, 1974. Bell tells Chase to wait until April 15, 1974 before signing an offer to purchase and Bell agrees. Adams
(a) can recover nothing.
(b) can recover from Bell.
(c) can recover from Chase.

(d) can recover from both Bell and Chase.

74. A broker, upon showing a client's property to a prospect, should
    (a) make an office memorandum.
    (b) confirm the interview by a memo to the buyer.
    (c) notify the seller as to the prospect's identity.
    (d) wait until the prospect makes the deal with the owner.
75. An owner told a broker that he would be pleased to obtain $15,000 for a house, left to him by an uncle. The broker sold it the next day, to a buyer, who resold it at $25,000, within three weeks. The owner can
    (a) recover the $10,000 profit from the first buyer.
    (b) can recover from the broker.
    (c) file a complaint with the licensing commission or department.
    (d) do nothing.
76. In the above case, the broker should have suggested to the owner
    (a) to obtain the assessment by the county.
    (b) to obtain an appraisal.
    (c) to obtain a statement of all annual taxes against the property.
    (d) to ask a local builder the probable market value.
77. A licensed broker, manager of large apartment buildings, bought quantities of supplies at wholesale prices, but he charged the various owners at retail prices. One apartment building owner discovered the situation and sued to recover $1,200, representing difference between retail and wholesale prices for one year. He sued the broker. The broker's defense was that for the one building he would be unable to obtain wholesale prices. The owner
    (a) can recover only interest on excess money spent.
    (b) cannot recover anything.
    (c) can recover excess cost.
    (d) can increase rental to cover excess costs.
78. The owner in the above case, has certain alternative remedies. Which one of the following is *not* available to him
    (a) terminate broker's management contract.
    (b) file a complaint with the Real Estate Commission.
    (c) file a complaint with the Public Housing Authority.
    (d) file a complaint with the Real Estate Board, of which the broker is a member.
79. Collins listed vacant property for sale with Ayers for $25,000, of which $3,000 was to be payable in cash and the balance by a purchase money note in monthly installments, secured by a deed of trust (mortgage). The broker was to receive all amounts in excess of $25,000. More than a year later, Collins sold the property to Ayers' prospect for $24,000,—$3,000 cash and $125 monthly on the mortgage plan. In a suit for commission, Ayers
    (a) can recover 10 per cent fee for selling vacant land.
    (b) cannot recover.
    (c) can recover on a "quantum meruit" basis.
    (d) can ask to have the dispute heard by a board of arbitration.
80. A net listing contract
    (a) generally favors the owner.
    (b) generally favors the broker.
    (c) is void as against public policy.
    (d) usually prevents a sale of the listed property.
81. Brown, a broker, represents to a young couple, with two grade school children, that the grade school is only two short blocks away. Actually, the school will be discontinued in September and become part of a grade school district, with the new school about 1 ½ miles distant. The buyers learn this in August, after the deal is closed
    (a) the buyers have no remedy.
    (b) the broker will be liable for the transportation charges to and from the school.

(c) the buyers can rescind the deal.
(d) obtain a refund of part of the purchase price.

82. A sales person, enroute to a sample house with a prospect, suffers injuries in an automobile accident. He is
    (a) protected for injuries against his broker, under the Workmen's Compensation laws.
    (b) he is not so protected.
    (c) he can only recover for his injuries under any accident policy he carries personally.
    (d) he can recover unemployment compensation against his employer for the period he is unable to work.
83. The Winthrop Clinic offered to pay a commission to Neil Smith, if he could purchase an adjoining lot, which they desired for parking. Smith obtains a listing and a sale is made to Helen Miller, a secretary to the clinic's manager. Three days later she conveys the lot to the clinic. In a claim for commission
    (a) Smith can recover from the clinic.
    (b) Smith can recover from the lot owner.
    (c) Smith can recover from both clinic and lot owner.
    (d) Smith can recover from no one.
84. Broker Stone showed a number of properties to Ann Simon. On seeing one of the properties, she told Stone that she had already seen the property with Broker Wolf. She contacted Wolf about three weeks later and signed an agreement to purchase the property. Stone contacted Wolf and Mrs. Simon and demanded one-half of the commission
    (a) Stone can recover one-half commission from Wolf.
    (b) Stone can recover one-half commission from Ann Simon.
    (c) Stone can recover a full commission from the owner.
    (d) Stone cannot recover from anyone.
85. Which type of contract affords the broker the greatest protection?
    (a) An open listing.
    (b) An exclusive listing.
    (c) A written listing.
    (d) An exclusive right-to-sell listing.
86. Whether to keep the forfeited earnest money, resell the property, or sue the buyer for performance, where the buyer defaults, is a matter to be decided by the
    (a) broker.
    (b) salesman.
    (c) court.
    (d) seller.
87. A broker, who sells a property to a purchaser recommended by a friend, should
    (a) thank the friend.
    (b) buy the friend a suitable gift.
    (c) give the friend half the commission.
    (d) pay the friend 5 per cent of the commission.
88. An example of fiduciary relationship is that which exists between
    (a) broker and prospect.
    (b) broker and anyone he talks to about real estate.
    (c) broker and client.
    (d) broker and the Real Estate Commission.
    (e) broker and salesman's prospect.
89. The broker must obey all instructions made known to him by his principal. Should the principal instruct the broker to violate the law, the broker should
    (a) do as instructed.
    (b) not do as instructed.
    (c) withdraw from the transaction.
    (d) sue the principal.
    (e) do nothing.

90. An owner converts a 3 story dwelling into 6 apartments, in violation of the zoning law. The owner lists the property for sale with a broker at $23,500. Should the broker
    (a) list the property at $23,500.
    (b) refuse to list the property.
    (c) suggest owner list property at $20,000.
    (d) obtain a buyer at $23,500 and have owner apply for a variation permit from the Zoning Board or Board of Adjustment.
91. Ash gives a written listing on certain property to broker, Brown, for sale on stipulated price and terms. Ash does not list this property with any other broker for 90 days.
    (a) Brown has an exclusive listing. T F
    (b) Ash cannot sell the property to a buyer obtained through his own efforts. T F
    (c) If Ash sold this property to a purchaser produced by a friend, he would have to pay Brown a commission. T F
    (d) This listing does not create a fiduciary relation between Ash and Brown. T F
92. Broker Martin advertised a dwelling for rent at $240 per month. A prospect inquired and wanted to see the property immediately. Martin was busy at the time, so he gave the prospect a key to the premises and demanded a $10 deposit for its return. The deposit was paid but the prospect never returned. Later, it was discovered that air conditioners were missing, worth $350.
    (a) Martin is liable for the loss.
    (b) Martin is not liable for the loss.
    (c) the loss will be made up out of the first two months rent.
    (d) no commission will be due on any lease negotiated by Martin during the first year.
93. Don Garwood listed his home for sale with the Fairview Realty Co. at $21,000, commission is to be 7 per cent. A buyer is obtained at $20,500, who gives the broker a deposit check for $750. Later, the buyer is unable to obtain financing for a $19,500 mortgage and refuses to complete the deal. The broker sues the owner for commission.
    (a) the owner must sue the buyer for specific performance.
    (b) the broker can keep the deposit money.
    (c) the broker can hold the owner to a full commission.
    (d) the broker cannot recover.
94. Clark is anxious to sell his house for $28,000. Clark mentions this fact to a friend, Wilson, who, in turn, tells his friend, Curtis. Curtis, in turn, introduces Stone to Clark, and purchases the property at $26,750. Curtis claims a commission from Clark.
    (a) he can recover.
    (b) he cannot recover.
    (c) he can file a complaint for services with the Consumers Protection Commission.
    (d) he can assign his claim to a licensed broker.
95. An owner gave a written exclusive listing to a broker on a dwelling at $50,000, commission to be 6 per cent. During the 90 day exclusive period, the broker produced a prospect who offered $45,000, which the owner refused. One month after the listing expired, the same prospect bought the property at $45,000. Under these circumstances the broker
    (a) can collect a commission from the seller.
    (b) cannot collect a commission from the seller.
    (c) can collect from both seller and buyer.
    (d) can bring an action of conspiracy against seller and buyer.
96. The terms of a written exclusive listing is for 60 days, and calls for a 7 per cent commission. At the expiration of the term, the owner, at the request of the broker, orally extends its duration for one month. During that month, broker brings a prospect, who purchases the property. Owner refuses to pay a commission, claiming the extension was not in writing. Broker sues.
    (a) broker cannot recover.
    (b) broker can recover.
    (c) broker can recover on a quantum meruit basis.
    (d) broker can recover from buyer and seller.

97. A salesman obtains a binding offer in writing and is given a deposit of earnest money.
    (a) He should immediately turn contract and deposit over to the employing broker. T F
    (b) Should the offer not be accepted by the owner, the money should be returned to the prospective buyer. T F
    (c) If the offer is accepted by the owner and the owner thereafter refuses to or cannot deliver title, the broker should keep the deposit, or part of it, to pay him for his trouble. T F
    (d) Should the owner accept the offer and the prospective buyer fail to complete the sale for reasons of his own, the money should be divided equally between the broker and owner up to the amount of what the broker's commission would have been had the sale been completed. T F
    (e) If the face amount of the offer is considerably larger than the price in the listing, only the price stated in the listing should be offered the owner. The balance should be divided between the salesman and broker. T F
98. A broker may lawfully receive a commission from
    (a) the owner. T F
    (b) a co-broker. T F
    (c) both buyer and seller. T F
    (d) a salesperson of a second broker. T F
99. A contract which provides for the payment of a commission to a broker, even though the owner makes a sale without the aid of the broker, is called
    (a) exclusive listing.
    (b) unilateral contract.
    (c) bilateral contract.
    (d) multiple listing.
    (e) exclusive right to sell.
100. A listing may be brought to an end in several ways. One of these is included in the following:
    (a) regulation.
    (b) reneging.
    (c) regurgitation.
    (d) renunciation.
101. An authorization to a person to act for and in behalf of another in a real estate transaction is called
    (a) an option.
    (b) a power of attorney.
    (c) a reconveyance.
    (d) an exclusive right of sale.
102. An unlicensed salesman negotiated the sale of real estate. The commission is payable to
    (a) the broker.
    (b) the salesman.
    (c) no one.
    (d) an escrow holder.
103. Weldin lists his three story dwelling for sale with Boone, a broker. It is in a district zoned for single families. Weldin had converted the second floor into a separate dwelling unit, by installing a kitchen and bathroom. Boone obtains a buyer, McLain. After the deal is closed, Weldin has moved to Canada. McLain is cited by the Zoning Board. What are McLain's rights?
    (a) He must pursue Weldin for damages.
    (b) He can look to Boone for damages.
    (c) McLain has no remedy.
    (d) The city's action is invalid.
104. Under an exclusive right to sell listing, an owner may list his property for sale with how many brokers?
    (a) One.
    (b) Two.

(c) Four.
(d) Any number.

105. How many copies of a listing should a broker make?
(a) One.
(b) Two.
(c) Three.
(d) Five.

106. Under an ordinary exclusive agency listing, with a definite expiration date, how many days of grace does the broker have in which to obtain a buyer after the termination date of the exclusive listing?
(a) 30 days.
(b) 90 days.
(c) 6 months.
(d) none.

107. A broker has a net listing of $70,000 to the owner. If the broker receives a firm offer of $70,000, the broker's commission would be:
(a) $3,500.
(b) $4,200.
(c) $4,900.
(d) Nothing.

108. If a net listing specifies the broker's commission, it is
(a) void.
(b) voidable.
(c) valid.
(d) unenforceable.

109. An attorney-in-fact is the holder of
(a) a certificate as an attorney-at-law.
(b) power of attorney.
(c) appointment by order of court.
(d) decree from a court.

110. Two rival brokers claim the commission in a real estate transaction. It should be paid to
(a) the broker with whom the property was first listed.
(b) the broker who was the procuring cause.
(c) the broker who makes the first claim.

111. A salesman may lawfully obtain listings when
(a) He obtains a broker who will employ him.
(b) The salesman's application has been filed.
(c) The broker receives the salesman's license from the Commission.
(d) The salesman has passed his examination.

112. A broker finds a purchaser, acceptable to his owner. After the agreements are signed, the buyer and seller agree not to consummate the deal. The broker
(a) is not entitled to a commission.
(b) is entitled to commission only upon the earnest money deposited.
(c) is entitled to a full commission from the buyer.
(d) can collect full commission from the seller.

113. An owner, who employs more than one broker at the same time, has given each broker
(a) unilateral listing.
(b) a multiple listing.
(c) an open listing.
(d) an exclusive listing.

114. Should the owner instruct the broker to misrepresent the existence of termites, the broker should
(a) do as instructed.
(b) not do as instructed.
(c) sue the owner.

(d) withdraw from the transaction.

115. Brown Realty Co., owned by Lee Brown, negotiates a sale for an office building. In order to make the deal, Brown Investment Co., also owned by Lee Brown, lends the buyer $100,000. In consideration thereof, the buyer gives Brown Realty Co. a written contract to manage the building for five years. At the end of one year, the buyer terminates the authority.
    (a) The contract is void, because it violates the statute of frauds.
    (b) The contract is terminated, because it involves personal services.
    (c) The contract is invalid, because it was not recorded.
    (d) The contract is valid, because it is an agency coupled with an interest.
116. The first active step necessary to recover a commission is to
    (a) find a buyer.
    (b) advertise the property.
    (c) have a contract of employment.
    (d) list it with the local Board's multi-list association.
117. Lawton, licensed as a broker, as an attorney and as an engineer, sued for a commission on the sale of a Dallas property. The property was listed verbally with him. (In Texas, a listing must be in writing).
    (a) He can recover as a broker.
    (b) He can recover as an attorney.
    (c) He can recover as an engineer.
    (d) He cannot recover.
118. Whelan, a broker, opened negotiations in November 1973 between the owner and a prospect upon property listed with his office, but failed to bring the parties to an agreement. The listing expired January 28, 1974. In June 1974, the owner sold the property to the buyer. The broker claimed a commission.
    (a) The broker can recover.
    (b) Broker cannot recover.
    (c) Broker can bring a conspiracy charge against owner and buyer.
    (d) Broker can file a lien against the subject property.
119. Gold gives Silver, broker, an oral listing on his residence. Silver obtains Brass, a buyer, upon Gold's terms. The agreement contains Silver's name as a witness to the Brass signature, and also has a notation in the lower left hand corner, "Silver, broker." The state of Nebraska requires a listing to be in writing. Silver sues for commission. Can he recover?
    (a) Yes.
    (b) No.
    (c) He can sue buyer.
    (d) He can sue both seller and buyer.
120. Albert listed a dwelling in Miami for sale with Curtis at $40,000, commission at 6 per cent. Curtis received a signed offer from Dale at $36,500 on June 21, 1974, which he submitted by air mail the same day to Alberts in Seattle. The letter was received by Albert on June 24, 1974. Albert accepted the agreement and air mailed a signed copy to Dale the same day, which was received by Dale, in Miami, on June 27, 1974. On June 24, 1974, Dale sent a telegram to Albert, revoking his offer, which was received by Albert on June 25, 1974. Under these circumstances,
    (a) there is a binding contract.
    (b) there is no binding contract.
    (c) Dale can sue for monetary damages.
    (d) Dale can recover any expenses incurred.
121. Helen Myers gave an exclusive right of sale to Jack Erler, broker, of a farm property at $2,000 per acre, or upon any other terms acceptable to the owner, for three years, with commission at 10 per cent of the sale price. Two years later, the owner sold the property to Dawson, who had been shown the property by Erler, 14 months earlier. The sale was at $1,650 per acre. In a suit the court held
    (a) that the 10 year listing was an unreasonable restraint on alienation.

(b) Erler could recover a 10% commission.
(c) Erler could only recover his expenses.
(d) could recover on a quantum meruit basis.

122. Is there any economic justification of a broker in society?
(a) Yes, since he renders services to the public.
(b) No, since he does not produce material goods.
(c) Yes, if he has other employment producing material goods.
(d) No, unless he has professional qualifications.

123. An "alter ego" relationship exists between
(a) a broker and his sales person.
(b) broker and owner.
(c) owner and sales person.
(d) broker and buyer.

124. Taylor, in writing, listed his property for sale with Ajax Realty, Inc. for 90 days. Taylor did not list this property with any other broker. Which, of the following, is true:
(a) Ajax Realty had an exclusive listing.
(b) Ajax Realty, Inc. had an open listing.
(c) if Taylor sells the property himself during the 90 day period, he owes Ajax Realty, Inc. a commission.
(d) if another broker sells the property during the 90 day period, Taylor owes Ajax Realty, Inc. a commission.

125. A broker's relation to an owner is governed by
(a) the law of equity.
(b) law of agency.
(c) respondent superior.
(d) investiture.

126. A printed advertisement for a new development, such as a subdivision is called a
(a) reservation.
(b) prospectus.
(c) nomenclature.
(d) origination.

127. A real estate salesman may lawfully accept an extra commission in a difficult sale from
(a) an appreciative seller.
(b) a thankful buyer.
(c) the broker-employer.
(d) the mortgage finance company.

128. Recovery of commission on a "quantum meruit" basis is commission expressed in
(a) a contract.
(b) what the broker deserves, as determined in a court action.
(c) the commission fixed by a local real estate Board.
(d) commission determined by an arbitration proceedings.

129. Where a broker acts as an agent for both buyer and seller, which fact is disclosed to both, he can collect commission from
(a) seller.
(b) buyer.
(c) seller and buyer.
(d) neither seller nor buyer.

130. Stone agreed to list a proposed subdivision tract, consisting of 30 lots with Clay, a broker, for a term of two years provided Clay lends him $1,500 for engineering expenses, for two years, without interest. After the lots are laid out and the plan is recorded, Clay sells 4 lots during the first six months at $3,000 each. Three months later, Stone notifies Clay that his listing is cancelled, since no further sales have been made. The cancellation is
(a) valid.
(b) invalid.
(c) the listing is renegotiable.

(d) Clay can recover commission on the unsold 26 lots.

131. A broker, who has earnest money in his escrow account, may, after the deal is closed
   (a) Retain the commission money in his escrow account indefinitely, without interest.
   (b) Retain the commission money in his escrow account, indefinitely, so as to earn interest.
   (c) May immediately withdraw his commission, even though the deed and mortgage have not yet been recorded.
   (d) Withdraw one-half of the commission money, and leave one-half in the escrow account.
132. An earnest money receipt recites a deposit of $1,000. The buyer gives the broker a post dated check in that amount. A Commission Auditor checks the broker's escrow account in the interim. The broker
   (a) should have placed the check in his escrow account.
   (b) should have opened up a special account in his accounting procedure.
   (c) deposit the check in his personal account.
   (d) should have notified the owner, when he received the check.
133. An investigator for the Real Estate Commission finds that Broker Williams has $1,000 in his escrow account. There are no real estate deals pending.
   (a) The escrow account will be approved and reported to the Real Estate Commission.
   (b) The escrow account will not be approved.
   (c) The escrow account will receive a qualified approval.
   (d) The investigator should await further instructions from the Real Estate Commission.
134. In accepting a note as a deposit from a buyer, the broker should
   (a) assume personal responsibility for payment of the note.
   (b) place the note in his safe deposit box.
   (c) state in the agreement that the deposit is in the form of a note.
   (d) discount the note with this bank and obtain cash.
135. Where a broker negotiates a deal for $18,000 and the agreement recites a $1,500 deposit, but the buyer has only $500 in cash, the broker should
   (a) obtain a "hold" check from the buyer for $1,000, dated one day before the closing date.
   (b) obtain a note for $1,000 due 10 days before the closing date.
   (c) re-write the agreement and state a $500 earnest money deposit.
   (d) do nothing and require the buyer to pay the full balance due at the closing.
136. Brooks negotiates a real estate deal between, Paige, seller and Gray, buyer. He receives a deposit of $1,000. An irreconcilable controversy arises at the closing between Paige and Gray. Each demands the $1,000 deposit. Brooks should
   (a) Return the $1,000 to Gray.
   (b) give the money to Paige.
   (c) turn the $1,000 in to the Real Estate Commission.
   (d) do nothing, await a suit and enter an interpleader.
137. A real estate listing is
   (a) real estate held for sale by auction.
   (b) a list of all property held by one person for tax purposes.
   (c) employment of a broker by an owner to sell or lease his property.
   (d) an offer to buy property owned by a political subdivision.
138. A real estate salesman may lawfully pay a part of his commission to
   (a) any person.
   (b) as a refund to the buyer.
   (c) as a bonus to the seller for selling.
   (d) another licensee.
   (e) no one.
139. Salesman Sloan is licensed under broker Klaus but wants to work for broker Fair, so he
   (a) may start selling for Fair as soon as he places his license on display in Fair's office.

(b) may start selling as soon as he notifies the Real Estate Commission of the change.
(c) may start selling if Klaus writes the Commission that he has no objection to the change.
(d) may start selling for Fair as soon as the Real Estate Commission reissues his license to Fair.

140. An example of fiduciary relationship is that which exists between
(a) broker and prospect.
(b) broker and client.
(c) broker and his salesman's prospect.
(d) broker and anyone.

141. Rose gave a written listing on certain property to broker Harris. Rose did not list this property for sale with any other broker for 90 days
(a) Harris had an open listing.
(b) Harris had an exclusive listing for 90 days.
(c) Rose cannot sell the property himself for 90 days.
(d) if Rose sold the property through another broker during the 90 day period, he would have to pay Harris a commission.

142. The Realtor Code of Ethics recommends an
(a) open listing.
(b) exclusive listing.
(c) net-listing.
(d) parol listing.

143. When a broker shows a prospect a house listed with him for sale, he should
(a) telephone the owner.
(b) post the premises.
(c) give the owner written notice of prospect's identity.
(d) send written notice to prospect.

144. A salesman can buy property listed for sale with his broker, where
(a) he takes title in name of another person.
(b) he takes title in name of his broker, in trust for the salesman.
(c) he discloses his intention to the owner.
(d) notifies the Real Estate Commission in advance.

145. Under the usual employment contract, a broker is entitled to his commission when
(a) the deal is consummated.
(b) He produces a ready and willing buyer, upon seller's terms, even though the seller refuses to sign the agreement of sale.
(c) He produces a ready and willing buyer at the listing price of the property, subject to a purchase money mortgage.

146. If a prospective seller asks a salesman at what price he should list his property for sale, the salesman should reply
(a) we will list at whatever price you suggest.
(b) at two and one-half times the assessed value.
(c) I will ask my broker to appraise it for you and list it at that figure.
(d) list it at 30 per cent above the present mortgage.

147. Whether to forfeit the deposit money, resell the property, or sue the buyer for performance, where the buyer defaults, is a matter for whom to decide?
(a) Broker.
(b) Vendor.
(c) Salesman.
(d) Independent agency.

148. Broker Dow negotiates a sale between Evans, seller and Fairchild, buyer, which contains a clause "Purchaser to obtain an F.H.A. insured loan in the amount of $10,100." The lending institute requires certain repairs. Evans orally agrees to make the repairs, but later refuses. The deal falls through. Dow sues for a commission. He can
(a) recover from Evans.

(b) recover from Fairchild.
(c) recover from Evans and Fairchild.
(d) no recovery from either Evans or Fairchild.

149. A broker receives a $1,000 earnest money deposit. At the closing, the seller demands the $1,000 deposit and refuses to pay the broker his commission, because of personal differences. The broker should
(a) withold the deposit in part payment of his commission.
(b) release the earnest money to the owner and sue him for the full commission.
(c) instruct the title company not to close the deal.
(d) file a complaint with the Real Estate Commission.

150. A broker owes certain duties to his principal. Which one of the following is not included
(a) loyalty to his principal.
(b) must obey instructions.
(c) maintain the property.
(d) account for money and property.

151. A broker is asked to prepare an agreement of sale and deed for seller and buyer, for which he makes a charge of $35.00. The broker can legally
(a) charge the seller only.
(b) charge the buyer only.
(c) charge both seller and buyer.
(d) charge neither seller nor buyer.

152. Where an agent breaches his duty to his principal, which one of the following would not apply
(a) civil suit for damages.
(b) equity suit for an injunction.
(c) complaint to the Real Estate Commission.
(d) terminate the contractual relationship.

153. A property was listed with a broker at $455,000 net to the owner. The broker obtained a buyer at that figure. The broker's commission is
(a) on a quantum meruit basis.
(b) 6%.
(c) 6% on the first $100,000 and then graduated.
(d) nothing.

154. A broker negotiates a sale, for which he is paid a commission. He prepares the deed and handles the closing. For these additional services, he may charge
(a) the seller.
(b) the buyer.
(c) both seller and buyer.
(d) neither seller nor buyer.

155. Ruth Stevens, owner, leased a property to the Sun Ray Oil Co. through Stone, a broker. The lease contained a "first right of refusal clause." Later she listed the property for sale with Stone, who procured a purchaser, Lemore, at $27,500. An agreement of sale was signed by the owner and the purchaser, Mr Lemore, which provided that if Sun Ray exercised its right to purchase at the same price, the agreement with Lemore was to be null and void. Sun Ray exercised its right to purchase the subject tract at $27,500. Stone sued for commission. Stone can
(a) recover from Stevens.
(b) Stone cannot recover from Stevens.
(c) Stone can recover from Stevens and Sun Ray.
(d) Stone cannot recover from anyone.

156. A principal (owner) may have more than one agent under
(a) a multiple listing.
(b) an open listing.
(c) exclusive listing.
(d) exclusive right to sell listing.

157. Albert lists property for sale with Broker Brown for $11,000. The broker obtains a prospective buyer, Chase, at $13,500. He has his mother-in-law buy the property at $11,000 and she deeds the property to Chase at $13,500. Albert paid Brown a commission of 6% on the $11,000 deal. In addition to recovering the commission paid and the profit, Albert could:
    (a) file a complaint with the Housing Authority.
    (b) file a complaint with the Real Estate Commission.
    (c) file an injunctive suit against Brown continuing to operate as a broker.
    (d) picket Brown's office.
158. Terry lists property for sale with Yancy, a broker. Yancy enlists an engineer, Wise, who is not licensed, to help him find a purchaser. Wise refers Thomas to Yancy, who purchases the property at $60,000. The agreement of sale states that a 4% commission is to be paid by Terry to Yancy and a 2% commission to Wise. Terry is liable to
    (a) Yancy for $2,400 and to Wise for $1,200.
    (b) Yancy for $3,600.
    (c) Yancy for $2,400.
    (d) no one.
159. A broker's listing contract may not be terminated by the owner before its expiration date, where
    (a) the broker negotiated the sale to the owner.
    (b) the broker has advertised the property.
    (c) the agency is coupled with an interest.
    (d) the owner desires to list the property with a more active real estate firm.
160. A property is listed with a broker at $8,500. He finds a prospect who is willing to sign an offer at $7,000, but will pay $8,500, if the owner declines the offer. The broker should
    (a) buy the property himself at $8,500.
    (b) submit the $7,500 offer.
    (c) persuade the buyer to make his $8,500 offer now.
    (d) refuse to submit the $7,500 offer.
161. Awarding a bonus to the salesman producing the highest volume of sales during the year is
    (a) a violation of the license law.
    (b) a good incentive.
    (c) contrary to public policy.
    (d) invalid, if paid in cash.
162. If the seller makes the misrepresentation to the broker, and the broker has no duty to check:
    (a) the broker is still liable.
    (b) the broker has no liability.
    (c) the seller and the broker are both liable.
163. Baker, a broker, receives a listing from Cooper to sell a commercial site at $45,000, at 6 per cent commission. He obtains Davis as a buyer. During the negotiations, he obtains a listing from Davis to sell a commercial site which he owns for $40,000. He sells this property to Edwards at the listing price. Both deals are closed the same day. Baker claims commissions from Cooper and from Davis.
    (a) Baker cannot recover from Cooper or Davis.
    (b) Baker can recover only from Cooper.
    (c) Baker can recover only from Davis.
    (d) Baker can recover from both Cooper and Davis.
164. A property is listed with Holmes. He places the listing in a multiple listing service to which he belongs. Fownes is a salesperson for Holmes, who contacts the ultimate buyer. Heath is a salesperson for Downes, also a broker member of the multi-list association. Heath obtains a signed offer and an earnest money deposit of $1,000. The check should be turned over to:
    (a) Holmes.

(b) Fownes.
(c) Downes.
(d) Should be held by Heath.

165. Broker Crane had a written exclusive right to sell listing from owner, Dean, which expired on May 31, 1974. Following that date, Dean knew that Crane was still trying to sell the property and permitted Crane to show the property to prospects. On August 19, 1974, Dean sold the property to King, who earlier was shown the property by Crane. Dean refuses to pay a commission. Under the circumstances:
I. Crane can recover from King.
II. Crane can recover from Dean.
(a) I only.
(b) II only.
(c) both I and II.
(d) neither I nor II.

166. Hugh Frank and Mary Frank, his wife, are the owners of a property. On May 1, 1974, they list the property for sale at $55,000, 6 per cent commission, with Stone, Realtor, for 90 days. The listing is signed by Hugh Frank, but Mary Frank, who is present, does not sign the listing. On June 24, 1974, Jim Sales procures a buyer at $55,000 cash. The Franks refuse to pay a commission:
I. Stone can recover from Hugh Frank.
II. Stone can recover from Mary Frank.
(a) I only.
(b) II only.
(c) both I and II.
(d) neither I nor II.

167. A listing contract provided that a commission would be paid to the broker, if (1) the sale was consummated or (2) if not consummated due to a title defect. A sale was made, but the buyer refused to close the deal. Under these circumstances:
I. The seller should sue the buyer for specific performance.
II. The broker can recover a commission.
(a) I only.
(b) II only.
(c) both I and II.
(d) neither I nor II.

168. A broker negotiated a sale and the agreement of sale, prepared by him, stated "Subject to satisfactory financing." Later, the buyer refused to go through with the deal and demanded the return of his deposit money:
(a) The buyer must complete the deal.
(b) The buyer can recover his deposit.
(c) The buyer cannot recover the deposit.
(d) The seller must provide adequate financing.

169. Where the buyer does not have sufficient money for the earnest money deposit:
I. The broker may loan him the broker's expected commission.
II. The broker may take a note from the buyer for the amount needed.
(a) I only.
(b) II only.
(c) both I and II.
(d) neither I nor II.

170. Steele, broker, negotiates a deal between Lynn, seller, and Marks, buyer, at $21,000. The parties sign an agreement to that effect. Marks requires a $20,000 mortgage, so Steele prepares a second agreement of sale, reciting a consideration price of $24,900, which is signed by the seller and buyer. The second agreement is submitted to a mortgage company for a $20,000 loan. Under these circumstances:
I. Steele is guilty of a criminal act.
II. Lynn and Marks are guilty of a criminal act.

(a) I only.
(b) II only.
(c) both I and II.
(d) neither I nor II.

171. Aiken, broker, negotiates a deal between Hendricks, seller, and Logan, buyer, at $120,000 for a vacant tract of land. The deal drags on for 15 months and then, is cancelled, because Logan is unable to secure the necessary financing for construction. Under these circumstances:
I. Aiken can recover commission from Hendricks.
II. Aiken can recover commission from Logan.
(a) I only.
(b) II only.
(c) both I and II.
(d) neither I nor II.

172. Adams gave an exclusive right to sell listing for property at $30,000 for a term of 6 months. Commission was to be 6 per cent. The property, during the listing period, was taken by the state by eminent domain. Under these circumstances:
I. The broker is entitled to a commission from Adams.
II. Broker is enitled to a commission from the state.
(a) I only.
(b) II only.
(c) both I and II.
(d) neither I nor II.

173. A broker had an exclusive right to sell the property for 90 days from the owner. During the 90 day period, the owner deeded the property to the mortgagee, because the latter threatened to foreclose the property, since it was in default. Under these circumstances, the broker can:
I. Recover his commission from the owner.
II. Can recover his commission from the mortgagee.
(a) I only.
(b) II only.
(c) both I and II.
(d) neither I nor II.

174. An agreement of sale, negotiated by a broker, was signed by his seller and buyer. The agreement names the broker, but he does not sign the agreement. Under these circumstances, the broker can recover commission from:
I. The buyer.
II. The seller.
(a) I only.
(b) II only.
(c) both buyer and seller.
(d) neither I nor II.

175. On February 15, 1974, Hadfield gave Baylor a 90 day exclusive listing on his home of $32,500, commission to be 7%. The listing had an extender clause for 6 months, commission to be paid if the property were sold to any person with whom Baylor had negotiated during the 90 day period. Baylor submitted the property to Rowland on February 21, 1974, but he did nothing further. Rowland purchased the property from Hadfield on July 13, 1974 at $30,000. Under these circumstances, Baylor can:
I. Recover a commission from Hadfield.
II. Sue Hadfield and Rowland for conspiracy.
(a) I only.
(b) II only.
(c) both I and II.
(d) neither I nor II.

176. Trojan Realty negotiated a $30,000 real estate deal. The listing agreement provides that any earnest money deposit is to be placed in the broker's escrow account. The broker received an earnest money deposit of $1,500. His commission agreement is 5%. At the closing, the owner refused to pay the commission and demanded the earnest money deposit. Under these circumstances, the broker should
   I. Keep the deposit money and await a suit by the seller.
   II. File a complaint with the Real Estate Commission.
      (a) I only.
      (b) II only.
      (c) both I and II.
      (d) neither I nor II.
177. Broker Flynn had a written listing from Simon, which expired on May 7, 1973. It was orally extended to August 7, 1973. Flynn continued negotiating with a prospect, with the knowledge and encouragement of Simon. In November, an agreement of sale was entered into between Simon and Flynn's prospect. The deal was closed. Flynn sued for a commission.
   (a) He can recover on a "quantum meruit" basis.
   (b) He can recover only his expenses and advertising costs.
   (c) He can recover his full commission.
   (d) He cannot recover.
178. Carl Gerold, a licensed broker, had a building management contract with the owner. The agent also had the sole exclusive right to sell or offer for sale, the property, if said property is sold or offered for sale during the terms of this agreement. The property was sold by the owner, during the term of this agreement for $212,500. Gerold sues.
   (a) He can recover.
   (b) He cannot recover.
   (c) He can bring a criminal action against the owner.
   (d) He can recover in a tort action.
179. Broker Moore employs Sharp as a salesperson, under a written agreement that if Sharp leaves Moore's employ, he can never engage in the real estate business in Jefferson County. One year later, Sharp opens his own business in an adjoining county.
   (a) The restrictive provision is binding.
   (b) The restriction is invalid.
   (c) Sharp can open an office 200 miles from Moore's office.
   (d) Moore can file a complaint with the Real Estate Commission.
180. Dunn lists his property for sale at $18,000 with Flood, a broker, who is a member of a multi-list association. Green, a broker-member of the same association, sells the property to Harris, who gives Green a check for $1,000, an earnest money deposit. Under these circumstances:
   I. Green should turn the check over to Flood, with consent of Harris.
   II. Flood, in turn, should turn the check over to the multi-list association, since both are members.
      (a) I only.
      (b) II only.
      (c) both I and II.
      (d) neither I nor II.
181. A licensed broker may lawfully pay part of his commission to which of the following:
   I. A licensed salesperson of another licensed broker.
   II. A licensed civil engineer.
      (a) I only.
      (b) II only.
      (c) both I and II.
      (d) neither I nor II.
182. Adams, an unlicensed salesman, employed by Baker, negotiates sale of property in behalf

of Clark, owner, to Davis, buyer. Davis now seeks to avoid the contract, on the grounds that Adams was unlicensed when the deal was made. Under these circumstances,
(a) the agreement can be rescinded by Clark.
(b) the agreement cannot be rescinded by Clark.
(c) the agreement can be rescinded, if Clark pays Davis a penalty.
(d) the salesman must obtain a license immediately in order to have a valid agreement.

Chapter 2

AGREEMENTS OF SALE

AN AGREEMENT of sale is a contract between two principals, one of whom is the seller and the other is the buyer. These parties are also known, respectively, as the vendor and vendee; and less frequently as the contractor and contractee. The broker prepares this contract, as agent of the party of the first part (owner). Although the broker is not a party to the contract, he may acquire important rights under it, if the agreement contains a clause which recognizes the broker as the one who negotiated the deal, and the seller agreed to pay him a commission for his services: *Herman v. Stern,* 419 Ia 272 (1965), *W. D. Nelson & Co., Inc. v. Taylor Heights Development Corp.,* 207 Va. 386 (1966).

The function of a broker is to negotiate a valid contract of sale between his principal, the owner, and the buyer. In this connection the broker prepares the agreement of sale, which, to a large extent, makes the law by which seller and buyer are governed.

It is important that a real estate broker or salesman be fully cognizant of the responsibilities which he assumes in undertaking to draw an agreement of sale. The instrument fixes legal rights and obligations of the seller and the buyer. It must adequately protect his principal, the seller, and at the same time, protect the buyer, who may be engaging in his first real estate venture. A poorly drawn agreement of sale may not only lead to dissatisfaction and controversy, but to expensive litigation as well. In addition, the broker, who prepared the faulty agreement of sale, may find himself the defendant, not only in an action at law, but also in proceedings for revocation or suspension of license, on the grounds of incompetency. In many respects, the agreement of sale is more important than the deed, because it dictates and determines what goes into the deed.

If the agreement, prepared by the broker, is within the actual or apparent scope of the agent's authority, any ambiguity will be resolved against the owner. The broker's fundamental duty of loyalty to the owner is based upon their principal-agent relationship. Invested with a license by the state, it attests to the broker's good repute and competency as a *professional.*

In *Yerkie, Jr. v. Salisbury,* 287 A. 2d 498 (Md. 1972), the court said:

> Brokers and their salesmen ought to have sense enough to realize that many contracts of sale are important legal documents, the preparation of which ought to be left to lawyers. Quite often there is a great deal more to the drafting of a contract for the sale of land than filling in the blank spaces on a printed form.

Under the Statute of Frauds, which exists in every state, a contract for the sale of real estate must be in writing, in order to be enforceable. The object of the Statute, passed in 1676 (29 Charles II), was to close the door to numerous frauds and perjuries in contracts which could be enforced only upon no other evidence than the mere recollection of witnesses: *Haddock Construction Co. v. Snedigar Dairy,* 510 P. 2d 752 (Ariz. App. 1973). However, partial performance of an oral contract to convey real estate may remove that contract from the operation of the Statute of Frauds where there has been an earnest money deposit, the purchaser has gone into possession and made improvements to the property. Under such circumstances, equity would intervene and entitle the buyer to a decree of specific performance: *Zaborski v. Kutyla,* 185 N.W. 2d 586 (Mich. App. 1971).

A written memorandum, to constitute an enforceable agreement, must disclose all essential elements of the sale of land, and cannot rest partly in writing and partly in parol. The court so stated in the case of *Colrodas v. Russell,* 289 So. 2d 55 (Fla. App. 1974), where the time of payment, manner of payment and whether cash or credit was omitted from the writing.

It is important to note that all prior committments are merged into the deed, unless, by express contract, certain matters are held open to be completed at a later time. However, the closing statement, accepted by the parties, may modify the sales contract insofar as the figures may be at variance with the sales contract: *S. G. Payne & Co. v. Nowak,* 465 S.W. 2d 17 (Mo. 1971).

A check for $1,000 from a purchaser to a seller, bearing only the notation "For lot 100 Earnest Money" did not constitute contract for sale of land, since 100 did not define subject matter of the transaction: *Kenimer v. Thompson,* 156 S.E. 2d 363 (Ga. 1973).

In a certain situation, a broker negotiated a $300,000 transaction and received a $10,000 deposit, which was to be the broker's commission. There was a $240,000 mortgage of record against the property. In referring to the mortgage, the broker stated in the agreement of sale, prepared by him, that the buyer was accepting the property "under and subject to the mortgage," in the amount then due of $240,000.

The seller's attorney tendered a general warranty deed to the buyer, at the closing. In referring to the unpaid mortgage, the deed stated it was "Under and subject to the mortgage balance of $240,000," which mortgagee, the grantee *assumed and agreed* to pay, as part of the purchase price. The buyer refused to accept the deed because it did not conform to the agreement of sale. The buyer was correct. The broker had rendered a disservice to his principal, the seller, from whom he expected a $10,000 commission. Under the broker's mortgage clause in the agreement, the buyer would have suffered no personal liability in event of a mortgage foreclosure sale, and a deficiency judgment was entered in favor of the mortgagee. Under the mortgage clause in the deed, which was tendered, the buyer *assumed* the mortgage, and if a foreclosure ensued, the buyer would have been obligated for any deficiency judgment. After a lengthy controversy, the deal fell through and the broker lost a $10,000 commission.

Once a deed is accepted, rights which the parties had under the agreement of sale, are merged into the deed. No further action arises under the agreement of sale: *Dillahunty v. Keystone Savings Association,* 363 N.E. 2d 750 (Ohio 1973). However, a closing statement, accepted by seller and buyer, may modify the agreement of sale if the figures are at variance with the sales agreement: *S. S. Payne & Co. v. Nowak,* 465 S.W. 2d 17 (Mo. 1971).

A dated memorandum signed by owners, reciting merely that they had received from purchaser the sum of $500 as deposit to purchase "Apt. at 20001 Conant, for $94,000" was sufficient to satisfy the statute of frauds. The court decreed specific performance: *Klymshyn v. Szarek,* 185 N.W. 2d 820 (Mich. App. 1971).

The Statute of Frauds does not require that a writing be one instrument. It may be created out of separate writing, connected with one another by the internal nature of the subject matter: *Lalone v. Modern Album and Finishing Co., Inc.,* 331 NYS 2d 889 (1972).

A contract for sale of realty was held too vague and indefinite with respect to time within which balance of purchase price was to be paid, where contract stated that $11,000 of purchase price was to be paid in three equal installments: *Cook v. Barfield,* 162 S.E. 2d 417 (Ga. 1968). An *oral* contract may give rise to an action for specific performance, where the buyer has paid part of the purchase price, gone into possession and made improvements to the property. *Walker v. Walker,* 448 S.W. 2d 171 (Tex. 1969). *Brotman v. Brotman,* 353 Pa. 570 (1946).

Authority of agent is limited

The broker is a *special* agent with *limited* authority. He is employed to obtain a purchaser for the owner. This employment, generally, cannot be enlarged to empower the broker to sign, as agent for the owner, a binding agreement of sale: *Peters v. Windmiller,* 314 Ill. 496 (1925). A listing contract, per se, containing the words of employment "to sell," does not confer such authority: *Gallant v. Todd et al.,* 111 S.E. 2d 779 (S.C. 1960). Some printed listing contracts do authorize execution of a sales agreement by the broker, using such words "and to contract in my name," or the like. Generally, this is not considered good ethical practice. Extenuating circumstances may dictate the use of such authority for the broker to sign as agent for the owner in the listing agreement,—where, for example, the owner is going abroad for an extended period of time, his itinerary is uncertain, and he is anxious to have the property sold.

An agent exceeds his authority when he permits a purchaser to take possession of the premises before the deal is closed, no matter how sympathetic he may be to the buyer's need. For example, where the buyer is moving from another state, and his furniture and household effects are already in transit. Often, the buyer will ask the broker permission to do some decorating, painting or to make minor repairs before the deal is closed. Should the deal fail to be consummated, the broker may find himself the defendant in an action for expenses and damages by the disappointed purchaser: *Cryder Well Co. v. Brown et al.,* 136 N.W. 2d 519 (Iowa 1965). If the buyer wants some special privilege, the broker should refer him to the owner for permission.

Ambiguity construed against owner

As stated earlier, since the broker is the agent for the owner, an ambiguous agreement of sale, executed by buyer and owner, would be construed most strongly against the owner. In the case of *Baker v. Leight,* 370 P. 2d 268 (Ariz. 1962), the defendant broker prepared a deposit agreement and receipt, which stated that the buyers were "to assume an existing mortgage of approximately $52,000, payable at approximately $518.39, including 7% interest . . ." The seller wrote in a modification, among others, viz. "5. The purchaser is to assume the legal obligation for the first mortgage." These modifications were accepted by the buyers. Later the parties became aware of the fact that the first mortgage in question contained the following clause:

> 16. It is expressly understood and agreed that this mortgage shall become due and payable forthwith at the option of the Mortgagee if the Mortgagors shall convey away the said premises or if the title shall become vested in any other person or persons in any matter whatsoever.

This mortgage was a matter of record prior to execution of the agreement of sale. When the buyers learned of the clause in question, they refused to go through with the deal. While other issues were also involved, the court said:

It was the seller's obligation to procure the waiver of clause 16 from the mortgagee and to come forward immediately upon being informed that the buyer elected to rescind because of the fact that clause 16 constituted a material breach of the contract. This the seller did not do. The buyer made out a prima facie case. It was reversible error to direct a verdict for the defendants.

The Supreme Court remanded the case for further hearing.

In the case of *Beattie-Firth, Inc. v. Colebank et al.,* 143 W.Va. 740 (1958), the broker lost his suit for a commission since his listing contract provided that he was to receive a commission (1) if a buyer was obtained and the sale was consummated, or (2) if the sale was not consummated by reason of any default of the seller. The broker obtained a buyer. The sales agreement, prepared by the broker, recognized the plaintiff as the broker in the deal and the seller agreed to pay him a commission, subject to the two conditions stated above. The *buyer* defaulted and the seller refused to sue the buyer for damages or specific performance. Since the deal was not consummated and the seller was not at fault, neither of the two conditions was satisfied and the broker could not recover. The court also held:

> . . . we would hesitate to enunciate a rule which would require a vendor whose promise is so conditioned to engage in expensive and perhaps fruitless litigation in order that a broker might become entitled to a commission. A burden so onerous cannot be imposed by implication.

Owner can recover for misconduct of broker

The law is well established in every state that the broker is a fiduciary and that the law exacts a high degree of loyalty and fidelity towards his principal. This rule also applies to a salesman and holds the broker responsible for the salesman's acts, where the broker connives with his salesman, is cognizant of what is going on, or benefits from an illegal transaction. The case of *Security Aluminum Window Mfg. Co. v. Lehman Associates, Inc. et al.,* 108 N.J. Super. 137 (1970), involved an action by seller against a broker and his agent for compensatory and punitive damages in relation to a sale of real property. The appellate court held, inter alia, that punitive damages should have been assessed against both the real estate broker and his salesman in relation to fraudulent scheme involving the sale of property in which the seller was led to believe that an offer of $25,000 had been made for the property where in fact an offer of $50,000 had been tendered by another party.

Legal requirements for agreement of sale

An agreement of sale is a contract *in writing* whereby one party agrees to sell and another to buy certain real estate under such terms and conditions as are therein set forth. It must be remembered that an agreement of sale is a contract. Hence, all the essential elements of a valid contract must be present; these are (1) offer and acceptance, (2) seal or consideration, (3) capacity of parties, (4) reality of consent, and (5) legality of object. Since the contract relates to real estate, an additional element, special formality, is also required. Offer and acceptance means there must be a "meeting of minds" upon the subject matter and terms of the contract. The terms of the contract must be precise and definite. It is the responsibility of the broker who undertakes to prepare the agreements to see to it that the form and substance of the contract will meet any legal challenge. Offer and acceptance may, and often do, arise from correspondence between the parties, so that a formal contract is never signed.

It is not necessary that any earnest money deposit be paid at the time the agreement of sale is signed, in order for the agreement to be valid and enforceable, as the mutual promise by the vendor to execute and deliver a deed and the concurrent promise by the vendee to pay for the same at the same time constitute good and sufficient legal consideration: *Cownan v. Allen Monuments, Inc.,* 500 S.W. 2d 223 (Texas 1973).

It is often difficult to determine whether a writing is a mere receipt or a sufficient agreement under the Statute of Frauds. If the memorandum contains the names of the parties and a definite enough description to identify the property and the terms of the sale, it will suffice.

Sometimes, a broker will have the parties sign a preliminary agreement, such as an offer to purchase, although the advisability of using two separate instruments to do a single job is questionable when one is sufficient. Where there are conflicting clauses in the two papers, trouble may ensue, and it does not always follow that the terms of the preliminary agreement are carried over into the later one.

The case of *Tomkins v. France,* 21 Ill. App. 2d 227 (1959), is pertinent. In that case, the preliminary agreement provided that the parties would execute the usual Chicago Real Estate Board sales contract form, embodying the terms, within five days. The contract submitted was not on the Chicago Board form and called for an earnest money deposit of $4,950, instead of $2,000, stated in the preliminary agreement to purchase. The court held that the buyer did not need to perform and he was entitled to a refund of his $2,000 deposit.

No particular form is necessary for an agreement of sale. It need only be signed by the vendor and need not be under seal. The memorandum or writing should contain the following information: (1) the names of the parties; (2) terms of the sale; (3) a description sufficient to identify the property; (4) the purchase price to be paid. A receipt for deposit money which embodies this data would suffice. Where the vendor is married, it is good practice to have the wife also sign even though the property is held in the name of the husband alone. This is true even if her name does not appear in the body of the agreement.

Sometimes, a broker will use a memorandum agreement initially and later he will prepare a complete agreement of the terms; even though the memorandum agreement is signed by both parties, it is not binding where the parties agree that the terms should be spelled out in a subsequent agreement. An agreement to make an agreement is not enforceable, where material terms are left to future negotiations: *Ripps v. Mueller et al.,* 517 P. 2d 512 (Ariz. 1973). It is a contradiction in terms and imposes no obligations on the parties: *Kenimer v. Thompson,* 196 S.E. 2d 363 (Ga. 1973).

A writing providing that particular piece of land, approximately 150 acres, to be conveyed is to be mutually agreed upon in a future agreement, was not enforceable: *Davison v. Robbins,* 517 P. 2nd 1026 (Utah 1973).

The case of *Boekelheide v. Snyder,* 71 S.D. 470 (1947) was an action for specific performance by the buyer. The writing, upon which the action was based read:

> Received of H. H. Boekelheide $50 to apply
> on purchase of house and property of the old
> Young house. Balance $650.
>
> Margaret Snyder

Does this memorandum satisfy the Statute of Frauds, as a written contract of sale? The Court held the writing insufficient. It must be complete in itself, containing all the terms of the contract. Oral evidence is not admissible to supply defects in a written contract, which must be in writing under the Statute of Frauds. Payment of $50 did not constitute part performance.

The offer and acceptance must be definite. In a certain case, a broker prepared an agreement of sale, and the buyer paid $1,000 deposit money, which was turned over to the seller. The buyer then sued the seller for the return of the money, claiming that the agreement of sale was inadequate, incomplete and ineffective. The provision in controversy related to a mortgage. The agreement said simply, "Subject to purchaser obtaining mortgage." It was silent as to the amount of the mortgage and all the related terms, such as the rate of interest, the duration of the mortgage, the size of monthly payments to be required, and whether or not the mortgagor had the right of anticipation. Clearly, the agreement lacked *definiteness,* the first essential in a meeting of the minds. It would have been preferable to have stated, "Vendee will pay cash to highest loan obtainable at 6 per cent." In this connection, a broker should be alert as to the responsibilities which he assumes when he, independently, represents or warrants to the buyer that he will obtain the necessary financing. If the broker is unable to produce the required mortgage with the result that the deal falls through and the buyer's deposit money is lost, the buyer has the legal right to sue the broker upon the latter's broken promise to produce the mortgage. It is considered unethical practice to require that the buyer finance the property through the broker *alone,* so that the buyer cannot look where he pleases for funds.

The same is true of the situation where the broker knows that the buyer must sell his present home in order to obtain funds necessary in the purchase of the new home. The broker, in good faith, may promise to sell the buyer's present home before the sale is consummated for the new home. If he fails to perform, the buyer can sue the broker, upon the latter's independent promise, for any loss he sustained. If the deal is contingent upon the buyer obtaining a mortgage or sale of his present home, the broker should write the contingency into the contract of sale, so that the owner will know that he has only a conditional sale, which may not materialize.

Truth in lending

Title I of the National Consumer Credit Protection Act (Truth-In-Lending Act) became effective on July 1, 1969 and immediately had an important impact upon every day real estate practice. It places duties to disclose upon seller, mortgagee and real estate licensee. The act attempts, among others, to eliminate undisclosed or hidden charges of a creditor in regard to the cost of financing a home purchase. The Act and/or Regulation Z, to implement the Act, can only be briefed as it relates to real estate financing. Regulation Z defines a creditor as "a person who in the ordinary course of business regularly extends or arranges for the extension of consumer credit." Regulation Z is specific in its requirement that the finance charge show the *total* of all finance charges imposed by the creditor upon the borrower in granting credit. Truthful advertising specifics rather than generalities are also important. It is important that licensees be familiar with the regulations.

Dual contracts

In connection with the necessary financing of a purchased dwelling, attention is called to a rather extensive and dangerous practice in real estate circles. It is the use of dual contracts, sometimes referred to as "kiting" or "ballooning." This is the situation where a purchase contract is executed by buyer and seller for the true consideration price of $16,000. Buyer requires a mortgage of $15,000. A second set of purchase contracts is then executed by the seller and buyer at a fictitious consideration price of $18,000. It is the $18,000 agreement which is submitted to the lending institution for a loan of $15,000. Very often the dual agreements are suggested by the real estate broker with the assurance to the parties that "it's done all the time."

Not only is this practice considered unethical and violative of the Realtor's Code of Ethics, but it constitutes a material violation of the license law, and is a criminal offense, as well. The broker, buyer, and seller and lending institution officer are all subject to criminal prosecution. Texas and Colorado make such practice a misdemeanor under State law. The Federal Act of June 25, 1948 makes it a federal crime for any person to make a false statement in applying for F.H.A. mortgage insurance, or *"to aid or abet"* such action. The seller, broker, buyer and even the mortgage lender, who are participants in a dual contract arrangement, are vulnerable to a criminal charge: *United States v. Hawkins et al.,* 295 F 2d 837 (Ky. 1961). *State Real Estate Commission v. Bongiorno,* 45 D & C 392 (Pa. 1968).

Offer may be revoked

An offer is not irrevocable. It can be withdrawn at any time before acceptance. An element in a preliminary offer to purchase contract is that it usually provides that the seller is to have a certain period of time within which to accept the offer—three, five, seven or ten days. The prospective buyer is not bound to keep his offer open for the designated period of time. He can withdraw the offer at any time, if the seller does not accept. Also, where a formal agreement of sale is prepared, which the buyer signs, it is still only a naked offer, which can be withdrawn at any time before acceptance. Thus, a broker should act promptly in seeing to it that his owner signs the agreement as soon as possible. It takes two parties to make the contract—signatures of buyer *and* seller.

It is equally important that a broker deliver the seller's signed agreement to the buyer as soon as possible. In other words, it is not only necessary that the seller accept the buyer's offer by signing the agreement, but the acceptance must be *communicated* to the buyer. Until the acceptance has been communicated, the buyer can withdraw his offer of purchase, even though he has signed the agreement of sale.

In the case of *Reynolds v. Hancock,* 53 Wash. 2d 682 (1959), a broker sued the buyer for a commission on the strength of a clause in an offer to purchase, which read:

> This offer is made subject to approval of the seller by midnight of March 27, 1957. In consideration of agent submitting this offer to seller, purchaser agrees with the agent not to withdraw this offer during said period or until earlier rejection thereof by seller.

After signing the offer to purchase, the buyer, prior to midnight of March 27, 1957, notified the seller, in California, that the offer was withdrawn. The Court held that there was no consideration to the buyers from the broker not to withdraw the offer prior to its expiration date. The broker could not recover. By using language that the offer is made *irrevocably* for a certain number of days may have some psychological effect, but it would not prevail in a suit at law.

Once the offer is signed by the owner, a binding contract is created. The offer must be accepted in order to have a binding contract. Thus, an offer may be accepted, or the offer may lapse through passage of a period of time (non-acceptance by seller); or it may be withdrawn before acceptance.

Anson on Contracts has compared an offer to a train of gunpowder. Once the match is applied, it produces something which cannot be undone or recalled, unless the gunpowder has lain until it has become damp, or the man who laid the train removes it before the match is applied; so an offer, once it is accepted, cannot be undone or recalled, but the offer may lapse through passage of time, or the man who made the offer may withdraw it *at any time* before acceptance. Thus a broker should stress to his owner the importance of signing the agreement upon his terms, as soon as possible. A counter-proposition is a rejection of the offer and an offer, once rejected, is gone forever unless the offeror reinstates it.

Prospective purchasers of certain property brought suit against the prospective seller to recover a $1,000 earnest money deposit in the case of *Stearns v. Western,* 252 N.E. 2d 126 (Ill. 1967). The offer to purchase was subject to the condition that vendees were able to obtain a $17,000 mortgage at interest not to exceed 5 3/4 per cent for not less than 20 years, within 10 days. The buyers were unable to obtain outside financing upon those terms within the 10 days. The vendor then offered a mortgage loan, specifying five additional conditions than the above, not shown to be matters of custom and usage. The court held this constituted a counter proposition and the buyers were entitled to a refund of the deposit money. *Pravorne v. McLeod,* 383 P. 2d 855 (Nev. 1963).

Where the buyer withdraws his offer before acceptance by the owner, he is entitled to a full refund of his earnest money or deposit, without any "strings" or conditions attached whatsoever. In one case, before returning the earnest money, the broker sought to have the buyer sign a memorandum that if he *ever* bought a property in the future, it would be through that broker. The memorandum is unethical and clearly unenforceable. In 8 Amer. Juris. 1060, Sec. 130, it is said:

> If earnest money is paid to a broker, and the contract is broken by the principal, the broker, notwithstanding that he has disclosed his principal, is liable to the buyer for a refund of the deposit money, unless he has in good faith paid it over to his principal. The fact that a broker has a claim against his principal is no justification for his refusal to return the deposit money. (*Gosslin v. Martin,* 56 Ore. 281, 107 P. 957.) (*Perry v. Thorpe Bros., Inc.* 267 Minn. 29 (1963).)

However, in order to avoid any charge against himself, the broker should not ignore the express instructions of his principal. In *Polette v. Wall,* 256 S.W. 2d 283 (Mo. 1953), the broker returned the deposit to the purchaser without the knowledge or consent of the sellers. The Missouri Court held that, by doing so, the broker exceeded his authority. In the Washington case of *Somers Co. v. Pix,* 134 P. 932 (1913), the broker waived his commission by allowing the purchaser to withdraw the earnest money, because of an objection to the title, which did not render it unmarketable.

If the offer to purchase is withdrawn before it is accepted by the owner, the buyer is entitled to a refund of his deposit *immediately.*

The case of *Hicks v. Howell,* 203 Va. 32 (1961) involved an action by a buyer against the owner and the broker to recover an earnest money deposit. The court held that the brokers who received the purchase money deposit as agent for the sellers could not apply such funds to the payment of commission where the vendors were unable to deliver a marketable title, as required. The brokers were held liable to the buyers for the amount of such deposit.

It is not necessary that any deposit money be paid at the time the agreement of sale is signed by the buyer and seller. The mutual concurrent promises that the buyer will pay a certain sum of money to the seller on a specific date and that the latter will execute and deliver a proper deed to the buyer on the same specified date, constitutes good, sufficient legal consideration. A broker or salesman would be rendering a disservice to the owner if he did not require a down payment from the buyer as evidence of his good faith. The deposit should be in a sufficient amount to afford the seller financial protection, in case the buyer defaults. And yet, too many licensees will accept a $500 deposit on a $25,000, or more, dwelling. Such a deposit falls far short of commission involved in the transaction. While it is true that the seller can sue the buyer for performance, the average seller is reluctant to engage in litigation. The size of the down payment should be commensurate with the amount of the consideration price for the property. A 10% earnest money requirement upon the signing of the agreement of sale is reasonable. The time for closing is also a factor to be considered in connection with the size of the hand money deposit. If the deal is to be closed more than 30 days from the date of the agreements, a larger down payment should be obtained as a protection to the seller, since the real estate market might change in that period. It often happens in real estate practice that a buyer does not have cash funds available for a 10% deposit, or even a 5% deposit. For example, in the purchase of a home for $17,500, the buyer does not have ready cash available for more than $200. It would be satisfactory for the broker to prepare a contract of sale at $17,500, with a cash deposit of $200, upon the signing of the contract. However, he should further provide that the buyer agrees to pay an additional sum of $1,300 or $1,800 within thirty days thereafter, *which date is of the essence of the agreement: Cownan v. Allen Monuments,* 500 S.W. 2d 223 (Texas 1973).

Earnest money deposit

The agreement should provide more than merely that the earnest money deposit shall be retained by the vendor as liquidated damages in case the buyer should fail or refuse to consummate the deal. The vendor should be afforded three alternative remedies:

1. sue the buyer for specific performance of the contract.
2. the right to resell the property and sue the buyer for any loss on the resale.
3. retain the deposit money as liquidated damages.

A suggested clause would read:

> Should the buyer fail to make settlement, as herein provided, the sum or sums paid on account of the purchase price, at the option of the seller, may be retained by the seller, either on account of the purchase price, the resale price, or as liquidated damages. In the latter case, the contract shall become null and void. In the latter event, all monies paid on account shall be divided equally between the seller and the broker, but in no event shall the sum paid to the broker be in excess of the usual rate of commission due him.

The case of *Simmons and Associates v. Urban Renewal Agency,* 497 S.W. 2d 705 (Ky. 1973) involved a suit to recover a deposit of $23,425 on the contract to purchase land for $475,000. The contract was dated April 25, 1965. The agency extended the time for submitting financing plans on eight separate occasions, over a period of 641 days. The court held that the retention of the deposit money as liquidated damages, under the contract, would be enforced.

Broker's responsibility for deposit money

It is important that the *listing* contract include a clause:

> The owner hereby agrees that all deposit money paid on account of the purchase price shall be retained by the within broker, in escrow, until the transaction is consummated or terminated.

The question of who is entitled to the earnest money or down payment frequently arises when the buyer defaults in performance. The broker mistakenly believes that, if he holds the deposit money, he is entitled to his commission out of this fund. It must be remembered that the broker is acting in a representative capacity, as agent for his principal, the owner. It thus appears that the money belongs to his principal. Under his employment by the owner, the broker has contracted to produce a purchaser, *ready, able,* and *willing* to buy. It would not appear that the agent has met his legal responsibilities if his purchaser is unwilling to complete the deal. It may be contended that, when the owner signs the agreement, he has placed his stamp of approval upon the purchaser, accepted him, and, upon the latter's default, must pursue him in a court of law for performance. The question is highly controversial although there are court decisions recognizing the broker's rights to his commission out of the deposit money held by him. However, if the buyer is pecuniarily unable to complete the transaction, litigation is futile, and the broker has not earned a commission. Where the agreement provides that the broker is to be paid his commission *upon delivery of deed,* he is not entitled to any sum under the circumstances outlined. Such a clause reads: "It is understood that Packer & Co. are the sole moving cause of this sale, and the vendors agree to pay said Packer & Co. a commission of five per cent of the full purchase price, said commission to be payable upon delivery of deed." The clause identifying the broker (Packer & Co.) as the broker negotiating the deed protects the broker against *both* buyer and seller, if the deal is completed, since it constitutes a *warranty* by both principals that Packer & Co. brought about the sale.

Many listing contracts in current use provide: "A deposit made, if forfeited by the buyer, shall first apply to the broker's commission; the balance, if any, shall belong to the owner."

While a broker is certainly entitled to a return for his efforts, good conscience requires that it shall not be at the expense of an innocent principal. Suppose the clause in question is used and the broker obtains a purchaser for a property at $10,000, and collects a deposit of $500. Later, the buyer defaults and forfeits the deposit money. Should the broker be permitted to retain the *entire* deposit as commission on the ground that the owner has a legal right to sue the defaulting buyer, even though litigation may prove futile? It is scarcely ethical that the broker should keep all the money paid on account of the purchase of the owner's property, and the latter required to pursue litigation, entailing additional expense of costs and attorney's fees, for recovery of a judgment which may be uncollectible. In addition, the property may be "tied up" for a considerable period of time from the date when the agreements were signed. Fair dealing requires that the down payment be divided equally between broker and owner, up to an amount where the broker receives full payment of his commission.

Deposit money in escrow account

Most states, by law, or by rule and regulation of the Commission, require that the broker keep all deposit monies in an escrow or trustee account. This does not mean that a broker must open a new account every time he receives an earnest money deposit. One trustee or escrow account will suffice, but it must be used only for the deposit of monies, belonging to others, which come into his hands through some real estate transaction. Such funds should be held inviolate until the deal is closed. A broker is not entitled to use such funds for personal uses. The theory that he may properly do so up to the amount of his commission in the particular deal, pending the final closing, conclusion or settlement of the transaction does not apply.

Mishandling of deposit money has been a prime source of complaints to Real Estate Commissions in recent years. As a result, states, by statute, rule or regulation, or both, regulate the subject. Guide rules laid down, require:

1. Broker must retain deposit money in a separate custodial account until transaction is consummated or terminated.
2. Every real estate salesman must promptly turn over deposit money received by him to his broker.
3. Under no circumstances shall a broker permit any advance payment of funds to be deposited in his business or personal account, or be commingled with any funds he may have on deposit.
4. Custodial or trust fund account must provide for withdrawal of funds without

previous notice.

5. Must keep complete records, showing the date and from whom he received deposit money, the date deposited, the dates of withdrawal and other pertinent information.
6. Broker executes a consent to bank permitting Commission representative to examine bank records.

One of the grounds relating to deposit money, contained in the Pennsylvania license law for disciplinary action is Sec. 10 (11) failure to comply with the following requirements . . . " (v) Every real estate broker shall keep records of all funds deposited (in escrow accounts) . . . All such records and funds shall be subject to inspection by the Commission." In the case of *State Real Estate Commission v. Roberts,* 271 A 2d 246 (Pa. 1970), the Supreme Court, in a 5—2 opinion, held that under the statute, the Real Estate Commission was authorized to suspend a broker's license who refused to permit an investigator to conduct an inspection of broker's escrow account, without a warrant or subpoena, and because no complaint had been filed by a member of the public.

Pursuant to this refusal, the Commission, upon its own initiative, issued a citation for hearing. The broker's contention was that the Commission violated his constitutional rights against self incrimination and unreasonable search and seizure. The court said:

> However, the statute clearly states that the Commission may upon its own motion . . . investigate any action or business transaction of any licensed real estate broker or real estate salesman. We believe "any action" means "any action," not just one where wrong-doing is suspected; otherwise the Commission could not properly exercise its function of the comprehensive regulation of the business of selling real estate to others. *Verona v. Schenley Farms Co.,* 312 Pa. 57, 167 A. 317 (1933).

The escrow of trust funds and maintaining records

Real estate brokers and their sales persons regularly come into possession of funds belonging to others and hence are trustees for such funds. Such trusteeship may exist for varying periods of time. As trustees, brokers have an exacting responsibility of handling such funds in a manner which will adequately protect the funds and so as not to destroy the trust nature of the funds, possibly making them subject to attachment as could happen to the broker's personal funds. To this end, most states have enacted legislation regulating, at least to some extent, the handling of other persons' funds. More than forty states require real estate brokers to maintain separate bank accounts as depositories for trust funds with such accounts clearly designated as trust or escrow accounts. The real estate commissions of many states make periodic examinations of real estate trust accounts.

The proper handling of trust funds requires adequate record-keeping. The complexity of the records required depends largely upon the volume of the broker's business and may range from computerized accounting to simple bookkeeping. A bookkeeping system which will clearly reflect the financial history of a real estate transaction is a necessity. A minimum system will include: (a) a separate bank account designated a real estate trust or escrow account; (b) pre-numbered checks for making disbursements from the trust account; (c) a pre-numbered receipt book for writing receipts when funds are received (other than funds received with an offer to purchase when such offer includes a receipt); (d) three-column bookkeeping forms for use in compiling a bookkeeping record for each real estate sale or for each principal for whom real property is managed.

Adequate trust account record-keeping begins with the drawing of an offer to purchase which should very accurately provide the details of any earnest money deposit. If the earnest money deposit is a check, it should be clearly stated; if cash, it should be recorded as cash; if a note, it should so state and include instructions about who will be holding the note and where it will be retained. When earnest money deposits are in the form of securities or other items of value, detailed instructions for holding and safeguarding them should be supplied. All of the details concerning the earnest money deposit should be fully disclosed to the seller at the time he considers accepting an offer. For example, should an offer state that the broker has received $500.00 cash as an earnest money payment when in fact he has received a check in the amount of $500.00 which the buyer does not want to be deposited until closing, then the seller does not have all of the information which he should have before considering the offer. Full disclosure of all financial details is basic to handling trust funds properly.

It should be noted that a bookkeeping system is a record of events as they occur and hence should be developed on a continuing basis with each entry being recorded at the time it transpires. There should be no delay in depositing cash or checks in a trust account. Such deposits should be made not later than the next banking day after they are received, unless, of course, an offer to purchase provides specific instructions about handling the funds.

Listing and selling broker in multi-list associations

Assuming that the broker, who listed the property for sale, and the selling broker, who negotiates the sale, are both members of the same multi-list the controversial question often arises, as to which broker should hold the earnest money deposit. Neither the seller nor buyer is a member of the organization, and, therefore, is not bound by the internal rules and by-laws of the organization. The owner has contracted with the listing broker; the buyer has dealt with the selling broker. If the listing broker is also the selling broker, no problem arises. If two brokers are involved and the deal is not consummated, or, if the selling broker absconds, a serious question is posed regarding the respective rights of seller and buyer.

The agreement of sale may provide that the earnest money deposit shall be paid by the buyer to the listing broker. This should be explained to the buyer, disclosing the name of the listing broker to him. For the protection of the selling broker, he should receive a *signed* acknowledgment to that effect from the buyer. If a check is tendered by the buyer, the selling broker should request that the listing broker be named as a payee.

Agreement subject to conditions

The agreement of sale must conform to any conditions in the listing contract, in order for a broker to collect a commission. It is also true that, independent of the listing agreement, if the agreement of sale is made subject to a condition or contingency, the broker cannot collect a commission unless the condition is satisfied. In the case of *Stovall Realty & Insurance Co., Inc. v. Goff,* 159 S.E. 2d 467 (Ga. 1968), a contingency in the sales agreement rested solely upon buyer's *procurement* of loan, not his ability to procure loan, or willingness of third party to make loan. The court held that performance of the contingency rested solely upon the act of the defendants in procuring the loan and, consequently, did not relieve the contract of the deficiency as to mutuality. The broker could not recover in his action for a commission.

Broker liable upon his independent promise

Where the broker knows that the buyer must sell his present home in order to provide funds for the purchase of his dream house, the broker or salesman should be aware of the responsibilities he assumes, if he guarantees to sell the buyer's present home, within the time for the closing on the new home, and he fails to do so.

The broker or salesman may be well intentioned, but if he is unable to fulfill his promise, he is personally liable to the buyer, for any loss which he may sustain. The same result is true, where the broker promises to obtain the necessary financing to make a real estate deal, and he fails to do so.

If the deal is subject to the sale of the buyer's present home, or to obtain necessary financing, a clause should be written into the agreement of sale to that effect. The owner may refuse to sign the agreement since it contains a conditional clause, but the broker then knows that he is taking a calculated risk, if the conditional clause is omitted and the broker has committed himself to selling the buyer's present home or obtaining mortgage financing.

Postdated checks for down payment

Sometimes a broker will accept a "postdated check" (bears a date subsequent to its delivery) which is not honored upon presentation to the bank. Unless the owner has consented to the acceptance of the check, the broker has violated his fiduciary responsibility to his principal and again jeopardizes not only his commission, but his license, which means his livelihood. A broker is within his rights in accepting an ordinary check for earnest money, even though the buyer immediately stops payment on the check because it is everyday business custom to accept a check in lieu of cash; but the broker who receives a check is duty-bound to deposit it *promptly* for payment. A postdated check, which is dishonored, or a check upon which payment has been stopped, has no effect upon the validity of the agreement of sale, if the seller takes action against the buyer to enforce it. Sometimes, instead of cash, the buyer will give the broker a short-term promissory note. A broker is guilty of bad faith and jeopardizes his license when he accepts a note instead of cash without disclosing this fact to his principal. The agreement is not void because of the default upon the note.

In the case of *Witherspoon v. Pusch,* 136 P. 2d 137 (Colo. 1960), suit by an owner for breach of written contract to purchase realty and to recover on check for down payment on which payment had been stopped. The Supreme Court held that parol testimony of buyer as to understanding with owner's *broker* that the offer to purchase was not a firm offer and that check for down payment was to be held until buyer had opportunity to investigate zoning restrictions and adaptability of the property to intended use, was admissible to show that there was no contract, and was not an attempt to vary terms of written contract. The plaintiff relied upon signed contract, and check for $1,500 marked "Payment Stopped." The Court said:

> The check itself stands or falls upon the existence of a good and sufficient contract between the parties. In this case, Mrs. Pusch (buyer) testified that the signing of the offer and the giving of the check was a convenience which would make it unnecessary for the parties to meet again, if she found upon the investigation that everything was satisfactory as to zoning classification, adaptability of the plumbing for conversion of the building into apartments made by the City and County of Denver.

The plaintiff contended that if these conditions were made between Mrs. Pusch and the broker, they were not binding upon her because the broker was not a party to the contract. The Court held that the broker was the agent of the owner and, therefore, there could be no recovery.

Where an agreement of sale has been signed and a check made payable to the broker, is given to the broker, as a deposit, and the buyer stops payment on the check, the owner cannot sue on the check, but the broker can. Under these circumstances, the court held, in the case of *Duncan v. Baskin,* 154 N.W. 2d 617 (Mich. 1969), that upon dishonor by the maker, and subject to any notice of dishonor or protest, the holder of a check has an immediate right of recourse against the drawer. Production of the check entitled the broker to recover, without submitting further proof of damages, subject to whatever proper defenses defendants raise.

In the case of *Staab v. Messier,* 264 A. 2d 790 (Vt. 1970), a contract of sale was executed, which recited "Deposit $500." This deposit was in the form of a $500 check given by prospective buyer to the broker "to be held, uncashed, by the plaintiff (broker) until Pepin (buyer) was able to ascertain whether or not he could raise the $15,000 purchase price by the closing date set forth in the contract." It was conceded that when the buyer gave the $500 check, he had insufficient funds in the bank to cover it. Broker lost his suit for a commission. The court quoted with approval the case of *Ellsworth Dobbs, Inc. v. Johnson,* 236 A. 2d 843 (N.J. 1967):

> The principle that binds the seller to pay commission if he signs a contract of sale with the broker's customer, regardless of the customer's financial ability, puts the burden on the wrong shoulders . . . It follows that the obligation to fulfill the monetary conditions of the purchase must be regarded as logically and sensibly resting with the broker.

Where a broker accepted a note instead of cash, as recited in the agreement of sale, the broker was unsuccessful in recovering a commission from the owner. *Slusser v. Brillhart,* 159 N.E. 2d 480 (Ohio 1958). The failure of the broker to acquaint his principal with the fact that he was holding a note, instead of cash, was fatal to a recovery. In *Mecklenborg v. Niehaus,* 85 Ohio App. 271 (1948), the court said:

> An agent owes a duty to his principal to inform him of all facts relating to the subject matter of the agency that would affect the principal's interest.

The facts should have been submitted to a jury to decide.

Where a broker signs a receipt for earnest money, which contains a notation that check is to be returned if purchaser cannot get a mortgage to cover balance (price of farm $4,200; balance $3,780), and no mention is made of the mortgage condition in the formal agreement of sale signed by seller and buyer, the broker is held personally responsible for the return of the down payment, if the mortgage is unobtainable: *Wartman v. Schockley,* 154 Pa. Superior Ct. 196 (1943).

A broker authorized to negotiate a sale of property has implied authority to accept the initial down payment but no implied authority to accept subsequent payments made on account of the purchase price. In the case of *Gerig v. Russ,* 200 Ore. 196 (1954), a broker in Salem negotiated the sale of 103 acres of land at $21,500 for Russ to Gerig. The earnest money receipt read:

> Received of David Gerig and Ellen I. Gerig the sum of $500.00 as earnest money on the following described property: Approximately 103 acres and building located east of Parkersville School. Purchase price, $21,500.00. Terms ½ down payment in cash, balance to be arranged by loan.

Between June 23, 1949 and July 22, 1949, the purchasers paid to the broker various sums, totalling $11,500.00 without the knowledge or consent of the sellers. The buyers brought suit for specific performance, tendering balance of $9,500.00. Sellers demanded balance of $21,000.00. The Court said:

> There is nothing in the language itself, "Terms: ½ down payment in cash, balance to be arranged by loan" implying the authority of the broker to receive such down payment . . . it was the duty of the purchasers to make the payments direct to the sellers rather than to the broker, and when they turned the money over to the broker, they did so at their own risk.

Personal check at closing

The agreement of sale usually provides that the balance of the consideration price shall be paid in cash at the settlement. The seller, usually, can refuse the personal check of the buyer at the closing. Such check may not be honored by the bank because of insufficient funds, or the buyer may die before the check clears the bank, upon which it is drawn. A bank cashier's check is always acceptable, as is a certified check. Under extenuating circumstances, a personal check may be acceptable. An attorney gave his personal check, for the buyer, at a Saturday settlement, when the bank was closed and he could not get it certified. The tender of the check was proper: *Southgate, Inc. v. Ecklini,* 207 N.W. 2d 729 (Minn. 1973).

Broker rights under signed agreement

When the broker obtains signed agreement of sale by buyer and seller, he has performed his contract of employment and, *generally,* can establish his right to a commission. Although the broker is not a party to the sales agreement or lease, his claim for a commission is clearly buttressed if he is named in the instrument as the broker who negotiated the transaction and a commission is to be paid to him by his principal.

Where the buyer causelessly defaults, the seller may forfeit the earnest money deposit and the broker is entitled to his commission. Where a seller and buyer, after execution of the agreement of sale, mutually agree to cancel the agreement, the broker is entitled to his commission upon the full consideration price. In the case of *Huber v. Gerahman,* 300 S.W. 2d 501 (Mo. 1957), the Court held that the broker was entitled to his commission where buyer and seller mutually rescinded an executed contract for the sale of a theatre; $2,500 deposit had been paid. The sales contract provided:

> Earnest deposit to be retained by Listing Agent, without interest; if sale is closed, earnest money to apply on sale commission. Forfeited earnest money shall go first toward reimbursing expenses of agent, and balance to go one-half to seller and one-half to agent.

The Court said:

> In these circumstances, the contracting parties were not free to direct the return of the $2,500 to the purchaser and ignore the contract rights of the broker in the earnest money deposit.

To avoid any question as to the broker's rights, it is advisable to provide in the listing agreement *and* in the agreement of sale, that in case any deposit money is forfeited, it will be divided equally between the seller and the broker, up to the amount of the broker's commission.

CAPACITY OF PARTIES

Not every person has *full* contractual capacity. In this category are minors, insane persons, corporations and, to a limited extent, in some states, married women. Today, there is an increasing number of states, which have lowered the age of majority from 21 years to 18 years. During minority, most contracts entered into by a minor are voidable at his option. Only contracts for necessaries are binding upon him. There is no hard and fast rule to define necessaries. They include more than those articles required for bare subsistence. Items which are useful and suitable to his station in life are included as necessaries. Certainly, maintenance, food, clothing, *lodging*, medical attention, and education in a reasonable amount, are included in the term. A voidable contract may be disaffirmed by the minor at any time during his minority or within a reasonable time after he attains his majority. Infancy is a defense personal to the infant alone. It cannot be pleaded by the other party to the contract as grounds for avoidance of his contractual liability. The appointment of an agent by an infant is generally void. In dealing with an infant owner of real estate, the other party should require the appointment of a guardian for the infant and deal with the guardian. A broker employed by an infant to sell property would be unable to collect his earned commission if the infant changed his mind and repudiated the contract of employment. It makes no difference that the sale arranged by the broker is advantageous to the infant. An infant may appear to be of full age, but this has no bearing upon his liability or freedom from liability in a contract. Even if he wrongfully misrepresents his age, the rule of law is the same, for he cannot make himself *sui juris* (of legal age) by falsifying his age. The infant could still disaffirm his contract. However, the injured party could sue the infant in a *tort* action of deceit.

An infant who elects to disaffirm his voidable contract must do so *in toto.* He cannot elect to ratify as much of the contract as will benefit him and reject that portion which operates to his disadvantage. For example, an infant who agreed to purchase a commercial property for $10,000 by paying $2,500 cash and giving the owner a purchase money mortgage for $7,500 could not compel the seller to deed the property to him upon payment of the $2,500 cash and then disaffirm his obligation to execute the $7,500 mortgage.

In 1970, the United States Congress enacted a law, permitting 18 year old persons to *vote* in federal elections. This does not permit 18 year old persons to enjoy full contractual capacity unless the state law emancipates them from a minor's incapacity to *contract.*

Insane persons

The law also protects persons mentally incompetent from their imprudent contracts. Mentally incompetent persons include insane persons and drunkards. To affect the contractual ability, the degree of mental derangement must be such as to render the person incapable of reasoning from cause to effect and thus understanding the effects of his acts. A person, mentally incompetent, is nevertheless liable for necessaries furnished himself, his wife, or children. Other contracts, if yet to be performed (executory), are voidable by him. The weight of authority is to the effect that where the contract has been executed so that the insane person has had the benefit and the parties cannot be restored to their former position, unaccompanied by any proof that the other knew or ought to have known of the insanity, the contract will not be voided. If the insane party has received no benefit, he may void the contract and recover what he has paid notwithstanding the other party's good faith. To be on the safe side, a guardian or committee for the estate of the incompetent should be appointed by the court and the sale of real estate made under the direction of said court. The test of whether a guardian should be appointed for the estate of a person is the degree of his mental unsoundness; if he is incapable of conducting the ordinary affairs of life so that to leave property in his possession and control would render him liable to become the victim of his own folly or designing persons, a guardian should be appointed.

Drunkards

An habitual drunkard may be regarded as an insane person and his capacity to contract is likewise limited. When a man loses his mind, he is entitled to legal protection whether such loss is occasioned by his own imprudence or otherwise. This is true even though the intoxication is voluntary and not procured by the intervention of another party.

Married women

The contractual powers of a married woman are based upon statute. Today a married woman is almost completely emancipated in her capacity to contract. She may generally transact business in the same manner as a single woman (a feme sole trader). In states where she cannot sell her own real estate without the joinder of her husband, he should join in the execution of an agreement of sale. Even in these states, if a woman, before marriage, enters into an agreement to sell her real estate and marries before the deal is consummated and the deed delivered, the courts will honor her agreement of sale and compel her husband to join in the deed. *Pepper v. Chatel* (D.C. No. 3056 1962).

Corporations

The contractual powers of most corporations are defined and limited by their charters and by the constitution and laws of the states where they are formed. They have those powers expressly stated in their charters and such implied powers as may be necessary and incidental to carry out those expressed powers. Where a corporation exceeds its powers, the act is *ultra vires* and unenforceable. An agreement for the sale of real estate by a corporation should be executed in pursuance of a resolution by the board of directors authorizing and directing the particular conveyance. When the agreement is made under a general resolution authorizing the officers to execute deeds for any property which they may sell, it is doubtful whether such a sale is valid since the price and terms are left to the discretion of the officers. Reference here is made to business and manufacturing corporations. Where the corporation is formed for the express purpose of dealing in real estate, requisite authority may be conferred upon its officers by general resolution to execute proper agreements and deeds as the occasions arise.

Aliens

In general, foreigners, whether citizens of another state or another nation, have full contractual authority. However, under the Federal law prohibiting trading with an enemy, an affidavit by the parties to a real estate deal may be necessary stating that they are not enemy aliens.

REALITY OF CONSENT

Mistake

A contract must be free from mistake, misrepresentation, fraud, duress, and undue influence. In other words, the consent to the contract must be *real.* To avoid a contract on the ground of mistake, the mistake must be mutual and substantial; that is, it must go to the heart of the agreement. Thus, where parties use ambiguous language and each has in mind an entirely different subject matter as the basis of the agreement, there is no contract. Where Ash owned considerable real estate, some of which was located on Jackson Street in Pittsburgh while another parcel was located on Jacksonia Street in the same city, an agreement was prepared for a parcel of real estate on Jackson Street. Due to the similarity in name, the buyer thought he was purchasing and intended to buy the tract on Jacksonia Street. The contract could be set aside on the grounds of mistake.

In the case of *Roy S. Ludlow Inv. Co. v. Taggart,* 509 P. 2d 818 (Utah 1973), a purchaser was not permitted to take advantage of a typographical mistake in an agreement of sale. Lot 22 was not included in a group of about 30 lots, which Taggart agreed to sell. However, Lot 22 was included, inadvertently, in the agreement of sale. Ludlow knew that Taggart wasn't the owner of Lot 22 because he had attempted to buy it from the *real* owner. Accordingly, no damages were allowed.

Misrepresentation and fraud

Misrepresentation and fraud are often confused. Misrepresentation is an innocent misstatement of a material fact, without intent to deceive, but which induces the contract. If Jones should sell Smith certain building lots and represent that the lots were on high ground and it later developed that they were not above tide level, Jones could not hold Smith to the contract even though he were honest in his representation. However, if the party to whom the misrepresentation was made did not rely upon it and made his own independent examination, he could not claim that the misrepresentation induced his contract. Misrepresentation must be as to fact and not a mere expression of opinion. If a broker represents to a customer that certain real estate *cost* $10,000 to build and it only *cost* $7,000, there is fraudulent misrepresentation present. Where the broker states, instead, that the property is *worth* $10,000, that is mere expression of an opinion and does not constitute misrepresentation.

If the following representations were untrue, they would constitute grounds for recision of the agreement of sale: that heating plant, plumbing, and electric wiring were in good condition; that an adjoining dilapidated house has been condemned by the city and would shortly be torn down; that there was sufficient land to sell a 60-foot lot off the property, for which lot an offer of $2,000 had already been made; that the cellar was dry and in good condition; and that the roof was in good repair. These representations are such that the truth cannot be readily determined from an inspection of the premises by one not skilled in the knowledge of home construction and plumbing. It has been held that plumbing, electric wiring, and heating are not generally ascertainable on viewing. The same is true of a roof. A sale is not dependent upon the fortuitous circumstance that a purchaser be available when rain or snow is falling so that he can inspect the roof and determine whether it is watertight and that the cellar is dry. An owner or broker must be circumspect in regard to the statements he makes.[1]

Whereas misrepresentation may be set up as grounds for the avoidance of a contract, it does not lay any basis for an action for damages, but only for actual incurred expenses. Fraud is a misstatement of a material fact made with intent to deceive or made with reckless disregard of the truth, which actually does deceive. It may also arise where a party conceals a material fact, disclosure of which is a duty. Fraud is a tort as well as a ground for avoiding a contract and will sustain an action for damages. Unless the seller does something to conceal a defect or throw him off

[1] Lake v. Thompson, 366 Pa. 352 (1950).

the inquiry, the buyer has only himself to blame if the purchase turns out less valuable than he anticipated. An owner, in selling a vacant lot to a person who desires to purchase it for the erection of a home, is not bound to disclose that the lot is "filled in" land unless the buyer makes inquiry and the owner, by word or deed, does something to disarm his suspicions and steer him away from the inquiry. By the same token, a buyer in negotiating the purchase of farm land, is not bound to disclose the presence of underlying coal land which is motivating the purchase in question. The parties deal "at arms length." It is wise to permit a prospective purchaser to make a thorough examination of the premises under consideration and then to insert a clause in the agreement of sale to the effect that the purchase is being made as a result of the buyer's inspection; or that he is buying the property "as is." As a general rule, the buyer takes the property subject to *patent* defects, *i.e.* those which are ascertainable upon view, or a reasonable inspection of the property; the buyer can rescind the contract, where he later discovers *latent* (hidden or concealed) defects which were not readily ascertainable upon view, such as a defective septic tank, plumbing or electrical lines.

In the case of *Dillahunty v. Keystone Savings Ass'n.,* 303 N.E. 2d 750 (Ohio 1973), the court held that the principle of caveat emptor applies to sale of real estate relative to conditions open to observations.

The rule of caveat emptor

The ancient rule of caveat emptor (let the purchaser beware) is fast being eroded, as court authority takes a broader view of a new social philosophy oriented towards consumer protection. Under the doctrine of caveat emptor, the buyer was supposed to examine the property he was purchasing to satisfy himself that it was fit, suitable and satisfactory for his purposes. Not so, today.

The case of *Rothenberg v. Oleno,* 262 A. 2d 461 (Vt. 1970), involved a new house under construction. A year after taking possession the buyers discovered that structural defects had appeared in the foundation. The walls were cracking and bulging; . . . nor the foundation properly water proofed which aggravated the damage to the foundation walls. The floors were uneven and hazardous and not finished in a workmanlike manner . . . The defendant relied upon the ancient doctrine of caveat emptor. The court said:

> The crucial question here is whether the doctrine of caveat emptor applies to the sale of a new house by a builder—vendor and it must be resolved on the basis of the particular facts presented in the case.

The court cited an English case, *Miller v. Cannon Hill Estate Ltd.,* 2 K.B. 113 (1931) where the defendant told the plaintiff that he would use the best materials and perform the work in the best workmanlike manner, but this was not written in the agreement. Some time after the plaintiff took possession, excessive dampness penetrated the house, due to faulty construction. The court decided in favor of the plaintiff, holding that where a purchaser buys a dwelling, under construction, there is an implied warranty that upon completion, the dwelling will be fit for the purpose intended and habitable. The Vermont court also cited a South Carolina case, *Rogers v. Scyphers,* 161 S.E. 2d 81 (1968), where the court said:

> While most courts still adhere to the proposition that in the usual, normal sale of land and old buildings, the ancient doctrine of caveat emptor, with respect to a vendor, who is also the builder of a new structure, the decided trend of modern decisions is to make a distinction. Where the vendor is also the builder he is today, by the weight of modern authority, held liable for damages and injuries occurring after the surrender of title and possession, based on the

theory of an implied warranty or an imminently dangerous condition caused by negligence in construction.

Other jurisdictions have adopted the implied warranty theory in *Vanderschrier v. Aaron,* 140 N.E. 2d 819 (Ohio 1957); *Glisan v. Smolenske,* 387 P. 2d 260 (Colo. 1943); *Jones v. Gatewood,* 381 P. 2d 158 (Okla. 1963); *Weck v. A.M. Sunrise Construction Co.,* 181 N.E. 2d 728 (Ill. 1966); *Staff v. Lido Dune, Inc.* 262 NYS 2d 544 (1965); *Bethlahmy v. Bechtel,* 415 P. 2d 698 (Idaho 1966); *Humber v. Morton,* 426 S.W. 2d 554 (Tex. 1968). The Vermont court said:

> The law should be based upon current concepts of what is right and just and the judiciary should be alert to the never ending need for keeping its common law principles abreast with the times. Ancient distinctions which make no sense in today's society and tend to discredit the law should be readily rejected as they appear to have been step by step in the cases cited . . . we find no rational doctrinal basis for differentiating between a sale of a newly constructed house by the builder—vendor and the sale of an automobile or any other manufactured product.

A Colorado Appellate Court held that the implied warranty doctrine does not apply when the house is bought from a previous owner, who is not the builder. In the case before the court, the defendants bought the house new and lived in it for 15 years. The house was represented to the buyers in July 1969 that it was in "good condition." In September of 1969, when the buyers attempted to operate the furnace, they found it was defective and they had to install a new furnace at a cost of $525. The appellate court reversed the lower court and found in favor of the seller: *Gallegos v. Graff,* 508 P. 2d 798 (Colo. App. 1973).

It may be said that implied warranty is the antithesis to caveat emptor.

In a Louisiana case, the Supreme Court held that the buyer of a used home could recover cost of repairs due to a *hidden* defect, even though the seller was unaware of the defect. There is no obligation on the part of a purchaser to inspect a property with *expertise,* particularly, in regard to termite damage: *Lorio v. Kaizer,* 277 So. 2d 633 (La. 1973).

In the case of *Pywell v. Haldave,* D. C. Court of Appeals (1962), the plaintiffs purchased a house from owners, through a broker, who represented the house to be in good or sound condition. Later, the house was found to be damaged by termites and the buyers brought suit for damages. The appellate court held the broker's representation that the house was in good or sound condition was merely the expression of an opinion and not a representation of material fact. The court said:

> Such a description of the premises, quite common in the parlance of sales, was so vague and general as to be incapable of particular application. The words were but indefinite generalities so plain that they cannot be supposed to have deceived any rational person.

In the sale of farm land or a ranch, a difference is to be observed whether the sale is "in gross or by acre." The difference is defined in 55 Am. Jur. Vendor and Purchaser, Sec. 127:

> A contract of sale by the acre is one wherein a specified quantity is material. Under such a contract the purchaser does not take the risk of any deficiency and the vendor does not take the risk of any excess. A contract of sale by the tract or in gross is one wherein boundaries are specified, but quantity is not specified or, if specified, the existence of the exact quantity is not material; each party takes the risk of the actual quantity varying to some extent from what he expects it to be. *Carrel v. Lux,* 101 Ariz. 430 (1966).

The case of *Witmer v. Bloom,* 288 A. 2d 323 (Md. App. 1972) involved the question whether the contract is for the sale of land in gross, or a sale by the acre. The agreement read "consisting of 26.6 acres more or less." The contract also provided "subject to survey of said property, to be made by buyer within 30 days . . ." The survey measurement showed slightly less than 21 acres. The court said:

> A sale in gross, sometimes called a 'contract of hazard', where specific designated parcels of ground are sold as whole and there is no warranty, express or implied, as to quantity, (2 Words and Phrases, Third Series page 446.) In determining whether a sale is by the acre or in gross as in other contracts, the intention of the parties is controlling and must be given effect.

In this case, the court reversed the lower court and held the sale was by the acre and the purchaser could rescind the deal.

In the case of *Peoples Furniture and Appliance Co. v. Healy,* 113 N.W. 2d 802 (Mich. 1962), a buyer sued for the return of a $5,000 deposit, when the buyer elected not to complete the deal, upon discovering there was a possibility of flooding. Plaintiff was unable to obtain flood insurance. The Supreme Court held that representation of agent with regard to slight possibility of flooding was material. The Court held that "the fact that plaintiff might have ascertained the situation from others is no defense if plaintiff had a right to rely on defendant's representation."

In the case of *Goggans v. Winkley et al.,* 465 P. 2d 326 (Mont. 1970), the purchasers sued the sellers for damages from alleged false representation by vendors in inducing purchase of land. The Supreme Court held that a provision in contract for deed that expense of surveying premises should be borne by purchasers did not preclude purchasers from attempting to prove that certain representations were made by real estate agent relative to a previous survey, and that these representations were properly relied upon and were incorrect.

Where a broker made certain misrepresentations concerning the gross income of a motel and the vendors made a correct disclosure prior to the time the transaction was closed, the buyers were not justified in relying on the previous misinformation furnished by the broker. Under such circumstances the broker cannot be held liable. If there had not been accurate disclosure before signing, the broker and vendors would have been jointly and severally liable: *Viebahn v. Gudim et al.,* 273 Minn. 504 (1966).

The case of *Isaacs v. Cox,* 431 S.W. 2d 494 (Ky. 1968) involved an action by purchasers for rescision and damages for alleged fraud and misrepresentation in obtaining a real estate contract. The complaint alleged that there were misrepresentations as to the water system, construction of the house and that the defendants represented that certain additional work and materials would be provided after the date of the deed and possession by the plaintiffs. It was also charged that this had not been done. The general rule of law is well settled that a principal is responsible for his agent's fraud in effecting a sale if made within the actual and apparent scope of his authority. The court held that misrepresentations, if any, made by the agent, as to water quality or supply, were material. The sellers contended that any statements made by them or their agent were not admissible in evidence, since the contract provides:

> We have read the entire contents of this contract and acknowledge receipt of same. We are not relying on verbal statements not contained herein. We further certify that we have examined the property described herein—above; that we are thoroughly acquainted with its condition and accept it as such.

The court said:

> Those cases (cited by defendants) held that the written terms of a contract of sale were controlling and that oral representations of a contradictory nature could not be introduced for

the purpose of varying the contract. The buyers offer the testimony, not for the purpose of varying the contract, but in order to prove misrepresentations which induced them to enter into it. Such testimony is admissible even though the contract contained the above quoted provision. The court remanded the case to the lower court for further hearing.

The parol evidence rule, upon which the defendants relied, provides that no oral testimony can be introduced to vary, contradict, add to or subtract from, the terms of a written contract, or change its legal import, except for fraud, accident or mistake. In spite of the "exoneration" clause in most agreements of sale that the buyer is not relying upon any verbal statements and it is being purchased as a result of personal inspection and examination, fraud can be introduced as grounds for overcoming and setting aside the clause in question: *Becker v. Lagerquist Bros. Inc.* 348 P. 2d 423 (Wash. 1960).

Fraud may also consist of concealing a material defect where there is duty to disclose. Silence, as to a condition, which the purchaser is not likely to discover (house built in a gulley, upon filled-in ground), may constitute fraud: *Lawson v. Citizens and So. National Bank,* 193 S.E. 2d 124 (S.C. 1972); *Webb v. Culver,* 509 P. 2d 1173 (Ore. 1973).

While it is the general rule that the agreement of sale is merged in the deed, this principle, however, will not prevent reformation upon showing of mutual mistake of fact, misrepresentation, or fraud: *Bicknell v. Barnes,* 501 S.W. 2d 761 (Ariz. 1973).

Closing Costs

A broker should furnish the buyer and seller a statement of *estimated* costs due at the closing. The statement to the buyer should include title insurance fees, mortgagee's charges (if applicable) cost of appraisal, credit report, origination and placement fees, mortgage service charge, survey, escrow fund (taxes and insurance), notary fees, pro-rata expense for unexpired insurance and taxes, state or local deed transfer tax, and recording fee for deed and mortgage. A statement of the estimated charges to be paid by the seller at the closing, should also be furnished to the seller before the agreements are signed. These would include cost of preparation of Deed, real estate commission, points if the buyer is obtaining a mortgage, if applicable, and Deed transfer stamps.

If the broker fails to acquaint the parties with the charges to be paid by the respective parties *before* the agreements are signed, difficulties may develop at the closing. The buyer may then find that he does not have sufficient funds available to close the deal and the seller may become disenchanted with the broker, when he finds for the first time that he is expected to pay points for the buyer's mortgage.

Undue influence

Undue influence is a mixture of fraud and force. Sometimes a person will enter into a contract in order to get rid of a persistent salesman. The mere fact that consent was obtained through nagging and importunity is insufficient to avoid the consequences of a contract. However, where the mind is enfeebled by old age, disease, or great distress, undue influence may be readily proved. Force is opposed to freedom. Free consent is the essence of every agreement. The question to be determined is whether the party was deprived of the exercise of his free will power.

In order to establish undue influence as basis for setting aside deed from parents to son, the law requires more than mere opportunity to exert undue influence or suspicions on part of those who feel aggrieved: *Hotchkiss v. Werth,* 483 P. 2d 1053 (Kan. 1971); *Gallegos v. Garcia,* 480 P. 2d 1002 (Ariz. 1971); *Hensley v. Stevens,* 481 P. 2d 694 (Mont. 1971).

Capacity to contract

In *Star Realty, Inc. v. Bower,* 169 N.W. 2d 194 (Mich. 1969), involving an action for specific performance brought by a buyer, the court denied specific performance. The court stated the well-settled test of mental capacity to contract, "is whether the person in question possesses sufficient mind to understand in a reasonable manner, the nature and effect of the act in which he is engaged. However, to avoid a contract it must appear not only that the person was of unsound mind or insane when it was made, but that the unsoundness or insanity was of such a character that he had no reasonable perception of the nature or terms of the contract."

In the case of *Watson v. Alford,* 503 S.W. 2d 897 (Ark. 1974), a vendor, 100 years of age and in feeble health, sold a property for $200, which was valued at $6,750. The court held that the vendor's physical condition and the gross inadequacy of price were sufficient to require cancellation of conveyance.

Duress

Duress may be defined as that degree of constraint or danger, either actually inflicted or threatened and impending, which is sufficient in severity to overcome the mind of a person of ordinary firmness. Mere threat of imprisonment or of a law suit is insufficient.

Legality of object

The object of the contract must be legal. If the purpose contravenes the Constitution, a statute, or a Federal treaty, the contract is void. Likewise a contract which tends to interfere with the public government or is injurious to the public at large, such as the perpetration of a nuisance, is unenforceable.

"Dummy" purchaser

Where the seller is accepting a mortgage in part payment of the purchase price, he should insist upon the real buyer signing the agreement. If the agreement is signed by a "straw" man or "dummy," the purchase money mortgage and accompanying note or bond add no value to the property security. In case of foreclosure at a future date, the seller would be unable to recoup any loss sustained between the sale price of the property at foreclosure and his debt.

Conditions in agreement

A written memorandum, in order to be effective as a sales agreement, must disclose all essential elements of the sale, and cannot rest partly in writing and partly in parol; e.g., time of payment, manner of payment, whether cash or credit.

Where the broker prepares the agreement of sale, he should ascertain from the owner's deed whether there are any conditions in the title which might affect the transferability of the property. Reference is made to oil, gas, coal and mining rights, rights of way, building restrictions, driveways, and the like. The agreement should be made subject to grants, rights, easements, covenants, and restrictions contained in prior deeds of record. If there is some question of encroachment or overlapping, the agreement description should be made subject to actual conditions shown by survey. These items, unless excepted, constitute encumbrances within the meaning of the term. Since the seller covenants that he will convey clear title, the buyer could refuse to consummate the deal and look to the seller for damages, unless the encumbrance in question was specifically excepted. A *definite* date for closing must be inserted in the agreement. If no date is specified for closing, the courts may well consider that the parties *intended* a reasonable time and would be governed accordingly.

A broker should not change or alter an agreement of sale after it has been executed, unless both parties agree *in writing.* The alterations may appear harmless but turn out differently.

An elderly seller agreed to sell his farm for $19,000—$1,000 earnest money deposit, $1,500 when the deal was closed, and the balance of $16.500 in a purchase money mortgage at the rate of $100 per month. The broker prepared the agreement of sale accordingly. The buyer inserted three small words "not less than" in front of "$100 per month." The seller refused to deal, because he wanted a monthly income in his old age and the buyer under the "not less than" clause could pay the entire mortgage or a substantial part of it at any time. The deal fell through and the broker lost a commission.

Exoneration clause or exculpatory clause

A great many agreements of sale, throughout the country, contain a clause, similar to the following:

> This agreement constitutes the entire agreement between the parties. There are no other conditions, terms or covenants agreed upon except those herein set forth, and the purchasers have not entered into this agreement in reliance upon any representations or statements not specifically set forth in this agreement.

The clause, however, cannot exonerate the broker, or his principal for any fraud or misrepresentation made by the broker, which *induced* the purchaser to enter into the agreement: *Ritz v. Mymor Houses, Inc.,* 213 N.W. 2d 470 (Iowa 1973).

The same defenses of fraud or misrepresentation could be asserted by a buyer as to hidden defects or damages, where the buyer purchases a dwelling "as is." The clause reads, more fully, as follows:

> It is understood by the parties hereto that the property herein sold has been inspected by the purchaser, or his or their agent, and the same is being purchased as a result of such inspection, in its present condition.

Date—essence of the agreement

If either party wants to insist that the closing be held absolutely upon the date specified, the date must be made a vital and material part of the agreement; thus, ". . . on Feb. 1, 1974, which date and time is of the *essence* of this agreement." If the date for closing is not made the essence of the agreement, both parties have a *reasonable* time after the date specified within which to close. There is no hard and fast rule to determine what constitutes a reasonable time. It depends upon a variety of circumstances—the activity of the real estate market, type of property involved, time of year, and the like. Thirty or sixty days in most cases would constitute a reasonable time.

Some printed real estate agreements of sale contain a clause reading:

> The said time for settlement and all other times referred to for the performance of any of the obligations of this agreement are hereby agreed to be of the essence of this agreement.

Should the vendor be indulgent and waive the strict time obligation in one respect, he may well be held to a waiver of the other time obligations by the buyer.

Any oral extension of time negotiated by vendor of "time is of the essence" clause in an agreement of sale is binding and need not be in writing under statute of frauds: *Kimm v. Anderson,* 313 A. 2d 46 (Me. 1974).

Tender and demand

Unless the buyer expressly waives tender of deed by the seller, in the agreement of sale, the latter, upon the buyer's failure to consummate the deal should make tender of an executed deed and demand for the balance of the purchase price. This can be done by the broker, for the seller, or by the attorney for the seller. This is especially important if tender of deed is not waived by the buyer in the agreement. This is necessary in order to establish that the seller is free from default and that he is ready and willing to perform. Tender may be excused where the buyer has expressed unequivocally an intention of renouncing the agreement. This is known as anticipatory repudiation. Tender would be a futile and meaningless gesture, but evidence of repudiation should be readily available before tender is omitted.

In the case of *Ward v. Doucette,* 301 N.E. 2d 256 (Mass. 1973), the court held that a letter from the buyer, through his attorney, to the seller that he was prepared to pay the balance due and requested that a deed be executed for delivery to him, did not constitute a legal tender. Accordingly, the defendant seller was not in default.

It is dangerous for a broker to re-sell the property for the owner, where there is a signed agreement outstanding, unless repudiation by the first buyer can be proven, or proper tender and demand can be shown to have been made by the vendor. Otherwise, the first buyer may appear and state that he is ready to perform. Even if he cannot prove a valid case, the seller may be put to harassment and expense.

It is imprudent to permit a buyer to take possession of premises under an agreement of sale which has not yet been consummated. In the absence of a lease, the buyer would be under no obligation to pay rent while in possession, if the deal were not consummated. When a buyer is allowed possession before the deal is closed, he should be required to execute a short-term lease. The rental might be increased substantially from month to month. The same precaution should be taken when the seller is permitted to remain in possession after the deal is closed. A broker should keep in mind the distinction between a specific date for closing and "at the time of the delivery of deed." Thus if taxes are to be apportioned as of the date specified—e.g., June 1, 1974—the buyer has the obligation for taxes from that date on even though the transaction is not closed until August 15, 1974, whereas, if taxes are apportioned as of the date of delivery of deed, the buyer's responsibility for taxes would not accrue until August 15, 1974.

Acknowledgment

It is not necessary to have the agreement of sale acknowledged. From the standpoint of the buyer, it is a good precaution to have the agreement acknowledged by the seller, particularly if a considerable time is to elapse before the deal is closed. Acknowledgment permits the agreement to be recorded and this constitutes a cloud upon the title until the agreement is merged into a deed or stricken from the record by some voluntary action upon the part of the buyer or by order of court.

Equitable conversion

With the signing of the agreement of sale, equitable (beneficial) title to the property vests in the vendee, and legal title continues in the vendor, until transferred by deed through the doctrine of equitable conversion. This means that any increase in the value of the property being sold, between the date of the sales agreement and the delivery of deed, inures to the benefit of the buyer.

Where the property is insured by the vendor, the vendee is entitled to the benefit of the insurance as a set off against the purchase price. In the case of *Dubin Paper Co. v. Insurance Co. of North America,* 361 Pa. 68 (1948), the court held that where the insured (owner) enters into an agreement of sale of the property covered by the insurance policy, and a fire loss occurs before the deal is consummated, and the insured receives the proceeds of the policy, he holds these as trustee for the buyer. "Conscience of equity" so requires, and is given expression by creating a constructive trust for the benefit of the buyer; *Beatty v. Guggenheim Exploration Co.,* 225 N.Y. 380.

In the case of *Insurance Co. of N.A. v. Erickson,* 50 Fla. 419 (1905), the Court stated:

> It has long been the law of Florida that under a binding executory contract for the sale of land, where the purchaser is regarded as equitable owner, the purchaser must ordinarily bear any loss that occurs . . . :

Sanford v. Breidenbach, 173 N.E. 2d 702 (Ohio App. 1960); *Skendzell v. Marshall,* 301 N.E. 2d 641 (Ind. 1973).

The minority view, followed in several New England states, holds that when the building is destroyed by fire, there is failure of consideration, under the law of contracts, and the loss falls upon the vendor: *Thompson v. Gould,* 20 Pick. 134 (Mass. 1838); *Libman v. Levenson,* 128 N.E. 13 (Mass. 1920); *Durham v. McCready,* 151 A. 544 (Me. 1930).

Where, after an agreement of sale is executed, and before the deal is closed, a building on the land is destroyed in whole, or in part, by fire, or other casualty, court decisions are not in accord as to which party to the agreement must bear the loss. The weight of authority holds that an accidental loss falls on the purchaser, and he must complete the deal according to the terms of the agreement: *Good v. Jarrard,* 76 S.E. 698 (S.C.); *Oakes v. Wingfield,* 95 Ga. App. 871 (1957).

A number of states, as in California and New York, have adopted the Uniform Vendor and Purchase Risk Act. The Act, in essence, places assumption of risk of loss upon the vendor, unless the buyer is in possession. Many agreements of sale in use, include a clause placing the risk of loss upon the seller, unless the buyer is in possession of the premises. It is a wise precaution for the purchaser to obtain insurance upon the property, *immediately,* upon the signing of the agreements, protecting him against loss by fire, casualty, or accident.

Equitable title—change in zoning

Under the equitable title doctrine, any change in the zoning ordinances of the municipality, affecting the property, are at the risk of the *buyer.* In the case of *Didonate v. Reliance Standard Life Ins. Co.,* 433 Pa. 219 (1969), "the crucial inquiry is which of the litigants (buyer or seller) bore the risk of loss attending the zoning change between the Agreement of Sale and the settlement." The court said:

> There appears to be no cogent argument for treating losses resulting from zoning changes occurring between the execution of the Agreement of Sale and settlement differently from casualty and other kinds of loss between those periods. The parties are always free to mold rights and responsibilities inter se (among themselves) in whatever fashion they desire. But when they are quiet, the law will speak in a voice of finality to set their dispute to rest.

In the case of *White Realty & Ins. Co. v. Moreland,* 259 A. 2d 461 (Pa. 1969), involving a suit for commission, the sales agreement contained the following controversial clause:

"Sellers warrant that the said location is zoned commercial at the time of settlement." The contract also provided that the seller was obligated to the broker for a commission "at or prior to the time of settlement, hereunder, a sales commission" of $2,670. The court held that the word "warrant" was not a promise by the sellers to secure a change in the zoning, but that it was an agreement "that the vendee's duties would be conditional on the future existence of the fact that the property was zoned as commercial property."

The court stated further:

> This interpretation is supported by the further principle *that contracts which tend to interfere with the administration of government are unenforceable.* (citing cases) *To contract for the accomplishment of something that is within the legislative discretion of a municipal body, is to be discouraged as against public policy.* (emphasis supplied)

No recovery by the broker. See also *Wright v. City of Littleton,* 483 P. 2d 953 (Colo. 1971).

In short, the agreement of sale should be made subject to zoning, permitting the use intended, upon delivery of deed. If a zoning change is required, the agreement should spell out whether the deal is contingent upon such change, and which party is to seek the change.

Agreement made subject to financing

If the agreement of sale is subject to mortgage financing, it is important that reference be spelled out in definite terms,—amount and type of mortgage, interest rate, commitment date for approval of mortgage; amount of appraisal required if FHA financing.

Should the mortgage be an FHA insured mortgage, the agreement should expressly provide that, notwithstanding any other provisions of the contract,

> the Buyer shall not be obligated to complete the purchase of the within described property or to incur any penalty by forfeiture of earnest money deposits, or otherwise, unless the Seller, or his agent, has delivered to Buyer a written statement issued by the Federal Housing Authority setting forth the appraised value of the property for mortgage purposes of not less than the amount specified above, (Purchase price) excluding closing costs, which statement Seller agrees to deliver to Buyer promptly, after such appraised value statement is available to Seller. Buyer may, however, have the option, within five days from the written notification to him of the FHA appraisal, proceed with the consummation of the contract according to its terms.

A Pennsylvania appellate court has held that where an agreement for sale of a $24,000 dwelling is made subject to the purchaser obtaining a mortgage in the sum of $16,000, that the purchaser had a right to expect a loan with a 20 year maturity and, upon his failure to obtain such a loan, he was entitled to a refund of his $2,000 deposit: *Tieri v. Orbell,* 192 Pa. Super. Ct. 612 (1960).

Marketable title

Marketable title, which the seller agrees to furnish the buyer, is one free from liens, encumbrances or clouds; it is such a title that a court could compel a buyer to accept. If the sale is subject to a mortgage, easement, or restriction, it must be noted in the agreement, and made subject thereto. If the owner submits an abstract of title, the buyer shall have a certain number of days (10 to 20) within which to submit any objections, in writing. The seller shall then have a certain number of days to clear up the objections. Charges for the abstract are assessed against the seller; examination of the title is at the expense of the buyer.

Title to be marketable (merchantable) need not necessarily be perfect, but a purchaser has a right to require that the title shall be of such a character that he will not be exposed to dangers of litigation as to its validity. If the facts throw a cloud on the title, rendering it dubious in the minds of reasonable men, it is not merchantable: *Ewing v. Plummer,* 308 Ill. 585 (1923).

Broker could recover a commission where he did not have knowledge of the seller's inability to deliver good title because of his wife's refusal to join in the listing contract. The broker's prospect was able to purchase the property: *Bryan, Appellant v. Jack Justice,* 287 So. 2nd 331 (Fla. 1973).

Blank vendee in agreement

Where the vendor knowingly signs an agreement of sale, with the name of the vendee not filled in, he impliedly gives his agent (the broker) authority to fill in the name of the vendee. When the vendee signs the agreement upon the terms set forth therein by the owner, it becomes an enforceable contract.

If the vendor is interested in the identity of the vendee, he should make inquiry as to his identity. If he signs the agreement first, without such inquiry, he cannot refuse to perform his contract, after it is signed by the undisclosed vendee: *McCrystall v. Connor,* 331 Ill. 107 (1928); *Oliver v. Wyatt,* 418 S.W. 2d 403 (Ky. 1967).

Assignment of leases

If possession is to be given by assignment of leases, the leases should be checked for parties, terms, and *expiration* date before the agreement of sale is signed. A provision should be incorporated in the agreement stating the expiration date in question. The leases should be properly assigned to the grantee at the closing, as well as any insurance policies which are to be assumed by the new owner, and the consent of the companies to the transfer endorsed thereon.

Personal property

The agreement of sale should recite in detail the specific articles of personal property which are included in the sale. These articles frequently include lighting fixtures, curtains, curtain rods, awnings, storm doors, screens, shrubbery, ranges, gas stoves, refrigerators, air conditioning units, carpets, mirrors attached to walls, coal, oil, and fireplace accessories. In the contract, the vendor should warrant that he has good title to the articles in question. At the closing the seller should execute a bill of sale for such personal property.

Assignability

Ordinarily, an agreement of sale is assignable by the vendee without any special notation to that effect. Very often a purchaser engages to buy a property without any intention of taking title but with the expectation that he will be able to sell (assign) the agreements at a higher price to a new buyer and pocket the difference. The seller cannot refuse to deed the property to the new purchaser unless he has agreed to take back a mortgage from the original purchaser in part payment of the purchase price, or unless the original buyer has assumed and agreed to pay an existing mortgage. This is based on the theory that a person has a right to select his debtor. It may make considerable difference to the seller whether the vendee, a person of financial stability, is indebted to him, or whether he must look to the vendee's assignee, a person financially irresponsible for payment. If the owner desires to deal exclusively with the original buyer in any event, then he should stipulate that "rights under the within agreement of sale are not assignable." In this connection, a person preparing an agreement of sale should be fully cognizant of the legal effect of several clauses used in regard to an existing mortgage. Let us assume that Adams is selling a property to Black for $10,000 and there is at present a mortgage against the property for $7,000 executed by Adams to the mortgagee, Crane, three years earlier. From Adams's standpoint it is to his advantage to insist that the buyer, Black, pay all cash or provide his own financing so that Adams's mortgage to Crane can be paid and satisfied. This is the only certain way that Adams can be relieved of any further obligation under the mortgage. If Black is to take the property, however, subject to the mortgage, caution must be exercised to see that the buyer, Black, not only takes the premises subject to the existing mortgage in favor of Crane, but also that he *assumes and agrees to pay it.* If a short form clause—such as "Under and subject, nevertheless, to a certain unpaid mortgage in the amount of $7,000 given by Adams to Crane, which mortgage dated July 1, 1974, is recorded in the office of the Recorder of Deeds of Blank County in Mortgage Book Vol. 2139 P. 422"—is used, the buyer is simply purchasing whatever equity there is in the property over and above the mortgage debt. If the property should subsequently be sold for default on the mortgage, Black would lose what money he has already paid on the property and no more.

Assumption of mortgage

Should the property at foreclosure sale be sold for less or be less valuable than the amount of Crane's claim, Black would not be liable for the deficiency of the mortgagee. Crane would have to look to Adams alone for payment. On the other hand, if the clause referring to the mortgage read exactly as it appears above, with this addition, "which mortgage the vendee expressly assumes and agrees to pay as part of the consideration herein," Crane, in event of a deficiency judgment, could look to Adams or Black, or both, for payment. If Crane collected the full deficiency from Adams, then Adams, in turn, could look to Black for reimbursement, by reason of the mortgage *assumption* clause. Of course, it is necessary that the same clause be inserted in the *deed* from Adams to Black.

Where an owner of a contract for deed assigns the contract to a new party, the question arises whether said purchaser is liable to the owner of the legal title according to the terms of the contract for deed. In the case of *Petersen v. Johnson,* 20 N.W. 2d 507 (Wis. 1972), the assignment did not contain a clause binding the assignee to pay the purchase price. In a foreclosure action, the original seller sought to obtain a deficiency judgment against the assignee. The court held that the seller could not recover from the assignee. He could recover from the original contractee.

Consent of mortgagee not necessary

The fact that there is an existing mortgage against the property does not prevent the owner from selling it; nor is it necessary, as a general rule, to secure the consent of the mortgagee to the sale. However, the mortgage may provide otherwise, to the effect that the debt will become due and payable, in event of a sale of the premises without the written consent of the mortgagee. In periods of high interest rates, this practice of accelerating the mortgage debt, in event of a sale, becomes more pronounced. As a result, the mortgagee is motivated to call the mortgage or renegotiate the mortgage with the buyer at the higher going rate of interest.

In the case of *Peoples Savings Association v. Standard Industries,* 275 N.E. 2d 406 (Ohio 1970), the mortgage contained a clause accelerating the due date of note in the event of a sale of the premises without the prior written consent of the mortgagee. The mortgagee instituted mortgage foreclosure proceedings against the buyer on the grounds that the violation of such acceleration clause constituted a default, permitting foreclosure. The purchaser contended that the provision for acceleration based on change of ownership was void as against public policy.

The court held that the right of the mortgagee to protect its security by maintaining control over the identity and financial responsibility of the purchaser is a legitimate business objective, and is not illegal, inequitable or contrary to public policy.

This is the prevailing rule. While court decisions permit a mortgagee to accelerate payment of the debt, *in case of a sale,* the California court held in the case of *La Sala v. American Savings & Loan Association,* 489 P. 2d 1113 (1971), that a clause in a deed of trust giving the mortgagee the right to accelerate the debt in event the mortgagor should obtain secondary financing on the property, was void. In the case of a sale of the property, it divests the owner of title and imposes obligations of taxation, maintenance and repair upon a new owner, with whom the mortgagee had no privity of contract.

Seller's damages for breach by buyer

If the seller intends to sue the buyer for damages resulting from the latter's breach, he should first attempt to receive a bona fide offer for the same property from another buyer. He should then notify the defaulting buyer as to the best price offered and advise the buyer that unless he can get the seller a higher price, the property will be sold at that price and the buyer will be held responsible in damages for the difference between the contract price and the best price that the seller could obtain.

A clause used in this connection would read:

> In the event of default by the Buyers, the Sellers may, at their option, elect to: (a) Retain the earnest money deposit and all monies paid on account of the purchase price as liquidated damages, in which event this Agreement shall become null and void and both parties shall thereupon be released of all further liability hereunder. It is hereby agreed that, without resale, Seller's damages will be difficult of ascertainment and that the earnest money deposit and all monies paid on account of the purchase price constitute a reasonable liquidation thereof and not a penalty.
>
> In lieu thereof, Seller may elect either or both of the following remedies: (b) Apply the earnest money deposit and all monies paid on account of the purchase price and proceed with an action for specific performance; (c) Apply said monies toward Seller's loss on the resale of said property and proceed with an action at law for all damages sustained by Seller; Provided, however, that no such election of (b) or (c) shall be final or conclusive until full satisfaction shall have been received.

Buyer's damages for breach by seller

Where the seller breaches an agreement of sale, the buyer's measure of damages depends upon whether the seller is guilty of fraud in the breach. If no fraud is present, the buyer can recover only his down payment and actual expenses. Where a borough ordinance is discovered, which provides for widening of the street upon which the property abuts, the buyer could rescind his contract to purchase and recover the deposit money and actual expenses. The same result would follow where a lot is of less width than contracted for, even though slight, and the buyer viewed the premises. False statements of value, or cost of the building, or the seller's arbitrary refusal to perform would constitute fraud and the buyer could then recover the full value of his bargain.

Usually, where a seller refuses to consummate the agreement of sale, the buyer will sue for specific performance to compel the seller to execute and deliver a general warranty deed to him.

Options

An option is a contract. It may be defined as an agreement, in writing, whereby the owner (optionor) gives to another (optionee) the exclusive right *for a limited period of time* to purchase (or lease) his real estate upon certain terms and conditions. *Johnson v. Worcester Business Development Corp.,* 302 N.E. 2d 575 (Mass. 1973). The option requires a consideration to support it, or it may be under seal. The consideration may be nominal, that is, $1.00. If the option recites a $1.00 consideration, that is sufficient, even though it has not actually been paid. Time is the very *essence* of an option agreement, and if not exercised prior to the expiration date, it automatically expires. Unlike an agreement of sale, there is no period of grace for performance beyond the expiration date. Where the owner is married, the wife's signature should be obtained to the option agreement of sale so that, if the optionee exercises the option, the wife of the optionor can be compelled to join in the agreement of sale. Death of the owner during the term of the option would not affect the optionee's rights under the agreement. Where the option is extended or renewed for an additional term, there *must* be additional consideration for the added term. An option is assignable in the same manner as the ordinary agreement of sale. The purpose of the option is to give the holder, in return for the consideration paid, a period of time to make up his mind whether he will elect to purchase the property in question. During the specified time, the property is withdrawn from other purchasers. If the optionee does not exercise the option, the money paid for the option is forfeited. However, the option agreement may specify that if the option is exercised, the money paid for the option shall be credited to the purchase price of the property.

Any rents paid during the period of the option belong to the owner, until the option is exercised and the deal consummated.

A letter from the optionee to the owner, during the option period, that he desires to exercise the option to purchase the property as therein set forth within the next 10 days, without tendering the purchase price, prior to the expiration date of the option, was fatal to the optionee's cause: *Adams v. Swift,* 500 S.W. 2d 437 (Tenn. 1973).

When an option is executed, it is a good precaution to prepare and attach the proposed agreement of sale, spelling out the terms upon which the option is to be exercised.

Installment land contracts

An installment land contract is also called either a contract for deed, or a conditional sales contract.

A purchaser, under a land contract for deed, or even in an agreement of sale is not required to sign the instrument. His *acceptance* of the instrument, signed by the seller, accompanied by the payment of a deposit, makes the contract bi-lateral: *Stachnik v. Winkel,* 213 N.W. 2d 434 (Mich. 1973).

In the promotion of subdivision tracts, many lots are sold on an installment basis. A modest down payment is made and then periodic monthly payments are made until the full consideration price is liquidated, at which time a deed is delivered.

Considerable improved real estate is also sold in the same manner. Should the buyer default in his payments, he forfeits the payments already made. In the alternative, the seller could also elect to hold the buyer to his contract. This method permits a family of modest means to acquire a home through periodic payments out of income. The monthly payments are usually first applied to interest and carrying charges and the balance to the unpaid principal indebtedness. Many such installment contracts, often termed "contract for deed," provide that upon payment of a certain amount of the purchase price (often 50 per cent), the vendee will receive a deed for the property. He, in turn, will then execute a purchase money mortgage to the vendor for the balance of the purchase price. The contract for deed usually provides that in the event the purchaser defaults, the balance of the purchase price, at the option of the seller, shall become payable forthwith. A clause may even be included which would permit the seller to confess judgment against the buyer for the full amount unpaid. An inherent danger in the installment contract, from the standpoint of the buyer, is that judgments may be entered against the seller during the long term the contract has to run. Such judgments, of course, would be a lien against the property.

Where vendors wrongfully rescinded a conditional sale contract for a motel property, the buyers were entitled to recover principal payments, as well as interest from date of wrongful ejectment. The vendors were not entitled to a set off in amount of rents and profits accruing to buyers while they were in possession: *Smeekens v. Bertrand,* 302 N.E. 2d 502 (Ind. 1973).

Often, it is a matter of choice, with buyer or seller, whether to use a land installment purchase contract, or a deed and mortgage. The seller's advantage in using the land contract lies in case of default, he can reclaim title to the property more readily than through foreclosure on a mortgage. The disadvantage to the seller is that in case he himself needs money quickly, the land contract cannot be sold as readily as a mortgage except, possibly, at a great financial loss.

An "instrument land contract" or so called "contract for deed" evidences a sale of land and an obligation of vendor to convey the land and of purchaser to pay the purchase price in installments over a period of time. It is essentially a security instrument, taking the place of a purchase money mortgage: *Hand L. Land Co. v. Warner,* 258 So. 2d 293 (Fla. 1972).

From the standpoint of the buyer, it appears preferable to require a deed and for the buyer to give the seller a purchase money mortgage for the balance due. To all intents and purposes, the buyer is the legal owner of the premises. Should the buyer default on the mortgage, title is not foreclosed to him summarily. He still has a period of grace to redeem the property, as provided for in the statute. Practical considerations, dependent on how much money the buyer has paid on account of the purchase price, may well dictate whether a land contract or a deed and mortgage should be used.

Where the land contract is used, the seller can protect himself by a clause in the contract, prohibiting assignment of the contract, mortgaging or leasing the property by the buyer, except upon the written consent of the seller. In the absence of a non-assignment clause in the land contract, the buyer would have these several privileges. If assigned, the assignment should be recorded.

Strict foreclosure upon default

On default upon a land contract, the remedy of strict foreclosure is frequently resorted to in some states. The vendor, thereby, foregoes any right to collect the full amount of debt. He cannot demand return of the land and also ask for the total purchase price. Strict foreclosure operates as a rescision, voiding or "calling off" of the contract by the vendor. The period of redemption is within the sound discretion of the court. Consideration should be given to ability of purchaser to redeem, his state of solvency. Value of the land and the likelihood of refinancing are deemed relevant facts. Also, taken into consideration are the size of the vendee's equity and the length of the default. The courts will attempt to do equity between the parties: *Kallenbach v. Lake Publications, Inc.,* 142 N.W. 2d 212 (Wis. 1966).

A vendee, under a land contract, became delinquent in his monthly payments during 1963. In 1966, the vendor started an action to quiet title. The vendee then offered to pay the entire balance due, plus interest. The vendor refused to accept payment. The vendee next sued for specific performance. The court decided in favor of the vendee, treating the land contract as a mortgage. The vendee had the right to redeem the property: *McFadden v. Walker,* 488 P. 2d 1353 (Cal. 1971).

AGREEMENT OF SALE

Date of this Agreement.......................... *April 4, 1974*..........................
Name of Seller.................................. HELEN L. LA PORTE, *unmarried, of the Borough of Zelienopie, County of Butler, and State of Pennsylvania*.................
Name of Buyer .... ROLAND GERARD, *of the City of Cleveland, County of Cuyahoga, State of Ohio*..
Name of Real Estate Agent .... *Ajax Realty Company*.................
WITNESSETH, that Seller, for the consideration hereinafter mentioned, does covenant, promise, grant and agree, to and with the said Buyer, by these presents, that Seller shall and will, on or before......................... *June 1, 1974*............... at the proper costs and charges of the Seller, by deed of....................... *general*......... warranty, well and sufficiently grant, convey and assure unto the said Buyer, in fee simple, clear of encumbrances, excepting coal, gas, oil and other mineral rights heretofore sold, reserved or leased, and existing building or use restrictions, if any, of record, the following described property:

ALL *that certain lot or piece of ground situate in the Borough of Mt. Oliver, County of Allegheny and State of Pennsylvania, being Lot No. 36 in the Crescent Hills Plan of Lots, of record in the Recorder's Office of Allegheny County in Plan Book Volume 29, pages 13 and 14, and being more particularly bounded and described by deed recorded in the Recorder's Office of Allegheny County in Deed Book Volume 2516, page 780.*

HAVING thereon erected a six (6) room, two (2) bath, brick and stone dwelling with integral garage, known as 3421 Hillmont Avenue.

TOGETHER with all and singular the buildings, improvements, and other the premises hereby demised, with the appurtenances, it being understood that gas and electric light fixtures, heating and plumbing systems, and laundry tubs installed in said buildings are included in this sale.

In consideration whereof Buyer doth covenant, promise and agree, to and with Seller, by these presents, that Buyer shall and will well and truly pay or cause to be paid unto the said Seller the sum of........... *Twenty-One Thousand ($21,000.00) Dollars in manner following: One Thousand ($1,000.00) Dollars evidenced by cash [ ], personal check [x], cashier's check [ ]........ as deposit on account of the purchase price, and the balance of Twenty Thousand ($20,000.00) Dollars, in cash, upon delivery of deed. It is understood and agreed that Buyer is to pay Pennsylvania Stamp Transfer Tax; Seller to pay local tax.*

Taxes, interest, and rents to be pro-rated as of........... date............ of delivery of deed.
For title references see Deed Book Vol........... *2516*........., page .... *780*..........
Possession to be given .... upon delivery of deed............. The buyer, at his own expense, agrees to place adequate fire insurance on the premises covered by this agreement.

Should the buyer fail to make settlement, as herein provided, the sum or sums of money paid on account of the purchase price, may, at the option of the seller, be (a) applied to the purchase price in an action for the purchase price; or, (b) may be applied to any loss suffered by the seller on the resale of the property without any advance notice to the Buyer of said proposed resale; or, (c) may be retained by the Seller as liquidated damages. In the latter case, this agreement of sale shall become null and void.

Should the Seller default in the performance of these agreements, the Buyer, may, at his option (a) waive any claim for loss of bargain and the Seller agrees to refund to the Buyer all sums of money paid on account of the purchase price, and any costs of expenses incurred: or, (b) sue for specific performance of the contract or, (c) sue in an action at law for damages.

The earnest money paid under this contract is to be held in escrow by the Broker. It is understood between the parties hereto that the property herein sold has been inspected by the Buyer, or his or their agent, and that the same is being purchased as a result of such inspection.

It is understood that....................... *The Ajax Realty Company* .... is acting as agent only in bringing the Buyer and Seller together and will in no case whatsoever be held liable to either party for the performance of any term or covenant of this agreement or for damages for non-performance thereof. Seller agrees to pay the said broker 7 per cent commission ($1470.00). This agreement shall extend to and be binding upon the heirs, executors, administrators, successors and assigns of the parties hereto. Whenever used in this agreement, the singular number shall include the plural, the plural the singular, and the use of any gender shall be applicable to all genders.

IN WITNESS WHEREOF, the said parties to this agreement have hereunto set their hands and seals, the day and year first above written.

SEALED AND DELIVERED IN THE
PRESENCE OF:

As to 1 .... *Ben Adams*.........
As to 2 .... *James Doyle* ....

1. *Helen L. La Porte* (SEAL)
(Seller)
2. *Roland Gerard* (SEAL)
(Buyer)

Questions on Agreements of Sale

1. Q. Who are the principal parties to an agreement of sale?
   A. Seller and buyer, commonly called vendor and vendee, respectively
2. Q. Can a broker acquire rights for a commission under an agreement of sale, since he is not a party to it?
   A. Yes, if the agreement states that the broker negotiated the deal and the seller owes the broker a commission.
3. Q. Is an oral agreement of sale invalid?
   A. It is invalid insofar as maintaining an action for specific performance is concerned, but it may give rise to an action for damages.
4. Q. If the date is omitted in an agreement of sale, is it invalid?
   A. No. A date is merely evidence of the time when the agreement of sale was signed, but it is not essential for the validity of the instrument.
5. Q. What information should an agreement of sale contain?
   A. Names of the parties, consideration price, description and terms of sale.
6. Q. Is a particular form required?
   A. No, so long as it contains the above information and clearly expresses the intention of the parties.
7. Q. Is an offer to purchase, in writing, which states that a formal agreement will be executed at a later date, desirable?
   A. No, because differences may arise as to what terms should be included in the formal instrument, so that, if the differences cannot be resolved, either party could withdraw from the deal.
8. Q. In order for an agreement of sale to be enforceable, how many elements of the law of contracts must be present?
   A. Six.
9. Q. What are they?
   A. Offer and acceptance; consideration (or seal, in some states); capacity of parties, reality of consent, legality of object and special formality.
10. Q. What is meant by reality of consent?
    A. The contract must be free from mistakes, misrepresentations, fraud, duress or undue influence.
11. Q. Chappel, seller, and Stone, buyer, enter into an agreement of sale for a farm, located in Erie County. The farm is located in the Harrison School District. Stone believes the farm is located in the Baldwin Township School District. It is located in Hays Township, three miles from the school. Can Stone rescind the agreement on the grounds of mistake?
    A. No, this is a unilateral mistake, not a mutual mistake, so that Stone is bound by his agreement to purchase the farm.
12. Q. What is the purpose of Statute of Frauds and when was it first enacted:
    A. It is an act for the prevention of fraud and perjury. It was first enacted in England, 29 Charles II, year 1676. It requires certain real estate contracts to be in writing.
13. Q. Define an agreement of sale.
    A. A written contract whereby the purchaser agrees to buy certain real estate and the

seller agrees to sell upon terms set forth therein.

14. Q. When a broker receives an earnest money deposit from a buyer, may he keep the money on file in his office pending the closing of the deal?
 A. No; he should deposit it immediately in his trust or escrow account.

15. Q. What recourse would a seller have against the broker, if the buyer backed out of the transaction before it was closed?
 A. None; the broker is not responsible for the buyer's default.

16. Q. Anthony gives Benson, a broker, a written exclusive contract to sell his property at $5,000. Benson procures Clark as a purchaser upon Anthony's terms. Clark signs an agreement but Anthony, the owner, refuses to sign. Does Clark have any right of action against Anthony?
 A. No. Anthony did not sign the agreement of sale. Anthony is not liable to Clark but would be liable to Benson for a commission.

17. Q. Wilson and Peters execute an agreement of sale for Wilson's property at $9,000, under and subject to a mortgage of $5,000 which Peters assumes and agrees to pay. Peters assigns the agreement to Crane. Wilson refuses to recognize Crane. Can Crane compel Wilson to execute a deed to him?
 A. No. Ordinarily an agreement of sale is assignable. However, where the financial responsibility of the buyer is involved, as here, the seller has a right to select his debtor.

18. Q. What conditions must be met in a memorandum in writing to comply with the Statute of Frauds?
 A. The writing must name the consideration, the property to be sold, and the terms, and it must be signed by the seller or by his lawful agent authorized in writing to do so.

19. Q. Beatty lists certain property with Coleman for sale at $40,000. He informs the broker that the property contains 3.5 acres. Coleman obtains a signed offer from Dixon at that price, which Beatty accepts. The agreement states 3.5 acres "more or less." The recorded deed description measures 2.5 acres. This is confirmed by a survey. Dixon demands a refund of his deposit money. Beatty refuses, relying on the "more or less" clause in the agreement. Decide.
 A. Dixon will win. "More or less" is no defense, where there is a substantial difference in the acreage. A one acre discrepancy in a three and one-half tract is substantial.

20. Q. Does the term "valuable consideration" mean only a money consideration?
 A. No. A valuable consideration may consist of services, chattels or anything which could be measured in monetary terms.

21. Q. Assume that after a sales contract has been written and executed, a slight change is made in the terms or conditions, and that the broker, in the presence of the interested parties, alters the writing to conform to the new agreement: what precaution should the broker take to protect himself against any future controversy?
 A. He should have all parties to the contract place their signature or initials in the margin opposite or nearest the alterations.

22. Q. Arnold agrees to sell a property to Winters for $10,000—$500 down and the balance in cash. Winters is unable to complete the deal and he obtains Summers, to whom the agreements are assigned. Two days later Summers finds that his wife disapproves the purchase, and he assigns the agreements to Davidson. Arnold, a business competitor of Davidson, refuses to execute a deed to him. Who will win?
 A. Davidson can compel Arnold to execute a deed to him as the agreement of sale was assignable.

23. Q. An agreement of sale is made out between Alfred Sims, vendor and Don Cosgrove, vendee. It is signed, however, by Alfred Sims and Elsie Sims, his wife, as well as by Don Cosgrove. The wife refuses to execute the deed on the grounds that she is not named as a party in the agreement proper. Must she join in the deed?
 A. Yes. Her signature is sufficient to show an intention on her part to be bound.

24. Q. Abrams signs an agreement to purchase Bell's property at $10,000 and pays $500 as deposit money. Later Abrams fails to complete the deal and Bell keeps the deposit money. Three months later Bell sells the same property to Clark for $9,000 and now sues Abrams for an additional $500. Can he recover?
A. No. When Abrams failed to perform, Bell could have sued for the purchase price. Since he elected to keep the $500 as liquidated damages, he has no other remedy.
25. Q. A buyer asks the broker not to deposit his earnest money check of $1,000 for ten days. The check is later deposited and returned on account of insufficient funds. The buyer fails to complete the transaction. Is the broker liable to the owner?
A. Yes. The broker is required to deposit the earnest money promptly, unless the owner knew and agreed to the delayed deposit.
26. Q. A broker negotiated the sale of a property for $40,000, his commission to be 6 per cent. The buyer deposited $4,000 as earnest money. Before the deal was closed, buyer and seller mutually agreed to call the deal off, the owner to keep the $4,000 deposit. The owner offers the broker a commission of 6% on the $4,000 deposit. The broker claims $2,400. Decide.
A. The broker is entitled to $2,400 as he fully performed his contract with the owner in obtaining a purchaser acceptable to the owner.
27. Q. How should a down payment clause be worded to protect the seller fully?
A. " $500 upon the signing of these agreements, receipt of which is hereby acknowledged, and which sum may, *at the option* of the party of the first part, be retained as liquidated damages in event of breach of any of the conditions contained herein by the party of the second part, and the balance of $9,500, in cash, upon delivery of deed."
28. Q. How large a down payment should the seller require?
A. At least 10 percent of the purchase price; a larger amount if the closing is at a date pretty far in the future or the responsibility of the buyer is questionable.
29. Q. An agreement of sale calls for the closing on Feb. 1, 1974. The buyer is unable to close at that time. Will he forfeit his earnest money (down payment) if he fails to close on Feb. 1, 1974?
A. No. The buyer has a reasonable time after Feb. 1, 1974 to close the deal. What is a reasonable time depends upon the circumstances of each case. 30 days is certainly a reasonable time.
30. Q. Suppose, in the preceding case, the seller has certain commitments on Feb. 1, 1974 and wants to be certain the deal will be closed on that date. How can the seller protect himself?
A. By providing that the date of closing is "of the essence" of the agreement.
31. Q. When a buyer defaults, what steps should a seller take?
A. Make a formal *tender* of the deed and *demand* of the consideration price.
32. Q. When is tender excused?
A. Tender is unnecessary where there is an anticipatory repudiation by the buyer; when the buyer has notified the seller before the closing that he will not go through with the deal.
33. Q. Is it necessary to have an agreement of sale acknowledged?
A. No. If acknowledged, the agreement can be recorded. The unexecuted agreement would then constitute a cloud upon the title.
34. Q. Kappel granted an option to Wilson to buy certain land for $50,000 for 60 days from June 15, 1974, "settlement to be made within 90 days from date the option is exercised." On August 3, 1974, Kappel entered into an agreement of sale with Cosgrove, subject to the rights of Wilson, who exercised his option on August 5, 1974, settlement to be made "one year" from that date. Cosgrove sues for specific performance. Will he succeed?
A. No. Cosgrove is not entitled to specific performance. Time is not of the essence in respect to the settlement date of an option contract. Wilson's right included the

right to renegotiate in good faith, a reasonable extension of the settlement date. Cosgrove's agreement was expressly subject to that right exercised by Wilson.

35. Q. If the agreement of sale makes no provision for the apportionment of taxes, whose responsibility is the taxes?
    A. The seller's, unless local custom dictates otherwise.
36. Q. Bunt agreed to sell certain land to Judd, a purchaser, brought by Rice, a broker. The terms as written in the sales contract were "Selling price $5,000; ½ cash balance 1 to 4 years, with interest at 6%." Is the contract enforceable?
    A. No; it is too vague and indefinite to be enforced, on account of the 1 to 4 year provision.
37. Q. What fixtures pass with the sale of real estate under an agreement of sale?
    A. Only those articles which may be considered as constituting a part of the freehold.
38. Q. Under what circumstances may an agent sign for his principal an agreement or contract required to be in writing?
    A. When he has a power of attorney duly recorded.
39. Q. Must an agreement for the sale of real estate be in writing?
    A. Yes, unless the purchaser has gone into possession, paid part of the purchase price, and made improvements.
40. Q. What should a broker do with down payments or earnest money that he has received?
    A. Deposit them in a trust account.
41. Q. Why is it important that a broker have the seller sign an agreement of sale and deliver a signed copy to the buyer as soon as possible?
    A. Because the purchaser may revoke his offer to purchase prior to the communication to him of the seller's acceptance of the offer.
42. Q. Can a contract for the sale of real estate be enforced if the description is not sufficient to identify the property?
    A. No.
43. Q. What is meant by a so-called "scavenger sale"?
    A. A sale of property which has reverted to the state because of nonpayment of taxes.
44. Q. Reed signs an agreement of sale to purchase certain real property from King on February 1, 1974 for $17,500. He pays $1,000 as a down payment and with King's consent, Reed moves in on February 15th. The deal was to be closed on March 15, 1974, but differences arose due to a faulty septic tank. The deal is not closed and Reed remains in possession until May 1, 1974. King claims a rental of $100 per month from February 15th to May 1st for use and occupancy. Can he recover?
    A. No. Reed did not move in under an express or implied *lease.* He simply took possession under the sales agreement and King cannot recover for use and occupancy. (Moral: If vendee is to take possession, have him sign a tight form lease for one month, with renewal on a monthly basis.)
45. Q. An offer to purchase is signed by a purchaser on January 28, 1974, and he pays $1,000 as a deposit at that time. It contains a clause to the effect that the buyer agrees to keep the offer open without fail for 5 days, within which time the seller may accept the offer. On January 29, 1974, the buyer notifies the owner that he is withdrawing the offer and demands the return of his $1,000. Can he do so?
    A. Yes; he can withdraw the offer at any time before it is accepted. The five days simply means that the offer will automatically expire at the end of that period unless accepted or previously withdrawn.
46. Q. What is the purpose of keeping a purchaser's deposit separate and apart from your own?
    A. The money does not belong to the broker. It is being held by him for the account of the owner and should therefore be treated as trust funds.
47. Q. A broker holding a listing on a property secures from a prospect a deposit and a signed agreement to purchase. What steps should be taken next?
    A. Four copies should be signed by buyer. He must leave one copy with the buyer, take

three copies to the seller and have him sign all three copies. He leaves one copy with the seller, delivers one copy bearing the seller's signatures to the buyer, and keeps one copy for his own file.

48. Q. Should a broker deduct his commission from a deposit for the purchase of property if the offer of purchase is declined by the owner?
    A. No. There has been no binding contract of sale. Any commission due the broker should be paid by the seller.

49. Q. What is a "binder" in real estate?
    A. Earnest money paid to show good faith until the sale is closed.

50. Q. What are the essentials of a valid contract for the sale of real estate?
    A. The date, names of the parties, description of the property, terms of the sale, and signatures of the parties.

51. Q. In a contract for the sale of real property, by what term is the party known who (1) is selling the property?(2) is buying the property?
    A. (1) Vendor. (2) Vendee.

52. Q. If you, as broker, sell a property for your client and he takes back a purchase money mortgage in part payment, is he a mortgagor or mortgagee?
    A. Mortgagee.

53. Q. If a vendor signs an agreement of sale for real estate and transmits it by messenger to a notary public, can the notary legally take the acknowledgment of the signature?
    A. No. The person making the acknowledgment (the affiant) must appear in person.

54. Q. What is meant by the clause commonly found in contracts for the sale of real property reading "rents, taxes, interest on mortgages, and all premiums on insurance policies in force at date hereof are apportioned" ?
    A. The items are prorated between buyer and seller as of the date of closing.

55. Q. A contract is made for the sale of real estate. Before taking title to the property and not being certain of the boundaries, the purchaser causes a (1) ______________ to be made. Upon inspection of this document he discovers that telephone poles are situated on the plot of land and that for this reason the telephone company has a (2) ______________ on the seller's land. He also discovers that one of the walls of a garage built on the rear portion of the land is situated on the adjoining property and this constitutes an (3) ______________ on the adjoining property. Disturbed by these physical facts of the property he is about to buy, the purchaser orders an (4) ______________ for the purpose of ascertaining the soundness of the title of the property.
    A. (1) survey.
    (2) right of way.
    (3) encroachment.
    (4) abstract of title.

56. Q. A broker receives a $1,000 earnest money deposit. The parties have a controversy at the closing and the deal is not consummated. Buyer and seller demand the $1,000 deposit. Who is entitled to it?
    A. Neither buyer nor seller. The broker is required to hold the deposit until the transaction is consummated or terminated. Since the matter may result in litigation, the broker should retain the money until court action is instituted. Then he should pay the money into court (interpleader) and enter a claim for his commission with the court.

57. Q. A broker had a $5,000 bond filed when he obtained his real estate license. The broker is sued on a furniture claim and the creditor recovers a judgment for $1,700. Can the creditor recover on the broker's real estate bond?
    A. No. The claim did not result from a real estate transaction.

58. Q. (1) Why is it advisable from the standpoint of the purchaser to have inserted in the real estate contract that he is taking the property subject to an existing mortgage, rather than that he is assuming payment of the mortgage indebtedness? (2) If the

purchaser does assume the mortgage indebtedness, does that relieve the original mortgagor of this obligation?

A. (1) Under this type mortgage clause (the short form) the purchaser is not liable to the mortgagee for payment of the mortgage indebtedness. The buyer can lose the property upon a mortgage default, but the mortgagee cannot collect a deficiency judgment from the purchaser of the property.
(2) No.

59. Q. In relation to real property, in what instances are the following terms employed? (1) "time is of the essence of this contract." (2) "to apportion as of the date of delivery of deed."

A. (1) Provision in agreement of sale which specifies the date for closing and makes it mandatory for the parties to perform on said date.
(2) Refers to prorating of taxes, rents, interest, and insurance.

60. Q. What is meant by an action of "specific performance"?

A. Court action to compel vendor to execute a deed to the vendee in accordance with the terms of the agreement of sale.

61. Q. Adams offers to sell his residence to Burns for $21,000 on a cash basis. Burns makes a counter proposition 5 days later, agreeing to buy the property for $20,000, if the deal is closed in 90 days, so that he can sell his home in the interim. Adams rejected the counter proposition. Burns sells his home three weeks later and agrees to buy the Adams home for $21,000. Burns signs the contract, originally prepared by Adams, at $21,000. Adams now refuses to sell. Can Burns compel Adams to honor the original agreement?

A. No, the counter proposition was a rejection of Adams' offer and an offer, once rejected, is gone forever, unless the offeror is willing to reinstate the offer.

62. Q. An agreement of sale includes the sale of all rugs and draperies. After the deal is closed and the buyer takes possession, he finds that the seller has removed the kitchen linoleum, which was not cemented to the floor. Does the buyer have any remedy?

A. No; the linoleum is personal property, which could be removed from the premises by the seller.

63. Q. Mary Richards sold her home to Adam Frey on February 15, 1974. The deal was to be closed on April 5, 1974. Mary Richards was moving into a new home, which was to be completed by April 1, 1974. Due to the contractor's difficulties, the house was not completed until May 17, 1974. Frey, at that time, has become disillusioned with his purchase, and refuses to close the deal and demands a refund of his deposit money. Will he win?

A. No. In the absence of a time is of the essence clause in the agreement of sale, Richards has a reasonable time after April 5, 1974 to close the transaction. The time of the delay should be reasonable.

64. Q. Keeping in mind the printed forms of real estate agreements of sale commonly used, list six of the items of information which should be inserted in the blank spaces.

A. 1. Name of the parties.
2. Date of closing.
3. Description.
4. Terms of the sale.
5. Apportionment of taxes, rent, interest, and insurance.
6. Date of possession.

65. Q. John Steele owns certain real estate clear of any mortgages or unpaid taxes. Name three other types of encumbrances which might cloud the title.

A. 1. Judgments.
2. A lease.
3. A right of way.

66. Q. Can the seller refuse to sign an agreement of sale when the broker insists upon

retaining his commission out of the down payment?

A. Yes. The broker should deposit the money in an escrow account.

67\. Q. In arranging for the closing of a real estate deal, enumerate at least ten items that a broker should look after or check.

A. 1. Have a copy of the agreement of sale at the closing.
2. See that tax receipts, sewer and water rent receipts are available.
3. Leases properly assigned to purchaser.
4. Endorsements for transfer of insurance policies.
5. Statement from mortgagee as to exact balance due upon mortgage; also receipt for last payment of mortgage interest.
6. Seller's old deed available for checking description in new deed.
7. Survey, if available.
8. Bill of sale for any personal property.
9. New deed to buyer.
10. Estimate of closing expense.
11. Purchaser has certified funds.
12. Transfer of keys.

68\. Q. Harris, owner of certain premises, executed an exclusive listing contract on January 2, 1974, in favor of Stewart, a broker, for a period of three months, with power "for me and in my name to sell and execute contracts of sale" for the property in question. Stewart signed an agreement of sale with Snyder, deal to be closed on Mar. 1, 1974. Harris refused to convey the property, contending that where the principal-agent relationship is limited to time, the agent is without authority to enter into a contract to be performed subsequent to the expiration of the agency contract. Snyder brought suit for specific performance. Who will win?

A. Snyder will win. Under the listing contract, Stewart is authorized to execute a binding agreement of sale for the owner, Harris. It is of no consequence that the agreement of sale will be consummated subsequent to the expiration of the listing contract.

69\. Q. Name five items which are usually adjusted at the closing of a real estate transaction between seller and buyer.

A. 1. Taxes.
2. Water rents.
3. Fire insurance premiums.
4. Rents.
5. Interest on mortgage.

70\. Q. What is meant by proration and what items are usually prorated?

A. Proration is the apportionment of certain items as of the date of closing the deal between seller and buyer. The items usually pro-rated are stated in the preceding answer.

71\. Q. *A* and *B* sign a binder for the sale of a parcel of real property, with the provision that a formal contract would be signed the next day. The following day *A* refuses to complete the transaction. Can *B* force *A* to go through with the transaction since no formal contract was signed?

A. No, since the terms of the contract have not yet been agreed upon. Courts do not make contracts for the parties.

72\. Q. You have obtained an offer to purchase and have an earnest money receipt signed by the prospective purchaser. You find that the property is owned by John Brown and Mary Brown, his wife, and Martha Brown, the mother of John Brown. The offer is acceptable to the Browns. Who would you have sign the earnest money receipt?

A. John Brown and Mary Brown, his wife, and Martha Brown, the mother. The listing is signed by John and Mary Brown.

73\. Q. In the above case you find upon contact with the owners of the property that Martha Brown, the mother, is away on a trip to California and not readily available. You, therefore, have the earnest money receipt signed by John and Mary Brown. Later, before any further steps are taken, the purchaser decides to cancel the deal and asks for his money back. Are you required to refund the earnest money deposit?

A. Yes; the offer has not been accepted by all parties who hold title.

74. Q. Suppose in the case above-cited it develops that the mother, Martha Brown, will not sign the deed transferring the property to the prospective purchaser. You have a buyer ready, willing, and able but cannot deliver. Can you collect a commission? If so, from whom?

A. Yes. You can sue John Brown and Mary Brown.

75. Q. The following earnest money receipt was submitted as evidence:

May 10, 1974. Received from John Doe $80.00 Eighty Dollars earnest money on lot and house number 960 Union Street. Price $5,000.00 Five Thousand and balance of $4,920.00 to be paid when papers and title insurance are completed. It is understood this deal would be closed and house vacated on or before June the 10th. All furniture except personal belongings included in this transaction.

Is this document binding upon the parties?

A. No; agreement is incomplete as it contemplates a subsequent instrument. In Oregon, omission of city considered fatal; in Pennsylvania, parol (oral) evidence permitted for purpose of giving a more precise description.

76. Q. An agreement of sale is made out between Ben Sharp, vendor, and Charles Lang. However, the agreement is signed by Ben Sharp and his wife, Myrtle Sharp. The wife, later, refuses to sign the deed. Can she be compelled to join in the deed?

A. Yes. Although her name does not appear in the body of the agreement, she has indicated an intention to be bound by the agreement by signing it.

77. Q. If a broker accepts a check for $1,000 from a buyer, who signs an agreement of sale, which is also executed by the seller, and then the buyer stops payment on the check, is the agreement of sale void?

A. No; the contract came into being when the agreement of sale was signed by both principal parties. The check is incidental or collateral to the contract and has no effect upon its validity.

78. Q. A broker prepared an agreement of sale, which recites a $1,000 cash deposit received. Actually, he received a 10-day promissory note to his order, which is unpaid at maturity. Upon ascertaining these facts, the seller decides to renounce the deal. Can he do so?

A. No; the buyer can hold the seller to the agreement as long as the buyer fully performs his part of the deal at the closing.

79. Q. A broker negotiates a real estate deal upon his oral promise that he will find "suitable or comparable" quarters for the seller. He fails to do so. Is he liable on his oral promise which is not contained in the agreement of sale?

A. Yes; the broker is personally responsible in damages to the seller for his failure to perform his promise.

80. Q. In order to prevent the assignment of an agreement of sale, what clause should be included?

A. "It is hereby agreed that rights under the within agreement are not assignable."

81. Q. A recorded agreement of sale constitutes a cloud on the title. How may it be removed?

A. 1. By a deed from vendor to vendee.
2. By a quit claim deed from vendee to vendor or vendor's purchaser.
3. By court decree.
4. By instrument of extinguishment.

82. Q. What is meant by equity when used in connection with real estate transactions?

A. The margin of value which the owner possesses between the price of the property and the indebtedness against it.

83. Q. A broker, John Steele, negotiates a real estate deal between Henry Cole, seller, and Marvin Hunter, buyer, at $30,000. The broker obtains a $2,500 deposit. The agreement contains a "time is of the essence" clause, and to be closed on March 27, 1974. Due to difficulties in obtaining financing, the settlement date is mutually postponed on several occasions to June 17, 1974. Hunter desires a further continuance and Cole refuses. Hunter demands the $2,500 deposit. What should the broker do?
A. Steele should invite a suit and interpleas, turning the $2,500 over to the court and file a claim for a commission.

84. Q. Identify the following, whether realty or personalty: (1) growing corn, (2) cut logs, (3) growing wheat, (4) growing meadow grass, (5) nursery trees, (6) window shades, (7) electric chandeliers, (8) linoleum glued to floor, (9) potted plants, (10) gas grate setting in fireplace.
A. 1-2-3-5-6-9-10 are personalty; 4-7-8 are realty.

85. Q. Where an offer has been mailed to the seller, is there a contract if the seller mails his acceptance, and due to some delay in the mail service, it does not reach the buyer for 15 days?
A. Yes. The contract came into being when the letter of acceptance was mailed. The mail service is considered the agent of the buyer since he used that medium in communicating the offer.

86. Q. What effect does an alteration to an agreement of sale by the broker or seller, after execution by buyer, have upon the instrument?
A. The buyer can repudiate the contract. Even if the alteration appears harmless, it may have some effect as to the buyer's desires and prejudice his purposes.

87. Q. What is the difference between cancellation and rescission of a contract of sale?
A. Cancellation is by mutual consent; rescission is by court action.

88. Q. Does a counter proposition enjoy the same rights of withdrawal (before acceptance) as the original offer to purchase?
A. Yes, since a counter proposition constitutes a new offer.

89. Q. What is meant by "earnest money"?
A. The deposit money paid by a prospective purchaser at the time of making his offer to purchase, as evidence of good faith. Also termed "hand money."

90. Q. D. Smith makes a written offer to purchase R. Lincoln's property for $18,000, with $1,000 down, $1,000 in 30 days and balance in 90 days. Lincoln makes a counter proposition to sell for $19,000 with terms of $2,000 down and balance in 60 days. This proposition is refused by Smith. Lincoln then agrees to accept Smith's original proposition, but Smith now refuses to deal. Is there a valid contract?
A. No. A counter proposition is the same as a rejection. An offer, once rejected, is gone forever, unless the other party is willing to reinstate it.

91. Q. To whose advantage is it to prorate taxes and rent from an income property as of the possession date, rather than the closing date?
A. Seller. He will continue to receive rents, which should exceed taxes and expenses.

92. Q. A husband and wife buy a home and take title, as such. Shortly afterwards, the husband leaves and his whereabouts are unknown. The wife cannot afford to keep up the payments. Can she sell the property?
A. No; unless she has him declared legally dead after the years specified in the statute.

93. Q. If a broker has good reason to doubt the competency of his owner, due to age and senility, and the owner wishes to sell, what protective steps can the broker take to avoid difficulty with some members of owner's family?
A. Have an interested party petition the court to appoint a guardian for the owner and have guardian sign agreement.

94. Q. In selling a home, can the seller take with him the bedroom unit air-conditioner, or does it belong to buyer?
A. The unit is considered the personal property of the seller.

95. Q. John Davis, 21 years of age, signs an agreement to purchase a house. He is drafted

before the deal is closed. He writes the owner to cancel the deal. Will he succeed?

A. Yes; as a practical matter. He is protected by law from any court proceeding on the contract during his military service. Rather than tie up the property indefinitely, the owner's interests would be served by selling the property to another party.

96. Q. An agreement of sale recites that the Friend Real Estate Co. is the broker in the deal and the owner agrees to pay him a commission of 7 per cent. Can Friend maintain a court action for a commission on the strength of this clause?

A. Yes; court decisions in Pennsylvania and Virginia have so held.

97. Q. A listing agreement dated Jan. 2, 1972 is given to a broker for 90 days. Will it expire in three months?

A. No. It will expire at midnight on the 90th day from Jan. 2.

98. Q. Can a salesman be held liable for earnest money that was turned over to his broker, who dies insolvent?

A. No. The salesman is required to turn over all deposit money to his employing broker.

99. Q. Clayton lists property with Moore Realty for $15,000. He obtains a prospect at $13,700. Clayton uses the offer of $13,700 to sell the property to his own prospect at $14,200. Is the broker entitled to a commission?

A. No. This is one of the "risks of the trade."

100. Q. Under what circumstances can a broker represent a buyer?

A. There is nothing to prevent a broker from representing a buyer and look to the *buyer* for a commission. However, he cannot, at the same time, represent the seller, unless both parties know it and agree to it.

101. Q. Should a broker quote any price other than the listing price to a prospect?

A. No. He can entertain a lower price offered by a prospect and submit it to the owner and thus negotiate.

102. Q. Can there be a verbal exclusive listing contract?

A. Yes; but it is difficult to prove and very unsatisfactory. In states requiring listings to be in writing, the answer is No.

103. Q. Is an agreement between salesman and broker legal that states that if salesman leaves the broker's employ, he will never again engage in the real estate business in that state?

A. No. Contracts in restraint of trade must be reasonable as to area and as to time.

104. Q. Alice Ritter agrees to sell her residence to James O'Donnell for $17,000 and agreements, dated June 17, 1974 are signed to that effect. The sale was to be closed on September 12, 1974. On August 14, 1974, O'Donnell agreed to sell the property to Steven Hill for $18,750 and assigned his agreement with Ritter to Hill. On September 14, 1974, Ritter is willing to deed to O'Donnell, but she is unwilling to do business with Hill. Can Hill enforce O'Donnell's agreement?

A. Yes. An agreement of sale is assignable, unless it contains a clause to the contrary.

105. Q. Saxman signs an agreement to sell vacant ground of 2 $1/2$ acres to Troop for $39,000, on June 23, 1974. Deal to be closed on September 10, 1974. The property is in a city zone which permits residential and commercial building use. Troop expects to erect retail store units, since none presently exist in the area. On August 9, 1973, the municipality adopts an ordinance, restricting the subject area to residences only. Can Troop rescind the deal because of the zoning change?

A. No. When he signed the contract to purchase the land, he became the equitable owner and as such is bound by the zoning change which affects the property.

106. Q. How could Troop have protected himself in the above case?

A. Troop should have included a clause in the agreement as to the proposed commercial use,—that the seller knew that the property was being purchased for that use.

107. Q. Blake enters into an agreement with Cobb on January 2, 1974, to sell a 3 story building for $55,000. The building has been vacant for three years and in need of major repairs. The deal is to be closed on March 28, 1974. On March 27, 1974, Blake receives a notice from the authorities, citing numerous violations of the housing

code and requiring correction immediately. Cobb refuses to close on that account and demands a refund of his deposit money. Will Cobb succeed?

A. No. Cobb became the equitable owner of the agreement on January 2, 1974, and it is his responsibility to make the corrections.

108. Q. Saxton is the owner of a dwelling, which he is selling to Ritter for $24,500. There is a mortgage debt against the property in the amount of $16,750, held by Mortgage Finance Co., in the original amount of $19,500, dated December 6, 1970. Is it necessary to obtain approval of the mortgagee for the sale, since Ritter is taking over the mortgage?

A. No. The property is security for the debt and the seller, Saxton, continues liable for payment of the debt.

109. Q. Is it improper for a broker to loan his commission to the buyer for use as the down payment ?

A. Yes. The practice would be unethical and cast doubts that he has an "able" buyer.

110. Q. In contracting with a builder for the construction of a new home, what precautions can the buyer take to protect his interest?

A. 1. Check contractor's responsibility, credit, and owners for whom he has built homes.
2. Require a performance bond.
3. Obtain mechanic's lien insurance from a title company.
4. Obtain a no-lien contract from the builder and file the same in the proper county office.
5. Make graduated payments to the builder at different intervals as the work proceeds.
6. If an expensive home, engage an architect to supervise the construction.

111. Q. Whom would you credit and for how many months or fraction thereof, if the seller paid this year's taxes and the settlement was held on April 15?

A. The seller; 8 1/2 months.

112. Q. Whom would you credit and for how many months if the taxes were not paid at the settlement on June 20?

A. The buyer; 5 2/3 months.

True and False

1. An agreement of sale is assignable. **T** F
2. An agreement of sale must always be closed on the date specified in the agreement. T **F**
3. The purpose of the statute of frauds was passed to prevent perjury. **T** F
4. An offer to purchase or an earnest money receipt can have the same effect as an agreement of sale. **T** F
5. Once an offer to purchase is signed by the buyer, and is signed by the broker, there is an enforceable contract. T **F**
6. Under the law, every agreement of sale is assignable, even though a clause states it is non-assignable. T **F**
7. Valuable consideration means that there must be a money consideration. T **F**
8. The marital status of the parties to an agreement of sale should be stated. **T** F
9. Every agreement must provide for a monetary consideration, or it is invalid. T **F**
10. The agreement of a minor to purchase a lot is voidable by the infant. **T** F
11. A buyer is entitled to the prompt refund of his deposit money if he withdraws his offer before the owner accepts it. **T** F
12. Hand money means the same as deposit money. **T** F
13. An offer to purchase is sometimes called a preliminary contract. **T** F
14. Provided the broker and the buyer agree, it is permissible not to cash the earnest money check until the deal is closed. T **F**
15. If agreements of sale are signed between the seller and buyer, it is not necessary

for the broker to prove that the buyer is ready, able and willing to buy. T F

16. The licensee can rely upon the seller's statement that the city will build a public garage next door to the listed property within one year and repeats this to a prospect. T F
17. A purchaser under a land contract usually takes possession of the premises. T F
18. In any real estate transaction, the broker is empowered to sign a contract of sale for the seller. T F
19. A contract for the purchase of real estate for cash may be assigned to another. T F
20. A vendor of real estate is sometimes called the seller. T F
21. Federal Revenue Stamps are not required on an agreement. T F
22. Either the salesman or broker must witness the purchase contract to make it valid. T F
23. The terms "option" and "listing" have the same meaning. T F
24. Title insurance offers protection against loss by fire if property is destroyed before the deal is closed. T F
25. An option contract must be bound by a consideration. T F
26. Conditional land contracts of sale may be assigned. T F
27. Chattel and personal property mean the same thing. T F
28. Deposit money held by a broker must be kept in a fireproof safe. T F
29. The amount of the consideration determines the amount of the earnest money deposit. T F
30. Agreements of sale are subject to the government "freeze" on wages and prices. T F
31. A real estate broker is not required to give the buyer a copy of the closing statement until the deed is recorded. T F
32. The earnest money check should be made payable to broker instead of to seller. T F
33. A broker has authority to acknowledge a purchase agreement since he is a neutral party. T F
34. Where the sole owner is a married woman, the husband's signature is necessary on a contract of sale. T F
35. Land divided into 6 parcels for purpose of sale is known as a subdivision. T F
36. Chattel is another name for the wife's interest in her husband's property. T F
37. Marginal land is land on the edge of a real estate development. T F
38. In an option, the optionor has the right to collect rents on the property during the life of the option. T F
39. A broker should close the deals negotiated by his salesmen. T F
40. The full consideration in any real estate deal must always be in legal tender. T F
41. A person, other than an attorney at law, may be given power of attorney. T F
42. Contracts to exchange real property need not be in writing to be enforceable. T F
43. A sales agreement must be acknowledged in order to be valid. T F
44. The purchaser cannot rescind the deal and receive his earnest money after the seller has orally approved the deal. T F
45. Real estate sold on "conditional sale contract" or "land contract" can be subject to liens for indebtedness of the seller. T F
46. There is no difference between a void and a voidable contract. T F
47. Any alteration to an executed contract of sale is proper, if it is initialed by all the parties. T F
48. It is important that the broker sign the contract of sale for real estate. T F
49. A sales agreement takes effect from the date it is signed by the buyer. T F
50. When a prospect submits to a broker an offer to buy real estate, the prospect cannot withdraw his offer until the owner has had an opportunity to act upon it. T F
51. Both parties to an agreement of sale should receive signed copies of the agreement. T F
52. An agreement of sale to be valid and binding must
    1. be entered into by competent parties. T F
    2. be bound by a consideration. T F

3. possess mutuality. T F
4. represent an actual meeting of minds. T F
5. cover a legal and moral act. T F
6. be oral. T F

53. A seller under an agreement of sale is known as the vendee. T F
54. One who has taken an option on certain real estate is bound to complete the purchase of property. T F
55. A contract of sale must be accompanied by a deposit to bind the transaction. T F
56. It is essential that a deal be closed on the date specified in the agreement. T F
57. The real estate broker is not a principal party to an agreement of sale. T F
58. An agreement of sale need only be signed by the vendor if the vendee pays a deposit. T F
59. A contract for the exchange of real estate must be in writing. T F
60. There must be at least three persons and a witness to form a binding agreement of sale. T F
61. An agreement of sale must be acknowledged by the vendor in order to be binding. T F
62. Upon the sale of a piece of property, the seller may remove and take with him:
    1. the gas range in the kitchen. T F
    2. a chandelier. T F
    3. shrubbery bordering a walk. T F
    4. the hall carpet. T F
    5. the furnace shovel and poker. T F
    6. the living room lamp. T F
    7. the awnings (specially fitted). T F
    8. gas or electric water heater. T F
63. An option should always be signed by the optionee. T F
64. A "bill of sale" is the instrument by which title to real estate is conveyed. T F
65. Once an agreement of sale is signed, the broker may file a lien for his commission, if not paid. T F
66. An attorney-in-fact who signs an agreement of sale must be an attorney at law. T F
67. Restrictions as to the use of property in an agreement are encumbrances but are not liens. T F
68. Fence posts are personal property. T F
69. An "abstract of title" guarantees a clear title. T F
70. An equity represents the actual amount of money a purchaser has paid on the property. T F
71. An option for which no consideration is given is not enforceable. T F
72. A power of attorney to sign an agreement of sale can be given only to duly qualified attorneys at law. T F
73. If a prospective purchaser revokes his offer in writing before he has received an accepted copy, signed by the seller, of the offer to purchase, he is entitled to the return of his deposit. T F
74. The sale of a property for cash automatically cancels a lease for less than one year. T F
75. An oral agreement for the sale of real estate, never reduced to writing, usually cannot be enforced. T F
76. An agreement of sale is subject to a zoning change made before the deal is closed. T F
77. Where money is actually paid as consideration for an option, the option cannot be assigned by the holder thereof. T F
78. A purchaser cannot rescind the deal and get his earnest money back after the seller has orally approved the deal. T F
79. If the earnest money received by a broker is represented by a note, it is essential that the earnest money receipt show that fact. T F
80. A tractor used to till a farm is considered real estate. T F

81. If a seller is married, it is the duty of the broker to procure the signature of the seller's husband or wife on the agreement of sale. T F
82. If a *slight* alteration is made in the earnest money receipt after it is signed by the purchaser, this does not invalidate the earnest money receipt. T F
83. Permanent buildings on real estate are not personalty. T F
84. Once the owner accepts an offer to purchase even on different terms from those contained in the offer, there is a binding contract. T F
85. The seller should pay for the continuation of an abstract of title. T F
86. The buyer should pay for an attorney's examination of the title. T F
87. The sale of land does not include buildings unless expressly stated. T F
88. A purchaser buying real estate under a land contract does not usually have title to the property. T F
89. A valid written sales contract is binding even if the seller dies. T F
90. An agreement signed on Sunday is enforceable. T F
91. If a person signs a joint and several note with other persons, it is possible that he may become liable for the entire sum of the note. T F
92. A contract of sale must be accompanied by a deposit to bind the transaction. T F
93. "Trade fixtures" means the brands, labels, names of products and the good will of a business. T F
94. There must be an agreement of sale in order to bring action for specific performance. T F
95. When a property is sold, all insurance policies then in effect should be immediately cancelled and new policies written. T F
96. An agreement of sale, which requires the purchaser to place his mortgage through the broker who negotiated the deed, is contrary to good ethics. T F
97. One who has taken an option on certain real estate may refuse to complete the purchase of the property. T F
98. If property is held by husband and wife as tenants by the entirety, neither may agree to sell to a third party his or her interest separately. T F
99. The reason for securing a deposit on the sale of real property is to guarantee the broker his commission in the event of a sale. T F
100. Unless expressly released in writing by the vendor, the vendee making an assignment of his interest in a land contract is not released from his liability for the unpaid balance of the contract. T F
101. When a husband is buying real property, it is not necessary for the wife to sign the contract to purchase as the husband's signature binds both of them. T F
102. Apportionment of taxes means prorating taxes between vendor and vendee as of time of closing. T F
103. All rights under an agreement of sale are merged in the subsequent deed. T F
104. The seller is always entitled to keep the earnest money if the buyer defaults without cause. T F
105. A tender of deed and demand for payment of the consideration is necessary in order to place the buyer in default. T F
106. Any item of movable property is called a chattel. T F
107. The closing on a sales agreement should be attended by the broker and not by the sales person, who made the deal. T F
108. A contract for deed and a land installment purchase contract are the same. T F
109. Anticipatory repudiation means that the buyer has not yet made up his mind to complete the deal. T F
110. The statute of frauds relates to unconscionable conduct by public officials. T F
111. A broker, employed by an owner "to sell" his property, has authority to sign a binding agreement for the owner. T F
112. If the buyer notifies the seller that he will not complete the deal, the buyer is entitled to a refund of his deposit money. T F

113. Time in an option is of the essence. T F
114. A deposit money check should be made payable to the sales person, who made the deal, and not to the seller. T F
115. Communication of the acceptance of an offer to purchase is essential to have an enforceable contract. T F
116. A counter-offer is the same as a rejection of the original offer. T F
117. There is a difference between a void and a voidable contract. T F
118. When title to real property is transferred, the insurance policies on the property are usually prorated at the closing. T F
119. An owner can refuse to sign a sales agreement for a store unless the buyer is sui juris. T F
120. A listing agreement should provide that deposit money shall be held by the broker in escrow. T F
121. Once the seller signs the sales agreement, he cannot later demand that the down payment be turned over to him. T F
122. A broker is not liable for any misstatements that he makes because he is not a party of the sales agreement. T F
123. A broker is personally responsible, if he promises the buyer that he will procure a mortgage and is unable to do so. T F
124. If the sale is contingent upon buyer selling his present home, the broker should include that fact in sales contract. T F
125. A broker is within his rights in accepting a "postdated" check even if sales agreement acknowledges cash. T F
126. It is acceptable practice for a broker to tell a salesman to attend the closing in his stead, even if the salesman did not negotiate the deal. T F
127. The broker attends the closing only to receive the commission or balance due him. T F
128. The broker attends the closing to settle any disputes that may arise between seller and buyer. T F
129. A broker should not compromise his commission claim in order to resolve a financial dispute between seller and buyer. T F
130. A broker cannot collect an earned commission if it is contingent upon a settlement, which does not materialize. T F
131. An offer-to-buy may be withdrawn after the prospective purchaser and the seller have signed the writing, but before the seller's signed copy is delivered to the buyer. T F
132. An habitual drunkard is considered insincere and his contractual capacity limited accordingly. T F
133. An oral contract to sell real estate is not void but unenforceable. T F
134. If a buyer defaults upon a contract of sale, the broker should turn the entire earnest money deposit over to the seller forthwith. T F
135. When the seller and buyer have an irreconcilable dispute as to the terms of a contract of sale and the deal is not closed, the broker should pay the earnest money deposit into court. T F
136. A broker should not advise a buyer as to his legal rights where there is a dispute between buyer and seller. T F
137. A listing agreement must be signed by both buyer and seller in order to be enforceable. T F
138. Hand money, deposit money and earnest money mean the same thing. T F
139. The sale of lands does not include buildings unless specifically stated. T F
140. Every state has a statute of frauds which requires real estate contracts to be in writing in order to be enforceable. T F
141. An acceptance of an offer to purchase after expiration of the time limit of the offer constitutes a "counter proposition." T F

142. The prime purpose for a broker attending a real estate closing is to obtain his commission T F
143. Where the buyer withdraws his offer after he has signed a contract of sale, he is liable to the broker for his commission. T F
144. A subdivision may consist of five or more lots. T F
145. If an agreement of sale does not have a date specified for closing, it is void. T F
146. Where the description in the contract of sale gives a street address and number, but no city, it is void. T F
147. Where a single woman, who is engaged to be married, executes a sales contract for her own property, it is necessary to have her fiance join. T F
148. An inmate of a home for the aged cannot execute a real estate sales contract without an order of court. T F
149. A land purchase contract is generally used to purchase real estate by people of limited means. T F
150. A buyer may rescind an agreement of sale, where the broker, without authority of the seller, has misrepresented the property. T F
151. Where the broker knows the property is infested with termites, and fails to disclose that hidden fact to the buyer, the latter can rescind the contract. T F
152. Rescission or avoidance of a contract is addressed to the equity side of the court. T F
153. A judgment or cognovit note, payable on demand, is the same as a cash earnest money deposit. T F
154. At the closing of a real estate, the seller can refuse to accept the buyer's personal check in payment of the consideration price. T F
155. A check from the buyer on a building and loan association account is acceptable as an earnest money deposit. T F
156. A broker should place a "SOLD" sign on a property when the agreement of sale is signed by both buyer and seller. T F
157. The vendee pays the cost of preparing the mortgage or deed of trust papers. T F
158. A broker is entitled to a fee for preparing the mortgage papers. T F
159. Action by a buyer for specific performance of a contract of sale must be brought within two years from the specified date for performance. T F
160. Where the closing date in a sales agreement is more than three months in advance, the broker should insist upon a much larger down payment than usual. T F
161. One co-owner can bind his other co-owner by signing an agreement of sale. T F
162. If the date in an agreement of sale is missing, the contract is void. T F
163. In signing a binder, the purchaser does not obligate himself for a future purchase agreement. T F
164. A broker can accept a note as a deposit so long as he is willing to make up the note, if unpaid. T F
165. An article can change from personalty to realty and then back to personalty. T F
166. Earnest money is money paid to close a real estate transaction. T F
167. In a land contract, the purchaser receives a deed and takes possession immediately. T F
168. The listing contract is usually the first instrument the buyer signs in purchasing property. T F
169. Trade fixtures are usually so affixed to the property that they become part of the property and may not be removed. T F
170. Property classed as real property can become personal property. T F
171. A thirty-day month is usually used in prorating real estate transactions. T F
172. A purchaser usually takes possession under a land contract. T F
173. Where a conflict arises, the written part of a contract usually prevails over the printed part. T F
174. The sale of land does not include the buildings unless expressly stated. T F
175. When rugs and drapes are included in the sale of a residence, title to these articles

is usually transferred by a chattel mortgage. T F

176. A salesman receiving a deposit of earnest money should turn it over to the owner. T F
177. A buyer under a land contract who erects improvements may remove the same if he defaults on his contract. T F
178. An escrow holder is considered the agent for both the buyer and the seller. T F
179. Fixtures, shelves, counters and merchandise in a grocery store do not pass with a transfer of the real property. T F
180. A bill of sale is used to convey title to appurtenances. T F
181. Hand money paid upon the signing of a contract of sale is called an option. T F
182. An agreement of sale is usually more detailed than an offer to purchase. T F
183. Under a land contract, the seller retains title until certain stipulated conditions are performed. T F
184. "Good will" has value but is never carried as an asset. T F
185. The salesman who negotiated the deal should attend the closing in order to collect the commission. T F
186. Under an exclusive right-to-sell listing contract, the broker has authority to sign an agreement of sale for the owner. T F
187. The consideration for a deed must always be shown in dollars and cents. T F
188. The sale of land does not include the buildings unless expressly stated. T F
189. The buyer pays for the abstract examination. T F
190. The broker pays for the loan closing costs. T F
191. An agreement of sale that requires the buyer to place his fire insurance through the selling broker as long as he owns the property would be considered unethical. T F
192. A contract of sale involving financial responsibility is not assignable. T F
193. Unexpired premiums on an insurance policy is a debit to the purchaser at time of settlement. T F
194. Unpaid city taxes, at date of settlement, is a credit item to the buyer. T F
195. In a purchase money mortgage, the buyer is the mortgagee. T F
196. The buyer is the vendee in an agreement of sale. T F
197. An owner is the optionee in an option. T F
198. A contract calling for a March 1, 1974 closing date must be closed on that date or the buyer forfeits his deposit money. T F
199. After terms of an escrow are agreed upon, they may not be later modified by mutual agreements. T F
200. A quit claim deed from vendee to vendor may be used to extinguish an agreement of sale. T F
201. A land instrument contract and an option are the same. T F
202. It is not necessary for all officers in a corporation to sign an agreement to sell real property. T F
203. Ordinarily, an optionee may collect rents on the optioned property, during the life of the option. T F
204. A purchaser may rescind the transaction and recover his earnest money even after the seller orally approved the sale. T F
205. The optionor can enforce the terms of an option contract by legal action. T F
206. $1 is sufficient consideration to support an option to purchase a property worth $1,000,000. T F
207. Under an installment land purchase contract, the seller upon default can enter judgment for the balance due. T F
208. An option is a bilateral contract binding upon both parties. T F
209. An agreement of sale controls the contents of the deed. T F
210. The first instrument a buyer signs in a real estate transaction is usually the offer to purchase. T F
211. Good consideration is always in monetary terms. T F
212. In order to make a joint tenancy deed, it is necessary for the agreement of sale

to so provide. T F

213. An agreement of sale may be enforceable by court action, even if no earnest money deposit is paid. T F
214. Acceptance is to an offer what a lighted match is to a charge of gun powder, in that it produces something which cannot be undone or recalled. T F
215. There is a difference between fraud and misrepresentation. T F
216. Co-insurance means that husband and wife are co-owners of an insurance policy. T F
217. A good way for a broker to obtain listings is to advertise free appraisals. T F
218. A licensed broker has the legal right to render an opinion on the validity of title to real estate. T F
219. If a sale is contingent upon a buyer selling his present home, this fact should not be included in the agreement of sale. T F
220. If the buyer is to obtain a mortgage, the agreement should specify amount, interest and term. T F
221. A post dated check, which is not paid, voids an executed agreement of sale. T F
222. Title insurance protects the buyer, if the property is destroyed by fire, before the deal is closed. T F
223. Gross inadequacy of the consideration price is always ground for rescission of an agreement of sale. T F
224. A water softener apparatus is real estate. T F
225. Laches and statute of limitations are the same. T F
226. An oral agreement, in the presence of two witnesses, accompanied by a handshake, will be enforceable. T F
227. A judgment note, endorsed by the mortgagee, is legal tender. T F
228. A contract for sale of real estate differs from a contract of sale of an automobile in that it must be in writing. T F
229. Consideration for the sale of real estate must be in money. T F
230. Time of the essence clause in an agreement of sale means that it must be signed on the date in the contract. T F
231. The real estate broker is an important signatory to the agreement of sale which he negotiates. T F
232. An option may be extended by mutual consent, without any additional consideration. T F
233. The terms in the agreement of sale control the terms of the deed. T F
234. If a dispute arises between seller and buyer, after agreements are signed, the broker should recommend that the buyer consult the broker's attorney. T F
235. Where a property is under contract by the owner, a widow, and she remarries, a broker can recover his commission, if husband refuses to sign deed. T F
236. If liquidated damages are construed to be a forfeiture, they will not be enforced. T F
237. A recorded agreement of sale constitutes an encumbrance on title. T F
238. Only a court of law can void a recorded agreement of sale. T F
239. A deed delivered by the vendor to vendee will, per se, extinguish a recorded agreement of sale between the same parties. T F
240. A seller can refuse to accept an assignee of the purchaser for any reason. T F
241. The statute of frauds prohibits assignment of agreements of sale. T F
242. A penalty clause is the same as a liquidated damage clause. T F
243. Courts abhor penalties in agreements of sale. T F
244. A broker, who is a notary public, should not take the acknowledgment of the seller in a deal he negotiated. T F
245. Disputes in regard to controversial terms in an agreement should be referred to the Real Estate Commission. T F
246. A broker should recommend that the buyer consult an attorney before he signs an agreement of sale. T F
247. A builder, *impliedly* warrants that the house he built is habitable. T F

248. A buyer can recover only deposit money and expenses where seller fraudulently breaches agreement of sale. T F
249. A buyer assumes risk of change in zoning, after agreement of sale is signed. T F
250. Threat of a law suit constitutes duress. T F
251. A "SOLD" sign is good advertising for the broker. T F
252. The consideration price and the earnest money deposit will appear in the same column of the closing statement. T F
253. Prorations of taxes, rents and insurance are made from the date the agreement of sale was signed. T F
254. The seller is charged with the marginal release of lien. T F
255. The buyer pays for preparing deed. T F
256. Tax on deed is paid by seller. T F
257. Pay-off figure on existing deed of trust is a credit to seller. T F
258. Buyer pays for recording deed of trust. T F
259. Loan commission is paid by buyer. T F
260. Survey charge is paid by seller. T F
261. Pro-rate clause of unpaid taxes is a credit to seller. T F
262. Credit report fee is a credit to buyer. T F

Multiple Choice

1. An agreement of sale, to be enforceable upon the owner, can be:
   (a) signed by the broker, for the owner, in the owner's absence.
   (b) signed by the broker, upon owner's verbal authorization.
   (c) signed by the recorded owner.
   (d) signed by the broker, for the owner by telephone call from the owner, in the buyer's presence.
2. An agreement of sale is a contract
   (a) between buyer and broker.
   (b) between seller and broker.
   (c) between buyer and seller.
   (d) between seller, buyer and mortgagee.
3. A buyer purchased a new dwelling from a builder. The contract of sale contained a provision that the builder would hold the buyer harmless "against seepage through foundation walls." After the buyer moved in, damage was caused from water coming through a door installed in the foundation wall leading to the rear yard. Under these circumstances, the buyer can:
   I. rescind the deal.
   II. recover expenses to make the door water tight.
   (a) I only.
   (b) II only.
   (c) both I and II.
   (d) neither I nor II.
4. Adams sells his home, which is 22 years old, to Baker in June 1973. Baker does not check the furnace nor does Adams make any representations concerning it. In January 1974, the furnace "quits." Under these circumstances,
   I. Baker must pay for a new furnace.
   II. Baker can collect from Adams the "junk" value of the old furnace.
   (a) I only.
   (b) II only.
   (c) both I and II.
   (d) neither I nor II.
5. Where a buyer causelessly defaults, the question whether to forfeit the earnest money deposit should be decided by
   I. the broker.
   II. the seller.

(a) I only.
(b) II only.
(c) both I and II.
(d) neither I nor II.

6. A statement of anticipated closing costs should be presented before signing of an agreement of sale
I. to the buyer.
II. to the seller.
(a) I only.
(b) II only.
(c) both I and II.
(d) neither I nor II.

7. Once an agreement of sale is signed, the purchaser has
(a) legal title.
(b) equitable title.
(c) ostensible title.
(d) naked title.

8. An earnest money deposit check should be made payable to
(a) owner.
(b) salesman.
(c) broker.
(d) mortgagee.

9. Adams executes a contract for the sale of his dwelling to Berger. Thirty-one days before the closing, Adams dies. The result is
(a) the deal is cancelled.
(b) Berger can compel Adams' executor or heirs to complete the sale.
(c) the deal is "in limbo" for one year.
(d) the deal is voidable at option of deceased's heirs.

10. A seller of real estate is also known as the
(a) vendee.
(b) grantor.
(c) vendor.
(d) grantee.

11. A charge against a property owner to cover the proportionate cost of a street paving is
(a) an ad valorem tax.
(b) a county tax.
(c) an assessment.
(d) equitable obligation.

12. Broker "A", in cooperation with Broker "B", made a sale, in which no deposit money was paid. The deal was closed and the buyer gave the broker the full amount due. The broker paid the net proceeds to the seller at the same time. The balance should be:
(a) Deposited in "A's" regular business account.
(b) Balance due "B" should be paid in cash.
(c) The balance should be run through "A's" trust account.
(d) "B's" share of commission should be drawn by "A" to "B's" trust account.

13. When legal title is transferred as the result of the sale of real estate, which is encumbered by a trust deed (a mortgage), it is always necessary
(a) to obtain the consent of the mortgagee.
(b) to pay off the mortgagee.
(c) for the grantor to deliver a deed.
(d) to completely refinance.

14. Gary, a Nebraska broker represents to Hill, a former mill worker from Steelton, Pa., that the 200 acre farm he is selling him is in good condition. In fact, it has been cash cropped

and the soil is in poor condition. Gary has been selling farms and ranches for 16 years and is a neighbor of the farm's owner. Upon learning the true facts, Hill can:
(a) Rescind the deal.
(b) Can do nothing.
(c) Keep the farm, but have the court reduce the price.
(d) File a complaint with the federal loan board.

15. Rushton enters into a contract for deed of a tract of land in Miami with the owner Alton. The consideration price is $40,000 and Rushton pays $5,000 on account. The balance is to be paid in installments of $300 a month, with interest at 8 per cent. This land contract is
I. In the nature of a purchase money mortgage.
II. In the nature of a warranty in future.
(a) I only.
(b) II only.
(c) Both I and II.
(d) Neither I nor II.

16. Broker Adams negotiated a transaction between Morgan, seller, and Ziegler, buyer. The agreement of sale provided for earnest money of $1,500, and that the date for performance, May 1, 1974, was "of the essence of the contract." At the oral request of the buyer, the broker agreed to an extension for performance to May 15, 1974. On May 10, 1974, the seller claimed that the agreement was breached and demanded the $1,500 deposit.
(a) The seller is entitled to the $1,500 deposit.
(b) The seller is not entitled to the $1,500 deposit.
(c) The buyer is entitled to a refund of the $1,500 deposit, less one-half of the broker's commission.
(d) The broker is entitled to his commission from the deposit money, and the balance is due the buyer.

17. Williams agreed to sell his residence to Gale for $40,000. Gale gave Williams a check for $1,000 which bore a notation "part payment on 2117 Bedford Avenue, Louisville, balance $39,000." Gale verbally agreed to assume an existing mortgage in the amount of $26,250. A week later, Gale reneged on the deal and demanded the return of his $1,000. Under these circumstances:
I. Williams can keep the $1,000.
II. Williams can compel Gale to complete the deal.
(a) I only.
(b) II only.
(c) both I and II.
(d) neither I nor II.

18. Bennett entered into an agreement of sale to sell his home to Randall. Deal to be closed on June 21, 1974. Time was of the essence and the agreement was subject to the buyer obtaining a mortgage. Randall made a $1,000 deposit on the purchase price. Since Randall was unable to obtain a mortgage by June 21, 1974, Bennett verbally agreed to extend the time for closing until August 1, 1974. Randall was still unable to obtain a loan by August 1, 1974. Randall demands the return of his $1,000. Under these circumstances:
(a) Randall can recover $1,000.
(b) Bennett can keep the $1,000.
(c) Randall can recover $1,000, less Bennett's expenses.
(d) Randall must continue efforts for a reasonable time to obtain financing.

19. Whenever all parties agree to the terms of a real estate contract, there has been
(a) legality of object.
(b) meeting of the minds.
(c) reality of consent.
(d) bilateral consideration.

20. At the time a buyer indicates he is ready to execute an agreement, the broker should obtain a
(a) trust deed.

(b) negotiable note.
(c) deposit.
(d) surety.

21. Unless there is a stipulation to the contrary, when real estate under a lease is sold, the lease
    (a) must be renewed.
    (b) is immediately cancelled.
    (c) remains binding on the new owner.
    (d) becomes a tenancy from month to month.
22. A property is listed with a broker for $17,500. He receives an offer from "A" at $15,000 cash, with closing in 90 days. An offer from "B" at $16,250, subject to the buyer obtaining a mortgage for $14,000; an offer from "C" at $16,900, subject to the owner taking back a purchase money mortgage for $15,000; an offer from "D" for $14,000, with closing in 30 days. The broker should submit to the owner only
    (a) the offer of "A."
    (b) the offer of "B."
    (c) the offer of "C."
    (d) the offer of "D."
    (e) all of the offers.
23. A broker receives a $5,000 deposit on January 2, 1974 on a $40,000 property, the deal to be closed on July 2, 1974. He should deposit the money:
    (a) in his checking account.
    (b) in his interest bearing savings account.
    (c) in his escrow account.
    (d) G.M.A.C. notes.
24. A real estate salesman, after receiving a deposit of earnest money, should immediately
    (a) turn it over to the seller.
    (b) deposit it in his personal account until the closing.
    (c) give it to his broker to deposit in a trustee account.
    (d) turn it over to seller's attorney.
25. Ames, a prospective purchaser, writes a letter to Brown on January 7, 1974, offering to buy certain described real estate owned by Brown for $20,000. Brown replies promptly by letter stating "I accept your offer contained in letter of January 7, 1974." Which of the following describes the situation?
    (a) There is an offer but no acceptance.
    (b) There is a valid contract between Ames and Brown.
    (c) There is an acceptance but no offer.
    (d) There is no contract between the parties.
26. Once the real estate transaction is closed, the closing statement, approved by seller and buyer should be
    I. recorded.
    II. filed with the mortgagee.
        (a) I only.
        (b) II. Only.
        (c) both I and II.
        (d) neither I nor II.
27. Tender of deed to the buyer is not necessary, where
    I. time is of the essence of the agreement.
    II. there has been an anticipatory repudiation.
        (a) I only.
        (b) II only.
        (c) both I and II.
        (d) neither I nor II.
28. When an agreement of sale is signed, the seller has
    I. equitable title.

II. naked title.
(a) I only.
(b) II only.
(c) both I and II.
(d) neither I nor II.

29. In pro-rating $200 rent paid for June 1974, agreements were signed on June 15, 1974, and the deal was closed on July 1, 1974, you would
(a) credit the buyer with $200.
(b) credit the buyer with nothing.
(c) charge the seller with $100 (half).
(d) charge the seller with $200.

30. A copy of the closing statement in a real estate transaction must be
(a) recorded.
(b) kept by the broker for 6 years.
(c) given to seller and buyer.
(d) given to the mortgagee.

31. Which of the following items should be included in the description of a sales agreement:
(a) Area of the house and floor plan.
(b) Legal description.
(c) City, street and number are sufficient.
(d) Names of adjoining property owners.

32. A promissory note for 60 days given to a salesman as an earnest money deposit under an agreement of sale
I. is acceptable with the broker's consent.
II. is acceptable with the mortgage lender's approval.
(a) I only.
(b) II only.
(c) Both I and II.
(d) Neither I or II.

33. Adams offers to sell his farm to Baker for $26,000. Baker makes a counter proposition to buy the farm at $25,000, provided Adams takes back a purchase money mortgage for $15,000 at 6% interest, maturity in 15 years. Adams refuses the offer and the same day sells the farm to Clay at $25,000, taking back a mortgage for $15,000 at 6% interest, payable in 5 years. The next day Baker accepts the original offer of Adams.
(a) Baker can compel Adams to convey to him.
(b) Baker cannot compel Adams to convey to him.
(c) Baker can record his agreement which would be a cloud on the title.
(d) Baker can compel Clay to assign his agreement to him.

34. An agreement of sale did not state when the transaction was to be consummated. The agreement is
(a) void.
(b) voidable at option of vendor.
(c) voidable at option of vendee.
(d) valid and enforceable, within a reasonable time.

35. One who has the right to sign the name of his principal to a contract of sale is
(a) a special agent.
(b) an optionee.
(c) an attorney-in-fact.
(d) an attorney at law.

36. When real property is sold on an installment contract, and a warranty deed to be delivered at a future date, the warranty deed should be placed in the custody of
(a) the real estate broker.
(b) the seller.
(c) the buyer.
(d) an escrow agent.

37. A purchaser, upon signing a contract of sale, has
    (a) equitable title.
    (b) a fee.
    (c) a legal title.
    (d) a reversionary title.
38. Which of the following instruments is not delivered to the buyer at the closing of the sale?
    (a) Deed.
    (b) Lease.
    (c) Affidavit of title.
    (d) Mortgage.
39. Under the usual form agreement of sale, the option to declare the deposit money forfeited belongs to
    (a) seller.
    (b) broker.
    (c) buyer.
    (d) Court of Equity.
40. A contract by which the owner agrees with another person that he shall have a right to buy the property at a fixed price within a certain time is called
    (a) an escrow agreement.
    (b) an exclusive.
    (c) an option.
    (d) the first right of refusal.
41. A purchaser's part ownership or interest in a parcel of real estate is called an
    (a) equality.
    (b) equity.
    (c) inheritance.
    (d) fee.
42. A property, owned by John Moore and Kay Moore, his wife, is being sold through Jay Stone, broker, to John Kottler. The buyer is giving a $1,000 judgment note. It should be made payable to
    (a) Jay Stone.
    (b) Jay Stone agent.
    (c) John Moore or Kay Moore, his wife.
    (d) John Moore and Kay Moore, his wife.
43. A contract of sale passes
    (a) an equitable title.
    (b) a fee simple title.
    (c) legal title.
    (d) an inchoate title.
44. To each sales agreement there must be
    (a) an offer and an acceptance.
    (b) earnest money payment.
    (c) notarial acknowledgment.
    (d) a recordation.
45. The tax on a given piece of real property is always determined by multiplying the tax rate by the
    (a) selling price.
    (b) assessed valuation of the property.
    (c) appraised valuation of the property.
46. When the contract for the sale of real property includes the sale of certain removable fixtures, such as refrigerators and radiator covers, upon delivery of the deed, the seller should also deliver a
    (a) bill of sale.
    (b) estoppel certificate.
    (c) chattel mortgage.

(d) satisfaction piece.

47. A broker, receiving a deposit of earnest money, should
    (a) tender it to the owner.
    (b) keep it, pending final closing of the deal.
    (c) use it to cover expenses on the sale.
    (d) deposit it in a trust account at the bank.
48. An agreement of sale becomes enforceable when:
    I. signed by the buyer.
    II. signed by the broker, as agent for the seller.
        (a) I only.
        (b) II only.
        (c) both I and II.
        (d) neither I nor II.
49. A licensed broker promises a buyer of a commercial property that a new pcst office will be built next door within six months. The post office is erected elsewhere.
    I. This is "puffing of goods."
    II. This constitutes a material misrepresentation.
        (a) I. Only.
        (b) II. Only.
        (c) both I and II.
        (d) neither I nor II.
50. The statute of frauds was passed to prevent
    (a) bribery.
    (b) forgery.
    (c) perjury.
    (d) embezzlement.
51. Where the buyer breaches an agreement of sale, the seller, under a recommended form of agreement can have, how many alternative remedies?
    (a) One.
    (b) Two.
    (c) Three.
    (d) Four.
52. If the seller breaches an agreement of sale because he cannot deliver good title, the buyer can recover
    (a) deposit money and expenses.
    (b) punitive damages.
    (c) exemplary damages.
    (d) full value of his bargain.
53. A broker negotiates a sale and receives a $1,000 post dated check (for 30 days) from the buyer. The broker should
    (a) deposit the check in his escrow account, after the 30 days have expired.
    (b) keep the check in his office safe until the closing.
    (c) open a special account in his accounting procedures.
    (d) none of these.
54. Broker Wallace negotiates a deal and receives a $1,000 judgment note payable in 30 days as a deposit. He should:
    (a) notify the prospective FHA mortgagee of this fact.
    (b) have the buyer notify the prospective mortgagee of this fact.
    (c) notify the seller that he has a 30 day note.
    (d) do nothing.
55. An option contract differs from a contract of sale in that
    (a) the option need not be consummated.
    (b) the option needs no consideration.
    (c) the contract of sale is enforceable by either party to it.
    (d) the contract of sale requires money consideration.

56. An article permanently attached or fastened to real property is considered to be
    (a) personal property.
    (b) real property.
    (c) a chattel.
    (d) private property.
57. John Mason signs a listing contract with Ben Baer Co. to sell his home. Baer, a licensed broker, obtains George Ryan, as a buyer, upon the terms of the listing, and Baer signs the agreement of sale "John Mason, by Ben Baer, Agent." Mason refuses to sign the deed. Ryan can
    (a) obtain a court decree for specific performance against Mason.
    (b) accept a valid deed signed "John Mason, by Ben Baer, attorney-in-fact."
    (c) record the agreement of sale to cloud the title.
    (d) do none of the above.
58. A contract for the sale of real estate becomes binding when signed by
    (a) the seller and broker.
    (b) the buyer and broker.
    (c) the seller and buyer.
    (d) the buyer only.
59. An owner delivers to Smith an option to purchase certain real estate upon Smith's payment of $10,000 within 30 days; the option recites that it is given in consideration of one dollar, the receipt of which the owner acknowledges; as a matter of fact, *nothing* is paid for the option. Under these circumstances the option is generally
    (a) valid.
    (b) void.
    (c) voidable.
    (d) unenforceable.
60. A contract of purchase or sale of real property should be signed by
    (a) the broker.
    (b) the agent and seller.
    (c) the seller only.
    (d) the buyer and seller.
61. Tender of deed is unnecessary where
    (a) time is of the essence.
    (b) the earnest money is less than 5 per cent.
    (c) date for performance has expired.
    (d) there is an anticipatory repudiation by buyer.
62. The amount of deposit money is
    (a) fixed by the real estate license act.
    (b) agreement of the parties.
    (c) a minimum of 5 per cent of consideration price.
    (d) determined by broker.
63. "Open housing" means:
    (a) a model house in a subdivision development.
    (b) a social party in a new subdivision.
    (c) celebration by purchaser of a new home.
    (d) prevention or elimination of discrimination in housing.
64. A "binder," accompanied by a deposit, binds the
    (a) buyer.
    (b) seller.
    (c) buyer and seller.
    (d) neither buyer nor seller.
65. The usual procedure is to deposit an earnest money payment
    (a) the next day after receipt.
    (b) within five days.
    (c) within one week.

(d) anytime before the closing.

66. Where the seller defaults, the deposit money or earnest payment
    (a) belongs to the broker.
    (b) should be returned to the buyer.
    (c) should be placed in an escrow fund.
    (d) should be paid into court.
67. An oral agreement of sale may be enforced where
    (a) the consideration price is less than $2,500.
    (b) there is a down payment of 20 per cent of the consideration.
    (c) the purchaser has gone into possession, paid part of the purchase price, and made improvements.
    (d) the broker guarantees performance.
68. Breach of an oral agreement of sale gives rise to
    (a) an action for specific performance.
    (b) an action for damages, if there is fraud by vendor.
    (c) a suit by broker against buyer for commission.
    (d) a suit for a written agreement of sale.
69. Upon the signing of agreements of sale
    (a) the legal title passes to purchaser.
    (b) the equitable title passes to purchaser.
    (c) no title to the real estate passes.
70. Anything that is fastened or attached to real property permanently is considered to be
    (a) personal property.
    (b) real property.
    (c) private property.
    (d) separate property.
71. A sewage disposal bill is an/a
    (a) easement.
    (b) lien.
    (c) encumbrance.
    (d) charge.
72. A contract based on an illegal consideration is
    (a) valid.
    (b) void.
    (c) legal.
    (d) enforceable.
73. The seller of real estate in a land contract is sometimes called the
    (a) vendee.
    (b) contractor.
    (c) grantor.
    (d) lessor.
74. A clause that the broker's commission is payable upon delivery of deed is construed to mean that
    (a) delivery of deed is a condition precedent to his payment.
    (b) the time when the broker is to be paid.
    (c) payable when seller signs the deed.
    (d) none of these.
75. When a purchaser withdraws his offer to purchase before it has been accepted by the seller, the broker should dispose of any deposit money received from the would-be purchaser in the following manner:
    (a) give it to the seller.
    (b) give it to the buyer.
    (c) keep it as his commission.
    (d) pay it into court.

76. An option without a valid consideration is
    (a) valid.
    (b) void.
    (c) revocable.
    (d) enforceable.
77. A payment made to bind a seller to the sale of real estate for a period of time is
    (a) a binder.
    (b) a bond.
    (c) an escrow agreement.
    (d) an option.
78. Deposit money paid upon the signing of an agreement of sale is called
    (a) an option.
    (b) a recognizance.
    (c) earnest money.
    (d) a freehold estate.
79. A note made payable to the order of the broker is
    (a) void.
    (b) non-negotiable.
    (c) negotiable.
    (d) voidable.
80. The description of land sold under an agreement of sale should
    (a) give the house number and street.
    (b) give a full legal description.
    (c) describe the improvements.
81. If, upon receipt of an offer to purchase under certain terms, the seller makes a counter offer, the prospective purchaser is
    (a) bound by his original offer.
    (b) bound to accept the counter offer.
    (c) bound by the agent's decision.
    (d) relieved of his original offer.
82. Insurance policy premiums on real property are prorated in escrow from the date the policy was
    (a) written.
    (b) recorded.
    (c) transferred.
    (d) cancelled.
83. Which of the following instruments would not belong in the same escrow with the others?
    (a) Mortgage.
    (b) Escrow instructions.
    (c) Warranty deed.
    (d) Deed of trust note.
84. When speaking of "improvements" regarding real estate, we mean
    (a) fences, wells, drains, roadways, etc.
    (b) everything affixed to the land.
    (c) additions to the original house.
85. An owner delivers to a party an option to purchase certain real estate upon payment of $5,000 within thirty days; the option states that it is given in consideration of good consideration, the receipt of which the owner acknowledges. Under these circumstances, the option is generally
    (a) valid.
    (b) void.
    (c) renewable.
    (d) not enforceable.
86. A sales agreement which provides that the broker involved should have the exclusive

right to place the fire insurance upon the property during the life of the building is
(a) allowed only if the broker is also licensed as an insurance agent.
(b) contrary to public policy.
(c) in the best interests of all.
(d) allowed if a copy is filed with the State Insurance Department.

87. It is necessary to set forth in a land contract
(a) the date the final payment is due.
(b) the purchase price and terms of agreement.
(c) amount of commission received by broker.

88. A tract of land described as the NE 1/4 of NW 1/4 of NW 1/4 of NW 1/4 contains:
(a) 20 acres.
(b) 10 acres.
(c) 5 acres.
(d) 2 1/2 acres.

89. At the time of closing a deal, the contractor—seller has not completed all of the landscaping, which will cost no more than $375. To insure prompt completion, this amount should be
(a) held by the broker.
(b) withheld by the buyer.
(c) placed in escrow.
(d) held by the mortgagee.

90. The document which conditionally conveys title to real estate is a
(a) mortgage.
(b) land installment contract.
(c) chattel mortgage.
(d) conditional bailment lease.

91. Dorothy Adams entered into a contract for the purchase of a home to be completed by Lemont, builder, on May 1, 1974. The house is not completed by that date and the buyer has "second thoughts" about the deal. Under these circumstances, the buyer:
(a) can call the deal off.
(b) the builder has a reasonable time to complete the dwelling.
(c) the buyer is entitled to reasonable damages for the delay.
(d) the buyer is entitled to a reduction in the price of the dwelling.

92. Hill hires Dale to build a custom house for $75,000. Before the house is completed, Dale became insolvent, and sub-contractors file liens against the property. What remedy does Hill have?
(a) Obtain a quit claim deed from Dale.
(b) Bring criminal charges against Dale.
(c) Sue the sub-contractors on the basis of unjust enrichment.
(d) Hill has no remedy.

93. Flynn, broker, negotiates the sale of a house at $17,000. The agreement recites a down payment of $1,000; Flynn receives $300 cash and a $700 note. The buyer seeks F.H.A. financing. Flynn certifies to the lending institution that he has received a $1,000 deposit from the buyer. Under these circumstances:
I. Flynn is guilty of a criminal act.
II. Flynn's license can be revoked.
(a) I only.
(b) II only.
(c) Both I and II.
(d) Neither I nor II.

94. A land sales contract contained a clause that in event of a sale of the property by the vendee, without the written consent of the vendor, the balance due would be accelerated. If the vendee sells the land contract, without consent of the vendor,
(a) balance of debt would be accelerated.
(b) seller can repossess the property immediately.

(c) the vendee can pay a penalty.
(d) the sale is void.

95. A financing arrangement by which the buyer does not become the owner of record would be a
(a) trust deed.
(b) land contract.
(c) purchase money mortgage.
(d) quit claim deed.

96. An option cannot legally be sold or assigned if the original consideration for the option was
(a) money.
(b) a promissory note.
(c) love and affection.
(d) a personal check.

97. A licensed real estate broker selling a property on which he holds an option must notify the purchaser that he is the
(a) optionee.
(b) optionor.
(c) holder in due course.
(d) lessee.

98. A contract for sale does not transfer
(a) possession.
(b) dower.
(c) curtesy.
(d) title in fee simple.

99. To determine the reasonable limit a man of ordinary income might be expected to pay for a home, his annual income is multiplied by
(a) 1.
(b) 2 1/2.
(c) 5.
(d) 10.

100. A bill of sale is used to convey title to
(a) an easement.
(b) personal property.
(c) life estate in real estate.
(d) real property.

101. A state deed transfer tax should be paid by the
(a) seller.
(b) buyer.
(c) broker.
d) mortgagee.

102. A contract which has no force or effect is said to be
(a) valid.
(b) void.
(c) voidable.
(d) revoked.

103. An item of personal property may be called a
(a) freehold.
(b) realty.
(c) tenure.
(d) chattel.

104. A statement that property is not termite-infested, if untrue, constitutes
(a) puffing of goods.
(b) sales talk.
(c) misrepresentation.

(d) caveat emptor.

105. Where a broker accepts a note in lieu of cash, as down payment in a real estate deal, and the note is unpaid, the owner can
(a) declare the contract void.
(b) bring a criminal action against the buyer.
(c) hold the broker responsible.
(d) file a complaint with the local credit bureau.

106. A purchaser should be notified by the broker, who has an option on the property being sold, that he, the broker, is the
(a) optionee.
(b) optionor.
(c) escrowee.
(d) lessee.

107. A broker should prepare how many copies of the agreement to purchase?
(a) Two.
(b) Four.
(c) Three.
(d) Five.

108. After an agreement to purchase has been prepared by the broker and signed by the buyer, the seller insists upon a slightly higher price and slightly different terms. The broker should
(a) delete the objectionable terms and insert the new terms, and then have the seller sign the contract.
(b) delete the objectional terms, insert the new terms and have buyer and seller write their initials in margin.
(c) prepare a new contract and have buyer and seller sign.
(d) have seller sign contract as originally drawn and send a memorandum to buyer as to changes.

109. Adams signs an offer to purchase Baker's property at $7,000. The broker with whom the property is listed at $7,500 submits the offer to Baker, but Baker wants $7,350. The broker prepares a new contract at $7,350. Adams refuses to sign. Baker then accepts Adams' offer at $7,000, but Adams has changed his mind about buying. There is
(a) a contract.
(b) no contract.
(c) due a commission by the seller to the broker.
(d) due a commission by the buyer to the broker.

110. The description of property sold under a contract of sale should
(a) state the size of lot in terms of feet—60 X 150 feet.
(b) give the house number and street.
(c) give location by approximation.
(d) give a full legal description.

111. Land that is divided into five or more parcels of lots for purpose of sale is defined as
(a) plottage.
(b) subdivision.
(c) a section.
(d) a hereditament.

112. An oral contract for the sale of real property is unenforceable because of
(a) laws of agency.
(b) statute of limitations.
(c) statute of frauds.
(d) licensing law.

113. Where a broker holds an option on a property and desires to sell the property, he must disclose that he is the
(a) optionor.
(b) trustor.

(c) optionee.
(d) assignee.

114. Which of the following is an element necessary to establish fraud or misrepresentation?
 (a) The broker knows the truth.
 (b) The party to whom the statement is made relies upon it to his detriment.
 (c) The property is worth so much money.
 (d) The property will resell at a certain price.
115. Under a land contract, who retains legal title until certain specific conditions are fulfilled?
 (a) Vendee.
 (b) Vendor.
 (c) Public trustee.
 (d) Recorder of deeds.
116. "A" conveyed a vacant one acre tract of land to "B." He received
 (a) 43,560 sq. ft.
 (b) 5,280 sq. ft.
 (c) 43,650 sq. ft.
 (d) 22,350 sq. ft.
117. The law which requires contracts for the sale of real estate to be in writing is known as the
 (a) statute of frauds.
 (b) statute of limitations.
 (c) adverse possession law.
 (d) parol evidence rule.
118. The term "sui juris" means
 (a) legal capacity to enter into a contract.
 (b) trial without a jury.
 (c) the acknowledgment to a legal instrument.
 (d) legal right to execute a will.
119. An agreement of sale is not enforceable if
 (a) it is unilateral.
 (b) there was fraud in its inducement.
 (c) it is unilateral and bilateral.
120. Marginal real estate is
 (a) yielding farm land.
 (b) waste land due to erosion, swamps and the like.
 (c) land which barely repays cost of operation.
 (d) the end lot in a subdivision.
121. An underground pipeline for irrigation of a farm is
 (a) personalty.
 (b) realty.
 (c) a riparian right.
 (d) an emblement.
122. Insurance policy premiums are prorated in escrow from the date the policy was
 (a) written.
 (b) recorded.
 (c) assigned.
 (d) cancelled.
123. A check is generally called a
 (a) time draft.
 (b) note payable.
 (c) negotiable instrument.
 (d) bill of attainder.
124. An option contract differs from an agreement of sale in that
 (a) the option needs no consideration to support it.

(b) the agreement of sale needs no consideration to support it.
(c) the option need not be consummated.
(d) the option automatically renews itself.

125. Which of the following does not usually appear as debit on the seller's closing statement
(a) pro-rating of insurance premium.
(b) pro-rating of taxes.
(c) interest on mortgage.
(d) cost of preparing deed.

126. An owner may sell the property to a second buyer where the first buyer has indicated
(a) that he will receive funds after the date fixed for closing.
(b) where first buyer complains dwelling is in disrepair.
(c) the buyer has declared an anticipatory repudiation.
(d) first buyer's credit rating is sub-par.

127. In order to take advantage of a capital gains tax on a real estate purchase and sale, the property must be held for at least
(a) six months.
(b) one year.
(c) three months.
(d) 30 days.

128. Zone R 1 usually refers to
(a) hospitals.
(b) single family dwellings.
(c) light industrial.
(d) commercial.

129. If there is ambiguity as to the meaning of any term in an agreement of sale, prepared by a broker, and signed by seller and buyer, it will be construed most strongly against
(a) broker.
(b) seller.
(c) buyer.
(d) lending institution.

130. Escrows are opened for protection of
(a) broker's commission.
(b) public.
(c) buyer and seller.
(d) mortgagee.

131. When real property is sold on an installment contract and a warranty deed is to be delivered at a future date, the deed should be placed in custody of
(a) the broker.
(b) the seller.
(c) the public trustee.
(d) an escrow agent.

132. Grove received an earnest money deposit check of $1,500. Which one of the following would be considered co-mingling of funds?
(a) Depositing the check in his escrow account.
(b) Placing it in his commercial account.
(c) Turning it over to the owner.
(d) Holding the check until the closing.

133. An option given without an actual consideration is
(a) enforceable.
(b) revocable.
(c) assignable.
(d) invalid.

134. When a real estate deal includes the sale of removable fixtures, such as a refrigerator, gas stove, etc., the seller should give to the buyer a
(a) bill of sale.

(b) chattel mortgage.
(c) chattel deed of trust.
(d) release.

135. A buyer made an initial deposit of $500 on a $10,000 house. He withdraws the offer before it is accepted by seller. The broker should dispose of the buyer's earnest money by
(a) turning it over to the seller.
(b) paying it into court.
(c) returning it to the buyer.
(d) keeping it for his commission.

136. When a seller accepts an offer to purchase, a salesman should deliver a copy of the signed acceptance to the
(a) lending institution.
(b) buyer.
(c) escrow agent.
(d) employing broker.

137. An option to purchase real estate is valid for how many days after the specified date
(a) thirty days.
(b) one month.
(c) none.
(d) ten days.

138. If a buyer fails to consummate a real estate deal, forfeiture of the deposit money is at the option of the
(a) seller.
(b) buyer.
(c) broker.
(d) salesman.

139. When a purchaser withdraws his offer to purchase before acceptance by seller, he is entitled to a refund of his deposit at what time
(a) immediately.
(b) after seller has had opportunity to accept agreement and declines.
(c) after broker keeps his commission.
(d) after buyer obtains court decree.

140. A sales agreement to be enforceable must have
(a) signature of wife of married seller.
(b) an earnest money deposit.
(c) competent parties.
(d) an attestation by a disinterested party.

141. Albert lists his home with Atkins, a broker, at $15,000. Adams makes a written offer of $13,500, with an earnest money deposit of $500; deal to be closed in 60 days. Albert refuses the offer but states he will take $14,000, with $1,000 deposit and deal to be closed in 30 days. This proposition is rejected by Adams. Albert then signs the original offer to purchase on Adams' terms. There is
(a) a contract.
(b) no contract.
(c) a cause for arbitration.
(d) an executory contract.

142. An installment purchase contract does not give the buyer
(a) possession.
(b) right to lease the property.
(c) title to the property.
(d) right to devise the property.

143. When real estate is sold on a land contract and a warranty deed is to be delivered at a future date, the warranty deed should be placed in the hands of
(a) the broker.

(b) escrow agent.
(c) buyer.
(d) no one.

144. Where a broker accepts a note, in lieu of cash, as a down payment on a real estate deal and the note is unpaid, the owner can
(a) hold the broker responsible.
(b) declare the deal void.
(c) bring a criminal action against buyer.
(d) file a complaint with the Real Estate Commission.

145. In fire insurance the most widely used coinsurance clause is
(a) 60%.
(b) 70%.
(c) 80%.
(d) 90%.

146. After an agreement of sale has been signed by the seller, the broker, at the request of the buyer, inserts the words "at least" before the words "$150 per month", referring to payments on a purchase money mortgage. The agreement of sale as executed is
(a) binding.
(b) binding at payments of $150 per month.
(c) invalid.
(d) a nudum pactum.

147. A land contract is preferable to a mortgage from the standpoint of
(a) the seller.
(b) the buyer.
(c) broker.
(d) mortgagee.

148. Under an acceleration clause in a land contract, seller can demand
(a) all arrearages due by buyer.
(b) arrearages for preceding 60 days only.
(c) entire unpaid balance on purchase price.
(d) due arrearages plus a percentage penalty.

149. The closing statement should be signed by
(a) the broker.
(b) the seller.
(c) the buyer.
(d) the buyer and seller.
(e) the title company.

150. Jones signs an agreement to sell his home to Brown for $27,000, subject to buyer obtaining a $22,000 mortgage. The mortgage money is available. Brown's wife refuses to sign the mortgage. Jones has an action for performance against
(a) the broker.
(b) wife.
(c) both husband and wife.
(d) no one.

151. Adams orally agreed to sell 40 acres of land to Bell at $100 per acre. Bell took possession, paid part of the purchase price, and made some improvements. Later, Adams sued to regain possession.
(a) Adams will succeed.
(b) Adams will not succeed.
(c) Adams will succeed, but must pay for improvements.
(d) the oral agreement must be reduced to writing.

152. The cost of examination of title for mortgagee and preparation of mortgage papers, at the closing, should be charged to
(a) the broker.
(b) the mortgagee.

(c) the seller.
(d) the buyer.

153. The cost for title insurance policy should be charged to
(a) seller.
(b) buyer.
(c) divided between seller and buyer.
(d) neither seller nor buyer, but to the broker.

154. Which one of the following will not terminate the principal-agent relationship by operation of law?
(a) Insanity of either principal or agent.
(b) Death of either principal or agent.
(c) Change of business address of broker.
(d) Bankruptcy of either principal or agent.

155. Which of the following items at a closing should not be pro rated?
(a) Sewer assessment.
(b) Taxes.
(c) Interest on a mortgage.
(d) Insurance.
(e) Rents.

156. An escrow account is terminated by
(a) withdrawal of offeree from the deal.
(b) withdrawal of offeror from the deal.
(c) consummation of the transaction.
(d) authorization by the broker.

157. Strict foreclosure is associated with
(a) land contract.
(b) mortgage.
(c) a conditional sale.
(d) offer to purchase.

158. Under the usual Vendors-Vendees assumption of risk act, loss by fire usually falls on
(a) the vendor.
(b) vendee.
(c) both vendor and vendee equally.
(d) partially on vendor but 80% on vendee.

159. In states which have the Uniform Vendor and Purchaser Risk Act, where the property under contract of sale is destroyed by fire before the deal is closed without fault of the buyer, who is not in possession, the assumption of risk falls upon
(a) the buyer.
(b) the seller.
(c) the lending institution committed to a mortgage.
(d) a governmental agency.

160. Where the agreement provides that the buyer inspected the property and purchased it "as is", but the electrical wiring is defective and dangerous, although not readily apparent, should the buyer
(a) hold the broker responsible.
(b) rescind the agreement of sale.
(c) is bound by rule of "caveat emptor."
(d) should relist the property for sale with the same broker.

161. "Caveat emptor" protects the buyer against
(a) patent defects.
(b) latent defects.
(c) a broken stairway.
(d) a bulging outside wall.

162. The party responsible for the payment of the title closing is determined by
(a) agreement of the parties.

(b) law.
(c) broker.
(d) title officer.

163. What happens when a deed has been delivered in escrow and the escrow holder dies before the escrow condition has been fulfilled?
(a) The deed is void.
(b) The deed is valid when the condition is performed.
(c) A new deed must be executed by the escrow agent's heirs.
(d) A new escrow must be set up.

164. An assumption of mortgage clause in an agreement of sale is most advantageous to
(a) seller.
(b) buyer.
(c) mortgagee.
(d) broker.

165. If an option for more than one year is exercised, the person liable for payment of taxes during the period of the option is
(a) the optionor.
(b) the optionee.
(c) the lessee.
(d) the assignee of the option.

166. Adams listed his property for sale with Wilkins, a broker, at $42,000. Wilkins obtained several offers below the listed price and one bona fide offer at $43,000 from Gordon. Adams, himself, obtained an offer of $40,000 from Bryant, a member of his country club, which he accepted. Gordon has
(a) an action for specific performance against Adams.
(b) no action against Adams.
(c) a cause of action against Wilkins.
(d) a cause of action against Bryant.

167. In the above case, Wilkins can collect a commission from
(a) Adams.
(b) Bryant.
(c) Adams and Bryant.
(d) neither Adams nor Bryant.

168. Adams writes a letter to Best on March 3, 1974 offering to buy Best's home for $22,000, "your acceptance to reach me by March 10, 1974". Best receives the offer on March 4, 1974 and writes Adams the same day accepting the offer. Due to a postal strike, the letter does not reach Adams until March 11, 1974. There is
(a) a contract.
(b) there is no contract.
(c) Best can sue Adams for damages, but not for specific performance.
(d) either party can refer the matter for compulsory arbitration.

169. An escrow, once opened, is
(a) revocable by either party to it.
(b) beyond the control of either party to it.
(c) terminates at the expiration of one year.
(d) held by the broker, as escrowee.

170. The person who cannot take an acknowledgment is
(a) a consul.
(b) a notary public.
(c) a justice of the peace.
(d) an interested party.

171. On March 21, 1974, Don Garwood, Santa Monica, California, writes to Henry Dolan in San Diego, California, offering to sell his home for $41,500. The letter is received on

March 23, 1974. On March 24, 1974, Dolan writes Garwood, accepting the offer and mails the letter. There is
(a) a contract.
(b) no contract.
(c) no meeting of the minds.
(d) a nudum pactum.

172. On March 21, 1974, Don Garwood, Santa Monica, California, writes to Robert Samuels in Sacramento, California, who had visited the property previously, offering to sell the property for $41,500. The letter is received on March 23, 1974. On March 24, 1974, Samuel writes Garwood accepting the offer. The letter is properly posted, but does not reach Garwood until March 28, 1974. Garwood signed an agreement to sell the property to Heinz on March 27, 1974. There is
(a) an enforceable contract by Samuels as of March 24, 1974.
(b) Samuels has an enforceable contract as of March 27, 1974.
(c) Samuels has no contract.
(d) Samuels now has a contract with Heinz.

173. A vendee becomes an equitable owner of real estate when
(a) the deal is consummated.
(b) the deed is recorded.
(c) the agreement is signed by the vendor.
(d) upon delivery of agreement, signed by the vendor, to the vendee.

174. After agreements are signed and the seller defaults, the earnest money
(a) belongs to the buyer.
(b) belongs to the buyer, less the broker's commission.
(c) should be returned to buyer.
(d) should be referred to Real Estate Commission for adjudication.

175. A broker is permitted to sign an agreement of sale for his owner because
(a) he is subject to discipline by the Real Estate Commission.
(b) authority is given in the license law.
(c) by Rule and Regulation of the Commission.
(d) verbal authority of the owner.
(e) none of these.

176. Where the license law requires broker to give owner a copy of listing contract, which broker fails to do, broker
(a) cannot collect a commission.
(b) is subject to disciplinary action.
(c) is deemed untrustworthy.
(d) is subject to criminal action.

177. In a real estate transaction, which one of the following instruments is not recorded?
(a) Deed.
(b) Land contract.
(c) Mortgage.
(d) Purchase money mortgage.
(e) Offer to purchase.

178. An agreement of sale, which has not been consummated, but has been recorded, can be removed by
(a) sale of property to another buyer.
(b) release by the broker who prepared the agreement.
(c) action to quiet title.
(d) order of the Real Estate Commission.

179. Where zoning precludes the intended use of the premises under contract of sale, the objection can be overcome by obtaining
(a) an order of court.
(b) a variance from the zoning adjustment board.
(c) a non-conforming use.

(d) a hardship permit.

180. Application for a change in zoning so as to permit intended use by buyer should be made by
    (a) broker.
    (b) seller.
    (c) purchaser.
    (d) broker and purchaser.
181. Where a salesman agrees to sell a buyer's present home in order to purchase a new house, he should
    (a) execute a memorandum to the buyer to that effect.
    (b) make such promise in the presence of two witnesses.
    (c) make a memo to the broker by whom he is employed.
    (d) incorporate a subject to sale clause in the agreement of sale for the new property.
182. The agreement of sale should provide that if the property is damaged or destroyed by fire, where the buyer is not in possession before the deal is consummated, the loss should fall upon
    (a) the seller.
    (b) the buyer.
    (c) equally upon buyer and seller.
    (d) make no reference to that possibility.
183. Where a buyer, after signing a valid agreement of sale asks the broker for permission to move into the property before the closing, the broker should
    (a) deny permission.
    (b) grant oral permission.
    (c) refer him to the owner.
    (d) have the buyer execute a temporary lease.
184. It is permissible for the broker to give a buyer permission, after the contract of sale is signed, but before the deal is closed, to make minor repairs, do some interior painting or decorating, if
    (a) he has received a substantial earnest money deposit.
    (b) receives an *additional* earnest money deposit.
    (c) he feels the property would be improved.
    (d) he receives permission from the owner.
185. An agreement of sale designates February 1, 1974 as the closing date. On March 1, 1974, the purchaser is ready to close the deal. State whether
    (a) he is too late.
    (b) he is guilty of laches.
    (c) the owner can sell the property on February 8, 1974.
    (d) the buyer can compel the seller to close the deal.
186. Where time is not of the essence of the agreement of sale, the buyer would have how much time to close the deal after the date specified in the agreement?
    (a) One year.
    (b) 30 days.
    (c) 90 days.
    (d) A reasonable time.
187. In determining what is a reasonable time the court would not take into consideration which one of the following conditions?
    (a) Type of property.
    (b) Time of year.
    (c) Condition of the real estate market.
    (d) Buyer's salary.
188. A broker's promise to obtain a change in the zoning of a property under agreement to sell is
    (a) binding upon the seller.
    (b) binding upon the broker.

(c) invalid as against public policy.
(d) a violation of the license law.

189. It is desirable that *all* listing contracts be in writing for the protection of
(a) owner and broker.
(b) owner.
(c) buyer.
(d) for the enhancement of real estate prestige.

190. An installment land contract is preferable where
(a) the property is overly priced.
(b) where the vendee has only a small amount of cash available.
(c) where the property will probably be taken by condemnation.
(d) where the property is in need of considerable repair.

191. "A" builds a custom house for "B", which is completed on May 15, 1974, and "B" takes possession on that date. "B" sells the house to "C" on December 6, 1974. Due to heavy rains, the filled in ground fails to support the house and there is considerable subsidence. "C" can recover for the damage from
(a) the seller.
(b) the builder.
(c) the city building inspector.
(d) no one.

192. A new house is completed on January 28, 1974, but landscaping, cement walks and some painting are not completed. To insure that all the items will be completed by April 15, 1974, the buyer should insist
(a) on a written memorandum from the builder to that effect.
(b) on taking out mechanic's lien insurance.
(c) to accept a promissory note from the builder for the cost of the items.
(d) on withholding money from the settlement to insure work will be done by April 15, 1974.

193. A commercial property in Los Angeles is listed with the Central City Realty at $70,000. Central City communicates with Woods in San Francisco, who is familiar with the property, and agrees to buy the property at that figure. Central City prepares an agreement of sale, which is signed by Downes, the owner, in Los Angeles. Copies are then mailed to Woods for signature, on May 31, 1974. The copies are received by Woods on June 3, 1974. He signs and mails the signed copies to Downes the same day. The copies are received by Downes on June 6, 1974. On June 4, 1974, Downes wired Woods "Offer withdrawn—property not for sale." Under these circumstances:
I. There is an enforceable contract.
II. Central City is entitled to a commission.
(a) I only.
(b) II only.
(c) Both I and II.
(d) Neither I nor II.

194. An agreement of sale provided it was contingent upon buyer's ability to obtain a $24,000 loan at $6\frac{1}{4}$ per cent for a 20 year maturity. The buyer, was unable to obtain a loan and sued to recover his deposit of $1,000. Under these circumstances:
I. It was incumbent upon buyer to show that he was unable to procure a loan after diligent effort.
II. Buyer could withdraw from agreement and recover deposit.
(a) I only.
(b) II only.
(c) Both I and II.
(d) Neither I nor II.

195. A buyer submitted an offer to purchase a dwelling upon condition that vendor install a water cooler. A deposit of $1,500 accompanied the offer. The seller agreed to the sale,

but stated that the buyer should pay for the installation. The buyer agreed, but changed his mind. Buyer sued for recovery of $1,500 deposit. Under these circumstances:

I. There was no valid contract.
II. Buyer is entitled to a refund of $1,500 deposit.
(a) I only.
(b) II only.
(c) Both I and II.
(d) Neither I nor II.

196. Clark signed an offer to purchase a dwelling from Grant for $29,000 on June 20, 1974. It stated "this offer shall remain open, irrevocably for a period of 5 days." On June 22, 1974, Clark informed Grant that he was withdrawing the offer. The next day, Grant signed Clark's offer to purchase and gave him the signed copy. Under these circumstances:

I. There is a valid contract.
II. Grant may sue for specific performance of the contract.
(a) I only.
(b) II only.
(c) Both I and II.
(d) Neither I nor II.

197. An agreement of sale provided that July 31, 1974 was of the essence of the agreement for the closing of the deal. On July 30, 1974, the seller orally agreed with the buyer to extend the closing date to August 30, 1974. On August 15, 1974, the seller notified the buyer that the latter had breached the agreement and that he was keeping the $1,000 earnest money deposit, as liquidated damages. Under these circumstances:

I. The buyer can recover the $1,000 deposit.
II. The buyer has until August 30, 1974 to consummate the deal.
(a) I only.
(b) II only.
(c) Both I and II.
(d) Neither I nor II.

198. On August 5, 1974, Boone, buyer, signed an agreement of sale to purchase Jordan's home, and paid a $500 earnest money deposit, deal to be closed on September 23, 1974. The agreement states that the buyer has examined the home and is purchasing it "as is." Before the closing, Boone has a termite inspection and learns the property is termite infested. Under these circumstances:

I. Boone can refuse to consummate the deal.
II. Boone can close the deal, but Jordan must allow a substantial discount on the purchase price.
(a) I only.
(b) II only.
(c) Both I and II.
(d) Neither I nor II.

199. Aiken verbally agreed to sell his property, consisting of 12 ½ acres to Beldin. The latter immediately made efforts to obtain financing and engaged an engineer to lay out lots and necessary streets. Beldin paid Aiken $1,500 on account of the purchase price of $10,500. Later, Aiken refused to consummate the deal and Beldin claims part performance, which satisfied the Statute of Frauds. Under these circumstances:

I. Beldin can compel Aiken to deed the property to him, upon payment of the balance of the consideration.
II. Beldin can recover his expenses.
(a) I only.
(b) II only.
(c) Both I and II.
(d) Neither I nor II.

200. Adams bought a new home from a builder, who, in the agreement of sale, guaranteed the roof against leakage for a period of one year. During the year, the buyer resold the dwelling to a purchaser, and the roof developed a leak. Under these circumstances:
I. The second buyer has a cause of action against Adams.
II. The second buyer has a cause of action against the builder.
(a) I only.
(b) II only.
(c) Both I and II.
(d) Neither I nor II.

201. Abbott agreed to sell his residence to Barnes on December 1, 1973 for $16,000. The deal was to be closed on May 1, 1974. In the interim, steps were taken by the state to condemn the property and the damages awarded for the property was $18,900. Under these circumstances:
I. The increase in price belongs to Barnes.
II. The increase in price will be divided.
(a) I only.
(b) II only.
(c) Both I and II.
(d) Neither I nor II.

202. Brown negotiates a sale for $18,000. The buyer needs a mortgage of $17,000 to close. Brown prepares two agreements of sale, one reciting consideration of $18,000; the second agreement recites $20,750. Brown has the seller and buyer sign both agreements. The $20,750 agreement is presented to the First Federal Savings and Loan for the loan. Under these circumstances:
I. Brown has committed a criminal act.
II. Brown's license can be revoked.
(a) I only.
(b) II only.
(c) both I and II.
(d) neither I nor II.

203. In the above case,
I. the seller is guilty of a criminal act.
II. the buyer is guilty of a criminal act.
(a) I only.
(b) II only.
(c) both I and II.
(d) neither I nor II.

204. An agreement of sale, signed by seller and buyer, provided that "in event of default by the buyer, the deposit money of $500 was to be retained by the seller, as liquidated damages. The buyer defaulted, without good reason. Under these circumstances, the seller could:
I. sue for specific performance.
II. re-sell the property and sue the buyer for any loss.
(a) I only.
(b) II only.
(c) both I and II.
(d) neither I nor II.

205. An agreement of sale specified May 3, 1974 as the date for consummation. Prior to that date, the broker called the buyer to tell him to bring a cashier check to the closing. The buyer told him that he would not be ready to close on that date. Neither the seller or the broker heard anything further from the buyer. On June 17, 1974, the broker negotiated a sale of the same property to another buyer. On June 24, 1974, the first buyer notified the broker that he was ready to close his deal. Under these circumstances:
I. the first buyer could compel the seller to consummate his agreement.
II. the seller would be liable to the second buyer for damages.

(a) I only.
(b) II only.
(c) both I and II.
(d) neither I nor II.

206. In the preceding case, the second buyer could:
I. recover damages from the broker.
II. file a complaint against the broker with the Real Estate Commission.
(a) I only.
(b) II only.
(c) both I and II.
(d) neither I nor II.

207. Hart entered into an agreement to sell his home to Benson for $26,000. Benson paid $1,000 as an earnest money deposit. Before the deal is closed, Benson's attorney discovers a borough ordinance which provides for widening of an abutting street. Under these circumstances, Benson can:
I. recover his $1,000 deposit.
II. recover exemplary or punitive damages.
(a) I only.
(b) II only.
(c) both I and II.
(d) neither I nor II.

208. Gage agreed to buy a residence from Hart for $40,000 and paid $2,000 earnest money deposit. The property is in Hart's name alone. Hart's wife refused to sign the agreement of sale, unless he bought her an expensive fur coat. Under these circumstances, Gage can:
I. compel Hart to place the $2,000 in the hands of an escrow agent, such as a trust company or abstract company.
II. record the agreement of sale immediately.
(a) I only.
(b) II only.
(c) both I and II.
(d) neither I nor II.

209. A buyer signed an agreement to purchase a home for $16,000, subject to satisfactory financing in the amount of $14,750. The seller received a $500 earnest money deposit. The buyer was unable to obtain satisfactory financing. Under these circumstances:
I. the seller can agree to take back a purchase money mortgage for $14,750.
II. the buyer can recover his $500 deposit.
(a) I only.
(b) II only.
(c) both I and II.
(d) neither I nor II.

210. John Steele and Henry Steele are unmarried brothers. John agrees to sell his summer cottage on Lake Bedford to Henry for $3,900. Henry gives John $250 in cash and they shake hands on the deal, in the presence of two friends. Under these circumstances:
I. Henry is obligated to pay $3,650 to John.
II. John is obligated to deliver a deed to Henry.
(a) I only.
(b) II only.
(c) both I and II.
(d) neither I nor II.

211. Young signed an agreement of sale to purchase Bell's residence on December 13, 1973, the deal to be closed on January 3, 1974. Between January 2, 1974, and March 28, 1974, Bell tried to contact Young, but was unsuccessful. On April 2, 1974, Bell sold the property to Hansen, who recorded his deed that same day. On April 22, 1974, Young notified Bell

that he was ready to close, when he learned the property had been sold to Hansen. Under these circumstances:

I. Young can compel Hansen to deed the property, upon refunding Hansen's consideration price.
II. Young has a valid right to join Bell and Hansen in an action to obtain title to the property.
(a) I only.
(b) II only.
(c) both I and II.
(d) neither I nor II.

212. Assuming in the above case that Hansen closed the deal with Bell on April 25, 1974 and Young recorded his agreement of sale on April 23, 1974,
I. the deed from Bell to Hansen would be invalid.
II. Young could compel Bell to convey the property to him, upon payment of the purchase price.
(a) I only.
(b) II only.
(c) both I and II.
(d) neither I nor II.

213. Adams, a broker, has a listing from Baker for his dwelling, at a $24,000 price, commission to be 6%. The listing is dated May 15, 1974 and runs for 90 days. Adams obtains a firm offer from Chase at $23,000 on May 21, 1974. Adams asks and receives an option to buy the listed property from Baker on May 24, 1974, for a five day period, at $20,500. Adams then exercises his option. Under these circumstances:
I. Adams can obtain title to the property from Baker at $20,500.
II. Chase can compel Adams to deed the property to him for $24,000.
(a) I only.
(b) II only.
(c) both I and II.
(d) neither I nor II.

214. Otis entered into an agreement of sale with Camp on March 21, 1974 to sell him a dwelling for $28,000. Camp gave Otis an earnest money deposit of $800. The deal was to be closed on April 29, 1974. Camp has failed to close the deal by July 3, 1974, and Otis has an opportunity on that date to sell the property to Edwards, at the same price. Under these circumstances:
I. Otis should tender a deed to Camp and demand the balance of the purchase price.
II. Otis should keep the $800 as liquidated damages and agree to sell to Edwards.
(a) I only.
(b) II only.
(c) both I and II.
(d) neither I nor II.

215. What type of real estate operation is exempt from displaying an Equal Housing Opportunity poster?
(a) Broker's place of business.
(b) A model house in a development.
(c) A real estate subdivision.
(d) A private dwelling which is for sale.

216. Broker Thomas negotiates a deal, and receives a $1,000 note, payable in 30 days, as an earnest money deposit.
(a) The broker has a duty to inform the prospective F.H.A. mortgagee of this fact.
(b) The broker has no duty to do so, since there is no privity of contract between the broker and the lender.

(c) The broker should ask the buyer—mortgagor to acquaint the mortgagee with this fact.
(d) The broker should ask the seller to inform the mortgagee of this fact.

Chapter 3

DEEDS
Real Property and Personalty Distinguished

AT THE OUTSET, it is important to remember that certain words and phrases in connection with real estate have a technical meaning and a different interpretation than is generally attributed to them by the average layman. The all-inclusive term "property" may be said to be the rights or interest which a person has in lands and chattels to the exclusion of all others. Blackstone defines land as comprehending all things of a permanent substantial nature. *Estate* means quantity of ownership, and *title* is the evidence of ownership. Estate stands for quantity and title refers to quality. Lands are *realty;* chattels are *personalty.* All property of whatever kind and description that is capable of being owned must fall into one of these two classes—realty or personalty. Realty, in turn, includes a twofold classification, *corporeal* realty and *incorporeal* realty. Personalty, likewise, may be divided into two groups, *tangible* (a desk) and *intangible* (copyright). "Corporeal" is derived from the Latin word *corpus,* meaning body.

Corporeal realty, like land, a building, or a tree, can be seen and felt. In other words, real property includes land and almost anything built upon, growing or affixed to the soil. Incorporeal realty includes rights issuing out of, annexed to, or exercisable within land, such as a right of way. It is frequently stated that realty includes lands, tenements, and hereditaments. The relationship of these three classes may be represented by three concentric circles. The smallest circle embraces lands; the next, tenements. Tenements, therefore, include lands and certain things which are realty but which cannot be described as land, such as a building. The largest circle contains whatever may be classed or inherited as realty. Hereditaments embrace lands, tenements, and certain other things, usually of an incorporeal nature, such as a right of way.

A tree growing upon land is real estate. When the tree is severed from the soil and cut into so many feet of boards, the lumber is personalty, and, when the lumber is fashioned into a dwelling, the lumber becomes real estate again. So too, when clay is part of the soil, it is realty. When it is removed and made into bricks, it becomes personalty. When these bricks are put together to form a building, they become realty again. Thus, many articles may change from realty to personalty and back again. When they are solidly fixed to land or to the structures built upon land, generally they are realty. However, there are many fixtures solidly fastened to buildings, such as heavy machinery bolted to a floor, which remain personalty. Then, there may be articles which have been annexed to the realty and were accidentally or wrongfully removed, which, nevertheless, retain their character of realty. Suppose that a storm blows down a garage or tree. The garage or tree may be no longer connected with the land, but it remains realty until the owner shows an intention to treat it as personalty. The key to a house is such a necessary part of the improvement that it would properly be considered realty.

As a rule, articles that have been brought upon land in order that they may become part of the improvement are not transformed from personalty to realty until they become an integral part of the improvement. For example, lumber and millwork delivered to a building job are not realty and would be subject to seizure as the contractor's personal property upon a judgment against the contractor, while deposited on an adjoining lot.

Realty and personalty distinguished

Thus, the distinction between realty and personalty is an important one because the law applicable to the two classes of property is radically different. The distinction is also a practical one, readily apparent in the sale of a house when a controversy arises between the interested parties as to whether certain articles, such as stoves, screens, wall mirrors, shrubbery, refrigerator, gas ranges, and other articles, pass with the sale of the house. Certain apparatus which was a constituent part of a rolling mill was held to be realty, although temporarily detached from the mill. The mere fact that the machinery could be unscrewed or otherwise removed without injury to the building would not constitute it personal property. The greater or less facility with which the removal could be accomplished would be too vague a test; the slightest tack or fastening would be sufficient to convert personalty into realty. If the possibility of removing an article without damaging the real estate were the test, the results would also be unsatisfactory. For example, an owner who sold a residence might lift the window shutter off the hinges without any damage to the building, but, in all fairness, it would seem that the shutters are a permanent part of the real estate and should pass with the sale. In the absence of an express stipulation in the agreement, the issue of realty or personalty may be determined finally only by recourse to the courts. The true test for determining whether an article, fixture, or piece of equipment or machinery is realty or personalty is the *intention* with which the article is affixed to the property, considered in the light of what is fair and reasonable under all the surrounding circumstances. In other words, each case must stand upon its own particular facts, but the main feature is "the intention" as disclosed by words or conduct of the owner when the installation was made, with due regard given to existing custom, if established. Custom plays an important part in determining what articles are realty and which are personalty. Most persons would be greatly surprised if the seller should detach and remove the chandeliers and radiators in a house. We have come to look upon such fixtures as an essential part of the premises, as are doors and windows. It is a broker's obligation to prepare a comprehensive and satisfactory agreement defining what shall pass with the conveyance of the premises.

Chattels which are distinctly furniture, as distinguished from improvements, and not particularly fitted or fastened to the property with which they are used, remain personalty. Chattels which, although physically connected with the real estate, are so affixed as to be removable without destroying or materially injuring the fixtures or the property to which they are annexed become part of the realty or retain their character as personalty, depending upon the intention of the parties at the time of the annexation. Chattels which are so annexed to the property that they cannot be removed without material injury to the real estate or to themselves are realty even if there is an expressed intention that they should be considered personalty.

In *Farmers & Merchants Bank v. Sawyer,* 163 So. 657 (Ala. 1937), a bathtub, built-in ironing board and lights were held to be fixtures by reason of their mode of annexation to the realty and were not removable by the seller.

In an apartment building, refrigerators and gas or electric ranges in the various units, are considered part of the realty. A sprinkler system in a factory or commercial structure is real estate.

Test to be applied

Court decisions are uniform in applying certain rules to determine the real or personal character of a fixture. They are:

1. Annexation to the realty; a built-in television set would be considered realty; likewise a roof antenna, a sprinkler system in a commercial building.
2. Adaptability or application, as affixed to the use for which the real estate is appropriated; a theatre sign or marquee, specially constructed storm doors or screens for a particular dwelling; a built-in organ in a church.
3. An intention of the party to make the chattel a permanent part of the freehold; lighting fixtures, radiators, laundry tubs.

A trailer, or mobile home, connected to a lot, with which it is sold as a "package" would be considered realty, and subject to taxation, as such. By being annexed to the land, the vehicle becomes real estate, although detached from the land, it would be personal.

Transfer of Title to Real Estate

TITLE TO real estate, the evidence of ownership, passes generally in several ways: (1) by purchase, through delivery of deed and (2) by descent, through a will or by inheritance. As will be seen later, title may also be obtained (3) through adverse possession and (4) by eminent domain.

Origin of title

It is of fundamental importance to know that the extent of the right which a person acquires in property can be no greater than that enjoyed by his predecessor in title. This means that one cannot buy more from the former owner than the latter had, despite the fact that he may give what purports to be a valid deed. If an owner gives a deed for a tract of land, 110 feet in depth, but he only owned 100 feet, it follows that the buyer obtains title only to 100 feet. Thus, in order to determine the exact extent of the rights of a present owner of property, a diligent and thorough search must be made in order to ascertain the rights which were handed down to him through a long line of former owners, and in many cases, it is necessary to trace the title back to its origin so as to ascertain the extent of the original grant which was made. This general principle, of course, is subject to certain modifications, for many laws have been passed, intended to cure or remedy defects in titles produced through carelessness or blunders. Title to a property has a very long life, extending back to the beginning of private ownership. Technically, titles emanated from a sovereign power or government, the exact source varying in the different sections of the country. For example, in New Jersey and Delaware, it is Lord Baltimore; in New York, it is the Duke of York, or his successor, the State of New York; in Pennsylvania, it is William Penn. In Kansas and Nebraska, it is the United States government, which secured title to the Great Western Domain through grants made by the thirteen original states, and subsequent negotiations with France for the purchase of the Louisiana Territory. A prudent purchaser of land, anywhere, will insist upon an Abstract of Title and opinion of title, or have the title insured by a title company, in order to obtain protection as to the quality of title to the land purchased.

Quality of title

The grantee is entitled to that quality of title, which will enable him to sell the property without objection or difficulty. Good title is said to be such title, free from encumbrances or clouds, which a court would compel a purchaser to accept. The doctrine of "doubtful title" is that a purchaser of land is entitled to a title that will not get him involved in litigation: *Baldwin v. Anderson,* 161 N.W. 2d 553 (Wis. 1968).

Formality of title transfer—by deed

The law has always regarded the transfer of real estate as one of the most solemn acts in which an individual can engage and thus a great deal of formality attends its transfer. In the early days of land tenure, transfer was accomplished by "livery of seizin," which, literally, means transfer of possession. The seller and buyer would go upon the land in question and there, in the presence of witnesses, the seller would take a clod of turf or a twig from a tree and hand it over to the buyer as a symbol or token of the transfer. The transfer was then made a matter of record by having the scrivener (the person in the community who could write) write out the transfer upon parchment or other durable matter, in order to prevent erasure or alteration; the scrivener wrote the name of the grantor (seller), and the latter affixed his personal seal. With the development of education, the emphasis has shifted, so that the signature is the all-important feature in the execution of a deed and the seal only incidental, usually printed upon the deed form. Although a deed is a contract between the grantor and grantee (buyer), it is not necessary for the latter to sign it, and, in fact, this would be unusual. The acceptance of the deed consummates the contract. It should be kept in mind that a deed is a contract and, therefore, all the essential elements of a valid contract must be present. It is also necessary to have special formality—that is, the deed must be in writing. There can be no such thing as an *oral* transfer of real estate. Under Spanish law, an oral deed, coupled with transfer of possession, was effective to pass title. A deed represents the formal completion of an agreement of sale previously executed by the parties.

In construing a deed, every attempt should be made to carry out the intent of the grantor, and *substance* rather than *form* should control: *Shulansky v. Michaels,* 484 P. 2d 14 (Ariz. App. 1971)

Where there is ambiguity of construction of a deed, it should be construed most favorably to the grantee, since the grantor prepared it: *Jones v. Johnson,* 307 N.E. 2d 222 (Ill. App. 1974).

Deeds are classified as warranty deed, bargain and sale deed and quit claim deed. There is very little real difference between a warranty deed and a bargain and sale deed. It is a distinction, without any real difference. A warranty deed conveys title to real estate to the same extent as a bargain and sale deed; and, the latter carries similar warranties as in a warranty deed.

Quit claim deed

A *quit claim* deed is used to clear clouds upon the title as in the case of a recorded agreement of sale or the release of a life estate or a contingent remainder. The grantee in the quit claim deed may already have or may claim a complete or partial title to the premises and the grantor has a *possible* interest that might constitute a cloud upon the title. A deed of *confirmation* is similar, in effect, to a quit claim deed. The operative words are "remise, release, and quit claim." The warranty is omitted entirely, and the grantor forever quits whatever interest he might have in the property. A wife, who has not joined in the bargain and sale deed, may subsequently sign a quit claim deed barring her potential dower right in the property. A quit claim deed conveys only such interest as the grantor is possessed at the time of the conveyance: *Chatham Amusement Co. v. Perry,* 216 Ga. 445 (1961).

A quit claim deed may be used to extinguish a recorded agreement of sale. The vendee (purchaser) would be the grantor in this deed.

Deeds—definition

Transfer of title by *deed* is the most common method of passing title to real estate. Blackstone defines a deed as a "writing or instrument under seal, containing some contract of agreement, and which has been delivered by the parties." Thus the word "deed," in a legal sense, may mean any sealed contract or instrument, such as a lease, mortgage, or bond. The popular sense restricts it to a conveyance of property. A deed may then be defined as a writing by which lands, tenements, and hereditaments are conveyed, which writing is signed, sealed, and delivered by the parties. The ordinary common warranty deed contains a number of clauses that have an important bearing upon the rights of the parties. A present day definition of a deed is of a similar tenor: *Williams v. Board of Education,* 201 S.E. 2d 889 (N.C. 1974).

For purposes of study, a deed may be divided into three component parts—the Premises, the Habendum and the Testimonium. The Premises includes the date, parties, consideration, granting clause, description, recital and appurtenances. The Habendum et Tenendum (to have and to hold clause) includes this clause and the Under and Subject or Mortgage clause. The Testimonium clause includes the Warranty and "In Witness Whereof," etc. This outline is valuable to remember so that a person may check a deed to ascertain that all clauses are included and, also, as an aid in preparing a proper deed. Now for a fuller discussion of the various parts.

Date

The date usually comes first but is not essential to the validity of a deed. When inserted, it indicates the time when the title passed; that is, when the deed was delivered; but it is only *prima facie* evidence, and the presumption of time of delivery may be rebutted by convincing testimony to the contrary. A deed dated on Sunday but delivered on a week day is good. A deed without a date or a date subsequent to that in the acknowledgment affidavit would not be void, but the party accepting the deed would have the burden, in case of litigation, of proving when the deed was actually delivered. If the date in the acknowledgment antedates the date in the deed, a technical examiner may require a new acknowledgment and re-recordation. If the grantor is dead or cannot be located, difficulty in this connection is readily apparent. Great care should therefore be exercised to examine the dates in the deed in order to avoid difficulty at a later date. If the date is inserted, the grantee would have the presumption in his favor that the deed was delivered on the date specified and the burden would then be upon the opponent of the deed to prove otherwise.

Parties

The names and residences of the parties to the deed immediately follow the date. The party selling the property is known as the *grantor;* the purchaser of the property is known as the *grantee.* Any uncertainty as to the persons intended would render the deed void. Where the parties have a middle initial, it should be inserted. A deed must be made to some certain person or else it is void. A deed to a fictitious or unincorporated community or corporation which has no legal existence, is void. Thus a deed to the Ajax Printing Company, which is a partnership consisting of two members, is void. The deed should have been made in the names of the two partners. A deed "to the employers of the school at Plum Creek" would also be invalid. Where a corporation is a party to a deed, a slight mistake in setting out its name will not vitiate the deed, if it is clearly apparent from the face of it that one certain corporation was intended. Thus, a deed written in the name of Boulevard Land and Development Company, Inc., would be upheld where the name of the corporation actually was Boulevard Land Development Company, Inc. However, in the case of *Alton Evening Telegraph v. Doak,* 296 N.E. 2d 605 (Ill. 1973), the word "Co." was omitted in the name. The court held that the action failed. Likewise, in *Arrow Ambulance v. Davis,* 306 N.E. 2d (Ill. 1974), failure to include "Inc." in the action, was held fatal.

Deed of bargain and sale—consideration

A deed of bargain and sale, which is the instrument adopted in most states to transfer real estate, requires consideration for the deed, although it need not be necessarily expressed. Consideration in the deed may be either good or valuable. A good consideration proceeds from love and affection or the like, and has no pecuniary measure of value. A valuable consideration is money or its equivalent, anything capable of being measured by a monetary standard. The practice of inserting a dollar as consideration is sufficient for the requirements of the law. Courts do not inquire into the adequacy of the consideration. The slightest consideration is sufficient to support the most onerous obligation. Thus a $1.00 consideration will support the transfer of a property worth $1,000,000. If the title is being transferred to a relative without any cash consideration, as from father to son, the deed should recite for "$1.00 and other good consideration." A deed made by an insolvent owner to a close relative or friend with the intent to disturb, delay, hinder or defraud creditors is void against a creditor.

Under statutes dealing with transfer of real estate by an insolvent debtor, or made with actual intent to defraud, the burden of proof is initially upon the one seeking to set aside the conveyance: *Sparkman & McLean Co. v. Derber,* 481 P. 2d 585 (Wash. App. 1971) Deeds from fiduciaries, such as trust companies, should recite the true consideration price rather than a nominal consideration. An error in stating the true amount of consideration will not affect the validity of the deed.

In consideration of support

An aged parent, in return for support and shelter from a son, may deed the home to him. Later on, differences arise between the two, and, sad to relate, the son orders the father from the home. Soon thereafter, the son sells the property to a bona fide purchaser. Unless the deed from father to son recites that the conveyance to the son was made in consideration of support during the father's life time, the conveyance to the third party will be upheld: *Wood v. Swift,* 428 S.W. 2d 77 (Ark. 1968); *Kinney v. Kinney,* 150 So. 2d 671 (La. 1963); *Mitchell et al. v. Wilcox et al.,* 139 N.W. 2d 203 (Neb. 1966).

Many states and some municipalities and/or school districts require a transfer tax. Usually, the seller absorbs one transfer tax, the state transfer tax, and buyer pays the local transfer tax. This is especially true where the state and local tax is in the same amount. For example, one percent of the consideration by each governing body.

Granting clause or operative words

The words used in the deed that transfer the estate from the grantor to the grantee constitute the granting clause and are termed the "operative words." These words are generally "grant and convey" or "grant, bargain, and sell." They usually precede the description but may be placed in any part of the deed. The necessity for technical words is no longer felt, and any words indicating an intention to convey will operate to transfer title. Following the grant and immediately preceding the description of the property are the words of limitation denoting the quantity of estate intended to be granted. The words ordinarily employed to pass a fee simple title are "heirs and assigns." A fee simple estate is the greatest estate which may be held in property, and at common law the words "heirs and assigns" were absolutely essential to pass a fee. Without the word "heirs" only an estate for life passes. It would not suffice to say that the "grantee is to have and to hold forever" or "to the grantee and his assigns forever," for this does not mean that the issue of the grantee acquire any vested interest in the land. The word "heirs" is said to be a word of *limitation,* rather than a word of *purchase,* and indicates a complete title of perpetual duration with power to sell to anybody; it does not give the issue or heirs of the grantee any rights in the property after the owner's death. Today, the operative words in a deed, "grant and convey," or either of them will generally be held to be effective to convey a fee simple title if the grantor had such title.

Fee simple title

A fee simple title is the highest and most complete ownership or enjoyment in real estate. It is sometimes referred to as ownership in fee or fee absolute. Where such owner executes a lease, he does not part with title. The person to whom the property is leased acquires a lesser, or leasehold estate. Likewise, if a person acquires a property for life, by deed, or will, he does not become a fee simple owner, but rather the owner of a transitory life estate, which ceases at his death. The person who succeeds to the title when the life estate terminates is known as the remainderman.

A property is conveyed to Mary Hardy for and during the term of her natural life and then the remainder to David Hardy, in fee simple. Upon Mary's death, title to the property would, of course, vest in David Hardy.

Description

The purpose of the description in a deed is to identify sufficiently the land to be conveyed, and no deed will be operative which does not contain a description sufficient for an exact identification of the property. The description need not necessarily be technically accurate but must be sufficiently precise to enable a surveyor to locate the boundaries. If the description is not sufficiently full, the deed will fail; verbal testimony will not be admitted to supply the deficiency unless such deficiency is the result of fraud, accident, or mistake, in which case the courts permit a reformation of the deed description.

A deed description calling for "about 8 acres to a lake" and "about 6 acres to a stake at road", without identifying stakes or giving beginning and ending points, was so indefinite as to be void: *Grand Lodge of Independent Order of Odd Fellows v. City of Thomasville,* 226 Ga. 4 (1970). The words "more or less" raises a presumption of sale by the acre; *Witmer v. Bloom* 288 A. 2d 323 (Md. App. 1972); *Allen v. Youngblood,* 200 S.E. 2d 758 (Ga. 1973).

Property description in deeds should be liberally construed to sustain rather than defeat a conveyance. In the Louisiana case of *Placed Oil Co. v. Young,* 246 So. 2d 306 (1971), the grantor conveyed "acres in S.W. corner of N.E. 1/4 of S.W. 1/4" of designated section, which was the same tract acquired by grantor under a partition agreement, the court held the description valid.

A real estate contract describing land only as "all that tract of Land Lot 112 of the 5th Dist. of Clayton County, Ga., being 36 acres on New Hope Road," was void and unenforceable for uncertainty: *Wallace v. Adamson,* 201 S.E. 2d 479 (Ga. 1973).

Parol evidence rule

The parol evidence rule generally applies. The rule is that verbal testimony cannot be introduced to vary, contradict, add to, or subtract from a written instrument, or to change its legal import, unless fraud, accident, or mistake is pleaded. However, should the deed refer to some other instrument, such as a previous deed, which accurately describes the premises, the new deed will be valid. All directions expressed as "northward" or "westward" mean due north and due west. There are four types of descriptions generally used:

1. Rectangular survey descriptions.
2. Lot number on plot or map.
3. Metes and bounds description.
4. Monuments.

Rectangular survey

The rectangular survey was adopted by Congress as early as May 20, 1785, and is used outside of the original thirteen states. In the *Real Estate Primer* issued by the State of Iowa[1] (1961 edition), the rectangular survey is explained and illustrated as follows:

This [rectangular survey] refers to a grid of north and south (meridians) and east and west (parallels) lines surveyed by the government. Identification of property is east or west so many ranges or vertical rows of checks from the north and south line called a "principal meridian" and so many horizontal rows of tiers or townships north of an east and west line called the "base line." Ranges run north and south and townships run east and west.

Distance between the parallels and meridians is twenty-four miles and the area contained therein is called a check. In this area are sixteen townships and the townships are further divided into thirty-six sections of a mile square each. The section is further divided into halves, quarters and smaller subdivisions.

Fractional sections on the north and west side of a township are due to corrections made of the survey lines for the curvature of the earth. This results in these sections having more or less 640 acres, depending upon corrections. In describing these sections the words "fractional sections" should be used.

SUBDIVISION OF A CHECK

1st Standard Parallel North

6 miles			T4N R1W				
Tier	3	North	T3N R1W				
			T2N R1W				
T1N R4W	T1N R3W	T1N R2W	T1N R1W	T1N R1E			

5th Principal Meridian

Range, East

24 Miles

Range 3 East

1st Guide Meridian East

24 Miles

Initial Point

Base Line

*TIN means "township 1 north R4W means "range 4 west"

In reading rectangular descriptions, for convenience one reads backwards from the general

[1] Permission of C. R. Galvin, Director.

part of the description to the specific part at the beginning. The general part of the description refers to the range and township and the specific to that part of a section.

Lot number

The lot number is used in urban centers where there has been a concentrated development of land. A property is transformed from farm or vacant land into a subdivision laid out in numbered lots. The plan, if approved, is accepted by the municipality and recorded. The property would then be identified as "Being all of Lot #162 in the Bower Hill Plan of Lots as laid out, and recorded in the office of the Recorder of Deeds of Dauphin County in Plan Book Volume 18, Page 113, being designated as Block 14J Lot 44 in the records of the Dauphin County Deed Registry Office."

SUBDIVISION OF TOWNSHIPS INTO SECTIONS

36	31	32	33	34	35	36	31
1	6	5	4	3	2	1	6
12	7	8	9	10	11	12	7
13	18	17	16	15	14	13	18
24	19	20	21	22	23	24	19
25	30	29	28	27	26	25	30
36	31	32	33	34	35	36	31
1	6	5	4	3	2	1	6

Adjoining sections are shown to give numbering.

Corrections for convergence are ordinarily made in sections 1, 2, 3, 4, 5, 6, 7, 18, 19, 30 and 31.

Metes and bounds

The oldest method of describing land is by "metes and bounds." Metes are measurements of length—feet, inches, perches (1 perch = 16 1/2 ft.); bounds are artificial and natural boundaries such as streets, roads, adjoining farms, roads and streams. Metes determine the certain quantity of land (acreage) while bounds confine that quantity within certain fixed limits. Such a description should have a definitely ascertained starting point, such as so many feet distant from the nearest cross street or at a definite lot dividing line, and then proceed clockwise, tracing the lines by directions and distances back to the point of beginning. A deed would be void in which the starting point was given as "a point on Bowman Street at the dividing line of property of B. Davidson" and a search of the title failed to locate any property owned or occupied by the said Davidson.

SUBDIVISION OF SECTION

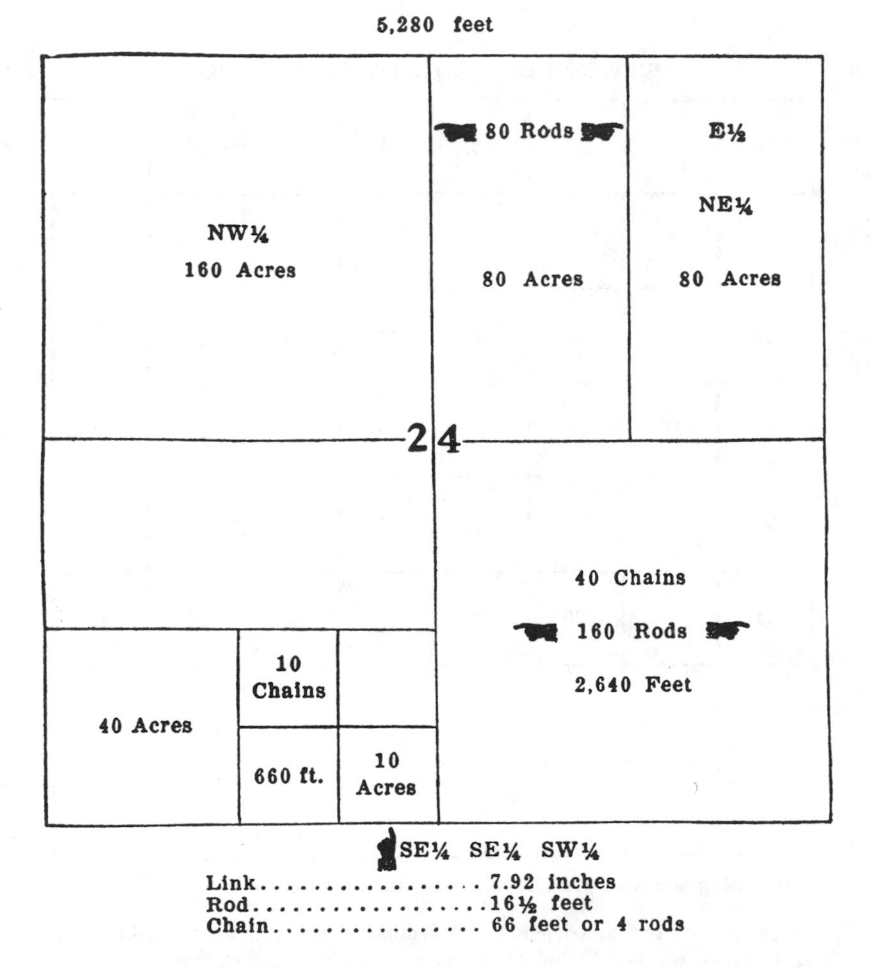

Link . . . . 7.92 inches
Rod . . . . 16½ feet
Chain . . . . 66 feet or 4 rods

The principle is well established that the courses and distances in a deed always give way to the boundary markers found on the ground or supplied by proof of their former existence when the marks or monuments are gone. Thus, a deed description "from said point, 40° 30' west a distance of 220 feet to the Revolutionary chestnut tree" would give the purchaser 230 feet, if that was the actual distance to the tree in question. This rule is to be used only in reconciling discrepancies.

Monuments

In rural areas, descriptions by monuments are still frequently used. At the end of the description it is customary to insert "containing 64 acres, more or less." The description by monuments does not lend itself readily to an examination of the title, particularly for one not familiar with the locale of the property. A description conveying "10 acres more or less" of other lands, and not locating the particular 10 acres, would be void, owing to uncertainity.

Fences

When the owners of adjoining land have acquiesced in the location of a fence for a length of time required by the statute of adverse possession, they are thereafter precluded from saying that the fence is not the true line. It then becomes immaterial to inquire whether or not the fence is on the original boundary line.

Roads

It is a general rule of law, well established by authority, that a conveyance of lands bounded by a highway gives the grantee title to the middle of the road if the grantor had title and did not expressly or by clear implication reserve the bed of the road to himself. This right to the middle of the road is always subject to the right of the public. Ownership becomes important only if the road is abandoned later.

Streams

Where a nonnavigable stream is given as a boundary, the grantee takes to the middle of the stream as in the case of a street. In the case of a navigable stream, the grantee takes absolutely to high water mark and, in a qualified sense, to low water mark. That is to say, in the area between high and low water, his rights are subject to the rights of the public for navigation purposes, which include all privileges necessary for such purposes. A navigable stream in law is one which is navigable in fact. The land between high and low water mark is known as flat land. A description in a deed read "five acres of marsh meadow *bounded by the River S.*" The boundary of the firm land *by the river* carried with it the adjacent flat land. The fact that the description states that the land is bounded "by" a stream or that it runs "along" a stream and names a monument on the shore does not necessarily show an intention to exclude the stream, and this is regarded merely as a statement of the point at which the boundary strikes the stream. It is impractical to place a marker in the stream proper.

An individual property owner has no absolute riparian rights of ownership in a navigable stream and to the land *below* high water mark, nor does he have littoral rights of ownership to land covered and uncovered by the flow and ebb of the sea tide. It has been held by the United States Supreme Court[2] that even the State of California has no title to the submerged land between the shoreline and the three-mile limit, but that title is in the Federal Government. The question of ownership is highly important because of valuable underlying oil deposits.

When a map, plan, or other survey is referred to in a deed, it becomes a material and essential part of the conveyance and is to have the same force and effect as if

[2] United States v. California, 332 U.S. 19 (1947).

copied in it. *Segaro v. Cornell,* 196 S.E. 2d 341 (Ga. 1973). Where there is a deed reference to a map of a highway to be dedicated in the future, there are two opposing rules. The New York rule holds that such a reference to an unopened highway raises a presumption of an intention to convey the land to the middle of the proposed highway as if the highway actually existed. The Massachusetts rule, on the other hand, states that the roadbed of the proposed highway is not included and the boundary is fixed at the side of the proposed highway. In Pennsylvania, the law seems to be that where the street is merely plotted upon the plan, the grantee takes only to the edge of the street, but when the street is opened, the grantee's title jumps to the middle of the street.

Calls in a deed are always to be controlled by lines on the ground. If the sale is made by lines staked and marked on the ground, such lines on the ground govern, if in conflict with the deed description.

Recital

The recital is a statement of facts interesting, or necessary, for persons examining a title to know. It tells how the grantor acquired title, or the reason why the deed is made, or some other explanatory remark. It usually follows the description, although when long, such as Trustee's or Executor's deeds made under an Order of Court, it usually comes after the names of the parties and commences with the word "Whereas." It can hardly be regarded as an essential part of the deed unless it contains something of a contractual nature between the parties to the instrument.

Appurtenances

The deed may contain the phrase "with the appurtenances and all the estate and right of the party of the first part [grantor] in and to said premises."

The right to the appurtenances goes with the property as a matter of law, so there is no real need for the above clause. All easements, rights, and incidents, which belong to the property conveyed and are necessary to its full enjoyment, pass as "appurtenances" without mention of them. What is merely convenient to the enjoyment does not. These include alleyways, water courses, light, and air. Thus, the deed should specify "together with" followed by a description of the rights intended to pass. What is appurtenant to a piece of land is appurtenant to every part thereof. Where a right of way is granted as appurtenant to a tract of land and the tract is later subdivided into smaller lots, each of the lot purchasers would be entitled to the same right of way. Also, where a property, bounded by a private alley is sold, and the alley is necessary to the premises sold, the right to use it passes as an appurtenance to the property unless there is something in the conveyance restricting the use solely to the grantor or expressly excepting the alley from the grant: *Westland Nursing Home, Inc. v. Benson,* 517 P. 2d 862 (Colo. App. 1974).

Habendum clause

The habendum clause (to have and to hold), where used, operates to define the quantity of estate which the grantee is said to have in the property granted. The habendum is not absolutely necessary. The estate granted may be limited in the earlier part of the deed and if the habendum contradicts the earlier limitation, it will have no effect. If the two can be reconciled, then effect will be given to both. Where the limitation in the premises is in general terms, as to Jones and his heirs generally, and the habendum limits the estate to Jones for and during the term of his natural life, the grantee takes a life estate.

Warranties

A seller, in conveying property, makes certain representations to the purchaser. He warrants that he has a fee simple title, that he has the right and power to convey it, and that there is no lien or encumbrance against the property. The seller is placed in the position where he personally guarantees the truthfulness of these statements and may be held personally responsible for them in case any of the statements are later proven false. Under the covenant of warranty the grantee may hold the grantor for any damage he has sustained. The three covenants of title relating to the ownership of a fee simple—the owner of the property in fee, the right to convey, and the freedom of the property from encumbrances—are known as covenants *in praesenti* (as of the present). The grantor also warrants that the grantee will quietly enjoy and that the grantor will make further assurances. These two warranties are known as covenants *in futuro* (as of the future). The quiet-enjoyment warranty means that the grantee will not be ousted by someone under a paramount title to his grantor. The further-assurances warranty provides that the grantor—if it is discovered at any time that, through an oversight or mistake in the deed, the grantee's title is imperfect—will voluntarily execute such instruments as are necessary to give the grantee the title which he thought he was receiving and which it was intended that he should receive. For example, a deed is improperly executed by the grantor. The grantee requests a new deed properly signed. The grantor cannot take the position that he is "through" with the deal and refuse to do anything more unless remunerated for doing so. Under the particular warranty the purchaser could enlist the aid of the court in compelling the seller to execute the necessary correction.

General and special warranty

The grantor also warrants the title and covenants to protect his grantee against any claimant. In a *general warranty* deed the grantor agrees with the grantee that he will "forever warrant and defend the property against every person or persons whomsoever lawfully claiming the same, or any part thereof." In other words, he agrees to protect or defend the buyer against the entire world.

The covenant of special warranty is not so sweeping in its grant. A man may not care to defend the title of a property against everyone. He may feel that he should be required to guarantee the title only against himself or anyone claiming under him. A *special warranty* is a promise or covenant on the part of the grantor to defend the grantee against all claims which may be brought by the grantor or his heirs, assigns, or anyone claiming under the grantor. The general warranty clause can be made into a special warranty by inserting the few words "by, from, through, or under him." If there are plural grantors, then use "them, or any of them." A purchaser of real estate has no right to expect a covenant of general warranty in his deed unless he bargains for it in the agreement of sale. He cannot refuse to take the deed merely because it contains a special warranty. Trustee deeds and deeds given in pursuance of an order of court are special warranty deeds. Where no warranty is expressed the court will hold there is an implied special warranty in favor of the grantee.

Execution—power of attorney

A deed may be executed by the grantor himself, or through his proxy under a power of attorney. A power of attorney has been defined as "an instrument, in writing, under seal, by which the party executing it appoints another to be his attorney and empowers him to act for him, either generally in all matters of business, or especially to do some specified act or acts, in his name and behalf." The power of attorney must be acknowledged so that it may be recorded in the county where the property is located; it must be recorded so that a purchaser may know that the particular execution was properly authorized. Death of the person executing the power of attorney automatically revokes the power of attorney even if the agent has no notice of the death. An attorney-in-fact has no right to delegate his authority unless the instrument by which he is appointed expressly authorizes the substitution. The signature of a deed by an attorney-in-fact should read as follows:

"John Steele
by Adam Taylor
his Attorney-in-fact"

However, the attorney or agent need not sign his own name; the name of the principal alone is sufficient. Better practice dictates the agent's name as well.

Signature

The object of a signature is to authenticate the genuineness of the document. It is not essential that the grantor himself should sign the deed. His mark, where he cannot write, or even where he can, if intended as a signature, will be sufficient. Signature by mark would be:

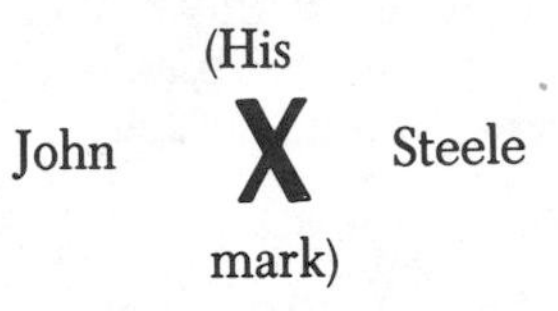

A signature by mark must be witnessed by two witnesses. Where the signing is done by a third person in the *presence* of the grantor and *at the direction* of the grantor, it amounts to a compliance with the requirements of the law. The ordinary situation is for property to stand in the name of one person. It is usual, however, where the title is in the name of the husband alone, to have the wife join in the execution of the deed. The wife joins for the purpose of extinguishing any claim which she may later have through her dower interest in the property.

A forged deed, unlike one procured by fraud, deceit or trickery, is void from its inception. In the latter event, the deed is voidable as between the parties thereto, but not as to a bona fide purchaser for value: *Harding v. Ja Laur Corp.,* 315 A. 2d 132 (Md. 1974).

Types of estates

We have already mentioned fee simple, which is the estate which can be created, and admits of the fullest and most complete ownership of real estate. Estates that are classified as to length of duration, for life or are inheritable, are termed freehold estates. In this category are: fee simple, life estates and estates upon condition (base fee). Estates less than a freehold comprise an estate for years; an estate granted for a limited or definite period of time (a leasehold) an estate at will and an estate at sufferance also fall in this category.

A life estate, as the name implies, is a conveyance to a person, to be owned by him, during the period of his natural life. Upon his death, the property reverts to the grantor or his heirs (reversion) or to the person named in the deed to succeed the life tenant (the remainderman). The life tenant is entitled to the benefits of the property, but he cannot suffer the property to go into disrepair or commit waste: *Gibbon v. Gibbon,* 287 S. 2d (Miss. 1974). A conditional fee estate is a conveyance of the property, to be used for a specified purpose, such as a school or church and, when that use is abandoned, the property reverts to the grantor or his heirs.

An estate from year to year is one for a definite period of time and then continues indefinitely until one of the parties elects to terminate it by giving proper notice. Thus, a lease for one year may continue for another year, at the expiration of the first year, unless either party has given the other party proper notice.

An estate at will is one which may be terminated at any time, without any formal notice.

An estate at sufferance is one where a person is in possession of premises lawfully,—under a lease for a *definite* term, and then continues in possession, at the expiration of the term, without the consent of the owner. Blackstone defines a tenancy at sufferance to be where one comes into possession of land by lawful title but keeps it afterward without any title at all. After the lease period has expired, the premises revert to the owner.

Dower

Dower is the right which a wife has in her husband's estate *at his death.* It is an inchoate or potential right which does not vest unless she survives her husband. It is personal to the wife alone and can only be asserted by her. It sometimes develops that a seller's wife refuses to sign the deed. She cannot be compelled to do so, unless she has signed the agreement of sale. In that event, an action can be maintained in court for specific performance to compel her to sign the deed. Thus, it is wise to have the wife join in the agreement, even though the property is in the name of the husband alone. If she does not sign the agreement of sale and refuses to join in the deed, the land remains subject to her dower interests in it. However, a husband ordinarily can mortgage his own real estate without the joinder of his wife. Sometimes a mortgage to the buyer is used to circumvent the wife's dower interests. If the wife can show fraud upon her, the transaction could be set aside unless the rights of a bona fide purchaser, without notice of the fraud, have intervened. The wife cannot prevent the sale of real estate by her husband, and she does not have any right of action against the purchaser until after the death of her husband, and then only in the case that she survives him. It sometimes happens that a man and woman contemplating marriage will enter into an agreement determining their property rights after marriage. This is known as an ante-nuptial agreement and is frequently used where one or both of the contracting parties are advanced in years. Under this agreement, the wife-to-be may surrender her rights in her husband's real estate, and he, in turn, agrees to relinquish any claim to her real estate after her death. Such agreements are not contrary to public policy, and if fair and conscionable, will be enforced. Thus, if a wife, prior to marriage, has entered into an ante-nuptial agreement and after marriage refuses to join in the agreement of sale or the subsequent deed to property owned by her husband alone, she may be compelled to execute her joinder by virtue of her previous agreement.

Dower is an encumbrance within the meaning of the term. If the wife refuses to sign, a purchaser has two alternatives. First, he can refuse to accept the deed signed by the husband alone and demand damages for the expense to which he has been put. Second, he can accept the husband's deed, in which event he is required to pay the full purchase price. He then assumes the risk of the wife predeceasing her husband or, if she does not, of paying her dower claim. Or, the husband and buyer may negotiate the purchase price and reduce the price by discounting the dower hazard. Dower, as such, has been eliminated in some states (Maryland 1969).

Deed by married women

In some jurisdictions (Alabama, Indiana, North Carolina, Texas), a deed by a married woman for real estate held in her own name is void unless her husband joins in the conveyance or unless she has been declared a feme sole (single woman). For cause shown, as where the husband has deserted the wife or is a profligate, the court, upon application of the wife, may declare her a feme sole, as if she were unmarried. She could then execute a valid deed by her signature alone. In Arkansas, Oklahoma, and other states, a married woman can convey her separate real estate without the joinder of her husband.

Where property is owned by a single woman who enters into an agreement of sale and, before the consummation of the deal, marries, the purchaser can compel the wife and her newly acquired husband to join in a valid deed. Since the married woman, prior to marriage, had contracted to sell the property, she retained only the bare legal title after the agreement of sale was signed, and her marriage was ineffective to enlarge her interest or to impinge upon the equitable title obtained by the purchaser under the agreement.

Estates by the entireties

Where property is held in the name of husband *and* wife, it is known as a joint tenancy and in some states as an estate by the entireties. In the Tennessee case of *Ballard v. Farley,* 226 S.W. 544 (1920), the Court held that a conveyance to a named person "and wife," without naming her was sufficient to create an estate by the entireties. It exists only in favor of husband and wife and has certain advantages to recommend it. A deed from John Steele to Adam Taylor and Anna Mae Taylor, his wife, would automatically create such an estate. Both signatures are absolutely essential in order to convey title. Where the parties are separated, neither spouse can convey or lease without joinder of the other spouse: *Schweitzer v. Evans,* 63 A. 2d 39 (Pa. 1949). Upon the death of one, the property immediately and automatically vests in the surviving spouse; no court proceedings are necessary. The property is usually free from state inheritance taxes, and in most states a judgment against one of the parties would not be a lien against the property, unless the debtor spouse survived. Both parties can join in a good conveyance of the property, free and clear of the judgment against the one party. A judgment entered against the husband, for example, would not be extinguished by such sale of the property. However, if a judgment exists against one spouse, and husband and wife desire to obtain a mortgage, they may experience difficulties. Since the judgment antedates the mortgage, the real possibility exists that the wife might die before the husband, and the judgment creditor would have precedence over the mortgage. The distinction between sale of the property, free from the judgment lien, and mortgaging the property, subject, in a qualified sense to the judgment, lies in the fact that a mortgage is only a *temporary* transfer of the property, and when paid off, title to the property reverts to husband and wife, as an estate by the entireties. Then, the judgment creditor must await the fortuitous circumstance that the wife die before the husband, in order for him to proceed against the property, to obtain payment of his judgment, by foreclosure proceedings. Most married couples, in states adhering to the estate by the entireties concept, prefer to hold property in this manner, because of the advantages offered. So long as there is a harmonious marital relationship, it should be recommended in most cases. Possibility of federal estate tax liability, if the husband is wealthy, might discourage this form of tenure. Both husband and wife *must* join in a deed to convey the property in order to convey a good title. Divorce will terminate the ownership by the entireties and each spouse will then own one-half of the property as tenants in common. Unless the parties can agree, amicably, to join in a deed for sale of the property, it would be necessary for the spouse desiring to sell to enter a court action for a sale of the property. The proceeds would then be divided equally between husband and wife.

Where a conveyance is made to two married persons and their spouses and it is intended that each couple shall hold by the entireties, the names and status of the respective parties should be set forth as follows.

THIS DEED, made the 10th day of June, 1971, between JOHN T. STEELE and FRANCES L. STEELE, his wife, of the city of Miami, County of Dade, and State of Florida,

A
N
D

WILLIAM C. GRAY, JR., and THELMA T. GRAY, his wife, and CARL T. FRYE and ALICE L. FRYE, his wife, of the same place, AS TENANTS BY THE ENTIRETIES AS TO THE RESPECTIVE SHARE OF EACH HUSBAND AND WIFE AND AS TENANTS IN COMMON OF THE WHOLE.

Sometimes a man and woman take title to property as husband and wife, when they are not so in fact. Such a tenure is not void, but they will hold title as joint tenants or as tenants in common, depending upon what the court could determine as their *intention* from all of the facts:

In the Maryland case of *Michael v. Lucas,* 152 Md. 512 (1927), property was deeded to Joseph H. Kuntz and Emily H. Kuntz, as tenants by the entireties, the survivor of them, his or her heirs, personal representatives and assigns. The grantees were unmarried. The court held the deed valid and upon the death of Joseph, the named Emily acquired title, as the survivor-joint tenant, since that was clearly the intention: *Adams v. Foster,* 466 S.W. 2d 706 (Mo. 1971).

Homestead

Homestead property resembles an estate by the entireties. Homestead laws exist in Alabama, Arkansas, California, Florida, Georgia, Iowa, Louisiana, Massachusetts, Missouri, Mississippi, Oklahoma, South Dakota, Texas, Virginia, West Virginia, Wisconsin and Wyoming. Property owned and occupied as a home, in a certain amount, is known as the family homestead. Both husband and wife must join in any deed or mortgage for this property. In the interests of public policy for the preservation of the family, homestead property cannot be sold to satisfy a judgment against the husband. Certain elements must be present to establish a homestead. There must be a family of two or more persons living together under a family head and actually occupying the land in question. The proper declaration must be filed that the property is actually occupied as a homestead. The homestead laws provide maximum areas and values of the homestead. In Arkansas, for example, the statute sets up two types of homesteads: first, the rural homestead, outside of any urban district, owned and occupied as a residence, consists of land not exceeding 160 acres, but no less than 80 acres, and not exceeding $10,000 in value; second, the urban homestead, in a city, town or village occupied as a residence, cannot exceed one acre of land, but no less than 1/4 acre, and not exceeding $2500 in value. It is not necessary for a person to live on a homestead in order to claim homestead rights, but there must always be an *intention* to return to the homestead. In Texas, property upon which the head of the family conducts his business is known as his "business homestead." In California, the exemption from execution on homestead property is $7500. In Florida, homestead exists as to 160 acres outside an incorporated city or town, and as to one-half acre if located within a city or town. In Wisconsin, not exceeding 1/4 acre residential; 40 acres rural can be held as a homestead.

Community property

Property acquired during coverture (marriage) other than by gift, devise, or descent is community property, and each spouse owns an undivided one-half interest, and each is entitled to dispose of his or her interest.

The basic concept of community property is that *whatever may be acquired during marriage by the efforts of either spouse belongs, on acquisition, in equal halves to both.* It was introduced into the United States through the Spanish-influenced laws of Mexico. The institution exists in California, Louisiana, New Mexico, Texas, and Arizona. It has likewise been incorporated into the statutes of Nevada (1865), Idaho (1867), Washington (1869), Oklahoma and Hawaii (1945), Michigan, Nebraska, Oregon, and Pennsylvania (1947).[3]

Enactments were prompted by a desire to reduce Federal income taxes payable by the income-producing husband. Court decisions are not uniform as to the allocation of income received by each spouse from different sources. Texas cases hold that *all* income received during marriage is community property, including income from a trust in which one of the parties has a life estate. In California, the Supreme Court held to the contrary, maintaining that a wife's income from her *separate* estate remained as her separate property.

Joint estates and estates in common

It has been stated previously that, where husband and wife own property together, the property is held by the entireties. In some states, as in Nebraska, it is termed a joint tenancy. Two or more persons may own property together; if they are not husband and wife, the ownership is joint or in common. In a joint tenancy, each party is possessed of an undivided part of the whole. In a tenancy in common, each is possessed of the whole of an undivided part. The language to create a joint tenancy must be clear and explicit; otherwise, the parties will be deemed to hold in common. In a joint ownership, a deceased party's interest in the property goes to the surviving owner or owners and not to the decedent's heirs or next of kin. A deed from Roger Harris to Carl Parsons and Edward F. Parsons, "as joint tenants, with the right of survivorship and not as tenants in common" would clearly create a joint estate. Upon the death of Carl Parsons, the property would vest absolutely in the surviving party, Edward F. Parsons, rather than in any surviving heirs or kin of Carl Parsons. If the conveyance from Harris were simply to "Carl Parsons and Edward F. Parsons," the grantees would hold as owners in common, and upon the death of Carl Parsons, his interest in the property would not go to the surviving party, Edward F. Parsons, but would vest in Carl's heirs. Where one joint owner dies, and there are two or more owners surviving, the property vests in all of the survivors until the last survivor, who succeeds to the entire estate. Joint owners must acquire ownership by a single deed. Husband and wife may hold property as tenants in common rather than by the

[3] Pennsylvania Act declared unconstitutional in case of Wilcox v. Penn Mutual Life Ins. Co., 357 Pa. 581 (1947).

entireties if the deed makes this clear. There must be present the four *unities* of time, title, interest and possession, in order to create joint ownership (joint tenancy).

In the case of *Zomisky v. Zomisky,* 449 Pa. 239 (1972), the grantor conveyed land to himself and his son as "joint tenants and as in common with the right of survivorship." Upon the father's death, the son claimed title to the land. The other children of the decedent brought suit, claiming that the deed created a tenancy in common. The Supreme Court, in affirming the lower court, held that the language in the deed was sufficiently clear to create a joint tenancy, with the right of survivorship.

A deceased joint owner's interest in real estate is subject to inheritance and estate taxes. Thus, if four persons hold title in this manner and one dies, tax liability would be based on one-fourth of the value of the property at the date of death. A sale by one of three joint owners of his interest would not destroy the joint ownership of the remaining two as joint owners of two-thirds. The purchaser of the one-third interest would become a tenant in common, to that extent, with the two joint owners.

A conveyance of a farm to Francis Lucas, a single man, and to Joseph and Matilda Lucas, husband and wife, raises the serious question whether each of the three grantees owns an undivided one-third interest, whether Francis owns a *one-half* interest, and Joseph and Matilda own the other half by the entireties, or whether Joseph owns a one-third interest and the married couple own the other two-thirds by the entireties. A broker preparing a deed is duty-bound to "spell out" the *intentions* of the parties, but he must first be cognizant of the applicable law under the circumstances. If the intention is not sufficiently manifested, a serious consequence may ensue. With no more language in the deed than indicated in the Lucas case above, Francis would own a *one-half* interest and Joseph and Matilda would own the other half interest by the entireties.[4]

A conveyance was made to James C. Miller, being unmarried, and Dimitri Katsowney and Elfena Katsowney, his wife, as joint tenants and not as tenants in common. James C. Millona (Miller) died. There was no question raised as to the Katsowneys holding an estate by the entireties. The issue was whether Miller, the co-grantee, became a joint tenant or a tenant in common. It is clear that Miller was a tenant in common and at his death the sale by the administrator, of his interest, was valid.

The Uniform Partnership provides for a special form of tenancy, called a "tenancy in partnership." Such property must be purchased with partnership funds and used for partnership purposes. A deed must clearly indicate that the conveyance is to a partnership, *as such;* otherwise, the grantees will be considered as tenants in common. In case one partner dies, his surviving widow would have no dower right or claim in such real estate. The value of the deceased partner's interest in the property, would become a part of his estate. If the two or more persons purchase real estate "as partners", this would not constitute partnership property, within the contemplation of the law. Instead, they would own the property as tenants in common.

Reading deed

Where a grantor signs a deed, he is presumed to have read it and to be familiar with its contents. Illiteracy is no defense to the validity of the instrument. If a person cannot read, the burden is upon him to have someone read the deed to him. A grantor cannot complain at a later date that the transaction has turned out differently than he anticipated, or that he was unaware of the full import of the deed, because he could not read. Where the illiterate grantor has been imposed upon and the deed content misrepresented to him, equity will grant relief and set the transfer aside.

---

[4] Heatter v. Lucas, 397 Pa. 296 (1951).

Witnessing

In most states it is not necessary to have the deed witnessed. In Georgia, the law requires two witnesses in order to record a deed, but without witnesses, the deed is valid between the grantor and the grantee. It is a good precaution in the event that a dispute arises, for the subscribing witnesses may be procured to testify as to the deed execution. The witness attests nothing but the signing and delivery of the deed. The date and other contents of the deed are matters which he does not attest and to which he seldom attends.

Acknowledgment

In addition to signing, sealing, and witnessing a deed, it is customary for the grantor to acknowledge it. The acknowledgment is a formal declaration made before a notary public, justice of the peace, alderman, or other official empowered to perform this service, affirming the genuineness of the signature on the deed. The acknowledgment accomplishes two things: first, it establishes the deed as *prima facie* evidence in any legal proceeding; that is, the deed will be accepted as evidence without any further proof of its genuineness; and second, *it permits the recording of the deed.* The acknowledgment contains the venue or county in which it is executed—"State of Illinois, County of Cook"—, the date, the name of the grantor, and the signature, seal, and expiration date of the commission of the officer taking the acknowledgment. It should state that the affiant is personally known or satisfactorily proved to be the subscriber. The grantor's marital status should also be indicated—"John Steele, unmarried," or "John Steele and Mary Steele, his wife," or "John Steele, unmarried, and Helen Steele, unmarried." In most states, only one acknowledgment need be taken for both husband and wife. In some states—Alabama, New Jersey, and South Carolina—separate acknowledgments are necessary for husband and wife. The married woman's acknowledgment must be taken apart from her husband—that she signed the deed freely and voluntarily. In North Carolina, a separate acknowledgment is necessary in a conveyance from a wife to her husband.

Delivery

Delivery is one of the most important steps in the transfer of title to real estate. A deed, signed, sealed, witnessed, and acknowledged, does not pass title until it is delivered by the grantor to the grantee, or to a third person for him: *Murphy v. Traylor,* 289 So. 2d 584 (Ala. 1974).

In *Fiori v. Fiori,* 405 Pa. 303 (1961), a deed was executed in 1940. It was not recorded until 1957. The grantor died in 1942. The court found that the grantor, at no time, told the grantee, or any member of his family, about the deed. The grantor controlled the property until his death. The court held that there was no presumption of delivery. An unrecorded deed, found by grantee among grantor's papers, after grantor's death, does not pass title, although grantee had said that it belonged to grantee: *Willingham v. Smith, et al.,* 106 S.E. 117 (Ga. 1921); *1st Natn. Bank of Gainesville v. Harmon,* 199 S.E. 223 (Ga. 1938); *Allgood v. Allgood* 196 S.E. 2d 888 (Ga. 1973).

As between the parties to a deed, it is necessary that there be delivery to grantee. Validity of the delivery depends upon intention of the grantor: *Proctor v. Forsythe,* 480 P. 2d 511 (Wash. 1971). When the deed is not "handed over," question of delivery arises. If delivery may be "presumed" from the circumstances, then title will pass. The question to be determined is the *intention* of the grantor. An executed deed, recorded by the *grantor,* would raise a strong presumption of delivery. Ordinarily, it may be said that retention of the deed by the grantor raises a strong presumption against delivery and possession by the grantee creates a presumption in favor of delivery. In both cases only a presumption is raised and is subject to rebuttal by proof.

Deposit of a deed with a third person to be turned over to the named grantee, upon death of grantor, constitutes a "delivery," only if grantor surrenders all control over deed, and conveys a present interest in the property. Intention can be construed through conversations and acts at time deed was delivered to third person: *Cain v. Morrison,* 512 P. 2d 474 (Kan. 1973).

Where decedent supplies purchase money for land, but took title in name of her cousin, who did not know of deed to him, title did not pass to him, after the death: *Caron v. Wadas,* 305 N.E. 2d 853 (Mass. 1974).

Delivery absolute

There are two kinds of delivery, delivery absolute and delivery in escrow. Delivery absolute occurs when made to a grantee or his agent without any conditions or stipulations attached. This is the usual situation.

In escrow

A delivery in escrow occurs when the deed is delivered to a third person and will take effect only upon the performance of some condition by one of the parties or the happening of some event. In an escrow delivery, the grantor loses all control over the deed, and he is powerless to recall it. The condition of the escrow must be stated *at the time* the deed is turned over to the escrow holder and not at some later date. The *time* for performance of the escrow condition should be definitely stated and, also, what happens if the condition is not performed. Otherwise, the delivery will be considered absolute and the escrow holder as agent for the grantee. The escrow holder should require that the condition of delivery be in writing, signed by the interested parties. A deed delivered in escrow will pass no title if it is stolen or otherwise fraudulently procured by the grantee or if delivered to him without fulfillment of the escrow condition, but a bona fide purchaser from the grantee, without notice, will obtain good title.

It should be remembered that the escrow holder must be some disinterested or impartial third person and the principals or their legal counsel are not such disinterested parties within the contemplation of the law. Nor is a broker a disinterested third party, because he is the agent of the owner from whom he receives compensation for his services in the form of a commission. A bank, title company or an escrow company should preferably be used as the escrow holder. A deposit of earnest money with a real estate broker should not be confused with an escrow.

Recording

When the deed has been signed, sealed, and delivered, the transfer of title is complete. Recordation is of no importance insofar as passing of title is concerned between grantor and grantee: *Huntington City v. Peterson,* 518 P. 2d 1246 (Utah 1974). However, in order for the purchaser to protect himself in the ownership, the law requires him to take one additional step. This consists in recording or registering his deed in the office of the Recorder of Deeds, Registrar, or Register of Deeds in the county where the property is located. The recording of a deed consists in having it transcribed in a proper book and indexed, so that the public at large may have notice of the transfer of title. The deed should be recorded promptly in order to protect the grantee against a subsequent conveyance of the same property by his grantor, or against a mortgage or judgment entered against the same grantor. Green delivers a deed to White on December 6, 1971 which is not recorded until March 21, 1972. A judgment entered against Green on February 21, 1972 would be a lien against the real estate in question. So also, a bona fide purchaser of the same land from Green would have a preferred claim to the property if he had no actual or constructive notice of the transfer to White. Actual notice is express or direct knowledge gained in the course of the transaction.

Constructive notice

Thus, Cox's knowledge that Adams at one time had mortgaged property to Brown would not be of itself actual notice to Cox unless he learned of it in the course of his negotiations with Adams for the purchase of the particular property. In most cases, notice of an unrecorded deed must be made out from a statement of facts that existed at the time and from which notice would be presumed to have been given to a cautious purchaser. This is what is known as "constructive notice." The rule concerning constructive notice is that notice can be presumed to have been given where there are circumstances which would make a prudent man suspicious and which would cause him to inquire whether the seller had not previously parted with his title. The chief test of constructive notice concerns *who was in actual possession of the land at the time of the sale.* If the land is not in the possession of the man holding himself out to own it but is occupied by the holder of the prior deed, then a little inquiry from the party in possession would readily reveal the duplicity of the original owner.

In *Weddell v. City of Atlanta,* 172 S.E. 2d 862 (1970), the court held that actual possession of the realty by a wife and children was sufficient to put all who might purchase from the husband on notice and on inquiry as to what interest or claim they might have.

Torrens system

A system of land registration was introduced in Australia in 1858 by Sir Robert Torrens. The system provided a permanent method of title registration with an assurance fund out of which losses due to title defects would be paid. Once the title is registered by an owner, subsequent transfers of the certificate of title registration could be readily effected at slight expense. The original Torrens system has not made any great inroad into the recording system in this country due to the initial expense involved, certain substantial objections inherent in the system, and the opposition of the title companies. Although adopted in varying forms in a number of states (California, (Repealed in 1955) Colorado, Georgia, Illinois, Massachusetts, Mississippi, Minnesota, Nebraska, New York, North Carolina, North Dakota, Ohio, Oregon, South Carolina, South Dakota, Tennessee, Utah, Virginia, and Washington), title searches are, in the main, still required. In Massachusetts and Illinois are found the most satisfactory applications of the Torrens system. Adaptations of the Torrens system require the registration of title ownership through court proceedings. The certificate of title issued by court authorization is conclusive insofar as the character of the title is concerned.

Adverse Possession

ORDINARILY, AN OWNER of real estate relies upon a "paper" title to establish ownership; that is, by deed from his predecessor, and which, when traced back, shows a continuity of title ownership to the source of title in the particular state. An examination of the public records establishes a "chain of title" upon which the occupier of land relies to prove ownership. Technically, title emanates from a sovereign power or government, the exact source varying in the different sections of the country. However, a resident of land may claim title to property without any deed or color of title at all. He may rely upon adverse occupation. Such title may be superior to that of the holder of the "paper" title if certain statutory requirements are met. This is known by title as *adverse possession.* The law governing adverse possession is now universal, being enforced in practically every state of the country. The purposes of these laws are identical. They are prompted in the first place by the demands of public policy which hold that a statute of this kind is necessary to prevent the abandonment of any portion of the territory. The law provides that where an occupier holds land and maintains actual, continuous, hostile, notorious, distinct, and visible possession for the required period of time, he is deemed to have the legal title as against one who holds a deed for the same land. The period varies from seven to thirty years. In Arkansas and Utah, 7 years is the statutory period; Mississippi, Missouri, and Oregon, 10 years; Connecticut, Kansas, Kentucky, Minnesota, and Oklahoma, 15 years; Illinois, Massachusetts, Maine, New York, 20 years; Pennsylvania, 21 years; Texas, 25 years; and in Louisiana, 30 years. The Adverse Possession Act is in a sense a statute of limitations in that it bars the legal owner from asserting his claim to the land where he has remained silent and done nothing to oust the adverse occupant during the statutory period. The theory of the law is that "no person ought to be permitted to lie by while transactions can be fairly investigated and justly determined, until time has involved them in uncertainty and obscurity, and then ask for an inquiry." An adverse claimant may petition a court for a decree to perfect his title. A party claiming title by adverse possession bears a heavy burden of proof: *Kerrigan v. Thomas,* 281 So. 2d 410 (Fla. App. 1973).

Actual possession

Incidents which help establish actual possession include building a dwelling or other structure, clearing brush, sowing crops, pasturing cattle, erecting fences, cutting timber, irrigating the land, constructing drainage ditches, planting orchards, and paying taxes. However, payment of taxes by an adverse possessor of land is not the controlling factor to establish title. In Florida, taxes must be paid by such adverse claimant for the requisite 7 year period, unless he has color of title, i.e., some written instrument or court decree: *Meyer v. Law,* 287 So. 2d 37 (Fla. 1973).

By actual possession is meant such a possession of the property as leaves no doubt in the mind of the ordinary person as to the nature of the occupancy. The law insists that the claimant must show the performance of adequate acts amounting to an open denial of the title of the recorded owner. It must not be inferred, however, that he is required to exercise force, as the law does not insist that a man should provoke a quarrel in order to demonstrate his ownership. Evidence of actual possession is to be taken from such facts as cultivating the land, erecting improvements upon it, fencing in the property, and payment of taxes. It has been said that the adverse claimant "must unfurl his flag on the land, and keep it flying, so that the owner may see, if he will, that an enemy has invaded his domains, and planted the standard of conquest." . . . The owner is, of course, chargeable with knowledge of what is openly done on his land and therefore calculated to attract attention. But a mere passive possession without intending to claim the property, is insufficient, regardless of the length of time it continues, or however open, notorious, or exclusive it may have been. (1 R.C.L. section 7, 693).

In a wooded area, indistinct markings, which consisted of a few strands of barbed wire, tacked to trees, but not on the claimed boundary line, would not give notice of an adverse claim: *Wales v. Lester,* 517 P. 281 (Or. 1973).

A tenant could never claim title by adverse possession no matter what improvements he might make nor how long he might be in possession, because he acknowledges the superior title of his lessor from the very beginning.

Where a party occupies property, under a permissive use, he cannot claim title by adverse possession: *Burns v. Owens,* 357 S.W. 2d 520 (Ark. 1962); *Dimmick v. Dimmick,* 374 P. 2d 824 (Cal. 1962). Payment of taxes alone, without actual residence and dominion over the property, would be insufficient to prove adverse possession. Payment of taxes is entitled to some weight in proving the adverse claim, but it is a contributing factor, not the controlling one: *Davis v. Mayweather,* 504 S.W. 2d 741 (Ark. 1974).

Constructive possession

It is not to be inferred that actual possession of a particular tract or area will cover a larger tract in its entirety. It is a well-recognized principle in the United States that a person having a "color of title"—that is, anything in writing concerning the title which serves to define the extent of the claim, no matter how imperfect the paper title is—is to be regarded in constructive possession of the whole tract although he is in actual residence of only a part of it. The entry of the owner would be barred to the entire tract after the lapse of the statutory period. This rule is founded on the theory that the person claiming adverse possession under "color of title" has a notorious possession by reason of the written instrument. A realistic interpretation of this doctrine must be made. It is doubtful whether possession of a few acres out of a thousand purported to be conveyed by the invalid deed would be held to be constructive possession of the whole. The rule concerning constructive possession applies when possession is taken, first, under a conveyance which is invalid either for want of title or capacity in the grantor or for want of proper formalities in the execution of the instrument, and second, under a void or voidable decree of court. However, if the paper title under which a person claims is a nullity, the adverse occupier acquires title only to so much of the land as has been actually occupied. One who enters into possession of a part of a tract of land under "color of title" is immediately, by construction of the law, in actual possession of the whole tract. But one who enters without "color of title" is a trespasser and acquires title only to the area actually occupied. In some states, where there is color of title, the period of adverse occupancy is materially reduced.

Continuous possession

The next requirement is that a claimant must have exercised continuous and uninterrupted possession for the statutory period. Any abandonment of the property would defeat the title. A man claiming title to a wood lot by adverse possession will be defeated if he shows that the only occupancy of the property has been an occasional visit to it for the purpose of cutting fire wood or for fence material. Likewise, a man cannot claim title by adverse possession to a coal mine to which he made only sporadic visits for a supply of coal. In the case of farm land, where the rigors of winter prevent its cultivation and the claimant temporarily abandons it to follow his trade so that he can obtain funds for the purchase of necessary farm implements, the continuity of his possession would not be broken.

Tacking

Where the possession has been continued for a number of years and has been handed down from one to another without any break or interruption, for a valuable consideration, or by descent as from parent to child, it is in some measure respectable. The right which the adverse occupier has in the property, although it has not ripened into title, may be sold. The purchaser can "tack" his seller's period of occupation to his own possession in computing the necessary statutory period. The possession is *connected* by privity of contract or by descent. For example, Adams takes possession of certain land in 1945 and sells his interest to Bell in 1953. Bell remains in possession until 1968. Bell can claim title to the land through the necessary period of adverse possession.

In order to take advantage of "tacking," it is advisable to indicate in the deed that the grantor is transferring all rights to any portion of the tract claimed by adverse possession to the grantee. Such a clause would read:

> The parties of the first part hereby convey any title by adverse possession to any property adjacent to the above described premises.

In the case of *Lewkowicz v. Blumish,* 442 Pa. 369 (1971), a dispute arose between adjoining property owners as to their respective use of a driveway. The defendant claimed a prescription right by adverse possession. The Pennsylvania requirement for adverse possession is 21 years. The defendant, who acquired title to his property only three months earlier, could only establish 12 years use by his grantor. Tacking on the 12 years to his 3 months use was far short of the 21 year requirement.

Party who had been in possession of tract since 1945 when he purchased it could not tack on possession of his ancestor, to satisfy the 30 year requirement, since the ancestor's possession was not hostile to plaintiff's claimed ownership: *Thibodeaux v. Quibodeaux,* 282 So. 2d 845 (La. App. 1973).

Hostile or notorious possession

The next requirement is hostile or notorious possession. The claimant must show that his possession has been hostile to the holder of the paper title, and not subordinate to it. The adverse possessor "must keep his flag flying," which means that he must exercise all the acts of dominion over the land, not only against the outside world but also against the owner in case the opportunity presents itself. If he recognizes the claim of the owner as superior to his own, he defeats his own claim because the element of hostile possession is lacking. Where the owner is absent or cannot be found, the question of hostility is purely one of invention. It may be said that hostile merely means occupation *foreign* to the paper title.

The doctrine of hostility, however, varies in different states. The Connecticut rule, frequently cited in other states, is that where two owners had located a line between their properties in an inaccurate manner, under an honest belief or mistake as to the exact boundary, with the result that one of them had occupied a strip of land which was, in reality, the property of the other, for the statutory period, without interruption, he should be given title to it even though there had been no intention to do wrong, or to exercise a hostile possession against his neighbor. The courts have decided, in effect, that *ground occupied under a mistaken belief is necessarily a hostile possession.* Other states follow the rule laid down in Iowa. Under the same facts the decision would be that the period of adverse possession would not begin to run until the mistake was discovered by the one encroaching. The *intention* of the party who took it and occupied the ground was the controlling factor. The intention could not arise until the mistake was discovered.

Visible possession

Possession must be visible. This requirement would preclude adverse possession to coal where the entrance took place beneath the surface and the entry was not readily noticeable to the owner or the public at large.

Distinct possession

The final requirement is that the possession of a claimant must be distinct. He cannot establish his claim to the ground unless he has laid claim to and exercised control over a definite piece of ground which can be sharply defined. He must exercise *exclusive* occupancy over it. Joint occupation would not satisfy the requirements.

Exceptions

The statute will not run against a remainderman until the termination of a precedent estate such as a life tenant. One owner in common could not claim adverse title against a co-owner: *Iverson v. Iverson, et al,* 213 N.W. 2d 708 (S.D. 1973). Neither will the statute run against the state nor against land owned by the United States Government, nor against any land used for a public purpose. In 1860 a railroad purchased a narrow strip of land, 700 feet in length by 75 feet in width. When the railroad attempted to make use of the land in 1911, it was found to be in possession of one Jones. An ejectment action was brought to recover possession. In the trail of the case the plaintiff railroad showed a *paper* title (deed) to the land in question. The defendant, in reply, set up a claim of the title by adverse possession in himself and his predecessors for more than 21 years. The pivotal question was whether title to land purchased by a railroad company outside its right of way for future railroad purposes can be acquired by adverse possession. Ordinarily, land used by a railroad as a right of way and for public purposes cannot be the subject of title by adverse possession. The same would be true insofar as land similarly used by any public utility. It is not true, however, where the land lies outside of the right of way. The railroad could not be heard to say, more than 40 years after the purchase, that it bought the land intending some day to use it for railroad purposes, but had not actively exercised this use. It was significant too, that the land in dispute was acquired by purchase rather than in the exercise of the company's right of eminent domain. The fact of condemnation, that is through eminent domain, indicates a public use, whereas in the case of a purchase, it indicates nothing and establishes nothing but title in the purchaser.[1]

[1] Delaware Lackawanna R.R. v. Tobyhanna Co., 228 Pa. 487.

Present-day significance

Where a person has complied with the adverse possession requirements, he obtains valid title to the land so occupied. While he has no deed to his property, yet he can give a deed to another. He can compel a purchaser from him to accept his deed. His rights and privileges differ in no respect from that of an ordinary owner.

Adverse possession has contemporary significance through many cases where fences, markers and buildings have been improperly located and the mistake not discovered for the period specified in the statute. Where the statutory period has expired, the claimant's subsequent abandonment of the property would not defeat his ownership unless some new occupier took over and maintained his occupation, in turn, for the necessary period.

Easements

An easement, such as a walk or right of way, can also be acquired by adverse use. It must be hostile in its inception in order to found a claim by adverse use. This is known as easement by prescription and the general rules of adverse possession apply. To acquire prescriptive rights, the use must be open and notorious: *Dickinson v. Pike,* 201 S.E. 2d 897 (N.C. 1974). Long, continued, uninterrupted use of roadway over farm land, creates an easement by prescription: *George v. Dickinson,* 504 S.W. 2d 658 (Mo. App. 1974).

In *Flynn v. Korsack,* 175 N.E. 2d 397 (Mass. 1961), the court held that the plaintiff had acquired the right to use a driveway between adjoining properties by prescription. The defendants were ordered to remove a chain link fence and all other obstructions in the driveway. The same ruling was made in the case of *Whytock v. Green,* 383 P. 2d 628 (Okla. 1963). In *Stewart v. Bittle,* 370 S.W. 2d 132 (Ark. 1963), a fence between two properties for more than 30 years was held to establish the boundary line.

It is sometimes difficult to determine whether the land itself has been acquired adversely, or merely a right of way over it. The owner of the land, in order to prevent the easement, must take adequate measures to prohibit the unlicensed use of his property. If a physical barrier is not effectual, application to court for injunctive relief should be made. Notice or threat of legal proceedings will not defeat the statute.

Thus, it may be seen that title to real estate may be acquired through descent (by will), through purchase (by deed), and through occupation (by adverse possession). Title to real estate may also be acquired through the involuntary act of the owner (by eminent domain).

Restrictive Covenants, Easements, Zoning

A COVENANT is generally defined as an agreement between two or more persons, entered into by deed, whereby one of the parties promises the performance or nonperformance of certain acts or that a given state of things does or does not exist. Covenants may arise by implication of law, from the conduct of the parties. They may be divided into two classes, personal covenants and restrictive covenants or covenants running with the land.

Restrictive covenants

Restrictions in a deed, as to limitations on the use of the property conveyed, have been in existence for a very long time. The restriction must be reasonable and it must not violate public policy. Restrictions have been employed to restrict type of building and/or to limit the use. Restrictive covenants have been productive of much litigation.

Restrictive covenants are not favored in the law. They are strictly construed and every doubt is resolved against the existence of the restriction.

Restrictions may arise by (1) express covenants, or (2) by implication (a) from the language of the deed, or (b) from the conduct of the parties: *Witt v. Sternwehr Development Co.,* 400 Pa. 609 (1960).

Restrictive covenants, as the expression is generally understood, are covenants running with the land. They are sometimes called "negative" covenants. They may be created in a number of ways. First, the limitations on the use of land may be explicitly set forth in the deed instrument. Second, the restrictions may be contained in a separate written instrument recorded or determined from a printed plan of the proposed development of the property. Third, restrictive covenants may be brought into existence by estoppel through oral representations alone. Thus, where an owner sells part of a subdivision tract under representations that his entire plan is restricted to the same extent, he thereby restricts use of remaining portion of his land to that extent.

The owner of a tract of land divided into lots sometimes imposes restrictions on some of the lots as sold. Such restrictions are not to be defeated merely because similar restrictions are not imposed upon the remainder of the lots. Where an owner of lots conveys one of them by a deed containing building restrictions with a covenant that he will impose the same restrictions in the deeds for the remainder of the lots, the deed is recorded, and he subsequently conveys the remaining lots by deed without such restrictions, his later grantee is bound by the terms of the deed to the former grantee, although he has no actual notice of such terms. In examining the record he is bound to read the whole of the former deed and if he fails to do so, he is affected by notice of all that it contains. In reading the deed he will thus have notice of the restrictions affecting all of the lots.

It is a well-recognized principle of law that every owner of land has the right to restrain its use by his grantees and to limit its appropriation to purposes which would in any way impair or lessen the value of that portion which he retains. Restrictions will be enforced by a court of equity unless they are against public policy. They are enforceable, if reasonable, commensurate with the quality and character of the development. Where a tract of land is conveyed to a person with restrictions and he afterwards subdivides the land and conveys the several lots to third persons *without* restrictions, his several grantees or their purchasers would have no right to enforce, *inter se* (among themselves) the restrictions in the deed to their common grantor. Where the restrictions are common to all the lot purchasers, each has a right to enforce the covenants and enjoin their violation. When a man sells lots in a plan with a 25-foot building line, the restriction is mutual to the extent that any lot owner may enjoin the violation of the building line restriction by any other lot owner.

A personal covenant is one binding upon the original party (covenantor) only, and when he dies, or disposes of the property, the restriction is at an end.

Restriction requirements

1. The language of a restriction must be clear as to its meaning. If ambiguous, it will be stricken down, for the courts are ever vigilant to protect the free alienation of property. Restrictions are strictly construed against persons seeking to enforce them and all doubts are resolved in favor of natural rights. All doubts must be resolved against the restriction and in favor of a free and unrestricted use of the property. Where the restriction limited an owner to one dwelling house upon a lot, the erection of a duplex dwelling was held not to be a violation. However, a restriction for the erection of a private dwelling house would prohibit the erection of an apartment building, housing a number of families. In the term "a private dwelling" the word "dwelling" restricts the character of building by eliminating all buildings for business or commercial purposes, such as stores, garages, warehouses, factories and the like. The word "private" further excludes buildings of a public character, such as hotels, dormitories, and apartment houses. A motion picture theatre was held not to violate a restriction against any building for "offensive occupation."
2. It is necessary to ascertain the *intention* of the grantor in order to determine whether the restriction is for the personal benefit or protection of the grantor or runs with the land. Where Jones owns tracts 1 and 2, and sells tract 2 to Brown, reserving a right of way across the tract sold, the covenant would be personal to Jones alone and upon Jones' death or sale of tract 1 by him, the restriction would cease. However, if Jones reserved the right of way to himself, his heirs and assigns, the language used would clearly indicate an intention to create the right of way over tract 2 in favor of tract 1, regardless of the ownership of the latter. In this example, tract 2 would be the *servient tenement,* the tract upon which the burden or privilege is imposed, and tract 1 would be the *dominant tenement,* the tract to which the privilege attaches. Any subsequent owner of tract 1 could enjoy the right of way.
3. Restrictions should be limited as to time—20, 30, or 50 years. If not so limited, the restriction would be perpetual and could become ineffectual due to resistless evolution effecting a radical change in the character of the neighborhood. The restriction would be tempered to conform to the "change of neighborhood," even before the time limit has expired.
4. Care should be taken in ascertaining how the restriction is to operate. Prohibiting an erection of a commercial structure will not operate to prevent the *use* of a residence for a commercial purpose. In order to prevent erection *or* use, the restriction clause should read:

That no building or said lot, or any hereafter erected, shall be erected for or *used* or *occupied* for business, trade, commerce, manufacturing, or for any offensive or malodorous occupation, or be used for any purpose other than that of a private dwelling house with private garage: *Jones v. Park Lane Home for Convalescents,* 120 A. 2d 535 (Pa. 1956).

5. The restriction must not be contrary to public policy. The courts have uniformly held that a prohibition by municipal *ordinance* effecting a racial restriction violates the Constitution and is invalid.

In the case of *Albino v. Pacific First Federal Savings & Loan Association,* 479 P. 2d 760 (Ore. 1971), all deeds in the subdivision prohibited all buildings except "a private dwelling house." An owner of two vacant lots sought to build an eight family garden type apartment building. He established that other apartment buildings were in the vicinity and a ball park had been erected across the road. A tremendous amount of traffic resulted. As a result, the city had changed the zone from single family to garden apartments.

The court held that the radical change of conditions in the area neutralized the deed restrictions.

Deed restrictions in a development provided that no temporary nor unsightly structures were permitted; also, anything offensive to a high class residential district was prohibited. An action was brought against the defendants, who moved their house trailer on a lot they had purchased in the plan. The court held that "temporary structure" included a house trailer or mobile home; *McBride v. Behrman,* 272 N.E. 2d 181 (Ohio 1971).

A subdivision developer told purchasers of lots that only one-family homes could be erected. A number of lots were sold and single family residences were constructed. The deeds contained no such restriction. Later, the developer decided to permit buyers to use the lots for trailer homes. Some of the original purchasers objected and brought an injunction action. The court held that oral testimony was admissible as the representations by the promoter constituted frauds. Relief was granted: *Burgess v. Putnam,* 464 S.W. 2d 698 (Tex. Civ. App. 1971); *Foro v. Deutsch,* 320 N.Y. 2d 778 (Sup. ct. 1971).

Enforcement

When considering relief by injunction against the breach of a restrictive covenant, the courts require due diligence upon the part of the plaintiff, and delay upon his part (laches) will ordinarily defeat his application; for instance, where an objector has permitted a violation to proceed without objection and the lot owner has incurred considerable expense in the building construction. Equity aids the vigilant and not the "sleeping." A person violating the restriction himself could not enjoin a similar violation by another owner. Where Jones converted a part of his residence into a store, in violation of a restrictive covenant, he would not succeed in enjoining Smith from using his building for a commercial purpose. Injunction is an extraordinary or special remedy addressed to the equity side of the court and "he who comes into equity must do so with clean hands." Injunction may be invoked or a building ordered to be torn down where a warning has not been heeded. Building restrictions are considered warranties rather than conditions. A breach generally gives rise to injunction or money damages rather than a forfeiture of the estate to the grantor as would be true if the restriction were construed as a condition. Release of restrictive covenants is not effective unless all persons who own property in restricted subdivisions join in release: *Amason et al, v. Woodman et al.,* 498 S.W. 2d 142 (Texas 1973). Restrictive covenants, being in derogation of the right of unrestricted use of property, will be strictly construed, and will not be extended by implication to anything not clearly and expressly prohibited by their plain terms: *Shea v. Sargent,* 499 S.W. 2d

871 (1973). However, other states observe "the modern trend", to the effect that restrictive covenants are not strictly construed because they are said to protect the land owner and the public rather than restrict the use of land: *Wallace v. St. Clair,* 127 S.E. 2d 742 (W. Va. 1962).

Easements

A restrictive covenant constitutes an incorporeal right. It is similar to an easement. An easement is defined as a liberty, privilege, or advantage which one proprietor may have in the lands of another, without profit in a material, physical sense. Easements may be classified as appurtenant—running with the land; and in gross—or personal to the individual owner, in the nature of a license. The best known easement is perhaps a right of way over another man's land. In origin, easements may be express or implied. Express easements are those which have been set forth in a deed or some supplementary writing, whereas the others arise as the result of a legal implication. With the opening up of the West, many situations arose where highways and boundaries between properties were laid down improperly, and, as a consequence, a man trespassed over other property in order to reach the main road. As a result, the courts invented the doctrine of implied easements, and this rule has been adopted throughout the country so that at the present time it is practically general.

Grant of an easement is the grant of a use and not a grant of title: *Park County Rod & Gun Club v. Dept. of Highways,* 517 P. 2d 352 (Mont. 1973).

Easement by necessity

The law is well settled that where property conveyed, is so situated that access to it cannot be had except passing over the remaining land of the grantor, then the grantee is entitled to an easement by necessity over the lands of the grantor: *Soltis v. Miller,* 444 Pa. 357 (1971). This use is not limited by the manner in which it was used at the time it was created, but to vary with reasonable needs, present and future.

An easement may be implied where the circumstances surrounding the case are such as to make such a course desirable in the interest of public policy. The implication under which the easement is created, however, must be based upon *necessity* and not mere *convenience.* It is difficult to lay down any general rule by which to judge the existence of necessity. The courts will judge that an easement is necessary in most cases where the facts show that an original arrangement, which is clearly in the nature of an easement, has existed and where the disturbance of this arrangement could be inequitable to the party claiming the right.

In *Oliver v. Ernel,* 178 S.E. 2d 393 (N.C. 1971), an easement by necessity was granted against a grantor, where the land conveyed was land-locked, and grantee has no other access to a public road: *Soltis v. Miller,* 444 Pa. 357 (1971).

Appurtenant Easements

One of the most important things to remember concerning appurtenant easements is that they are not personal grants which die with the death of the person in whose favor they were made, or become extinguished when he parts with the property. They belong, instead, to the land, and pass with it to all subsequent holders, unless excepted by the express provisions of the deed. It is also important to remember that the right of an easement belongs to all and every part of the land. The holder of any portion of the original tract, no matter how small a tract, is entitled to all the rights that he would possess if he owned the entire tract. The courts will permit the burden to be made greater where the additional servitude is due to the more complete development of the dominant tenement. The right of way which one farm possesses over another may be used very seldom so long as the tract is used for farming; but, when the ground is subdivided into lots, it is readily seen that the burden of the servient tenement is considerably increased; however, so long as the use is confined to those who are holders of any part of the original property, the courts will not intervene to release the servient tenement of any part of the extra burden. This is so because the easement right belongs to the property and to limit the full use and development of the property would be contrary to public policy: *Garam v. Bender,* 55 A. 2d 353 (Pa. 1947); *Fristoe v. Drapeau,* 215 P. 2d 729 (Cal. 1950); *Ragonaud v. Dimaggio,* 249 N.Y.S. 2d 705 (1964); *Westland Nursing Home, Inc.,* 517 P. 2d 862 (Colo. 1974).

Implied easement

Another example of an implied easement is where the owner of two properties constructs a building upon one lot, and a cornice, roof, or spouting encroaches over the other parcel. If he sells the unimproved property to another, the purchaser takes it subject to the open, visible, permanent, and continuous servitude which has been placed upon it by the encroachment, and he cannot later demand the removal of the encroachment. It is necessary, however, in order to create an implied easement in favor of the improved property, to show that the advantage which is claimed satisfies these requirements: *open, visible, permanent,* and *continuous.* In other words, it is such a burden as could readily be seen by the intending purchaser before he has paid for the property and he thus takes the property subject to the existing encroachment. However, if the dwelling with the encroaching cornice burned down or was destroyed, the owner would not be permitted to rebuild so as to continue the encroachment. He would be required to contain the *entire* building within his own property limits. It should be noted, too, that an implied easement cannot be extended to include land.

In the case of *Rice v. Reich et al.,* 186 N.W. 2d 269 (Wis. 1971), the purchaser sued a broker and owner to recover a $1,000 earnest money deposit, because of an existing driveway (easement) which served the subject property and the adjoining property. The executed agreement of sale required the seller to convey the property "free and clear of all liens and encumbrances." In view of the court's finding that the buyers knew of the existence of the joint driveway at the time they executed the contract of sale, they could not recover. An easement which is fully known to a purchaser before he makes his contract of purchase, or which is so open, obvious and notorious that he must have known of it, is not an incumbrance within the meaning of such a convenant: *Taxman v. McMahan,* 124 N.W. 2d 68 (Wis. 1963). In the latter case, the court held that a party wall constitutes "an encumbrance" which will render the title to real estate defective, where there is a covenant to maintain and rebuild the wall.

The doctrine of implied easement will not be enlarged to deprive an owner of the right of use or possession of his property. Circumstances may temper this principle, as where the case involves a *slight* encroachment of a building upon or near the dividing line, or where the use of the encroachment upon land is claimed as a real necessity, the deprivation of which would cause a severe hardship.

Where easement in deeds used the term, "ingress and egress," without limitation, the easement was designed to serve a specific piece of property, rather than being personal to the grantor: *Westland Nursing Home, Inc. v. Benson,* 517 P. 2d 862 (Colo. App. 1974).

Finally, it should be remembered that the easement does not in any way give its beneficiary title to the property which is subservient to it. It simply gives the right of use and not of possession. The owner of the servient tract can sell the land over which his neighbor has certain rights, in the same way as though those rights did not exist; and if, by mutual agreement, the easement is cancelled, it is not necessary that the strip which has been subject to the servitude be deeded back to the owner of the servient tenement since he already possesses title to it. An easement is an encumbrance and a purchaser could refuse to accept a deed subject to a right of way or other privilege unless the agreement of sale provided that the conveyance was to be subject to the right.

Usufructory right in water

Property rights in water and in the use and enjoyment of it are well established as rights in the soil over which it flows. But water, from its very nature, does not readily adapt itself to possession as does land so that a property right in water is really only a usufructory right, a right of use. If the natural channel of a watercourse lies along or through the lands of different owners, the water therein is the common and indivisible property of all. They have equal privileges to it in all respects insofar as a right to its use for domestic or business purposes. An upper owner, whose land is traversed by the stream, cannot so exercise his use as to deprive the lower owners of a similar enjoyment. That is to say, he cannot divert the water, dam it up, or interfere with its natural flow. If, however, in the ordinary, normal, and reasonable exercise of his right to use, the result is to prevent a subjacent owner of a similar use, the lower owner has no redress. This is the common law rule of the doctrine of riparian rights. A mining company would be liable if pollution of the stream results from an artificial diversion of the stream.

In *Tyler v. Vanelst,* 512 P. 2d 760 (Wash. App. 1973), the defendants were working with a bulldozer to clear brush which caused the waters of Cozy Nook Creek to be muddied upstream from plaintiff's diversion system. The mud, silt and debris dislodged thereby caused problems with plaintiff's water system. The defendants were enjoined from such interference.

In a number of the western states the common law rule has been rejected, where, by reason of the arid condition of the land, the necessities of the people compel a change in the rule. The policy there permits a diversion of the stream water from its natural course and protects the *first* appropriation as a recognized proprietary right. Three elements must exist for a valid appropriation: (1) intent to appropriate the water to some beneficial use existing at the time or contemplated in the future; (2) an actual diversion from the natural channel by means of a ditch, canal, or other conduit; and (3) the practical application of the water within a reasonable time to some useful purpose. The appropriation, intention, the use, and the beneficial purposes are the test by which the right to divert a stream are determined.

The question of liability is frequently raised relative to the overflow of water from one property on to another. The law is clearly established that the first owner may not obstruct a natural channel for the flow of the water or a channel that has acquired the character of an *easement,* nor may he gather surface water into a body and discharge it upon adjoining land. He may not act negligently in directing the flow so as to do unnecessary damage to others. But so far as he acts upon his right to the enjoyment of his own property, any accidental damage to a neighbor is, in the eyes of the law, *damnum absque injuria* (injury without wrong). In other words the injured party has no legal remedy.

Zoning

Closely allied to building restrictions, which result from voluntary agreement of the parties, are zoning restrictions.

We have already discussed the limitations upon a property owner's free use of property through the medium of building restrictions contained in deeds and by special agreement. They are designed to insure the uniform character of a development. Further restrictions upon the use of property may arise through zoning regulation. Zoning is the creation by law of districts in which regulations, differing in various districts, prohibit injurious or unsuitable structures and uses of structures and lands. Zoning, if reasonably exercised, represents a valid exercise of the police power of the state. The zoning, however, is not done by the state but by the municipality in pursuance of an enabling act of the state, permitting the municipalities within the state to adopt zoning codes or ordinances. The general purpose of zoning laws requires that such regulations shall be made in accordance with a comprehensive plan—designed to lessen congestion in the streets, to secure safety from fire, panic, and other dangers, to promote health and the general welfare, to provide adequate light and air, to prevent the overcrowding of land, to avoid undue concentration of population or traffic flow. Closely identified with zoning is the creation of planning commissions by municipalities. They regulate the over all development of a community. Zoning and planning must be made with reasonable consideration, among other things, to the character of the district and its peculiar suitability for particular uses, and with a view to conserving the value of lands and buildings and encouraging the most appropriate use of land throughout the particular political subdivision. Regulation under the guise of zoning, which results in the destruction or confiscation of property, must necessarily fail. Courts, in the interests of justice and equity, may pertinently inquire into the valid or invalid exercise of the police power, keeping in mind whether the challenged ordinance is necessary *for the public health, safety, morals, or general welfare.* The reasonableness of the ordinance is for judicial determination. It is not the duty of the courts to fix district lines or to usurp the place of zoning authorities, but the work of such authorities is subject to review and, if its application is found, upon judicial examination, to be unreasonable and confiscatory, to be set aside. The United States Supreme Court has declared that: "the inclusion of private land in a residential district under a zoning ordinance with resulting inhibition of the use for business and industrial buildings to the serious damage of the owner, violates the Fourteenth Amendment, if the health, safety, convenience, or general welfare of the part of the city affected will not be promoted thereby."

Zoning ordinances will be held inoperative when based upon purely aesthetic considerations. They must have a substantial relation to the public good. Civic-minded real estate operators and brokers are in accord that reasonable zoning regulation is essential to maintain and promote the attractive character of a city or town. To permit the unbridled development or use of land in accordance with the selfish interest of an individual owner is bound to be reflected in the depreciated value of surrounding properties. Legislation in the form of "spot" zoning so that the zone of one particular property is changed is not favored but may be allowed under special circumstances. [1]

Nonconforming use

Zoning laws have no application to the location of properties or their use prior to the enactment of the zoning measure: *Norton Realty & Loan Co., Inc. v. Gainesville,* 224 Ga. 166 (1968); *Walworth County v. Hartwell,* 214 N.W. 2d 288 (Wis. 1974). This is known as a nonconforming use. A zoning ordinance is not an encumbrance within the meaning of the term, which would enable a purchaser to renounce his agreement

[1] Christopher v. Mathens 362 Mo. 242 (1951).

of sale. However, a title insurance policy will except any existing zoning ordinance from the title insurance contract. A broker's responsibility to the prospective purchaser or lessee should require him to ascertain the use to which the property is to be put and whether the proposed use conforms to zoning provisions. Zoning ordinances excluding the use of property by certain races are clearly illegal. Where a zoning ordinance is in force, a property owner who desires to erect a structure must first obtain a building permit from the city building inspector or department. If the proposed building meets the requirements of the building code of the municipality and is not violative of any zoning restrictions, the desired permit will be issued and posted upon the property. Where the use contemplated does not adhere to the zone set up for the particular location, the permit will be refused. An appeal by any aggrieved party may then be taken to the board of adjustment, or as it is sometimes called, the zoning board. The board has power to hear and decide appeals where it is alleged there is error in the decision of an administrative official, to hear and decide special exceptions to the terms of the ordinance, and to authorize, in special cases, a variance from the terms of the zoning ordinance. The board can take cognizance of special conditions where a literal enforcement of the ordinance provisions will result in unnecessary hardship. Further appeal to court is permitted, and ordinarily an appeal from the decision of the board operates to stay the proceedings upon the decision appealed, but the court may, on application, grant a restraining order, upon cause shown and upon the petitioner posting a bond as in other cases seeking injunctive relief.

In the case of *Nickola v. Township of Grand Blanc,* 209 N.W. 2d 803, the plaintiffs bought the subject property for the purpose of building and maintaining a mobile home park. The site was zoned single family residences other than mobile homes. The plaintiffs relied upon the representations by the township supervisor that rezoning for a trailer park would be no problem. A two year delay ensued upon plaintiff's petition to build. One reason was it was anticipated that part of the land would be condemned for highway purposes, and thus the damages would be considerably increased. Another reason was the lack of sanitary sewers. Plaintiffs were led to believe that when these two factors no longer existed, rezoning would be granted. The court said:

> . . . prospective purchasers and their counsel (should) be aware of the general unenforceability of such claimed representations. It would be well for purchasers to heed the ancient adage of *caveat emptor* in this area of law, and *get their rezoning problems adjudicated before purchase and not after."* (emphasis supplied) The court added, however, that in the instant case: ". . . we cannot possibly see how a mobile home park vis-a-vis single family residence can possibly affect Grand Blanc Township's morals, health or safety on the land in question.

The ordinance was held invalid.

It frequently happens that an owner will convert a three story dwelling into apartments on the upper floors, in violation of an ordinance, permitting only one family residences. A broker aware of this situation, in selling such a property to a buyer for investment is doing the buyer a disservice, since the buyer could be compelled to restore the building to its original use.

Even where a property is converted into a multiple family use, *before* the ordinance was passed, should the property be destroyed by fire, he could not rebuild for multiple family occupancy: *Goldfarb v. Dietz,* 506 P. 2d 1322 (Wash. App. 1973).

In the United States Supreme Court case of *Village of Belle Terre et al v. Bruce Boraas et al* (No. 73-191-April 1, 1974), a village ordinance which restricted land use to one-family dwellings and defined the word "family" to mean one or more persons related by blood, adoption, or marriage, or not more than two unrelated persons, living and cooking together as a single-housekeeping unit, was challenged as unconstitutional. The owner of a house was cited by the village, who had leased the property to six unrelated college students. The Court held that the ordinance was reasonable and not arbitrary and bears "a rational relationship to a (permissible) state objective." The ordinance was upheld as a valid land-use legislation addressed to family needs.

Zoning classifications

Municipalities follow different zoning classes, depending upon their requirements and the size and area of the municipality. All ordinances have classifications of residential, industrial, and commercial zones. A higher use classification is usually permissible in a lower use classification. In urban centers, industrial classification is divided into heavy and light industrial zones. Even under the lowest classification of heavy industrial zone, certain uses are sometimes prohibited. Prohibited uses would include abattoirs, manufacture of animal fertilizer, gun powder or explosive manufacture or storage, garbage disposal plants, or stockyards. Any of these operations would be offensive or dangerous to the population if carried on within the city limits. A dwelling, except living quarters for the use of watchmen employed upon the premises, could also be excluded. A commercial district can also be separated into classifications to take care of special needs in a neighborhood retail district as well as the downtown commercial zone. Residential zones are often classified into several districts. In a class "A" residence district, for example, one-family or more dwellings, including apartment buildings, are permitted, as well as educational or charitable institutions, churches, greenhouses, or schools. In a "B" residence district, multiple family (more than two) or apartment buildings would be prohibited, while in a "C" residential district, only a single family dwelling use might be permitted. A large part of zoning ordinances is devoted to height limitations and front, rear, and side yard areas.

A situation arises where a buyer purchases a tract of land on the strength of an existing zone classification, obtains a building permit, and makes expenditures, to find that the zoning code has been amended to prohibit his intended use of the tract. This situation was before the Supreme Court, the case of *Gulf Oil Co. v. Fairview Township Board of Supervisors,* 438 Pa. 457 (1970). The court laid down the following rule quoted in *Penn Township v. Yecko Bros.,* 217 at 2d A. 171 (Pa. 1966):

> A property owner who is able to demonstrate (1) that he has obtained a valid building permit under the old zoning ordinance, (2) that he had obtained it in good faith (without "racing"), to get it before a proposed change is made in the zoning ordinance, and (3) that in good faith he spent money or incurred liabilities in reliance on his building permit has acquired a vested right and need not conform with the zoning ordinance as changed.

Dedication

Dedication is the setting aside of private property for public use and acceptance by the municipality of the tract for public use. It may be intended as a parklet, a sports area or a beach. It may be intended for the use of the public at large, or, in a subdivision, it may be intended for the use of the owners in the subdivision. If intended for public use and accepted by the municipality, the owner is exempt from taxes and other liability. As an alternative to dedication, the tract may be deeded to the municipality.

In order to constitute a dedication of a public road by implication, there must exist clear and unequivocal intention to do so by the land owner *and* acceptance by the public: *Hudson v. Gaines,* 501 S.W. 2d 734 (Tex. 1973).

Eminent Domain

EMINENT DOMAIN may be defined as the power of the state to take private property for public use. Under the 5th Amendment to the Constitution of the United States, the Federal Government is prohibited from taking private property for public use without just compensation and, under the "due process" clause of the 14th Amendment, the prohibition is extended to the several states. The right is expressly given to the state by constitutional provision. Even though the state constitution contained no such provision, the right could, nevertheless, be exercised by the state as eminent domain is an inherent attribute of state sovereignty. The state government is the supreme power in the state, and private rights are held under such supreme power and may be said to represent an indulgence by the sovereign power. The right of eminent domain exists not only in favor of the state but also for the benefit of any municipal subdivision of the state. In fact, any public corporation or any private corporation vested with a public use may exercise this extraordinary power when necessary for the public good. Appropriation of private property does not mean confiscation of such land, for the owner is entitled to fair and just compensation for the taking. Ordinarily, a public utility embarking upon a program of expansion, or a municipality in the development of a needed civic project, will endeavor to purchase the required properties for what is considered a fair consideration price. It is only when private bargaining fails that resort is made to condemnation through eminent domain proceedings. The court, upon failure of the interested parties to agree upon the sale price or to accept an award of court-appointed viewers, will then determine a just price for the property in question.

If the right to eminent domain did not exist, a single obstructionist property owner in a key position for a planned improvement could successfully stay the betterment and progress of a whole community with his refusal to sell or his unwillingness to sell at any but a prohibitive price.

In *State of Hawaii v. Midlsiff*, 516 P. 2d 1250 (1973), the court said:

> "Just compensation, in a non-realignment case, may be summed up by the formula: Just compensation = (value of the land taken plus severance damages) minus special benefits. (3 Nichols Eminent Domain Sec. 8.6206 at 90 3d ed. 1965). Each of these three elements of just compensation should be independent of the others."

Frequently, a land owner will receive a higher price through court condemnation proceedings than was offered to him for a voluntary conveyance of the same land. Just compensation is held to be the fair market value of the land and the improvements thereon. Where, however, only a part of the owner's tract is condemned, differences and difficulties arise as to the amount of compensation. Certainly, the claimant is entitled to the fair market value of the part taken and it is equally well accepted that he is entitled, as an element of damage, to the depreciation in value, if any, caused by the improvement to the land retained by him. These two elements constitute his highest possible damage.

Where only part of property is taken, measure of severance damage is difference between market value of remainder before and after the taking: *Defnet Land and Dev. Co. v. State,* ex Cel Herman 480 P. 2d 1013 (Ariz. App. 1971).

Award of $93,500 for taking 21 acres out of tract consisting of 196.32 acres, part of which was in flood plain and part of which was hilly and in an industrial area, together with taking of right of direct access to highway, was fair and did not evidence bias, passion, or prejudice: *State Highway Commission v. Crooks,* 282 So. 2d 232 (Miss. 1973).

Factors to consider in a total taking of a dwelling under eminent domain are comparative data and reproduction. *State of Louisiana v. Carmouche,* 155 So. 2d 451 (La. 1963).

In an eminent domain proceedings, the burden is upon the property owner to establish that public use is the direct and proximate cause of the damage complained of, and not merely such as is possible, as may be conceived by the imagination, or as merely affects the feelings of the property owner: *Frank v. Mercer County,* 186 N.W. 2d 439 (N.D. 1971); 4 Nichols on Eminent Domain Sec. 14.24.

Unsightliness of farm property caused by construction of transmission lines was held to be a proper element of damage: *Missouri Public Service Co. v. Garrison,* 454 S.W. 2d 628 (Mo. App. 1969).

Existence of valuable deposits including sand, gravel, and lime stone is a proper element in ascertaining value of land in an eminent domain proceedings: *Seaboard Coast Line R.R. v. Harrelson,* 202 S.E. 2d 1 (S.C. 1974).

Owners were not entitled, as an element of compensation, to the increase in value of property prior to taking and attributable to proposed improvement: *Pozin v. State Dept. of Transportation,* 281 So. 2d 73 (Fla. App. 1973). The enhancement of the value of the property caused by the proposed improvement cannot be considered. However, a limitation to the foregoing rule, as stated in case of *Levit v. State Dept. of Transportation,* 248 So. 2d 542 (Fla. App. 1971), is, as follows:

> Such enhanced value is generally peculiar only to land lying adjacent to the improvement and within close proximity to the interchange exits and entrances leading to and from intersecting roads and highways.

Loss of liquor license is not compensable in condemnation proceeding, as such license is not "property" which is protected by constitutional guarantees. It is only a limited permit to engage in an enterprise which, otherwise, would be unlawful: *Restaurants, Inc. v. City of Wilmington,* 274 A. 2d 137 (Del. 1971).

Generally, a condemnee is not entitled to compensation for personalty used in land taken. (e.g. restaurant equipment). However, depreciation in value of personalty, in addition to physical damage, should be allowed. *State of Alaska v. Ness,* 516 P. 2d 1212 (1973).

Benefits assessed against the taking

Should not the owner, by the same logic, be taxed for the benefit resulting to the remaining tract because of the improvement? The cases on this question are not uniform throughout the country. Sound logic would seem to dictate that *special benefits* received by the owner should be charged against the price paid to him. Lewis, on Eminent Domain, summarizes the law on benefits as follows (Sec. 687):

> The law in regard to benefits is now pretty well settled in every State, either by the decisions of its courts, or by its statutes, or its constitution. While different and conflicting rules prevail in the different States under precisely the same constitutional provisions, it is evident that there can be but one absolutely correct rule. In taking private property for public use, the State acts

rightfully and not as a wrongdoer. It guarantees just compensation and nothing more. In arriving at what is just compensation, the matter is to be viewed in the same light as though the State had bargained with the owner for a portion of his land and had agreed to make him just compensation therefor. It is self-evident that, where a part of a tract is taken, the just compensation cannot be determined without considering the manner in which the part is taken, the purpose for which it is taken, and the effect of the taking upon that which remains. All the authorities concede this so far as damages to the remainder are concerned, and the justice of so doing may be taken for granted. But what justice is there in considering the effect insofar only as it produces damage? If a railroad is constructed through a farm and drains a valuable spring whereby the remainder is depreciated five hundred dollars, it is conceded that just compensation must include this five hundred dollars. But if, instead of draining a valuable spring, it drains a marshy tract so as to make it worth five hundred dollars more for actual use, the same sense of justice requires that this five hundred dollars of benefits should be considered.

It is true, of course, that the entire municipality profits and benefits by the improvement of streets and other public service and indirectly, the entire tax-paying population participates in the maintenance of the original improvement. But where, for example, a street which serves only a limited number of properties is changed from a dirt street to one of brick, it is fair that only the immediate properties benefited should be assessed for the improvement.

Urban renewal is a substantial state interest that can justify taking property dedicated to religious use: *Pillar of Fire v. Denver Urban Renewal Authority,* 509 P. 2d 1250 (Colo. 1973). In short, church property is private property which can be taken by eminent domain for permanent public use.

A property owner is entitled to severable damages, if it is shown that the property taken is part of a larger tract, which has been adversely affected by the taking: *Babinec v. State,* 512 P. 2d 563 (Alaska 1973).

In recent years, special authorities were created by the Congress and the state legislative bodies for erecting public housing projects. These projects, intended to supply badly needed housing and to improve the standard of living for low income groups, have had an important effect upon the economic and social well-being of a large segment of our industrial population. In the fulfillment of the housing program, blighted areas have been condemned and destroyed and new structures erected. In this development, it is often necessary to resort to condemnation of an entire zone or district. This is known as *zone condemnation* and is the only practical and effective method of clearing slums. Zone condemnation is for a specific purpose. Even in public condemnation the cost is great, but the benefits of better health of the inhabitants and the elimination of crime are readily commensurate with the cost involved. The United States Government in the exercise of its broad war powers has, in the interests of flood control, condemned extensive areas throughout the country. Today state legislatures have created public authorities with the right of condemnation for housing, sanitation, parking, and public utility purposes.

Excess condemnation

Excess condemnation, as the name implies, is the taking of land in larger measure than actually necessary for the improvement proper. Special constitutional authority is necessary for exercising this extraordinary right. The earlier court decisions have held that statutes for excess condemnation, enacted under the general constitutional provision, were invalid. Recent social philosophy may well influence the judicial view that public use, liberally interpreted, may often permit excess condemnation. A street is laid out and land on each side of the proposed street is taken in excess of the area actually needed to confine the street. The control of the excess part by the municipality, whether in the case of a street, park, or other development, insures the usefulness of the improvement and is conducive to the better channelling of municipal growth. Better city planning is bound to ensue.

Title taken under the right of eminent domain ordinarily carries with it a fee simple title to the land, so that the condemnor has as absolute a title as if it were acquired by purchase. But land taken for roads is usually a base fee. It is governed by statute.

Under a base, or qualified fee, when the use for which the property has been taken is abandoned, title to it reverts to the original owner or his heirs. In other takings of land, a fee simple title is acquired.

Value of raw land is subdivided land

Generally, the value of a farm land, on the outskirts of a growing town is worth less than the value of such land, converted into a subdivision, on a lot basis. Of course, the subdivider must have taken forward steps to make the change by the time of the taking. Incidents of such transformation would include such items as engineering, promotion of sales, advertising, plotting, and recording: *United States v. 147.47 Acres of Land,* 352 F. Supp. 1055 (Md. Pa. 1972).

Lessee's Right to Damages

Examination of a commercial lease should determine what understanding exists, under the lease, in regard to a taking of the leased property under eminent domain. If the lease does not foreclose the lessee's right to damages, all elements affecting the value of the leasehold must be determined.

In the case of *Barnini 161 Conn. 59* (1971), the plaintiff's property was taken for highway purposes. The property was under lease to the defendant for a service station, with option to renew. The court said:

> The value of the lease is properly arrived at in the case of a complete taking by subtracting the rent provided for under the lease, from the fair market value of the lease. In a determination of what this amount should be, all elements legitimately affecting the value of the lease should be considered.

A lessee may be entitled to the reasonable market value of the unexpired period of the lease, unless they are obsolete at the time of the taking: *State Highway Commission v. Samborski,* 463 S.W. 2d 896 (Mo. 1971).

Federal Open Housing Legislation: Anti-Discrimination

IN RECENT YEARS, repeated crises have plagued many of our large cities, and small ones, too. Riots, "sit-ins," racial incidents, dissatisfaction with the war in Vietnam, strikes by school teachers and public employees, together with other factors, have all contributed to some extent to crime, violence and disorders. Many books have already been written as to the underlying causes and suggested remedies. Poverty and discrimination are always given as basic causes, from which crime and violence erupt. City, state, and federal programs, combined, were found wanting as a cure to the nation's ills. Equally important as a basic cause of the nation's turbulent times is racial discrimination in the housing field, particularly against Negro citizens, although other minority groups are also affected.

Under the President's Executive Order of November 20, 1962, housing, which related to or was aided by Federal assistance, came under an anti-discrimination mandate. The Order included new F.H.A. or V.A. mortgage construction, public housing, housing assisted through urban renewal, and Federally-owned housing. Since then, statutes have been passed in a number of states, augmented by ordinances in some cities, making it illegal to discriminate against a purchaser on the grounds of race, color, religion or national origin or background. These regulatory measures vary as to their provisions and effectiveness.

On April 11, 1968, President Johnson signed an open housing law that is vitally important for all those in the housing and mortgage business. The law prohibits racial discrimination by most sellers and renters of dwellings, and also bans discrimination by all those who make loans to buy or improve residential property. For sellers and renters, the law takes effect in three stages, but for lenders its effective date is January 1, 1969. The agency charged with administering and enforcing the law is the Department of Housing and Urban Development (HUD); the Department of Justice will also play a role in those instances where violations reach the courts.

It is important to note that, by some state statutes, or by amendment to existing state license laws, conviction of a real estate broker or salesman as being a party to a discriminatory act, constitutes grounds for disciplinary action by the Real Estate Commission.

The problem of housing is nationwide, and the states look to the Federal Government for leadership and guidance in alleviating the complex difficulties. The Congress acted and passed an Open Housing law, which was signed by the President on April 11, 1968. A capsule analysis of the important provisions of the law follows, (taken from Prentice-Hall, Inc.,—*Federal Aids to Financing Report,* with permission):

The law prohibits discrimination on the grounds of race, color, religion, or national origin in the sale, rental, or financing of dwellings. This includes setting harsher terms for publishing discriminatory advertising, telling a person that a dwelling is not available for sale or rental when in fact it is, or "block-busting" (attempting to get a person to sell or rent by representations that people of a particular race, color, religion or national origin are entering or are about to enter the neighborhood).

The law became effective in two stages:

(1) In 1968, it banned discrimination in the sale or rental of housing insured or guaranteed by the Federal Government or located in a Federally assisted urban renewal or slum clearance project. The ban applies to all such housing backed by the Government after November 20, 1962 (the date of the Executive Order banning discrimination in government-backed housing), unless payment was made before the date of enactment, namely, April 11, 1968.

It also covers dwellings owned or operated by the Federal Government and dwellings built with the aid of loans, advances, grants, or contributions made by the Federal Government.

(2) Effective January 1, 1969, the ban applies to all dwelling units, no matter how financed, with these two exceptions:

(a) Single-family homes, provided the owner does not own more than three single-family homes at one time. If the owner is a non-occupant of a single-family home he sells, he gets the exemption for only one sale within a 24-month period. (b) One-to-four family dwellings, if the owner occupies one of the units.

Loans: Also effective January 1, 1969, banks, savings and loan agencies, mutual savings banks, insurance companies and other lenders cannot discriminate in making loans on apartment buildings or homes—whether for purchase, repairs, or construction. Also forbidden is discrimination in setting the terms of the loans, such as the amount of the mortgage, the interest rate, and so on.

Enforcement of the Act is in the Secretary of Housing and Urban Development (HUD). The Secretary, or his assistant, is limited in his powers in handling complaints to "education, conciliation, and persuasion." In this connection, he can investigate complaints, issue subpoenas, and hold hearings, before issuing a final order. He cannot issue a "cease and desist order," nor fine an offender. For punitive damages for violation of the law, a complainant must file a suit in a Federal district court. If there is a "substantially equivalent" local or state fair housing law, the Federal Court generally will direct that a complaint be filed in the state or local forum.

The law gives the government the right to inspect the records of anyone charged with discrimination.

In addition to the enforcement provisions, the Attorney General can bring action in cases where there is a general pattern of discrimination or an issue of general public importance.

On June 17, 1968, the United States Supreme Court handed down its land mark decision on open housing, in the St. Louis case of *Jones v. Mayer Co.,* 392 U.S. 409 (decided June 17, 1968), involving the purchase of a homesite in a subdivision called Paddock Woods. The Supreme Court held that an Act of Congress passed in 1866 forbade racial discrimination in the sale or rental of housing in the United States. In a majority (7-2) opinion, Mr. Justice Potter Stewart said, inter alia,

> Negro citizens North and South, who won in the Thirteenth Amendment a promise of freedom—freedom to go and come at pleasure and to buy and sell when they please—would be left with a mere paper guarantee if Congress were powerless to assure that a dollar in the hands of a Negro will purchase the same thing as a dollar in the hands of a white man.

The Act of 1968 contains many exemptions, including specifically single-family residential units sold without an agent. The Act of 1866 contains no such exemption and it lacks the federal enforcement machinery and other remedies available under the 1968 Act.

The law is comparatively new and it is not yet court tested as to any ambiguities or conflicts in its provisions, particularly in its relationship to the Act of 1866 and the recent Supreme Court decision. A number of legal experts are in accord that the Supreme Court opinion in the Jones case has the effect of eliminating the several exceptions contained in the Act of 1968, without voiding the law itself. In support of this view, they call attention to the language of the 1866 Act, which states:

> All citizens of the United States shall have the same right, in every state and territory, as is enjoyed by white citizens thereof to inherit, purchase, lease, sell, hold, and convey real and personal property.

It would appear that a party plaintiff could petition for injunctive relief in a federal district court, on the basis that there is no irreconcilable conflict between the Act of 1968 and the Act of 1866. The total effect of the Supreme Court decision is to bring all property, personal as well as real, under anti-discriminatory regulation. In real estate, the decision creates an "open housing" law throughout the country. However, it should be noted that buyers or renters can still be rejected for reasonable *cause,* but the grounds for rejection must apply equally to *all* persons.

Questions on Deeds

1. Q. What do you understand by air rights?
   A. The ownership of the rights to use, occupy or control the air space over a specified property.
2. Q. What is the basic test for determining whether an article is realty or personalty?
   A. The *intention,* with which the article was affixed to the realty, considered in the light of what is fair and reasonable under the surrounding circumstances.
3. Q. Is it necessary for the grantee to sign the deed?
   A. No; acceptance of the deed by the grantee is sufficient.
4. Q. What is meant by a curative statute in reference to deeds?
   A. An act of the legislature to validate defective acknowledgments.
5. Q. A deed is written with a life interest to Adam, and upon Adam's death, the property vests in Bennett. What is Bennett's interest in the property called?
   A. A remainderman.
6. Q. Which is preferable, a general warranty deed or a special warranty deed?
   A. A general warranty, because the grantor agrees to protect the grantee against the world; whereas, in a special warranty deed, the grantor limits his protection to anyone claiming under him or through him.
7. Q. What kind of a warranty of title does the grantor make in a quit claim deed?
   A. None.
8. Q. What does real property include?
   A. Lands, tenements and hereditaments.
9. Q. What is meant by tenements and hereditaments?
   A. Tenements include land and anything affixed permanently to the land such as a building. Hereditaments include lands, tenements and things of an incorporeal nature, such as a right of way.
10. Q. Do all titles emanate by patent from the U. S. government ?
    A. No. In the 13 original states, title originated from the Proprietor (under grants from the King of England) or from the sovereign states.
11. Q. Under a fee simple deed, what is the legal concept of land which a purchaser acquires?
    A. The surface land, to an indefinite extent upwards and down to the center of the earth.
12. Q. How would you define a "property right" ?
    A. The right to enjoy lands and chattels to the exclusion of all others.
13. Q. Into what two classes is property divided ?
    A. Realty and personalty.
14. Q. Into what two classes can realty be divided ? Give examples.
    A. Corporeal realty (lands and buildings); incorporeal realty (right of way; an easement).
15. Q. Name four ways by which good title to real estate may be acquired.
    A. Deed, Will, Adverse Possession, Eminent Domain.
16. Q. What estate is of potentially indefinite duration and is fully transferable and inheritable?
    A. Fee simple.

17. Q. What is a deed?
    A. A deed is a writing by which lands, tenements and hereditaments are conveyed, which writing is signed, sealed and delivered between the parties.
18. Q. What is meant by a merchantable title?
    A. A title free from any clouds or defects.
19. Q. Name four types of legal description of land.
    A. 1. Rectangular survey. 2. Metes and bounds. 3. Monuments. 4. Recorded map—lot and block number.
20. Q. What is a Warranty Deed?
    A. It is a Bargain and Sale deed *with* covenants—that the grantor has a fee simple title, free from encumbrances and that the grantor will forever warrant and defend the grantee against any claims.
21. Q. Name at least three classifications of estates.
    A. Inheritance, life, years at will.
22. Q. When real estate is held in the husband's name, why is it necessary for the wife to join with the husband in deeding the property to another?
    A. In order to extinguish her dower right.
23. Q. What is meant by a Government Patent?
    A. Original and initial conveyance of real property from the United States Government to individuals, or from a state to an individual.
24. Q. What defect is there in the following property description:
    "Property next to Marvel Gasoline Station, City limits, Andrews County, Texas, official records in Recorder's Office of Andrews County, also known as the 500 block on Main Street in the City."
    A. The description is fatally defective because the name of the City does not appear.
25. Q. What are the requirements usually necessary in determining whether an article is a fixture?
    A. 1. Actual physical annexation to the realty.
    2. Application or adaptation to the use or purpose to which the realty is devoted.
    3. An intention on the part of the person making the annexation to make a permanent accession to the land.
26. Q. Who are the parties to a deed?
    A. The grantor and the grantee. The grantor is the one who sells the property and signs the deed. The grantee is the purchaser, who receives the deed.
27. Q. Real Estate ownership is said to consist of a "bundle of legal rights." Name six "rights."
    A. 1. To lease. 2. To sell. 3. To will. 4. To regain possession at end of lease—reversion. 5. to build thereon—destroy improvements—maintain—control use within the law. 6. To mortgage.
28. Q. What is a quit claim deed?
    A. A deed used to clear clouds upon the title. The operative words are "remise, release, and quit claim." There is no warranty of title in this form of deed. A wife who has not joined in a warranty deed may sign a quit claim deed in order to bar her dower interest in the property.
29. Q. What does the word "title" mean when referring to property?
    A. Title is the evidence of ownership in land.
30. Q. Why is it necessary for a deed to be in writing?
    A. Statute of frauds passed in England in 1676 in order to prevent unscrupulous persons from swearing under oath that property had been deeded or leased verbally for a long period of time at a ridiculously low rental. It requires contracts for the sale and transfer of real estate to be in writing. The statute of frauds has been adopted in the various states.
31. Q. For what purposes is a special warranty deed most generally used?
    A. It is the usual form of conveying a tax title. It is also used by fiduciaries or trustees

in conveying title to real estate.

32. Q. What are the principal types of deeds used in real property transfers?
    A. General Warranty Bargain and Sale, Special Warranty, Quit Claim.
33. Q. Name five kinds of entries or instruments found in an "abstract of title."
    A. 1. Deeds. 2. Mortgages. 3. Releases. 4. Foreclosures. 5. Delinquent Taxes.
34. Q. What are the two most common methods of title closing?
    A. Escrow and delivery of deed.
35. Q. Is a date essential to the validity of a deed?
    A. No. It indicates the time when the deed was delivered. It is only prima facie evidence: i.e., appears to be sufficient to establish the time of delivery but may be rebutted by stronger proof.
36. Q. Is a deed dated on Sunday void?
    A. Not if delivered on a week day.
37. Q. Is consideration necessary in a deed?
    A. Yes. Good or valuable consideration.
38. Q. What is good consideration?
    A. Good consideration arises from love and affection and has no pecuniary value.
39. Q. What is understood by a valuable consideration?
    A. Money or its equivalent measurable in monetary terms.
40. Q. Is a $1.00, or nominal, consideration valid?
    A. Yes. Courts do not inquire into the adequacy or inadequacy of the consideration.
41. Q. What parties have limited or qualified right to contract?
    A. Infants, insane persons, corporations, and aliens.
42. Q. Is a deed from husband to a wife valid where the husband has been made the defendant in a lawsuit involving a substantial sum of money?
    A. No. Any conveyance made with intent to disturb, delay, hinder, or defraud creditors may be set aside as fraudulent.
43. Q. Is a joint estate the same as an estate by the entireties?
    A. An estate by the entireties, which may be held only by husband and wife, enjoys advantages over a joint tenancy. In some states, as in Nebraska, husband and wife hold as joint tenants, similar to an estate by the entireties.
44. Q. What are "appurtenances" in a deed?
    A. Rights which pass as incidental to the premises; anything necessary to the enjoyment of the property. Land ordinarily cannot pass as appurtenant to land, but a right in land may.
45. Q. What are a husband's rights in his wife's property called?
    A. Curtesy.
46. Q. Is a deed by a married woman for her own property valid, void, or voidable?
    A. Valid in most states, but void in others, unless she has been declared a "feme sole."
47. Q. Who is a "feme sole"?
    A. A single woman. A married woman may be declared a feme sole by court decree where her husband has deserted her or is a drunkard, or there is other good cause.
48. Q. What is meant by "estate by the entireties"?
    A. The ownership of property by husband and wife. The tenancy exists only in favor of husband and wife.
49. Q. What are the advantages of an estate by the entireties?
    A. 1. Upon death of one party the property forthwith vests in the surviving spouse.
    2. No probate or other court proceedings are necessary.
    3. Not subject to state inheritance tax.
    4. A judgment against one spouse will not be a lien.
50. Q. What is the main disadvantage of such an estate?
    A. Unless both parties join in a deed, court action is necessary to partition the estate.
51. Q. What is the difference between "joint tenancy" and "tenancy in common"?
    A. In joint tenancy, where one of the parties dies, the property vests in the surviving

party or parties. In a tenancy in common, each of whom is considered as being possessed of the whole of an undivided part, upon death of one, his interest goes to his heirs.

52. Q. Brother and sister are purchasing a residence. Brother is a widower, with two children, and sister is a widow with no children. What kind of a deed should issue if she is to have a $1/3$ interest and he is to have a $2/3$ interest?
A. A deed as tenants in common.

53. Q. What are the purposes of the acknowledgment?
A. 1. The deed will be accepted as prima facie evidence in any court proceedings.
2. The deed may be recorded.

54. Q. Is it necessary for the grantee to acknowledge or sign the deed?
A. No.

55. Q. Jones conveys certain real estate to Brown and Smith as joint tenants, and not as tenants in common. Subsequently, Brown dies, and Smith claims property. Brown's son claims title to the same property. Who will win?
A. Smith, the survivor. The deed to Brown and Smith expressly created a joint tenancy.

56. Q. Adams conveys certain real estate to Black, Carr, and Dean as tenants in common. Black later dies, and in a contest among Carr, Dean, and Black's widow for Black's share in the property, who will win?
A. The widow. The conveyance to Black, Carr, and Dean established a tenancy in common.

57. Q. White conveys property to Smith and Jones as joint tenants. Can Smith sell his interest to Green? If so, would Green then become a joint owner with Jones?
A. Smith can sell or alienate his interest in the property to Green. Green does not become a joint owner with Jones, but Green and Jones now hold the property as tenants in common. (Alabama, Indiana, North Carolina, Pennsylvania, Texas.)

58. Q. Various covenants designed to limit, restrict or prohibit the use, improvement or occupancy of real estate are sometimes incorporated in deeds to real estate. Name at least three different types.
A. Buildings must be of a certain height; certain minimum cost; set back from street; they cannot be used for commercial purposes; liquor cannot be sold upon the premises.

59. Q. What is a tax deed?
A. A deed issued for property which has been sold for taxes.

60. Q. Is a title that is acquired by purchase at a treasurer's sale for unpaid municipal taxes, good and marketable?
A. No, the owner still has right of redemption.

61. Q. Name three types of encumbrance which might cloud the title to real estate.
A. Unpaid taxes, judgments, a right of way.

62. Q. What is the meaning of the words "more or less" in many deed descriptions?
A. Intended to indicate that a slight variation in dimensions of the tract would not void the contract.

63. Q. What is a tax title?
A. Title by which one owns land purchased at a tax sale.

64. Q. Where are deeds to real estate officially recorded?
A. In the Office of the Recorder of Deeds, or Register of Deeds.

65. Q. Does an abstract of title guarantee a clear title?
A. No; it merely gives a summary as to the conditions of the title.

66. Q. What is the purpose of a correction deed?
A. A correction deed, often called a deed of conformation, is used to correct an error in a deed. This is usually done with a quit claim deed containing explanations.

67. Q. Is it correct to state that a lease on a property being sold constitutes an encumbrance on that property?
A. Yes.

68. Q. What are the dangers in not having a deed recorded promptly?
    A. The deed may be destroyed or lost; judgments may be entered against the previous owner, which would constitute a lien against the property; the previous owner might deed or mortgage the property to someone else, who, by recording his instrument promptly, would have priority.
69. Q. What is included in the execution of a deed?
    A. The execution includes the signing, sealing, witnessing and acknowledgment of the instrument.
70. Q. Is it necessary for the grantor himself to sign the deed?
    A. Good practice requires the grantor's personal signature, but a deed signed by another for the grantor in the grantor's presence and at his direction would be a sufficient compliance with the requirement for signature, if proved.
71. Q. If the grantor cannot write, how should the deed be signed?
    A. The grantor should make his mark in the presence of witnesses and the grantor's name should then be appended by someone for him. The signature would appear "John (his X mark) Steele." There must be two witnesses to the mark.
72. Q. Can a grantor later repudiate a deed because he is illiterate and could not read the instrument?
    A. No. The burden is upon the grantor to have someone read the deed to him; unless fraud has been practiced on the grantor.
73. Q. Can a husband and wife make a single acknowledgement of a deed?
    A. In most states, yes. In Alabama, New Jersey, North Carolina and South Carolina, it is necessary to have separate acknowledgment of the wife.
74. Q. What information does the acknowledgment contain?
    A. The venue, place where the acknowledgment is taken (state and county); the name of the grantor and his marital status, as John Steele, single; the signature of the person taking the acknowledgment, his official capacity, expiration date of his office, and official seal.
75. Q. Must the grantors appear in person before the officer taking the acknowledgment?
    A. Yes. An acknowledgment should never be taken in absentia.
76. Q. Can a deed be executed by an agent under a power of attorney from the owner?
    A. Yes. The power of attorney, however, must be recorded.
77. Q. When should a proxy or power of attorney be used?
    A. Only in rare cases and under special circumstances as when the grantor is uncertain as to his whereabouts at the time of closing the deal and does not want to execute the deed beforehand. The attorney-in-fact should be a person in whom the grantor reposes the highest trust and confidence.
78. Q. When does title to the property pass?
    A. When the deed is delivered to the grantee or his agent.
79. Q. What kinds of delivery are there?
    A. 1. Delivery absolute, where the deed is handed over to the purchaser without any conditions.
       2. Delivery in escrow, where the deed is delivered to a third person until the performance of some act or condition by one of the parties.
80. Q. Arthur delivers a deed in escrow to Cox until certain items in the title are cleared up. The purchaser, Bell, turns over the consideration price at the same time to the escrow agent, Cox. Two days later Arthur notifies Cox to return Bell's money to Bell and to return the deed to Arthur. Must Cox comply with these instructions?
    A. No. Once the deed is delivered to the escrow agent and the condition of delivery is specified, the grantor is powerless to recall it.
81. Q. Suppose that Abbot delivers a deed to Cooper in escrow for Brown, to be handed over to Brown once he has paid Cooper the balance of the consideration price. Later in the day, Brown visits Cooper's office during Cooper's absence and sees the deed on Cooper's desk. Brown takes the deed and records it. Does Brown get good title?

Suppose that after recording the deed Brown conveys the property to Quinn for a valuable consideration. Will Quinn obtain a valid title?

A. Brown will not obtain good title because of his fraudulent act, and Abbot could have the deed stricken off. However, Quinn, an innocent purchaser for value, would obtain good title, for he had no notice of Brown's fraud, assuming, of course, that the transfer from Brown to Quinn was made before Abbot took any legal proceedings to set Brown's deed aside.

82. Q. Anthony executes a deed to Burger and delivers it to Conway, to be delivered to Burger upon the death of Anthony. Will Burger get good title upon the death of Anthony?

A. Yes. If the title does not pass until Anthony's death, it cannot do so at the death. This would seem to defeat Anthony's purpose. But the law comes to the rescue and considers the passing of title as "relating back to the date of direct delivery," which was, of course, prior to Anthony's death. This is known as the doctrine of relation. When finally delivered to the grantee, it operates as from the date of first delivery, which was, of course, prior to Anthony's death.

83. Q. Ash executes a deed to Burke and places it in his inside coat pocket. The coat is hung in Ash's cupboard. Ash is killed in an explosion that afternoon. The deed is intact. Does Burke obtain title to the real estate?

A. No. The deed was not delivered.

84. Q. Jones executes a deed to Brown and records it. Later Jones seeks to set the conveyance aside, claiming that there had been no delivery to Brown. Will he succeed?

A. No. In cases like this, delivery is presumed from recording.

85. Q. Is it necessary to have the deed recorded?

A. As concerns grantor and grantee, title passes upon delivery and it is not necessary to record it. However, in order to protect the grantee against a lien or a subsequent deed by the grantor for the same property, the law requires the grantee to record his deed. This constitutes constructive notice.

86. Q. Adams delivers a deed to Black on December 6, 1971, which Black records on January 21, 1972. Adams deeds the same property to Clark on January 14, 1972; Clark records his deed the same day. Who owns the property?

A. Clark. The person who gets his deed on record first, providing he had no notice of a prior deed, is deemed the owner.

87. Q. Suppose that in the preceding case, Black took possession on December 6, 1971. Would the decision be the same?

A. No. Clark would have notice of Black's ownership, and he would then be a purchaser with notice.

88. Q. Brown owns two adjoining tracts of land. He conveys one piece to Evans and reserves a right of way across the rear in order to reach a side street. Later he sells the other tract to Case. Subsequently, Evans and Case have differences, and Evans refuses to permit Case the use of the right of way across his land. Can Case enjoin Evans from interfering with his use?

A. No. The original right was personal to Brown, and when Brown conveyed the property, the right was extinguished. If Brown had reserved the right to himself, "his heirs and assigns," Case would be successful.

89. Q. Williams owns two parcels of real estate. A house is built upon one tract, with the cornice encroaching upon the other. Williams sells the second tract to James. Nothing is mentioned in the deed about the encroachment. Later, James, notifies Williams that he is trespassing by the encroachment and demands that he remove the objectionable cornice. Will James succeed?

A. No. Williams has an implied easement in James's land to the extent of the encroachment. The condition was open, visible, continuous, and permanent at the time James purchased the property and accordingly, he takes it subject to the existing condition.

If the house were destroyed by fire or other cause, Williams could not rebuild so as to continue the encroachment.

90. Q. What are the granting words or operative clauses used in a deed to pass a fee simple title?
A. Grant and convey.

91. Q. Smith's deed to a farm is made subject to a right of way in favor of Jones' farm. The Jones' farm, 12 years later, is subdivided into lots. The lot owners attempt to use the same right of way and Smith objects to the increase of use. Will Smith succeed?
A. No. The right of way exists for the benefit of every part of Jones's farm and the increased use represents a normal and logical development of the farm.

92. Q. Adams, without Black's consent, uses a shortcut across Black's farm. From time to time, Black places an obstruction across the path, which Adams removes. The use, under these conditions, continues for more than 21 years. Black now erects a cable fence across the path and Adams takes legal action to prevent Black's interference with his use of the right of way. Who will win?
A. Adams. In order to defeat the statute of adverse possession, Black's interference or objection must be effective. Since the barriers during the 21-year period were not effective in preventing the use, Adams will win. Black should have obtained a court decree enjoining the trespass.

93. Q. As used in legal descriptions of real estate, what is (a) a section, (b) a township, (c) a range, (d) the 5th Principal Meridian? Where is this meridian?
A. Refer to definitions and text.

94. Q. What is the "Torrens system"?
A. It is a system of land registration introduced in Australia by Sir Robert Torrens about 1858. It is a system for the registration of land titles whereby the state of the title, showing ownership and encumbrances, can be readily ascertained from an inspection of the "register of titles" without the necessity of a search of the public records. It is used to a modified extent in some states in this country.

95. Q. In 1960, an owner made a contract with the owner of an adjoining residence for the joint use of an automobile driveway, half of which lay on each lot. In 1972, the owner made a contract to sell and convey his lot free of all encumbrances. When the title was searched, the joint users' agreement, which had been recorded, came to light. Under such circumstances, would the buyer have had the right to refuse to go through with the deal?
A. Yes. The joint driveway is an easement, constituting an encumbrance within the meaning of the term.

96. Q. Upon the closing of title to real property, where the purchaser, as part of the purchase price, gave a purchase money mortgage, the seller, upon receipt of said purchase money mortgage, and the buyer, upon the receipt of the deed, have each taken the respective two documents and placed them in a bank safe deposit vault for safe keeping. By doing so, have the two individuals committed anything detrimental to their interests with respect to the two documents? Why?
A. Both grantor and grantee have taken an unwarranted risk. The mortgage and deed should be recorded so that the grantee will be protected against a subsequent deed or mortgage for the same property given by the grantor and so that the grantor will be protected against a subsequent mortgage or lien given or suffered by the grantee before the deed is recorded.

97. Q. Would you prefer a general warranty deed with merchantable title or a court deed?
A. A general warranty deed with merchantable title. The court deed would not guarantee the title.

98. Q. Adams, residing in Dade County, Florida, owns a lot in Broward County. Adams asks where he must legally record the deed to his lot.
A. Broward County. Recordation of the deed must be in the county where the property is located.

99. Q. Harris conveys certain real estate to his son, John, "for and during the grantee's life." What kind of an estate does John obtain?
    A. John obtains a *life estate* only.
100. Q. A deed is executed by Alfred Sims to the First Presbyterian Church, of which he is a member. The Church is not an incorporated body. Does the Church obtain good title to the property?
    A. No; the deed is void because the grantee is incapable of taking title to real estate.
101. Q. What is meant by a homestead?
    A. The homestead consists of the dwelling house in which the claimant resides, together with outbuildings, and the land on which the same are situated. Declaration of homestead must be filed in the Recorder's Office.
102. Q. What information must be given in the declaration filed?
    A. 1. A statement showing that the claimant is the head of a family.
    2. If claimant is married, the name of the other spouse.
    3. That claimant is residing on the premises and claims them as a homestead.
    4. A full description of the premises.
    5. An estimate of their actual cash value.
103. Q. What advantages accrue to homestead property?
    A. Such property is protected from execution and foreclosure sale against most creditors.
104. Q. What claims will not be defeated by a homestead?
    A. 1. Judgments which became liens before the declaration was recorded.
    2. Mechanics' liens for work or materials furnished upon the premises.
    3. Mortgages and trust deeds executed and acknowledged by husband and wife or by an unmarried owner.
    4. Mortgages and trust deeds recorded before the declaration was recorded.
105. Q. How may a homestead be terminated?
    A. By a conveyance or by recorded instrument of abandonment.
106. Q. Does removal from the premises effect an abandonment of a homestead?
    A. No.
107. Q. Wherein does a sale of real estate differ from a sale of personal property?
    A. A sale of real estate is effected by a formal deed, duly signed, acknowledged, delivered, and recorded. A sale of personalty is effected by a bill of sale delivered to the purchaser.
108. Q. What federal income tax advantage do residents of community property states have?
    A. The husband's income may be divided equally between husband and wife for income tax purposes. The income tax law permits this division of income in all states which have community property.
109. Q. What is the difference between (1) an abstract of title, (2) a certificate of title, and (3) a title insurance policy?
    A. 1. An abstract of title is a document setting forth a brief synopsis of all matters of record affecting the title to the real estate in question.
    2. A certificate of title gives the net result of the examination of title, showing the name of the owner and the encumbrances and defects of title as of the date of the certificate.
    3. A title insurance policy insures the title in a given name, subject to noted exceptions and encumbrances listed in the policy and renders the insurer liable to compensate the insured for loss arising from errors of search and legal interpretation, in an amount not exceeding that stated in the policy.
110. Q. What is the purpose of recording a deed?
    A. To give notice to the public of the transfer of title, thus protecting a subsequent purchaser or mortgagee from the same grantor.
111. Q. John Lake has been designated by William Gardner as his attorney in-fact. Indicate

how Lake would sign a deed on behalf of Gardner.

A. William Gardner (Seal)
By his attorney-in-fact,
John Lake (Seal) The power of attorney must be recorded.

112. Q. Paul Simon conveys a lot in the Holliday Plan to Miles Jones. The deed recites a number of building restrictions and a provision to the effect that all other lots in the plan will be sold subject to the same restrictions. Without any mention of the restrictions, Simon sells a lot to Woodruff who attempts to erect a store. Jones files suit to enjoin the violation.

A. Jones will win. Woodruff is bound to examine the deeds of record and has notice of the restrictions in Jones' deed. Jones has an implied easement to the extent that the same restrictions apply to all lots in the plan, which he can enforce.

113. Q. Helen is married to Michael. The property is only in Michael's name. Should Helen sign the agreement and deed?

A. Yes; she should sign the agreement so that she can be compelled to sign the deed. She should sign the deed in order to extinguish her dower right.

114. Q. What is the bulk sales law and what is its purpose?

A. It is a law which requires that the seller of certain personal property give a list of all outstanding obligations prior to the completion of the sale and that the creditors be notified of the sale. It is intended to protect the purchaser of certain types of personal property, such as merchandise purchased in bulk, and arises frequently in connection with sale of business opportunities.

115. Q. What is the size of a Section of Land?

A. One square mile or 640 acres.

116. Q. How many sections of land in a Township?

A. Thirty-six.

117. Q. How many acres of land in SE $1/4$?

A. One hundred sixty.

118. Q. For the purpose of legal description of urban real estate, how is land usually divided?

A. In lots, blocks, and plan of lots.

119. Q. Is the street address of a property one and the same thing as "legal description"?

A. No.

120. Q. Are town lots any part of a Section, Township, or Range?

A. Yes.

121. Q. Point out three *errors* in the following description:
"Beginning at the North-West Quarter of lot numbered Eleven in Blank addition to the City of Poe, Roe County, Missouri; thence running South a distance of 202 feet; thence West a distance of 300 feet; thence North a distance of 202 feet to the point of beginning, containing five acres more or less."

A. 1. Beginning at North-West Quarter is wrong; should be North-West *corner.*
2. Tract does not close out—should go East 300 feet.
3. Size of tract is considerably less than five acres. Tract 202 X 300 feet would total only 60,600 square feet.

122. Q. Adams owns a tract of land which is traversed by a stream of water. The source of the stream is a spring-fed lake about two miles distant. Baker owns land between the lake and Adams's tract. Baker diverts the stream in order to make a pond about a quarter mile away from the stream channel. Adams learns of Baker's intention and gets an injunction against Baker prohibiting him from diverting the stream. Will the injunction stand? If so, why?

A. Yes; an upper owner merely has a usufructory right (right to use). He may not divert the stream from its natural channel so as to deprive a lower owner of his right to use the stream.

123. Q. *A,* who owns a house and lot, has contracted to sell it to *B.* He wishes to remove the

following articles from the premises. Indicate which of the following items will pass as real estate.

A. (x) Small evergreen trees and bushes.
( ) The coal range in the kitchen.
(x) The living room chandelier.
( ) The furnace shovel and poker.
( ) The living room lamp which is attached to a wall plug.
( ) The stair carpet.
( ) Awnings, unless specifically fitted to the dwelling.

124. Q. An electric light company has the right to erect its poles and run its lines along the rear five feet of a lot. What sort of a property right is this?

A. An easement.

125. Q. There are a number of restrictions usually found in deeds to property in high class subdivisions. Name two of these and state the reason for such restriction.

A. 1. Floor space restriction which determines minimum size house which can be built.
2. Price restriction which determines minimum amount which can be spent for dwelling.

126. Q. Lawrence conveys the coal under his farm to the Acme Coal Company. Finney purchases the farm and lays out a subdivision. Later, Finney sells a lot to Jordan giving a general warranty deed and no mention is made of the coal conveyance. Jordan builds and subsequently attempts to sell to Reed who refuses to complete the deal because of the coal conveyance. Does Jordan have any claim against Finney?

A. Yes, since Finney gave Jordan a general warranty deed, he warranted that title was absolute and complete and guaranteed the purchaser against all claimants.

127. Q. Watson conveys certain real estate to Lee "subject to coal and mining rights conveyed by prior deeds of record." Later, damage is caused to the house because of a surface cave-in due to the removal of the coal by the Ajax Coal Company. Does Lee have any action for damages?

A. He would not have any right of action against Watson because the deed to Lee was made subject to coal mining rights previously conveyed. It depends upon the language of the deed to the coal company whether he would have any cause of action against the Ajax Coal Company. The general rule of law is that all property in this country is held under the implied obligation that the owner's use of it shall not be injurious to the community. Thus, failure of the mineral owner to render support to the surface will make him liable to the surface owner. However, the United States Supreme Court has held (260 U. S. 392) that the owner may relinquish, by deed or agreement, his right to surface support. Most coal deeds now provide, "WITHOUT LIABILITY UNDER ANY CIRCUMSTANCES WHATEVER FOR DAMAGES DONE TO THE SURFACE OF SAID LOT OR TO THE IMPROVEMENTS NOW ERECTED OR HEREAFTER TO BE ERECTED THEREON." A state statute may abrogate this clause.

128. Q. William McKee and Fred Starr are partners doing business as McKee and Starr. They have acquired real estate for the firm purposes with partnership funds. Subsequently, the property is sold to Lowell Baker. Both McKee and Starr are married. Is it necessary for their wives to join in the deed?

A. No. Since the real estate was partnership property and held *as such,* the joinder of the wives is unnecessary.

129. Q. A tract of land was settled by Miller who lived on it for nine consecutive years. Due to conditions of health, he moved away for a six-year period. He then moved back to the same land and occupied it for six years. At the end of this period, or twenty-one years from his first occupancy, he claimed title by adverse possession. Will he succeed?

A. No. The possession must be continuous. Since he moved away for six years, the continuity has been broken, which is fatal to his claim. His adverse occupation has continued only for the last six years.

130. Q. Dolan owns certain real estate, upon which there is a mortgage held by Walsh. The mortgage is in default and in lieu of foreclosure, the mortgagee agrees to accept a voluntary deed from Dolan.
1. Does Walsh get a good title?
2. Is the mortgage extinguished?

A. 1. Walsh gets no better title than Dolan has. If there are judgments against Dolan, they will continue as liens against the property.
2. The deed, per se, does not extinguish the mortgage. The deed should recite the *intention* of the parties—that the mortgage is cancelled.

131. Q. A deed of farm land describes the land as running from a certain defined point nine hundred feet to the Revolutionary chestnut tree. The tree in question has long been identified and known in the neighborhood as such. The actual distance to this tree is 987 feet. Is the purchaser entitled to 987 feet or 900 feet?

A. 987 feet. In reconciling distances in a deed with distances shown by monuments upon the ground, the latter govern.

132. Q. Where a single woman owns real estate and sells the property after marriage, how should the deed refer to her as the grantor?

A. "Mary Steele, formerly Mary Sone." The notarial acknowledgment should read the same way.

133. Q. Is an oral deed, accompanied by occupancy by buyer, valid?

A. No.

134. Q. If a property is encumbered by a mortgage, would it be a merchantable title?

A. No.

135. Q. What is "escheat" in reference to lands?

A. The lapsing or reverting of land to the state, which occurs usually for failure of heirs or lack of legal ownership.

136. Q. What type of deed is preferable from the buyer's standpoint?

A. A general warranty deed, because the grantor warrants to protect the grantee against any claimant.

137. Q. Local planning commissions have an area of jurisdiction, in addition to the most common ones—land use through zoning, community subdivision, design and flood control. Name at least three of these other fields.

A. 1. recreation 2. streets and highways 3. sewage disposal and drainage.

138. Q. Name four different ways in which an owner of real estate may have secured title to it.

A. Purchase, gift, inheritance, adverse possession.

139. Q. If a warranty deed has been executed and delivered to a purchaser, is it necessary to have it recorded in order to make it a valid conveyance?

A. No.

140. Q. What is the danger in not recording a deed promptly?

A. Judgments may be filed against previous owner; also, previous owner may sell or mortgage the property to someone else.

141. Q. May a life estate be sold?

A. Yes; purchaser would hold during the life of his grantor (per auter vie).

142. Q. Who is the legal owner of a piece of property when the deed to it is delivered but not recorded?

A. The grantee (purchaser).

143. Q. What is a Condominium?

A. An individual ownership of a single unit in a multi-family structure.

144. Q. How does it differ from ownership in a co-operative apartment?

A. A condominium can be bought, sold or mortgaged and is taxed separately. In a co-op, the owner usually purchases stock in the corporation and holds possession under a long-term, renewable lease.

145. Q. Smith conveys one-half of a tract of land to Ellis, reserving to himself a right of way across the rear ten feet. On April 24, 1969, Smith sells his one-half to Lawrence. Later Ellis attempts to restrain Lawrence from using the right of way. Will he succeed?
 A. Yes. The right of way was reserved to Smith as a personal covenant. To permit Lawrence to use it, the reservation should have been made to Smith, "his heirs and assigns."

146. Q. Is it necessary to affix United States Revenue Stamps to a deed?
 A. No. Not since January 1, 1968.

147. Q. Is there a difference in making a deed "under and subject to a mortgage" and in making deed "under and subject to a mortgage, which the grantee assumes and agrees to pay"?
 A. Yes. In the first clause, the grantee does not *personally* assume any obligation to pay the debt; in the second clause, he does and he would be personally liable for any deficiency judgment, i.e., the difference between the amount of the debt and the amount realized at a foreclosure sale.

148. Q. A deed is signed in blank by the owner and left with a broker, with the request that broker make the best deal possible. The broker sells the property to a friend at a price lower than the market price. Is the deed valid?
 A. Yes. The deed is good unless there was some "connivance" between broker and buyer. The broker can be held accountable to the owner for his lack of good faith.

149. Q. At a closing, a seller refuses to pay a broker's commission and demands that the deal be closed. Can the closing officer ignore the broker's claim and disburse the funds?
 A. Yes; the broker has only a collateral claim in the deal between buyer and seller.

150. Q. One year after a closing, an unpaid special assessment of $540 is discovered. Is the broker or owner responsible to the buyer, or neither?
 A. The owner is responsible to the buyer for the assessment, and costs, under a general warranty deed.

151. Q. What are the five governmental limitations on land?
 A. Police power, eminent domain, zoning, taxation and escheat.

152. Q. What is meant by venue?
 A. This is the acknowledgement of the deed, stating the state and county where the deed is signed.

153. Q. Suppose the property is located in Dade County, Florida, and is acknowledged in Cook County, Illinois, what formality is required?
 A. A certificate of the clerk of courts that the notary public is authorized to take acknowledgments, is usually required.

154. Q. Can a United States Consul in Liverpool, England, take an acknowledgment to a deed for property in the United States?
 A. Yes.

155. A. What precaution should be taken in the acknowledgment as to the date?
 A. Care should be taken that the date in the acknowledgment is not earlier than in the deed.

156. Q. Allen signs an agreement of sale to sell a lot, zoned residential, to Barnes, who desires to erect a dwelling. Before the deal is closed, the city changes the zone to commercial. Barnes seeks to rescind the deal. Will he succeed?
 A. No. Under the doctrine of equitable conversion, Barnes assumed the risk of change in zoning.

157. Q. Does an eight-unit townhouse complex violate a deed restriction which read "owners and occupiers of certain lots shall not at any time hereafter erect more than one dwelling house?"
 A. The appellate court held that the restriction was valid and prohibited the eight-unit

complex, since it would have the appearance and character of the eight party wall houses and could not be considered "one dwelling house": *Shapiro v. Levin,* 223 Pa. Super. 535 (1973).

158. Q. James MacDonald and Margaret MacDonald, his wife, acquired title to their residence, by the entireties, in 1965. In 1970, Margaret obtained an absolute divorce from James. The same parties re-married in 1973 and James died on October 2, 1974. The widow, Margaret, claims title to the entire property. Irene, a daughter of James by a previous marriage, claims a one-half interest in the property. Decide.

A. Irene is entitled to a one-half interest. Upon divorce in 1972, Margaret and James became the owners of the subject property as tenants in common, and each then owned a one-half interest. The subsequent re-marriage did not convert the ownership into an estate by the entireties. To create an estate by the entireties a *new* deed would have been necessary to James and Margaret, his wife.

True and False

1. A deed is a bilateral contract. **T** F
2. One party only signs the deed (the grantor). **T** F
3. Livery of seisin is sufficient to pass title. T **F**
4. An oral deed, coupled with possession and making improvements is sufficient to pass title. T **F**
5. In a tenancy in common, each co-owner possesses an equal share. T **F**
6. Title, under a quit claim deed, is not insurable. **T** F
7. A marketable title is one free from liens and encumbrances. **T** F
8. Burden of establishing marketable title is on the grantor. **T** F
9. A creditor of a wife can assert her dower interest. T **F**
10. Title to real estate may pass without consent of the owner. **T** F
11. Merchantable title is title free from liens. T **F**
12. Under a "government survey" the size of a check is 24 by 24 miles on each side of the square. **T** F
13. A life tenant cannot sell the property to another. T **F**
14. A deed to real estate cannot be assigned. **T** F
15. An abstract of title guarantees clear title. T **F**
16. The full consideration in any real estate transaction must always be in legal tender. T **F**
17. In a tenancy in common, one person may own $\frac{1}{5}$th interest and another person may own a $\frac{4}{5}$th interest. **T** F
18. When the tide water is a boundary in the deed, title to the ordinary high water mark is conveyed. **T** F
19. The passing of title to real estate or an interest therein from one person to another is called a conveyance. **T** F
20. Escrow is another name for a husband's interest in his wife's estate. T **F**
21. Constructive notice is knowledge charged by law to one who has no actual knowledge. **T** F
22. A warranty deed to real estate may be assigned. T **F**
23. If Albert owns real estate, he can create a tenancy in common by conveying to Blake an undivided interest in such real estate. **T** F
24. Recorded restrictions in a deed may be enforced by any citizen of the community. T **F**
25. The cost of extending an abstract is generally paid for by the purchasers. T **F**
26. Urban real estate is always described by sections. T **F**
27. A deed should state the marital status of parties. **T** F
28. Recording of a deed is a proper charge against the seller. T **F**
29. A conveyance of the title to property for the duration of the life of the grantee is called a life estate. **T** F

30. A deed cannot be recorded unless it is signed by the grantee. T F
31. A deed is of no effect until it has been recorded. T F
32. A quit claim deed ordinarily conveys a good and merchantable title. T F
33. A special warranty deed is preferable to a general warranty deed. T F
34. The grantor in a deed may impose restrictions as to the use of real property. T F
35. Zoning restrictions, once established, cannot be changed. T F
36. Community clubhouses, parks, and public buildings are "community property" in the real estate sense of the term. T F
37. A quit claim deed may serve the same ends as a suit to quiet title. T F
38. In land descriptions, the "Rectangular System" was first used in the Northwest Territory. T F
39. The house number and the name of the street is one of the best legal descriptions there is. T F
40. Land with the improvements thereon, is described as "real property." T F
41. Fee simple estate is the greatest estate in real estate. T F
42. Real property may be held in joint tenancy only by husband and wife. T F
43. The passing of title to real estate or an interest therein from one person to another is called a conveyance. T F
44. A deed without a date is void. T F
45. A deed dated on a Sunday but delivered on Monday is invalid. T F
46. An oral deed is void. T F
47. Only related persons may be joint tenants of real estate. T F
48. A deed to real estate does not pass title until it is recorded. T F
49. An oral deed is valid if the grantee takes possession. T F
50. A deed must be recorded in the city where the property is located. T F
51. A remainder estate is one that has been inherited by a person to hold during his lifetime. T F
52. The original source of ownership for most land in the United States was in the form of a grant known as a patent. T F
53. Vertical rows of townships are called ranges. T F
54. In a recorded plan, a lot within the plan is usually described by metes and bounds. T F
55. There is no difference between a condominium and a co-operative apartment. T F
56. It is lawful to deed real estate to a minor. T F
57. A deed has no legal effect until it is delivered to the grantee. T F
58. Delivery of a deed to grantor's agent passes title to real estate. T F
59. Better title is conveyed by a warranty deed than by a quit claim deed. T F
60. Good title to real estate and a good title of record are the same. T F
61. Real property must be free and clear of all encumbrances to be declared as a "homestead." T F
62. The recording of a deed is the obligation of the grantor. T F
63. A deed recites a consideration of $1.00; the actual price is $100,000. The deed is void because of fraud on the public in misrepresenting the selling price. T F
64. In joint ownership, if one of the parties dies, his interest goes to the surviving parties and not to the decedent's heirs. T F
65. Failure to attach the proper amount of State Revenue stamps renders the deed void. T F
66. A person under 21 years of age cannot hold title to real estate. T F
67. A valid deed must contain a granting clause. T F
68. A quit claim makes no warranty of title. T F
69. The legal description in a deed can be enlarged by oral testimony in court. T F
70. Escrow is another name for a wife's interest in her husband's property. T F
71. A deed takes effect only upon delivery. T F
72. A forged deed is void and does not convey good title under any circumstances. T F
73. The lot and block system of land description is a description by metes and bounds. T F

74. In describing lands by metes and bounds, a course described as being "North 45 degrees east" runs in a northeasterly direction. T F
75. Title to real estate is passed by delivery of the abstract of title. T F
76. The term "tenants in common" refers to several persons who lease and occupy the same property. T F
77. Certain parts of condominium ownership are held as tenants in common. T F
78. Any person sui juris may be given power of attorney. T F
79. A person unable to write could not own real estate since he would be unable to sign a deed. T F
80. A typewritten signature to a deed is void. T F
81. After a deed has been recorded, the grantee will lose the property if he loses the deed to it. T F
82. A "set-back" ordinance regulates the minimum distance allowable between street line and front of new buildings. T F
83. In the sale of real property, the seller is known as the grantee. T F
84. In describing lands by metes and bounds, a course may be described by trees, rocks and woods. T F
85. In order to create a joint tenancy, there must be present the four unities of time, title, interest and possession. T F
86. Clouds on title to real estate are removed by obtaining title insurance. T F
87. The most common form of land measurement in eastern rural areas is by metes and bounds. T F
88. A gift deed must always have a monetary consideration. T F
89. A quit claim deed warrants and guarantees nothing. T F
90. Title to real property without improvements may be conveyed by the issuance of a Bill of Sale. T F
91. A township is one mile square. T F
92. Property may be held in joint tenancy only by husband and wife. T F
93. A tenancy in common carries with it the right of survivorship. T F
94. A deed is of no effect until it has been signed, sealed, and delivered. T F
95. A single person and a married person may hold title to real estate as joint tenants. T F
96. A deed is recorded to give notice to the public that the party named in the deed has a vested right or interest in the property described. T F
97. One instrument often used to remove a cloud on a title to real estate is an escheat. T F
98. Real estate may be defined as any property not considered personal. T F
99. The buyer should pay for an attorney's examination of the title. T F
100. In the escrow of a deed, it is desirable for the broker to act as the escrow holder. T F
101. Assessments on real estate for tax purposes are made every even year. T F
102. A public utility company always has an easement in any property by act of the legislature. T F
103. An action to quiet title is used to remove a cloud on the title. T F
104. A married woman who acquired title before marriage should sign a deed only in her maiden name. T F
105. It is proper to give a quit claim deed even though your interest in the property is negligible or questionable. T F
106. An abstract of title guarantees a clear title. T F
107. When one owns real estate, his warranty deed gives no better protection than his quit claim deed would give. T F
108. A deed may sometimes be recorded without being acknowledged. T F
109. One who receives the deed is called the grantee. T F
110. An escrow agent is the agent for *both* buyer and seller. T F
111. A deed by a minor is voidable at his option. T F
112. A deed takes effect only from the date it is recorded. T F

113. Real estate taxes are levied only upon the owner's equity between the assessed value and the mortgage encumbrance. T F
114. Chain of title is the succession of conveyances from some accepted starting point whereby the present holder of real property derives his title. T F
115. A grantee receives no better title than his grantor had. T F
116. The owner of real property becomes the grantor when he sells the property. T F
117. An easement is an encumbrance on real estate. T F
118. An estate in severalty is an estate owned by one person alone. T F
119. It is necessary to itemize in the deed all improvements affixed to the real estate being conveyed if they are to be sold with the real property. T F
120. A Bill of Sale is the instrument by which the title to real estate passes. T F
121. Upon the death of one of two tenants in common to real estate, the interest and title in the land of the deceased owner descends to his heirs and not to the surviving party. T F
122. The terms "tide lands" and "shore lands" apply to the same land. T F
123. Tenancy in common refers to ownership rather than occupancy. T F
124. When a grantor faultily executes a deed, he can be compelled to sign a corrected deed. T F
125. A trustee's deed is generally a warranty deed rather than a special warranty deed. T F
126. A chain of title refers to a unit of land measurement. T F
127. A good title and a marketable title generally mean the same thing. T F
128. Real estate and real property generally mean the same thing. T F
129. A community apartment house is considered a subdivision. T F
130. Where one is negligent in asserting his legal rights, he is guilty of estoppel. T F
131. Metes and bounds is a system of land description by measure and direction. T F
132. A beneficiary under a trust must always join in the deed by the trustee. T F
133. A deed by the officers of a corporation must be made in pursuance of a resolution of the board of directors authorizing the particular sale. T F
134. A deed to farm property will include the sale of all machinery and farm implements. T F
135. The recording of a deed guarantees its validity. T F
136. If a deed has been recorded and the consideration price has not been paid in full, the deed is void. T F
137. Title insurance offers protection against loss by fire. T F
138. An unpaid tax lien is an encumbrance on title. T F
139. A sheriff's deed is a general warranty deed. T F
140. No personal property can ever become real property. T F
141. A good and a valuable consideration are legally the same. T F
142. A declaration of homestead is of no effect until recorded. T F
143. Two brokers can own community property. T F
144. Real property in name of wife is presumed to be her separate property. T F
145. On death of father, children inherit one half of community property. T F
146. A quit claim deed generally conveys fee simple title. T F
147. An abstract of title is a summary or digest of all instruments affecting the title. T F
148. A deed to husband and wife creates an estate by the entireties. T F
149. Property may be owned by more than two joint tenants. T F
150. Recording a deed is the obligation of the grantor. T F
151. A grantor of a deed may impose restrictions as to the use of real property. T F
152. Building restrictions which run perpetually are invalid. T F
153. Zoning restrictions and building restrictions are the same. T F
154. A minor cannot void a real estate transaction if he misrepresented his age. T F
155. To be valid, a deed must always be signed by both the grantor and the grantee. T F
156. A habendum clause is essential in a deed in order to pass a valid title. T F
157. The date in the beginning of the deed should not be subsequent to the date in

the acknowledgment. T F

158. The clause in the deed which indicates who is to give the property and who is to receive the property is called the covenant of seizin. T F
159. Attestation means witnessing the deed. T F
160. A deed may be acknowledged by a justice of the peace or a notary public. T F
161. In the conveyance of real estate, all permanent buildings must be described in the warranty deed. T F
162. A quit claim deed does not convey fee simple title. T F
163. A deed need not be in writing if grantor and grantee appear before the County Recorder of Deeds and swear that the transfer is voluntary and for consideration. T F
164. The actual selling price of real property must be shown in the deed. T F
165. A property owner may use his property as a surety bond for another person's obligation. T F
166. Joint tenants with right of survivorship means literally that the building is being operated as a "joint" with police protection. T F
167. An unrecorded deed is good and valid as between the parties to the instrument. T F
168. A fee tail estate affords greater protection to a grantee than a fee simple estate. T F
169. A "deed" takes effect during the grantor's lifetime and a "will" at the testator's death. T F
170. The actual selling price of real property is never shown in the deed. T F
171. In the conveyance of real estate, all auxiliary buildings are described in the warranty deed. T F
172. Fractional sections of farm land are always caused by errors in survey. T F
173. A judgment lien against a grantor renders the title unmarketable. T F
174. Title insurance guarantees the owner against all defects in title. T F
175. An error by the Recorder's Office in recording the deed will render the deed invalid. T F
176. A Judge of a court of record may take acknowledgments. T F
177. A general warranty deed gives the same protection as title insurance. T F
178. The right to continue a non-conforming use may be lost through destruction of the building. T F
179. A non-conforming use may be terminated by a new zoning law. T F
180. The law of caveat emptor has been strengthened through court decisions. T F
181. A person who has real estate devised to him is said to acquire title by adverse possession. T F
182. "Metes and bounds" has reference to the topography of the land. T F
183. Zoning ordinances are enacted primarily to define "no-parking" zones. T F
184. A deed given in return for domestic services has legal consideration. T F
185. An interest in ownership of personal property is usually termed an estate in fee simple. T F
186. A City Zoning Ordinance has reference to the local postal zones. T F
187. The recording of a deed to real property is the obligation of the grantee. T F
188. Torrens Land Titles is a state operated land title system based upon registration of title. T F
189. The full consideration in any real estate transaction must always be in legal tender. T F
190. The execution of a deed means that it was properly signed and acknowledged by the grantee. T F
191. A grantor impliedly warrants that he has fee simple title to the property. T F
192. The sole purpose of an acknowledgment to a deed is to promote the security of the title. T F
193. A purchaser at a foreclosure sale usually receives a bargain and sale deed. T F
194. The "Chain of Title" is found in the "Abstract of Title." T F
195. Real property includes everything that is not personalty. T F

196. One who dies holding tenancy in common may will his interest to his next of kin. **T** F
197. A septic tank system is a private sewage disposal system for individual homes. **T** F
198. A Sheriff's Deed and a Tax Deed are usually considered to have the same effect. **T** F
199. Title to property may pass to another by adverse possession. **T** F
200. Title by adverse possession is just as valid as title by deed. **T** F
201. A suit for specific performance is an action to quiet title. T **F**
202. In directions in a deed, east is always to the right of north. **T** F
203. Real estate may include more than just land. **T** F
204. Real Estate Commissioners are authorized by the license law to take acknowledgments. T **F**
205. A section of land contains 360 acres. T **F**
206. A $1.00 consideration is sufficient for an option. **T** F
207. One who has taken an option on certain real estate must complete the purchase of the property. T **F**
208. The consideration in an option is always applied to the purchase price, if the option is exercised. T **F**
209. Zoning regulations limit the use of real estate. **T** F
210. Failure to record documents has no effect on their validity. **T** F
211. It is usually false economy to fail to secure a title search when purchasing property. **T** F
212. If you include your piano and television set in the sale of your home, they become a part of the real estate. T **F**
213. A property may be transferred by deed when the consideration is only love and affection. **T** F
214. The term "fee simple" means that it is the usual commission for the sale of real estate. T **F**
215. An easement means making the payment easier on a mortgage. T **F**
216. A warranty deed is used to convey title to chattels. T **F**
217. A power of attorney can be given only to duly qualified attorneys at law. T **F**
218. A deed to partnership property sold by the partners need not have the joinder of the wives of the partners. **T** F
219. Two or more persons who take title to property by a single deed hold it as partners. T **F**
220. It is not necessary to require a title search when conveying property worth less than $1,000.00. T **F**
221. It is legal to describe property by lot, block, and tract number if sold from a recorded plan. **T** F
222. Laws passed by a governing body whereby certain described sections are set aside for certain purposes are known as zoning laws. **T** F
223. The deed which is executed in a foreclosure action is an Executor's Deed. T **F**
224. The terms "real estate," "realty," and "real property" mean practically the same thing. **T** F
225. An agreement under which an instrument or money is deposited with a third person to be delivered upon the performance of a condition is called a power of attorney. T **F**
226. The ownership of real estate by two or more persons, each of whom has an undivided interest, without the "right of survivorship" is called a Tenancy in Common. **T** F
227. It is not necessary to require a title search when buying a vacant lot. T **F**
228. "Beneficiary," "Trustor," and "Trustee" are the legal designations of the parties to a trust deed. **T** F
229. Upon the death of the father and mother, the children inherit one half of the community property. T **F**
230. A "conditional sales contract" on real property can be recorded only if it has been

acknowledged by the buyer. T F

231. A final decree of divorce has the effect of an abandonment of a declaration of homestead. T F
232. Dating a deed is necessary to make it valid. T F
233. If a husband alone signs a listing on community property, the broker cannot collect a commission if the wife refuses to sell. T F
234. In a standard township, section 31 is located in the southwest corner. T F
235. Fee simple title is all the bundle of rights in real estate. T F
236. A standard township contains 23,040 acres of land. T F
237. A "Power of Attorney" is a title examiner who closes real estate transactions. T F
238. A ground rent is real estate. T F
239. Title by adverse possession is just as valid as title by a written instrument. T F
240. An easement is real estate. T F
241. A deed must be recorded in the county where the property is located. T F
242. A deed, once recorded, if lost, has no effect on the title. T F
243. The major objective of the Homestead Law is to protect against execution to satisfy debts. T F
244. A grantor who has improperly executed a deed, which has been recorded, cannot be required to execute a new deed. T F
245. Restrictions in a deed are desirable in order to maintain value of the property. T F
246. A restriction and an easement mean the same thing. T F
247. A grantee who delays in recording a deed is subject to a penalty. T F
248. Courts do not inquire into the sufficiency of the consideration price. T F
249. The warranty clause in a deed and the testimonium clause mean the same thing. T F
250. A recital of title is essential to the validity of a deed. T F
251. It is the obligation of the grantee to see that the deed is properly indexed. T F
252. A deed executed in a foreign country should be acknowledged before a minister or consul of this country. T F
253. Where a judgment note has been given in payment of the consideration and the note is not paid at maturity, the deed is void. T F
254. Either parent, by operation of law, is duly authorized to execute a deed for a minor child. T F
255. The sale of land includes all appurtenances thereto. T F
256. Building restrictions, as specified in the deed, are not encumbrances against the property. T F
257. The only essential unity in a tenancy in common is the equal right of possession. T F
258. A list of furniture included in a sale of property should be stated in the deed. T F
259. A deed by a partnership should be executed in the partnership name only. T F
260. A corporation deed should always recite the resolution of the board of directors, authorizing the conveyance. T F
261. Where property is sold within one year, it is not necessary to have the title examined. T F
262. A road through a private property used by another with permission of the owner is an appurtenance. T F
263. It is possible to exchange properties even though both are subject to existing mortgages. T F
264. Interest on delinquent real estate taxes always accrues at the rate of 1%. T F
265. In a standard township, section 30 is in the southwest corner. T F
266. A sheriff's deed and a tax deed are the same as far as warranties. T F
267. A deed to "John Saxman or Andrew Erbel" is valid. T F
268. A merchantable title is one free from clouds or defects. T F
269. A covenant of seizin is the grantor's guarantee that he is the owner of the property and has the power to convey title thereto. T F
270. There are no covenants to be found in a quit claim deed. T F

271. Signing a deed does not transfer title. T F
272. Failure to record a deed or a mortgage has no effect on its validity. T F
273. Alluvium and Avulsion are synonymous terms. T F
274. A fee simple estate and a fee simple absolute estate are the same. T F
275. An executed deed transfers title to real estate. T F
276. An encumbrance is anything which affects the title to real estate. T F
277. Every fixture is a chattel. T F
278. In a rectangular survey a check is sixteen townships. T F
279. A title insurance policy excepts conditions shown by actual survey. T F
280. A quit claim deed of a husband need not be signed by his wife. T F
281. Condemnation of private property for public use is called acquisition. T F
282. A co-operative apartment ownership generally is more advantageous than in a condominium. T F
283. Tenancy in common refers to ownership. T F
284. A restrictive easement is one which runs with the land. T F
285. "Spot" zoning is permissible in hardship cases. T F
286. The total land area of a homestead is limited by statute. T F
287. A person having a freehold interest in land to be held during the life of another is a leasehold estate. T F
288. A tract (of land) and a check can be used interchangeably in measurement terms. T F
289. The habendum clause and the testimonium clause in a deed are similar and can be used interchangeably. T F
290. An irrigation ditch on a ranch is personal property. T F
291. A and B may own a 1/8 and 7/8 interest, respectively, as tenants in common. T F
292. A single man and a husband and wife may own property as joint tenants. T F
293. A husband and wife may own real estate only as community property. T F
294. Personal property is never held by tenants in common. T F
295. Title to real estate may pass without consent of the owner. T F
296. When the tide water is a boundary in the deed, title to the ordinary high water mark is conveyed. T F
297. A freehold interest is ownership of a fee simple or life estate. T F
298. Tenancy in common may be created by destruction of a joint tenancy. T F
299. As between the parties, a deed is invalid without subscribing witnesses or acknowledgment. T F
300. The recording of a deed guarantees its validity. T F
301. Alluvial land is generally unproductive land on which the return over cost of production is practically nil. T F
302. Horizontal rows of townships are called tiers. T F
303. Chain is a unit of measurement—16 1/2 feet. T F
304. The United States Internal Revenue Tax was repealed on January 1, 1966. T F
305. Condominium ownership is a stabilizing factor in maintaining urban population. T F
306. Condominium ownership has greater safeguards to the individual owner than that of a co-op apartment. T F
307. Condominium ownership is less than 25 years old in this country. T F
308. An owner of a condominium must obtain approval of his fellow owners as to type of flooring and decor, in order to maintain uniformity. T F
309. Owner of a condominium unit is unable to obtain F.H.A. financing. T F
310. Condominium ownership is the result of a state enabling statute. T F
311. An estate is the interest one has in property. T F
312. A system of land registration by which the state guarantees the title is known as the Torrens system. T F
313. Rights which are incidental to the land and "go with the land" are encroachments. T F
314. A reconveyance deed is used in connection with a trust deed. T F

315. There are 20 acres included in the S $1/2$ of the NW $1/4$ of the SE $1/4$ of a section of land. T F
316. Title to a vacant tract of land may be conveyed by a bill of sale. T F
317. A devise is the reversion of real estate to the State when the testator dies intestate. T F
318. An appropriation of land by an owner for some public use and acceptance for such use is called a dedication. T F
319. Reformation is an action to correct an error in a deed. T F
320. A devise of real estate may be changed by the maker of the will at any time before death. T F
321. An oral gift of real estate to take effect after death, made in the presence of two disinterested witnesses, is valid. T F
322. A fence existing for more than six years will be regarded as the true boundary line between two farms. T F
323. Ownership of a condominium unit is the same as ownership of a dwelling. T F
324. Constructive knowledge is knowledge charged by law to one who has no actual knowledge. T F
325. Delivery in escrow is where a deed to real estate is delivered to a third person pending the performance of some condition. T F
326. The cost of any required state documentary transfer stamps are charged to the seller. T F
327. Harry Jones, a single man, and Mary Steele, a married woman, may own property as joint tenants. T F
328. The cost of any state documentary transfer tax may be deducted from the Federal Income Tax. T F
329. The statute of frauds is the same as the Truth in Lending law. T F
330. A fee simple absolute estate is the same as a fee simple estate. T F
331. State documentary (excise) stamps are necessary on both deeds in an exchange of real estate. T F
332. A deed can include an easement which was not included in the agreement of sale. T F
333. A deed is of no effect unless it has been signed, acknowledged, delivered and recorded. T F
334. A deed can be signed for the grantor by another person at the grantor's direction and in his presence. T F
335. The grantor may impose restrictions as to the sale of real property to persons other than that of the Caucasian race. T F
336. The 1866 Act of Congress forbidding discrimination in real estate sales is still in force. T F
337. In recording a deed, it must be recorded in the city or town where the property is situated. T F
338. If Adams owns real estate, he can create a tenancy in common by conveying an undivided $1/10$ interest. T F
339. If you include the ancient grandfather's clock in the sale of your house, it becomes a part of the real estate. T F
340. A grantee may require the grantor, who claims title to real estate by adverse possession, to obtain a court decree first. T F
341. A deed in escrow passes title to the grantee immediately upon delivery to the escrow holder. T F
342. If a deed is delivered in escrow and the grantor dies on the following day, the deed is void. T F
343. An unrecorded deed is good as against a subsequent recorded mortgage against the grantor. T F
344. An action to quiet title is brought to remove a cloud on the title. T F
345. Real property may be owned jointly by persons other than husband and wife. T F

346. In order to hold a power of attorney, the person must be an owner of real estate. T F
347. In order to convey property, the grantor must produce the deed to him. T F
348. A wife cannot become a tenant in common with her husband. T F
349. A tax rate of one mill is the same as a rate of one-tenth of one per cent of the assessed value of the property. T F
350. Two persons who own undivided interests in a piece of real property without the right of survivorship own the property as joint tenants. T F
351. A person who makes, signs, or issues any taxable instrument shall affix and cancel the documentary stamps. T F
352. Two or more persons may together own property in severalty. T F
353. The rectangular survey system is the United States governmental survey system. T F
354. Metes (in a description) are measurements of distance. T F
355. A fee simple title is the most comprehensive ownership in land. T F
356. A building permit, issued by a city, which violates a zoning law is a nullity. T F
357. A zoning ordinance excluding singles from a one-family residence zone is unconstitutional. T F
358. Verbal testimony is generally admissible to explain the contents of a deed. T F
359. A quit claim deed may be assumed by endorsement by the grantor. T F
360. Tenancy at will is equivalent to tenancy in common. T F
361. A cul de sac in a subdivision creates less traffic and noise. T F
362. A trust account serves the same purpose as an escrow account. T F
363. The burden of proof in an eminent domain proceedings is upon condemnor. T F
364. Eminent domain is an inherent right of state sovereignty. T F
365. In an easement of a right of way, the servient tenement receives the benefit. T F
366. An easement in gross is appurtenant to the land. T F
367. An implied easement is enforceable. T F
368. In a quit claim deed to extinguish a recorded agreement of sale, the vendee is the grantor. T F
369. If the date in the acknowledgment antedates the date in the deed, the deed is void. T F
370. The date in the deed always determines when title passed. T F
371. If a grantor signs a deed without reading it, the deed is invalid. T F
372. A deed, naming the Lutheran Church as grantee, is void. T F
373. A deed to two individuals, John Steele and Henry Adams, "as partners," would not create a tenancy in partnership. T F

Multiple Choice

1. A restrictive covenant in a deed must not be contrary to
   (a) The real estate license.
   (b) public policy.
   (c) statute of frauds.
   (d) opinion of the state attorney general.
2. The United States governmental survey system is
   (a) metes and bounds.
   (b) recorded plat.
   (c) rectangular survey system.
   (d) none of these.
3. Bates conveys a fee simple title to the Avon Baptist Church, by deed, to be used for church purposes, in 1950. In 1974, the church abandons the property, due to environmental changes. Title to the property will:
   (a) Remain in the church.
   (b) Escheat to the state.
   (c) Revert to Bates.
   (d) Be owned by the church and Bates, as joint tenants.

4. Probate means an action to:
    (a) Cure a defect by a quit claim deed.
    (b) Prove title by adverse possession.
    (c) Process a will, to establish its validity.
    (d) Obtain access to a safe deposit box.
5. The construction of a mobile home in a commercial use zone,
    (a) violates residential restrictions.
    (b) does not violate residential restrictions.
    (c) violates a city public health code.
    (d) is a violation, per se.
6. Which type of deed limits the covenants of the grantor when he conveys real estate?
    (a) Quit claim.
    (b) Special warranty.
    (c) General warranty.
    (d) None of these.
7. The voluntary transfer of title to real estate is
    (a) divestiture.
    (b) adverse possession.
    (c) alienation.
    (d) surrender.
8. Trees on land become personal property by
    (a) conversion into lumber.
    (b) sale of the land.
    (c) appropriation by eminent domain.
    (d) foreclosure on a mortgage.
9. Which one of the following is not necessary for a valid transfer of title to real estate?
    (a) Signing.
    (b) Acknowledgement.
    (c) Delivery.
    (d) Recording.
10. A man devised his residence to his widow and upon her death, it was to go to two of his three children. The widow received a
    (a) life estate.
    (b) partial estate.
    (c) remainder estate.
    (d) leasehold.
11. Tenancy in common refers to
    (a) occupancy by two or more persons.
    (b) survivorship.
    (c) ownership.
    (d) a lease that has restrictive covenants to tenants.
12. Real estate occupied as a home, by an owner, who enjoys special rights and privileges is
    (a) a freehold.
    (b) a homestead.
    (c) a joint tenancy.
    (d) unjust enrichment.
13. Timber on land becomes personal property by
    (a) sale of the land.
    (b) written declaration of owner.
    (c) severance.
    (d) eminent domain.
14. The water table is the
    (a) measure of water flow.
    (b) rate for cost of water.

(c) depth where water is found.
(d) average rainfall per month.

15. An estate at will is a
    (a) form of co-ownership.
    (b) tenancy of uncertain duration.
    (c) inheritance of property by will.
    (d) life estate.
16. An area of land set off by municipal authorities for a specific use is called
    (a) a cul de sac.
    (b) a subdivision.
    (c) a zone.
    (d) territory.
17. Alice Nichols, a married woman, and Henry Steele, single, may not own real estate as
    (a) tenants in common.
    (b) joint tenants.
    (c) tenants by the entireties.
    (d) as remainder devisees.
18. A conveyance is made to John Smith, his heirs and assigns
    (a) Smith has a life estate.
    (b) Smith has a fee simple estate.
    (c) Smith's heirs have a remainder estate.
    (d) Smith's heirs have a reversionary estate.
19. Andrew Erbel, a single man, and William Rushton, a single man, wish to take the title to real property so that each will own a one-half interest, and if either of them dies, the other will own the entire property. The Grantee clause should read:
    (a) Andrew Erbel, a single man, and William Rushton, a single man, each an undivided one-half interest as tenants in common.
    (b) Andrew Erbel and William Rushton, single men, as joint tenants.
    (c) Andrew Erbel, a single man, and William Rushton, a single man, jointly and severally.
    (d) Andrew Erbel and William Rushton, single men, as co-owners.
    (e) none of the above is correct.
20. In order to record a deed, it must be in writing and
    (a) signed by grantee.
    (b) recite the actual purchase price.
    (c) acknowledged.
    (d) be free of all liens.
21. The most comprehensive ownership of land at law is known as
    (a) estate for years.
    (b) life estate.
    (c) fee simple.
    (d) defeasible title.
22. James Steele and Mary Steele, his daughter, buy a tract of ground for all cash and the property is deeded to them "with right of survivorship." James and Mary are:
    (a) joint tenants.
    (b) tenants by the entireties.
    (c) tenants in common.
    (d) none of the above.
23. In a tenancy in common, each person owns
    (a) the whole of an undivided part.
    (b) an undivided part of the whole.
    (c) an equal share.
    (d) a pro rata share in severalty.
24. Clauses in a deed are dictated by
    (a) the recorded deed.

(b) the listing agreement.
(c) the oral agreement of the contracting parties.
(d) the agreement of sale.

25. An estate of inheritance, or for life is known as
    (a) freehold.
    (b) less than a freehold.
    (c) greater than a freehold.
    (d) none of these.
26. A wall erected on the line between two adjoining properties belonging to different persons which serves as an outside wall of both buildings is a
    (a) party wall.
    (b) community wall.
    (c) line wall.
    (d) share wall.
27. The largest estate or ownership in real property is
    (a) a fee tail estate.
    (b) a fee simple estate.
    (c) a homestead.
    (d) a littoral right.
28. A land description reading: The N $1/2$ of the S $1/2$ of the SW $1/4$ of the NW $1/4$ contains
    (a) 15 acres.
    (b) 10 acres.
    (c) 7 acres.
    (d) 20 acres.
29. From the standpoint of the grantor in a deed conveying real estate which of the following types of deed creates the least liability?
    (a) Special warranty.
    (b) General warranty.
    (c) Bargain and sale.
    (d) Quit claim.
30. Land acquired by husband or wife by their labor after marriage in Arizona, Arkansas, California, Florida or Texas, is
    (a) separate property.
    (b) real property.
    (c) community property.
31. Community property is owned by
    (a) the church.
    (b) father and son.
    (c) the city or community.
    (d) a housing authority.
    (e) husband and wife.
32. The instrument which conditionally conveys title to real estate is a
    (a) conditional bailment lease.
    (b) chattel mortgage.
    (c) mortgage.
    (d) land purchase contract.
33. A means of acquiring title where the occupant has been in actual, open, notorious, exclusive and continuous occupation of property for the statutory period by
    (a) reversion.
    (b) adverse possession.
    (c) fee simple.
    (d) fee absolute.
34. The recording of a warranty deed
    (a) passes the title.
    (b) insures the title.

(c) guarantees the title.
(d) gives constructive notice of ownership.

35. The four unities required for joint tenancy are
    (a) possession.
    (b) time.
    (c) husband and wife.
    (d) title.
    (e) location.
    (f) interest.
36. The clause in a deed which sets forth or limits the extent of the interests in the title being conveyed is
    (a) the demising clause.
    (b) the testimonium clause.
    (c) the habendum clause.
    (d) the indenture clause.
37. A person who has real property devised to him by a will is said to acquire title by
    (a) reversion.
    (b) release.
    (c) inheritance.
    (d) adverse possession.
38. A deed to be valid need not necessarily be
    (a) signed.
    (b) written.
    (c) sealed.
    (d) delivered.
39. By will, Calhoun devises his property to his daughter, Mary Calhoun, for life, and at her death to "her children." At Calhoun's death, Mary, 30 years of age and unmarried, deeds a fee simple estate to Davis. The title is
    (a) valid.
    (b) invalid.
    (c) Davis obtains a fee tail estate.
    (d) Davis is a tenant.
40. The type of deed which creates the least protection to the grantee is a
    (a) quit claim.
    (b) general warranty.
    (c) special warranty.
    (d) deed to tenants in common.
41. A distance in a recorded deed description is inadvertently omitted. The grantee has a buyer for the property, who raises questions about the incomplete description. The original grantee
    (a) must file court suit for reformation of the deed against the Recorder (Register) of Deeds.
    (b) Merely record a copy of the deed, with the proper description inserted.
    (c) compel the buyer to accept the deed since it conforms to the original deed description.
    (d) can compel the original grantor to execute new deed with proper description.
42. In which of the following, would an innocent purchaser for value be held not to require title?
    I. Under a forged signature to a deed.
    II. Under a quit claim deed.
        (a) I only.
        (b) II only.
        (c) Both I and II.
        (d) Neither I nor II.

43. A person to whom real estate is devised by will acquires title by
    I. Inheritance.
    II. law of remainderman.
    (a) I only.
    (b) II only.
    (c) both I and II.
    (d) neither I nor II.
44. The 1968 federal housing act relates to open housing and related mortgages. It deals with:
    I. Multiple listing associations.
    II. Racial discrimination.
    (a) I only.
    (b) II only.
    (c) Both I and II
    (d) Neither I nor II.
45. A clause in a deed limiting the use and enjoyment of property is:
    I. A hereditament.
    II. A restriction.
    (a) I only.
    (b) II only.
    (c) Both I and II.
    (d) Neither I nor II.
46. The largest ownership in real estate is:
    I. Fee simple.
    II. Life estate.
    (a) I only.
    (b) II only.
    (c) Both I and II.
    (d) Neither I nor II.
47. In zoning, a use established after passage of a zoning ordinance, and in violation of it, is called
    (a) a non-conforming use.
    (b) a variance.
    (c) illegal.
    (d) spot zoning.
48. Which one of the following debts is subject to the Homestead Exemption?
    (a) The purchase price of the Homestead property.
    (b) Services rendered by a laborer or mechanic.
    (c) $1,000 promissory note to a bank.
    (d) Street assessment.
49. Describing land boundaries, setting forth the lines together with terminal points and angles, is termed description by
    (a) acreage.
    (b) metes and bounds.
    (c) perimeter.
    (d) lot and block number.
50. A document which transfers possession of real property, but does not transfer ownership is
    (a) a deed.
    (b) a mortgage.
    (c) a lease.
    (d) a deposition.
51. When a deed which is delivered but not recorded is lost or destroyed, the legal title to the property described therein
    (a) remains in the grantee named in the last deed.
    (b) reverts to the last former owner of record.

(c) escheats to the state.

52. The party to whom a deed conveys real estate is called the
    (a) grantee.
    (b) grantor.
    (c) beneficiary.
    (d) recipient.
53. The word "escrow" refers to
    (a) a young crow.
    (b) deposit of legal documents with a third person to be delivered upon the fulfillment of certain conditions.
    (c) deposits of money in a bank, subject to withdrawal by depositor.
    (d) safe deposit box where deed is placed.
54. A quit claim deed conveys the interest of the
    (a) grantee.
    (b) mortgagee.
    (c) grantor.
    (d) lessee.
55. When real estate under lease is sold the lease
    (a) expires.
    (b) remains binding upon new owner.
    (c) must be renewed.
    (d) is broken.
56. An acquired legal privilege or right of use or enjoyment falling short of ownership which one may have in the land of another is known as
    (a) a devise.
    (b) an abstract.
    (c) an easement.
    (d) a riparian right.
57. Property held in joint tenancy, upon the death of one of the tenants, passes to the
    (a) landlord.
    (b) state.
    (c) heirs of the deceased.
    (d) surviving owner.
58. A conveyance of title with the condition that the land shall not be used for the sale of intoxicating beverages or liquors creates
    (a) a nuisance estate.
    (b) an estate on condition subsequent.
    (c) an estate on condition precedent.
    (d) a reservation.
59. The only essential unity in a tenancy in common is
    (a) equal right of possession.
    (b) ownership to survivor.
    (c) equal rights to heirs.
    (d) none of these.
60. An absolute conveyance of real property would be by
    (a) quit claim deed.
    (b) assignment.
    (c) warranty deed.
    (d) deed of extinguishment.
61. Which of the following is necessary to the validity of the deed?
    (a) Signing.
    (b) Acknowledgment.
    (c) Recording.
    (d) Delivery.

62. An encumbrance is anything which affects the
    (a) grant deed.
    (b) transfer of ownership.
    (c) loan value.
    (d) title.
63. If you contracted to sell the southwest quarter of the southwest quarter of the northwest quarter of a section of land, how many acres would pass by the deed?
    (a) 15 acres.
    (b) 10 acres.
    (c) 40 acres.
    (d) 160 acres.
64. Deeds are recorded in the
    (a) County Courthouse.
    (b) City Hall.
    (c) State Capitol building.
    (d) office of the title company.
65. Restrictions in a deed are created by
    (a) order of court.
    (b) grantee.
    (c) grantor.
    (d) by the municipality.
66. An instrument which transfers title to real estate may be
    (a) assigned by the grantor.
    (b) invalid, if not recorded within six years.
    (c) valid if signed and recorded by grantee.
    (d) valid if signed and delivered by grantor.
67. The appropriation of land by an owner to some public use together with acceptance for such use by or on behalf of the public, constitutes
    (a) eminent domain.
    (b) dedication.
    (c) condemnation.
    (d) adverse conveyance.
68. Land description by measure and direction in a deed is known as description by
    (a) survey.
    (b) lot and bounds block plan.
    (c) monuments.
    (d) metes and bounds.
69. If title to real property remains in the seller's name after it is sold on a monthly payment plan, the buyer would have purchased it under
    (a) an F.H.A. mortgage.
    (b) a conventional mortgage.
    (c) a real estate contract.
    (d) a V.A. approved mortgage.
70. A deed must
    (a) contain the street address identification.
    (b) state nature of the improvement on the land (dwelling).
    (c) contain adequate description to identify the premises.
    (d) state total area in the tract.
71. At the closing of a deal, which item is generally charged to the seller?
    (a) Recording fee for deed.
    (b) Fire insurance.
    (c) State revenue stamps.
    (d) Attorney's examination.
72. Title to real property passes by voluntary alienation by
    (a) quit claim deed.

(b) grant deed.
(c) court decree.
(d) trustee in bankruptcy.

73. North and south boundaries of townships are created by
(a) state surveyor.
(b) metes and bounds descriptions.
(c) court decree.
(d) base lines.

74. A riparian owner is one who owns land bordering on
(a) a wild orchard.
(b) sub-marginal land.
(c) existing subdivision.
(d) a river or lake.

75. The person who cannot take an acknowledgment is
(a) an alderman.
(b) a Justice of the Peace.
(c) an interested party.
(d) a judge.

76. A government official who evaluates property for tax purposes is an
(a) assayer.
(b) assessor.
(c) administrator.
(d) surveyor.

77. Fraud is to truth as concealment is to
(a) statute of frauds.
(b) misrepresentation.
(c) disclosure.
(d) duress.

78. The overhang of a porch or balcony beyond the established line of a parcel of land is known as
(a) an easement.
(b) an encroachment.
(c) right of way.
(d) freeway.

79. The instrument which conveys title to a trustee is
(a) a mortgage.
(b) trustee's guaranty.
(c) an indenture.
(d) trust deed.

80. An article may be changed from realty to personalty by
(a) attachment.
(b) detachment.
(c) written declaration.
(d) order of court.

81. Adams deeds (fee simple) a property to Burns. The acknowledgment is defective
(a) the deed is void.
(b) the deed is valid.
(c) Adams can require Burns to pay additional consideration for a corrected deed.
(d) Burns can compel Adams to execute a correct deed.

82. Clauses in a deed are dictated by
(a) agreement of sale.
(b) the mortgagee.
(c) the F.H.A.
(d) Real Estate Commission.

83. What is the maximum number of grantees that can be named in a deed?
   (a) Two.
   (b) Any number.
   (c) Four.
   (d) Ten.
84. Property is identified in a conveyance instrument by the
   (a) habendum.
   (b) consideration.
   (c) description.
   (d) the warranty.
85. A proper escrow, once established, should be
   (a) held by a licensed broker.
   (b) voidable at the seller's option.
   (c) voidable at option of either buyer or seller.
   (d) beyond the control of any one interested party.
86. First grant or patent in chain of title is issued by
   (a) a sovereign power.
   (b) U.S. Government Patent Office.
   (c) the recorder of deeds.
   (d) the grantee of a fee simple deed.
87. A widow who is willed the use of the family home for the rest of her natural life, with provision that it shall go to the children upon her death, holds
   (a) no interest in the property.
   (b) a fee simple estate.
   (c) a leasehold.
   (d) a life estate.
88. Chain of title means
   (a) a measurement used by a surveyor.
   (b) a listing of all recorded instruments affecting the subject title.
   (c) certificate of title.
   (d) heirs named in a will to inherit property after death of testator.
89. The right of a water company to lay and maintain water mains along a designated line in the rear of a lot would be called
   (a) an encroachment right.
   (b) an easement.
   (c) adverse possession.
   (d) an appurtenance.
90. A title insurance policy, standard form, insures
   (a) that there are no judgment liens against the property.
   (b) that the property is free and clear of all encumbrances.
   (c) the title only as it appears of record, subject to stated exceptions.
91. Property of a person who dies intestate, leaving no heirs, passes to the state by
   (a) escheat.
   (b) eminent domain.
   (c) adverse possession.
   (d) condemnation.
92. A section of land is
   (a) 360 acres.
   (b) 6 miles square.
   (c) 6 square miles.
   (d) 1 square mile.
93. Dolan executed a deed to his nephew, Wright, which recites the consideration as "love and affection." Wright orally promised to pay Dolan's living expenses, but failed to do so. Under these circumstances,
   I. the deed is invalid.

II. the deed can be reformed.
(a) I only.
(b) II only.
(c) both I and II.
(d) neither I nor II.

94. Bates, owner of a property, serviced by a drive-way, entered into a bilateral agreement with his neighbor, Carter, to use the driveway, if Carter would remove stone steps to his sun parlor, which abutted the driveway. Under this agreement, Carter had
I. an appurtenant easement.
II. an easement in gross.
(a) I only.
(b) II only.
(c) both I and II.
(d) neither I nor II.

95. A restriction in a deed stated that "no temporary trailer nor any mobile home" would be erected on the property. Under this provision,
I. the buyer could place a house trailer.
II. the buyer could erect a mobile home.
(a) I only.
(b) II only.
(c) both I and II.
(d) neither I nor II.

96. Under a zoning ordinance of the Harbor Estates Village, recreational uses was described as including golf courses, boat harbors and bathing beaches. Adams asked for a permit for a drive-in theatre, which was refused.
(a) The permit should be granted.
(b) The promoter should post bond to protect the municipality against damage suits.
(c) The ordinance should be repealed.
(d) Enforcement of the ordinance should be waived.

97. The party appointed by a court to settle a deceased person's estate is
(a) a trustor.
(b) a trustee.
(c) a guardian.
(d) an administrator.

98. A description reading: the S 1/2 of the SE 1/4 of the NW 1/4 of the NE 1/4 of a section of land contains
(a) 15 acres.
(b) 12 1/2 acres.
(c) 10 acres.
(d) 5 acres.

99. A valid declaration of homestead may be filed on a home by
(a) the lessee.
(b) trustee.
(c) mortgagee.
(d) head of family.

100. The number of square feet in an acre of ground is
(a) 5,280.
(b) 25,120.
(c) 43,560.
(d) 50,560.

101. Townships and ranges are characteristic of
(a) subdivisions.
(b) government surveys.
(c) municipalities.
(d) title insurance.

102. In the West a township is
    (a) an incorporated city.
    (b) a 640-acre plot of land.
    (c) five square miles.
    (d) six miles square.
103. Which of the following are incompetent to execute a deed?
    (a) Minor.
    (b) Widow.
    (c) Intoxicated person.
    (d) Single woman.
    (e) Insane person.
    (f) Man over 80 years of age.
104. Deeds are acknowledged
    (a) to make them legal.
    (b) to enable them to be recorded.
    (c) because of ancient custom.
    (d) to establish legal capacity.
    (e) to terminate a lease by tenant.
105. A "quit claim" deed is used to
    (a) correct a defect in description.
    (b) convey a life estate.
    (c) pass an absolute fee simple estate.
106. Which of the following forms of deeds have one or more guarantees of title?
    (a) Quit claim deed.
    (b) Warranty deed.
    (c) Executor's deed.
107. Creating an easement refers to
    (a) cost or design of dwelling.
    (b) set back from street.
    (c) giving someone the right, privilege or advantage to use the property.
    (d) renting it on a temporary basis.
108. A system of registration by which the state guarantees the title to the land is called
    (a) Torrens system.
    (b) Land Registration.
    (c) Land Equalization System.
    (d) Land Protection System.
109. Which of the following are essentials to a deed of real estate?
    (a) Covenant of seizin.
    (b) Description.
    (c) "Habendum" clause.
    (d) Signature of seller.
    (e) Signature of buyer.
110. A deed which carries with it the implied rights of survivorship is called a
    (a) warranty deed.
    (b) grant deed.
    (c) joint tenancy deed.
    (d) power of attorney.
111. Title to real estate passes to the grantee at the time the deed is
    (a) written.
    (b) delivered.
    (c) notarized.
    (d) signed.
112. Real property owned by husband or his wife prior to their marriage is presumed to be
    (a) community property.
    (b) separate property.

(c) personal property.
(d) tenancy in common.

113. A quit claim deed conveys only the interest of the
(a) grantee.
(b) property.
(c) claimant.
(d) grantor.

114. A declaration of homestead is an instrument recorded in the Recorder's office for the purpose of
(a) acquiring title to property.
(b) conveying property to another.
(c) exempting property from execution.
(d) satisfying a debt.

115. An authorization to a person to act for and in behalf of another in his absence is called
(a) an option.
(b) an easement.
(c) a power of attorney.
(d) a release.

116. Which of the following are real estate and pass under a common warranty deed?
(a) Chandeliers in a house.
(b) Awnings.
(c) Furnace.
(d) The fence surrounding the property.
(e) A portable gas stove.
(f) The rock garden.

117. The right to cross over property owned by another is called
(a) adverse possession.
(b) an easement.
(c) a homestead.
(d) a lien.

118. Unpaid taxes on real estate become
(a) a lien.
(b) an easement.
(c) a judgment.

119. If the city wishes to take property for public improvements, it may acquire title by action based on
(a) attachment proceedings.
(b) right of eminent domain.
(c) suit to quiet title.
(d) adverse possession rights.

120. The relinquishment of some right, claim or interest to a person who already has some interest in the property is known as a
(a) forbearance.
(b) extinguishment
(c) release.
(d) remainder.

121. Where a life tenant conveys real estate during his lifetime to another, the grantee is known as
(a) the sub-tenant.
(b) the junior tenant.
(c) tenant per auter vie.
(d) remainder tenant.

122. Taking of property for public use is
(a) zoning.
(b) condemnation.

(c) escheat.
(d) reversion.

123. An instrument which requires recordation to be legally effective is a
(a) mechanic's lien.
(b) agreement to sell real estate.
(c) will.
(d) deed.

124. An easement is *not* extinguished by which one of the following:
(a) decision of the property owner.
(b) when necessity no longer exists.
(c) release.
(d) abandonment.

125. Which one of the following applies to ownership of land
(a) tenancy in common.
(b) tenancy at will.
(c) tenancy for years.
(d) tenancy of sufferance.

126. John L. Davis Jr. and Marie E., his wife, own property jointly. In deeding it, the wife should sign
(a) Mrs. John L. Davis Jr.
(b) Marie E. Davis Jr.
(c) Marie E. Davis.
(d) in her maiden name (Marie E. Dutch), now Mrs. John L. Davis Jr.

127. A charge levied against real estate for municipal functions is
(a) an assessment.
(b) a tax.
(c) a lien.
(d) a judgment.

128. In order for a buyer to be certain that the property he is purchasing has no encroachment, he should obtain
(a) purchaser's policy of title insurance.
(b) survey.
(c) certificate of no defense.
(d) warranty deed.

129. The grantor's guarantee that he is the owner of the property and has the power to convey title is called the covenant of
(a) further assurance.
(b) seizin.
(c) quiet enjoyment.
(d) warranty.

130. Eminent domain is
(a) a public park.
(b) a country home.
(c) property owned by the federal government.
(d) power to take property for public use.

131. A person who has real estate devised to him by a relative is said to have acquired title by
(a) adverse possession.
(b) inheritance.
(c) reversion.
(d) release.

132. Condemnation of private property for public use is called the right of
(a) eminent domain.
(b) municipalities.
(c) acquisition.

(d) acquirement.

133. The rights to the water thereon of a person owning land containing or bordering upon a stream are called
  (a) water rights.
  (b) riparian rights.
  (c) eminent domain.
  (d) a reservation.
134. A clear title to real estate may be assured by securing
  (a) a warranty deed.
  (b) an abstract of title.
  (c) a policy of title insurance.
  (d) a guarantee of title.
135. Brown purchases property from Adams. Adams later gives another deed to Clark. Notice of Brown's interest may exist because of
  (a) possession of abstract of title.
  (b) possession of property by Brown.
  (c) possession of adjoining property by Brown.
  (d) possession of deed by Brown.
  (e) Adams's not paying taxes.
136. A quit claim deed is of as much practical value to the grantee as a warranty deed would be
  (a) if the grantee is insolvent.
  (b) if the grantee is not given an abstract.
  (c) if the title is not good and merchantable.
  (d) if the grantor is not financially able to back up his warranty.
  (e) if the grantee loses his deed.
137. A policy of title insurance "purchaser's form" insures the record title in the name of
  (a) the mortgagee.
  (b) a broker.
  (c) the grantor.
  (d) the grantee.
138. One who acquires property under a deed is
  (a) an optionee.
  (b) a vendee.
  (c) a grantee.
  (d) a trustee.
139. Severalty ownership is ownership
  (a) by several persons.
  (b) by title passing to the survivors upon death of one.
  (c) of an undivided interest in property.
  (d) by one person only.
140. A homestead right is surrendered by recording
  (a) a satisfaction.
  (b) an abandonment.
  (c) a release.
  (d) a reconveyance.
141. Which of the following is generally true of easements?
  (a) created by verbal agreement.
  (b) cannot be revoked.
  (c) are of temporary duration.
  (d) are purely personal rights and do not run with the land.
142. Owner of an undivided interest in land with no right of survivorship owns it by
  (a) joint tenancy.
  (b) severalty.
  (c) absolute ownership.

(d) tenancy in common.

143. Title to fixtures, shelves, counters, and merchandise is transferred or conveyed by
   (a) deed.
   (b) bill of sale.
   (c) chattel mortgage.
   (d) escrow.

144. The tax on a given piece of real estate is determined by multiplying the tax rate (millage) by
   (a) the selling price.
   (b) appraised value of the property.
   (c) insured value.
   (d) assessed valuation.
   (e) market value, less depreciation.

145. The legal rights which a wife has in her husband's property at his death are known as
   (a) curtesy.
   (b) dower.
   (c) share by entirety.
   (d) share by survivorship.

146. The title to land held in absolute ownership is called
   (a) estate for years.
   (b) a leasehold.
   (c) fee simple.
   (d) a base fee.

147. In order to accurately determine the boundaries of real property, one should obtain
   (a) a title policy.
   (b) a survey.
   (c) an abstract.
   (d) a decree of court.

148. The state of ownership in real property by which the husband and wife hold title to real estate and in which the right of survivorship cannot be destroyed by either party is known as
   (a) estate in joint tenancy.
   (b) estate by entirety.
   (c) estate in common.
   (d) estate by dower right.

149. The law which requires certain contracts to be in writing in order to be enforceable is called the
   (a) written instrument law.
   (b) parol evidence law.
   (c) statute of limitations.
   (d) statute of frauds.

150. A roadway over Taylor's land existed for 25 years. Wagner sought a court decree for a perpetual easement and an injunction against interference. Heretofore, Taylor gave permission for its use to people asking permission. Under these circumstances, the court should:
   I. Grant a decree for an easement.
   II. Grant a perpetual injunction, preventing Taylor from obstructing the roadway or interfering with Wagner's use
      (a) I only.
      (b) II only.
      (c) Both I and II.
      (d) Neither I nor II.

151. A policy of title insurance in favor of the mortgagee will also insure
   (a) the owner.
   (b) the buyer.

(c) the buyer's purchases.
(d) no other person.

152. An absolute conveyance of real property would be by a
(a) mortgage deed.
(b) general warranty deed.
(c) quit claim deed.
(d) gift deed.

153. When a notary public or other qualified official attests to the signature on a deed or mortgage, it is called an
(a) authorization.
(b) acknowledgment.
(c) execution.
(d) authentication.

154. At the closing of a deal, which item is generally chargeable to the seller?
(a) Recording deed.
(b) Title insurance.
(c) State Deed Transfer stamps (if required).
(d) Survey.

155. Mrs. Elsie M. Sims, wife of Alfred D. Sims, should sign a deed to real estate in which manner?
(a) Elsie M. Sims.
(b) Mrs. Alfred D. Sims.
(c) Mrs. Alfred D. (Elsie M.) Sims.

156. When speaking of "improvements" regarding real estate, it means
(a) fences, wells, drains, roadways, etc.
(b) everything except the land.
(c) additions made to the original house.

157. Creating an easement means
(a) restricting the style or cost of a house which can be built in a subdivision of lots.
(b) placing a dwelling over your property line onto another's property.
(c) giving someone the right, advantage, or privilege to use your land.

158. The owner of an undivided part of the whole is a
(a) tenant in common.
(b) joint tenant.
(c) remainderman.
(d) partner.

159. In order for a would-be buyer of real estate to be certain of the validity of the title, he should order
(a) a survey.
(b) a title search.
(c) an estoppel certificate.

160. If Jane White and James White, her husband, are living together on property legally described, a deed conveying the property to a purchaser, signed only by the wife, Jane, may be valid when
(a) it is recorded.
(b) property was acquired by wife before marriage (in community property states).
(c) the husband is out of the state.
(d) all liens are paid.

161. An encumbrance on real estate may be
(a) unpaid broker's commission.
(b) live stock.
(c) easement granting another a right of way over land.
(d) a building.

162. If you wish to have a driveway over your neighbor's yard, which instrument would you

use?
(a) A quit claim deed.
(b) Easement.
(c) Assignment of contract.
(d) Estoppel certificate.

163. For which reason or reasons is a deed recorded?
(a) Insures certain title.
(b) Gives notice to the world.
(c) Required by the state.
(d) Save title insurance cost.

164. Tenancy in common is holding by several persons by unity of possession and also by
(a) several and distinct titles.
(b) unity of time.
(c) owning to the same interest.
(d) right of survivorship.

165. Ownership of property is transferred
(a) when grantor signs the deed.
(b) when the grantor's signature has been notarized.
(c) when delivery of the deed is made.
(d) when the correct documentary stamps are put on deed and cancelled.

166. The deed to a purchaser must include
(a) legal description of property.
(b) survey.
(c) title report.
(d) a recital how grantor obtained title.

167. A valid deed must contain
(a) the grantee's signature.
(b) an acknowledgment.
(c) evidence of recordation.
(d) a granting clause.

168. A notice of abandonment is recorded to release a
(a) mortgage.
(b) chattel real.
(c) declaration of homestead.
(d) listing.

169. A widow who is willed the use of the family home for the rest of her natural life, with provision that it shall go to the children upon her death, holds
(a) no interest in the property.
(b) a fee simple.
(c) a leasehold.
(d) a life estate.

170. Chain of title means
(a) a measurement used by a surveyor.
(b) the last deed of record.
(c) a part of the history of all instruments affecting the particular tract of ground.
(d) a secured policy of title insurance.

171. A charge levied by a local government to finance street paving is
(a) an ad valorem tax.
(b) a zoning charge.
(c) an equalizer.
(d) an assessment.

172. The sovereign power in determining title to land is
(a) the municipality.
(b) the State.
(c) the Attorney General.

(d) the Real Estate Commission.

173. In an escrow which document would not properly belong?
    (a) contract of sale.
    (b) warranty deed.
    (c) trust deed note.
    (d) insurance binder.
174. Deed is to property as a will is to
    (a) heir.
    (b) probate.
    (c) estate.
    (d) court.
175. A deed delivered in escrow is given to
    (a) the buyer's attorney.
    (b) the seller's attorney.
    (c) the mortgagee.
    (d) a neutral third party.
176. A perch or rod is a unit of land measuring
    (a) 16 ½ feet.
    (b) 66 feet.
    (c) 12 feet.
    (d) 21 ½ feet.
177. Et Ux is an abbreviation for "et uxor" meaning
    (a) and husband.
    (b) and father.
    (c) and wife.
    (d) parties of the second part.
178. A quarter section of land is
    (a) 240 acres.
    (b) 160 acres.
    (c) 440 acres.
    (d) 250 acres.
179. An agreement of sale was signed by Hays, before marriage. Later, the wife refuses to sign the deed, but the deed, signed by the husband above, is accepted by the buyer. One year later, the husband dies. Under these circumstances:
    I. The deed is valid.
    II. The widow is entitled to the value of her dower interest.
        (a) I only.
        (b) II only.
        (c) Both I and II.
        (d) Neither I nor II.
180. Alberts purchased a restaurant and building in a municipal zone permitting restaurants. The zoning code prohibited the service of alcoholic beverages in the same retail district. The state liquor control board issued a license to Alberts. Under these circumstances:
    I. The liquor control board's license to Albert is valid.
    II. The municipality should repeal the law, excluding sale of alcoholic beverages.
        (a) I only.
        (b) II only.
        (c) Both I and II.
        (d) Neither I nor II.
181. The city of Adelphia passed an ordinance defining a one-family residence, which excluded unmarried persons. Four college students rented one apartment. The city claimed the occupancy was in violation of the ordinances. Under these circumstances:
    I. The ordinance should be amended.
    II. The ordinance is discriminatory and illegal.
        (a) I only.

   (b) II only.
   (c) Both I and II.
   (d) Neither I nor II.

182. A deed was made to John Steele and wife, without naming her. The deed creates
   (a) an estate in severalty.
   (b) a tenancy in common.
   (c) an estate by the entireties.
   (d) the deed is invalid.
183. A deed description refers to a plat of the property recorded in the County Recorder of Deeds Office. Under these circumstances:
   I. The deed description would be valid.
   II. The deed would have to be redrawn.
      (a) I only.
      (b) II only.
      (c) Both I and II.
      (d) Neither I nor II.
184. A notary public's commission expires on January 31, 1974. He may take a valid acknowledgment
   (a) if he applies for renewal before Jan. 31, 1974.
   (b) within 30 days after Jan. 31, 1974.
   (c) no time after Jan. 31, 1974.
185. That covenant which is construed to mean that the grantor covenants that he has the exact interest in the property that the deed purports is a
   (a) covenant of further assurance.
   (b) covenant of warranty.
   (c) covenant of the right to convey.
   (d) covenant of seizin.
186. The addition of one's land by the gradual deposit of soil through natural causes is
   (a) annulation.
   (b) sedimentation.
   (c) accretion.
   (d) ademption.
187. The voluntary parting with the ownership of real property is
   (a) adverse possession.
   (b) alienation.
   (c) forfeiture.
   (d) eminent domain.
188. That which gives the appearance of title, but is not title in fact is
   (a) exoneration.
   (b) redemption.
   (c) color of title.
   (d) subordination.
189. A grantor limits his liability to the grantee to anyone claiming, by, from, through or under him, with a
   (a) special warranty deed.
   (b) a quit claim deed.
   (c) a general warranty deed.
   (d) a sheriff's deed.
190. Devise is a
   (a) sum of money for real estate.
   (b) gift of real estate by will.
   (c) method to obtain title without deed, in a court action.
191. Any interest in, or right to, land by third persons, adversely affecting the value of the property is an
   (a) encumbrance.

(b) encroachment.
(c) appurtenance.
(d) escrow.

192. An instrument which transfers possession of real property but does not transfer ownership is a
(a) deed.
(b) mortgage.
(c) satisfaction piece.
(d) lease.

193. Tender of deed is unnecessary where
(a) time is of the essence.
(b) date for performance has expired.
(c) comprehensive insurance policy has expired.
(d) there is an anticipatory repudiation by buyer of the sales agreement.

194. Limitations on the use and enjoyment of property are called
(a) remainders.
(b) hereditaments.
(c) tenements.
(d) restrictions.

195. Which of the following would be held to be void and pass no title even in favor of an innocent purchaser?
(a) A quit claim deed.
(b) A forged deed.
(c) A bargain and sale deed.
(d) A trustee's deed.

196. Under the early English common law, transfer of title to real property by delivery of possession was called
(a) livery of seizin.
(b) adverse possession.
(c) chancery.
(d) laissez-faire.

197. Adams hands deed to Beal with the intent to pass title, but with an oral request not to record the deed until after Adams's death.
(a) Beal must comply or the deed will not be valid.
(b) Valid delivery has occurred.
(c) Delivery will not occur until Adams's death.
(d) The deed is void.

198. Where an agreement of sale has been recorded, and a quit claim deed is used to extinguish it, the deed should be signed by
(a) the vendor.
(b) the vendee.
(c) the notary public who took the acknowledgment.
(d) the broker, who prepared the sales agreement.

199. Abstract of title is a
(a) contract for deed.
(b) condensed history of the title.
(c) guarantee of title.
(d) rough painting of the property.

200. A quit claim deed may also be known as a
(a) special warranty deed.
(b) bargain and sale deed.
(c) reformation deed.
(d) satisfaction claim deed.

201. The right to light and air accompanied by the transfer of title ownership to the land is

called an
(a) alienable right.
(b) restriction.
(c) appurtenance.
(d) easement.

202. It is the usual function of City Planning Commissions to pass upon
(a) new homes.
(b) new apartment buildings.
(c) new garages.
(d) new subdivisions.

203. A zoning ordinance is a
(a) restriction.
(b) easement.
(c) lien.
(d) appurtenance.

204. An area of land set off by local ordinance for a specific use is called
(a) a subdivision.
(b) a zone.
(c) public improvement.
(d) cul de sac.

205. A freehold interest in land that is to end with the life of the grantee is known as
(a) an estate at will.
(b) an estate sufferance.
(c) life estate.
(d) annuity.

206. Lines of meridian run
(a) east and west.
(b) any direction depending upon location of property.
(c) easterly or westerly from baselines.
(d) north and south.

207. The column of townships running north and south is referred to as
(a) checks.
(b) ranges.
(c) divisions.
(d) tracts.

208. A wall erected on a line between two adjoining properties belonging to two different persons is a
(a) share wall.
(b) party wall.
(c) live wall.
(d) community wall.

209. Anything that is permanently fastened or attached to real estate is
(a) an attachment.
(b) real estate.
(c) personal property.
(d) a chattel.

210. A purchaser should obtain which one of the following to be sure there is no encroachment
(a) title insurance policy.
(b) survey.
(c) declaration of no set off certificate.
(d) each of the above.

211. An owner of land containing or bordering upon a stream, has rights to the water known as
(a) water rights.
(b) riparian rights.

(c) alluvion rights.
(d) allodial rights.

212. In a joint ownership, which one of the following unities is not present
(a) possession.
(b) time.
(c) title.
(d) location.
(e) interest.

213. In numbering a township, section 6 is always on the
(a) northeast corner.
(b) southeast corner.
(c) northwest corner.
(d) southwest corner.

214. If a municipality wishes to obtain title to property from an owner unwilling to sell, it can proceed by
(a) right of eminent domain.
(b) attachment proceedings.
(c) action to quiet title.
(d) adverse possession.

215. Words of conveyance are essential in the
(a) listing contract.
(b) agreement of sale.
(c) deed.
(d) bill of sale.

216. The S $1/2$ of the SE $1/4$ of the NW $1/4$ of a section contains
(a) 20 acres.
(b) 40 acres.
(c) 80 acres.
(d) 160 acres.

217. The section in the northwest corner of a township is
(a) section #1.
(b) section #7.
(c) section #6.
(d) none of these.

218. Partners usually own real property as
(a) tenants by the entireties.
(b) joint tenants.
(c) tenants in common.
(d) tenants in severalty.

219. Owner of an undivided interest in land with no right of survivorship owns it as
(a) tenant in common.
(b) joint tenant.
(c) tenant in futuro.
(d) none of these.

220. Zone R-1 is restricted to
(a) refrigeration plant or the like.
(b) rolling mill plant or the like.
(c) single family homes.
(d) hospital or school.

221. An example of involuntary alienation is where title to real estate passes by
(a) quit claim deed.
(b) trustee deed.
(c) grant deed.
(d) sheriff's deed.

222. Which of these may not be considered an appurtenance
   (a) bar.
   (b) garage.
   (c) orchard.
   (d) Revolutionary chestnut tree.
223. A light company lays and maintains concealed electric along an agreed-upon line with owner. It does so by right of
   (a) eminent domain.
   (b) condemnation.
   (c) an easement.
   (d) a sub-surface appurtenance.
224. John Cooke and Mary Cooke, wife, have owned their home by the entireties. On Sept. 17, 1974, they were divorced. The property is now owned
   (a) each owns property in severalty.
   (b) each is a tenant in common.
   (c) they own property as joint tenants.
   (d) they own property as partners.
225. Which of the following is usually paid by the buyer
   (a) recording the deed.
   (b) acknowledgment to the deed.
   (c) cost for preparing deed.
226. Ownership by an individual is ownership in
   (a) severalty.
   (b) joint tenancy.
   (c) inchoate.
   (d) severance.
227. The summary of the most important parts of all instruments comprising the record title of the seller, arranged in chronological order is known as
   (a) indenture.
   (b) abstract of title.
   (c) certificate of title.
   (d) history of title.
228. Where property is acquired by Marie Davis, a single woman, and later conveys it after her marriage to John Saxman, she should sign the deed
   (a) Mrs. John Saxman.
   (b) Marie Davis Saxman.
   (c) Marie Saxman, nee Marie Davis.
   (d) Marie Davis.
229. Where a conveyance is to Patti Sims, unmarried, and Alfred Sims and Elsie Sims, his wife, Patti will own
   (a) one-third of the property as a tenant in common.
   (b) one-half of the property as a tenant in common.
   (c) the property as a joint tenant with Alfred and Elsie.
230. A property is deeded to John Gates, "his heirs and assigns." By will, Gates leaves the property to his nurse, Lucy Gibbons. Two sons, Adam and Earl, claim the property upon John's death.
   (a) Each son now owns a one-half interest.
   (b) Each son now owns a one-fourth interest and Lucy owns one-half.
   (c) Lucy owns the entire property.
   (d) The property escheats to the state.
231. Words of conveyance is an essential element in a (an)
   (a) bill of sale.
   (b) deed.
   (c) contract of sale.
   (d) exclusive listing contract.

232. The party responsible for payment of the title closing costs is determined by
   (a) agreement of the parties.
   (b) broker.
   (c) title officer.
   (d) local Real Estate Board.
233. A law which prohibits certain legal actions from taking place during a period of emergency is called
   (a) statute of limitations.
   (b) bill of rights.
   (c) declaration relief.
   (d) moratorium.
234. Trust deeds are used to
   (a) transfer stock certificates to a seller.
   (b) protect sub-contractors.
   (c) borrow money.
   (d) transfer property from one co-owner to another co-owner.
235. Delinquent taxes are considered to be
   (a) easements.
   (b) personalty.
   (c) liens.
   (d) attachments.
236. The dominant tenement is the property
   (a) upon which the burden is imposed.
   (b) in whose favor the burden is created.
   (c) the top story in an apartment building.
   (d) owned by a person having the largest interest.
237. Where the state requires documentary transfer stamps, the stamp must be affixed to a
   (a) bill of sale.
   (b) agreement of sale.
   (c) warranty deed.
   (d) mortgage.
238. The number of square feet in an acre is
   (a) 46,530.
   (b) 43,650.
   (c) 43,560.
   (d) 36,350.
239. The person for whom the beneficial trust in a deed is held in a trust instrument is the
   (a) grantee.
   (b) grantor.
   (c) escrowee.
   (d) cestui que trust.
240. A, B and C own property as joint tenants. C dies and B sells his interest in the property to D. The property is now owned
   (a) as joint tenants by A, D and C's widow E, his sole heir.
   (b) A and D as joint tenants.
   (c) A and D as tenants in common.
   (d) none of these.
241. A and B, husband and wife own their home as tenants by the entirety. B obtains a divorce from A, one year after the purchase. The property is now owned
   (a) by A and B in severalty.
   (b) by A and B as joint tenants.
   (c) A and B continue to hold title by the entireties.
   (d) A and B as tenants in common.
242. A, single, and B, married, who are partners, acquire property with partnership funds and

take title in the partnership name. Shortly thereafter, A marries C and subsequently A died. The property is now owned by
(a) B and C as tenants in common.
(b) by B.
(c) by B and C as joint tenants.
(d) none of these.

243. Et al is an abbreviation for
(a) and wife.
(b) and another.
(c) and so forth.
(d) as follows.

244. The total area of a homestead is limited by
(a) agreement of seller and buyer.
(b) law.
(c) partition proceedings.
(d) zoning.

245. In order to take advantage of a capital gains tax on a real estate purchase and sale, the property must be held for at least
(a) 30 days.
(b) 6 months.
(c) one year.
(d) two years.

246. In a recorded plan, the lots are usually described by
(a) metes and bounds.
(b) lot number.
(c) zone.
(d) street and number.

247. The initial conveyance of real property from the Federal Government to an individual is by
(a) Act of Congress.
(b) deed from Secretary of the Interior.
(c) U. S. Register of deeds.
(d) patent.

248. Which one of the following, if any, would be grounds for voiding a deed because of the recital of an improper consideration? The property sold for $20,500.
(a) $21,000.
(b) $1.
(c) $20,000.
(d) none of these.

249. Actual notice to a prospective buyer of ownership would occur where
(a) the mortgagee told the prospect the identity of the owner.
(b) tenant in possession gave name of absent owner.
(c) adverse claimant in possession claims title.
(d) recorded deed to vendor.

250. A husband separated from his wife and children listed a property for sale with a broker. The wife and children are in possession of the premises. Upon obtaining a signed agreement, the wife refuses to sign the deed or move. The buyer sues for specific performance. He cannot recover because
(a) he had actual notice of wife's occupancy.
(b) the buyer failed to record the agreement of sale.
(c) the broker should not have listed the property.
(d) the state inheritance laws prevent.

251. A deed executed and delivered, but not recorded, is
(a) void.
(b) voidable.

(c) valid.
(d) unenforceable.

252. Hereditaments include
(a) the lands and chattels used thereon.
(b) property inherited under intestacy laws.
(c) lands, buildings and easements.
(d) real property acquired by court decree.

253. An escrow, once established, is
(a) subject to withdrawal by either party.
(b) subject to rescision only by the seller.
(c) subject to rescision only by the buyer.
(d) none of these.

254. A base or qualified fee is
(a) a sale of land with a number of easements.
(b) a sale for a particular use or purpose (school or church) and where such use is ended, property reverts to grantor.
(c) tenure by adverse use until real owner brings court action to reclaim title.
(d) a term in description of land acquired by patent.

255. A base or qualified fee results
(a) purpose for which the property was granted is abandoned.
(b) when life tenant dies.
(c) property is leased for an uncertain term.
(d) none of these.

256. In zoning, a use granted in violation of an enacted ordinance is
(a) void.
(b) non-conforming.
(c) variance.
(d) spot zoning.

257. In real estate transactions in Wisconsin all of the following documents except one are usually recorded in the appropriate office of the Register of Deeds:
(a) deed.
(b) land contract.
(c) offer to purchase.
(d) mortgage.
(e) purchase money mortgage.

258. Bates developed a subdivision in 1940. Each deed to the purchaser contained a restriction "no building except a private dwelling house shall be erected on said lot." Curtis, a purchaser of two lots, sold them to Bacon in 1973. On February 21, 1974, Bacon started to excavate for the erection of a four story garden type apartment building. Since 1960, the street has been widened to a four lane artery, a pony league baseball park has been built across the street, flanked by several business establishments. Under these circumstances:
I. The apartment building will be permitted.
II. The apartment building will be permitted upon damages in favor of the protesting property owners.
(a) I only.
(b) II only.
(c) Both I and II.
(d) Neither I nor II.

259. In determining whether an article is realty or personalty, the test to be employed is:
I. Manner of annexation to the dwelling.
II. Intention of the grantor when the item in question was installed.
(a) I only.
(b) II only.
(c) Both I and II.

(d) Neither I nor II.

260. The City of Garden Valley passed an ordinance, prohibiting "For Sale" signs in residential areas. Broker Hal Forbes sues to have the ordinance voided, as unrelated to the public good or welfare. The ordinance is:
(a) valid.
(b) invalid.
(c) should be amended.
(d) zone should be changed.

261. Albert's will devises his property, one-half to his son, Bert, one-sixth to a nephew, Harold, and two-sixths to a niece, Mabel, as tenants in common. The Acme Motor Co. has a judgment lien against Bert and sells his share in the property at Sheriff's sale to satisfy its judgment. The effect of the sale is:
I. The sheriff's sale is void.
II. The Acme Motor Co. becomes an owner in common with Harold and Mabel.
(a) I only.
(b) II only.
(c) Both I and II.
(d) Neither I nor II

262. The state of Texas has taken all of Hester's property for a four lane highway. Under these circumstances:
I. The condemnee is entitled to moving expenses, as well as other expenses incurred by the relocation.
II. The state must pay such expenses directly to the creditors.
(a) I only.
(b) II only.
(c) Both I and II.
(d) Neither I nor II.

263. A property owned and used by the owner, was taken by the City of Wilmington, Delaware. The owner claimed damages for the loss of his restaurant business and loss of liquor license, as well as the real estate.
I. The owner is entitled to damages for loss of the restaurant business, as such.
II. Owner is entitled to damages for loss of liquor license.
(a) I only.
(b) II only.
(c) both I and II.
(d) Neither I nor II.

264. In an eminent domain proceedings, the owner claimed damages for noise due to construction of a freeway, for which part of his land was taken.
I. The owner can recover that noise was an element of damage.
II. The damage due to the item of noise must be valued separately from the land.
(a) I only.
(b) II only.
(c) Both I and II.
(d) Neither I nor II.

265. A property was listed with a broker for sale by the owner at $30,000, commission to be 7 per cent. During the exclusive period, the property was condemned by the state and paid the owner $30,000 for the property. Under these circumstances:
I. The broker is entitled to a commission from the state.
II. The broker is entitled to the commission from the owner.
(a) I only.
(b) II only.
(c) Both I and II.
(d) Neither I nor II.

266. Where legal title is transferred in the sale of real estate, encumbered by a deed of trust,

it is always necessary to:
I. obtain the consent of the beneficiary.
II. for the grantor to deliver a deed.
(a) I only.
(b) II only.
(c) both I and II.
(d) neither I nor II.

267. Tom Burton devised his residence to his wife, Elizabeth, and upon her death, the property was to go to their son, Edward. Elizabeth died one day after her husband. Under these circumstances, Edward received:
I. an estate in expectancy
II. a remainder estate.
(a) I only.
(b) II only.
(c) both I and II.
(d) neither I nor II.

268. Ray Upton and Opal Upton, his wife, conveyed their property to Opal Upton and a daughter, Nancy Upton. The deed recited that the deed was expressly made with the right of survivorship between the grantees. The deed created
(a) a tenancy in common.
(b) a void estate.
(c) a joint tenancy.
(d) a life estate for Opal, the mother.

269. A promoter of a subdivision dedicated a street in the plan for public use, with the reservation that if the street were ever abandoned, it would revert to the promoter (a corporation), its successors and assigns. The street was subsequently abandoned. The street now reverts to
(a) the municipality.
(b) the state.
(c) each abutting property owner owns to the middle of the street.
(d) the original promoter.

270. An easement in gross is created in favor of George Sampson by his neighbor, Adam Otis, for use of a driveway, separating their two properties. Five years later, Sampson sells his property to M. Fairchild. The easement in question is
(a) continued for benefit of Fairchild.
(b) Sampson may use the driveway any time he visits Fairchild.
(c) the easement is terminated.
(d) an easement by necessity is now created.

271. George Costello used a roadway over land of Stewart Sloan for ingress and egress to his land, for over 30 years, with permission of the latter. Sloan sold his property to McKee, who erected a barricade, preventing Costello's use. In a suit to enjoin interference with Costello's use,
(a) he will win.
(b) he will not win.
(c) the court will assess damages for the continued use.
(d) the court will remand the case to an arbitration panel.

272. John Harris and Mary Harris own a property by the entireties. Due to domestic difficulties, John moves out. Two years later, he brings suit for partition, to have the property sold and the proceeds divided between them.
(a) John will win the suit.
(b) John will not win the suit.
(c) The court will require Mary to pay John one-half the rental value.
(d) The court will decree that John and Mary now own the property as tenants in common.

273. Title to property is taken in the names of Thomas Gilson and Elsie Gilson, his wife. They have never been married, and Elsie is married to Nick Cullen, whereabouts unknown. Thomas died. The property will go to:
(a) Elsie.
(b) The heirs of Thomas.
(c) One-half of the proceeds of a sale to Elsie and the other half to heirs of Thomas.
(d) The property will escheat to the state.

274. Mrs. White, a widow, entered into an agreement with her neighbor, Stone, whereby she could use his driveway, which abutted her land, and she would remove four inches of stone steps on the side of her dwelling, which would benefit Stone's driveway in winter use of the driveway. The easement read "an easement for the benefit of Kay White." She has
(a) an appurtenant easement.
(b) a license.
(c) an easement in gross.
(d) a revocable easement.

275. George Crow, owner of a tract of land, occupied 10 feet over on Delbert's land upon the erroneous belief as to the true boundary. During this adverse occupation, Delbert notified Crow that he was a trespasser. The period for adverse possession passed and Delbert now sues Crow
(a) Crow now owns the subject 10 feet.
(b) Delbert continues to own the land since he gave effective notice to Crow.
(c) Crow must pay Delbert the reasonable value of the 10 feet.
(d) Crow can occupy only one-half of the 10 feet, or 5 feet.

276. Plaintiffs and their predecessors in title used defendant's adjoining farm land for 30 years as ingress and egress to their farm. Defendants claimed that such use was permissive in the beginning and the land so used was unproductive waste land
(a) the use will be enjoined.
(b) the plaintiff now owns the land.
(c) the plaintiff now has an easement by prescription.
(d) the plaintiff must pay the reasonable value for a continued use.

277. Davis claimed title to several vacant lots. Davis and George derived title from a common grantor. The Davis deed was recorded first. Davis and his predecessors never paid taxes or other assessments for 40 years. George had paid taxes on these lots, and other assessments and for removal of weeds levied by the city. Who has title to the lots?
(a) George has title to the lots by adverse possession.
(b) George has title by laches on part of the plaintiff.
(c) George because of the "clean hands" doctrine.
(d) Davis has title to the lots.

278. The disability of the principal, requiring a wheelchair
(a) will terminate the agency.
(b) will not terminate the agency.
(c) will require a new power of attorney from the principal.
(d) will be voidable at principal's election.

279. The L P S partnership is deeding a tract of land to Sam Simon. The partnership is composed of 3 brothers, one of whom is not active in real estate transactions.
(a) The acknowledgment to the deed can be taken by S.
(b) The acknowledgment can be taken by L or P.
(c) The acknowledgement can be taken only by all three members.
(d) The acknowledgement to the deed cannot be taken by any of the three members.

280. A developer subdivided land and orally represented each purchaser of a lot that only one family residences could be erected, and prohibiting mobile or trailer homes. Only eight lots were sold in the subdivision of 40 units. After six years, the developer sold two lots to persons who were permitted to use the lots for trailer homes. The deeds to the first

purchasers contained a clause that all representations, covenants and agreements were expressed therein. The original owners have a cause of action

(a) against the trailer owners.
(b) criminal action against the land developer.
(c) injunctive relief against developer.
(d) civil suit for damages against developer.

281. A buyer agreed to purchase a vacant lot on November 30, 1973 for $3,500, payable at the rate of $50 per month. Payments were made irregularly until $1,650 was paid. On July 22, 1970, the buyer informed the seller that he was ready to pay the balance. A deed was executed by the seller in February 1974, but it was never tendered to the buyer. The buyer now sues to recover the $1,650 paid by him.

(a) Buyer can recover.
(b) Seller can recover balance due.
(c) Seller must tender a deed.
(d) Action of buyer is premature.

282. In 1970, Adam Steele and Mary Steele, his wife, acquired title by the entireties to their home. Mary obtained a divorce from Adam in 1972. On June 15, 1974 Mary and Adam re-married. Under these circumstances,

I. Adam and Mary again own the residence by the entireties
II. Adam and Mary are owners of the property as tenants in common

(a) I only
(b) II only
(c) Both I and II
(d) Neither I nor II

283. Which of the following is true?

I. A deed always grants the exact extent of ownership
II. A title search is necessary to ascertain exact extent of ownership

(a) I only
(b) II only
(c) both I and II
(d) neither I nor II

Chapter 4

THE FINANCING OF REAL ESTATE

THE TERM "money market" is sometimes used in referring to those institutions whose function it is to make available money and credit to borrowers. The whole business structure of the United States is based upon the assumption that credit will be available to those who need it and can show the ability and willingness to repay.

The money market

At any one time various segments of our economy are competing for the investor's dollar. The investors on the other hand are competing with each other to obtain the best investments at the most favorable rates.

The investor gives up the privilege of spending his money when he lends it to another. In return for giving up the money and privilege of spending it, he exacts a promise from the borrower to repay it at a future time. He also requires that the borrower pay a certain amount for the use of the money. This is called interest. It is really rent for the use of the money.

The rate of interest which investors ask and get is determined by many complex economic factors. One of the most important of these factors is the availability of lendable funds, and the current demand for and supply of "mortgage money." Another is the risk involved in making the loan. A third is the business outlook for the future. These are only a few of the economic forces which determine the rate of interest in general and in a specific locality.

The supply of money through our banking system is controlled to a great extent by the Federal Reserve System and the local banks. The funds available for investment in real estate, however, are made up principally from the savings of firms and individuals.

Banks, for instance, cannot use funds deposited by their customers in their checking accounts to make long-term loans on real estate. Only funds deposited in savings accounts are available for such use. Savings and loan institutions and insurance companies also lend funds which are really the savings of individuals. Since these institutions are lending the money of others, the Federal and state government have required of them a high degree of responsibility for the funds placed in their care.

What investments compete for these savings?

One of the basic principles of investment is that a person should never put all of his savings in one type of investment. By diversifying his investments, he is able to minimize the over-all risk of loss. At any time an investor can put his money into government bonds, corporate bonds, savings accounts, mortgages, land contracts, real estate, savings and loan institutions, or into the preferred or common stocks of several hundred corporations. The investor, therefore, has before him at all times a wide range of investment media from which to pick and choose according to his likes and dislikes.

Mortgages

Almost since the beginning of written history we have records of a debtor pledging some property as security for a loan. If the debt were not paid, the property pledged was taken over or sold to satisfy the debt.

In real estate financing the borrower gives a note in which he unconditionally promises to pay a certain amount of money. This is the debt instrument that sets up the obligation of the debt. The borrower also gives to the creditor a mortgage which pledges certain property as security for the loan. It is sometimes called a "dead pledge" because as long as the debtor carries out his promises and obligations the mortgage has no effect. However, if the borrower defaults on any of his promises, the pledge "comes to life" and gives the creditor the right to have the property seized and sold to satisfy the debt. The mortgage, however, does not prevent the sale of the real estate.

People often say they are "paying on a mortgage" but this is misleading because actually they are paying on the note.

Banks as money lenders

Commercial banks have been a traditional source of funds for the financing of real estate. National Banks are restricted by law as to the amount which they may lend on real estate and as to the time limit of such loans. If the installment payments are sufficient to amortize the entire principal of the loan within the period ending on the date of its maturity, nationally chartered banks may lend up to 90% of the appraised value of the real estate at the time the loan is made. The maximum term for a National Bank mortgage loan is 30 years for a conventional loan. F.H.A. or G.I. loan regulations are those set forth by the government agencies having jurisdiction. The total loans that the bank may hold on real estate may not exceed, at the time of making the loan, the unimpaired capital plus the unimpaired surplus of the bank, or 70% of its time and savings deposits, whichever is greater. The large increase in time and savings deposits have made banks much more active in the field of real estate financing.

Savings and loan associations

The savings and loan associations originated as a cooperative attempt to help members of the organization finance their own homes. Members could subscribe to shares in the organization and make payments on these shares. When they had paid in a sufficient amount, they were allowed to borrow from the association. Dividends were paid on the funds invested in the organization. However, these dividends depended upon profits and were subject to wide fluctuations.

Over the years, savings and loan associations have changed in character, so that today they are thrift organizations catering to the small and medium sized investor. Although they specialize in loans on single family residences there has been a trend to invest a portion of the assets in loans on multi-unit dwellings to serve the housing needs of the country. Federal Savings and Loan Associations are permitted, within certain limitations, to make loans secured by multi-unit dwellings and other investment type properties in addition to home mortgage loans; that is, one to four family dwelling units.

Individual savings and loan associations have, in recent years, also engaged in participating as groups in larger loans which are beyond their individual capacities. This lending method has provided them greater yield and diversification of investment which are major considerations for all investors.

Savings and loan associations were pioneers in the use of amortizing loans on homes. Years before other lending institutions used this type of loan, savings and loan associations were advertising the advantages of such loans to both the borrower and lender.

Savings and loan associations have grown to be the largest single factor in mortgage financing. At the end of 1972 they accounted for 36% of total mortgage loans outstanding according to the Federal Reserve Board and the Federal Home Loan Bank Board. Their total investment was in excess of $206 billion. Of this $206 billion, almost $166 billion was invested in mortgage loans secured by one to four family residences.

Life insurance companies

Life insurance companies are one of the largest sources of funds for real estate loans. Because of our increased population, longer life expectancy, group insurance as a fringe benefit in labor contracts, the life insurance companies have found themselves in possession of increasing amounts of funds and for longer periods of time.

The increase in assets of life insurance companies in this country has been nothing short of phenomenal. In 1920, total assets were less than $8 billion; in 1961, the assets were in excess of $141 billion. In recent years their assets have been increasing dramatically to the present level, at October 31, 1973, of $251.590 billion, according to the Federal Reserve Board.

An examination of the assets of these companies reveals that real estate mortgages make up their second largest investment. At October 31, 1973 (according to the Federal Reserve Board), their mortgage portfolios in total amounted to $79.516 billion or over 31% of their total assets. The only other larger investment was that in corporate securities which accounted for about 47.5% of life insurance companies total assets.

Almost all of the loans made by these companies with real estate as security are of the amortizing type. This means that the borrower starts to pay back the loan at the end of the first month. To be distinguished from the "amortizing" loan are mortgage loans on which interest only is paid or the loan type wherein the payment is "ballooned" after a period of time.

The loan which does not amortize, that is, on which interest only is paid, is called a "standing" loan. This type of loan is generally very short (up to 5 years), because consideration must be given to the depreciation in value of the real estate due to normal wear and tear.

"Balloon" in mortgage lending refers to the loan contract which requires amortization over a longer period than the loan term. A loan term is set at the end of a relatively short period, but payments against principal are made as if the loan were to be repaid over a longer period. For example, a loan may have a maturity of 15 years with an amortization period of 30 years.

There are advantages to both borrower and lender; the borrower has a lesser "constant" payment than might otherwise be required and the lender has an opportunity for renegotiation of the loan at a later date.

Some major insurance companies have taken an equity, that is ownership, position in certain income producing properties in order to acquire a hedge against inflation. These companies will then benefit from increases in the value of the real estate or the increases in rental income. Another method of providing for increases in income, in addition to the interest on the loan, is the charging of a percentage of the rents over a specified minimum amount as additional interest. That is, a figure is set as the projected gross or net rental income and a charge is made in addition to the interest, which charge is a percentage of the income achieved over that which has been projected. Both these methods result in a potentially greater overall yield on the loan to the lender.

Mutual savings banks

Most mutual savings banks are in the eastern part of the United States. They were set up in many cases to promote thrift by encouraging people to invest. Originally they invested in mortgages in their own immediate geographic area. With the advent of FHA and VA loans they started to invest nation-wide.

Mutual savings banks, like most financial institutions, are restricted as to the types of investments permitted to them. Of the permitted investments mutual savings banks (according to the Federal Reserve Board) invest the preponderance of their assets in mortgage loans. The statistics for the period ending October 31, 1973 show that their investments in mortgage loans are in excess of $72 billion out of total assets for all mutual savings banks of $105.5 billion. The major share of mutual savings bank mortgage investment (over $60 billion) was in residential lending.

Mutual savings banks as a form of financial institution direct the major share of their efforts to real estate mortgage lending, and as can be seen from the statistics quoted above, they are very important to the support of such activities in the United States.

Pension funds

Pension funds in the "Private non-insured" category are showing a decreasing interest in mortgage loans as investments. The Statistical Bulletin of the United States Securities and Exchange Commission for April, 1973 reports preliminarily that at the end of 1972 the book value of investments in mortgage loans were $3 billion compared to $3.68 billion one year earlier or a decline of $68 million. Investments in common stock have increased over the periods mentioned while mortgage investments have declined. Over the period from 1962 to 1972, private non-insured pension funds had shown an increasing interest in mortgage investments until 1971 when the interest lessened.

Private lenders

Many individuals with funds to invest are willing to lend and take back mortgages as security. This preference for mortgage loans is at least to some extent brought about by their desire to see the property which is pledged as security.

Individuals will often loan on real estate on which institutional lenders will not or cannot legally lend. Thus private money sometimes fills a need for loans which would not otherwise be made. Many such loans entail more than average risk and therefore carry a higher interest rate than those made by institutional lenders. Individuals may also be willing to make short-term loans which ordinary lenders would not consider because of the cost of placing the loan.

Loans made by individuals, however, comprise only a small segment of all loans. But they help to round out the loan market and fill in gaps left by the organized lenders. Vital as this is, they do not actively compete with the institutional lenders.

Responsibility of institutional lenders

Institutional lenders are actually lending other people's savings. Because of this, laws controlling such institutions require of them a high degree of responsibility and business judgment. They also have certain responsibilities to the borrower and to the public.

In their fiduciary capacity they must see that the loans they make are economically sound and that there is adequate security in the property covered by the mortgage. From the standpoint of the borrower they must see that he is obtaining property which fills his needs and that the schedule of payments is such that he will be able to make them without undue hardship. If there is a default the borrower may lose all of the equity he has built up in the property. In medium and low income classes the home usually constitutes the only savings a family has other than Social Security. Therefore, a lending institution has a double responsibility to see that the loans which are made are economically sound for both the lender and the borrower.

G.I. loans[1]

Mortgage loans which are guaranteed or insured under Title 38, United States Code (formerly the Servicemen's Readjustment Act of 1944, as amended), are usually called G. I. loans. Under this law the Veterans Administration may guarantee or insure home and farm loans to World War II veterans, veterans of the Korean conflict, eligible post-Korean veterans and certain other servicemen. The loans are made by lending institutions and the loan guarantees, which are provided by the Veterans Aministration, are for the benefit of those lenders. The lenders are benefitted in the event the veteran-borrower defaults in repayment of the loan. In addition to the guarantee or insurance of loans for veterans, the Veterans Administration has a program for the making of direct loans where mortgage lenders do not function effectively.

Under present laws, each eligible veteran has an aggregate entitlement of $12,500, that is, the Veterans Administration may guarantee or insure loans against default up to this amount. The most common type of loan assistance provided by the Veterans Administration is through the "guarantee" program for mortgage loans.

The "guarantee" program permits the Veterans Administration to assure the lender that up to 60%, but not more than $12,500, of a mortgage loan will be paid to a lender if the loan to the veteran is defaulted. For example, a lending institution which lends $10,000 to a veteran under the "guarantee" program receives a guarantee of $6,000, that is, 60% of the loan. A further example is the case of a lending institution which provides a loan in the amount of $30,000 and obtains a guarantee of 41.6% of the $30,000 loan ($12,500 is the limit and is 41.6% of $30,000).

The guarantee or insurance of loans by the Veterans Administration is for the purpose of assisting eligible veterans in purchasing only one home. However, there are cases wherein the veteran may use this program to its fullest more than once. The used loan entitlement may be restored to a veteran upon request if he or she has been forced to sell the home purchased with assistance provided by the Veterans Administration. This "restoration of entitlement" is a matter for individual consideration by the Veterans Administration.

If the veteran defaults in payment of the loan and the lender resorts to the guaranty or insurance, the Veterans Administration has certain options with respect to the guaranty or insurance. It may elect to pay the portion of the loan which has been guaranteed or insured, and the lender may then dispose of the property to recapture the balance of the loan. Or, the Veterans Administration may elect to pay the loan off in full and purchase the foreclosed property from the lender.

The veteran must keep in mind that although he or she obtains assistance in purchasing a home, the loan must be repaid in accordance with the contract. The Veterans Administration assists the veteran through guarantee or insurance, but does

[1] G.I. loan is the same as a V.A. loan—one guaranteed by the Veteran's Administration.

not otherwise intervene in the fundamentals of the loan contract. If a veteran defaults in repayment of the loan and the Veterans Administration loses money in the transaction, the veteran is held liable for the loss; therefore, the government provides assistance, but does not make a gift to an eligible veteran.

Loans guaranteed or insured by the Veterans Administration had a statutory ceiling until 1968 when the establishment of the maximum rate was placed under the control of the Secretary of Housing and Urban Development in consultation with the Administrator of Veterans Affairs. This action permitted a response to the conditions prevailing in the money market and was an effort to provide a continuing source of funds for loans to veterans. From time to time, as interest rates increased generally, the G. I. loan availability was lessened or eliminated for a time because the maximum rate fixed for G. I. loans was less than the market for other competing investments. In mid 1974, the maximum rate fixed for loans guaranteed by the Veterans Administration was 9%, that is, no mortgage loan to a veteran under the provisions of Title 38 of the United States Code could provide for an interest rate in excess of 9%.

In addition to fixing the maximum interest rate, the Veterans Administration also provides protection to the veteran against paying in excess of the market value of the home to be purchased. The Veterans Administration provides this protection to the veteran by requiring that all properties be appraised by qualified real estate appraisers. In the event the purchase price exceeds the appraisal, that is, the Certificate of Reasonable Value, the veteran who wishes to complete the purchase contract must:

1. Restrict the loan amount to not more than the reasonable value as determined by the Veterans Administration.
2. Must pay in cash from his own sources the difference between the purchase price and the reasonable value plus proper closing costs.
3. The veteran must sign a certificate acknowledging that he understands the purchase price is higher than the determined value and that he will pay the excess in cash from his own resources.

Certain geographical areas of the United States have been designated as housing credit shortage areas. In these parts of the country, the Veterans Administration provides direct loans to veterans. The direct loan program is not available where there is a supply of funds for VA guaranteed or insured mortgage loans.

In addition to the requirement that the geographical area be designated as one experiencing housing credit shortage, the Veterans Administration places other requirements for qualifications under the direct loan program:

1. The loan must be for the purpose of buying, building or improving a home to be occupied by the veteran.
2. The loan may be for the purpose of purchasing a farm where there is a residence to be occupied by the veteran.
3. The loan may be for the purpose of building a residence on a farm, but again the veteran must occupy the residence.
4. The loan may be for the purpose of refinancing an existing loan secured by the Veteran's residence.
5. If the veteran has full entitlement, the loan is permitted to be a maximum of $25,000. If the entitlement has been partially used, the loan is reduced.

If a veteran desires to sell his property after purchase, he may do so without repaying the loan. In the event of sale without repayment, the veteran has the following choices:

1. He or she may sell the property "subject to" the mortgage loan, that is, the veteran remains liable for the debt, but transfers title to the real estate and receives payment for the difference between the sale price and the outstanding balance of the mortgage loan.
2. The purchaser may assume the veteran's liability for repayment of the loan and the veteran will no longer be held responsible for the repayment of the debt by either the lender or the Veterans Administration. In this instance the purchaser's credit must be approved by the Veterans Administration and the lender in order to accomplish the desired release from liability.
3. The purchaser may assume the veteran's liability without release by the Veterans Administration or the lender, that is, a contract for assumption of the obligation exists between the veteran and the purchaser, but there is no approval or concurrence by the lender or the Veterans Administration.
4. The veteran may also be released from liability by the Veterans Administration, but the liability to the lender is retained.

The veteran who desires to sell his property subject to the Veterans Administration guaranteed or insured loan is always well advised to consult his lender, the Veterans Administration and legal counsel. Such a sale can have far reaching future effects on the veteran's assets and his credit standing.

The Veterans Administration programs for the purpose of providing assistance to eligible veterans have been very effective since their beginning in 1944 with millions of veterans being served and lenders protected in making high ratio mortgage loans.

The Home Owners' Loan Corporation

In 1933, the Home Owners' Loan Corporation was authorized to assist home owners who were in default. This occurred during the Great Depression when the typical home owner was two years delinquent on mortgage payments and three years delinquent on real estate taxes. Foreclosures of residential real estate were being filed at the rate of almost 1000 each day.

The Home Owners' Loan Corporation was set up to "bail out" both the home owners and the lending institutions which had made the loans. The H.O.L.C. made loans rather than provide loan insurance.

The Federal Housing Administration loans

In 1934, the Federal Housing Administration was formed with the idea of insuring the loans of lenders so that they would be more willing to lend to home owners. There are several parts or titles to the original act but the section of most interest to real estate people is Title II which makes provisions for insuring loans on one- to four-family dwellings, and Title I loans which are for improvement and repairs. The F.H.A.[2] sets up the requirements which the borrower and the property must meet before the loan will be insured.

In general the standards of F.H.A. are rather high. They have devised a pattern of rating risks that attempts to evaluate all the factors that affect the property including the qualifications and credit of the buyer. They have also been leaders in the attempt to standardize appraising procedures.

A lending institution, in order to qualify for making insured loans, must be a corporation with total assets in excess of $100,000. It must also file an application and

---

[2] F.H.A.—Federal Housing Authority; federal government agency that insures real estate loans.

be accepted by the F.H.A. as a qualified lender. The fact that a lending institution has qualified for making insured loans does not mean that all the loans it makes are insured. It can make insured loans or conventional loans as it sees fit. The advantage to the lender of making insured loans is that the risk involved decreases; but because the interest rate decreases with the lesser risk, the lender will receive a lower yield.

The interest rate applicable to F.H.A. insured mortgage loans is fixed by the Secretary of Housing and Urban Development (HUD) under authorization by the Congress. The maximum rate permitted by the Secretary in mid 1974 was 9%. In addition to this interest rate the borrower is required to pay an insurance premium of 1/2% to the mortgage lender. The lender periodically remits this insurance premium to the Federal Housing Administration. The borrower is also required to make monthly deposits for payment of real estate taxes and hazard insurance in order to be certain that these obligations are paid when due.

For the purpose of providing the benefits of home ownership and improved housing to low income families, Sections 235 and 236 of the Housing Act were enacted by Congress. These two sections of the Act were suspended due to abuses which occurred in their use and the need to restudy the programs.

At this writing, the Federal Housing Administration, which made a major contribution to home ownership for forty years, has declined in importance. This decline came about because of the aforementioned abuses in certain areas, but also because of the rising importance of private mortgage insurance companies. These private mortgage insurance companies, as will be discussed later in this chapter, are taking the place of importance maintained for so long by the Federal Housing Administration. No attempt is made to forecast the future of the F.H.A., except to say that it appears that changes in its operations will occur.

Qualifying for an F.H.A. loan

A home buyer may choose any approved lending institution in applying for a loan, and file his application on the approved F.H.A. forms. On these forms he gives a description of the property. He also outlines his financial status and gives a short personal history and an employment record unless he is self-employed.

The lending institution will then examine the application to see whether to submit it to the F.H.A. for approval. The lending institution, having made many such loans, can judge quite accurately the chances the potential borrower has of having his loan approved. If the lender feels that the loan will be approved, the application is forwarded to the regional F.H.A. office. The F.H.A. will then examine the application, appraise the property, and apply the mortgage pattern for the area. If the application meets the requirements for insurance, a Commitment for Insurance is issued. When this is received by the lending institution, the loan is made.

Some lending firms do not originate F.H.A. loans but prefer to purchase mortgages which have been made by other institutions. This buying of mortgages by a firm which did not originate them is known as the secondary mortgage market. If there is an active demand for loans, the originating firm can liquidate some of its loans and in this way have available funds for further lending. Without the secondary mortgage market, lending firms would have to wait to make further loans until collections or additional investments were made when they had loaned out the total of available funds.

In many cases, the originating firm in selling its mortgages to another firm continues to collect the payments on the mortgage and is paid a small fee for this service. This is an advantage to both because the originating firm has the history of the borrower and often knows local conditions better than the secondary firm. It relieves the buying firm of the detail work of collection. The secondary firm can also buy large blocks of mortgages without the cost of originating the loans.

During the period it has been in operation, the F.H.A. has foreclosed on only about 1 per cent of the real estate on which insured mortgages were placed. The loss to the insuring corporation has been only a small fraction of 1 per cent. This indicates that the lending practices outlined by the F.H.A. are sound.

It is generally felt that the F.H.A. has stabilized the lending market. By its standardization of procedure and consideration of the credit of the buyer as well as the security offered by the property, it has strengthened the whole mortgage market. The higher loan ratio under this program has reduced junior financing a great deal. The overall effect has also been to reduce interest rates and to make the amortizing mortgage a standard lending instrument.

Conventional loans

A conventional loan is one that is neither guaranteed nor insured. Several years ago such loans would have been non-amortizing and would have had maturities from three to five years. Today, due to the changes brought about by F.H.A. and V.A. practices, the typical conventional loan is also an amortizing loan. For the most part, conventional loans carry a slightly higher interest rate and the maturities are shorter than the F.H.A. and G.I. loans.

Conventional loans are made by lending institutions and by individuals as well. The interest rates charged are determined by local market conditions and by the risk involved. As indicated earlier in this chapter, individuals often make real estate loans on property which lending institutions cannot or will not make. In some cases the loan is really a form of credit loan because the property pledged does not have a ready market. Such loans often carry a relatively high interest rate due to the extra risk involved. On the other hand, loans made on new construction may be competitive with insured and guaranteed loans.

Private mortgage insurance corporations

The laws of most states permit lending institutions to lend above statutory ratio of loan to value if the excess is insured by an acceptable insuring agency. The amount of this excess is usually 10 per cent to 15 per cent of the loan. The main purpose of this insurance is to supply additional security to financial institutions seeking higher yields from investments through mortgage loans of maximum loan-to-value ratios.

First in this private field was Mortgage Guaranty Insurance Corporation, known as MGIC. Others have since entered the field.

An additional feature which has developed in the area of insurance of conventional loans has been the insurance of payments by tenants under leases. This type of insurance has permitted more lenders to enter the field of financing, other than single family residences. The insurance of the leases has provided not only a limitation on risk, but also a more expert underwriting approach. Smaller associations with limitations on staff now can use the underwriting expertise of the private mortgage insurance corporations. The staffs of these insurance companies, because of the benefits of specialization, are able to determine with greater exactness the possibilities for success or failure of a large project. Therefore, the smaller associations and larger ones too, benefit through insurance of a part of the loan plus the review of the proposed investment by qualified experts in the field of mortgage financing.

Other financial instruments

The Land Sales Contract. The land sales contract, previously discussed, is also used as a junior financing instrument. For example, a man has an existing mortgage on a house that he wishes to sell. The lending institution will not allow a second mortgage to be placed on the property and the prospective buyer cannot buy out the equity of the owner with his down payment. To illustrate, the sales price is $15,000 and the existing mortgage is $9,000 leaving $6,000 to finance. The prospective buyer has only $2,000 to pay down. Under the circumstances, the seller may be willing to take back a land sales contract for the remaining $4,000. This does not constitute a second mortgage on the property. The buyer then pays on the mortgage to the lending institution and to the seller on the land sales contract. In this way, the sale can be made without violation of the first mortgage.

The Purchase Money Mortgage. Another way in which a seller may finance the sale of property is by means of a purchase money mortgage. The seller agrees to sell to a buyer for a stated price. The purchaser agrees to pay a certain amount down on the purchase price. The seller then agrees to take back a purchase money mortgage for the remainder of the sale price.

Pledges

In recent years the plan of using pledges with savings and loan associations to increase the loan amount over and above the amount of a permitted real estate mortgage has been used. Under this plan the lending institution combines two lending privileges.

First: The amount of mortgage it can lend based on its statutory regulation of ratio of loan to value.

Second: A loan on a savings account. The pledge is against this savings account.

In a typical case the seller will open a savings account. This account will be pledged against a loan to the buyer which is over and above the mortgage. The seller does receive dividends on his savings account. He cannot withdraw the full amount until the original mortgage is reduced to a certain amount.

There are many plans for pledged accounts. Two basic plans are:

1. Mortgage $8,000, pledged account $1,000, total borrowing $9,000. The total amount is paid off at a level monthly payment rate. Under this plan, $100 will be released from the pledged account for each $200 paid off on the mortgage.

2. A plan for accelerated pay-off of the pledged account. In the case of an $8,000 mortgage and $1,000 pledge the mortgage will be amortized by a level monthly payment over a period of 20 or 25 years. The $1,000 will be paid off in 3 years or 5 years. The pledged account may be withdrawn after the three- or five-year period and the monthly payments of the borrower would be reduced accordingly.

Most lending institutions agree to notify the pledgee if there is a default on the mortgage so he can step in to protect his interest.

Discounts

V.A. and F.H.A. mortgage loan interest is determined by government regulation. In a case where interest is fixed, the yield is often not attractive enough to secure a ready market for funds. A good example of this is government bonds with interest rates below that which can be obtained from an insured savings account in either a bank or savings and loan association. These bonds do not have a ready market because of the fixed yields unless they are sold at a discount.

A rule of thumb used to determine yield on mortgages with an estimated life of

12 years is this: a four point or four per cent discount increases the yield of the mortgage loan approximately 1/2 of 1 per cent. Although most mortgage loans are for a longer term than 12 years, the average life of a loan is approximately 12 years. To determine yield you may refer to a Prepayment Mortgage Yield Table. Based on a term of 25 years and an interest rate of 7% you will achieve the following yields by charging a discount at the inception of the loan:

25 Year Loan Prepaid In

Price	8 yrs.	10 yrs.	12 yrs.	To Maturity
95 (5% discount)	8.03	7.91	7.84	7.71
96 (4% discount)	7.84	7.75	7.69	7.59
97 (3% discount)	7.66	7.59	7.55	7.47
98 (2% discount)	7.48	7.43	7.40	7.35

Very complete tables are published with regard to mortgage yields and are a very necessary tool in the business of real estate financing. Yields are so carefully scrutinized that they are computed within one-one hundredth of one per cent. Each one-hundredth of one per cent is referred to as a "basis point" so that an increase or decrease of one per cent in yield may be referred to as a change in yield of "one hundred basis points."

Constant payment tables

In order to simplify the calculation of payments in the field of mortgage financing, a method of computation has been developed to express the payment in terms of percentage of the total loan. Given the rate of interest and the term of the loan, a person may refer to such a table and quickly acquire the percentage of the loan needed to repay the loan on a fully amortized basis. For example, the constant annual per cent needed to repay a 25 year loan at 7% is 8.49%. Therefore, on a loan of $100,000 the annual payment is $8,490 per year. To compute the monthly payment simply divide by 12. The following is the problem in simple form:

$100,000 X .0849 = $8,490 ÷ 12 = $707.50 per month

GNMA securities

On February 19, 1970 a major new contribution to the field of mortgage financing occurred with the issue of the first Government guaranteed mortgage-backed security. This is a method by which mortgage lenders may accumulate pools of F.H.A. insured or V.A. guaranteed loans and for an initial fee of $500.00 plus an annual fee of either .04% or .06% paid to the Government National Mortgage Association may obtain the guaranty of the Government National Mortgage Association. This guarantee is backed by the full faith and credit of the United States Government.

These securities have revolutionized the approach of lenders to mortgage financing and it is expected that the program will help to level out the supply of mortgage funds. These funds have characteristically been extremely vulnerable to increases in interest rates.

This program, referred to as "Ginnie Mae" mortgage backed securities permits the sale of fractional interests in blocks of mortgages to investors. The investors have yields which compare very favorably to high grade corporate issues and receive interest and principal payments each month. The securities are practically risk-free, since they are backed by the full faith and credit of the United States Government. The issuer (mortgage company, bank, savings and loan association, or other mortgage lender) reaps large benefits through servicing fees, escrow deposits and other collateral benefits. Hopefully, the prospective buyers of houses have a constant supply of mortgage funds and the construction industry does not suffer injury to it by money market fluctuations. Obviously, these are important considerations as our country looks forward to a continuing need for additional housing in the future.

Truth in lending

On May 29, 1968, President Lyndon Johnson signed into law the Truth in Lending Act, Title I of the Consumer Credit Protection Act. This law required that effective July 1, 1969, those people engaged in lending must disclose certain information to their borrowers. The purpose of the Act was to permit prospective borrowers to make adequate comparisons of the charges of the various lenders. It does not in any way limit charges for credit, but simply provides for disclosure of the charges related to the loan.

This law was implemented by the Board of Governors of the Federal Reserve System as Regulation Z and is known as "Truth-in-Lending" or "Regulation Z" to those involved in lending money. The regulation gives the lending institutions the information they need in order to comply with the law; it tells them how to meet the requirements.

The law applies to all persons who are involved in regular extensions of credit, such as: banks, savings and loan associations, department stores, credit unions, finance companies. Truth in Lending, as implemented by Regulation Z of the Federal Reserve System, then covers the financing of real estate.

The typical disclosure statement required pursuant to the Truth in Lending Act, as it applies to real estate financing, contains information to the borrower with regard to:

1. Total prepaid finance charges such as origination fees, discount points, construction loan fee, loan insurance fees to F.H.A.
2. Items not included in Finance Charge such as real estate transfer charges, filing and recording fees.
3. A statement that fire insurance coverage is required, but the borrower may choose the seller of such insurance.
4. The fact that the disclosure statement does not reflect many of the borrower's closing costs such as title examination fees, legal fees, credit reporting fees and others.
5. The costs of life and health and accident insurance with a statement that it is not required as a condition of making the loan.
6. The amount of the delinquency charge.
7. The charge for early prepayment.
8. The property in which the lender has acquired a security interest.

The Truth in Lending Act is a complex matter requiring study of the various specifics for the lender desiring to lend and acquire a security interest in real estate.

Variable interest rates

Of growing importance is the need of the lender to be able to maintain a favorable spread between money cost and interest earned, and of the potential borrower to be able to find mortgage financing when it is needed. The concept of the "variable rate" is now in the process of development with methods that can only be judged after they have stood the test of time. The fundamental procedure is to tie the interest rate applicable on the loan to a money market instrument which compares in maturity to a mortgage loan and permit the rate to float during its life. There has not been a general acceptance of the concept at this writing, however, there is a distinct acknowledgment of the need for more rapid change and response to market conditions.

Of particular interest in this regard is an act of the Pennsylvania Legislature in early 1974 which fixes the maximum rate at 2.5 per cent over long term government bonds with the month's maximum rate to be announced during the month preceding. This Pennsylvania method fixes the rate for the term of the loan, but permits a quick response to market conditions. The conditions which brought about this legislation are solidly rooted in the problem of usury rates and the flight of mortgage funds from Pennsylvania to other states and into investments other than single family house mortgages.

Real Estate Investment Trusts

This financial intermediary has had outstanding growth since the passage of legislation in 1961 which made it particularly desirable to investors. The principle is not new since real estate investment trusts have been in existence for many years. However, the passing of the previously mentioned legislation required the payment of at least 90% of its income to its owners of shares as a return on investment in order to escape the payment of federal income tax.

The REIT as it is known invests in real estate either as owner or lender or is involved in both these activities. The REIT is known as either an equity or mortgage trust or a combination trust.

Construction and development lending have been the most important activities of these financial intermediaries as a group. They have invested funds available to them in relatively large projects and have not been a factor in residential lending because of lower yields available in that sector and the management problems which attend it. They lend money to developers who have not yet acquired permanent financing, and who are desirous of taking a project to the "permanent" mortgage market after completion, because a completed and operating shopping center, apartment building, office complex or other real estate venture usually finds a higher permanent mortgage loan than one which is proposed. The interest cost is higher without a permanent loan arranged before construction starts, but the loan benefits are anticipated to be greater.

They have also invested in standby, second mortgage and gap commitments.

The standby commitment is that type of assurance of permanent financing which permits the developer a permanent loan at a rate higher than the usual permanent loan. It is at least a source of permanent funds and permits the developer to seek out troughs in interest rates which will provide the best possible permanent financing vehicle.

The second mortgage loan provides to the borrower-developer a source of funds at a higher rate than the first mortgage which will assure funds for the project to be completed without the need for a cash investment by the developer.

The "gap" commitment is that type of financing vehicle which provides for a loan to the borrower-developer in the amount of the difference between the floor loan (the amount to be advanced by the permanent lender without occupancy of the structure) and the greater amount to be advanced after a certain income level has been achieved by rent-paying occupancy.

Real estate investment trusts sell shares to the general public to acquire equity capital. With this equity capital as a base, they seek out commercial banks and other financial institutions which lend additional funds for the loans the REIT's make to their borrowers. The funds borrowed from these financial institutions are at least, theoretically, invested in mortgage loans at a higher rate with the difference between the borrowing and the lending rate becoming income.

This type of investment by the share purchaser is considered as having substantially more risk than investment in other types of money market instruments and is comparable to common stock.

The real estate investment trust is managed by an "advisor." This advisor is owned by a financial institution, such as an insurance company or a commercial bank holding company, or perhaps by a company without other financially related activities. The advisor is paid prearranged fees by the REIT for its services and by this means provides income to the sponsoring company.

The recent popularity of this type of real estate concentrated financial intermediary has forced changes in the underwriting practices of financial institutions who had previously pursued a more conservative course for their investments.

Summary

The preceding pages are but an introduction to a science which is constantly developing and changing. New methods are brought to the forefront, tried for a time, and then replaced. The basic principles remain the same, however, and a thorough knowledge of these will permit the practitioner to have an understanding of the field as change occurs with emphasis provided by sociological, political or economic factors.

Questions on the Financing of Real Estate

1. Q. Financial intermediaries are those institutions and businesses that accept money from savers and lend it to borrowers. Name five financial intermediaries that invest in mortgage loans.
   A. Commercial banks, mutual savings banks, savings and loan associations, life insurance companies and pension funds.
2. Q. Name some of the choices an investor has with regard to investments.
   A. Government bonds, corporate bonds, savings accounts, mortgages, land contracts, real estate or stocks.
3. Q. Does the appraisal by the VA determine the purchase price the veteran can pay for a house?
   A. No. An amendment effective May 7, 1968, changed the former law. The veteran must pay the difference in cash if the sales price exceeds the reasonable value.
4. Q. What procedure should you pursue if the VA appraisal value is less than contract price?
   A. Try to adjust the sales price to the VA value or pay difference in cash.
5. Q. Explain the term "Secondary Mortgage Market"—"Secondary Financing."
   A. Secondary mortgage market refers to the resale market for existing loans. This has no connection with the meaning of the term "Secondary financing" which refers to junior loans such as are made on second deeds of trust (mortgages) and the priority of such security on the loan is second to that of the senior first deed of trust (first mortgage).
6. Q. A real estate broker prepares an earnest money receipt wherein it is shown that cash has been received by the seller, when in fact, the said payment is represented by a note. The deal is to be F.H.A. financed. Does the broker have any liability in this connection?
   A. Yes; subject to a Federal criminal prosecution, with a penalty of $5,000 fine, up to 2 years imprisonment, or both.
7. Q. Does the F.H.A. permit secondary financing?
   A. No; at the closing, the mortgagor certifies on the front of the F.H.A. commitment that he will not have outstanding any other unpaid obligations contracted in connection with the mortgage transaction. An untruth constitutes a violation of the U. S. Criminal Code.
8. Q. In its relation to real property, what is the meaning of the term "amortization?"
   A. The liquidation of a financial obligation on real property by payments at regular stated intervals, or on an installment basis.
9. Q. Does the F.H.A. require a penalty for early pre-payment of the insured mortgage loan?
   A. No. A pre-payment penalty of 1% of the original loan amount was once required, but has been eliminated.
10. Q. A broker accepts a deposit on a property and arranges for original F.H.A. financing. The appraisal does not come up to the prescribed amount. What should the broker do with the deposit money?
    A. ( ) retain the deposit.
    ( ) deliver deposit to seller.

(x) return the deposit to buyer.
( ) substitute a new buyer.

11. Q. What does the term "money market" mean?
A. The money market is made up of those institutions whose function is to supply money and credit to borrowers.

12. Q. To what extent is business dependent on the availability of loanable funds?
A. Our whole business structure is built upon the assumption that funds will be available to those who can show ability and willingness to repay their loans.

13. Q. How do investors and the lending institutions compete in the money market?
A. At any time the different parts of our economy that need loans are competing with each other for the available funds. On the other hand, the investors are competing with each other for the best investment and the most favorable rate of return.

14. Q. How are interest rates determined for different kinds of loans?
A. The interest rate at any time is the result of the different forces which are competing for the investor's money. Supply and demand have a great effect on the rate. The risk involved is also a determining factor. The final rate is the result of supply in relation to demand, the risk involved, the business outlook, and many more economic forces.

15. Q. How do the banks make loans on real estate?
A. Banks may loan out a certain percentage of the deposits which they have in the savings accounts of their customers. They cannot make real estate loans out of their checking deposits.

16. Q. Do banks create the credit with which to make real estate loans?
A. No. It is impossible for a bank or savings institution to create the credit. The funds loaned are the savings or investment of individuals or firms.

17. Q. How does an investor attempt to minimize the risks of investment?
A. By spreading his investments over different types of investments, he is able to decrease the overall risk of investment.

18. Q. What is a mortgage?
A. A mortgage is an instrument by which the owner of certain property pledges it as security for a loan.

19. Q. Is a mortgage a debt instrument?
A. No. It is only the instrument that pledges the property as security for the loan. The debt instrument is the note or bond signed by the borrower. Although both the note and the mortgage could be combined in one instrument, they are usually separate.

20. Q. Explain what is meant when the mortgage is called a "dead pledge."
A. As long as the borrower makes his payments and fulfills all that he agreed to do in the mortgage, the instrument has no effect; it is inoperative. Only when the borrower fails to keep his promises or make proper payments does the mortgage "come alive" and make it possible for the creditor to seize the property.

21. Q. What do people mean when they say they are "paying on a mortgage?"
A. They mean that they are paying on a note or bond which is secured by a mortgage on their property.

22. Q. Does a mortgage on a piece of real estate prevent the owner from selling it?
A. No. The owner may sell the property whenever he wishes but he would still be responsible for the unpaid balance of the note he has signed. The buyer of the property would also have the mortgage as a lien against the property and in case of a foreclosure, he might lose his equity.

23. Q. What restrictions are placed on national banks as to their lending on real estate?
A. National banks may lend only up to 90 per cent of the appraised value of real estate. They also may not make loans for a longer period than 30 years. These limitations do not apply to F.H.A. or G.I. loans but only to conventional loans.

24. Q. What percentage of total assets of a national bank could be loaned on real estate?

A. A national bank may not hold loans on real estate in excess of 70 per cent of its time or savings deposits.

25. Q. How do savings and loan associations differ from banks?
A. Savings and loan associations are unlike banks in that the funds deposited with them are not subject to check. They merely take the deposits of customers and loan them out. Although funds deposited with a savings and loan association can be withdrawn, the funds are not withdrawn by check, as are bank funds.

26. Q. How have savings and loan associations helped to encourage the use of amortizing loans?
A. The savings and loan associations were pioneers in the use of the amortizing loan. They were the first to point out the advantages of such loans to both borrower and lender.

27. Q. Why have savings and loan associations had such a growth in recent years?
A. The savings of the average family in the United States have increased a great deal in recent years and the savings and loan associations have catered to the small investor. They have encouraged thrift by taking very small deposits. As a result, many families have chosen these institutions in which to invest their savings.

28. Q. Why are life insurance companies one of the leading sources of mortgage loan money?
A. In recent years more and more life insurance has been purchased by the typical family. The life span of the average person has also been materially extended in the past twenty years. As a result of these two factors, the insurance companies have had an ever-increasing amount of funds to invest and real estate loans constitute their second largest investment—about 31% of the total investment.

29. Q. What type of real estate loans do the insurance companies make?
A. Insurance companies make practically all types of real estate loans to individuals. They make the three most common types: F.H.A., G.I., and conventional loans. Almost all of these loans call for the complete amortization of the loan over the loan period.

30. Q. Why is it said that insurance companies have a kind of "revolving fund" out of which to make loans?
A. Most of the loans made are amortizing and as a result the borrowers start to repay the loan at the end of the first month and make payments each month until the debt is repaid. This creates a stream of repayments flowing back to the company and these funds must be reinvested.

31. Q. How are mutual savings banks unlike commercial banks?
A. Mutual savings banks are savings institutions and do not offer checking facilities as do commercial banks.

32. Q. Are mutual savings banks one of the principal sources of mortgage loans for the financing of real estate?
A. Yes. Out of total assets at the end of October, 1973, these financial institutions, as a group, had invested over $72 billion out of total assets for all mutual savings banks of $105.5 billion.

33. Q. Why are private individuals often willing to make loans on real estate?
A. Many people feel that real estate loans are more secure than are other similar investments. They also can see the property which is mortgaged as security for the loan and make their own decisions as to the quality and value of it. Land will not wear out or be destroyed by many common hazards.

34. Q. Explain why private loans on real estate often carry higher interest rates than loans made by institutional lenders.
A. Private lenders are often willing to accept loans which institutional lenders will not make. However, such loans are more risky and the lenders ask for and get a higher interest to pay them for the extra risk.

35. Q. What are some of the responsibilities of institutional lenders?
A. Institutional lenders have greater responsibility than private lenders because they

are lending the savings of others. Therefore, they are responsible for seeing that the loans are sound investments for the borrower as well as the lender. They also have a responsibility to the public to be sure that the loans they make are economically sound. They must require that adequate security is maintained throughout the life of the loan.

36. Q. What responsibility does the lending institution have toward the borrower?
A. The lender should make sure that the loan meets the individual's needs, but at the same time is not so large that the payments are a burden on his available income.

37. Q. What are some of the responsibilities of an appraiser for a lending institution?
A. The appraiser for a lending institution has a great deal of responsibility to both the lender and the borrower. His duty is to make a sound estimate of the loan value of the property under appraisal. Assigning too high or too low a value is not fair to either party involved. Therefore, an appraiser should use all the skills and techniques available as well as good sound judgment in arriving at a loan value of a property.

38. Q. What is meant by the statement that a G.I. loan is guaranteed?
A. A lending institution makes a loan to a qualified veteran. In the event the loan is not paid off the Veterans Administration will guarantee a certain amount of the loan.

39. Q. For what purposes may a veteran get a loan?
A. To buy or build a home. To buy a farm and equipment or to purchase a business.

40. Q. Can a commission fee be charged a veteran for obtaining a G.I. loan?
A. No commission may be charged the veteran although the lender may charge the borrower reasonable closing costs. The lender may also charge a reasonable flat fee for originating the loan.

41. Q. Who is eligible for a G.I. loan?
A. Under the Servicemen's Readjustment Act of 1944 and subsequent legislation, each honorably discharged veteran of World War II, the Korean conflict, and post Korean veterans are entitled to receive G.I. loans, if qualified. There is no time limit on eligibility.

42. Q. What is meant by an entitlement?
A. The rights of a veteran to mortgage loan benefits.

43. Q. Would a widow of a veteran be eligible for a loan?
A. An unmarried widow of a veteran who was eligible but who did not use his entitlement would be eligible for a loan.

44. Q. Are children of a deceased veteran eligible?
A. No, only the unmarried widows.

45. Q. In a case where both man and wife are eligible, may they buy property together and in this way increase the amount which may be guaranteed?
A. Guarantee may not exceed 60% with a maximum of $12,500 on a home loan or 50% with a maximum of $2,000 on a non-real estate loan.

46. Q. May a veteran join with a non-veteran in obtaining a loan?
A. Yes, but the guaranteed part only applies to that share of the loan belonging to the veteran and does not guarantee any part of the non-veteran's loan.

47. Q. How much can a veteran borrow and still have the loan guaranteed?
A. There is no limit on how much of a loan may be made by a lending institution to a veteran. However, real estate loans for home purposes are guaranteed only up to a maximum of $12,500. Real estate loans for farms or business purposes may be guaranteed only to a maximum of $4,000.

48. Q. For how long a period of time may a G.I. home loan be made and still be guaranteed?
A. For any period up to 30 years.

49. Q. Can a veteran get a longer term on a farm-real estate loan than on a home or business real estate loan?
A. Yes. Up to 40 years.

50. Q. For how long can a G.I. get a guaranteed loan to go into business?
    A. Such loans can be made up to ten years unless real estate is involved.
51. Q. Can a G.I. use his full entitlement for each of the three types of loans?
    A. No, he can use his entitlement only once.
52. Q. May a veteran obtain a loan in one state to buy real estate in another state?
    A. Yes. However, most lenders will not make a loan if the funds are to be used in another state.
53. Q. Could a veteran obtain a G.I. loan to be used in a foreign country?
    A. No. The property which is security for the loan must be located in the United States, its territories, or possessions.
54. Q. May a veteran qualify for a loan while attending school and receiving educational benefits?
    A. Yes, if he can qualify with the lending institution.
55. Q. Could a veteran obtain a loan to buy a farm or business which he intends to operate on a part-time basis?
    A. Yes, if the lending institution is willing to make the loan.
56. Q. What circumstances gave rise to the formation of the Home Owners' Loan Corporation?
    A. The Home Owners' Loan Corporation was formed to refinance real estate loans which were in distress during the depression in the 1930's. The government felt that the refinancing of these loans would not only aid the home owners but also the lending institutions which held the mortgages.
57. Q. How widespread were defaults on home mortgages during the depression?
    A. It has been estimated that as much as 80 per cent of the home loans were in trouble at some time during the depression.
58. Q. In what way was the Home Owners' Loan Corporation related to the Federal Housing Administration?
    A. The Home Owners' Loan Corporation was set up to refinance existing loans on real estate. The function of the F.H.A. was to encourage the lending of money to home owners by insuring the loans made by the lending institutions.
59. Q. What parts of the F.H.A. Act are of the most interest to home owners or those who are interested in home ownership?
    A. Title I of the law makes provision for insuring loans to home owners for the improvement or repair of existing buildings. Title II is concerned with the insuring of loans made by qualified lenders on one- to four-family dwellings.
60. Q. How high are the standards set by the F.H.A. for insuring loans?
    A. In general, the standards set by the F.H.A. are quite high. Not only must the property qualify, but also the credit rating of the borrower is also investigated and approved before the loan is accepted for insurance.
61. Q. Name some of the accomplishments of the Federal Housing Administration.
    A. The F.H.A. has made the amortizing loan the standard procedure on home loans. It has standardized appraising processes. It has also been instrumental in raising the construction standards, and in better planning and land utilization. The second mortgage has almost disappeared due to the high loan-to-value ratio made possible by insured loans. The mortgage market has also been extended and stabilized by the F.H.A.
62. Q. How does a lending institution become approved for making F.H.A. insured loans?
    A. The lending institution must apply to the F.H.A. for approval and answer certain questions about the firm and its practices. It must also be a corporation with assets in excess of $100,000.
63. Q. Must all loans made by an approved lending institution be F.H.A. insured loans?
    A. No. An approved lending institution has merely qualified to make insured loans, but it may make as many conventional or G.I. loans as it wishes.
64. Q. How does the insuring of loans benefit the lending institution?
    A. The insuring of loans reduces the risk of the lending firm. This makes it possible for

the lenders to make a higher percentage loan and to make longer maturity loans than would otherwise be possible.

65. Q. Does the government pay the cost of the insurance on F.H.A. loans?
A. No. The borrower pays for the cost of the insurance at a rate of ½ per cent per annum of the unpaid balance of the loan.

66. Q. What is meant by a budget loan?
A. A budget loan is one in which the monthly payments made by the borrower not only cover interest and a payment on the principal, but also one-twelfth of such expenses as taxes, insurance, assessments and other charges against the property. The lending firm keeps these payments in a reserve account and pays the charges as they become due.

67. Q. What is meant by the term "variable interest rate" in mortgage lending?
A. This term refers to that interest rate which fluctuates in relation to a certain money market instrument.

68. Q. What is the procedure for applying for an F.H.A. loan?
A. The borrower chooses an approved lender and fills out the F.H.A. forms, and indicates the location of the property to be purchased. He also gives information as to his financial condition and a short history of his employment.

69. Q. How does a prospective home buyer choose a lending institution from which to obtain a loan?
A. The buyer may choose any local institution which is qualified to make F.H.A. loans. This is just a matter of personal choice.

70. Q. What is the procedure after the application for an F.H.A. loan is filed?
A. The lending institution will look over the application to see if it is complete and also to appraise the possibility of having the loan approved. If it is satisfactory, it will be sent to a regional F.H.A. office.

71. Q. Could an approved lender purchase F.H.A. mortgages from other firms rather than originate the loans?
A. Yes. A firm could purchase insured mortgages rather than make the loans, if it prefers to do so.

72. Q. What is the secondary mortgage market?
A. The secondary mortgage market is made up of those firms who buy mortgages from the firms who originate them.

73. Q. How does the government participate in this secondary mortgage market?
A. The Federal National Mortgage Association was authorized by Congress in 1938. It was formed to provide a secondary market for insured mortgages. It is known as "Fanny May" and has the power to buy insured mortgages from lenders who need additional funds to make further loans.

74. Q. What is a conventional loan?
A. A conventional loan is any loan which is not insured or guaranteed by a governmental agency.

75. Q. How do conventional loans compare with insured and guaranteed loans as to interest rates and length of maturity?
A. Conventional loans usually have about ½ per cent to 1 per cent higher interest rates and shorter maturities than comparable insured and guaranteed loans.

76. Q. Can a lending institution refuse to make F.H.A. loans if it has funds available for loans?
A. Yes. A lending institution may refuse to make F.H.A. loans if it wishes to do so.

77. Q. What is a land sales contract, also known as a land contract?
A. The prospective purchaser of a piece of property enters into a contract with the owner of the property, whereby he agrees to purchase the property at a stated price and the owner agrees to sell. The owner gives up possession to the buyer but does not give him the title until the final payment is made. Upon the final payment being made, the owner gives the buyer a deed which completes the transfer.

78. Q. What rights would a seller under a land sales contract have in case the buyer defaulted on his payments?
A. He may dispossess the buyer and recover possession of the property. The contract usually has a clause that states that in case the owner repossesses the property all of the payments made by the buyer shall be considered rent for the period of time he was in possession.

79. Q. To what extent is the owner financing the deal under a land sales contract ?
A. The owner is actually financing all of the deal except for the down payment which the purchaser makes when he first takes possession of the property.

80. Q. Could a land sales contract be used to finance a deal where the buyer is assuming a mortgage but does not have enough cash to buy out the owner's equity?
A. Land sales contracts are often used where the buyer is assuming a mortgage which states that a second lien cannot be placed on the property, yet the purchaser does not have enough cash to buy the equity of the owner. The seller takes back a land sales contract for the difference between the selling price and the down payment and the mortgage is assumed by the buyer. If the owner wishes to "cash out," he can sell the land sales contract.

81. Q. Under what circumstances is a purchase money mortgage given?
A. A purchase money mortgage is used where the seller of the property is willing to finance the deal for the buyer. The seller takes the down payment of the buyer in cash and takes a note and a purchase money mortgage for the remainder of the selling price. It is necessary for the purchaser to record the deed before the seller records the purchase money mortgage or it will appear on the records as if the buyer were mortgaging property which is recorded in the seller's name.

82. Q. Are the rights of a mortgagee under a purchase money mortgage the same as under other mortgages?
A. In many states, the rights of the mortgagee of a purchase money mortgage are the same as any other. However, it would constitute a second lien if there were an existing mortgage on the property at the time of the sale. In other states, the rights of the mortgagee are limited. The most common limitation is that in case of foreclosure where the property did not sell for enough to cover the unpaid balance of the purchase money mortgage, the holder of the mortgage could not get a deficiency judgment on the remainder.

83. Q. Do purchase money mortgages carry about the same interest rates as other mortgages?
A. The interest rates on all mortgages vary with the risk involved; this also applies to purchase money mortgages. Since such mortgages are often used to finance deals which would not be accepted by institutional lenders, the rates may be somewhat higher.

84. Q. Why do lending agencies usually prefer a conventional mortgage over a V.A. mortgage?
A. Because the interest returns are higher.

85. Q. Can a purchaser from a veteran assume the existing mortgage?
A. Yes.

86. Q. What is the difference between a conventional loan, an F.H.A. loan and a G.I. loan?
A. In a conventional loan, the mortgagee deals on its own and is not protected in any way by any government agency. In an F.H.A., the lending institution, the government, (F.H.A.), reduces the risk of the lending firm. In a G.I. loan, if the loan is not paid, the V.A. will guarantee a certain amount of the loan. The money in each case is loaned by the lending institution.

87. Q. What are the two basic reasons for discount points?
A. 1. To allow the lender to compensate for different risks.
2. Attract money that would not otherwise be available at a fixed rate of interest.

88. Q. How can a veteran be certain that the buyer of his home will assume the veteran's debt responsibilities?
    A. The veteran should include a provision in the sales contract that the purchaser will assume all his loan obligations and that the sale will not be consummated unless the V.A. and the lender approve the income and credit of the purchaser.
89. Q. How can this be accomplished?
    A. The veteran should include a provision in the sales contract that the purchaser will assume all his loan obligations and that the sale will not be consummated unless the V.A. approves the income and credit of the purchaser.
90. Q. What type of mortgage loan is not guaranteed or insured by an agency of the United States government?
    A. A conventional mortgage loan.
91. Q. What is the financial intermediary which has most recently gained prominence?
    A. The real estate investment trust.
92. Q. What share of its income must a real estate investment trust return to the owners of its shares?
    A. 90%.

True and False

1. The interest in or value of real estate in excess of mortgage indebtedness is called an equity. **T** F
2. A V.A. loan is insured by the Federal Housing Administration. T **F**
3. A borrower must make application to the local F.H.A. director for an F.H.A. loan. T **F**
4. A private lender is prohibited from lending more than 80 per cent of the market value of the property. T **F**
5. Building and loan associations generally lend only on conventional loans. **T** F
6. The building and loan associations were the first to amortize mortgage loans. **T** F
7. The mortgagee pays the costs of financing the loan. T **F**
8. Variable interest rates are interest rates which change in relation to certain instruments of the money market. **T** F
9. The "money market" is made up only of banks who lend on real estate mortgages. T **F**
10. The whole business structure of the country is based upon the assumption that responsible persons who have the ability and willingness to repay can borrow money. **T** F
11. In normal times there is not much competition for the investor's dollar. T **F**
12. At any time investors are competing with each other to obtain the best investment at the most favorable rates. **T** F
13. Interest paid for the use of money could be thought of as rent for the use of the money. **T** F
14. The interest rate which a lender can charge is usually fixed by the Federal Government. T **F**
15. The rate of interest on mortgage money at any time is determined by many complex economic factors. **T** F
16. The risk involved and the future business outlook do not materially affect the interest rate on mortgages. T **F**
17. At any time the amount of money available in our banking system is controlled to a considerable extent by the Federal Reserve System. **T** F
18. The funds which commercial banks use to lend on real estate come from the checking accounts of their depositors. T **F**
19. Banks are allowed to make loans on real estate from the savings of individuals, which are deposited in the savings accounts. **T** F
20. The funds which savings and loan associations use for real estate loans are the savings of individuals. **T** F
21. Investors tend to put their savings into the same type of investment regardless

of business conditions. T F

22. Lending institutions that lend out the savings of individuals are held to a high degree of responsibility and business judgment. T F
23. One of the principles followed by investors is to diversify their investments by putting their savings into several types of investments in order to reduce the risk. T F
24. The making of loans to individuals backed by a mortgage on real estate as security has been in common use for only about 50 years. T F
25. A mortgage is a pledge instrument that gives the mortgagee the right to seize and sell the property in case of default. T F
26. A mortgage is a debt instrument. T F
27. A mortgage and a note might be incorporated into one instrument. T F
28. A mortgage gives the mortgagee certain rights in the real property of the mortgagor. T F
29. A mortgage could be called a dead pledge for it is inoperative as long as the owner of the property makes the payments and does not violate the covenants of the mortgage. T F
30. An owner of property who has a mortgage on it could not sell the property without paying off the debt. T F
31. If a buyer purchases a property "subject to" an existing mortgage, he would be liable for the debt as well as the original mortgagor. T F
32. A purchaser of a residence "assumed" an existing mortgage. He could be held responsible for the unpaid balance by the mortgagee. T F
33. When real estate is sold and the buyer assumes the mortgage, both the seller and the purchaser are liable on the unpaid balance of the mortgage. T F
34. National banks are allowed to lend up to 90% of the appraised value of a piece of real estate on a conventional loan. T F
35. National banks can make loans for only ten years or less on conventional loans. T F
36. Due to the legal restrictions placed upon national banks, they are quite conservative in their loan policies. T F
37. Savings and loan associations are much like banks because they offer checking services for their depositors. T F
38. The early savings and loan associations were conceived as a cooperative attempt to help members finance their homes. T F
39. Savings and loan associations still hold to the policy of making loans only to their own members. T F
40. The savings and loan associations were pioneers in the use of the monthly payment amortizing loan. T F
41. Savings and loan associations no longer encourage the small investor to deposit his savings with the firm because the cost of keeping the accounts is too great. T F
42. Savings and loan associations would be considered thrift organizations rather than banking institutions. T F
43. Most lending institutions feel that amortizing loans are beneficial to both lender and borrower. T F
44. Life insurance companies make only a small percentage of the real estate loans. T F
45. Life insurance companies are an important factor in providing funds for investment in mortgage loans. T F
46. Total assets of savings and loan associations are greater than those of life insurance companies. T F
47. Real estate mortgages make up the largest single type of investment held by insurance companies. T F
48. Most insured and guaranteed loans made by life insurance companies are for 25 years or longer. T F
49. Most insurance companies make both insured and conventional loans. T F
50. The present-day amortizing loans make it necessary for insurance companies to

continually make loans in order to keep their funds earning interest. T F

51. In recent years insurance companies have not increased their investments in mortgages as much percentagewise as some of their other investments. T F
52. Mutual savings banks are the smallest group of lending institutions that make loans on real estate. T F
53. The mutual savings banks pioneered the use of the long-term amortizing loan. T F
54. The mutual savings banks are true banks because they accept checking deposits as well as savings used for loans. T F
55. People who have funds to loan are often more willing to lend it on real estate because they feel it is more secure than on many other investments. T F
56. Private lenders will seldom accept loans on real estate if institutional lenders have turned down the loan. T F
57. Loans made by private individuals are often at higher rates of interest than those made by institutions due to the extra risk involved. T F
58. Institutional lenders are supervised by government agencies because of the responsibilities they undertake with regard to investment of funds belonging to others. T F
59. Firms which make loans on real estate have little responsibility to the public because they represent only the investor. T F
60. Veterans of both World War I and II are eligible for G.I. loans. T F
61. Each eligible veteran has a total entitlement of $7,500 for home loan purposes. T F
62. G.I. loans are made by the Federal Government directly to the individual. T F
63. The government guarantees only 60% of a loan on a home. T F
64. G.I. loans cannot carry more than a 5 1/4% interest rate. T F
65. The purchase price of a property on which a G.I. loan is granted can be slightly higher than the appraised value of the property. T F
66. If a veteran defaults on a loan and the government must pay some of the loss, he is indebted to the Veterans Administration for the amount of the loss. T F
67. A non-veteran cannot purchase a property from a veteran and assume the G.I. loan. T F
68. In case of default and foreclosure on a G.I. loan, the Veterans Administration will pay in cash the guaranteed percentage of the loss to the lender. T F
69. The unmarried widow of an eligible veteran who had not used his entitlement would be eligible for a G.I. loan. T F
70. A lender cannot charge a veteran closing costs on a loan even though the costs appear to be reasonable. T F
71. A veteran could obtain a G.I. loan to buy either a home or a farm. T F
72. A lending institution cannot refuse to give a veteran a loan if the veteran has a certified entitlement. T F
73. A veteran could get a G.I. loan to buy a duplex if he were going to live in part of it. T F
74. Only one entitlement is allowed even though both husband and wife are veterans. T F
75. The government role in mortgage financing is principally that of guarantor or insurer for the purpose of protecting the lender. T F
76. A lending institution may make G.I. loans for any period up to 30 years. T F
77. A veteran could not be receiving education benefits and obtain a G.I. loan at the same time. T F
78. Veterans' loans are the budget type where each monthly payment includes payment on such things as insurance, taxes, etc. T F
79. A lending institution cannot require a down payment if the veteran is buying a new house. T F
80. The Home Owners' Loan Corporation was set up during the depression to insure loans of individuals who wanted to build or buy a home. T F

81. The F.H.A. makes loans directly to home owners. T **F**
82. Most home loans which are insured by the F.H.A. are made under Title II of the Act. **T** F
83. Title I provides for unsecured home improvement and repair loans. **T** F
84. The F.H.A. believes that the principal security for a loan is in the property itself. T **F**
85. The government pays the cost of insuring F.H.A. loans. T **F**
86. F.H.A. loans are budget type loans in which each monthly payment includes part payment of taxes, insurance, and other such expenses. **T** F
87. A borrower may choose any approved lending institution from which to obtain an F.H.A. loan. **T** F
88. Lending institutions cannot refuse to accept an application for an F.H.A. loan if they have available funds to loan. T **F**
89. The "Fanny May" organization was set up by the government to create a secondary mortgage market to which lending institutions could sell insured mortgages when they needed funds for additional loans. **T** F
90. The F.H.A. has been forced to foreclose on only about 1% of the real estate on which it has insured loans. **T** F
91. The purpose of the discount in real estate financing is to increase the yield to the lender. **T** F
92. Conventional loans are made by both individuals and lending institutions. **T** F
93. A conventional loan could not be an amortizing loan. T **F**
94. The F.H.A. considers the credit rating of the individual as well as the security of the property when approving a loan to be insured. **T** F
95. Conventional loans usually carry a higher interest rate because they are not insured or guaranteed. **T** F
96. A conventional loan could not be a budget mortgage. T **F**
97. A land sales contract is just another type of mortgage. T **F**
98. Title to property financed by a land sales contract remains in the seller or in the hands of the escrow agent until the final payment is made. **T** F
99. The interest rate on land sales contracts is usually higher than on most mortgages. **T** F
100. The seller of a piece of property under a land sales contract could not sell the contract because the buyer of the property might object. T **F**
101. Land sales contracts are sometimes used to finance deals where the lender on the existing mortgage will not allow a second mortgage. **T** F
102. If a deal using a land sales contract is closed through escrow, the seller would give a deed to the escrow agent made out in the name of the buyer. **T** F
103. When a mortgage has been paid off, the mortgagor should have the mortgagee sign a satisfaction of the mortgage and record this in order to clear the title of the lien. **T** F
104. Most firms who make construction loans do it in order to obtain a "permanent" loan on the property when the building is completed. **T** F
105. A construction loan requires little supervision by the lender because the builder has agreed to build according to plans and specifications. T **F**
106. The ability of a broker to find adequate financing for his prospects is one of the most important factors in making sales. **T** F
107. The government by using its controls over the mortgage market should attempt to promote an orderly market and to prevent too much or too little available mortgage money. **T** F
108. If a note given in a mortgage transaction is later outlawed by the Statute of Limitations, it would also extinguish the mortgage. **T** F
109. Profit on the sale of real property which has been held six months or longer may be classified as a capital gain and maximum Federal Tax would be about 25 per cent. **T** F
110. Congress regulates the interest to be charged upon F.H.A. loans. **T** F

111. An F.H.A. mortgage gives the purchaser greater security as to construction than does a conventional mortgage. T F
112. Endowment funds may not be loaned out on individual mortgages. T F
113. A single mortgage can be part conventional and part F.H.A. T F
114. A mortgage is similar to a land purchase contract in that it permits the purchase of a property through periodic payments. T F
115. It is possible to procure a G.I. loan to purchase livestock and equipment for a farm. T F
116. A residence subject to a lien resulting from a G.I. guaranteed loan may not be sold except to another qualified veteran. T F
117. The agency of the Federal Government which insures a V.A. loan is the Veterans Loan Association. T F
118. Under all circumstances an F.H.A. insured loan may be paid in full before maturity without the payment of a "bonus" charge. T F
119. The agency which insures an F.H.A. loan is the Home Owners' Loan Corporation. T F
120. A minor part of the funds invested by savings and loan associations comes from checking accounts. T F
121. Insurance companies operate under such restrictive laws that they are of minor importance in mortgage lending. T F
122. Savings and loan associations are major factors in mortgage lending because this is the reason for their existence. T F
123. The large increase in recent years in time and savings deposits of commercial banks have made them much more active in the field of real estate financing. T F
124. Commercial banks are prohibited by federal regulations from acting as mortgage loan correspondents for other investors. T F
125. In addition to the F.H.A. and V.A. regulations which govern such mortgages, the state laws are restrictive as to interest rate and term of loan. T F
126. Savings and loan associations cater primarily to investors of large sums of money. T F
127. Savings and loan associations specialize in loans secured by single family residences. T F
128. Savings and loans are prohibited by law from investment in loans secured by apartment houses. T F
129. Yield and diversification of investment are major considerations for all investors. T F
130. In 1920 assets of life insurance companies were $8 billion and, toward the end of 1973, their assets had increased to over $250 billion. T F
131. Real estate mortgages as a group are the major investment of life insurance companies. T F
132. Real estate mortgages compose one group of the major investments of life insurance companies. T F
133. Corporate securities are the major investment by groups of life insurance companies. T F
134. Life insurance companies, because they are regulated by government, need not concern themselves if loans are not repaid. T F
135. In spite of longer mortgage terms, that is, up to 30 years, mortgage loans have an average life of 12 to 13 years. T F
136. Yearly pay off and amortization of real estate loans held by life insurance companies requires reinvestment. T F
137. During the past two or three years prior to 1971, life insurance companies have favored mortgage loans. T F
138. Rate is only secondarily important in the investment of mortgage funds. T F
139. Some major insurance companies are taking equity positions in some of the larger loans they place on income producing properties. T F
140. In addition to charging interest on mortgage loans, life insurance companies sometimes require a percentage of the rents received by the owner-borrower

over a specified minimum. T F

141. Charges in addition to interest which increase yield are not a hedge against inflation. T F
142. Mutual savings banks are for the most part located west of the Mississippi River. T F
143. Mutual savings banks invest nationwide in accordance with the regulations under which they operate. T F
144. Although the smallest group of lending institutions, mutual savings banks are major contributors to mortgage lending. T F
145. Pension funds are decreasing their mortgage investments. T F
146. Institutional lenders lend the savings of other people. T F
147. Conscientious, careful lending benefits borrower and lender. T F
148. VA guaranteed loans carry a greater risk than F.H.A. insured loans. T F
149. Even though a veteran uses his entitlement to a G.I. loan, it may be "recomputed" for a valid reason. T F
150. Veterans who default on G.I. mortgage loans cannot be held liable for the loss incurred. T F
151. G.I. loans and F.H.A. loans require appraisal approval by the respective agency of the government for the protection of the purchaser only. T F
152. The Secretary of Housing and Urban Development (HUD) sets the maximum rate on FHA loans within the limits of the authority given him by Congress. T F
153. The Veterans Administration does not guarantee mortgage loans which exceed "reasonable value." T F
154. Legal maximum rates as set for V.A. and F.H.A. loans become in reality "minimum" rates. T F
155. Variable interest rates refer to those rates charged by different lenders. T F
156. Regulation Z implements the "Truth-in-Lending Act." T F
157. The term "floating" rate refers to that interest rate used in financing ocean-going vessels. T F
158. The F.H.A. Digest of Insurable Loans provides an overall view of the National Housing Act. T F
159. Private mortgage insurance corporations are an important factor in providing savings and loan associations with substantial benefits from careful underwriting of loans. T F
160. A "basis point" is equal to $^{1}/_{100}$ th of one per cent. T F
161. Constant payment tables refer to a method of computation of periodic payments of interest and principal. T F
162. G.N.M.A. securities have revolutionized the approach of lenders to mortgage financing. T F
163. The use of Ginnie-Mae backed securities discourages the sale of fractional interests in blocks of mortgages. T F
164. Investors in G.N.M.A. mortgage-backed securities secure yields comparable to those offered by high grade corporate issues. T F
165. G.N.M.A. mortgage-backed securities are backed by the full faith and credit of the United States government. T F
166. Certified entitlement to a V.A. mortgage guarantees the G.I. a mortgage. T F
167. The secondary mortgage market deals in second mortgages. T F
168. An F.H.A. mortgage is one usually held by a private lending agency and insured by the government. T F
169. A simple mortgage can be part F.H.A. and part V.A. T F
170. The annual interest rate on a \$5,000 loan is $7\frac{1}{2}\%$ when the quarterly payments to principal and interest are \$139.55 and the term of the loan is 15 years. T F
171. A broker should advise a buyer as to his legal rights where there is a dispute between buyer and mortgagee. T F
172. At the closing of a real estate transaction, the seller can refuse to accept the

buyer's personal check in payment of the consideration price. T F

173. A broker is entitled to a fee for preparing the mortgage papers. T F
174. Real Estate Investment Trusts were designed only for ownership of real estate. T F
175. Real Estate Investment Trusts are owned by "advisors." T F
176. Owners of shares in Real Estate Investment Trusts may be compared to owners of common stock in a corporation. T F
177. Points on the mortgage are paid by the buyer. T F

Multiple Choice

1. The form of mortgage often used in mortgage financing is
   I. The open-end mortgage.
   II. The blanket mortgage.
   (a) I only.
   (b) II only.
   (c) both I and II.
   (d) neither I nor II.
2. The best way for a home owner to liquidate a mortgage debt is
   I. Employer withholding monthly payments from the mortgagor's salary.
   II. Amortization on a monthly basis.
   (a) I only.
   (b) II only.
   (c) both I and II.
   (d) neither I nor II.
3. Construction loans for apartment buildings are paid off
   I. Through amortization.
   II. By means of permanent financing at the end of construction.
   (a) I only.
   (b) II only.
   (c) both I and II.
   (d) neither I nor II.
4. One of the following does not apply to personal risk in mortgage lending
   I. Character.
   II. Call loan.
   (a) I only.
   (b) II only.
   (c) both I and II.
   (d) neither I nor II.
5. In lending funds in the mortgage market, the mortgagee must guard particularly against
   I. Obsolescence, whether functional or economic.
   II. The inability of the borrower to repay the debt.
   (a) I only.
   (b) II only.
   (c) both I and II.
   (d) neither I nor II.
6. Funds for conventional single family mortgage loans are supplied by
   I. "Fannie Mae."
   II. Savings and loan associations.
   (a) I only.
   (b) II only.
   (c) both I and II.
   (d) neither I nor II.
7. The greater risk to a mortgage lender is found in
   I. Construction loans.
   II. Permanent loans.
   (a) I only.

(b) II only.
(c) both I and II.
(d) neither I nor II.

8. Amortization of mortgage loans was first developed by
   I. F.H.A.
   II. Commercial banks.
   (a) I only.
   (b) II only.
   (c) both I and II.
   (d) neither I nor II.
9. Forces which determine interest rates for mortgage loans are
   I. Economic.
   II. Local.
   (a) I only.
   (b) II only.
   (c) both I and II.
   (d) neither I nor II.
10. Banks lend money for long term mortgage loans from
    I. Demand deposits.
    II. Time deposits.
    (a) I only.
    (b) II only.
    (c) both I and II.
    (d) neither I nor II.
11. Federal Savings and Loan Associations make a major contribution through their lending activities to
    I. Standardized underwriting requirements.
    II. Housing for the population of the United States.
    (a) I only.
    (b) II only.
    (c) both I and II.
    (d) neither I nor II.
12. The largest sources in single-family home financing on a conventional basis are
    I. National banks.
    II. Savings and loan associations.
    (a) I only.
    (b) II only.
    (c) both I and II.
    (d) neither I nor II.
13. Generally, insurance company mortgage lending is restricted to a maximum of
    I. 75% of appraisal.
    II. 66 ⅔% of appraisal.
    (a) I only.
    (b) II only.
    (c) both I and II.
    (d) neither I nor II.
14. "Overage" in the contract for a mortgage loan refers to
    I. Properties over 45 years old.
    II. That yield on the loan which exceeds the interest rate and has its basis in the achievement of rental income by the borrower-owner in excess of a set minimum.
    (a) I only.
    (b) II only.
    (c) both I and II.
    (d) neither I nor II.

15. Nationwide, which catagory of financial institutions has the smallest total dollar investment in mortgage loans
    I. National banks.
    II. Savings and loan associations.
    (a) I only.
    (b) II only.
    (c) both I and II.
    (d) neither I nor II.
16. Mortgage loans entailing more than average risk are usually made by
    I. Pension funds.
    II. Private lenders.
    (a) I only.
    (b) II only.
    (c) both I and II.
    (d) neither I nor II.
17. Under Title 38, United States Code (formerly the Servicemen's Readjustment Act of 1944, as amended), each eligible veteran has an entitlement for loan purposes in the aggregate amount of
    I. $12,500.
    II. $15,000.
    (a) I only.
    (b) II only.
    (c) both I and II.
    (d) neither I nor II.
18. The amount of loan guarantee provided by the Veterans Administration is restricted to a $12,500 maximum, but not more than what percentage of the loan
    I. $66\frac{2}{3}\%$.
    II. 75%.
    (a) I only.
    (b) II only.
    (c) both I and II.
    (d) neither I nor II.
19. The statutory rate of interest for VA guaranteed (G. I.) loans under the present regulations is
    I. 8%.
    II. A rate to meet the mortgage market.
    (a) I only.
    (b) II only.
    (c) both I and II.
    (d) neither I nor II.
20. Effective July 8, 1974, VA and FHA interest rate ceilings were set at
    I. 9%.
    II. $8\frac{1}{2}\%$.
    (a) I only.
    (b) II only.
    (c) both I and II.
    (d) neither I nor II.
21. Regardless of the term stated in the single family mortgage contract, these loans are usually paid off in
    I. 5 to 10 years.
    II. 20 years.
    (a) I only.
    (b) II only.
    (c) both I and II.
    (d) neither I nor II.

22. If a non veteran purchases a property encumbered by a VA guaranteed or insured mortgage, the loan
    I. Must be repaid.
    II. Can be assumed by the purchaser.
    (a) I only.
    (b) II only.
    (c) both I and II.
    (d) neither I nor II.
23. Entitlement to a G. I. loan for veterans
    I. Expires for World War II veterans on July 15, 1982.
    II. Expires for veterans of the Korean conflict on January 1, 1999.
    (a) I only.
    (b) II only.
    (c) both I and II.
    (d) neither I nor II.
24. For certain eligible post war veterans, eligibility
    I. Expires on January 1, 1999.
    II. Has no time limit.
    (a) I only.
    (b) II only.
    (c) both I and II.
    (d) neither I nor II.
25. Commercial banks are classified as either
    I. Nationally chartered.
    II. State chartered.
    (a) I only.
    (b) II only.
    (c) both I and II.
    (d) neither I nor II.
26. Many states permit lending institutions to lend above the statutory ratio
    I. If the excess above the statutory limit is insured against default.
    II. If the loan is exceptionally well collateralized.
    (a) I only.
    (b) II only.
    (c) both I and II.
    (d) neither I nor II.
27. A land sale or instalment purchase contract can sometimes be used as a
    I. Vendor's lien.
    II. A junior financing instrument.
    (a) I only.
    (b) II only.
    (c) both I and II.
    (d) neither I nor II.
28. Discounts or "points" in mortgage lending refer to
    I. A charge to the buyer.
    II. A reduction in the price of the real estate purchased.
    (a) I only.
    (b) II only.
    (c) both I and II.
    (d) neither I nor II.
29. "Points" are determined by
    I. The American Bankers Association.
    II. Conditions in the money market.
    (a) I only.
    (b) II only.

(c) both I and II.
(d) neither I nor II.

30. In order to qualify as an approved FHA lender, a corporation must have assets of
I. At least $50,000.
II. At least $100,000.
(a) I only.
(b) II only.
(c) both I and II.
(d) neither I nor II.

31. Mutual savings banks are closely allied in method of operation to
I. Commercial banks.
II. Savings and loan associations.
(a) I only.
(b) II only.
(c) both I and II.
(d) neither I nor II.

32. Life insurance companies are interested in mortgage loans as investments because of
I. Yield.
II. Security.
(a) I only.
(b) II only.
(c) both I and II.
(d) neither I nor II.

33. Pension funds as mortgage lenders are a force in the mortgage market. During recent years, their position with regard to this type of lending has
I. Increased.
II. Decreased.
(a) I only.
(b) II only.
(c) both I and II.
(d) neither I nor II.

34. If your responsibility was the investment of funds for a life insurance company, you would be primarily interested in
I. Returning funds available for investment to the geographic area where they were generated.
II. Debentures of large companies.
(a) I only.
(b) II only.
(c) both I and II.
(d) neither I nor II.

35. The secondary mortgage market refers to
I. Sources of second mortgage loans.
II. Investors who provide mortgage funds by purchasing them from originators.
(a) I only.
(b) II only.
(c) both I and II.
(d) neither I nor II.

36. Under the VA guaranty program, upon foreclosure, the Veteran's Administration may
I. Purchase the property.
II. Pay the guaranty.
(a) I only.
(b) II only.
(c) both I and II.
(d) neither I nor II.

37. The FHA insurance of mortgage loans provides protection to the
    I. Lender.
    II. Borrower.
        (a) I only.
        (b) II only.
        (c) both I and II.
        (d) neither I nor II.
38. The FHA made major contributions to mortgage lending by
    I. Provided underwriting standards.
    II. Helped to provide a secondary mortgage market so that funds available in capital surplus areas could be invested in areas of capital shortage.
        (a) I only.
        (b) II only.
        (c) both I and II.
        (d) neither I nor II.
39. FHA credit underwriting of loans for insurance has been responsible for
    I. Low foreclosure rates.
    II. The decreased quality of housing.
        (a) I only.
        (b) II only.
        (c) both I and II.
        (d) neither I nor II.
40. In the case of a land sales contract, a seller of real estate may
    I. Foreclose on the mortgage instrument.
    II. "Cash out," that is, sell the instrument.
        (a) I only.
        (b) II only.
        (c) both I and II.
        (d) neither I nor II.
41. A purchase money mortgage is
    I. That which is taken back by the seller from the buyer at the time of the sale.
    II. Of no value.
        (a) I only.
        (b) II only.
        (c) both I and II.
        (d) neither I nor II.
42. Discounts in the field of mortgage financing may be defined as
    I. A percentage of the mortgage amount paid by a seller to a lender in order to increase the lender's yield on the loan.
    II. Useful in meeting market conditions where the interest rate is fixed by law.
        (a) I only.
        (b) II only.
        (c) both I and II.
        (d) neither I nor II.
43. The yield on mortgage investments is controlled by
    I. The FHA.
    II. Individual states through usury laws.
        (a) I only.
        (b) II only.
        (c) both I and II.
        (d) neither I nor II.
44. The use of pledges is common to
    I. Savings and loan associations.
    II. Commercial banks.
        (a) I only.

(b) II only.
(c) both I and II.
(d) neither I nor II.

45. The use of pledges has been
 I. Eliminated.
 II. Of benefit as a financing vehicle for real estate.
 (a) I only.
 (b) II only.
 (c) both I and II.
 (d) neither I nor II.
46. Conventional mortgage loans
 I. Are sometimes insured in part by private mortgage insurance companies.
 II. Are insured by the Federal Housing Administration or guaranteed by the Veterans Administration.
 (a) I only.
 (b) II only.
 (c) both I and II.
 (d) neither I nor II.
47. With respect to encouraging the growth of the fully amortized loan, the Federal Housing Administration has
 I. Made a major contribution to mortgage lending.
 II. Been able to regulate conventional financing.
 (a) I only.
 (b) II only.
 (c) both I and II.
 (d) neither I nor II.
48. The Federal Housing Administration was formed in
 I. 1900 and known as the Home Owners Loan Corporation.
 II. 1913 and a subsidiary activity of the Federal Reserve System.
 (a) I only.
 (b) II only.
 (c) both I and II.
 (d) neither I nor II.
49. In the case of a V.A. guaranteed or insured loan, the owner-borrower may
 I. Sell the property subject to the loan.
 II. Not repay the loan ahead of schedule.
 (a) I only.
 (b) II only.
 (c) both I and II.
 (d) neither I nor II.
50. A mortgagee, in the case of a G. I. loan, is required to
 I. Report all costs to the Veterans Administration.
 II. Appraise the real estate.
 (a) I only.
 (b) II only.
 (c) both I and II.
 (d) neither I nor II.
51. The Veterans Administration will now guarantee loans wherein the purchase price exceeds the reasonable value if
 I. The veteran pays in cash from his own resources the difference between purchase price and appraisal (reasonable value) and the loan does not exceed the appraisal.
 II. Signs the required certification.
 (a) I only.
 (b) II only.
 (c) both I and II.

(d) neither I nor II.

52. A prospective home buyer desiring an F.H.A. insured loan applies to
    I. The F.H.A.
    II. An insured savings and loan association or a commercial bank.
    (a) I only.
    (b) II only.
    (c) both I and II.
    (d) neither I nor II.
53. An authorized agent appointed by a secondary market mortgage lender to process and service its mortgage loan investments is described as
    I. A loan investigator.
    II. A mortgage loan correspondent.
    (a) I only.
    (b) II only.
    (c) both I and II.
    (d) neither I nor II.
54. A requirement of a borrower under an F.H.A. insured loan is that he
    I. Not have other than the mortgage debt in connection with the transaction.
    II. Certify that he will occupy the premises if that is a condition of the FHA approval.
    (a) I only.
    (b) II only.
    (c) both I and II.
    (d) neither I nor II.
55. Mortgage lending is a dominant factor in the development of
    I. Highway systems.
    II. City and rural communities.
    (a) I only.
    (b) II only.
    (c) both I and II.
    (d) neither I nor II.
56. The following refers to those institutions which function to make credit available to borrowers
    I. Financial intermediaries.
    II. F.H.A., V.A., G.N.M.A. and F.N.M.A.
    (a) I only.
    (b) II only.
    (c) both I and II.
    (d) neither I nor II.
57. Rent for the use of money is called
    I. Monthly finance charge.
    II. Interest.
    (a) I only.
    (b) II only.
    (c) both I and II.
    (d) neither I nor II.
58. The rate of interest on a mortgage loan charged to a customer is determined by many complex economic, social and legal factors. Those most important are
    I. Applicable state usury laws.
    II. The Federal Reserve System.
    (a) I only.
    (b) II only.
    (c) both I and II.
    (d) neither I nor II.
59. Funds for real estate investment are principally obtained from
    I. Savings of firms and individuals.

II. The Eurodollar market.
(a) I only.
(b) II only.
(c) both I and II.
(d) neither I nor II.

60. Banks are restricted from using one of the following sources of funds for investment in real estate mortgage loans
I. Checking accounts.
II. Capital.
(a) I only.
(b) II only.
(c) both I and II.
(d) neither I nor II.

61. One of the basic principles of investment is
I. Invest all funds available.
II. Diversification.
(a) I only.
(b) II only.
(c) both I and II.
(d) neither I nor II.

62. A borrower who gives a creditor a mortgage which pledges property as security may be said to have
I. Sold his property.
II. Given a "dead pledge."
(a) I only.
(b) II only.
(c) both I and II.
(d) neither I nor II.

63. One reason for increased activity on the part of commercial banks in real estate financing is
I. Desire for more secured loans.
II. Changes in Comptroller and Federal Reserve regulations.
(a) I only.
(b) II only.
(c) both I and II.
(d) neither I nor II.

64. Savings and loan associations have changed in character over the years so that they are now
I. Functioning like commercial banks.
II. A major source of single family mortgage lending.
(a) I only.
(b) II only.
(c) both I and II.
(d) neither I nor II.

65. Savings and loan associations were pioneers in
I. Use of amortizing loans.
II. Functioning as financial intermediaries to assist purchasers of single-family houses and to serve the relatively small investor.
(a) I only.
(b) II only.
(c) both I and II.
(d) neither I nor II.

66. During recent years, the assets of life insurance companies have changed. That change has been
I. Brought about by regulation.

II. A phenomenal increase in assets.
(a) I only.
(b) II only.
(c) both I and II.
(d) neither I nor II.

67. The availability of life insurance funds for mortgage lending is directly affected by
I. Bond and direct placement yields.
II. Applicable laws.
(a) I only.
(b) II only.
(c) both I and II.
(d) neither I nor II.

68. Some major insurance companies have taken equity positions as part of the loan contract. This applies to
I. Residential loans.
II. Loans on small shopping centers.
(a) I only.
(b) II only.
(c) both I and II.
(d) neither I nor II.

69. Mutual savings banks are concentrated in the eastern United States. They widened their area of investment
I. With the advent of FHA and VA guaranteed loans.
II. After World War I.
(a) I only.
(b) II only.
(c) both I and II.
(d) neither I nor II.

70. Institutional lenders, because they undertake the responsibility for lending the savings of others are
I. Carefully controlled by law.
II. Evidence a high degree of responsibility.
(a) I only.
(b) II only.
(c) both I and II.
(d) neither I nor II.

71. Once a veteran uses his eligibility for a VA guaranteed or insured loan, he can acquire another such loan if he is eligible for
I. Reenlistment in the armed forces.
II. Disability compensation.
(a) I only.
(b) II only.
(c) both I and II.
(d) neither I nor II.

72. After foreclosure by a lender of a VA guaranteed or insured loan, the Veterans Administration may
I. Pay the guaranteed portion of the loan to the lender and permit the lender to dispose of the property.
II. Purchase the property from the lender for the unpaid balance of the loan.
(a) I only.
(b) II only.
(c) both I and II.
(d) neither I nor II.

73. The buyer of a property subject to a mortgage loan
I. Assumes complete liability for repayment of the debt.

II. Does not assume any liability unless he enters into a contract of assumption between himself and the seller-borrower.
(a) I only.
(b) II only.
(c) both I and II.
(d) neither I nor II.

74. A buyer who assumes a mortgage loan
I. Takes responsibility for repayment of the debt.
II. Needs financial assistance.
(a) I only.
(b) II only.
(c) both I and II.
(d) neither I nor II.

75. In 1933, the Home Owners Loan Corporation was formed to help in refinancing mortgage loans in default. Foreclosure filings were then
I. Being handled by the F.H.A.
II. Almost 1000 per day.
(a) I only.
(b) II only.
(c) both I and II.
(d) neither I nor II.

76. The Truth-in-Lending Act, implemented by Regulation Z, was passed by Congress in order to
I. More clearly disclose costs of borrowing to potential debtors and give them an opportunity to compare such costs.
II. Protect lenders from unscrupulous borrowers.
(a) I only.
(b) II only.
(c) both I and II.
(d) neither I nor II.

77. A publication by the Federal Housing Administration, which gives an overall view of the FHA programs, is
I. FHA Underwriting Manual.
II. Digest of Insurable Loans.
(a) I only.
(b) II only.
(c) both I and II.
(d) neither I nor II.

78. F.H.A. insured loans provide insurance coverage against default to
I. Both borrower and lender.
II. Lender only.
(a) I only.
(b) II only.
(c) both I and II.
(d) neither I nor II.

79. F.H.A. foreclosures are
I. High because of the low downpayments.
II. Low because of effective underwriting.
(a) I only.
(b) II only.
(c) both I and II.
(d) neither I nor II.

80. It is the opinion of some students of mortgage lending that the FHA has contributed materially to
I. Local building codes.

II. Standardization of mortgage loan underwriting.
(a) I only.
(b) II only.
(c) both I and II.
(d) neither I nor II.

81. In the field of conventional mortgage lending, private mortgage insurance companies have made important contributions. These are
I. Provided a review of the proposed investment by qualified underwriting specialists.
II. Provided insurance of a portion of the loan against default.
(a) I only.
(b) II only.
(c) both I and II.
(d) neither I nor II.

82. In order to simplify the calculation of mortgage payments, we have available a set of tables which express payments of interest and principal as a percentage. These tables are called
I. Constant payment tables.
II. Interest percentage tables.
(a) I only.
(b) II only.
(c) both I and II.
(d) neither I nor II.

83. Determining the needs and abilities of the prospective purchaser with a suitable property is known as
I. Underwriting the risk.
II. Qualifying the prospect.
(a) I only.
(b) II only.
(c) both I and II.
(d) neither I nor II.

84. When the FHA insures a lender against default, the insurance
I. Carries the full faith and credit of the United States Government.
II. Is backed by the insurance fund established by the Federal Housing Administration.
(a) I only.
(b) II only.
(c) both I and II.
(d) neither I nor II.

85. A mortgage loan made by a private lender is always a
I. Conventional mortgage loan.
II. An open mortgage.
(a) I only.
(b) II only.
(c) both I and II.
(d) neither I nor II.

Chapter 5

MORTGAGES

MORTGAGES CONSTITUTE a very important phase in the development and growth of home ownership. They represent an extension of long-term credit, and the function of mortgage-lending may be said to be to promote the economic, social, and financial welfare of the community. Mortgages are also recognized as a dominant factor in the development of city and rural communities through promotion of home, farm, commercial, industrial, and investment ownership.

Definition and history

A mortgage is a pledge of real estate as collateral security for the repayment of money or the performance of some act. Since early days the practice of pledging property for repayment of a debt has been prevalent. The mortgage grew out of the pledges of land for debt by the Anglo-Saxons. The early encumbrances operated in a very summary manner. If the debtor failed to meet his debt upon the exact day due, the pledged land became the absolute property of the creditor. A wide difference between the value of the land and the amount of the debt was of no consequence. This resulted at times in such injustice and hardship that the courts began to interfere. The legal principle, Equity of Redemption, was then developed which permitted the debtor, within a statutory period, to repay the debt together with a penalty in the form of interest and to reclaim his property. The pendulum of justice now swung to the other extreme, and a creditor taking property for nonpayment of a debt found it difficult to dispose of the same because a purchaser was reluctant to buy or improve since the debtor might turn up and demand the return of his property. The courts again stepped in and allowed the creditor to file a bill to foreclose the debtor's equity of redemption, and a day was fixed on or before which the debtor was required to pay up or suffer his property to be lost.

This period, by statute, was usually six months or one year. Upon foreclosure on the mortgage the property is sold at public sale by the sheriff. Under a procedure, known as *strict foreclosure,* if the debtor did not redeem his property by payment to the mortgagee, the latter then became the absolute owner. This procedure now exists in the states of Connecticut and Vermont. This modification was the forerunner of the present-day mortgage. The term mortgage comes from the old French *mort* (dead) and *gage* (pledge).

Transfer of title—lien—deed of trust

In some states a mortgage is actually a *transfer* of title to real estate upon condition, as security for the payment of a debt. Between owner and mortgagee, it is a conveyance of real estate; as to third parties, it is a lien. In other states, a mortgage is considered and treated strictly as a lien. A lien is a hold or claim which a person has upon the real property of another, as security for some debt or charge. A lien is an encumbrance and a person purchasing real property, encumbered by a mortgage, takes the property subject to the lien. In both cases of transfer of title, or lien, possession of the premises remains in the owner-debtor.

In a number of states, a deed of trust is used in lieu of a mortgage instrument. (California, Colorado, Idaho, Illinois, Minnesota, Missouri, New Mexico, Tennessee, Virginia, West Virginia and the District of Columbia). A "deed of trust" is in legal effect, a mortgage with power to sell upon default; *Johnson v. Snell,* 504 S.W. 2d 397 (Tex. 1973).

Trust deeds have the same function as a mortgage on real estate. There are three parties to a trust deed—the debtor, the lender, and the trustee, to whom the property is conveyed, as security for the accompanying promissory note of indebtedness. The note is a direct obligation from the debtor to the creditor. The primary difference between a trust deed and a mortgage is in the method of foreclosure. Upon payment of the debt, the lender, who is also known as the Beneficiary, completes a form, "Request for Full Reconveyance," the cancelled note and other instruments relating to the loan transaction. In the deed of trust, the parties are: (1) the Trustor, who is the debtor-owner, who conveys the subject premises by a Trust Deed, as security for the payment of the debt; (2) the Beneficiary, who advances the money (creditor), for whose benefit the Deed of Trust is executed; (3) the Trustee—a third person, to whom the "naked" legal title to the real estate is transferred by the Deed of Trust. In form, the Deed of Trust resembles the warranty deed to the extent that it contains such operative or granting words as "grant, bargain, sell and convey" with the limitation "to the Trustee, in trust, with power to sell", in event of a default or breach by the grantor (debtor), to reconvey the premises to the party entitled thereto. The grantor (owner), who has borrowed the money, also executes a promissory note, in the amount of the debt. The note is evidence of the debt and the deed of trust (mortgage) is security for the debt.

Upon the grantor's failure to comply with the terms of his indebtedness, the Trustee may foreclose the mortgaged property by newspaper advertisement and sale, following the prescribed statutory requirements, such as 120 days of notice of default (may vary in different states), before the sale takes place.

The proceeds of a Trustee sale are first applied to the expenses of the sale, to the obligation secured by the Trust Deed, other liens of record; and the balance, if any, to the original grantor or the owner at the time of the foreclosure.

If the mortgage debt is paid off at or before maturity, the debtor-grantor will ask for a "Request of Reconveyance". This is an authorization by the beneficiary (creditor) to the Trustee to reconvey to the grantor, or other parties entitled thereto (a purchaser from the grantor). The Trustee then makes the necessary reconveyance, and the deed is recorded. A lending institution, such as a savings and loan association, a bank authorized to conduct a trust business, title insurance or abstract company is usually selected as the Trustee.

The chief advantage to the lender is the short period necessary for foreclosure. This is important since it is an incentive to an out-of-state lending institution to make funds available for financing in that particular state. Availability of considerable funds, obviously, is a benefit to the borrower. The procedure under the Trust Deed also protects the debtor against the possibility of a deficiency judgment, and the right to cure a default at any time prior to the sale, by making the indebtedness current.

Where note secured by trust deed contained provision that if default was made in any installments, holder could declare all indebtedness due on default in any payment: *Long v. Manning,* 455 S.W. 2d 496 (Mo. 1970).

In some estates, as in Alabama and Florida, a seller has a vendor's lien for the balance of the unpaid purchase price. A vendor's lien is the right of the seller to subject the land as security for the unpaid purchase price. The lien may be enforced by a bill in equity to sell the property for the amount due. It is not good against subsequent creditors or purchasers, unless they have actual notice of it, or reference to the lien is contained in the recorded deed from seller to buyer.

Parties

There are essentially two parties in a mortgage transaction: the *mortgagor,* who is the borrower and the owner of the property and who executes a mortgage upon the property as security for payment of his debt; and the *mortgagee,* who is the lender of the money and the creditor and who receives the mortgage.

In many states, the obligor also executes a judgment note (cognovit note), in the amount of the indebtedness, as evidence of the obligation. Upon default, the creditor-mortgagee proceeds to obtain judgment on the note and then forecloses the mortgaged property, at sheriff's sale, to obtain satisfaction on the judgment. Should the mortgagee die, judgment could not be entered upon the note, but the property could be sold through court proceedings upon the mortgage.

A mortgage is a contract and the law of contracts is generally applicable. The same care urged in the preparation of a deed should also be exercised in the case of a mortgage. The mortgage instrument is comprised of two parts, the conveyance of the property and the defeasance. The latter clause provides that if the debt is repaid and the other covenants are performed by the mortgagor, then the conveyance to the mortgagee shall be null and void.

The existence of a mortgage does not prevent the property from being sold by the debtor-owner; he does not have to obtain the consent of the mortgagee-creditor. The mortgagee can look to the property as security for the debt no matter who owns it, so long as the debt remains unpaid.

However, the mortgage instrument may provide that upon the sale of the mortgaged premises, the mortgage debt shall, thereupon, become due and payable. The purchaser of land encumbered by a mortgage is called the terre tenant in a foreclosure proceedings.

Acknowledgment

It is necessary for the mortgage to be acknowledged by the mortgagor, and, like a deed, it should be recorded immediately by the mortgagee.

In the case of *Insurance Co. of America v. Holliday,* 214 N.W. 2d 273 (Neb. 1974), a mortgage was executed and acknowledged by only one of three owners of the real estate. It was signed by a second owner, but not acknowledged. The court held that it was entitled to be recorded.

Liability of purchaser of land

What liability does the purchaser of the mortgaged premises assume? Liability depends upon the type of clause used in the deed to refer to the mortgage. The clause used is a "short" or "long" form and liability differs accordingly.

Short- and long-form mortgage clause

As stated previously, the short-form clause is usually as follows: "Under and subject, nevertheless, to a certain mortgage in the present unpaid amount of $5,000.00, given by John Steele, the grantor herein to the City National Bank, dated June 16, 1971 and of record in the Recorder's Office of Piedmont County in Mortgage Book Vol. 2117, Page 316." The long-form mortgage clause reads exactly the same, with this addition: "which mortgage, the grantee expressly assumes and agrees to pay as part of the consideration herein." It must be remembered that the property is always liable for the debt. But it frequently happens, particularly in times of depressed real estate values, that the property value at a foreclosure sale is less than the mortgage indebtedness.

Deficiency judgment

During the depression years, 1931-1938, the mortgagee was entitled to a deficiency judgment for the difference between the sale price at the foreclosure sale and the mortgage debt. Very often the property was sold to the plaintiff mortgagee at a nominal price (costs and taxes) as there were no other bidders and the deficiency judgment was considerable.

The legislatures and courts, motivated by a social consciousness, recognizing the unfairness of this situation that permitted a mortgagee to acquire the property and to obtain a judgment for practically the entire debt as well, decreed that a debtor should have credit for the fair value of the property at the date of the foreclosure sale as an offset to the debt. Thus, today, if the property is sold to the plaintiff mortgagee for a nominal bid, the debtor would be liable only if the amount of the debt were in excess of the fair value of the property. But the possibility of a deficiency judgment, in *some* amount, is still very real. The mortgagee can look to the original owner for this deficiency, no matter through how many hands the property may have passed, because the original owner (mortgagor) is liable upon his contract obligation to repay the debt. Under the short-form clause the mortgagee has no right of action against the purchaser of the mortgaged premises, as there is no privity of contract, i.e., relationship, between the mortgagee and the purchaser of the property. The only way the original mortgagor could be relieved of all personal liability would be for him to insist that his purchaser do his own financing and have the original mortgage paid off and satisfied and the accompanying note returned and cancelled. If the original mortgagor actually pays the judgment entered against him by the mortgagee, he would have the right of *indemnification* against his purchaser, but not otherwise. Under the long-form clause, the mortgagee is considered a third party or creditor beneficiary under the deed contract between the owner and purchaser and would have a right to sue the purchaser of the mortgaged premises for the deficiency, proceed against the original debtor, or both. The principle of law has been stated to be: "where the contract is purely one of indemnity, the indemnitee [seller] cannot recover until he has suffered actual loss or damage; the mere incurring of liability gives him no such right; but where the contract is to protect against liability, the indemnitee may recover as soon as his liability has become fixed and established even though he has sustained no actual loss or damage at the time he seeks to recover."[1] Where the buyer takes over an existing mortgage, the protection of the seller requires the use of the long-form clause in the deed. Since the deed is the formal consummation of an agreement of sale previously entered into, it behooves the broker or attorney preparing the agreement of sale to exercise adequate care in drawing the mortgage clause in the sales agreement.

Industrial property mortgage

In the case of industrial property the mortgage covers not only the real estate but the fixtures and equipment contained therein. It will also cover under its lien such machinery—fixtures and equipment added subsequent to the execution of the mort-

[1] American and English Encyclopedia of Law, 2nd Edition, p. 178.

gage—as is necessary to the functioning of the complete plant. The fact that the additional equipment is installed long after the mortgage was given will not prevent its becoming additional security for the benefit of the mortgagee.

Blanket mortgage

Where a mortgage is given to include more than one parcel of real estate, the mortgagee cannot be required to release any one parcel from his *blanket* mortgage upon the payment of a pro-rata share of the mortgage debt. The contention that the remaining property is ample security is unavailing. The mortgagee is entitled to payment of the mortgage in full and to have all the properties as security until that time.

Release and postponement distinguished

Where a property is released from the lien of a mortgage, the rights of the creditor are forever barred insofar as the tract of land which he has released is concerned.

It is preferable for such creditor to postpone the lien of his judgment, rather than release it. Suppose "A" has a judgment for $1,000 against "B," who owns three tracts of land. "A's" judgment is a lien against all three tracts. "B" desires to build on tract No. 3 and requires a $10,000 mortgage. A bank will be unwilling to make the loan since its mortgage will not be a first lien. Thus, "B" may persuade "A" to postpone the lien of his judgment in favor of the bank's first mortgage as to tract No. 3. "A" may have ample security as tracts 1 and 2 are still subject to his lien. Or, "A" may require that "B" pay him a partial payment on his $1,000 judgment for the accommodation.

Closed and open mortgages

A mortgagee cannot be required, in the absence of a condition to the contrary, to accept payment of the indebtedness before the maturity date. Thus, a "closed" mortgage is one which cannot be paid off before maturity (e.g. "payable at the expiration of five years from the date hereof"). The mortgagee can accept payment before maturity only if he is so inclined. Some lending institutions will accept prepayment upon payment of a premium. Mortgagees, insured under the Federal Housing Act, require one per cent of the original mortgage debt as a premium if the purchaser pays off the mortgage debt with borrowed funds. An open mortgage is one which is payable "within" a certain time (within five years from the date hereof) and can be paid off at any time. Building and Loan Associations will usually permit payment of the debt at any time.

Rights of mortgagor

The rights of the mortgagor and mortgagee depend, in the main, upon the provisions of the mortgage contract. Even under the conveyance theory of mortgages, the mortgagor is regarded as the real owner of the premises. As such, he has certain fundamental rights in the property. The most important right is that of possession and the accompanying right to sell the property subject to the mortgage. He may lease the premises and is entitled to the rents, profit, and revenue arising from the property. He may dispose of the property by will, subject to the mortgage. Where the mortgagee has taken possession, the mortgagor is entitled to an accounting during his stewardship.

Rights of mortgagee

Usually the mortgagee is not entitled to possession so that his rights in the property are few. He is entitled to payment of interest and installments of principal as they become due.

Mortgagee in possession

Where the property is income-producing, the creditor may, upon default, exercise his right of *mortgagee in possession.* This is accomplished simply by notifying the tenants in possession that the mortgage is in default and demanding payment of future rents to the mortgagee. A tenant will be protected against any claim of his lessor-owner by payment to the mortgagee. If the lease antedates the mortgage, the mortgagee, in those states subscribing to the conveyance theory of a mortgage, can compel the tenant to pay future rents to the mortgagee and upon the tenant's refusal can issue a landlord's levy to collect the rent. Upon subsequent foreclosure of the property, the purchaser at the sale takes the property subject to the prior lease. If the mortgage antedates the lease, the tenant cannot be compelled to pay rent to the mortgagee, but if he does so (attorns), he must continue to pay rent during the mortgagee's tenure in possession. Should the tenant refuse the mortgagee's demand for rent, the latter's only recourse would be to foreclose the property and thereby terminate the lease. Even if the lessee attorns to the mortgagee, the plaintiff mortgagee, upon foreclosure at a later date, could nevertheless void the lease. His status as a mortgagee in possession is separate and independent from his status as owner as a result of the foreclosure proceedings.

A mortgagee in possession may also become liable for damages to a person injured on or about the mortgaged premises. If the mortgagee takes over such control and dominion of the property as to supplant the owner, then he also assumes tort liability to third persons. Mere receipt of rentals is insufficient, but actual control and possession are necessary to make a mortgagee liable. Courts in Kentucky, New York, and Pennsylvania have so held. "Actual control and possession" means collecting rents, negotiating leases, paying taxes, and authorizing necessary repairs. In short, it is necessary to establish that the mortgagee exercised those acts of dominion over the property which any owner of a similar property would do under the circumstances.[2]

Assignment of mortgage

Just as the mortgagor-owner can sell the premises subject to the mortgage, so the mortgagee can sell the mortgage. This is effected by assignment. The purchaser of the mortgage, the *assignee,* acquires the same title and interest in the mortgage which his *assignor* had, but no better title. An assignee is said to stand in the shoes of his assignor. Any claim, demand, or setoff which the mortgagor had against the mortgagee he can set up with equal facility against the mortgagee's assignee. Thus, if the mortgagor had paid the mortgagee $1,000 upon a $5,000 mortgage debt, which mortgage the mortgagee had sold to his assignee for $5,000, the mortgage purchaser could recover only $4,000 from the debtor.

Certificate of no defense, declaration of no setoff, estoppel certificate

In order to protect himself against this possibility the purchaser should obtain a statement from the mortgagor acknowledging the full indebtedness. This is known

---

[2] Miner's Saving Bank v. Thomas 140 Pa. Super Ct. 5 (1940).

as a Certificate of No Defense, an Estoppel Certificate, or a Declaration of No Setoff, by which the mortgagor admits that he owes the debt and must pay it in full at maturity. The Certificate or Declaration also serves notice, and acknowledgment of notice upon the debtor of the transfer of the mortgage. Otherwise, he would be protected in continuing payments to the original creditor. The assignee of a mortgage should also require the mortgagee to turn over to him the mortgage instrument, the accompanying note, fire insurance policy, and any other papers relating to the mortgage transaction. The mortgagee should acknowledge upon the margin of the recorded mortgage the transfer to the purchaser or execute and record an assignment. The original mortgagor can compel the mortgagee to assign the mortgage to him upon tender to the creditor of the mortgage debt. It may be expeditious to make such a tender in order to avoid the possibility of a judgment deficiency in the future.

Particularly so, if a depression should ensue, and property values diminish considerably.

Voluntary deed

It frequently happens that a mortgagor, in order to avoid foreclosure and the possibility of a deficiency judgment against him, will agree to convey the property voluntarily to the mortgagee in settlement and satisfaction of the mortgage. It is important that the deed recite that the conveyance is *intended* as a satisfaction of the debt, as the deed, per se (by itself) will not have that effect. The debtor should insist that the mortgagee satisfy the mortgage of record and return the mortgage and any other evidence of the debt to him. The mortgagee, in accepting a voluntary deed for the property, should have the records examined to make sure that he is acquiring the property free and clear of any judgments or liens. Under a voluntary conveyance, the mortgagee would acquire no better title than the mortgagor had, whereas through foreclosure proceedings, he could divest liens and judgments entered of record subsequent to his mortgage.

Sheriff's foreclosure

Upon default in any of the mortgage terms the creditor is entitled to institute foreclosure proceedings against the mortgaged property. At the public sale, the property is sold by the sheriff to the highest bidder. The deed is executed by the sheriff and gives no assurance or guarantee as to the validity of the title. The equity of the debtor is effectively wiped out. If the property brings an amount in excess of the debt, and there are no other liens to be paid, the mortgagor is entitled to the excess fund. Where a Deed of Trust is used, the instrument prescribes the procedure for sale of the mortgaged property.

Payment and satisfaction

A mortgage is usually terminated by payment and satisfaction. Where the debtor tenders payment of the debt, he is entitled to have the mortgage marked "Satisfied in full" of record and the mortgage papers returned to him. The mortgagee can personally satisfy the mortgage of record or he may do so by executing a *Satisfaction Piece,* which is a separate instrument, and duly recording it to show that the debt has been paid. After 20 years a mortgage is *presumed* to be paid and the burden of proving otherwise is upon the mortgagee. Where an old mortgage is of record and no payment or demand for payment has been made for more than 20 years, a party in interest can petition the court for an order satisfying the mortgage of record.

Chattel mortgages

There has been some activity for a "package mortgage," which will include not only the real estate but also the refrigerator, laundry equipment, furniture, and even the family car. Most states provide for mortgaging of personal property by a chattel mortgage, which is generally used to finance the purchase price of furniture, household appliances, and commercial equipment. The chattel mortgage is recorded. Title is transferred to the purchaser, and he in turn can convey title to the article in question to a new buyer, but the title is subject to the balance due under the chattel mortgage. In an examination of the title of real estate, search should also be made for chattel mortgages. A chattel mortgage differs from a conditional sale in that, while possession passes in both cases to the buyer, title, in a conditional sale, remains in the seller until the last installment is made.

Acceleration of debt

High interest rates present a problem for an owner of mortgaged premises to sell the property, contingent upon the buyer assuming and agreeing to pay the mortgage. For example, if the owner had mortgaged his property in 1970, at a mortgage rate of six percent, and the owner desires to sell his property in 1974, it is clearly apparent that it would be to the buyer's advantage to assume the mortgage, since mortgage interest rates in 1974 are eight per cent to nine and one-half per cent. To offset this possibility, many mortgages in recent years include a clause to the effect that if the mortgagor (owner) should sell the property without first obtaining consent from the mortgagee, the entire principal debt should become immediately due and payable at the option of the mortgagee. In the case of *Gunther v. White* 489 S.W. 2d 529 (Tenn. 1973), the mortgagor alleged that the acceleration clause was an illegal restraint on his right of alienation, to sell his land upon his best possible terms. The court held the acceleration clause valid.

In an earlier case of *Peoples Savings Association v. Standrd Industries, Inc.,* 257 N.E. 2d 35 (1970), the Ohio Court of Appeals held that the "due-on-sale" clause of acceleration was not illegal, inequitable or contrary to public policy.

Somewhat different is the California case of *La Sala v. American Savings and Loan Association* in 91 Cal. Rptr. 238 (1970). The mortgage, in addition to the acceleration clause, also included a restriction against encumbering the property. In this case, the mortgagor gave a second mortgage on the property and the mortgagee claimed there was a default and the debt could be accelerated to the full amount. The Appellate Court held that the subject clause was not an illegal restraint upon alienation.

Questions on Mortgages

1. Q. Why does a borrower execute a note when he executes a mortgage?
   A. The note is evidence of the debt and expedites the entry of judgment (by confession) in case of default.
2. Q. Is the consent of the mortgagee necessary in order for the debtor-owner to sell his property?
   A. Usually not; the mortgage instrument, however, may make such consent necessary.
3. Q. What two theories are there in regard to mortgages?
   A. In some states, a mortgage is a conveyance of real estate; in other states, it is considered merely a lien, similar to a judgment.
4. Q. Do all commercial banks belong to an association, which promulgates rules for lending money on mortgages?
   A. No.
5. Q. Why does a broker render a disservice to his owner when he stresses to the buyer that there is a mortgage on the property, which the buyer can assume, so that the buyer will not have to do any financing?
   A. Because the owner will continue potentially liable on the mortgage as long as it is unpaid.
6. Q. What is the difference between a first and second mortgage?
   A. A first mortgage is the one which is first recorded and has priority in distribution of funds at a foreclosure sale. A second mortgage is subordinate to a first mortgage.
7. Q. What is the difference between an open mortgage and a closed mortgage?
   A. An open mortgage can be paid off at any time before the maturity date while a closed mortgage cannot be paid off before the expiration date unless the mortgagee is willing to accept payment.
8. Q. Who are the parties to a mortgage?
   A. The mortgagor, who owns the property and borrows money upon the security of the property, and the mortgagee, who lends the money. The mortgage is executed by the mortgagor in favor of the mortgagee.
9. Q. What economic functions do mortgages serve?
   A. Mortgage credit has made possible the wider distribution of home ownership and the promotion of the economic, social, and financial welfare of the community.
10. Q. Name six sources of mortgage funds.
    A. Individuals, banks, insurance companies, savings and loan associations, endowment funds, Federal farm loan system.
11. Q. What is a junior mortgage?
    A. A mortgage in which the lender's claims against the owner's rights are subordinate to the claim of the first mortgage holder or to other liens.
12. Q. What additional security does a borrower give in addition to the mortgage proper?
    A. A note undertaking to repay the debt as specified and a warrant of attorney authorizing an attorney at law to appear for and confess judgment against the debtor in event of default.
13. Q. Can a minor mortgage real estate owned by him?
    A. Yes, but the mortgage could be disaffirmed by the infant during his minority or

within a reasonable time after attaining his majority. The creditor should deal only with the legally appointed guardian of the minor. A minor's warrant of attorney to confess judgment is absolutely void.

14. Q. What is a deed of trust?
    A. A written instrument, signed, sealed and acknowledged wherein a property owner pledges his property as security for a debt by conveying title to one or more trustees for the purpose named in the deed of trust.
15. Q. What are two functions of trustees named in a deed of trust?
    A. To foreclose in case of default under any of the terms of the deed of trust and to release the property upon payment or satisfaction of the debt.
16. Q. How many trustees are required to be named in a deed of trust?
    A. One or more. Sometimes a corporation is used as a single trustee. When individuals are used as trustees, generally two are named.
17. Q. How could a property be foreclosed or released under the terms of a deed of trust in which two trustees are named:
    (a) in the event of the death of one of the trustees?
    (b) in the event of the death of both trustees?
    (c) in the event of refusal of one or both trustees to act?
    A. (a) The surviving trustee could act.
    (b) Petition the court for the appointment of a substitute trustee or trustees.
    (c) Same as (b).
18. Q. What is meant by "first deed of trust" and "second deed of trust"?
    A. The distinction is merely the order in which they have been recorded. The one recorded first is the first deed of trust, and the one recorded next is the second deed of trust, and the priority of lien is thus established.
19. Q. What is a "deferred purchase money" deed of trust?
    A. A deed of trust pledging real estate as security for the payment of that part of the purchase price which has been deferred.
20. Q. Can a corporation execute a mortgage?
    A. Yes, if in the ordinary course of its business, but not for the purpose of increasing its indebtedness.
21. Q. Does a married woman have power to execute a mortgage on real estate owned by her?
    A. Generally a married woman can. In some states, she cannot unless she has been declared a feme sole trader.
22. Q. What is meant by the debtor's "equity of redemption"?
    A. A period of grace, *after default,* in which the debtor may redeem his property, provided it has not been foreclosed. Equity of redemption should not be confused with right of redemption which is the right the debtor has to redeem property after it has been sold for taxes.
23. Q. What indicia determine that an instrument is a mortgage rather than a conditional sale?
    A. 1. The fact that the transaction originated in an application for a loan of money.
    2. The fact that the grantor retained possession.
    3. The fact that grantor continued to pay taxes and made repairs and improvements.
    4. Gross inadequacy of price.
24. Q. Johnson has a mortgage on three contiguous tracts of equal value owned by Lee. The mortgage is for $9,000. Lee desires to sell one tract for $5,000 and asks Johnson to release the tract upon payment of $3,000. Johnson refuses. Can Lee compel Johnson to release the tract in question?
    A. No. Johnson has a "blanket mortgage" upon the three parcels and is entitled to the full security until the debt is paid. If he doesn't choose to accept a partial payment and release the tract, he cannot be compelled to do so.

25. Q. What rights does the mortgagor have?
 A. 1. The right of possession.
 2. The right to lease, deed, or will the property subject to the mortgage.
 3. The right to an accounting if the mortgagee is in possession.
26. Q. What are the rights of the mortgagee?
 A. 1. Right to interest and principal as due.
 2. Right to prevent the mortgagor from committing waste so as to lessen the mortgagee's security.
 3. Right to possession in case of a default.
27. Q. What is meant by amortization of a mortgage?
 A. Liquidation of the debt through regular periodic payments.
28. Q. What is the purpose of the Federal Farm Loan Act and how does it operate?
 A. It provides capital for agricultural development. First mortgage loans only are made. Amount of loan limited to 85% of appraisal; proceeds must be used to pay off an existing indebtedness or in farm production; debt is payable in monthly, annual or semiannual installments of principal and interest; mortgage term is from 5 to 40 years; rate of interest is not limited. Loan amount varies from $100 upward.
29. Q. Saunders owned certain premises subject to a mortgage to Thurston for $8,000. Saunders leased the premises to Stevens for 10 years. Later Saunders desired to obtain possession of the premises. He purchased the mortgage from Thurston in the name of Smith and foreclosed the property. Smith then notified Stevens to vacate. Who will win?
 A. The tenant, Stevens, will win. Since Saunders is the lessor, he cannot commit any act to interfere with the tenant's quiet and peaceful enjoyment of the premises.
30. Q. What is an F.H.A. mortgage as the term is commonly used?
 A. A loan that is guaranteed to the mortgagee-lending institution by the Federal Housing Administration.
31. Q. What is meant by an acceleration clause in either a mortgage or contract?
 A. A clause giving the mortgagor or vendee the right to pay more than the regular payments or to pay the mortgage or contract in full at any time. It is also used to indicate that a mortgagee can accelerate the balance due under a mortgage or lease immediately after any default.
32. Q. What is a chattel mortgage?
 A. A mortgage upon personal property such as livestock, equipment, or fixtures. It must be recorded.
33. Q. What is the difference between a note and a mortgage?
 A. A note is the evidence of indebtedness and the promise to repay; a mortgage is a pledge of specific realty as a security.
34. Q. If there is a discrepancy between the note and mortgage as to the amount of the debt of the time of its repayment, which will prevail?
 A. The note.
35. Q. Does the purchaser assume personal liability for the mortgage debt?
 A. It depends upon the mortgage clause in the deed. If the purchaser buys the property "under and subject to the mortgage," he assumes no personal liability. If he buys "under and subject to the mortgage, which he assumes and agrees to pay," he is personally liable for the payment of the mortgage debt.
36. Q. Ross executes a deed to Bonfield, "under and subject to the payment of a certain mortgage for $5,000 in favor of the First National Bank, dated January 3, 1968 and of record in the Recorder of Deeds' Office of Harkins County in Mortgage Book Vol. 2117, page 360." On June 1, 1974, the bank forecloses and the property is sold at the sheriff's sale for $4,100. What are the respective liabilities of Ross and Bonfield to the bank?
 A. Ross is liable for any deficiency judgment to the bank. Bonfield is not liable to the bank, because he did not assume and agree to pay the debt. If Ross is required to

pay the judgment to the bank, he, in turn, would be entitled to indemnification from Bonfield.

37. Q. Given the preceding facts, if Bonfield signed an extension agreement with the bank extending the term beyond the maturity date and agreeing to make the payments, what liability would ensue?
 A. The bank could hold Ross or Bonfield for the deficiency because there is now privity of contract between Bonfield and the bank. Ross remains liable so long as the debt is unpaid.
38. Q. Who pays the premium on an insurance policy with a mortgage clause?
 A. The mortgagor, to protect the mortgagee, to the extent of his interest, in case the mortgaged premises are destroyed or damaged by fire, or other casualty.
39. Q. Why is it important that a deed of release be promptly recorded after the debt has been paid or satisfied ?
 A. To guard against carelessness or accident which might result in loss of the cancelled note, which loss would cause serious consequences.
40. Q. Adams purchased a tract of land from Baker. The property is encumbered by a past due mortgage, which Baker gave Conway when Baker purchased the property from Conway. Conway is willing and does extend the mortgage for another period of five years.
 1. Should the extension of mortgage be entered into between Adams, the new owner, and Conway, the mortgagee, or should the extension agreement be signed by Baker and Conway?
 2. After the extension of mortgage is signed by Conway, is Baker relieved of his obligation as the maker of the original mortgage?
 3. What liability, if any, does Adams, the new purchaser, now have in connection with the mortgage?
 A. 1. Adams and Conway, since Adams is now the owner of record of the property.
 2. No. Baker is still responsible for conditions of the mortgage as of the date of the extension.
 3. Adams, the new owner, is responsible for any new condition which may arise after the extension of the mortgage.
41. Q. What is the function of the Federal Housing Administration in the mortgage loan field ?
 A. It insures loans that are made by F.H.A. approved lending agencies.
42. Q. What is a reduction certificate?
 A. A certificate showing the balance due on a mortgage at the time of closing a sale.
43. Q. Ogden, a real estate broker, is employed by Whitney, a mortgagee, to collect interest on a mortgage due him from Crane, the mortgagor. Ogden collects the interest payments for three years and remits to Whitney, deducting a commission for his services. In 1974 Crane pays the mortgage debt of $4,000 to Ogden, who uses the money for his own purposes. Ogden dies two months later and his estate is hopelessly insolvent. In a contest between Whitney and Crane, who will suffer the loss?
 A. The loss falls upon the mortgagor, Crane, for Ogden had no authority to collect the principal, and the responsibility was upon Crane to ascertain the extent of the agent's authority.
44. Q. Where a mortgagor makes extensive improvements to the property, can he set off the cost against the mortgage debt in case of a foreclosure?
 A. No. All improvements become part of the freehold and go to increase the mortgagee's security for the debt.
45. Q. Is a mortgage assignable?
 A. Yes, but the purchaser gets no better title or claim than the mortgagee had.
46. Q. What steps should the purchaser take or require in purchasing a mortgage?
 A. 1. Transfer of mortgage and other papers to him.
 2. Note the assignment upon the record.
 3. Obtain a declaration of no setoff, estoppel certificate, or certificate of no defense

from the mortgagor.

47. Q. Green executed a mortgage to Brown in 1968. Green leased the property to White for 5 years from May 1, 1972. Green failed to pay taxes or interest on the mortgage in 1973, and Brown notified White to pay the rents to him. White did so, and Green instituted an action for the rent against White. Will Green win?
    A. No. White is protected in paying the rent to Brown, who, upon Green's default, can exercise his right of mortgagee in possession. White may attorn to Brown; that is, recognize Brown as his lessor.
48. Q. Given the same facts, suppose White refused to honor Brown's request for rent but continued his rent payments to Green. What redress does Brown have?
    A. Brown cannot compel White to pay the rent; he would have to foreclose the property and obtain title, in which case he could then terminate White's lease.
49. Q. Suppose, given the preceding facts, that White paid the rent to Brown for a period of seven months and then Brown foreclosed the property and obtained title to it. Brown now notifies White that his lease is terminated. Can Brown do so?
    A. Yes. Although Brown recognized the lease previously by accepting rent payments from White, he is not estopped from cancelling the lease after he becomes owner of the property. Brown's status as a mortgagee in possession is entirely different and apart from his rights as owner after foreclosure. This is true where the mortgage antedated the lease, as here.
50. Q. Is a valid oral lease assignable?
    A. Yes, but not desirable.
51. Q. Mitchell exercises his rights as a mortgagee in possession under a mortgage from Adler. Mitchell collects the rents from the six tenants, pays the taxes, makes necessary repairs, and generally exercises dominion over the property. A pedestrian is injured due to a defective sidewalk and sues Adler, who brings in Mitchell as an additional defendant. Is Mitchell liable?
    A. Yes. The mortgagee in possession assumes the status of an owner when he exercises control, direction, and dominion over the property.
52. Q. What is the purpose of a "mortgagee clause" attached to a fire insurance policy?
    A. To protect the mortgagee against destruction of the mortgaged premises, as the mortgagee's interest may appear. The insurance policy is kept by the mortgagee and a policy certificate is furnished the owner. The mortgagor pays the insurance premiums.
53. Q. Can a mortgagee accept a voluntary deed from mortgagor in lieu of foreclosure?
    A. Yes, but the mortgagee should make certain that there are no liens or encumbrances entered subsequent to his mortgage as he will take the property subject to them.
54. Q. When a mortgagee has made two assignments of the mortgage, which assignment will take effect?
    A. The first assignment will prevail. However, in the assignment of a specialty such as a mortgage, transfer of the instrument itself is the controlling factor in determining ownership of the mortgage.
55. Q. What should be done when the mortgage is paid off?
    A. The mortgagee should acknowledge payment and satisfaction upon the record or execute a satisfaction piece and record it. The mortgagor should require the return of all the mortgage papers executed by him and the fire insurance policy.
56. Q. What is a mortgagee's remedy for the failure of the mortgagor to pay interest upon the principal of the mortgage debt as agreed?
    A. If the property is revenue-producing, he can step in as mortgagee in possession and require the tenants to pay him the rent; or he can foreclose the property and sell it for his debt.
57. Q. A property on which there is a first mortgage of $4,000, a second mortgage of $4,000 and a third mortgage of $2,000, is sold under foreclosure, bringing a price of $5,000. What sum of money would each mortgagee receive if sold by first mortgagee?
    A. The first mortgagee would receive $4,000; the second mortgagee, $1,000; and the

third mortgagee, nothing. The purchaser at the foreclosure sale would receive the property clear of the three mortgages.

58. Q. What is the name of the clause inserted in a contract when it is desired by the purchaser of real property to place a mortgage at a later date on the property to take precedence over a purchase money mortgage given at the time of purchase?
    A. A subordination clause.
59. Q. Who executes a "Certificate of No Defense" or an "Estoppel Certificate" relating to a mortgage? For what purpose is it asked?
    A. By the mortgagor. It is asked when the mortgagee sells or assigns the mortgage so that the purchaser will have the mortgagor's assurance that the debt is owing and unpaid.
60. Q. Who executes the deed to real property when it is sold by the court in an action to foreclose a mortgage?
    A. The sheriff.
61. Q. Archer executes a mortgage to Hood for $5,000. Later Hood purchases merchandise from Archer for $750 and agrees to permit Archer to set the amount off against the mortgage debt. Subsequently Hood sells the mortgage to Cox. At maturity Archer refuses to pay more than $4,250 on the principal. How much can Cox collect?
    A. Only $4,250 as Cox received no better title to the mortgage than Hood had. Cox should have obtained an Estoppel Certificate or Certificate of No Defense from Archer when he purchased the mortgage.
62. Q. Ash obtained a mortgage from the Peerless Mortgage Co. for $6,000. On the same day, the Peerless Mortgage Co. assigns the mortgage to the Traders' Bank, and Ash executes an Estoppel Certificate (same as a Certificate of No Defense or a Declaration of No Setoff). Later the Traders' Bank assigns the mortgage to the Rex Tile Co. for value. At maturity Ash refuses to pay more than $5,250, claiming that he has made payments of $750 to the Traders' Bank. If Ash can establish this fact, how much can the Rex Tile Co. collect?
    A. Only $5,250. The tile company should have obtained a *new* estoppel certificate when it purchased the mortgage from the bank.
63. Q. A mortgage with amortization provisions and in the original sum of $10,000 is offered for sale two years after its inception. Name two legal documents to be used in effecting a proper transfer of the mortgage to the purchaser.
    A. 1. An assignment of the mortgage by the mortgagee.
    2. An Estoppel Certificate by the mortgagor.
64. Q. An owner of five parcels of real estate is seeking a mortgage loan and offers all of the five parcels as security for the loan. The owner wishes to reserve the right to repay portions of the money borrowed at stated intervals before the due date of the mortgage and upon each payment to eliminate from the mortgage one of the five parcels covered by the mortgage. What is the name of the mortgage the owner will be required to execute, and what is the name of the document the owner will require from the mortgagee to free one of the parcels upon making a payment as stated above?
    A. The mortgage is a *blanket* mortgage. The mortgagee will be required to execute a *release*.
65. Q. What is the difference between a *purchase money* mortgage and a *blanket* mortgage?
    A. A purchase money mortgage is one given by the buyer to the seller in part payment of the consideration price. A blanket mortgage is one mortgage covering a number of properties.
66. Q. If you borrow and give an F.H.A. mortgage, is the loan made by the Federal Government?
    A. No. The loan is made by a bank or other lending institution and guaranteed by the Federal Government.

67. Q. An F.H.A. mortgage is referred to as an insured mortgage. Whom does the insurance protect, the mortgagor or mortgagee?
    A. The mortgagee.
68. Q. Is it necessary to record a mortgage in order to have a valid mortgage?
    A. No, as between the two original parties, mortgagor and mortgagee. The mortgagee must record the mortgage in order for it to be a valid lien against the property ahead of a subsequent creditor, or in case of sale of the property by the mortgagor.
69. Q. In case of the death of the mortgagor, does the mortgage become immediately due?
    A. No, the mortgage continues in accordance with its terms, if it is not delinquent and the property continues as security, no matter who inherits it.
70. Q. Does the death of the mortgagee have any effect upon the mortgage?
    A. No; it passes as personal property in the estate.
71. Q. What is an "open end" mortgage?
    A. The mortgagor has the right, after he had paid off part of the debt, to borrow additional funds from the mortgagee up to the original amount, at any time during the mortgage term.
72. Q. Abbott owes the Greenbacks Mortgage Co. $14,000 on a mortgage on his home. In 1971, he sells the home to Cabot for $17,000, and Cabot assumes and agrees to pay the mortgage. In 1972, Cabot sells the same residence to Lodge for the same price, "under and subject to the mortgage." In December 1973, Lodge sells the property to his brother-in-law, Stoner, at $16,000 and Stoner assumes and agrees to pay the mortgage in the then amount of $12,890. Stoner defaults, and the mortgage company realizes only $11,200 at a foreclosure sale. Can it collect the deficiency from (a) Abbott (b) Cabot (c) Lodge (d) Stoner the deficiency?
    A. (a) The mortgage company can collect from Abbott upon his original obligation (note). (b) It can collect from Cabot because he assumed and agreed to pay the debt. (c) It cannot collect from Lodge, because he did not assume the debt. (d) It cannot collect from Stoner because Stoner's promise to assume and pay the debt was made to Lodge, who was not liable to the mortgage company.
73. Q. What is the main reason for a lender to require a provision in the mortgage that failure to pay the taxes when due constitutes a default of the mortgage?
    A. The lien created by unpaid taxes has priority over a mortgage on the property.
74. Q. What is the difference between "recording a mortgage" and "releasing a mortgage"?
    A. Recording a mortgage benefits the mortgagee in that it is public notice of the existence of the mortgage; releasing a mortgage benefits the mortgagor, because the mortgage is no longer a lien against the particular property which is released.
75. Q. What are the essentials of a mortgage upon real property?
    A. (1) In writing (2) Competent parties (3) Purpose must be stated (4) A mortgaging clause (5) Description (6) Mortgagor's covenants (7) Signed by the mortgagor (8) Acknowledged by the mortgagor (9) Delivered to the mortgagee.
76. Q. What is the main difference between a mortgage and a deed of trust?
    A. A mortgage has a one year redemption period after default. A deed of trust can be foreclosed in 120 days, unless reduced by agreement or by statute.

True and False

1. An acceleration clause in a mortgage advances the maturity date. T F
2. The date when the mortgage was executed determines its priority. T F
3. The mortgagor pays the title insurance fee on a mortgage. T F
4. The law requires the consent of the mortgagee in order for an owner to sell his property subject to the mortgage. T F
5. A mortgagee is protected by the recording acts. T F
6. A mortgagee is bound to accept payment of the mortgage at any time offered. T F
7. A mortgage must be recorded to become a lien on property. T F

8. The date of recording determines the priority of a mortgage. T F
9. A lending institution cannot refuse to give a veteran a loan if the veteran has a certified entitlement. T F
10. A seller must obtain a court order to sell mortgaged property. T F
11. A minor cannot affirm his purchase of a property and disaffirm his purchase money mortgage. T F
12. A mortgagee is concerned more with the financial responsibility of the debtor than the security of the property. T F
13. A deed of trust is usually conveyed to a Trustee. T F
14. An escrow account must be forfeited by the seller when the purchaser assumes his mortgage. T F
15. Taxes have priority over recorded mortgages. T F
16. A blanket mortgage is one upon a dwelling which has two or more bedrooms. T F
17. The mortgagee should have possession of the Abstract of Title and fire insurance policies. T F
18. In a joint estate, either party can execute a valid mortgage. T F
19. There are no covenants to be found in a mortgage. T F
20. In the sale of real property, it is more advisable to sell the property with a clause that buyer assumes the mortgage than merely "under and subject to mortgage." T F
21. An acknowledgment is necessary on the note accompanying the mortgage. T F
22. A veteran purchaser is not allowed to pay the V.A. appraisal fee. T F
23. A mortgage is released upon the records by filing a deed of "reconveyance." T F
24. It is lawful for a purchaser to give a second lien to the owner and assume the outstanding balance of an F.H.A. mortgage. T F
25. The evidence of a personal obligation which is secured by real estate is called a mortgage. T F
26. A deficiency judgment may be taken against the mortgagor in the foreclosure of a purchase money mortgage. T F
27. A chattel mortgage is used to borrow money on farm lands. T F
28. When a mortgage is overdue, and it is the desire of the owner to negotiate the continuance of the mortgage to a later date, he negotiates an extension agreement. T F
29. A mortgagor is the party who has loaned money on real property. T F
30. The word "amortization" as applied to a mortgage or deed of trust means a reduction of the debt which they may secure by the payments of regular installments. T F
31. An F.H.A. loan on real estate means that the Government of the United States has made a direct advance of money to the owner and has taken a mortgage or deed of trust as security. T F
32. A mortgage is a lien on specific real estate. T F
33. There is no difference between a purchase money mortgage and one given to secure a loan. T F
34. A mortgage is personal property. T F
35. Usury means charging more than the legal rate of interest. T F
36. A mortgage on personal property is called a chattel mortgage. T F
37. F.H.A. loans are never made for more than 60% of the appraised valuation of the property. T F
38. An open mortgage is one upon vacant land. T F
39. A mortgage terminates an existing lease on the property. T F
40. A construction mortgage is one for a limited period of time. T F
41. An F.H.A. loan is the same as a V.A. loan. T F
42. In an estate by the entireties, either husband or wife can execute a valid mortgage. T F
43. When a loan is made to a veteran, the money loaned does not come from the

United States Government. **T** F

44. It is possible to procure a G.I. loan to purchase livestock and equipment for a farm. **T** F
45. When a G.I. loan is obtained, it is lawful for the borrower to give a second mortgage, where there is an F.H.A. first mortgage. T **F**
46. It is lawful for the borrower upon an F.H.A. mortgage to give a second mortgage on the same property covered by the F.H.A. mortgage. T **F**
47. At the present time an F.H.A. loan may be paid off in full without penalty if it is paid from the borrower's own funds. T **F**
48. It is unlawful to sue on a note secured by a mortgage on real estate without first starting to foreclose the mortgage. T **F**
49. There is a substantial difference between buying property subject to a mortgage and buying the property and assuming a mortgage thereon. **T** F
50. A purchaser of property at a foreclosure sale on a mortgage receives a general warranty deed. T **F**
51. Where an applicant for a mortgage loan is an excellent moral risk, a higher appraised value of the real estate is permitted than if the applicant is a poor risk. T **F**
52. A mortgagor cannot, at foreclosure, set off against the debt the value of improvements made by him during the mortgage term. **T** F
53. A mortgagee is bound to accept a voluntary deed from the mortgagor in lieu of foreclosure. T **F**
54. In the purchase of real property, it is more advisable to buy the property subject to an existing mortgage than to assume payment of it. **T** F
55. A "junior mortgage" will take precedence over the first mortgage or trust deed, if no interest is paid on the first mortgage for the period of the calendar year. T **F**
56. The operation of paying off a mortgage by periodic payments is called the prepayment of the mortgage. T **F**
57. A mortgagor is bound to obtain the consent of the mortgagee before he can sell the mortgaged premises. T **F**
58. A mortgagee in possession must account to the mortgagor for all revenue received by him from the property. **T** F
59. The so-called "blanket mortgage" is one that includes attached fixtures and appliances, as well as the real estate. T **F**
60. A mortgage clause which permits the mortgagee to advance the maturity date of the principal is called an acceleration clause. **T** F
61. A chattel mortgage is used to borrow money on a right of way. T **F**
62. A mortgage can be transferred from one person to another. **T** F
63. Where a mortgagee takes over control of the mortgaged premises, he, and not the owner, is liable for injuries on the premises. **T** F
64. An "estoppel certificate" is the same as a "certificate of no defense." **T** F
65. A mortgage for more than 20 years is void. T **F**
66. A mortgage must be paid off before the property can be sold. T **F**
67. Even though a mortgaged property is sold more than 3 times, the original mortgagor continues liable upon his note, until paid off. **T** F
68. Where the mortgagee enters into an extension agreement with the new purchaser of the mortgaged premises, the original mortgagor is discharged from liability. T **F**
69. Where a purchaser of mortgaged premises "assumes and agrees to pay" the debt, he is liable to the mortgagee for full payment. **T** F
70. Where a purchaser of mortgaged premises "assumes and agrees to pay" the debt, the original mortgagor is no longer liable for the full debt. T **F**
71. An agent appointed to collect interest on a mortgage has authority to collect the principal. T **F**
72. An administrator of an estate has no authority to execute a mortgage upon real

estate belonging to the decedent. **T** F

73. A person inheriting real estate subject to a mortgage must pay off the mortgage immediately. T **F**
74. A sound conventional loan should be for not more than two-thirds of the property value. **T** F
75. The Home Owners Loan Corporation gave its assistance to distressed property owners during the depression. **T** F
76. The mortgagor pays the fee for recording the mortgage. **T** F
77. A first mortgage is always a first lien. T **F**
78. Subordinating or postponing the lien of a mortgage is always more advantageous to the mortgagee than releasing the lien. **T** F
79. A minor is not permitted to own a mortgage. T **F**
80. The mortgagee should have possession of the fire insurance policy. **T** F
81. The mortgagor is required to pay the fire insurance premiums. **T** F
82. A "satisfaction piece" means that the mortgage has been partially paid off. T **F**
83. The mortgagor's "equity of redemption" is a period of grace for payment of the debt. **T** F
84. Any excess of funds realized at a foreclosure sale belong to the mortgagor. **T** F
85. A mortgage represents a liquid asset of the mortgagee. T **F**
86. Payment to the borrower of the money loaned under a construction loan is made when the construction of the improvements on real estate is completed. T **F**
87. There is no difference between a mortgage release and a mortgage satisfaction. T **F**
88. The obtaining, by a lender, directly or indirectly of more than the statutory rate of interest is called an assessment. T **F**
89. The person who lends money and to whom the property is mortgaged, is called the mortgagee. **T** F
90. Paying off a mortgage by regular periodic payments is called the reduction of a mortgage. T **F**
91. It is to the seller's advantage to have a buyer obtain a new mortgage rather than to assume and agree to pay the existing mortgage. **T** F
92. When a mortgage is overdue and it is the desire of the owner to negotiate the continuance of the mortgage to a later date, he negotiates an Estoppel Certificate. T **F**
93. A blanket mortgage is a single mortgage on two or more parcels of land as security for a single loan. **T** F
94. A debtor who gives five properties of equal value to a lender as security for a mortgage loan can require the lender to release any one parcel upon payment of one-fifth of the mortgage debt. T **F**
95. Where a mortgagor makes an addition to a dwelling after the mortgage has been placed, he can receive credit for the cost of such addition in event of a mortgage foreclosure sale of the dwelling. T **F**
96. Certain real estate was sold in a foreclosure sale bought by the first mortgagee for $5,400. There was a first mortgage of $6,000 and a second mortgage of $2,400. The second mortgagee will receive $1,800. T **F**
97. In the preceding case, the second mortgagee will receive nothing. **T** F
98. The debtor is protected in making mortgage payments to the original mortgagee, even though there is an assignment of the mortgage to a new person duly recorded. **T** F
99. Where a mortgage has been assigned, the law requires the debtor to give the assignee a Declaration of No Setoff, or a Certificate of No Defense. T **F**
100. If the mortgage is past due, it cannot be assigned. T **F**
101. The monthly payments on an amortized loan include the interest. **T** F
102. When a mortgage debt is past due, and unpaid, and the holder of the mortgage wishes to force the sale of the property to satisfy the debt, he starts an action for

Specific Performance. T F

103. A Certificate of No Defense is obtained from the mortgagee by the purchaser of a mortgage. T F
104. Property on which there is an F.H.A. mortgage can be further encumbered by a judgment. T F
105. In all cases, the redemption period of the mortgagor is six months after foreclosure sale. T F
106. The holder of a mortgage may sell or transfer the mortgage to a third party; the new holder obtains no greater interest than that which the original holder had at the time of transfer. T F
107. A mortgage which is taken back as part of the selling price is called a Blanket Mortgage. T F
108. A borrower, under a mortgage, is allowed one year in which to redeem the encumbered property after mortgage foreclosure sale. T F
109. A mortgage may be satisfied by full payment or foreclosure. T F
110. A mortgage note is personal property. T F
111. A trust deed does not take priority over a previously recorded mortgage. T F
112. A mortgage is executed by the mortgagee in favor of the mortgagor. T F
113. An instrument which transfers possession of property but does not transfer ownership, is a mortgage. T F
114. A majority of a commercial bank's investments are in mortgages. T F
115. A mortgagee in possession may be liable for sidewalk injuries to a pedestrian. T F
116. A mortgage on an industrial plant covers the machinery and equipment necessary to operate the plant. T F
117. Where the mortgage is in default, it is more advantageous to the mortgagor to give a voluntary deed than to suffer foreclosure by mortgagee. T F
118. As real estate activity increases, mortgage foreclosures increase. T F
119. Interest rates on mortages in comparison with yields from other investment, determines the supply of available mortgage funds. T F
120. A purchase money mortgage is one taken by the seller in part payment of the purchase price. T F
121. Where a mortgage calls for "not less than $66.00 per month," it can be paid off at any time. T F
122. It is now customary to place the mortgage on record, before the mortgagee releases the funds to the mortgagor. T F
123. The closing statement to the seller should reflect all of the mortgage costs to the buyer. T F
124. It is the obligation of the seller to pay for the cost of preparing the mortgage papers. T F
125. Title insurance for the amount of the mortgage affords the owner no protection after the loan is paid off. T F
126. An owner's title insurance policy, in a mortgage case, can be obtained at a small additional cost. T F
127. The "pay-off" figure on an amortized mortgage changes from month to month. T F
128. The proceedings to discharge an old mortgage, upon which no payments have been made for more than 20 years, is an action to quiet title. T F
129. Assignment of a mortgage is the same as negotiability of a promissory note. T F
130. A mortgagee can enjoin the removal of a building from the mortgaged premises. T F
131. Waste is an action by the mortgagee which lessens the value of the property. T F
132. Of the parties to a trust deed, the trustor is the "lendor." T F
133. A trust deed may be satisfied of record by marginal release. T F
134. Defeasance clause in a mortgage nullifies the conveyance. T F
135. A G.I. loan and a V.A. laon mean the same thing. T F
136. The evidence of a personal debt which is secured by a lien on real estate is called

a mortgage. T F
137. A mortgage is considered satisfied when an offset certificate has been filed. T F
138. If a person "assumes" a mortgage, the most he can lose, in the event of foreclosure, is the amount of his equity in the property. T F
139. A Certificate of Reduction of Mortgage is generally required when the mortgage is sold. T F
140. A recorded mortgage binds all and any real property subsequently acquired by the mortgagor. T F
141. In order that a note be legally enforceable it must be properly acknowledged. T F
142. The clause which permits the placing of a mortgage at a later date which will take priority over an existing mortgage is the subordination clause. T F
143. A mortgage should be properly acknowledged and recorded. T F
144. Redemption is the right which a mortgagor has to redeem his property after the expiration date. T F
145. A chattel mortgage is never recorded as it is not secured by real estate. T F
146. An acceleration clause in a mortgage speeds up mortgage payments. T F
147. An interest rate of 12 per cent is considered usurious. T F
148. The legal compensation received from the use of real estate is called equity. T F
149. The recording of a "Satisfaction Piece" is the only way a mortgage record can be released. T F
150. The mortgagor is required to pay fire insurance premiums. T F
151. Most interests in real property can be mortgaged. T F
152. A property subject to a G.I. guaranteed mortgage cannot be sold except to another qualified veteran. T F
153. A mortgage covering two or more lots in a recorded subdivision is a double mortgage. T F
154. It is possible to exchange one mortgaged property for another mortgaged property even though the mortgage amounts are unequal. T F
155. A title mortgage title insurance policy insures the mortgagor as well as the mortgagee. T F
156. The amount of a construction loan mortgage must be in the same amount as the permanent mortgage. T F
157. An Extension Certificate and an Estoppel Certificate mean the same thing. T F
158. The monthly interest on a mortgage is usually paid at the end of the month and not at the beginning. T F
159. Every mortgage is a Purchase Money mortgage. T F
160. Strict foreclosure is available where a mortgage is involved. T F

Multiple Choice

1. The instrument which conditionally conveys title to real estate is a
   (a) chattel mortgage.
   (b) conditional bailment lease.
   (c) escrow deed.
   (d) mortgage.
2. The grantor in a trust deed is
   (a) the mortgagor.
   (b) the mortgagee.
   (c) the trustee.
   (d) an escrow holder.
3. The instrument used to remove the lien of a deed of trust from the record is called a
   (a) redemption of equity.
   (b) satisfaction.
   (c) certificate of no defense.
   (d) deed of reconveyance.

4. A provision in a mortgage requiring prior written notice to the mortgagee and the mortgagee's approval, in event of sale of the mortgaged premises, is
   (a) contrary to public policy.
   (b) valid.
   (c) violates the statute of frauds.
   (d) has illegality of object.
5. The right of a mortgagor to redeem the property by paying the debt after maturity is called
   (a) reversion.
   (b) ademption.
   (c) redemption.
   (d) recapture.
6. The interest or value which an owner has in the property over and above the mortgage debt is known as
   (a) an escrow.
   (b) an equality.
   (c) an equity.
   (d) a surplus.
7. A purchase money mortgage is
   (a) a mortgage given to the seller or third person by the purchaser as part of the purchase price.
   (b) a partial release of the first mortgage.
   (c) a mortgage on personal property purchased.
   (d) used in a land contract transaction.
8. The Trustor in connection with a trust deed is the party who
   (a) lends the money.
   (b) receives the payments on the note.
   (c) signs the note.
   (d) holds the property in trust.
9. A clause in a deed of trust or mortgage or accompanying note or bond, which permits the creditor to declare the entire unpaid sum due upon certain default of the debtor, is
   (a) an acceleration clause.
   (b) an elevator clause.
   (c) a forfeiture clause.
   (d) an excelerator clause.
10. A deed of trust is usually conveyed to the
    (a) grantor.
    (b) broker.
    (c) public trustee.
    (d) mortgagor.
11. A mortgage is released by
    (a) reversion.
    (b) reconveyance.
    (c) quit claim deed.
    (d) satisfaction.
12. The money for making F.H.A. loans is provided by
    (a) qualified lending institutions.
    (b) any governmental agency.
    (c) the Federal Housing Administration.
    (d) the Federal Deposit Insurance Corporation.
13. An agreement to waive prior rights in favor of another is called
    (a) subordination.
    (b) subjugation.
    (c) subjacent.
    (d) none of these.

14. One mortgage theory is that a mortgage is a lien. The other is
    (a) an escrow.
    (b) an estate in fee tail.
    (c) a transfer of title.
    (d) a reversionary estate.
15. Which of the following pays the one per cent handling charge on an F.H.A. mortgage?
    (a) The lending institution.
    (b) The borrower.
    (c) The seller.
    (d) The broker who negotiated the loan.
16. A chattel mortgage is given to secure
    (a) an eviction.
    (b) chattels.
    (c) a lease.
    (d) money borrowed on real property.
    (e) a loan on personalty.
17. A reduction certificate is required when
    (a) the mortgage is assigned.
    (b) the property is sold.
    (c) a new mortgage is placed.
    (d) the mortgage is being extended.
18. A Veterans Administration loan is guaranteed by the
    (a) mortgage company.
    (b) F.H.A.
    (c) Veterans Administration
    (d) broker who made the deal.
19. The owner of five parcels of real property desires a mortgage loan and offers all five parcels as security. The mortgage he will be required to execute will be
    (a) a purchase money mortgage.
    (b) an amortizing mortgage.
    (c) a blanket mortgage.
    (d) a building and loan mortgage.
20. A mortgage is usually released of record by recording
    (a) quit claim deed.
    (b) satisfaction piece.
    (c) reconveyance.
    (d) estoppel certificate.
21. In the event that a penalty is being charged in the prepayment of an F.H.A. loan it is
    (a) $50.00.
    (b) $75.00.
    (c) 1 per cent of the face of the mortgage.
    (d) 2 per cent of the face of the mortgage.
22. A loan issued by the F.H.A. is usually borrowed from the
    (a) government.
    (b) lending institution.
    (c) seller.
    (d) county.
    (e) Federal Housing Administration.
23. A blanket mortgage covers
    (a) farm property.
    (b) more than one parcel of real estate.
    (c) personal property.
    (d) a coal or gas furnace.
24. In the sale of a mortgaged property, it is necessary
    (a) to obtain the consent of the mortgagee.

(b) to pay off the mortgage.
(c) for the grantor to deliver a deed.
(d) to obtain a court order.

25. An F.H.A. mortgage is one which is
(a) so known because the principal is reduced monthly.
(b) financed by F.H.A. money.
(c) insured by a Federal Government agency.
(d) on property owned by a veteran.

26. An agreement to waive prior rights in favor of another is called
(a) redemption.
(b) subjugation.
(c) subordination.
(d) estoppel.

27. When a mortgage is given as part of the consideration price a mortgage clause will be written in the
(a) insurance policy.
(b) equity of redemption.
(c) deed.
(d) mortgage.

28. Amortization is the process of
(a) liquidation of a debt.
(b) depreciation.
(c) winding up a business.

29. Where a purchaser assumes and agrees to pay an insured mortgage debt, it is most advantageous to the
(a) mortgagee.
(b) purchaser.
(c) mortgagor.
(d) F.H.A.

30. Where a lease antedates a mortgage, the mortgagee in possession has a right to
(a) evict the tenant.
(b) collect the rent.
(c) foreclose the property and terminate the lease.

31. The existing mortgage which is taken back as part of the selling price is called
(a) a blanket mortgage.
(b) an assumed mortgage.
(c) a subordinated mortgage.
(d) an extension of mortgage.

32. An estoppel certificate is required when
(a) the mortgage is sold by the mortgagee.
(b) the property is sold.
(c) a new mortgage is placed.
(d) the property is being foreclosed.

33. In the absence of an agreement to the contrary, the mortgage normally having priority will be
(a) the one for the highest amount.
(b) the one which is a first mortgage.
(c) the one that was recorded first.
(d) the one that is a construction loan mortgage.

34. The mortgage on real estate that includes items such as refrigerators, ranges and electric washers is referred to as a
(a) blanket mortgage.
(b) package mortgage.
(c) participation mortgage.
(d) private mortgage.

35. A mortgage which has both personalty and realty as security is a
    (a) chattel mortgage.
    (b) package mortgage.
    (c) blanket mortgage.
    (d) an open end mortgage.
36. The mortgage covenant which permits the mortgagee to advance the due date of the principal of the mortgage is called
    (a) prepayment clause.
    (b) foreclosure clause.
    (c) acceleration clause.
    (d) demising clause.
37. The owner of a property places a bank mortgage on it. He later sells the property with the buyer assuming and agreeing to pay the existing mortgage. In the event the bank later forecloses and sells the property at an amount less than the balance of the mortgage, which statement is correct?
    (a) Only the original owner is liable for the deficiency.
    (b) Only the buyer is liable for the deficiency.
    (c) Neither is liable. The bank can only collect what it realized on the sale of the property.
    (d) The bank could look to the buyer or seller, or both for payment of the deficiency.
38. A chattel mortgage is usually given in connection with
    (a) real property.
    (b) farm lands.
    (c) a trust deed.
    (d) personal property.
    (e) commercial property.
39. The instrument which may conditionally convey title is
    (a) an option.
    (b) a patent.
    (c) a mortgage.
    (d) a quit claim deed.
40. Trust Deeds are used to
    (a) finance purchase of stocks.
    (b) secure a judgment.
    (c) borrow money.
    (d) to bond an administrator of an estate.
41. A "satisfaction piece" is a writing that
    (a) records payment of a deed of trust indebtedness.
    (b) records and acknowledges a paid-off deed of trust (mortgage).
    (c) pays a landlord for damages to his property.
    (d) renders satisfaction to a lessor for personal damages.
42. A "balloon" payment on a deed of trust refers to the
    (a) first payment.
    (b) final payment.
    (c) middle payment.
    (d) second payment.
43. An owner who desires a deed of trust loan and offers three properties as security will be required to execute which type of deed of trust
    (a) blanket.
    (b) F.H.A.
    (c) conventional.
    (d) building and loan.
44. A mortgage which is past due and subject to foreclosure at any time is called
    (a) an open mortgage.
    (b) a senior mortgage.

(c) a primary mortgage.
(d) a closed mortgage.

45. Money realized at a foreclosure sale on a mortgage in excess of the mortgage indebtedness belongs to
    (a) purchaser at sheriff's sale.
    (b) sheriff.
    (c) mortgagee.
    (d) mortgagor.
46. The usual term of a mortgage in the $20,000 price for dwellings is
    (a) 12 years.
    (b) 35 years.
    (c) 20 years.
    (d) 10 years.
47. The borrower under a Trust Deed is the
    (a) grantor.
    (b) grantee.
    (c) cestuique trust.
    (d) none of these.
48. A clause releasing one lot in a mortgaged subdivision is
    (a) release.
    (b) an exoneration.
    (c) prepayment clause.
    (d) an equity.
49. When a mortgage is foreclosed, any lease made after the date of the mortgage is
    (a) terminated.
    (b) binding upon tenant, but not the mortgagee.
    (c) not affected in any way.
    (d) binding upon purchaser at the foreclosure sale, but not upon tenant.
50. The mortgagor's right to reestablish ownership, after delinquency, is known as
    (a) a statute of allowances.
    (b) unjust enrichment.
    (c) equity of redemption.
    (d) acceleration.
51. The Federal National Mortgage Association purchases
    (a) chattel mortgages.
    (b) F.H.A. mortgages.
    (c) government-insured mortgages.
    (d) conventional mortgages.
52. Which one of the following statements is false?
    (a) The Federal Government supplies the funds to the lending agency.
    (b) The Federal Government insures the lending agency against losses.
    (c) F.H.A. may insure either apartment house project or a residence mortgage.
    (d) V.A. is limited to G.I. mortgages.
53. A G.I. loan is the same as
    (a) an F.H.A. loan.
    (b) a V.A. loan.
    (c) a d.s.b. loan.
    (d) a co-insured loan.
54. The usual remedy on a defaulted mortgage is
    (a) issue a court citation.
    (b) sequestration.
    (c) foreclosure sale.
    (d) eviction.
55. In all cases of an open end mortgage, the promise to repay the advances is made:
    (a) at the time the mortgage is given.

(b) before each advance is paid to mortgagor.
(c) may be made at any time within one year of the date of the mortgage.
(d) must be made 30 days before any advance is paid.

56. A clause in a mortgage whereby the mortgagee waives his rights in favor of another party is known as a subordination. Under these circumstances,
I. the first lien holder is called an assignee.
II. the first lien holder has no further security.
(a) I only.
(b) II only.
(c) Both I and II.
(d) Neither I nor II.

57. Adams holds a mortgage on Abbott's property. Adams is now selling the mortgage to Chance. Under these circumstances, it is necessary for
I. Chance to obtain a Certificate of No Defense (an Estoppel Certificate) from Adams.
II. necessary to obtain such a certificate from Abbott.
(a) I only.
(b) II only.
(c) Both I and II.
(d) Neither I nor II.

58. The purpose of a mortgagee clause in a comprehensive insurance policy is
I. to make the mortgagor first beneficiary of the insurance proceeds, in event of a fire loss.
II. to make the lender liable for the payment of premiums.
(a) I only.
(b) II only.
(c) Both I and II.
(d) Neither I nor II.

59. Where a property is foreclosed upon a mortgage and the mortgagee buys the property at a foreclosure sale, he should receive a deed from
I. the owner.
II. The sheriff.
(a) I only.
(b) II only.
(c) Both I and II.
(d) Neither I nor II.

60. A mortgage purportedly executed by husband and wife, was acknowledged before the husband, a notary public. The wife's signature was a forgery.
(a) The mortgage is void as to H and W.
(b) The mortgage is void as to W.
(c) The mortgagee can collect only.
(d) The mortgage is a nudum pactum.

61. Kline is the owner of three separate tracts of land, A, B and C. He gives a single mortgage of $9,000 on all three tracts to Young. Later, Kline sells tract "A" to Hoyle for $4,000 and takes a purchase money mortgage from Hoyle for $3,000. Young gives a subordination agreement to Kline. Under these circumstances,
I. Young still has a blanket first mortgage against tracts "B" and "C."
II. Kline has a first mortgage on tract "A."
(a) I only.
(b) II only.
(c) both I and II.
(d) neither I nor II.

62. Lewis entered a judgment of $400 on December 6, 1973 against Brown, who owns a tract of land. Brown gave a mortgage for $1,500 to Carlson on January 3, 1974. The mortgage

is in default on August 2, 1974, and Brown agrees to deed the property to Carlson in satisfaction of the mortgage debt. Under these circumstances,

I. the deed is valid.
II. Carlson will take the property subject to the judgment of Lewis.
   (a) I only.
   (b) II only.
   (c) both I and II.
   (d) neither I nor II.

63. Stevens gives Thomas a mortgage for $5,000. Later, Thomas purchases a piano from Stevens for $1,100 and agrees to offset the purchase price against the mortgage debt. Subsequently, Thomas sells the mortgage to Queens for $5,000. Under these circumstances,
   I. Queens can collect $3,900 from Stevens.
   II. Queens can collect $1,100 from Thomas.
      (a) I only.
      (b) II only.
      (c) Both I and II.
      (d) Neither I nor II.

64. Adams gave a mortgage for $4,000 to Haines. He gave a second mortgage to Hill for $3,000 and a third mortgage for $2,000 to Green. Hill forecloses. The property brings $6,250 at sheriff sale. Under these circumstances,
   I. each mortgagee will receive $2,000.
   II. the purchaser will take the property subject to Haine's mortgage.
      (a) I only.
      (b) II only.
      (c) both I and II.
      (d) neither I nor II.

65. A mortgage contained a clause, making the entire debt due, if the mortgagor conveyed title to the property to a third person. The property was conveyed. The mortgagee brought an action to accelerate the debt.
   (a) The mortgagor will win.
   (b) The mortgagee will win.
   (c) The purchaser will be held liable.
   (d) The acceleration clause is void as against public policy.

66. An obligation in a deed of trust (mtge.) secured by a promissory note calling for monthly payments of $80 per month. The debtor paid $100 monthly from June 15, 1971 to December 15, 1973. He then ceased making payments. On Feb. 16, 1974, the creditor brought foreclosure proceedings.
   (a) The foreclosure is invalid.
   (b) The foreclosure is valid.
   (c) Creditor must wait three months before instituting action.
   (d) The obligation is now void.

Chapter 6

JUDGMENTS

FROM EARLY times (1688) lands of debtors have been subject to liens as security for debts. Although almost every person is interested in judgments from viewpoints of creditor and debtor, very few people are sufficiently conversant with the legal principles that apply. In the first place, what is a judgment? In legal parlance, it may be defined as a decree of a court of competent jurisdiction declaring that one individual (the debtor) is indebted to another (the creditor), and fixing the amount of such indebtedness. A verdict obtained in every court is not necessarily a judgment. Some further step may be necessary to reduce the verdict to judgment; hence the qualification in the definition, "of a court of competent jurisdiction."

In personam and in rem

Judgments fall into two main classes, judgments *in personam* (against the person) and judgments *in rem* (against the thing or particular property). A judgment *in personam* may be termed a general lien; a judgment *in rem* may be called a specific lien. Most judgments are against the person, and as such, bind *all* his real estate. Adams sues Burns on a contract (in assumpsit) and obtains a judgment; or Jones sues Smith for damages due to an automobile accident (in trespass) and obtains a judgment. Both are *in personam.* A tax lien, an assessment for a street improvement, and a mechanic's lien are judgments *in rem.* That is, the judgment binds only the particular piece of real estate for which the tax was due, or benefited by the street improvement, or upon which the work was performed and for which materials were furnished by the mechanic or material supply dealer. It is a judgment against the particular person by reason of his being the owner of that particular piece of real estate. The effect of a judgment is that a lien immediately attaches against the debtor's real estate upon the entry of the judgment. It automatically binds all the real estate located in the county where the judgment is entered. That is what is meant by the *lien* of the judgment. A lien may be defined, in technical language, as a hold or claim which one person has upon the property of another as a security for some debt or charge. It is the right which the creditor has under the law to have the debt satisfied out of the debtor's property. If the creditor merely has a claim, not reduced to judgment, the debtor can sell or mortgage his property, free and clear of such unsecured claim. If the creditor has reduced his claim to a judgment, a lien is thereby created against the real estate. A purchaser would then take the property subject to the lien and stand in the place of the debtor.

A judgment, other than a judgment *in rem,* binds every freehold interest in the land. A judgment entered against a life tenant will bind his interest in the property, which may be sold to satisfy the judgment. The purchaser would take the property for or during the lifetime of the debtor, as a tenant *pour autre vie* (for the life of another).

Lien on personal property

Judgments are not liens on the personal property of the debtor as they are on his real estate. A debtor may convey good title to a bona fide purchaser of his automobile or other personal property even though there is a judgment of record against him. Personal property may, however, be seized in satisfaction of a judgment debt. This is done by levy or attachment upon directions to the sheriff, the executive officer of the court, to seize and sell the described property. A mortgage, while it deals with real estate, is personalty, but the court can direct the sheriff to levy on a mortgage belonging to the debtor and sell it. The same is true of a leasehold. In other words, a creditor is entitled to proceed against any property of his debtor to recover his debt. In a sense, a debtor is a trustee for his creditors.

Release of judgment

It is always important to remember that a judgment attaches and adversely affects real estate of a debtor, as a lien, just as soon as it is entered of record. The judgment is a lien against all of the real estate owned by the debtor at the time the judgment is entered. The owner cannot give a purchaser good title to any part of the real estate owned by him. No prudent buyer would accept title thus encumbered, nor could the creditor be compelled to release any part of the debtor's real estate upon payment of any sum short of the full debt. A release is a matter of indulgence by the creditor. The real estate released should be noted on the margin of the recorded judgment.

In a subdivision property, with a mortgage against the entire property, it is the usual practice to include in the mortgage a clause that upon the sale of any lot, the mortgagee will release the particular lot sold, upon payment to him of (X) dollars.

When the debtor pays the judgment, he is entitled to have the judgment marked "satisfied in full" of record.

Lien period

The lien of a judgment does not last forever. As between the original debtor-owner and judgment creditor, execution may be had against the debtor's property at any time, so long as the debtor continues to own it and rights of mortgagees or other judgment creditors have not intervened. The lien of the judgment lasts for a limited period of time, and, if the judgment is not revived within the prescribed period of time, the lien against a subsequent purchaser, mortgagee, or judgment creditor is lost. In Pennsylvania, the lien of the judgment lasts five years. If the judgment is for longer than the statutory period and no action taken to revive it, a purchaser from the debtor takes the property free from the judgment. In other jurisdictions, the judgment is a lien for ten years,

Judgments arise in several ways, among which are court decision, default, and confession. Since litigation is always prevalent, a great many judgments arise through court action. Where the litigation takes place in a minor judiciary court such as a Justice of the Peace, a transcript of the verdict or judgment can be filed in the proper County Court so as to be a lien. A judgment by default arises where the law requires a person to take some sufficient legal step and he fails to do so. For example, Thompson sues Bryan and serves him with a copy of his statement of claim. Bryan is then required to file an answer within a certain period of time, say 20 days, and he fails to do so. Thompson can enter judgment against Bryan because of Bryan's default. The great majority of judgments probably arise through confession, authorized in a note, bond, or lease. They are known as judgments DSB, which stands for *debitum sine brevi* and means "debt without a writ or declaration."

By confession

A judgment by confession is as conclusive as a judgment on the verdict of a jury. The main distinction between a promissory note and a judgment note is that upon a default in payment of a promissory note, the holder must sue the maker before he can obtain a judgment, while in a judgment note, the holder may enter up judgment upon a default, without any suit. This is so by reason of the language of the instrument which authorizes and empowers

> . . . any Attorney of any Court of Record within the United States or elsewhere to appear for (me), and with or without declarations filed, confess judgment against (me) and in favor of said payee, his executors, administrators, or assigns, as of any term for the above sum with costs of suit, etc.

In fact, the holder of the note may confess judgment at any time, even before default or maturity, but no execution can issue until default. If the obligor is deceased, judgment may not be confessed against him as death revokes the agent's power to confess. Where one joint obligor dies, the note can be entered as a judgment against the survivor; it is irregular to enter the note against all of the obligors including the decedent. Judgment by confession operates in a very summary manner, and very often the debtor is unaware that a judgment has been entered against him until he tries to sell his property or place a mortgage upon it. If the debtor claims that the entry of the judgment is unjust, he may petition the court to open up the judgment; and if the court, in the exercise of its sound judicial discretion, believes that the debtor should be permitted to make a defense, it will open up the judgment and then the case is heard *de novo* (anew) to determine whether the plaintiff is entitled to his judgment.

A petition to set aside a default judgment is addressed to the sound discretion of the court, and must be supported by clear, strong and satisfactory evidence of mistake, inadvertence, surprise or neglect: *Edwards v. Edwards,* 481 P. 2d 432 (Colo. App. 1970): *Ute, Inc. v. Opfel,* 518 P. 2d 156 (Nev. 1974). If the judgment appears erroneous upon its face, the proper proceeding is to strike it off by motion. The court will examine the record to ascertain the form of the judgment but will not go into the merits of the debtor's claim as in a petition to open up the judgment. A great volume of judgments on notes or bonds accompanying mortgages are confessed. If there is a genuine issue of fact, a summary judgment is inappropriate: *Williams v. N.C. State Board of Education,* 201 S.E. 2d 889 (1974). A judgment, of course, can only be collected for the real debt due. Deficiency judgments have been discussed in connection with mortgage foreclosures. Although the majority of an infant's contracts are voidable at the infant's election, nevertheless a warrant of attorney by a minor to confess judgment against him is absolutely void. A judgment so confessed will be vacated upon a motion to strike it off. Since the confession is void, a minor is deemed incapable of ratifying it. A summary judgment may not be entered where there is disputed question of fact, which is material to the disposition of the case: *Borough of Monroeville v. Effie's Ups and Downs,* 315 A. 2d 342 (Pa. Cmwlth. 1974); *Cardente v. Travelers Ins. Co.,* 315 A. 2d 63 (R.I. 1974). Default judgments are looked upon with disfavor: *Girkin v. Cook,* 518 P. 2d 45 (Oklahoma 1973).

In the Federal Court case of *Swarb v. Lennox,* 314 F. Supp. 1091 (1970), the court held that the confession clause was a violation of the due process clause of the Constitution for persons having incomes less than $10,000. The United States Supreme Court, in the same case 405 U.S. 191 (1972) affirmed part of the lower court decision, holding that it was not unconstitutional to enforce the confession of judgment against those earning over $10,000.

It has been previously stated that a judgment is a lien against all of the real estate which the debtor owns at the time the judgment is entered against him. It does not bind property he acquires by purchase or by will after the date of entry of the judgment. Such after-acquired property can be brought under the lien of the creditor's judgment by reviving the lien of the judgment. This can be done at any time. After-acquired property, sold by the debtor before revival of the judgment, would pass clear title to a purchaser without notice.

A judgment creditor may take the necessary legal action to foreclose the property in order to obtain satisfaction of the debt and the costs of the sale. Frequently, however, the creditor may do nothing since foreclosure proceedings necessitate an advance of costs and payment of any delinquent taxes against the property. The creditor may feel, rather, that in time the debtor will desire to sell or mortgage the property and will then have to make peace with the creditor and pay him off. This often happens. The creditor should be ever alert, however, that the lien of his judgment is not lost through passage of time. The creditor instituting foreclosure proceedings must be circumspect in complying with all legal requirements as to notice and advertisement of the property for sale. The property is put up at competitive public sale and sold to the highest bidder. Any excess funds realized at the sale, over and above the debts of record and costs, belong to the debtor-owner. Where there is more than one creditor, the funds are distributed in the order of priority of liens. The creditor who initiates the sheriff's sale obtains no preference on that account, but takes his place in distribution of funds according to the date when his judgment was entered. Where there is a first mortgage against the property, which is a first lien, and the property is sold on a later judgment lien, the first mortgage is not divested. The purchaser at sheriff's sale takes the property subject to the first mortgage. If the property is sold on the first mortgage, all liens would be divested, and the purchaser would obtain clear title. Where there are two or more mortgages of record, without any prior or intervening judgments, sale on a subsequent judgment would not divest any of the mortgages. The sheriff makes no warranty or guaranty of title. The risk and responsibility are entirely upon the purchaser.

Fraud on creditors

A property sold, mortgaged, or liened in an effort to hinder, delay, or defraud a creditor may be set aside by a creditor's petition to court for relief. A judgment entered the same day as a conveyance or mortgage of the property would constitute a prior lien against the property. In practice, a mortgagee may record his mortgage one day and disburse the funds the next day so as to have sufficient time to examine the records and ascertain that no judgment, mortgage, or adverse conveyance has been entered.

Mechanic's lien

A mechanic's lien is given to contractors, laborers, and material men, by statute, for work performed or materials furnished. It is really special class legislation, but has nevertheless been sustained by the courts. There must be strict compliance with the legal requirements as to serving the notice of intention to file the lien. A distinction as to time for filing a mechanic's lien is made as between new construction and repairs and as between a contractor and subcontractor. The contractor may enter into a "No Lien Contract" with the owner, and, as the name implies, no mechanic's liens can be filed for work or materials furnished on the job for the owner. If the "No Lien Contract" is recorded, sub-contractors are bound by its terms, even though they had failed to take the precaution of examining the records. This does not give the owner, however, "letter perfect" protection. If after the "No Lien Contract" is filed, the terms of the contract are materially changed between owner and contractor, the "No Lien Contract" filed would be inoperative.

If there is no "No Lien Contract" filed, a sub-contractor, in Pennsylvania and other states, would have the right to file a mechanic's lien for his labor, even though the owner has made his required payments to the contractor. An irresponsible contractor often visits an unjust hardship upon the owner in this connection. A licensing law for contractors has been agitated in a number of states in order to make a contractor responsible to an owner under a building contract. In some states, a sub-contractor can recover only the balance due and owing by the owner to the general contractor under the building contract. The owner after receiving notice from a sub-contractor as to the value of his services is privileged to hold out such amount from the contract price and pay it directly to the sub-contractor. Notice from the sub-contractor is imperative. This is known as the "New York system."

In most states a mechanic's lien dates back to the beginning of the construction job. Thus mortgagees are apprehensive lest the mortgage be consummated and recorded before ground is broken. A prudent mortgagee will take the precaution to have photographs made of the site before any building or excavation has been performed at the time the mortgage was executed. This would be convincing evidence that no work had been done nor any materials used.

The sub-contractor has priority over a mortgage if the mortgage was recorded after the work started, even though the sub-contractor—a plumber, for example—did not render any service until after the building was well advanced. The time for serving notice of intention to file a mechanic's lien dates from the time when all the work is completed. An owner can protect himself by requiring the general contractor to post a performance bond or by reserving to the owner the privilege of paying sub-contractors' claims upon certification of the architect that the work has been satisfactorily performed.

A purchaser from a contractor relies upon a release of liens, which must be executed by every sub-contractor and material man who did work or furnished materials on the job. Unfortunately, in too many cases all of the material men or sub-contractors have not executed the release. They may file a claim at a later date, which the purchaser must pay even though full payment of the purchase price has already been made to the builder. Also, the purchaser may be deceived by an unscrupulous builder who furnishes a release, for example, signed by a lumber company that furnished only a small portion of the lumber used. The buyer may mistakenly believe that all claims for lumber have been paid, whereas the lumber company that furnished the bulk of the lumber has not signed a release nor has it been requested to do so. In purchasing a new building, it is recommended that title insurance be purchased insuring against mechanic's liens as well as defects in title.

Where carpet and carpet pad were installed directly over slab on ground floor and directly over unfinished plywood on second floor, glue used to hold down carpet was a long lasting glue and tacks were used with great frequency, the court held that carpeting and pads were lienable items: *United Benefit Life Ins. Co. v. Norman Lumber Co.,* 484 P. 2d 527 (Okla. 1971). In the case of *Hartford Fire Ins. Co. v. Balch,* 350 P. 2d 514 (Okla. 1960), involving an insurance claim, the court found that the carpet was loosely tacked and glued in place; that the glue was merely intended to keep the carpet from slipping, and therefore, was personal property. Thus, the two cases are distinguishable.

A Minnesota case, *Reuben E. Johnson Co. v. Phelps,* 156 N.W. 2d 247 (1968) held that an architect, in preparation of plans for improvement and the work of a surveyor in doing a preliminary survey of the property, on which a mortgage is to be placed, did not permit liens filed after the mortgage, to attach and take effect as of the date of the plans and preliminary survey.

A bulldozer operator could not file a mechanic's lien for work performed in removing brush and trees from subdivision since the court held the work was done "to" the land and not "upon it." *Lambert v. Newman,* 431 S.W. 2d 480 (1968).

Marshalling

Where a creditor has two or more funds out of which to satisfy his debt, he cannot so elect as to deprive another creditor of his security who has but one fund. This is known as marshalling. For example, Benson entered judgment against Archer for $1,700 on June 16, 1968. Archer owns three parcels of improved real estate. On January 3, 1970, Chance places a mortgage on one tract for $1,500. Then, on March 20, 1972, Benson issues execution against the mortgaged tract. Chance can compel Benson to proceed first against the other two properties owned by Archer. Of course, if, upon the sale of the other two tracts, Benson does not receive the amount of his judgment in full, he may then proceed against the parcel upon which Chance holds his mortgage.

Indexing judgment

In concluding judgments, attention is directed to the necessity of identifying the debtor accurately in the judgment index. Omission of the middle initial of the debtor's name may prove fatal. The question is whether the debtor's name in the index is such as to put the searcher upon inquiry. Where property was held in the name of Daniel J. Murphy and judgment entered against Daniel Murphy, a court held the judgment was not a lien. Where land was owned by W. A. Black and judgment was entered against W. *G.* Black, the court held no lien. However, a judgment entered against Rosie Reustle was held a good lien against property owned by Rosie *C.* Reustle. Rosie Reustle and Rosie *C.* Reustle were one and the same person, and the only person by that name in the county. A judgment against Caroline Kerl was a binding lien against real estate owned by Caroline *C.* Kerl. Each case necessarily depends upon its concomitant circumstances. The Pennsylvania Supreme Court,[1] in determining what constituted sufficient constructive notice, said:

> It is not necessary that the name of the judgment debtor as docketed and indexed should be letter-perfect, nor do the cases hold that the omission of the middle initial in the entry of a judgment automatically and inevitably vitiates the entry and subordinates it to subsequent judgments more accurately docketed. Each case must depend upon concomitant circumstances.

Omission of a middle name may be misleading or harmful in cases where the surname is a relatively common one. The first or Christian name must be correct in the judgment. Title in name of Kathryn Steele, judgment entered against Catherine Steele held invalid.

Assignment

A judgment is personal property. It is readily assignable in the same manner as a note or mortgage may be assigned. The judgment creditor, who transfers the judgment is the assignor. The party to whom the judgment is assigned is the assignee. The assignee takes no better title than the assignor had. The assignee takes subject to all

[1] Coral Gables, Inc. vs. Kerl, 334 Pa. 441, 6 A. 2d, 275 (1939).

equities existing between the original parties: *L. C. Russell Co. v. Pipeguard Corp.*, 504 S.W. 2d 596 (Tex. 1973).

Questions on Judgments

1. Q. What is the effect of a recorded judgment on the real property of the judgment debtor?
   A. It is a lien upon all real property of the judgment in the county where it is recorded.
2. Q. What is a deficiency judgment?
   A. A judgment entered for the difference between the amount of the debt owed and the amount realized from the sale of the debtor's real property at foreclosure sale.
3. Q. In searching for liens on real estate what would you look for?
   A. Mortgages, judgments, mechanic's liens, delinquent taxes, liens for certain city improvements, and delinquent vendor's liens.
4. Q. Does compliance with the Bulk Sales Law, in selling a business, relieve purchaser of all liability for outstanding indebtedness?
   A. No. It does not protect the purchaser against back sales tax which may be due and owing by the seller and which constitutes a prior lien against the assets of any business.
5. Q. Define a judgment.
   A. A judgment is a decree of a court of competent jurisdiction determining that one individual is indebted to another and fixing the amount of such indebtedness.
6. Q. What kinds of judgment are there?
   A. Judgments are of two kinds, *in personam* and *in rem.* Judgments which bind the person against whom they are rendered and all of his real estate are judgments *in personam,* and judgments which bind a particular piece of real estate only and are against a particular person because he is the owner of that property are judgments *in rem.*
7. Q. Do judgments bind personal property?
   A. Not in the sense that the judgment is a lien on the personal property of the debtor. Personal property, however, may be sold in satisfaction of a judgment.
8. Q. Is a judgment a lien on a mortgage?
   A. No. A mortgage is personal property and not realty.
9. Q. Jones obtains a judgment for $500 against Brown. The debtor, Brown, owns an automobile which he sells to Cox. Does Cox get good title to the automobile?
   A. Yes. The automobile is personal property.
10. Q. Suppose Adams obtains a judgment for $900 against Brant who owns tracts 1, 2, and 3. Can Brant sell tract 3 to Chalmers so that Chalmers will get a free unencumbered title to the property?
    A. No. Adams' judgment is a lien against *all* of Brant's real property.
11. Q. In the preceding case, suppose Brant offers to pay Adams $300 on account of the judgment and demands that Adams release tract 3 from the judgment so that Chalmers can obtain clear title. Must Adams release the lot?
    A. No. Execution of a release is a matter of accommodation by the creditor. He cannot be compelled to execute a release even though partial payment of the judgment is tendered.
12. Q. Is a judgment a lien on property acquired by a debtor after entry of judgment?
    A. No. Such after-acquired property can be brought under the lien of the judgment

only by reviving the judgment.

13. Q. In what ways may judgment be entered?
    A. By verdict, default, or confession.
14. Q. Ash sells a tract of ground to Boone on November 26, 1973, and on November 27, 1973, Crane secures a judgment against Ash. Boone records his deed December 6, 1973. Will Crane's judgment be a lien against the property?
    A. Yes. The records showed Ash was the owner of the property when the judgment was entered.
15. Q. Suppose, in the preceding case, that Ash conveys the property to his wife on November 26, 1973. Could the deed be set aside?
    A. Yes. The conveyance is a clear fraud upon creditors.
16. Q. How long does a judgment remain a lien?
    A. Five years in some states, ten years in other states. (In Indiana, for example, the lien period is ten years.)
17. Q. Atkins secures a judgment against Burke for $600 on June 16, 1961. Can Atkins on March 21, 1974, sell the property on his judgment?
    A. Yes. Although the lien period has expired, Atkins can still sell the property so long as a new purchaser's rights, or those of a creditor, have not intervened.
18. Q. White enters into an agreement of sale for the purchase of certain real estate on October 2, 1973. Black enters a judgment against White on October 4, 1973. The property is conveyed to White on November 26, 1973. Is Black's judgment a lien against this real estate?
    A. Yes. White's equitable title or interest in the real estate can be bound by the lien of a judgment.
19. Q. Is a lease of years subject to lien of a judgment?
    A. No. A lease of years is personalty. However, if there is an option to purchase, the leasehold can be sold in execution.
20. Q. Suppose the following liens and encumbrances exist against Martin's property:
    (a) Fielding's mortgage for $4,000 entered on June 16, 1972.
    (b) Pope's judgment for $2,250 entered on December 16, 1973.
    (c) Swift's mortgage for $1,000 entered on February 2, 1974.
    (d) Gray's judgment for $750 on February 4, 1974.
    The property is sold on Gray's judgment on March 1, 1974. The costs and taxes amount to $710. The property is sold for $3,650 to Williams. How will this fund be distributed, and subject to what liens, if any, will Williams, the purchaser, take the property?
    A. The costs and taxes of $710 will be paid first, leaving $2,940 for distribution. Pope will be paid in full. Swift will receive the balance of $690. Gray will get nothing. Williams will take the property subject to Fielding's mortgage. Where the first mortgage is a first lien and the sale takes place upon a subsequent lien, the mortgage is not divested.
21. Q. Suppose the following liens and encumbrances exist against Jones' property:
    Benson's mortgage for $25,000 entered on October 2, 1973.
    Conover's mortgage for $5,000 entered November 26, 1973.
    Dodd's mortgage for $1,000 entered April 25, 1974.
    Evans' judgment for $7,500 entered April 26, 1974.
    Franklin's judgment for $1,200 entered May 3, 1974.
    The property is sold on Evans' judgment and brings $9,750. The cost and taxes amount to $850. How will the $9,750 be distributed and subject to what liens, if any, will the purchaser, Johnson, take the property?
    A. Costs and taxes will be paid first, leaving $8,900 for distribution. Evans will receive $7,500, Franklin will receive $1,200, and the balance of $200 will go to Jones, the owner. Johnson will take the property subject to the three mortgages of Benson, Conover, and Dodd. Where there are two or more mortgages against a property and

no prior or intervening judgment, and a sale takes place upon a subsequent lien, none of the mortgages is divested.

22. Q. In the event that Grafton had a judgment of $150 entered on October 1, 1964, revived in 1968, show how the fund in the preceding case would be distributed and subject to what liens, if any, Johnson would take the property.
    A. After payment of costs and taxes, Grafton would receive $150 and the balance of $8,750 would be paid to Benson. Conover, Dodd, Evans, and Franklin would receive nothing. The purchaser would take the property free and clear of all liens. The judgment, being the first lien, divests all the mortgages and judgments.
23. Q. How could Benson and the other creditors have protected themselves?
    A. By appearing at the foreclosure sale and bidding the property up to cover their liens.
24. Q. Is title acquired by purchase at a treasurer's sale for unpaid municipal taxes good and marketable?
    A. Ordinarily, a title insurance company will not insure a tax sale title. The title is, thus, not good and merchantable. Besides, the owner of the property usually has one year's time within which to redeem the property.
25. Q. What is the best way for the purchaser of a new home from a contractor to protect himself from the filing of mechanic's liens against the property?
    A. Title insurance is the best protection. He could require a surety bond for performance or completion; a release of liens from all sub-contractors and material men; have the general contractor file a "no-lien" contract; pay out the money as the work progresses.
26. Q. Special tax assessments (or liens) are levied against city property. Name four things for which special assessments may be levied.
    A. Street paving, curb, sidewalk, sewer.
27. Q. A lien filed against real property by the contractor for labor or material is called a
    A. ( ) labor lien.
       ( ) completion notice lien.
       (x) mechanic's lien.
       ( ) builder's lien.
28. Q. A property is sold in a foreclosure sale at $5,000. There was a first mortgage against the property for $4,600 and a second mortgage lien of $1,000. Unpaid taxes amounted to $400. Show the distribution of the $5,000 sale upon first mortgage.
    A. Taxes will be paid first in amount of $400. First mortgagee will get $4,600. Second mortgagee will receive nothing.
29. Q. What is the difference between a promissory note and a judgment note?
    A. In a promissory note, if it is not paid at maturity, the holder must *sue* the maker to obtain a judgment. In a judgment note, if it is not paid at maturity, the holder can forthwith *confess* judgment against the maker of the note.
30. Q. Who is a holder in due course of a note?
    A. A person who has obtained a note for a valid consideration, before maturity, without knowledge of any defect in the instrument, or of any set off to the debt.

True and False

(Judgments)

1. A charge by a water company, if unpaid, is a lien on real estate. T F
2. A judgment must be recorded to become a lien against real estate. T F
3. A lien is always an encumbrance. T F
4. In a "joint and several" obligation, suit must be entered against all of the obligors. T F
5. The duty is upon the creditor to see that his judgment is properly indexed. T F
6. An unsecured creditor can reduce his claim to a judgment by filing his claim in the clerk or prothonotary's office. T F
7. A prothonotary is the chief clerk of the county or district court. T F
8. The lien of a judgment binds real estate only. T F

9. A mechanic's lien is a general lien. T F
10. Personal property may be sold upon a judgment. T F
11. Postponing a lien is preferable to releasing a lien. T F
12. A judgment is not a lien on a mortgage. T F
13. A first mortgage is always a first lien. T F
14. Where a debtor owns two properties of equal value, a judgment creditor can be compelled to accept one half of the debt and release one property. T F
15. A DSB judgment is one entered by confession. T F
16. Where there are a number of judgment creditors, the one who institutes foreclosure is paid first out of the proceeds. T F
17. Where one joint obligor dies, the note can be entered as a judgment against the survivor. T F
18. Death of the obligor prevents a judgment being confessed against the decedent. T F
19. Execution may not be issued upon a judgment against a municipality. T F
20. A property can never be sold where there is a judgment against it. T F
21. A judgment entered by confession against a minor is void. T F
22. A leasehold is subject to the lien of a judgment. T F
23. A judgment against a husband will operate as a lien against property owned by husband and wife. T F
24. A judgment is protected by the recording acts. T F
25. A judgment is void after the lien period has expired. T F
26. A judgment is non-assignable. T F
27. Previous payment to the creditor is a good defense to suit by the assignee of the judgment. T F
28. Any excess of funds realized at a foreclosure sale belongs to the owner. T F
29. After a "notice of completion" is properly filed, no one can record a valid mechanic's lien. T F
30. A chattel is a mortgage on personal property. T F
31. A right to or interest in real estate that diminishes its value is called an encumbrance. T F
32. Tax liens have priority over a previously recorded trust deed or mortgage. T F
33. A recorded easement is considered an encumbrance but not a lien. T F
34. The obligee is the creditor. T F
35. Negotiability is the same as assignability. T F
36. Property conveyed to a close relative in contemplation of a judgment, but before the judgment is actually entered, can be set aside. T F
37. A judgment entered against the seller of real estate, but before the deed to the purchaser is recorded, will be a lien against the real estate. T F
38. Judgments are only entered in the courts of the county. T F
39. A verdict before an alderman or Justice of the Peace constitutes a judgment. T F
40. Judgments entered on a note accompanying a mortgage date from the date when the mortgage was executed. T F
41. The effect of a mortgage is to create a lien. T F
42. An *in rem* judgment is a specific lien against one property only. T F
43. The lien of a judgment is 20 years. T F
44. When a suit for damages is filed, the plaintiff has a cautionary judgment against the defendant. T F
45. A suit in equity for real estate operates as a cloud against the real estate when the suit is filed. T F
46. Judgments bear interest at five per cent until paid. T F
47. Upon payment of a judgment, the creditor is required to satisfy the records. T F
48. Where the judgment has been assigned of record, the debtor must pay the assignee and not the original creditor, even if he has not been notified of the assignment. T F

49. Liens against real estate are satisfied in the order in which they are executed. T F
50. A property, against which a judgment has been entered, must be sold within ten years or the judgment will be void. T F
51. Property sold on a first mortgage which is a first lien will discharge all judgments against the same property. T F
52. A judgment has priority over all other liens. T F
53. An "encumbrance" is always a "lien." T F
54. The lien of a trust deed is released by the recording of a properly executed deed of reconveyance. T F
55. Judgment entered against Catherine Lynn is a good lien against property owned by Katherine Lynn. T F
56. The lien of a judgment does not have priority over all other liens. T F
57. A real estate broker may file a lien for his commission against the property sold, if he is not paid. T F
58. Lis Pendens is a form of public notice filed against a named property that a suit is about to be filed. T F
59. A contractor, who is not paid, may file an injunction against the subject property. T F
60. A judgment is always an encumbrance against all the property the defendant owns. T F
61. A property can be sold even if there are judgments against it. T F
62. Current unpaid real estate taxes constitute a lien against the real estate. T F
63. In Wisconsin, homestead is exempt from execution to the extent of $5,000. T F
64. A judgment entered by a Justice of the Peace in favor of a plaintiff constitutes a lien. T F
65. A defendant's automobile may be sold to satisfy a judgment. T F
66. A firm, furnishing paint to an owner in the repair of his home, may file a mechanic's lien, to protect its claim. T F
67. When a deed of trust note is secured by a deed of trust, the latter but not the former should be recorded. T F

Multiple Choice

1. Judgments are entered by
   (a) an Alderman.
   (b) court of competent jurisdiction.
   (c) real estate Commission.
   (d) a Justice of the Peace.
2. The majority of judgments are entered by
   (a) court decisions.
   (b) default.
   (c) confession.
   (d) insurance companies.
3. When a firm furnishes materials for a house, and is not paid, it may file
   (a) a mechanic's lien.
   (b) a deficiency judgment.
   (c) a lis pendens.
   (d) an estoppel certificate.
4. A deal is closed on February 15, 1974 and the buyer, Jones, does not record the deed until April 24, 1974. A judgment for $1,200 is filed against the grantor, Adams, on April 19, 1974. The judgment
   (a) is a lien against the property.
   (b) is invalid against the property.
   (c) Jones can rescind the deal.
   (d) constitutes a judgment inchoate.
5. A judgment entered of record, is a lien on the debtor's
   (a) automobile.

(b) residence.
(c) bank account.
(d) wages.

6. A judgment takes effect from the time
   (a) the debt is incurred.
   (b) suit is decided.
   (c) verdict of a jury is given.
   (d) it is entered of record.
7. If a debtor owns three pieces of real estate and a judgment is entered against him, it will be a lien against
   (a) the property first acquired by him.
   (b) the property last acquired by him.
   (c) all three properties.
   (d) homestead property only.
8. The period of lien of the judgment is determined by
   (a) statute of state.
   (b) law of Congress.
   (c) plaintiff.
   (d) court.
9. The type of property of a debtor which can be sold on execution of a judgment is
   (a) real property only.
   (b) real or personal.
   (c) incorporeal real estate.
   (d) personal property only.
10. Holder of a cognitive or judgment note can confess judgment
    (a) after default only.
    (b) after execution and delivery of the note.
    (c) after 30 days default.
    (d) decree of court.
11. Judgment notes can be confessed for a debtor by
    (a) an attorney-in-fact.
    (b) an agent.
    (c) a Justice of the Peace.
    (d) an attorney at law.
12. A mechanic's lien can be filed against an owner by
    (a) a salesman against a broker.
    (b) a lumber company furnishing materials.
    (c) an abstracter.
    (d) the building superintendent after completion of building.
13. A judgment entered against a person who owns property would not be good against which one of the following:
    (a) a life estate.
    (b) tenancy in common.
    (c) leasehold.
    (d) estate by the entireties.
14. A judgment was entered against John Stone on May 3, 1969. The judgment would *not* be a lien against which one of the following:
    (a) property purchased on April 25, 1960.
    (b) property acquired by devise on November 25, 1968.
    (c) property purchased on Jan. 14, 1972.
    (d) property acquired by gift on March 17, 1969.
15. Property acquired by a debtor after judgment has been entered against him will be liened by the issuance of
    (a) an action to quiet title.
    (b) *scire facias* proceedings.

(c) filing a civil suit in assumpsit.
(d) suit to annul a debtor's exemption.

16. Postponing a judgment, instead of releasing a judgment benefits
(a) the debtor.
(b) no one, since they are the same.
(c) the creditor.
(d) a third party.

17. A judgment may be satisfied by sale of personal property through
(a) levy and attachment proceedings.
(b) filing a creditor's bill
(c) bill of interpleader.
(d) sequestration proceedings.

18. A judgment *in rem* binds only debtor's
(a) personal property.
(b) real property.
(c) household effects and furniture.
(d) automobile.

19. Judgments prevent the debtor's property from being
(a) sold.
(b) leased.
(c) mortgaged.
(d) none of these.

20. Adams has a judgment against Austin dated March 21, 1974. Austin owns two properties, designated Tracts 1 and 2. Clark holds a mortgage against Tract 1, dated April 24, 1969. Adams, in order to satisfy his judgment must proceed
(a) against Tract 1.
(b) against Tract 2.
(c) must wait until Austin sells Tract 1.
(d) must wait until mortgage is paid or foreclosed.

21. Alberts deeds property to Forster on January 3, 1974. The deed is recorded on January 15, 1972. Boone enters judgment against Alberts on January 10, 1974. Which of the following is true:
(a) the judgment is now a lien against Forster.
(b) the judgment is a lien against the subject property.
(c) the deed is invalid.
(d) Forster can have the sale rescinded.

22. With a judgment entered on December 6, 1968, a first mortgage entered on January 21, 1969, a second mortgage entered on February 14, 1969, and a second judgment entered on March 4, 1974, in a foreclosure action brought by the second judgment creditor, the first judgment creditor would be paid
(a) first.
(b) second.
(c) third.
(d) fourth.

23. Where, at a sheriff's sale upon a delinquent mortgage, the amount realized is more than the indebtedness, the excess belongs to
(a) the mortgagor.
(b) the mortgagee.
(c) sheriff's office.
(d) the purchaser.

24. Stevens, a retail shoe merchant, entered judgment for $3,000 upon a note given to him by Hilton, a wholesale shoe dealer, on March 21, 1974, for a loan. On May 3, 1974, Stevens purchased shoes from Hilton for $850, and agreed that Hilton could apply this sum on the debt due him by Hilton. Stevens assigned his judgment to Rhodes on May 21, 1974.

The assignment is recorded. Hilton tenders $2,150 to Rhodes, in full satisfaction of the debt, which Rhodes refuses to accept. Under these circumstances

I. Rhodes can recover only $2,150 from Hilton.

II. Rhodes can recover the $850 from Stevens.

(a) I only.
(b) II only.
(c) both I and II.
(d) neither I nor II.

Chapter 7

LANDLORD AND TENANT

A LEASE is a non-freehold, or as is often stated, it is less than a freehold estate: "a leasehold." It is an estate for a specified period of time and upon expiration of the lease term, the estate terminates.

The relationship of landlord and tenant is that which arises from a contract, express or implied, by which one person occupies the real property of another with his permission and in subordination to his rights; the occupant being known as the "tenant" and the person in subordination to whom he occupies is the "landlord." *McNeill v. McNeill,* 456 S.W. 2d 800 (Mo. App. 1970). It is created by a lease. The two parties to a lease are the lessor, who is the owner, and the lessee, who obtains possession of the premises for a specified period of time. The term landlord is used interchangeably with the term lessor, and the same is true of the lessee, who is often referred to as the tenant. The lessor's interest is called a reversion. Strictly speaking, the two prime parties to the lease should be called lessor and lessee. Where the lessee sublets a portion of the leased premises to another person, he becomes the landlord and the sub-lessee is the tenant. However, in every day parlance among laymen and licensees, the relationship of lessor-lessee is called a landlord-tenant relationship.

The lease contract, voluntarily entered into by the parties, largely determines the law by which the parties are governed. The lease contract may be verbal or in writing. The verbal lease is just as binding and of great legal efficacy as the written contract, providing that the term of the lease is not in excess of the period prescribed by the Statute of Frauds. The Statute of Frauds requires certain contracts to be in writing, particularly those relating to real estate. Contracts which cannot be performed within one year, as a rule, must be in writing. Thus, a lease for more than one year, in most states, as in California, must be in writing in order to be enforceable.

In an action to collect rents under a three year lease, signed only by the *lessee,* for property in California, the court held that the lease violated the California Statute of Frauds in that a lease for more than one year must be in writing and signed by the party to be charged (lessor). The lessee, a resident of Oregon, where the suit was brought could not recover: *Palmer v. Wheeler,* 481 P. 2d 68 (Ore. 1971). The period runs from the date when the contract is entered into, rather than from the date the lease term commences. In Pennsylvania, a lease in excess of three years must be in writing. For obvious reasons, a written lease is preferable to a verbal one. The tenure of human life is uncertain, and one or both of the parties to the contract may die during its term. In case of controversy or litigation, the surviving party would not be permitted to testify as he is a party in interest, and the other party is deceased.

Where lessee occupies premise under oral lease fixing no duration, either lessor or lessee can terminate lease at expiration of any month by giving written notice: *Branch v. Watkins Realty Corp.,* 289 So. 2d 381 (La. App. 1973).

The lease must be definite, and free from ambiguity: *Russell v. Valentine,* 376 P. 2d 548 (Utah 1962).

An agreement to contract for lease in the future must be definite and specific as to terms of the lease; otherwise it is unenforceable. A contract to lease which did not fix rental, and which was conditioned upon obtaining financing and adequate parking facilities (which were not met) was unenforceable; *Kapetan v. Kelso,* 481 P. 2d 24 (Wash. App. 1971).

The essence of a lease is the payment of rent. A lease may be defined as a contract, oral or written, for the *possession* of lands and tenements, on the one hand, in return for a recompense of rent or other income, on the other hand. A license is a personal privilege. It is not an estate in land, and it is not usually assignable. In deciding whether a writing was a lease or a license for pin ball machines, the court held that the test is whether exclusive possession of premises is given or merely possession to use: *Timmons v. Cropper,* 172 A. 2d 757 (Dela. 1961). A license may be termed a tenancy at will, which can be terminated at any time.

Term

A tenancy for years is one for a fixed period of time, whether it is a month, year, or longer. A tenancy from year to year or month to month is one that continues for an indefinite number of definite terms. The estate continues indefinitely until one of the parties elects to terminate it by giving proper notice. Usually the lease is for a specified term, one month or one year.

Generally, when a lease for a certain term expires, a lessee is not entitled to crops planted at such time that they do not and cannot mature before expiration of the lease; nevertheless, a lessee is entitled to the crop, where lessor knew the crop could not mature during the term and still consented to acquiescence in the planting or cultivating: *Beken v. Elster,* 503 S.W. 2d 408 (Texas 1973).

Holding over

An implied renewal of a tenancy by the holding over of the tenant after the expiration of the lease, is presumed in case nothing is said in the lease to the contrary. All the terms and conditions in the former lease, therefore, will continue in force. Where the lease is for one year, from May 1, 1973 to April 30, 1974, it expires at 12:01 A.M. on May 1, 1974, Where the tenant holds over and continues to occupy the premises during all of the day of May 2, 1974, he will be liable for the whole rent for the second year. It would be no defense to claim that he occupied the premises during May 2nd under a mistake of law as to the time the lease expired. This would be the case even though the lessee previously had given written notice of his intention to quit the premises. Of course, a lessee cannot stay over after the expiration of the lease term for an additional few days and then claim he is entitled to possession for an additional year. The holding over must be *lawful,* i.e., with the consent of the lessor.

A tenant, who holds over after expiration of the lease term is liable for reasonable rent. Under Florida law, the tenant, may, in fact, be liable for double rent; *Nelson v. Growers Ford Tractor Co.,* 282 So. 66 (Fla. App. 1973).

Tenant at will; tenant at sufferance

A tenancy at will is in the nature of a license, to be ended at the instance of the owner. A tenant at sufferance is no tenant at all since he holds over without the consent of the landlord, which is essential to a landlord—tenant relationship. He is a wrongdoer and the lessor may bring an action in ejectment to recover possession: *Kilbourne v. Forester,* 46 S.W. 2d 770 (1970).

In the case of *Custis v. Klein,* 127 A. 2d 268 (D.C. 1962), the court held in a lease, for month to month, notice given in April to vacate premises on April 30 was defective and lessee was entitled to possession for full month of April.

In the case of *Housing Authority of Pittsburgh v. Turner,* 191 A. 2d 869 (Pa. 1963), the termination of a month to month lease by Housing Authority, without giving any reason, was held no abuse of due process. Where the lease is for five years and the tenant remains in possession after the expiration of that term with the consent of the lessor, he cannot claim a new term for *five* years. The lease would be extended only for an additional *one* year, and so on from year to year until terminated by either party. The lease may be for one year, with a clause in the contract that if the tenant holds over lawfully, it shall be in force for another *month* and so on from month to month. The lease provision determines the rights of the parties.

The lease may be automatically continued in force in the absence of written notice of termination required under the lease, as follows:

> From and after the expiration of the term hereby created, this lease and all its terms, provisions, covenants, confessions, and remedies shall be deemed to be renewed and in force for another year, and so on from year to year unless either party shall have given to the other written notice to terminate said tenancy sixty (60) days prior to the expiration of the current term.

Parties

The names of the parties are inserted in the lease for the purpose of identification. A mistake or omission in setting forth the parties, if it is not material or does not cast doubt upon the parties intended, will have no effect upon the validity of the contract. Generally speaking, anyone who is capable of making a contract is capable of making a lease. A lease may be executed by the owner of the property himself or by a properly authorized agent acting in his behalf. If the lease must be in writing under the Statute of Frauds, then the agent's *authority* to execute the lease must be *in writing.* A lease signed and sealed by an agent in his *own name alone* would be open to attack by lessor or lessee. The execution of a lease by an agent must be carefully made. An agent may execute a lease, *as agent,* for an undisclosed principal, in which case the agent is considered as the lessor. It would be signed "John Steele, agent." The best execution, from the standpoint of the agent, is to include the name of the lessor, as

Adam Taylor
by John Steele, agent

An agent who is appointed merely to collect rents has no authority to negotiate a lease for the owner.

If a *minor* leases land, the same rules apply as in the case of any other contract executed under a similar condition. Such a lease, in other words, is not void but only voidable by the minor, and may be disaffirmed by him during his minority or within a reasonable time after attaining his majority. A *guardian* of a minor stands, however, in exactly the same position that he would had he himself owned the property, so far as his power to lease is concerned. He has been appointed for the purpose of administering the affairs of the minor, and consequently possesses all the power which may be necessary for executing the lease. In the same way, a *trustee* may grant leases which are unimpeachable so long as the trustee has remained within the powers granted to him by the deed of trust. The trust instrument should be examined to ascertain the extent of the trustee's authority. An *administrator* cannot lease. He has been appointed for the purpose of winding up the estate and has nothing to do with the renting of real estate. An *executor,* for the same reason, unless he has been made a trustee of the real estate, cannot lease any of the estate property. A *married woman* has full capacity to execute a lease for property owned by her. Where the property is owned by the entireties, in the name of husband and wife, either spouse can execute a valid lease upon the property owned by both. The lease benefits inure to both spouses.

It is important to note that the wife is for all practical purposes a co-beneficiary of the lease. An owner in common has no authority to bind his co-owners by a lease. In order to bind all, the lease must be executed by all the owners: *Needleman v. American Clothing Co. Inc.,* 63 A. 2d 201 (Vt. 1949).

Description

In making a lease it is not necessary to insert a minute description of the premises which is the subject of the property. The lease should provide that the premises are leased "as is"; that is, in their present condition. If the premises are in good repair, a statement to that effect should also be included. In case of commercial or industrial property, a full description should be used. In renting a furnished house, it is important to have a list of the furniture or other articles which are to pass with the house, attached to the lease. A clause should be inserted giving the lessor the right to make an examination of the articles in order to ascertain the condition of the furniture, which the tenant is bound to preserve in good order.

Warranties

Upon execution of a lease, there is an implied warranty that the condition of the premises described in the lease shall remain the same between the time of the execution of the lease and the beginning of the term. If a material change has taken place in the character of the premises, the tenant is not bound to take possession, for the premises tendered are not those described in the lease. Where a landlord rented a city property, and, before the lessee took possession at the commencement of the term, he allowed a third party to dump earth on the premises without the consent of the tenant and thereby changed the character of the leasehold, the landlord could not recover in an action for rent.

A lessee should require the lessor to covenant that the tenant will obtain possession of the premises at the commencement of the term, for otherwise the tenant can recover only damages for the delay in obtaining possession. Frequently, a lessee cannot obtain possession because of the unlawful holding over of the previous lessee. In a commercial establishment, this may result in considerable damage to the new tenant. Whether the new tenant can consider the breach sufficient to terminate the lease depends upon the circumstances. Adams' lease of dairy store premises from Brown had a 90-day sales clause. Brown sold the property to Clement, who immediately leased the premises to Denton for a dairy store at a considerably higher rental. The lease term was for five years, beginning February 15, 1971. Adams leased other premises about a half block distant but could not get possession until May 1, 1971. On April 1, 1971, Denton notified Clement that he would not honor the lease because of Clement's inability to give him possession. Denton claimed that he suffered irreparable harm since he could not take possession until after Adams was able to enter in active competition with him. Denton expected to obtain a considerable portion of Adams' present trade, which *induced* him to sign the lease and was, in a sense, a condition precedent. Here, possession on February 15th was distinctly understood as a material element in the contract and Clement could not hold Denton to the lease. Clement could have protected himself from this situation by a provision that:

> Lessor or his agent shall not be liable in damages, or otherwise, for failure to deliver posses-

sion of the demised premises to the lessee at the commencement of the term, where such failure is due to the unlawful holding over by a prior tenant or occupant; this lease shall, nevertheless, remain in full force and effect, with an abatement of rent to the lessee until the date possession is made available to him.

Eight months delay in giving tenant possession, due to failure to complete building, permitted tenant to rescind the lease: *Hartwig v. 65 Realty Co.,* 324 N.Y. S. 2d 567 (1971).

Rent

One of the characteristics which distinguishes a lease from a license is the payment of rent. Rent may be payable not only in money but in provisions, chattels, or labor. When no time is fixed for the payment of rent in a lease for a term, such as a year, the rent is not payable until the end of the term. If a specified time is provided, the rent is due and payable at that date.

In most cases, the lease contains a clause stipulating that the rent shall be paid monthly in advance. It is considered good practice to insert an express covenant in the lease by which the tenant binds himself to pay the amount agreed upon. This is valuable because of the fact that while an implied agreement can be presumed in all cases for the tenant to pay the agreed rental, yet if there is an express covenant and the tenant should subsequently assign the lease, even with the lessor's consent, the first tenant would still be liable for the rent. The only way in which he can be relieved from this responsibility is by the formal release by the landlord of the tenant. This practically amounts to the cancellation of the first lease and the creation of a second agreement with the new tenant. If the tenant is of questionable financial responsibility, a landlord can protect himself by insisting that the tenant provide a satisfactory surety to guarantee the terms of the lease; or the landlord may require that the tenant put up a substantial sum of money as evidence of good faith, which shall be applied to the *rent for the last several months of the lease term.*

In the case of *Martinique Realty Corp. v. Hull,* 166 A. 2d 803 (N.J. 1960), the tenant had made advance payment of rent for the full term. The property was sold during the term. The court held that it was the duty of the purchaser to ascertain the lease arrangement, and that he was bound by the pre-paid rentals.

It is also good practice to insert a clause in the lease of an apartment or furnished house, that all or part of said deposit may be used by the lessor to compensate him for any damage caused by the lessee to the furniture or premises during his occupancy.

It is a principle of law that a leased store will remain in the same condition between the date when the lease was signed and when the lease term begins.

Security Deposits

It is a general practice, in urban areas, for the landlord, upon signing a lease for an apartment, to require the tenant to pay a full month's rent, as a security deposit. This deposit is in addition to a month's rent, which the landlord may require as a guarantee for payment of rent during the term of the lease, which is applied to the last month's rent. The security deposit is held by the landlord until the tenant vacates the apartment. It is intended to reimburse the landlord for any damage to the premises during the tenant's occupancy. The tenant will also be charged, as an offset to the deposit, for any expense incurred by the landlord, in "cleaning up" the premises, or in obtaining a new tenant during the unexpired term of the lease: *Pyrimid Enterprises, Inc. v. Amadeo,* 294 N.E. 2d 713 (Ill. App. 1973). It also acts as an incentive to the tenant to keep the premises in good order, reasonable wear and tear excepted.

The question arises, —who is entitled to interest on the security deposit, held by the landlord during the term of the lease, which is often successively renewed for a number of years? The Illinois law provides that the lessee is entitled to 4 per cent interest upon deposit money held for more than six months. The New Jersey law provides for interest, less one per cent to the landlord for administration expenses. In the absence of a statute, the lease should contain a provision as to which party is entitled to interest on the deposit money.

Commercial use of the premises

The particular commercial use to which the leased premises are to be put should be spelled out with clarity. While courts will not make contracts for the parties, they will lend their aid in ascertaining the *intention* of the parties from the language used in the lease instrument.

In the case of *Anderson v. Busoda,* 180 A. 2d 130 (D.C.) the lease prohibited the use of the premises "for any other purpose than laundry service." The tenant, after several months on the premises, added a "dry cleaning service." He changed the name from "Normandy Laundry" to "Astro Laundry and Cleaners." The court held there was a violation of the lease, pointing out that, "In ordinary and popular usage there is a vast and distinct difference between laundry service and dry cleaning service, both in the methods used and the results accomplished." It is obvious that the "use" clause is of great importance in shopping center leases.

Shopping center leases

The preparation of leases in shopping center developments calls for expert knowledge in that particular area of real estate practice. The services of an experienced real estate attorney are strongly recommended if the owner or developer of the shopping area is not knowledgeable in the field. Practically all leases provide a stated minimum monthly rental payable up to a certain volume of sales. Then, the rental is based upon a percentage of gross sales,—the percentage decreases as the volume of gross sales increases. The lease usually provides that the lessee shall pay, as additional rent, increases in taxes upon the subject property during the lease term, a provision for a renewal of the lease, at the option of the lessee upon new terms of rental, and the lessee's liability for increased insurance premiums due to his occupancy as well as contributions according to a formula, for his participation in any program for promotion or advertising the particular shopping area for the advantage of all tenants.

In order to promote harmony, sightliness and good business practices, the lease will embody necessary rules as to days and hours of operation, parking for employees, types of fronts, signs, awnings, outside displays, deliveries and trash collections. The lessor is responsible for the location, marking and maintenance of the parking areas, policing, lighting and cleaning. It is customarily found that the tenants in a large shopping center will implement the rules embodied in a lease, by organization of all the lessees into a Merchants Association to their mutual advantage.

A shopping center leased a store for a retail bakery, donut shop and snack bar. The lease contained a prohibition against a lease for similar use within a designated distance. The lessee, later, received permission to sell sandwiches and other allied items usually sold. Subsequently, an adjoining vacant store was leased for a Mexican-type restaurant. The court held that the restaurant use violated the first lease: *Anderson v. Blondo Plaza, Inc.,* 186 N.W. 2d 114 (Neb. 1971); *Carousel Snack Bars v. Crown Construction Co.,* 439 F 2d 280 (1971).

Apartment leases

It is not unusual in leasing a unit in an apartment building to implement the lease contract by a set of rules and regulations, which, by reference to them, become a part of the lease proper. The rules are intended to prevent a tenant from becoming obnoxious or a nuisance to other tenants or to the public.

One prohibition, in particular, prohibits the maintenance of any domestic or wild animal in or about the premises except with the written consent of the lessor. In the case of *Margolin et al. v. Richards,* 70 D & C 380 (Pa. 1949), confession for possession was entered against a tenant who kept a small dog in his apartment of a recently completed building. Several tenants had complained. The lessee contended that before he signed the lease, the building manager told him that "he might surreptitiously bring the dog in and out the cellar door." The court held that "there was nothing to indicate the manager had any authority to waive any provision in the lease, and, furthermore, whatever oral agreements or conversations were made before signing a contract are merged in the written agreement."

The importance of a lease of an apartment is not to create a tenurial relationship, but rather to arrange the leasing of a habitable dwelling. This means that there are no latent defects in facilities vital to the use of the property for residential purposes and that these essential facilities will remain during the entire term in a condition which will make the property livable. *Marini v. Ireland,* 265 A. 2d 526 (N.J. 1970).

The very object of the letting was to furnish the defendant with quarters suitable for living purposes. This is what the landlord at least impliedly (if not expressly) represented he had available and what the tenant was seeking. "The warranty of habitability which we hold exists in such a case is imposed by law on the basis of public policy. It arises by operation of law because of the relationship of the parties, the nature of the transaction, and the surrounding circumstances." In *Kline v. Burns,* 276 A. 2d 248 (N.H. 1971), a tenant brought an action against his landlord to recover all rent paid during occupancy on grounds that premises were in violation of city housing code. The landlord then brought an action for possession and to recover the unpaid rent.

Adoption of this view makes available to the tenant the basic contract remedies of damages, reformation and rescission. *Lemle v. Breeden,* 51 Hawaii 426 (1969). The tenant can obtain relief by instituting an action for breach of warranty or by offsetting his damages against a claim made against him by the landlord.

Increased adoption of implied warranty doctrine

The trend of the implied warranty principle of law, has been held, in a number of jurisdictions, to apply to leasing dwellings and apartments. The thrust of these decisions is that the leased premises must be habitable. The opinion of Justice Tobriner, in the case of *Green v. The Superior Court of the City and County of San Francisco,* 517 P. 2d 1168 (Cal. 1974), gives a very lucid and comprehensive discussion for justification of the implied warranty of habitability for residential leases. The opinion states:

> "Under traditional common law doctrine, long followed in California, a landlord was under no duty to maintain leased dwellings in habitable condition during the term of the lease. In the past several years, however, the highest courts of a rapidly growing number of states and the District of Columbia have re-examined the bases of the old common law rule and have uniformly determined that it no longer corresponds to the realities of the modern urban landlord-tenant relationship. Accordingly, each of these jurisdictions has discarded the old common law rule and

has adopted an implied warranty of habitability for residential leases.[1] In June 1972, the California Court of Appeal reviewed this emerging out-of-state precedent in the case of *Hinson v. Delis,* (1972) 26 Cal. App. 3d 62, 102 Cal. Rptr. 661, and, persuaded by the reasoning of these decisions, held that a warranty of habitability if implied by law in residential leases in California. We granted a hearing in the instant case, and a companion case, to consider the Hinson decision and to determine whether the breach of such implied warranty may be raised as a defense by a tenant in an unlawful detainer action.

For the reasons discussed below, we have determined that the Hinson court properly recognized a common law implied warranty of habitability in residential leases in California, and we conclude that the breach of such warranty may be raised as a defense in an unlawful detainer action.

First, as the recent line of out-of-state cases comprehensively demonstrate, the factual and legal premises underlying the original common law rule in this area have long ceased to exist; continued adherence to the time-worn doctrine conflicts with the expectations and demands of the contemporary landlord-tenant relationship and with modern legal principles in analogous fields. To remain viable, the common law must reflect the realities of present day society; an implied warranty of habitability in residential leases must therefore be recognized.

Second, we shall point out that the statutory "repair and deduct" provisions of Civil Code section 1941 et seq. do not preclude this development in the common law, for such enactments were never intended to be the exclusive remedy for tenants but have always been viewed as complementary to existing common law rights.

Finally, we have concluded that a landlord's breach of this warranty of habitability may be raised as a defense in an unlawful detainer action. Past California cases have established that a defendant in an unlawful detainer action may raise any affirmative defense which, if established, will preserve the tenant's possession of the premises. As we shall explain, a landlord's breach of a warranty of habitability directly relates to whether any rent is "due and owing" by the tenant; hence, such breach may be determinative of whether the landlord or tenant is entitled to possession of the premises upon nonpayment of rent. Accordingly, the tenant may properly raise the issue of warranty of habitability in an unlawful detainer action. . . . "

In the case of *Mannie Joseph, Inc. v. Stewart,* 335 N.Y. S. 2d 709 (1972), the owner refused to make repairs in a tenement building, so that the tenants would move, and he could release the units more profitably. Mrs. Stewart failed to move, although she suffered from absence of heat, gas, no hot water, and other inconveniences. She stopped paying rent, and the owner sued for delinquent rent. The court refused to allow a recovery of rent. The cases, heretofor, generally held that the tenant's remedy in these circumstances is to vacate the premises. Another significant New York case, along similar lines, is *Granford Realty Corp. v. Valentine,* 337 N.Y. 2d 160 (1972).

Repairs

The tenant is bound to make tenantable repairs, but he cannot be forced to make lasting and general repairs to the structure, which would put the property in a better condition than it was when he took possession. Generally, a tenant cannot be bound to make good such deterioration as arises from necessary wear and tear incidental to

---

[1] See Pines v. Perssion, (1961) 14 Wis. 2d 590, 111 N.W. 2d 409; Lemle v. Breeden, (1969) 51 Haw. 426, 462 P. 2d 470; Javins v. First National Realty Corp., (1970) 138 U.S. App. D.C. 369, 428 F. 2d 1071, cert. den. 400 U.S. 925, 91 S. Ct. 186, 27 L. Ed. 2d 185; Marini v. Ireland, (1970) 56 N.J. 130, 265 A. 2d 526; Kline v. Burns, (1971) 111 N.H. 87, 276 A. 2d 248; Jack Spring, Inc. v. Little, (1972) 50 Ill. 2d 351, 280 N.E. 2d 208; Mease v. Fox (1972) Iowa, 200 N.W. 2d 791; Boston Housing Authority v. Hemingway, (1973) Mass., 293 N.E. 2d 831.

the proper and ordinary use of the property: *Lensing v. Carlisle Motor Sales, Inc.*, 189 A. 2d 307 (Pa. 1963).

Ordinarily, there is no obligation upon the landlord to make repairs. If, due to an existing defect, the tenant, a member of his family, or an invitee is injured, does the injured party have a right of action against the owner? The general rule of law is that a landlord who is entirely out of possession and control is not liable for an injury sustained by the tenant or by one visiting the tenant if the defect responsible for the accident was a patent one. The principle of law is fairly well established that, where the tenant rents the entire premises, the owner is not liable for any injury to the tenant or his invitees by reason of any dangerous condition existing at the time the tenant took possession. "The lessee's eyes are his bargain" and he takes the property "as is" with all existing faults. However, the landlord may be liable, depending upon extenuating circumstances in the particular case under an implied warranty.

A landlord is responsible where he conceals or fails to disclose a dangerous condition of which he had knowledge and one which a tenant was not likely to discover upon examination. A hidden, or latent, defect does impose a liability upon the landlord. He is also liable when he leases premises in a dangerous condition for a public use and has reason to believe the tenant will not first correct the defect. The lease of a theatre or a stadium is in this classification. In other words, where an owner leases public premises which constitute a nuisance, then, whether he is in or out of possession is immaterial insofar as relieving himself of liability is concerned.[2] A department store or a public garage would not fall in the described category. Although a landlord may not be required to make repairs, nevertheless, if he undertakes repairs voluntarily, he becomes responsible for any accident occasioned by the negligent manner in which the work is performed. Where a landlord has covenanted to make repairs and fails to do so, and someone is injured as a result of such failure, the agreement to repair does not operate as a resumption of control by the landlord and he is not liable for the injury. Of course, in an action of assumpsit on the contract, the landlord would be liable for damage suffered by the tenant. He would not be liable in a tort action for negligence. Where a landlord has promised to make repairs as an inducement to the execution of a lease, the tenant should insist that the repairs be written into the lease contract. If verbal only, and if the landlord later refuses to perform, the tenant would run into difficulty in compelling performance under the parol evidence rule.

Sidewalk injuries

What has been stated relative to liability relates to accidents upon the premises. Another important question arises in connection with sidewalk injury cases. Here, again, an owner out of control and possession is not liable. An owner who rents out a portion of the premises or who rents out separate parts to different tenants is held to remain in possession and control of the sidewalk, stairways, and corridors and is, therefore, responsible if any injury occurs in these areas. *Leary v. Lawrence Sales Corp.*, 442 Pa. 389 (1971). Where the municipality notifies the owner to repair a sidewalk and an injury results before the repair is made, the owner would be liable. A mortgagee in possession who exercises control and dominion over the leased premises is held to occupy the same role as the owner. In order to recover damages the injured party must establish the existence of a dangerous condition and that the owner had notice of it. The claimant must also be free of contributory negligence. Dangerous conditions include an accumulation of snow or ice, a missing brick, an

---

[2] Folkman v. Laver, 244 Pa. 605 (1914); Webel v. Yale University 7A Fd. (Conn. 1939).

elevation or depression causing an uneven surface, an accumulation of debris concealing an uneven pavement or gutter, an accumulation of oil causing a slippery surface, a hole in the sidewalk, and faulty position of basement outlets or doors to the pavement.

In the case of *Richardson v. Weckworth,* 509 P. 2d 1113 (Kan. 1973), the landlord agreed to repair a broken sidewalk. He failed to do so for several months. The tenant fell, suffering serious injuries. The tenant sued. The landlord's defense was that the defective sidewalk had been in existence for one year, the tenant knew it and, therefore, the tenant has assumed the risk, and was guilty of negligence. The landlord was held liable for the tenant's injuries.

Notice

Where an owner is sued for injuries, the owner must have had notice of the defective conditions. Notice to the owner may be *actual* or *constructive.* Actual notice is knowledge of the owner through observation or proximity. Constructive notice is where the defect has existed for such a long time that it will be presumed that the owner saw it or could have seen it with a reasonably frequent inspection. Since the municipality owes a duty of protective safety to its citizenry, the person injured will usually sue the city in the first instance. The city will then bring in the property owner as an additional defendant. The owner, in turn, may bring in the tenant as an additional defendant if the responsibility lies with the tenant.

In the case of the lease of an apartment, it is interesting to note that the New Hampshire Supreme Court has pronounced principles, which represent a radical departure from the common law. In the case of *Kline v. Burns,* 276 A. 2d 248 (N.H. 1971), a tenant brought an action against his landlord to recover all rent paid during his occupancy of an apartment on the grounds that the premises were in violation of the City Housing Code. The landlord, in turn, brought an action for possession and to recover unpaid rent. The language of the Supreme Court is significant. The Court said:

"The following are factors to be considered in the appraisal of the legal principles to be applied to the present day relationship of landlord and tenant: (1) Our legislature has recognized (RSA ch. 48-A) that the public welfare requires that dwellings offered for rental be at the beginning, and continue during the tenancy to be, in a safe condition and fit for human habitation. (2) Common experience demonstrates that the landlord has a much better knowledge of the conditions of the premises than the tenant. Furthermore housing code requirements and violations are usually known or made known to the landlord. *Marini v. Ireland,* 56 N.J. 130, 142, 265 A. 2d 526, 533 (1970); 44 Denver L.Q., 387, 398 (1967); *see* RSA 48-A:3(III) (supp.). It follows that the landlord is in a better position to know of latent defects, such as some of those involved in this case, which might go unnoticed by the tenant who rarely has sufficient knowledge or expertise to see or discover defects in wiring, fusing, or venting of gas appliances or furnaces. *See Reste Realty Corp. v. Cooper,* 53 N.J. 444, 452, 251 A. 2d 268, 272 (1969). (3) It is appropriate that the landlord who will retain ownership of the premises and any permanent improvements should bear the cost of repairs necessary to make the premises safe and fit for human habitation. 1 American Law of Property s. 3.78, at 347-48 (1952). In today's housing market, the landlord is usually in a much better bargaining position than the tenant which results in rental of poor housing in violation of public policy. A. B. Foundation, Model Residential Landlord-Tenant Code 9 (Tent. Draft 1969); 50 B.U.I. Rev. 24, 38, 39 (1970).

"In our opinion the above considerations demonstrate convincingly that in a rental of an apartment as a dwelling unit, be it a written or oral lease, for a specified time or at will, there is an implied warranty of habitability by the landlord that the apartment is habitable and fit for living.... *Marini v. Ireland,* 56 N.J. 130, 144, 265 A. 2d 526, 533 (1970); *Javins v. First Nat'l*

Realty Corp. supra; Lemle v. Breeden, 51 Hawaii 426, 433, 462 P. 2d 470, 474 (1969); *Lund v. MacArthur,* 51 Hawaii 473, 475, 482 P. 2d 461, 463 (1969). The warranty of habitability which we hold exists in such a case is imposed by law on the basis of public policy. It arises by operation of law because of the relationship of the parties, the nature of the transaction, and the surrounding circumstances. . . . "

Additions, alterations, improvements

An important covenant contained in leases of business property is one which provides that all alterations, additions, and improvements made by the lessee upon the property shall remain until the end of the lease, at the option of the lessor. It is frequently further provided that the lessor shall have the option of requiring the tenant to restore the premises to their original condition. The meaning of these three words, "alterations, additions, and improvements," has been the source of much friction, and it is practically impossible to lay down a general rule which would be applicable in all cases. The conflicts usually arise between the parties over machinery and other fixtures annexed to the freehold. The tenant claims that such equipment is trade fixtures, and as such, personal property, which may be removed by him at the expiration of the lease. The landlord on the other hand contends that such property is included within the phrase "alterations, additions, and improvements." For example, if a tenant leased a store and installed shelving at considerable expense, which shelving enhanced the value of the building for renting purposes, the landlord would be within his rights in maintaining that such shelving constituted additions, alterations, and improvements, and in requiring that it be left upon the premises at the expiration of the lease. On the other hand, if the shelving installed were of little value and would cost more to remove than it was worth, the landlord could insist that the tenant remove such fixtures and restore the premises to their original condition in accordance with the terms of the covenant in the lease.

Forcible entry in tenant's absence

Sometimes, a landlord or his agent, in the tenant's absence, will change the locks on a dwelling or apartment to prevent the tenant from obtaining re-entry. The rent may be delinquent. Even so, the landlord cannot take the law into his own hands. In the case of *Edwards v. Investment Co.,* 272 N.E. 2d 652 (Ohio 1971), the lease contained a clause that in event of tenant's default in rent or other provisions of the lease, the landlord may, without notice or demand, terminate the lease and remove, store or dispose of tenant's property at the risk and expense of the tenant. The court held the clause was against public policy and, therefore, void. A landlord must resort to law and legal methods, and not resort to self help, to obtain possession of premises, when tenant fails to make rental payments: *Bass v. Boltel & Co.* 217 N.W. 2d 804 (Neb. 1974).

Sub-letting and assignment

One of the most important covenants frequently found in leases is one forbidding the tenant to sub-let. All covenants against sub-letting in a lease are strictly construed. A covenant against *assignment* will not be construed to include *sub-letting.* In exactly the same way, should the lease contain a proviso that the premises should not be sub-let, the tenant will not be prevented from assigning his lease to anyone to whom he sees fit. To prohibit sub-letting entirely, it is important to provide "or any part thereof." Since the lessor usually prepares the lease, any ambiguity will be construed against him, in accordance with the legal principle that an instrument, if ambiguous, is most strongly construed against the person who prepared it. A tenant, in sub-letting a portion of the leased premises, should see to it that the sub-tenant's rights do not rise higher than his own. In fact, a special clause should be inserted to the effect that the lease is made subject to the terms and conditions of the landlord's lease from the owner. In renting out a portion of a business or commercial floor, it is advisable to insert a clause that the sub-tenant shall observe the same hours of opening and closing his business as the landlord follows. Also that the sub-tenant, his employees, customers, and invitees will refrain from committing any act or conduct which may be construed as a nuisance.

Surrender of premises

Whether a tenant is liable for damage caused by fire, the elements, "an act of God," or an inevitable casualty depends upon the language of the lease. If he agrees to return the premises at the expiration of the lease, reasonable wear and tear alone expected, he must restore the premises if damaged by fire or other accident. If fire is excepted, the tenant would still be responsible for damage caused by flood, tornado, or other "act of God" or by an inevitable accident. Act of God and inevitable accident are not synonymous. Even if the clause is sufficiently comprehensive so as to exclude a liability for rebuilding, the tenant would still be liable for the payment of *rent,* unless there was a clause abating the rent. This is the common law rule, but it has been modified by statute in some states to the effect that the rent ceases until the property is repaired by the lessor. However, if the premises are only partially destroyed by fire and the tenant remains in possession, the rent does not abate. It is not uncommon in a commercial lease, to include a provision for the abatement of rent due to destruction of the leased premises, as follows:

> It is understood and agreed by and between the parties hereto, that if during the term of this lease and any renewal hereof, the building is damaged or injured by fire, Act of God, or other casualty so that the demised premises are rendered unfit for occupancy to the extent that said premises cannot be repaired within ninety (90) days from the happening of such injury, then this lease shall cease and determine from the date of such injury. In such case, the Tenant shall pay the rent apportioned to the time of injury, and shall immediately surrender the leased premises to the Lessor, who may enter upon and repossess the same. If any such injury can be repaired within ninety (90) days thereafter, Lessor shall enter and repair, and this lease shall not be affected except that the rent shall be apportioned and suspended while such repairs are being made; but if said premises shall be so slightly injured by fire, Act of God, or other casualty, so as not to render same unfit for occupancy, then the Lessor agrees that the same shall be repaired with reasonable promptitude, and in that case the rent accrued or accruing shall not cease or determine.

Where the lessee has made extensive repairs at his own expense preparatory to taking possession, his investment should be protected by adequate fire insurance and a clause relative thereto, incorporated in the lease. The lease provision should read: "The proceeds of any fire insurance carried in both the Lessor's and Lessee's names and paid for by the Lessee, shall inure to the sole benefit of the Lessee."

Termination

There are various ways by which a lease may be terminated—by performance, agreement, or breach. The usual method is, of course, by performance; that is, the lease normally terminates at the expiration date.

Option and first right of refusal clauses

Where a lease contains an "option" clause, the lessee has the privilege of purchasing the leased premises at a *specified* price, during the term of the lease. The lessee knows exactly what price he must pay. In a lease, containing "right of first refusal", it means that the lessee has the right to meet any bona fide offer made by a third party for the purchase of the leased premises. It differs from an option in that the lessee does not know what the price offered will be: *King v. Dalton Motors, Inc.,* 109 N.W. 2d 51 (Minn. 1961); *LoCicero v. Demers,* 186 N.E. 2d 604 (Mass. 1962); *Hamel v. Altman,* 317 N.Y. S. 2d 722 (1971).

In an option, the time element is of the very essence of the contract. An option *expires* if not exercised within the time limit. In the case of *Cities Service Oil Co. v. National Shawmut Bank of Boston, Adm. et al.,* 172 N.E. 2d 104 (Mass. 1961), the lessee had an option to purchase the leased premises during the 10 year term, expiring August 31, 1959. A letter, purporting to exercise the option was mailed from New York on August 31, 1959, at 8:30 P.M., to the lessor, in Boston. It was received by the lessor on September 1, 1959. The court held that the mailing in New York "at such a late hour was not a proper giving of notice." The court held, in effect, that it is the majority rule that notice to exercise an option is effective only upon its *receipt* by the party to be notified, unless the parties otherwise agree. (citing numerous cases).

In *Schlussberg v. Rubin et al.,* 435 S.W. 2d 226 (Tex. 1971), the court held that a lease provision, giving lessee first refusal to renew lease at price *to be agreed upon,* or to meet any bona fide offer was not definite and certain, and was, therefore, unenforceable. A case of a similar tenor is: *Playmate Club, Inc. v. Country Clubs, Inc.,* 462 S.W. 2d 269 (Tenn. 1970).

Surrender of lease

The parties may mutually agree to terminate the lease before the expiration date. This is called a surrender. It is not necessary that such an agreement be in writing or in any particular form, and no consideration need be included in order to make the contract binding upon the parties, the presumption being that the advantage accruing to both parties is sufficient to give it full force and effect. In order, however, to make a surrender complete, it is necessary that it be specifically accepted by the landlord.

In the case of *Estate of Wm. O. Barnes, Deceased,* 37 N.Y. Misc. 2d 833 (1962), the court held that turning over keys to superintendent of building did not constitute a surrender.

Proof of acceptance must be clear and explicit. A lease may be terminated by breach of condition. Where one of the parties violates some important covenant in the lease, the other party may plead such act as grounds for the termination of the contract.

Gray, owner of a commercial building, operated a shoe store. He later sold the stock and fixtures to Dean, leasing the store to Dean for 5 years. Dean was unsuccessful in operating the business after six months, and decided to quit. He sold the stock and Gray agreed to buy the fixtures, cash register, etc. on July 1, 1968. At the end of the day, Dean placed the keys in the cash register and abandoned the premises. Three months later, Gray sued Dean for the intervening months rent. The court held there was a surrender of the lease since the owner used the premises to store the fixtures there: *Sanden v. Hanson,* 201 N.W. 2d 404 (N.D. 1972).

Eviction

Where the landlord is guilty of a violation of the lease, such breach is termed an eviction. It is a violent assertion of a right by the landlord as opposed to the rights which the tenant possesses. In other words, it is an unwarrantable ousting of the tenant by the landlord. The distinction between an eviction and an ejectment rests primarily upon this point. An eviction is a wrongful dispossession of the tenant. The action of ejectment is used to test, or establish, the title to real estate. An eviction has a somewhat different meaning from that generally attributed to it by the layman. It need not necessarily be a forcible ousting or removal of the tenant by the landlord from possession of the premises. As used here in connection with the law of landlord and tenant, it means the violation of any material covenant by the landlord which interferes with the tenant's quiet and peaceful enjoyment of the premises. Suppose, for example, a landlord should go upon the premises for the purpose of making repairs, there being no provision in the lease giving the landlord such right; the tenant could plead such action as sufficient grounds for cancelling the lease agreement. It is immaterial that the repairs to be made would benefit the tenant.

It must be remembered that the act complained of must be committed by the *landlord or an agent* representing the landlord or acting for him. The only ground upon which a tenant can plead eviction by a third party is in case the one whose act he complains of was exercising a right which he secured under a *paramount title to that of the landlord.* For example, if Jackson leased to Finch and afterward it turned out that the title was vested not in Jackson but in Chase and Chase should proceed to dispossess Finch, the action of Chase would amount to an eviction. If, however, the party whose acts were complained of proceeded under a questionable or defective title, the tenant could not plead immunity on the grounds that an eviction occurred. An overt act committed by a third party is not an eviction in contemplation of law. Anderson, the owner of a building, had leased the upper wall of the building to Brown for a term of three years for advertising purposes. Brown had erected an advertising sign upon the wall which could be seen by people passing in the vicinity. At the expiration of one year, Chambers, the owner of the adjoining property, a one-story building, erected an addition on the building in such a way that the view of Brown's wall was completely hidden from the eyes of passers-by and its value for advertising purposes destroyed. Consequently, Brown refused to pay rent on the grounds that an eviction had occurred, but the court disallowed the claim on the grounds that the injury had been inflicted neither by the owner nor by one having paramount title to the wall upon which the advertising was displayed, but by a third person, over whose action Anderson had no control. Entry by the city, or repairs ordered by the municipality, would not constitute an eviction. Eviction by the State, under its power of eminent domain, would not sustain a cause of action against the landlord.

A lessee may be entitled to damages for taking of the leased property, by condemnation, unless he waives this right. In a commercial lease, especially for a long term, provision should be inserted for the protection of the lessee in this situation.

In a long term leasehold, the lessee's interest may be more valuable than the lessor's land: *State of Tennessee v. Burkhart et al.,* 370 S.W. 2d 411 (Tenn. 1963), where the verdict was for ten times as much for the lessee, as it was for the owners. However, the lease may provide, as was the case in *Sugarman v. City of Baltimore et al.,* 191 A. 2d 240 (Md. 1963), that:

> In the event that condemnation proceedings are instituted against the premises hereby demised, and title taken by any Federal, State or Municipal body, then this lease shall become null and void, and the lessee shall not be entitled to receive any part of the award which may be received by the Lessor.

Fisk leased certain premises to Martin. They were part of a double house. Crum, the owner of the other half of the dwelling, had the party wall torn down after complying with the legal requirements. Martin claimed an eviction and refused to pay rent since he only had three walls on the leased premises. The tenant was held liable for rent. In another case. Appleby owned certain premises subject to a mortgage in favor of Eastman. Appleby then leased the premises to Crane for five years. Regretting his bargain, and seeking to get rid of Crane, Appleby purchased the mortgage from Eastman and took an assignment in the name of a "straw" party. The assignee then foreclosed and sought to eject Crane from possession. Appleby lost sight of the fact that under his lease to Crane the covenant for quiet possession protected the tenant not only from direct acts of the lessor and his agent, but also from those of persons holding a paramount title. Thus, the lessor is liable in damages to the tenant if the mortgagee asserts his rights to put the tenant out of possession. If the lessor becomes the holder of the mortgage, his exercise of the right of possession would at the same time subject him to a liability for so doing. The same result would follow if he brings action in the name of another (a "straw" party).

A mortgagee in possession must be cognizant of the fact that the mortgagor might pay off the debt during the term of a lease given by the mortgagee to the tenant, terminate the lease, and thereby subject the mortgagee to a cause of action for eviction damages by the tenant. In order to avoid this possibility, a mortgagee in possession, when leasing property owned by the mortgagor, should include a provision in the lease as follows:

> The lessee herein understands and agrees that the lessor is executing this lease under rights as mortgagee in possession of said premises and does not in any way or manner, covenant, agree, promise, or guarantee to the lessee, his heirs, or assigns, possession, quiet enjoyment or otherwise as against any person having a paramount title or interest to the within leased premises, anything contained in the written lease to the contrary notwithstanding.

On the other hand, if the lessee entertains any doubts or suspicions as to the lessor's legal right to lease the premises, he should insist upon a provision that:

> The lessor hereby certifies and represents that he has full right and authority to make and execute this lease and further certifies and represents that the demised premises are at the time of entering into this lease, free and clear from any mortgage, lien, or other encumbrance, which, if proceeded upon, might or could divest this lease.

Just as in the case of a sale of property, a broker should be familiar with zoning laws applicable to an intended lease by a prospective lessor. In the case of *Hoff v. Sander,* 497 S.W. 2d 651 (Mo. App. 1973), the lessor and lessee both believed that the leased property could be used for boarding horses, dogs and other pets. The city zoning ordinance, in fact, did not permit that use. The court held that the parties were charged with knowledge of zoning applicable and could not procure rescission of lease or damages on account of mutual mistake. Contracting parties are presumed to know the law and have it in mind when drawing their agreement: *Dill v. Poindexter,* 451 S.W. 2d 365 (Mo. App. 1970).

Tenant's remedy

If an actual or constructive eviction occurs and the tenant chooses to terminate the agreement, all of the rent which is past due and payable becomes an obligation which must be settled by the tenant upon demand. This action on the part of tenant terminates any right which the landlord has to demand rent after the date of the eviction. It is important to note that if the landlord should evict a tenant from a portion of the property, the tenant could, on this ground, evade the duty of paying rent on the portion which still remains to him. An eviction by landlord from part of the premises is, in the eyes of the law, an eviction from all of the property.

An important modification of this rule, however, exists in the case where a tenant is evicted from part of the premises by a paramount title invoked by a third party. In this case, the rent would be apportioned so that he would have to pay rent for that portion of the premises which still remained to him. If, however, the lessee takes the property with knowledge of the defective title of the lessor, it is then impossible for him to plead eviction as a defense against the payment of rent. After an eviction has occurred and the tenant remains in possession of the premises and takes no action which would indicate that he intends to hold the landlord responsible for the overt act, his continued occupation would constitute a waiver of the injury. When an eviction occurs, the tenant should promptly assert his rights in the matter. There are two courses which he may pursue: first, he may terminate the contractual relation between himself and the landlord by moving out and bringing suit for damages which he has sustained; or secondly, he may remain in possession of the premises and, after promptly notifying the landlord of the injury suffered and stating that he will hold the landlord responsible for the damage, he may bring suit for the amount he claims to have lost. In this event, however, it is necessary for him to continue to pay rent in exactly the same manner as though no breach had occurred.

Where a tenant is temporarily away from the premises, the landlord takes a grave risk when he padlocks the premises and prevents the tenant's re-entry: *Pitman v. Griffith,* 200 S.E. 2d 760 (Ga. 1973).

Forfeiture

Corresponding to the tenant's right to terminate the lease by reason of breach of covenant by the landlord, is the landlord's right to terminate the lease where the tenant is guilty of a violation of a material covenant. This is known as a forfeiture. Under the common law, if a tenant should disclaim, disaffirm, or impugn the landlord's title by some positive act, he thereby forfeits all rights under the contract. The reason for this is obvious. If the landlord could not terminate the contractual relation, it might be possible for the tenant to work great harm to the property, not only by violating the spirit and letter of the agreement but also by going so far as to claim title to the property by adverse possession after continuous occupation for the statutory period. The law, therefore, provides that the landlord has the option of declaring the lease forfeited upon the breach of any material covenant by the tenant. The landlord then has the right to enter and take possession of the property unless it can be shown that he has by some act waived the breach which has occurred. Suppose, for example, that a landlord should accept rent from a tenant for a period subsequent to the commission of the acts in controversy; in this case, he would have waived his right to declare the contract forfeited by permitting the tenant to continue in possession. The most usual breach by the tenant is non payment of rent.

Landlord's levy

It is important to note in this connection that distraint instituted for rent in default constitutes a technical waiver of the forfeiture which has occurred and permits the tenant successfully to maintain his right to possession under the terms of the lease. A landlord's levy is one of statutory enactment entirely. Under the common law, the landlord had no lien on the chattels of the tenant on leasing the premises or to the crops raised thereon. They were the absolute property of the tenant. It is in statutory law that the landlord has a method by which he can secure a lien upon the chattels and goods of the tenant. The right to distrain, however, exists in favor of the landlord only upon a claim for rent due and accrued.

Distraint defined

Distraint may therefore be defined as the right of a landlord to levy upon a tenant's goods and chattels for rent *in arrears.* The right does not reside in the landlord until there has been a default in rent, but he can bring this action the day after the rent is due.

Rent in arrears

If the rent is due on the first day of the month, as is generally true, and is not paid on that date, distraint proceedings may be instituted against the tenant on the second day of the month.

Penalty clause

Some leases provide that the rent shall be $100 per month, due and payable on the first day of the month, and if not paid by the tenth of the month, then the rent, in that case, shall be $110 per month. Since the rent is not in arrears until after the due date, the important practical question arises as to when the rent is in default; is it on the second day of the month or must the landlord wait until the eleventh day before instituting his right to distrain, or is the rent not in arrears until the first day of the following month ? It would appear that even though the lease provides for the payment of rent on the first day of the month, the effect of the second due date is to avoid the responsibility of payment on the first day, and the tenant is, therefore, within his rights in tendering the correct amount of rent at any time during the month. No lawful levy can be made until after the month has elapsed. It would make no difference whether a discount or penalty clause is used. The question becomes particularly vexatious during the last month of the lease, as the landlord may be fearful that the tenant may remove without payment of the rent; yet he is powerless to act.

A landlord may estop himself from insisting upon the punctual payment of rent where he has indulged a tenant and accepted rent after the due date. Suppose the lease from Adams to Brown provides for the payment of rent on the first day of each month during the lease term from May 1, 1973 to April 30, 1974. Brown pays the May rent on the first day, but after that he makes his rent payments anywhere from the 15th to the 25th of the month. In October, 1973, Adams could not distrain for the month's rent on October 2, because of his previous conduct in accepting the rent late. The doctrine of estoppel could be invoked against him. In order to reassert his right to punctual payment of rent, it would be necessary for Adams to notify Brown of his intention to hold him to punctual payment of the rent in the future.

The lessee need not tender payment in money when he has on previous occasions tendered a check which was accepted as payment of rent. If the landlord desires to insist upon payment in cash, the lessee is entitled to notice. Where rent is delinquent and the tenant makes a partial payment, the payment generally will be applied to the rent which first accrued. Rent paid "on account" will not give rise to the presumption that it was paid for the current period. The lessor may apply it to the most delinquent rent. This rule, of course, may be modified by agreement between the parties.

Where lessee paid all overdue rent before receipt of notice to quit, lessor had no right to terminate lease for failure to make *timely* payment of rent: *Village Development Co., Ltd. v. Hubbard,* 214 N.W. 2d 178 (Iowa 1974).

Penalty and forfeiture clause

A broker and salesman should be familiar with the legal difference between liquidated damages and a penalty clause. It has been noted that "liquidated damages" is frequently used in an agreement of sale where the vendee fails to consummate the transaction and earnest money deposit may be forfeited on that account. It is a sum of money agreed upon for breach of contract by the vendee. Liquidated damages, in an amount certain, is upheld by the courts, where the amount of damages sustained by the aggrieved party cannot be definitely ascertained. Where the damages flowing from the breach can be ascertained with some certainty, then the sum agreed upon as liquidated damages, if greater than the actual amount of damages, will be considered a penalty and unenforceable.

As applied to a lessor-lessee relationship, an example frequently found in leases will illustrate. In the lease from Adams to Baker is a provision that the lessee is to pay all water and sewer charges, as they become due quarterly. The lease further provides that upon failure to do so, Baker shall pay Adams the sum of $100 as "liquidated damages." Baker fails to pay the water and sewer charges for the fourth quarter of 1971 in the amount of $24.70. The lease expires on January 1, 1972. Adams can collect only $24.70, the actual charges, rather than the agreed upon sum of $100.

A lessor may prefer to oust a delinquent tenant rather than struggle with him periodically to recover the rent. Under a "tight" form lease, which contains a confession of judgment clause for possession, a non-paying tenant can be evicted promptly. Likewise, a tenant who holds over unlawfully (without the consent of the lessor) after the expiration of the lease, may be dispossessed in the same manner.

Effect of mortgage

Where a lease antedates a mortgage, the mortgagee takes the property subject to the lease if the mortgage is foreclosed at a later date. The lease cannot be terminated. In order for the mortgage to have precedence, it would be necessary to stipulate in the lease that it is subject and subordinate to any mortgage of record or which may at any time be placed upon the property. The tenant should have the right to pay any delinquency on the mortgage and apply such payments to the rent obligation. Ordinarily, a mortgage placed upon the premises before the execution of a lease would have priority. The lease could be terminated by the mortgagee, upon his acquisition of the property through foreclosure. This is true even though the mortgagee accepted rents from the tenant during a period prior to foreclosure when the former was a mortgagee in possession. In other words, his rights as *owner* are separate and independent from his rights as *mortgagee in possession.*

Leased housing program

The "Leased Housing Program" is a program of Federal assistance to provide habitable living quarters for large low-income families in dwellings leased from private owners and real estate companies. It is designed to provide "instant" dwellings for these low-income groups more rapidly than through new housing; to make better use of and rehabilitate present structures and thereby upgrade neighborhoods. The prime object is to encourage private interests to undertake this civic program by governmental guaranty of the income to such developers. This is accomplished by having the owner lease the structure to the Housing Authority of a city for a rent return and the Authority then sublets the unit to the individual tenants. The relationship between the owner and the Authority is upon the usual and ordinary relationship of Lessor and Lessee. Necessary mortgage financing is facilitated upon the strength of a "letter of intent to lease" from the Housing Authority to the owner. Rent is guaranteed by the Housing Authority to the owner even if the property is unoccupied—payable monthly. Since the program is intended to provide housing for large families, the dwellings or apartments should have a minimum of three bedrooms. The Housing Authority will adopt a rental scale according to the tenant's income and if less than the rent in the prime lease, the difference is paid by the Housing Authority. The lease term may vary from one to five years. Since the Authority is the principal tenant, it is responsible to return the premises at the expiration of the lease term in the same condition as at the commencement of the term, reasonable wear or tear or accident by fire excepted. Public liability is controlled pretty much by the law applicable to the usual relationship of landlord and tenant.

Questions on Landlord and Tenant

1. Q. What is the tenancy called where the lessee holds the land at the will of the lessor?
   A. Tenancy at sufferance; in some states, a tenancy at will.
2. Q. What is the obligation of the renting agent to the owner?
   A. To obtain the owner the greatest income, for the longest period of time, with the least expense on the property managed, keeping in mind the well-being of the tenant.
3. Q. Can a lease be enforced when the consideration is expressed in terms of farm products instead of money?
   A. Yes.
4. Q. In computing the income from an apartment house, there are several major items taken from the gross income in order to arrive at the net income. Name at least six (6).
   A. (1) taxes (2) insurance (3) repairs (4) depreciation on building (5) depreciation on furniture (6) collection of losses (7) management expenses (8) reserve for replacements (9) utilities (10) license fees.
5. Q. In a long term lease, what provision should be included relative to taxes?
   A. In a lease for 5 or 10 years, there should be a clause that the tenant agrees to pay any increase in taxes during the term of the lease.
6. Q. In the management of property, name four duties which an agent owes to his owner.
   A. (1) collect rents (2) keep proper records (3) remit net proceeds promptly (4) maintain and repair property.
7. Q. When a leased property is sold, and the lease does not expire for seven months after the sale takes place, at what time can the purchaser take physical possession of the property?
   A. Upon expiration of lease (7 months).
8. Q. What do you understand by a sub-lease?
   A. A lease granted to another person by the lessee.
9. Q. Distinguish between an assignment of a lease and the sub-letting of a lease.
   A. In a sub-lease or sub-letting of a lease, the lessee becomes the lessor and the sub-lessee becomes the tenant. Calls for a new lease. An assignment of a lease is a transfer by the lessee of his rights under the terms of the original lease.
10. Q. Name the essentials of a valid written lease.
    A. Parties, description, rental, term, demising, (leasing) signatures and delivery.
11. Q. In regard to lease terminology, what is the difference between an option and a first refusal?
    A. An option gives the lessee a definite right to buy the leased property at a designated price and within a specified time. A first refusal gives the tenant the first right to purchase the property at a price offered by a third party.
12. Q. In the investigation of a prospective tenant to determine his desirability, what information should be ascertained?
    A. Size of family, occupation, approximate income, previous address and former rental agent. A credit report is also recommended.
13. Q. What information should a rent receipt contain?
    A. Date paid, amount, address of property, rental period covered by payment, signa-

ture on receipt.

14. Q. Write an ordinary receipt for rent.
    A.

Des Moines, Iowa.
January 3, 1972.

Received of Henry Thompson .... Sum of Seventy-five ....
.... ($75.00) Dollars, for rent for month of January, 1972, for property at 1334 Capitol Street, Des Moines, Iowa.

Des Moines Realty Corporation,
Agent for James Black, Lessor.
By C. E. Prentice, Secretary.

15. Q. Where the tenant defaults in the payment of rent, can the landlord terminate the lease and evict a sub-tenant as well as the tenant?
    A. Yes, the sub-tenant's rights rise no higher than those of the tenant.
16. Q. Arthur verbally leases certain premises to James on February 1, 1970, for a one-year term from May 1, 1970, to April 30, 1971, with an option of two additional years at an increased rental. On April 1, 1971, Arthur notifies James that the property has been leased to Black. Does James have any cause of action against Arthur?
    A. No. Under the Statute of Frauds, the lease from Arthur to James had to be in writing in order to be enforceable. In most states, the period is one year from the making of the lease, or from February 1, 1970. In Pennsylvania, the period is three years.
17. Q. A lease is made by the Rapid Realty Co. agent to John J. Flynn for a term of five years. The lease is approved by the owners. Prior to the expiration of the five-year term, the Realty Co. executes a new lease for an additional five-year period. Three months before the expiration of the original term, the owners notify Flynn to vacate the premises at the end of that term. The tenant insists he has a lease for another five-year term. Is he correct?
    A. No. The agent's authority to execute a lease beyond the period fixed by the Statute of Frauds must be in writing, and it does not appear that the agent had such written authority.
18. Q. An agent executed a lease to Jenks, as John Steele, agent. Upon the tenant's default in rent, judgment is confessed against Jenks in the name of the owner, Adam Taylor. Jenks petitions the court to have the judgment stricken off. Will Jenks succeed?
    A. Yes. The judgment was improperly entered as the owner was not a party to the lease.
19. Q. If, in the preceding case, the lease bore a notation "Approved by Adam Taylor," would Jenks succeed?
    A. Yes. The notation does not establish Taylor as the owner and a party in interest. To all intents and purposes, he is a stranger to the instrument.
20. Q. Rogers leases premises to Pike for a one-year term. The lease provides that if Pike lawfully holds over after the expiration of the term, he would be a tenant "from year to year" and so on from year to year. The original lease term ends on April 30, 1972. On April 20, 1972, Rogers notifies Pike to vacate the premises at the end of the current term, April 30, 1972. Pike refuses. Can Pike claim possession for another year?
    A. Yes. Rogers should have given Pike statutory notice (30-90 days, depending upon state).
21. Q. Jones leases premises to Brown for one year. The lease provides that if Brown remains over he shall be a tenant from month to month. After 14 months' occupancy, Jones gives Brown 30 days' notice to vacate. Brown claims he has a lease for an additional 10 months. Is Brown correct?
    A. No. The lease contract determines Brown's rights. It specifically provides that upon

Brown's holding over, the tenancy shall be upon a monthly basis and this provision will be enforced.

22. Q. A store lease provides that in event of sale, the lessee "agrees to vacate the said premises at any time upon receiving—O—days' notice in writing so to do, in case of sale of said property." Archer sells the property to Connor, who notifies the tenant, Benson, to vacate the premises in 30 days. Benson claims that he has a right to remain in possession until the expiration of the lease term, a period of 20 months. Who will win?

A. Benson will win. It is a matter of intention of the parties, and it is inconceivable that the lease could be terminated in advance of the expiration date without any previous notice at all.

23. Q. Lloyd leased certain premises to Barnes in February 1972, effective May 1, 1972. Before Barnes took possession, Lloyd permitted Cox to dump earth on the premises so that Barnes later refused to take possession. Can Lloyd collect rent from Barnes?

A. No. Upon execution of a lease, there is an implied warranty that the condition of the premises described in the lease shall remain the same between the time of the execution of the lease and the beginning of the term.

24. Q. Adams leased certain premises to Thomas and executed a release in favor of Clark, relinquishing his right to distrain upon certain articles owned by Clark and stored upon the premises. Later Adams sold the property to Dwight, who distrains for delinquent rent due him, upon Clark's property. Clark claims his property is exempt from levy because of Adams' release. Decide.

A. Dwight can sell Clark's property, because Adams' release is personal in its nature and not binding upon Dwight. A new release should have been obtained from Dwight.

25. Q. Can a tenant for life make a valid lease?

A. Yes, if it does not extend beyond the term of his own life. Since the life tenancy is uncertain, the joinder of the remainderman or reversioner should be had.

26. Q. A bank is a mortgagee in possession. It executes a lease to Casey for a two year term. During the lease term the mortgage debt is paid by Boone, the mortgagor, who ousts Casey from possession. Does Casey have a cause of action against the bank?

A. Yes. The landlord guaranteed the tenant quiet and peaceful enjoyment of the premises which was broken by Boone asserting a paramount title.

27. Q. How could the bank have protected itself?

A. By inserting a proper clause in the lease such as: "The lessee herein understands and agrees that the lessor is executing this lease under rights as mortgagee in possession of said premises and does not in any way or manner covenant, agree, promise, or guarantee to the lessee, his heirs, or assigns, possession, quiet enjoyment, or otherwise as against any person having a paramount title or interest to the within leased premises, anything contained in the within lease to the contrary notwithstanding."

28. Q. What are the interests of the lessor and lessee in a lease called?

A. Lessor's interest is called a "reversion." The interest of the lessee in the leasehold is usually an "estate for years."

29. Q. Ashley leases certain premises to Bridger for a motion-picture theatre for 10 years, with the right of assignment. Bridger expressly covenants to pay rent. Later Bridger forms a corporation and assigns the lease to the corporation. Upon the subsequent insolvency of the corporation, Ashley seeks to hold Bridger personally liable. Will he succeed?

A. Yes. By virtue of Bridger's express covenant to pay rent, he continues liable during the term of the lease. Assignment of the lease does not toll Bridger's liability. He would be relieved of liability only if his lease were cancelled and a new lease made to the corporation.

30. Q. A banking corporation leased certain premises to an oil company. Later the oil

company refused to pay rent claiming that the banking corporation's lease was *ultra vires* (beyond the powers of the corporation). Will it succeed?

A. No. The contract is executed so the *ultra vires* doctrine would not apply. In addition, it is a long-established rule of law that a lessee cannot impeach the title of his lessor for any cause except fraud.

31. Q. What is the difference between a tenancy at will and at sufferance?

A. There is no real difference. A tenancy at will is where a party is in possession of property under a mere license while a tenancy at sufferance is where one comes into possession of land by lawful title but keeps it afterward without any title at all. A tenant in possession under a lease from the mortgagee in possession would be a tenant at sufferance, after the property is foreclosed insofar as the new owner is concerned.

32. Q. Allen leased certain premises to Beck for a period of one year beginning on March 2, 1971. The lessee remained in possession through March 2, 1972. Is Beck liable for another year's rent?

A. Yes. The lease expired at midnight on March 1, 1972. Where the lessee holds over and continues to occupy the premises during all of the day of March 2 of the following year, he will be liable for the whole rent for the second year.

33. Q. Ash leases certain premises to Blake for a three year term at $200 monthly. At the expiration of three months, a flood damages the premises to such an extent that the premises are uninhabitable for five months. What, if any, is Blake's liability?

A. He is liable for rent for the five-month period. If the lease has no Act of God clause, Blake would also be liable for the cost of repairing the premises, unless exempted by statute.

34. Q. Appel owns certain premises leased to Brent. There is also a mortgage against the property, which is in default, and Cooper, the mortgagee, as well as Appel, demands rent from the tenant. To whom should Brent pay the rent?

A. To Cooper. The mortgagee in possession, where the mortgage is in default, is entitled to the rent.

35. Q. A guest fell upon a landing in front of an apartment, due to a hole in the flooring. Is the lessor or tenant liable?

A. The lessor. In an apartment building, the lessor is bound to make necessary repairs to stairways, landings, and the like.

36. Q. Archer leased certain premises to Barnes. There is no provision in the lease requiring Archer to make repairs. The city orders the owner, Archer, to make extensive repairs. Can Barnes plead Archer's entry as unlawful?

A. No. It would not constitute an eviction even if the action of the city was unconstitutional. The act complained of was not due to any voluntary conduct on the part of the lessor.

37. Q. In the following list of terms, which four pertain to leasing?

A. *Covenant,* equity, prospectus, *assignment, distraint,* eminent domain, easement, lien, foreclosure, *eviction.* (The terms applying to leases are italicized.)

38. Q. What is the compensation or income received for the use of real property called?

A. Rent.

39. Q. What type of property, as a general rule, may be distrained on the rented premises in order to collect delinquent rent?

A. All property upon the premises irrespective of ownership unless specifically exempted by statute or previously released by the lessor.

40. Q. Jones leased certain store premises to Bogg, who purchased equipment under a conditional sales contract, duly recorded. Can Jones distrain upon such equipment for delinquent rent?

A. Yes. The owner of the equipment should have obtained a release from Jones before making the sale to Bogg; or unless specifically exempted by statute, with notice to owner (lessor).

41. Q. When a tenant becomes in arrears in his rent, what action can be taken to protect the landlord's interest?
A. A distraint proceedings may be instituted to collect the rent, and, if there is a "tight" form written lease, confession of judgment for possession may be entered.
42. Q. What is meant by a "percentage" lease?
A. A lease which provides that the rental shall be a percentage of the gross volume of business done upon the leased premises, for example, 3 per cent. The lease usually provides first for a guaranteed minimum monthly rental.
43. Q. What is meant by a "surrender" of the lease?
A. A mutual agreement to cancel the lease before the expiration date; it must be specifically accepted by the landlord.
44. Q. Where Anders leases property to Brown, a person of dubious financial responsibility, for a term of five years, what steps can Anders take to protect his interest?
A. 1. Require a surety on the lease.
2. Require Brown to pay 6 months' rent in advance to be applied to the last 6 months of the lease term.
45. Q. Axton leased the roof of a building to Barnes for three years for the purpose of erecting advertising signs. At the end of one year, Colfax, who owned adjoining property, erected an addition upon his property which obstructed the view of Barnes' signs. Barnes refused to pay further rent. Can Axton collect?
A. Yes. The lessor was in no way responsible for the interference. It is a "bad bargain" on Barnes' part.
46. Q. If a tenant refuses, at the expiration of the lease term, to sign a new lease upon different terms, can the landlord oust him from possession?
A. Yes.
47. Q. If a member of the tenant's family is seriously ill or the premises are quarantined at the expiration date of the lease, what redress does the lessor have?
A. None, until the condition abates.
48. Q. If a property is leased at the time it is being sold, why should mention be made of it in the agreement of sale?
A. Because a lease is an encumbrance within the meaning of the term.
49. Q. An owner of real estate, which is mortgaged, leases it to a tenant. The mortgagee forecloses and obtains title to the property. He then ousts the tenant from possession. Does the tenant have a right of action against the owner under such circumstances?
A. Yes. The owner has violated the lease covenant of quiet and peaceful enjoyment to the tenant.
50. Q. Where a leased property is sold, who assigns the lease to the purchaser—the lessor or lessee?
A. The lessor.
51. Q. Who is ordinarily liable for the payment of the utilities for leased premises?
A. The lessee.
52. Q. In commercial leases what important clauses should be included for the lessor's protection?
A. 1. Tenant to pay any increased insurance premiums due to lessee's use or occupancy of premises.
2. Tenant to pay any increased taxes during term of lease.
3. Subordination clause so that lessor may place a first lien mortgage upon the premises.
4. Tenant to carry plate glass insurance.
53. Q. A lease is drawn between P. Kelly and Kay Semel, beautician, for certain premises. Her father, Joseph Semel, has signed the lease as surety. Miss Semel, with the consent of her landlord, sub-leases the entire premises to Dorothy Adams. Is Miss Semel relieved from liability for the rent?
A. No. As the original lessee, she continues liable for rent during the term of the lease.

as she expressly covenanted to pay rent under the lease executed by her.

54. Q. In what ways may a lease be terminated?
A. 1. By performance; automatically terminates at expiration of term.
2. By surrender; mutual cancellation of lease before expiration of term.
3. By breach; act of lessor is known as an eviction; act of lessee is known as forfeiture.

55. Q. Under the terms of a valid lease, must the landlord keep his tenant safe from trespassing of others upon the leased premises?
A. No; it is the duty of the tenant to enjoin such trespass.

56. Q. A property was held in the name of James Patz alone. He leased it to a tenant with an option to purchase. The wife of Patz did not sign the lease. The tenant exercised the option, but before consummation, Patz died. The wife refuses to execute a deed. What are her status and rights?
A. Since the wife did not sign the lease containing the option, she could not be compelled to execute a deed. The tenant, accepting a deed from the executor, would take it subject to the widow's dower right. Of course, he can refuse to take such a deed, subject to the encumbrances of dower, and either sue the estate for damages or recover any money paid on the sales contract.
Moral to Tenant:—Have lessor's wife join in a lease containing an option to purchase clause.

57. Q. Can a tenant after leasing property for 25 years claim ownership by adverse possession against the heirs of the original lessor?
A. No; occupancy was permissive throughout and not hostile or adverse.

58. Q. What articles belonging to others are usually exempt from a landlord's levy for delinquent rent?
A. Leased articles, such as furniture, soda water apparatus, ice cream cabinets, shoe repair machinery, cigarette vending machines, beauty and barber shop equipment, certain electrical apparatus and pianos, are exempt in some states, provided that notice of the leased article is given to the lessor.

59. Q. Whose liability is protection of plate glass windows?
A. Usually that of the lessee.

60. Q. Joseph Gray leases a neighborhood store to the Craft Cleaning Company. Due to a labor dispute, violence occurs and the premises are damaged. Who is liable for the repairs?
A. The tenant.

61. Q. Albert leases certain premises to Bold for a cigar store. In six months the place is raided five times as a "numbers joint." Court action is taken to padlock the premises. What is the status of rent for the unexpired period of the lease?
A. The tenant would be liable for the rent. If the landlord had guilty knowledge that the premises were to be used illegally, the courts would not enforce the lease.

62. Q. Make up a rent receipt in which the Paul N. Smith Agency is the broker-agent and Helen Gardner is the tenant at 1223 Maple Lane, Salt Lake City, Utah. The rent is $90 per month, with a $5 discount if paid by the 10th of the month. The rent is payable on the first of the month and the March 1974 rent is being paid March 6, 1974.

A.

Salt Lake City, Utah
March 6, 1974

Received of Helen Gardner. . . . .
Sum of. . . . . Eighty-five . . . . ($85). . . . . Dollars,
for rent for month of March 1974 . . . .
for premises located at 1223 Maple Lane, Salt Lake City, Utah.

Paul N. Smith Agency, Inc.
by Adele Trumper, Secretary

63. Q. What is an exculpatory clause in a lease?
    A. It is a clause which releases and relieves the landlord from damages and claims, e.g. liability for injuries resulting in injuries to tenant upon the leased premises. It is a question for a jury whether there was such disparity in bargaining power between landlord and tenant as to make such clause void, as against public policy.
64. Q. Where a member of a minority group has been refused a lease on that account, can he recover damages for mental anguish?
    A. Yes. (*Hinish v. Meier & Frank Co.,* 115 P. 2d 438 (Ore. 1941).

True and False

1. A lease is a contract. **T** F
2. A valid oral lease is assignable. **T** F
3. A lease given by a lessee to a third party is a release. T **F**
4. Leases may include fixtures along with the real estate. **T** F
5. A tenancy from month to month may be terminated at any time without notice. T **F**
6. An estate for years and a tenancy from year to year mean the same thing. T **F**
7. Every lease must be signed by the tenant. T **F**
8. The terms "tenant" and "lessee" are generally used in the same sense. **T** F
9. A "tenant by sufferance" is one who is unable to remove from the premises at the end of the term because of serious illness. T **F**
10. Where a tenant has been transferred to another city by his employer, he may terminate his lease. T **F**
11. A sales clause in a lease means that the lease can be terminated in event of sale of the property by giving notice to tenant. **T** F
12. Where a sales clause has been exercised, the tenant is entitled to moving expenses. T **F**
13. An oral lease favors the tenant. **T** F
14. "First right of refusal" is the same as an option to purchase the property under a lease. T **F**
15. All leases over three years must be recorded. T **F**
16. A tenant of a fourth floor apartment finds that the elevator service is permanently discontinued. The tenant may move on that account. **T** F
17. If the tenant fails to pay his rent when due, such action immediately terminates the lease. T **F**
18. Joint tenancy means ownership of real estate, not the leasing of it. **T** F
19. There are no covenants to be found in a lease. T **F**
20. If the monthly rental is to remain the same, a long-term lease on real property need not be in writing to be enforceable. T **F**
21. A lease stated that the rent was to be paid monthly, but did not specify that the rent should be paid in advance. In that case, the rent was due and payable on the last day of the month. **T** F
22. When a lease of a store does not provide who shall make necessary repairs to the premises, the cost of such repairs falls upon the lessor. T **F**
23. A lease is a *nudum pactum.* T **F**
24. A lease for five years, signed and sealed only by an agent, does not bind the owner. **T** F
25. An oral lease for one year is valid. **T** F
26. Sale of a property terminates an existing lease. T **F**
27. Lease of a property in disrepair constitutes a violation of law. T **F**
28. A lessee is the tenant. **T** F
29. An agent's authority to execute a lease for more than three years must be in writing. **T** F
30. A lease usually favors the tenant. T **F**
31. A married woman has authority to execute a lease to property owned by herself

and her husband. **T** F
32. A lease must be for a money rental. T **F**
33. An administrator of an estate cannot execute a lease for 5 years. **T** F
34. The beneficiary of a trust estate must always join in the lease by the trustee. T **F**
35. A lease for three years automatically renews itself for three more years if the tenant remains on the premises. T **F**
36. A lease is assignable if there is no clause in the lease to the contrary. **T** F
37. Sub-letting and assignment are the same. T **F**
38. In an assignment the original lessee continues liable for the rent payments. **T** F
39. A sky lease is one for space in a building above the 25th floor. T **F**
40. A tenant is liable for ordinary repairs. **T** F
41. The landlord is liable for repair of frozen water lines. T **F**
42. A tenant can refuse to pay rent where the owner has failed to make repairs agreed upon. T **F**
43. A lessor is liable for injuries where he leases any premises in a defective condition. T **F**
44. A lessor is not liable for damages where he voluntarily makes repairs and does so negligently. T **F**
45. A lease for five years need not be in writing if the tenant pays a substantial amount of rent in advance. T **F**
46. The lease of a tenant in a store building expires if there is a change of ownership of the property. T **F**
47. A lease on a property being sold constitutes an encumbrance on that property. **T** F
48. A percentage lease is one based upon a percentage of the assessed valuation. T **F**
49. On a percentage lease the monthly rental is always the same and does not vary. T **F**
50. If a tenant does not pay his rent when due, the landlord may immediately treble the rent. T **F**
51. A lease for less than one year need not be in writing to be enforceable. **T** F
52. When a lessee rents to another a part of the property which he holds under lease, he is "sub-letting." **T** F
53. City property may be leased for any period from one to ninety-nine years. **T** F
54. In condemnation proceedings, the tenant is entitled to compensation for loss of his lease. **T** F
55. A 22-year lease on farm land is valid. **T** F
56. A lease is a bilateral contract which conveys the right of possession to real property. **T** F
57. A release clause is used when a tenant has secured an option to renew the lease for an additional term. T **F**
58. Where leased property is condemned by the municipality, the lessee has a right of action against the lessor for damages. T **F**
59. A landlord must keep his tenant safe from trespassing of others upon the leased premises. T **F**
60. A tenant in an apartment building must pay rent if the building is destroyed by fire. T **F**
61. A tenant in possession of the entire building is liable for injuries suffered upon the leased premises. **T** F
62. A lessor has no right to go upon the leased premises to show prospective purchasers the property unless the right is reserved in the lease. **T** F
63. A tenant is always entitled to the first right to purchase the leased property if it is for sale. T **F**
64. Where the landlord violates the lease, it is termed an eviction. **T** F
65. An estate for years is for some determinate period. **T** F
66. Where the leased property is taken under eminent domain, the tenant can recover for the value of his lease from:
    (a) the lessor. T **F**
    (b) the body or corporation condemning the property. **T** F

67. Rent is in default the day after it is due. **T** F
68. Where a lessor accepts delinquent rent for five months, he cannot refuse to accept rent for the next month because it is after the due date. **T** F
69. Rent controls apply to all leased properties. T **F**
70. A sales clause in a lease refers to the period of time a tenant must be given in order to terminate the lease. **T** F
71. Any dwelling lease can be terminated before its term if the property is purchased by a veteran. T **F**
72. A tenant for one year who holds over after the term would be a tenant for an additional year. **T** F
73. A verbal lease for one year with an option to renew for three years must be in writing. **T** F
74. A mortgagee in possession of leased premises cannot collect the rent unless he has written assignment from the owner. T **F**
75. A lessor may levy for rent upon a stranger's goods found upon the premises. **T** F
76. A tenancy at will can only be terminated by the tenant. T **F**
77. In case of ambiguity in a lease, it is construed most strongly against the person who prepared it. **T** F
78. Where the premises are destroyed by an Act of God, the tenant is relieved from rebuilding. **T** F
79. On levying for delinquent rent, the lessor, or his agent, may break open an outer door in the tenant's absence. T **F**
80. Rent controversies are determined in a special "people's court." T **F**
81. A landlord is not liable for injuries suffered by the tenant due to a hidden defective condition of the premises. T **F**
82. A landlord is liable for injuries to a guest suffered in the collapse of a public building such as a grandstand. **T** F
83. Where the tenant defaults in the payment of rent, the landlord can terminate the lease and evict a sub-tenant as well as the tenant. **T** F
84. Where a landlord distrains for rent, he cannot, at the same time, terminate the lease. **T** F
85. The first floor tenant of an apartment house is liable for snow removal. T **F**
86. The law requires all leases to be in writing. T **F**
87. A leasehold is considered an estate for years. **T** F
88. Sale of a property for cash automatically cancels a month to month lease. T **F**
89. The term "tenants in common" refers to several persons who lease and occupy the same property. T **F**
90. A tenant who continues to occupy the premises after the expiration of the lease is called a hold-over tenant. **T** F
91. A landlord may send mechanics into leased premises to make alterations even though the lease contains no specific authority to do so. T **F**
92. Goods exempt from a landlord's distraint arise from statute. **T** F
93. A mortgagee in possession cannot lease the mortgage premises. T **F**
94. A lease by a mortgagee in possession can be terminated by the owner if he pays off the mortgage debt. **T** F
95. A lessor has a reversionary interest in the leased premises. **T** F
96. Act of God and accident by fire are the same. T **F**
97. A tenant is required to repair frozen water pipes. **T** F
98. The rule of "caveat emptor" applies to the tenant in leasing a property in a state of disrepair, if it is habitable. **T** F
99. A straight monthly rental, by tenant, is preferable to a percentage lease with a minimum monthly rental. T **F**
100. Where a lease contains a "first right of refusal" clause the tenant is certain as to what he will have to pay for the property if he elects to purchase it. T **F**

101. There is an implied warranty that the lessee will enjoy quiet and peaceful possession during the term of the lease. T F
102. All goods found upon the leased premises are subject to a landlord's levy for delinquent rent. T F
103. A mortgagee in possession of leased premises has the same rights to distrain as an owner. T F
104. A mortgagee in possession must account to the owner for all rents received. T F
105. Tenancy at will refers to ownership rather than occupancy. T F
106. A freehold is an estate in real estate held under a lease. T F
107. A broker has the right to assign a lease for the owner to the purchaser, if the property is sold. T F
108. A broker's right to commission for rents ceases under a lease prepared by the broker containing a sales clause, when the property is sold. T F
109. An owner would be liable for injuries to a pedestrian injured due to a fall over a trap door. T F
110. Broken windows in a leased property are the tenant's responsibility. T F
111. A mortgagee of leased premises is more interested generally in the term of the lease than in the rental. T F
112. Before leasing premises to an unknown applicant, the broker should check with the applicant's previous lessor or renting agent. T F
113. A lessor is better protected by accepting a lease from a new tenant of presently leased premises than by permitting the present tenant to assign the existing lease. T F
114. The terms "leasing" and "listing" are used interchangeably. T F
115. A writing which transfers possession of real estate, but does not transfer ownership is a lease. T F
116. The manager of an apartment building has authority to vary terms of a written release, upon complaint of a tenant. T F
117. An option to purchase clause in a lease is generally preferable to a first right of refusal clause, from the lessor's standpoint. T F
118. A tenant who installs a fancy chandelier in a rented property and destroys the old one, is permitted to remove it at the expiration of lease term. T F
119. A deposit accepted by a broker on a vacant apartment obligates the owner to lease it to the party making the deposit. T F
120. An eviction corresponds to a forfeiture as to breach of a lease. T F
121. A tenant who continues to occupy the premises after the expiration of the lease is called a squatter. T F
122. A release clause is commonly used in a lease. T F
123. Failure by a tenant to pay his rent when due does not constitute a termination of his lease automatically. T F
124. The terms of a written lease cannot be changed by oral agreement. T F
125. In order that a landlord have the right to send mechanics into leased premises the lease must contain this authority. T F
126. A lease given by a lessee is called a re-lease. T F
127. "Tenancy at sufferance" is leasing by one tenant to another. T F
128. Dispossession of a tenant by a landlord is known as an eviction. T F
129. Eviction is the violation of a material lease provision by the lessor. T F
130. A landlord may send a carpenter into leased premises to make repairs even though the lease contains no specific authority to do so. T F
131. A tenant who assigns a lease to a third party is still liable for rent, even though lease permits the assignment. T F
132. In promoting social justice, more courts require leased premises to be habitable, despite provisions in the lease exonerating lessor. T F
133. A lease of property which requires the lessor to pay all property charges through ownership is called a net lease. T F

134. No lease is assignable unless it expressly grants this right to lessee. T F
135. Ground rent is rent paid by an *owner* and not by the *tenant.* T F
136. In community owned property, a husband alone can not execute a valid lease for more than one year. T F
137. A "demising" clause may be found only in leasing contracts. T F
138. "Graduated" lease can provide for a change in the rent to be paid, either lowering or raising the rent. T F
139. A three day notice to vacate is all that is necessary to evict a tenant who fails to pay his rent. T F
140. A lease cannot be recorded unless it is acknowledged by lessor. T F
141. A tenant at will can assign his lease. T F
142. A tenant at sufferance can assign his lease. T F
143. A lessee is one who gives a mortgage upon his property in return for a loan. T F
144. "Tenancy at sufferance" is one in possession of property at the discretion of a court. T F
145. Accident by fire and inevitable casualty do not mean the same thing. T F
146. A fixture under a lease and a fixture in the sale of a residence mean the same thing. T F
147. Ground rent is real estate. T F
148. The legal return received from the use of property is called rent. T F
149. An owner can compel a tenant to remove store shelving at the end of the lease term. T F
150. The gross money expectancy from any income property is the gross income less the operating expenses. T F
151. A writ of restitution must be obtained to evict a tenant for non-payment of rent. T F
152. A sub-lessee, who sub-lets to another person is said to hold a sandwich lease. T F
153. A lease given by an owner to a tenant is considered personal property. T F
154. A lease may be terminated by lessor, where the premises are padlocked by court order for illegal sale of liquor. T F
155. Parol testimony can always be introduced to explain the terms of a written lease. T F
156. Under a net lease, the lessee is liable for increased property taxes. T F
157. The manager of an apartment building is entitled to keep rebates on supplies purchased. T F
158. If a tenant fails to surrender possession at the expiration of a lease term, he is always considered a tenant by sufferance. T F
159. Rules and regulations in an apartment lease are of a contractual nature. T F
160. Death of the lessor, during the term, terminates the lease. T F

Multiple Choice

1. A lease for 50 years would be considered:
   (a) personalty.
   (b) realty.
   (c) a remainder estate.
   (d) a freehold estate.
2. Which one of the following will not terminate a lease?
   (a) Performance.
   (b) Breach.
   (c) Surrender.
   (d) Vacancy.
3. Which one of the following types of tenancies does not apply to a lessor-lessee relationship?
   (a) Tenancy at will.
   (b) Tenancy in common.
   (c) Tenancy for years.
   (d) Tenancy at sufferance.

4. When a leased property is sold, the sale has the following effect upon the tenant:
   (a) Tenant must record lease in recorder's office.
   (b) Tenant must obtain assignment from purchaser.
   (c) No effect.
   (d) Tenant must move out after 30 days' notice.
5. A tenancy at will is a
   (a) form of partnership.
   (b) tenancy of uncertain duration.
   (c) inheritance of property by will.
   (d) life tenancy.
6. Under a net lease, who is liable for the payment of increased property taxes?
   (a) Lessor.
   (b) Lessee.
   (c) Sub-lessee.
   (d) Both lessor and lessee.
7. The legal compensation or income received from the use of real property is called
   (a) ground rent.
   (b) interest.
   (c) rent.
   (d) owner's equity.
8. The owner of real estate who leases it to another is called
   (a) vendor.
   (b) lessee.
   (c) lessor.
   (d) optionee.
9. Which one of the following is ordinarily not essential to the validity of a month to month lease?
   (a) Offer and acceptance.
   (b) Consideration.
   (c) In writing.
   (d) Reality of consent.
10. A clause, in a lease, by which the lessor agrees with the lessee that the latter shall have the first right to purchase the property at the same price, as offered by a prospective purchaser is called
    (a) an option clause.
    (b) first right of refusal clause.
    (c) an election clause.
    (d) a prime clause.
11. A lease cannot be recorded unless it is acknowledged by the
    (a) lessee.
    (b) lessor.
    (c) vendor.
    (d) seller.
12. A landlord rents a store to a men's clothier on a "percentage lease." On which of the following is the percentage usually based?
    (a) Market value.
    (b) Assessed value.
    (c) Tenant's gross sales.
    (d) Tenant's net income.
13. When real estate under lease is sold, the lease
    (a) expires.
    (b) is broken.
    (c) must be renewed.
    (d) remains binding upon new owner.

14. When a lease antedates a mortgage, and the mortgagee becomes the mortgagee in possession, the tenant must pay the rent to
    (a) mortgagee.
    (b) landlord.
    (c) court.
    (d) himself and hold until foreclosure sale.
15. Adams leases property to Baker for a cigar store and pool room. Baker is arrested and convicted of permitting gambling on the premises and is fined $500. This action
    (a) has no effect on the lease term.
    (b) the lease can be terminated by the lessor.
    (c) lessor can sue for damages.
    (d) Baker can assign the lease to Chase for use as a grocery.
16. When a tenant is delinquent in his rent under a written lease, the owner may have him evicted by
    (a) notifying the real estate commission.
    (b) having the Office Housing Expeditor take legal action.
    (c) giving tenant 30 days' notice.
    (d) bringing court action.
17. Where a guest is injured on a leased dwelling, he may bring action (in most states) against
    (a) lessor.
    (b) lessee.
    (c) broker, who collects the rent.
    (d) person, who has equitable title.
18. A lease should be in writing
    (a) to make the agreement binding.
    (b) to avoid misunderstandings.
    (c) to benefit the tenant.
    (d) to benefit the landlord.
19. Under a lease for 3 years, if the tenant remains in possession after the expiration of the term, the lease is
    (a) cancelled.
    (b) renewed for 3 years.
    (c) renewed for 1 year.
20. Where a leased property is changed to a different zone by the city
    (a) the tenant must continue to pay rent.
    (b) the lease is terminated.
    (c) the lessor must provide other accommodations.
21. A lease to be binding must be signed by the
    (a) broker.
    (b) beneficiary.
    (c) lessor and lessee.
    (d) lessee and broker.
22. Distraint is a proceedings to
    (a) prevent a tenant from removing.
    (b) collect delinquent rent by lessor.
    (c) impeach the lessor's title.
    (d) prevent lessor from showing property to a sales prospect.
23. A lease may be terminated
    (a) if the lessor interferes with tenant's quiet enjoyment.
    (b) if property is sold by lessor.
    (c) if lessor becomes delinquent in his mortgage payments.
24. A lease by an infant lessor is
    (a) void.
    (b) voidable by lessee.
    (c) voidable by lessor.

(d) not renewable.

25. A pedestrian injured due to the negligent accumulation of snow and ice in front of an apartment building can recover damages from
    (a) the municipality.
    (b) the real estate broker who negotiated the lease.
    (c) the first floor tenant.
    (d) the lessor.
26. In a distraint for rent, leased counter equipment can be
    (a) claimed by owner of equipment.
    (b) sold by lessor.
    (c) claimed by tenant as his debtor's exemption.
27. Pedestrian traffic counts are usually taken to determine
    (a) urban population.
    (b) size of shopping area.
    (c) rental value of a location.
    (d) average age group.
28. "Spot zoning" is usually determined by
    (a) lease contract.
    (b) owner of property.
    (c) city law department.
    (d) Board of Adjustment.
29. A lease gives the tenant an option to purchase the property at $40,000. The owner receives an offer from a third party at $45,000.
    (a) Tenant can purchase property at $45,000.
    (b) Tenant can buy at $40,000.
    (c) Third party can buy it.
    (d) Owner must pay tenant $5,000.
30. A sub-lease is for
    (a) basement premises.
    (b) a new tenant of the entire premises.
    (c) a portion of the leased premises.
31. Leases cannot be recorded unless they are acknowledged before a proper official by the
    (a) lessee.
    (b) lessor.
    (c) assignee.
    (d) vendor.
32. Where a tenant's furniture is damaged by water due to the negligence of an upstairs tenant, he can
    (a) refuse to pay rent until made whole.
    (b) move out if this happened before.
    (c) complain to the city officials.
    (d) bring a civil action against the upstairs tenant.
33. Where a tenant is delinquent in rent for many months, it is preferable for the lessor to
    (a) confess judgment for amount of rent.
    (b) institute a landlord's levy.
    (c) confess judgment for possession of premises.
    (d) notify local credit association.
34. Where a 4 room apartment is leased to a young couple and later the parents of the couple move in, the landlord can
    (a) do nothing.
    (b) terminate the lease.
    (c) increase the rent proportionally.
    (d) require tenant to post bond against any damage.
35. Where a husband owner of real estate leases property for five years and dies shortly

afterwards, the
(a) lease is terminated.
(b) lease is carried out by Probate or Surrogate's Court.
(c) lease is taken over by devisee of leased property.
(d) court appoints licensed broker to administer lease.

36. A lease which requires the tenant to pay all expenses of the property in addition to his rent is called
(a) a gross lease.
(b) an assigned lease.
(c) a percentage lease.
(d) a net lease.

37. Alberts verbally leases certain premises to Underwood for a term of one year. This lease is
(a) void.
(b) enforceable.
(c) only a month to month lease.
(d) non-renewable.

38. When a commercial property is being offered for sale, and a tenant wishes to renew a long term lease, the managing broker should renew the lease with
(a) a percentage clause.
(b) a cancellation clause.
(c) a distraining clause.
(d) an elevator clause.

39. According to the Statute of Frauds, a verbal lease for five years is
(a) enforceable.
(b) not enforceable.
(c) assignable.
(d) renewable.

40. When a lease of a store does not provide who shall make necessary repairs to the premises, the cost of such repairs is borne by
(a) the lessee.
(b) the lessor.
(c) the legatee.
(d) the insurance company.

41. Under a "net" rental agreement, the tenant generally meets all but one of the following charges
(a) taxes.
(b) mortgage interest.
(c) assessment.
(d) liability insurance.

42. A percentage lease is a lease
(a) which provides for a percentage of rents to be paid to the broker as a commission.
(b) covers only a certain percentage of property, where there are two or more persons sharing the premises.
(c) where rent is based on percentage of tenant's receipts.
(d) covers the lending of money and interest charged thereon.

43. A lease for less than one year
(a) may be oral.
(b) must be in writing.
(c) may be oral, but must be reduced to writing within one year.

44. A tenancy at will is
(a) tenancy for a specified duration.
(b) possession of property under a will.
(c) life estate.
(d) none of the above.

45. A chain store firm in determining value of a site is motivated by
    (a) spot zoning.
    (b) pedestrian count.
    (c) traffic count during and between 8:00 A.M. and 8:00 P.M.
    (d) latest census figures.
46. Where a lessee holds farm property at the will of the lessor, he has a
    (a) tenancy at sufferance.
    (b) freehold estate.
    (c) common of pasturage.
    (d) holdover tenancy
47. Where the lease fails to state when the rent is due and payable, it is due
    (a) on the first day of each month.
    (b) on the first day of the lease term.
    (c) on the last day of the lease term.
    (d) on the last day of each month.
48. Taking property into custody, or seizure of goods by due legal process is called
    (a) an eviction.
    (b) a forfeiture.
    (c) an attachment.
    (d) none of these.
    (e) an action in trespass.
49. Cancellation of a lease by mutual consent of lessor and lessee is called
    (a) Action of Rescission.
    (b) Action of Revocation.
    (c) Surrender and Acceptance.
    (d) Lis Pendens action.
50. A real estate broker usually represents
    (a) the lessor.
    (b) an adverse party.
    (c) lessor and lessee.
    (d) lessee.
51. A document which transfers possession for recompense, but not ownership is
    (a) a special warranty deed.
    (b) option.
    (c) easement.
    (d) lease.
52. An oral lease for five years is unenforceable under
    (a) the statute of frauds.
    (b) statute of limitation.
    (c) under an Act of Congress.
    (d) the common law.
53. The Statute of Frauds is a law
    (a) requiring certain contracts to be in writing.
    (b) requiring a license to operate as a broker or salesman.
    (c) regulating escrow accounts.
    (d) regulating estates owning real estate.
54. Ground rent is a fixed rental
    (a) paid for vacant property.
    (b) rental paid on a parking garage.
    (c) rental paid by a grantee to his grantor.
    (d) paid by an upper tenant to first floor tenant.
55. A tenant spends $10,000 in improving the landlord's property. Annual taxes are then increased $240. The tenant
    (a) is liable for the tax increase.
    (b) is liable for one-half of the tax increase.

(c) depends upon lease provisions.
(d) the lease is terminated.

56. A lease which provides for a step-by-step increase in rentals at regular intervals is called
    (a) an instalment lease.
    (b) a percentage lease.
    (c) an open lease.
    (d) a graduated lease.
57. A lease basing rental on portion of gross sales with a guaranteed minimum is
    (a) percentage lease.
    (b) net lease.
    (c) acceleration lease.
    (d) and ad valorem lease.
58. Net return on investment property is computed by deducting all expenses from
    (a) gross annual income.
    (b) gross annual income less depreciation.
    (c) appraised value.
    (d) market price.
59. Fixtures under the ordinary lease, at the expiration of the lease will be the property of
    (a) lessor.
    (b) lessee.
    (c) mortgage.
    (d) ground rent owner.
60. Accepting rebates on purchases of materials for an office building is unlawful for which ones of the following:
    (a) owner.
    (b) tenants.
    (c) broker managing property.
    (d) building manager.
61. A lease of part of the premises by a tenant to another party is
    (a) assignment of lease.
    (b) a release.
    (c) subletting.
    (d) an eviction.
62. The unlawful taking of possession of real estate from a person in possession is known as
    (a) an ejectment.
    (b) an eviction.
    (c) ouster.
    (d) recapture.
63. Under the law of landlord and tenant where the property is sold during term of lease, who is entitled to emblements?
    (a) Landlord.
    (b) Tenant.
    (c) Both landlord and tenant.
    (d) New owner.
64. Dispossession of a tenant by a landlord unlawfully, entitles tenant to a
    (a) surcharge.
    (b) penalty.
    (c) damages.
    (d) reimbursement.
65. A life tenant may convey
    (a) a fee simple title.
    (b) a perpetual easement.
    (c) a tenancy per auter vie.
    (d) none of these.

66. An "exculpatory" clause in a lease releases which one of the following, for water damage from bursting pipes?
    (a) lessor.
    (b) sub-tenant.
    (c) lessee.
    (d) assignee of lease.
67. A lessor has the right to show the premises to a prospective purchaser, because
    (a) implied right under law of landlord and tenant.
    (b) provision in the lease contract.
    (c) he has a bona fide prospect.
    (d) the showing is between 10 A.M. and 5 P.M.
68. A lease may be terminated:
    I. By performance.
    II. By breach of either party.
    (a) I only.
    (b) II only.
    (c) By either I or II.
    (d) Neither I nor II.
69. Under a 10 year commercial lease, the lease can provide that the tenant:
    I. Pay increased taxes.
    II. Pay for repairs.
    (a) I only.
    (b) II only.
    (c) Both I and II.
    (d) Neither I nor II.
70. Which one of the following applies to a landlord-tenant relationship?
    (a) tenancy in common.
    (b) tenancy at sufferance.
    (c) joint tenancy.
    (d) tenancy by the entireties.
71. A 10 year lease which provides for specified increases in rent from year to year is a
    (a) percentage lease.
    (b) acceleration lease.
    (c) graduated lease.
    (d) a unilateral lease.
72. The income received by the owner under a lease is known as
    (a) interest.
    (b) ground rent.
    (c) profit.
    (d) rent.
73. Johnson leased a dwelling to Adams for two years. At the end of six months, Adams abandoned the premises. Under these circumstances
    I. Johnson can demand rent for the balance of the lease term.
    II. Johnson can relet the premises to another tenant.
    (a) I only.
    (b) II only.
    (c) both I and II.
    (d) neither I nor II.
74. Adams was a tenant in an industrial building. Due to the loud noises from printing presses in the space of an overhead tenant, he refused to pay rent, claiming a constructive eviction. The landlord sued for rent. Under these circumstances
    I. the landlord can recover the rent.
    II. the landlord must abate the nuisance.
    (a) I only.
    (b) II only.

(c) both I and II.
(d) neither I nor II.

75. A property was leased to a tenant for a "supermarket." During the term, the tenant assigned the lease for use as a ladies' apparel store. The landlord sued to evict the subtenant. Under these circumstances
I. the subtenant can be evicted.
II. the original tenant can assign the lease to another supermarket.
(a) I only.
(b) II only.
(c) both I and II.
(d) neither I nor II.

76. An owner sued a tenant for nine months unpaid rent under a lease "for the street level floor only." A fire occurred, rendering the leased space totally untenantable. Under these circumstances
I. the tenant is liable for the rent.
II. the tenant must restore the leased premises.
(a) I only.
(b) II only.
(c) both I and II.
(d) neither I nor II.

77. A lease for a bowling alley did not require the landlord to make any repairs. A severe rain storm flooded the building three feet deep. The bowling alleys were damaged beyond repair. The building itself suffered only minimal damage and could be repaired within one week. Under these circumstances
I. the tenant continues liable for rent.
II. the owner must restore the alleys.
(a) I only.
(b) II only.
(c) both I and II.
(d) neither I nor II.

78. Aiken, owner of a shopping center, leased the entire complex, consisting of 30 units, to Balfour. Balfour, in turn, leased 26 units to separate subtenants. The prime lease contained a clause for assignment of rents of subtenants to Aiken. On May 2, 1974, Balfour was three months delinquent in his rent. Aiken, on that date, gave Balfour notice of cancellation of his lease. Balfour had deposited rents collected from subtenants in the Chelsea City Bank. Balfour owed the bank $12,000 on several promissory notes, which were overdue. On May 15, 1974, the bank offset the money on deposit against Balfour's debts. Under these circumstances
I. the bank can offset the notes against the money on deposit.
II. Aiken will receive the money for the unpaid rent.
(a) I only.
(b) II only.
(c) both I and II.
(d) neither I nor II.

79. A tenant abandoned the premises used for manufacturing purposes, before the term has expired, but he continued to pay rent. The tenant left a water cooling system and certain electric systems, which he had installed and used in his manufacturing processes. The landlord contended that the equipment were fixtures, which became a part of the leased premises. Under these circumstances
I. the fixtures belong to the tenant.
II. there was no abandonment of the lease.
(a) I only.
(b) II only.
(c) both I and II.
(d) neither I nor II.

80. An apartment was rented for one year. The tenant remained over for a second year. Near the end of the second year, the owner notified the tenant and the other eleven tenants to vacate their units at the end of the month, as the leases would not be renewed; and that eviction would be brought if they remained for a third year. The tenant claimed that the owner was retaliating against them, because they had filed complaints alleging city housing and building code violations. In a suit:
    (a) Owner will win.
    (b) Tenants will win and the lease will be renewed for one year.
    (c) Tenants can remain over for only one month.
    (d) The rent of the tenants will be reduced on a quid proqui basis.
81. A 2 year lease provided that the lessor could terminate the lease upon 5 days written notice for non-payment of rent. During the first year of the lease, lessee was frequently delinquent in his monthly payments, but they were accepted by the lessor, without objection. Subsequently, upon a default, the lessor gave written notice by certified mail to the lessee that the lease was terminated for non-payment of rent. Lessor sought to evict the lessee.
    (a) The lessee will win.
    (b) The lessor will win.
    (c) The lessor can only recover the rent plus a penalty.
    (d) The lease will become a month to month lease, and lessor can collect the delinquent month.
82. A tenant was delinquent for four weeks in rent on a one year lease with rent payable weekly. During the tenant's absence, the landlord entered the premises and changed the entrance lock. The tenant was unable to enter her apartment. She sued for damages.
    (a) The tenant cannot recover.
    (b) The tenant can recover.
    (c) The tenant will have free rent for the remainder of the term.
    (d) The tenant can recover nominal damages, since she suffered no physical harm.

Chapter 8

VALUATION AND APPRAISAL[1]

Basic Valuation Concepts[1]

PROPERTY valuation may be considered as the heart of all real estate activity. Only a practical understanding of real estate valuation will enable real estate brokers and salesmen to carry out their functions in a useful and dependable manner in serving their clients and in meeting their obligations to the general public.

Even though they may not qualify as expert appraisers, brokers and salesmen should be familiar with the theoretical concepts of value, the forces which influence values and the methods by which such values may best be estimated. Such a knowledge is essential in arriving at a logical solution as to the highest and best, and hence the most profitable use of property.

It is a daily occurrence for the real estate broker to be asked by clients as to the fair market value, a fair price, a fair rental, a fair basis for trade, or a proper insurance coverage for property. He needs to know how to answer such questions intelligently. To be successful in business, he must determine whether he can profitably spend his time in trying to sell a property at a listing price which the owner sets. In this regard he must keep in mind that in accepting a listing he obligates himself to put forth his best efforts to find a buyer for the property.

Value designations

There are many different designations or definitions of value. They may be divided into the following two main classifications: (1) *Value in use*—or, the special value to the owner or user. This frequently is termed *subjective* value, and it includes a valuation of amenities which attach to a property. (2) *Market value*— or value in exchange. This is the price at which property can be sold or exchanged at a given time or place as a result of market balancing. It is based on a "willing-buyer" and "willing-seller" concept. This is frequently termed the *objective* value.

Value of property most generally means the market value. Market value is said to be the price in terms of money for which a property would sell in the open market, seller not being obliged to sell, the buyer not being obliged to buy, with a reasonable length of time to effect the sale. This also supposes that both seller and prospective buyer are fully informed of all uses to which the property is adapted and for which it is capable of being used. Value is what the property is worth. Price is what someone actually paid for the property. It may or may not be the same as the value.

Among the various types of value that have been designated from time to time are book value, tax value, market value, cash value, capital value, speculative value, par value, true value, exchange value, reproduction or physical value, replacement value, insurance value, investment value, rental value and cost value.

[1] The text material on Valuation and Appraisal, in the main, has been taken from the State of California Reference Book and Guide with permission of the California Real Estate Commissioner, Hon. Robert W. Karpe.

Value can be distinguished from "cost" as well as from "price." The principal differences may be explained as follows:

(a) Value has to do with the combined factors of present and future anticipated enjoyment or profit. The value sought in the appraisal of property may be said to be the present worth of all desirable things (benefits) which may accrue from a skillful use of it. A conclusion in regard to these things will clearly be a matter of opinion—an intelligent estimate based on a thorough analysis of all available influencing factors and on reasonable and more or less warranted assumptions.

(b) Cost represents a measure of past expenditures in labor, material or sacrifices of some nature. While cost may be, and frequently is, a factor upon which value is partially based, it need not be, as it does not control present and future value. An example of this fact is the value of an oil well, which in one case may prove to be a big producer and of great value, while in another case may prove to be a dry hole and of no value, although both may have cost the same to develop and drill.

(c) Price is what one pays for a commodity. Usually it is considered to be the amount of money involved in a transaction. Whether we receive in value more or less than what we pay for will depend on the soundness of judgment in appraisal of value, or upon fortuitous future developments. Under an efficient market structure, prices will usually tend to equal values, varying only as buyers and sellers have unequal knowledge or economic strength.

Purposes and characteristics of value

The purpose of an evaluation or an appraisal is usually indicated in the value concept employed, for example: assessed value, condemnation value, liquidation value, cash value, mortgage loan value, fire insurance value, etc. The type of value sought frequently dictates the valuation method employed and influences the resulting estimate of value.

There are only three elements of value, all of which are essential. These are utility (the capacity to satisfy a need or desire), scarcity and demand (coupled with purchasing power). None alone will create value. For example, a thing may be scarce but, if it has no utility, there is no demand for it. Other things, like air, may have great utility and may be in great demand, but are so abundant as to have no commercial value. Likewise, the commodity must be transferable as to use or title to be marketable. Generally speaking, a commodity will have commercial or marketable value in proportion to its utility and relative scarcity. Utility creates demand, but demand, to be effective, must be implemented by purchasing power.

Fundamental to the concept of value is the idea of the "highest and best use." This can be defined as follows: The highest and best use is that use which is most likely to produce the greatest net return over a given period. Sometimes "net return" takes the form of amenities, but more usually it is thought of in terms of money. The "given period" may be dependent on the purpose for which the property is desired. For example, the "given period" to be analyzed would be shorter for a speculative venture than for a long-term investment.

Location is also a factor. For example, a site in a downtown district of a city which could most profitably be used for a time as a parking lot without improvements might later become more desirable as a location for a new commercial structure. In addition, any analysis to reach a decision as to the "highest and best use" must include consideration as to the future supply and demand for such use within the area and a possible oversupply with attendant decrease of market value.

Special forces influencing value

The value of real estate is created, maintained, modified and destroyed by the interplay of the following four great forces:

(a) Social ideals and standards. Examples of social forces include: population growth and decline, marriage, birth, divorce and death rates, attitudes toward education, recreation, and other instincts and yearnings of mankind.

(b) Economic adjustments. Examples of economic forces include: natural resources—including location, quantity and quality, industrial and commercial trends, employment trends, wage levels, availability of money and credit, interest rates, price levels, tax loads, etc.

(c) Political or governmental regulations. Examples of political forces include: building codes, zoning laws, public health measures, fire regulations, government guaranteed loans, government housing, credit controls, etc. Each and every one of these many social, economic and political factors affects cost, price, and value to some degree. The three of them interweave and each one is in a constant state of change.

(d) Physical forces. Examples of physical forces include: climate and topography, soil fertility, flood control, mineral resources, soil erosion, sub-surface conditions, etc.

Factors influencing value

Directional Growth. In any estimate of value, attention should be paid to "the city directional growth." The city directional growth refers to the manner and direction in which the city tends to grow. Properties in the direction of growth in different sections of the city tend to increase in value, especially if the growth is steady and rapid.

Location. This includes access. This factor of valuation is often measured by traffic counts, which, in turn, have to be interpreted in purchasing power as well as volume of traffic. A property must have access by street, right-of-way, easement, alley or other means, to have value.

Utility. This is the capacity to satisfy a need or desire. This important factor involves judgment as to the best use to which a given property may be put. Building codes, zoning ordinances, and other public and private restrictions affect utility.

Size. The width and depth often determine the possibilities and character of use.

Shape. Parcels of land of irregular shape cannot usually be developed as advantageously as rectangular lots.

Thoroughfare Conditions. The width of streets, traffic congestion, condition of pavement all affect the value of those properties fronting any given street.

Action of the Sun. The south and west sides of business streets are usually preferred by merchants, because the pedestrian traffic seeks the shady side of the street in warm weather, and merchandise displayed in the windows is not damaged by the sun.

Character of Business Done. The larger cities develop retail, financial, wholesale, and commission-house districts, and women's and men's shopping sections, for the cheap, medium and high-grade trade.

Social Atmosphere in Residential Districts. The quality of the neighborhood has a direct bearing upon the values of properties within it.

Plottage. This is the *added* value of several parcels of land when brought under one ownership making possible a higher utility than could be found for the parcels considered separately.

Proportion of Depth to Width. This is important in determining the best uses to which a given property may be put. A lot must be of usable width and depth to have value.

Character of the Soil. Almost always a critical factor in agricultural property and frequently important in other types of properties.

Conspicuousness. Largely a factor of publicity value, and becomes of great importance to businesses depending upon advertising.

Grades. These vary from level land to hillside properties.

Obsolescence. A form of depreciation (loss of value reproduction or replacement cost new). It is divided into *functional* obsolescence, caused by changes in types of construction, design and/or interior arrangement, and *economic* obsolescence, caused by factors outside the property itself. Functional obsolescence can be either curable or incurable; whereas, economic obsolescence is almost always incurable.

Appreciation. A sustained trend of rising costs in labor and materials has caused appreciation in nearly all cases to be more rapid than total accrued depreciation.

Building Restrictions and Zoning. These sometimes operate to depress values and at other times to increase values. For example, there may be a vacant lot on a residential street which will sell for only $50 a front foot for residential use, but would sell for $300 per front foot as an apartment site. Or a vacant lot in a zoned area may sell for more per foot as a business site because of the supply of business sites being restricted by zoning. Many other examples might be given.

Residential property

In appraising single family residences, the most important consideration is the market comparison (also known as the "market data" or "comparable sales" approach, i.e., comparing the property to be appraised with similar or "comparable" properties which have been sold recently.

The "cost approach" may also be used under proper circumstances, especially where the structure is fairly new. This approach involves estimating the reproduction or replacement cost of the improvements, deducting the accrued depreciation (loss of value) and adding the land value.

Industrial property

Industrial lands are usually valued on an area basis,—small plots by the square foot and larger tracts by the acre.

Topography. The topography of undeveloped land is of importance, and consideration should be given to the cost of grading, if required.

Subsoil. The character of the subsoil is frequently overlooked, and yet may be vital. Quicksand, rock, or other characteristics may make a certain site impossible for a given industry. Drainage also may be a vital factor.

Plottage Value. There is an added or plottage value from assembling lots into a reasonable-sized industrial site, but on the other hand, it is generally recognized that an area of unusual size has a lesser unit value, in the same way that the value per square foot of a commercial lot decreases, according to any of the published tables, with increased depth.

Track Layouts. In the study and valuation of unimproved, but potentially valuable, industrial lands, the assistance of a competent engineer, familiar with plant and track layouts, is frequently a decided advantage.

Agricultural or farm lands

In estimating the value of agricultural land, the nature and long-term trend of prices for the crop which is grown or intended to be grown is probably the chief determining factor. If the property is to be used for a dairy farm, then the character of the soil, whether suitable for hay and grain, water supply for the cattle and crops, proximity to markets, climatic conditions, labor conditions in the district, breed of cattle and their general conditions are extremely important. If the land is to be used for fruit growing, then it is essential to ascertain if the water supply is ample, if the land is suitable for the type of crops to be grown, if the cost of water is not excessive, a full knowledge of climatic conditions, with special reference to frosts and production against frost, age and condition of the trees, their past production, market conditions, labor conditions, and the price of produce in past years.

If the land is to be used for vineyard or root crops such as truck gardens, then consideration must be given to suitability of the soil, water supply, the cost of water, proximity to markets, labor supply and climatic conditions.

Generally, in agricultural land evaluation, it is also well to remember that all fruit and nut trees under four years of age from time of planting in orchard form, and all grape vines under three years old from time of planting in orchard form, and all growing crops are exempt from taxation.

Farm land valuation is highly specialized and often requires the assistance of soil and crop experts.

Appraisal methods and techniques

Definition of appraisal

To appraise means to arrive at an estimate of the value of a property. An appraisal is the appraiser's opinion of the value, as defined by the appraiser, of a parcel of property as of a specified date. It is a conclusion which results from the analysis of facts.

Real estate appraising is being definitely standardized by virtue of the experience and practice of men in organizations in all parts of the country who encounter the same class of valuation problems, and who, by various methods and processes, succeed in solving them in a scientific way. It is natural that differences of opinion exist as to the value of real estate and the means of estimating its value in specific cases.

Methods of appraising properties

It is generally accepted that there are three ways to approach a value estimate. These methods or types of approach are:

1. *Comparison (or Market Data) Approach.* A comparison is made as to market level, location and physical characteristics, in relation to other comparable properties sold recently.
2. *Cost (or Summation) Approach.* In this approach, accrued depreciation is deducted from the cost of reproducing or replacing the improvements. To this depreciated value is added the value of the land, estimated by means of the comparison (market) method or any other recognized technique.
3. *Capitalization (or Income) Approach.* In this approach, value is estimated on the basis of its relationship (capitalization rate) to the net income which the property produces or ought to produce.

Frequently, the skilled appraiser will use all three methods in appraising a given property. No single method of approach by itself can always be depended upon to produce reliable estimates. Each appraisal must be solved after analyzing the special problem which is being presented.

Not only does every piece of real estate differ in some respects from all other properties, but there are many different reasons for which an appraisal may be made. The specific type of value sought will also affect the valuation. For example, insurable value, used for insurance purposes, will invariably be higher than fair market value. The nature of the property, whether non-investment, investment, or service; the purpose of the purchase, whether for use, investment, or speculation; and the reason for the appraisal, such as sale, loan, taxation, insurance and the like, all constitute matters which will influence the approaches used and the weights accorded them.

The first step in any appraisal procedure is to have a clear understanding of the reasons for making the appraisal and the objective to be sought. The adequacy and reliability of available data also are determining factors in the selection of the specific approach method or methods to be employed. A lack of certain pertinent or up-to-date information may well eliminate an otherwise possible approach method.

In other instances, proper procedures may call only for an appropriate discounting of conclusions drawn from such data. Thus, based on its adaptability to the specific problem, one method is usually given greater weight than the other approach methods.

In most appraisals, all three approach methods will ordinarily have something to contribute. Each approach method is used independently to reach an estimated value. Then as a final step, by applying to each separate value a weight proportionate to its merits in that particular instance, conclusions are reached as to one appropriate value. This procedure is known as correlation.

For the real estate broker or salesman dealing primarily in single family residences, a good understanding of the advantages and disadvantages as well as the limitations of the market data (comparison) approach is especially desirable. However, there will be situations where this approach cannot be relied upon exclusively for reaching a reasonable estimate of value. Consequently a reasonable understanding of the proper procedures and application of all three approaches is necessary for the well-qualified real estate broker.

We will now proceed to elaborate on and examine more closely the three approaches to value.

Market Comparison (Comparable Sales)

This approach is most generally adaptable for use by real estate brokers and salesmen. It lends itself well to the appraisal of land, buildings, and residences which exhibit a high degree of similarity, and for which a ready market exists. It is also particularly applicable as a check against the other methods of appraising all types of properties where the market value is the end result being sought.

The mechanics of the process involves the use of market data of all kinds in order to compare closely the property being appraised with other similar properties. The sources used include actual sales prices, listings, offers, rents and leases, and an analysis of social and economic factors affecting marketability.

Some of these prices are obtainable from the appraiser's own records, financial news services, classified advertisements, abstract companies, and state revenue stamps. In the latter case, while a price may be calculated from the value of the revenue stamps, this figure must be accepted with caution. It may not represent the actual price because no maximum limit is set as to the number of stamps which may be purchased. Thus, to create the impression of high prices, more stamps may have been used than are actually required. On the other hand, the price paid may be much more than is indicated by the stamps used as these may represent only the equity consideration involved. Again, in cases of property exchanges, it may be to the mutual advantage of the interested parties to understate or overstate the transaction price for tax or other purposes.

Listing prices may often indicate the probable top market value, while bid prices may normally indicate the lowest probable value. Both are subject to variation based on motivation, but a reasonable number of such figures will provide a bracket within which a current fair value will be found. Offers are likely to approach market values more closely than are listings which frequently are made to test the market. However, an offer to purchase is not usually a matter of common knowledge.

The procedure used in the market data (comparison) approach method is to assemble data concerning sales and other market data of comparable properties. The greater the number of good comparisons used, the better should be the conclusions which may be drawn therefrom. The approach is based on the assumption that property is worth what it will sell for in the absence of undue stress, if reasonable time is given to find a buyer. For this reason, the appraiser should look behind sales and transfers to ascertain what influences may have affected sales prices—particularly if only a few comparisons are available.

Proper comparisons between properties should be based on an actual and thorough inspection of such properties. For nearly comparable properties, penalties should be assessed, against the property being appraised, for poor repair, freakish design, existing nuisances, etc. Conversely, additional values should be imputed to the subject property for attractive design, view, special features, better condition, higher quality of materials, landscaping, and the like. Unless the sales being compared are of recent date, consideration must also be given to adjusting values in keeping with changes in the real estate market since such dates.

Some of the advantages of using this approach method are as follows:

1. It is the simplest of the various methods to learn and to use. The factor of economic obsolescence of the neighborhood presumably is included in the value as set by the market.

2. It is particularly applicable for appraisal purposes involving the sale, exchange and loan transaction of single family residences. These make up the great bulk of real estate transactions. It is valuable as a check against the values determined by the other approach methods.

Some of the disadvantages of the comparison approach method are as follows:

1. Its reliability is greatly reduced by the lack of suitable comparisons. These must be adequate in number, reliable as to source, and sufficiently recent to justify reasonable conclusions to be drawn from them.

2. Being based primarily on current or short-term values, it is influenced by temporary market fluctuations, and may not satisfactorily forecast long-range values.

3. Scattered comparison may exaggerate or disregard special influences that have affected sales prices.

4. Individuals using this approach frequently neglect to make enough inspections to get a true comparison of values between the properties being used for this purpose.

Cost (or summation) approach

In estimating the cost of reconstructing the improvements on the date of the appraisal, the appraiser may estimate either their reproduction or their replacement cost. There are advantages and disadvantages to both methods.

Reproduction cost is the cost of faithfully reconstructing the improvements precisely as they are; it is the cost of reconstructing the exact improvements being appraised. However, because of the changes which have taken place in design, materials and construction methods since the building was erected, reproduction cost will usually include a measure of functional obsolescence which must be considered in the estimate of depreciation. The older the building, the more obsolescence of this type will have occurred.

Replacement cost, on the other hand, is the cost of replacing the building being appraised with one having equivalent utility and amenities. It is the cost of erecting a building of its type, employing the design, materials and construction methods normally used in construction on the date of appraisal. Substituting modern construction features for the obsolete ones in the building being appraised has the advantage of eliminating the necessity for estimating functional obsolescence. On the other hand, it is open to the criticism that, although it does represent how this building would probably be erected on the date of appraisal, it is not the actual building being evaluated. This criticism is particularly applicable if the building has considerable age.

The result of the respective advantages and disadvantages of the reproduction and replacement cost methods is that appraisers variously use one or the other.

The cost approach is based upon the principle that people will ordinarily not pay more for a property than it would cost to duplicate it in its condition on the date of appraisal.

Sequential steps in the cost approach are as follows:

(a) An independent estimate is made as to the value of the land. This is always the current market value of the land, considered as vacant and available for improvement to its highest and best use. This value is not necessarily related to the actual cost when purchased.

(b) An estimate is made as to the reproduction or replacement cost new (as of the effective date of the appraisal) of all improvements on the property. Accuracy requires the application of principles of building cost estimating, including the taking of an inventory of the materials and manufactured equipment making up the property and then applying to this inventory the current prices of similar materials, equipment, labor costs and all overhead costs which would be necessary to construct a suitable replacement of the improvements as of the appraisal date. The methods used in such estimates vary from the very technical and detailed procedures used by contractors and mortgage loan companies, to the simpler shortcut methods such as the comparison methods, which are used by most appraisers.

To use the simpler methods, an estimate of total cost is made by comparison with other similar buildings whose costs are known and have been reduced to units per square foot of floor area of living space or per cubic foot of the building content. Applying these costs to the actual area or content of the property under appraisal will give an approximate undepreciated (new) valuation, provided the data as to costs are accurate and the buildings and improvements are similar as to quality and design. Corrections must be made for such differences as well as for changes in cost levels which may have taken place between the date of basic costs and the date of the new estimate.

Cost figures are also obtainable from local contractors or from numerous services which publish building costs. Actually, building costs will vary considerably, based on the efficiency of the builder and the amount of profit which is included in such costs. There is a great variation also in the quality and design of structures, so that unless the appraiser is experienced in such matters, his estimate of value may be inaccurate.

(c) The third step in the cost approach method is to determine the accrued depreciation of the property. This amount must be deducted from the reproduction or replacement cost new to determine the depreciated value of all improvements. The difficulties of correctly estimating depreciation tend to increase with the age of the property and require skill, experience, and good judgment. A value determined by using the cost approach is no more reliable than is the estimate of depreciation. There is no justification in assuming that improvements necessarily depreciate at a rate corresponding to their age, although all too frequently this simple method is employed by the inexperienced appraiser.

(d) The final step in the cost approach method is to add the value of the land, as determined in (a) above, to the depreciated cost, (b) and (c) above. This is the source of the term, "Summation Approach."

The cost approach is particularly appropriate for appraising newly-built properties where depreciation is incidental. It is also the most appropriate approach method for public service properties, such as schools, hospitals, libraries, etc. These have no active market, and thus lack market data which can be used for a comparison approach, and there is no income on which to base an income or capitalization approach.

Capitalization (Income) Approach

The income approach is concerned with the present worth of future benefits of property. This method is particularly important in the valuation of income-producing property, although rarely can it be taken as the only pertinent approach. It is usually measured by the net income which a fully informed person is warranted in assuming the property will produce during its remaining useful life. An exception, where gross income may be used rather than net income, is found in the appraisal of one or two family residences by using a gross rent-multiplier. Such property normally is not considered as income property, as this was not its original purpose or function.

The procedure used in the capitalization approach involves the following three main steps:

(a) A net annual income is derived, preferably over a period of years, by deducting total expenses from gross income. Unless such figures have remained fairly constant, it is important that trends in income and expenses be taken into account in forecasting future net income. The existence of current excessively high profits should indicate the probability of early competition and the lessening of future profits.

(b) A selection is made of an appropriate capitalization rate or present worth factor. This is the crux of the matter and is a most important step.

The rate is dependent upon the return which investors will actually demand before they will be attracted by such an investment. The greater the risk of recapturing the investment price, the higher will be the accompanying rate as determined in the market for such properties. By analyzing market prices, these rates can be approximated at any given time.

A variation of only 1 percent may make a substantial difference in the capitalized value of the income. For example, based on an annual net income of $30,000, and a capitalization rate of 5 percent, the resultant capitalized property valuation would be $600,000. Capitalizing this same income at a rate of 6 percent would result in a value of only $500,000 in valuation due to a difference in the capitalization rate of only 1 percent.

(c) The final step after having determined the net income and the capitalization rate is to capitalize the income. This may be merely a mathematical calculation of dividing the income by the rate if an overall rate is used. For example, the valuation of property which has an annual income of $30,000 and a capitalization rate of 5 percent is $600,000. The lower the rate, the greater the valuation and the greater the assumed security of the investment. So-called annuity tables are used in capitalizing fixed incomes for fixed periods.

An important element in all capitalization rates is provision for a return of the investment in the improvements to the property during their remaining economic life. This may be called an amortization or "recapture" of such investments. It may be provided for by straight-line depreciation, which recovers a definite sum every year for the period of years estimated to be the economic life of the improvement, at the end of which time the cost of replacement will be accrued. It may also be provided for by other methods, such as establishing "sinking funds", or a declining balance depreciation. These are more technical procedures which are used by professional appraisers.

In the hands of those who are familiar with its use, the capitalization approach may be helpful in determining the value of vacant land. This is accomplished by calculating probable incomes that would result if the property were used for different purposes and permits a determination of the most profitable or highest and best use of the land.

The technique used is known as the "land residual process." It seeks the capitalized value remaining in property after deductions are made for a return *on* and a return *of* the investment in the improvements alone.

The capitalization approach is particularly advantageous where insufficient market data are available for proper use of the market data approach.

Income (capitalization) approach applied. In determining the value of an income-producing property, one method that the appraiser may use is:

1. Estimate the adjusted gross income of the land and buildings, making proper allowances for vacancies and collection losses;
2. Ascertain the correct amount of all taxes;
3. Ascertain the annual cost of adequate insurance;
4. Estimate the annual stabilized operating expenses (utilities, maintenance, management, etc.);
5. Estimate an annual amount of reserve funds for necessary replacement of equipment or furnishings prior to the end of the estimated economic life of the building;
6. Compute the net income of the entire property before recapture by deducting items 2, 3, 4, and 5 from item 1;
7. Capitalize the remainder at a reasonable rate according to the risk involved, which will result in a valuation of the property as a whole.

Example: 10-unit apartment house—4 years old. Each apartment presently leased at $100 per month.

10 × $100 = $1,000 per month or $12,000 per year
Proven vacancy factor—10 percent
10 percent × $12,000 = $1,200 per year

$12,000
− 1,200
$10,800 Effective gross income (adjusted for vacancy factor)

Expenses (annual)—	Management	$1,200
	Taxes	960
	Insurance	240
	Utilities	600
	Reserve for Replacements	+ 400
		$3,400

$$\begin{array}{l} \$10{,}800 \text{ Gross Income} \\ \underline{-\ 3{,}400} \\ \$\ 7{,}400 \text{ Net Income before recapture} \end{array}$$

$$\text{Overall Capitalization Rate—8 percent} \quad \frac{\$7{,}400}{.08} = \$92{,}500 \text{ Valuation}$$

If it is desired, a valuation for the land alone may be arrived at through the following additional steps:

8. Compute the interest on the value of the improvements today, at a reasonable rate, according to the risk involved in the building investment only;
9. Compute annual "recapture" necessary to return owner's investment in improvements to him.
10. Deduct items 8 and 9 from item 6 above and capitalize the result at a rate justified by the risk involved in the land investment only, which will result in a value for the land alone.

In computing the net income from an apartment house there are several major items for deduction from the gross income to indicate the net income. Major items are:

(a) Taxes;
(b) Insurance;
(c) Repairs;
(d) Depreciation on furniture (if furnished);
(e) Vacancies and collection losses;
(f) Management;
(g) Reserve for replacements.

Gross multipliers

Since much of the business in real estate has to do with the sale of middle-aged and older residential property, the real estate broker and salesman should understand the use of the "gross multiplier" to assist in appraising such rent properties on the basis of value in capitalization. This method is based upon the market relationship between rental value and the sale price of such properties. For instance, a certain type of property might be generally sold at 100 times the monthly gross income. Prices determined by gross multipliers are usually considered as general indications of value only and not as a substitute for actual appraisal.

In summarizing it may be said the market data (comparison) method is the most widely used of all valuation methods. Investment property is frequently appraised by the income capitalization method while the replacement or reproduction cost method lends itself to special valuation problems. The methods are sometimes used independently and at other times concurrently as modifiers or checks.

Depreciation

In connection with the appraisal of real property, depreciation is defined as "loss in value for any cause from reproduction cost new." It is customarily measured by estimating the difference between the current reproduction cost new and the estimated value of improvements as of the date of appraisal.

Depreciation includes all of the influences that reduce the value of a property below its replacement cost new. The principal influences are often grouped under three general headings and sub-divided as follows:

1. Physical deterioration, resulting from:
   a. Wear and tear from use;
   b. Negligent care (sometimes termed "deferred maintenance");
   c. Damage by dry rot, termites, etc.
2. Functional obsolescence, resulting from:
   a. Poor architectural design and style;
   b. Lack of modern facilities;
   c. Out-of-date equipment;
   d. Capacity (in relation to site).
3. Economic and social obsolescence, resulting from:
   a. Misplacement of improvement;
   b. Zoning and/or legislative restrictions;
   c. Detrimental influence of supply and demand;
   d. Change of locational demand.

The first two groups are considered to be inherent within the property itself. The third group of depreciating influences consists of economic and social factors which are extraneous to the property itself.

Depreciation is deducted from the current new replacement or reproduction cost of the building involved to arrive at the current value of improvements. The resulting figure is then added to the appraised value of the land to obtain the total appraised value of the property. Accrued depreciation may be classified either as curable or incurable. The latter classification includes those instances that would require complete replacement or excessive repair costs and thus be too costly to remove and replace, or to repair.

Three methods may be used to estimate "accrued depreciation."

The first is the observed-condition method. Under this method the accrued depreciation is usually determined by establishing the total cost of making all repairs to correct curable physical deterioration and functional obsolescence, plus the estimated loss in value due to incurable physical deterioration and functional and economic obsolescence.

The observed-condition method is the most widely used in actual practice.

The second method is known as the age-life method. This is based on depreciation tables which have been developed to reflect age-life experience in the depreciation of structures of various types and uses, assuming average care and maintenance. Some depreciation tables, such as those published by the U. S. Treasury Department, Bureau of Internal Revenue, under the title "Income Tax Depreciation and Obsolescence Estimated Useful Lives and Depreciation Rates," reflect not only normal physical deterioration but also all economic and functional obsolescence as well.

The third method is a technical one used by appraisers as a by-product of the capitalization approach to value. It is known as the building-residual technique. Under this method the land is valued independently of the building and the fair annual net return on the land is deducted from the estimated net annual income of the property (land and building). The residual amount is said to be attributable to the depreciated building and is capitalized to indicate the building value. The depreciation figure is the difference between the residual value of the building as shown above and that of a new structure of similar type. It provides a good check on the cost approach appraisal.

Accrual for depreciation

Future depreciation or recapture is the loss in value which has not yet occurred but will come in the future and is of significance in the capitalization of income method. In the income approach to valuation, it is based on the remaining economic or useful life during which time provision is made for the recapture of the value of improvements. It is the return "of" the investment—as differentiated from the return (interest and profits) "on" the invested capital. Under the income approach this depreciation may be measured by one of two different methods. These are:

Straight-line depreciation, a definite sum deducted from the income each year during the total estimated economic life of the building to replace the capital investment.

Sinking-fund method, which also includes a fixed annual depreciation deduction from income, but with yearly reserves set up from such funds which at compounding interest will offset the depreciation. Accruals for future depreciation to replace the capital investment are in addition to and essentially different from both maintenance charges and reserves for periodic replacement of curable depreciation. Should there be any estimated salvage value to the property at the end of its economic life, this amount need not be returned through the annual depreciation charge under either the straight-line or the sinking-fund method.

Recapture usually is recognized as a proper charge against income. It is an authorized expense for investment property or property used in trade or business, where the property is subject to fair wear and tear. Under income tax regulations depreciation is not an authorized expense for residential property unless such property is used for rental income. The rate of depreciation, for income tax purposes, may be determined by several different methods.

Book depreciation

It should be understood that differences exist between "book" depreciation as computed by an accountant and estimated loss in value as determined by a professional appraisal. The former is a theoretical figure adopted for accounting purposes. The latter is based on observed conditions and engineering and economic analysis as of the date of appraisal.

In accruals for future depreciation where both estimates are based on theory, since the accountant and the appraiser select rates of depreciation for different purposes, they may vary considerably. While both estimators may use the same period as to the remaining economic life of the property and may also use the same method, additional considerations may affect the resultant rate. Whereas the accountant may be restricted because of accounting conventions, the appraiser is under no such restrictions. The real estate agent who is estimating values should understand the necessity for following proper appraisal procedures and should not rely on book values either to estimate accrued depreciation or for future depreciation accruals.

Contrasting with depreciation is *appreciation* of values which result from inflation or from special supply and demand forces relating to the specific property. Appreciation may reduce or offset entirely a normal anticipated decrease of value due to depreciation.

In concluding this chapter on concepts, valuation and appraisal techniques, let us wave three warning flags. It is to be noted that there is no real difference between the words *valuation* and *appraising.* The first is broader, tends to be economic in origin and emphasizes theory; whereas the latter refers more to practice, methods and techniques. Next, anybody can make an appraisal, even a layman, but the *worth* of an appraisal report is determined by the experience, compensation, qualifications, and motives of the man behind it. And, finally, let us not be deceived by any broad statement that appraising is an exact science. It is a science as is any of the other social sciences, but people and property cannot be appraised with the exactness and accuracy reached by the mathematical and physical sciences.

Questions on Appraisals

1. Q. What is an appraisal?
   A. An expression of opinion of the value of a property as of a given date and under certain limiting conditions. It is an estimate of the present worth of future benefits.
2. Q. Explain why cost differs from price and value.
   A. Cost is the amount of expenditure necessary for, or incurred in, the creation of a thing whereas price is the amount it sold for. Value is (1) the power to command other commodities in exchange or (2) the present worth of future benefits arising from ownership.
3. Q. Distinguish between value and market value.
   A. Value is (1) the present worth of future benefits arising from ownership or (2) the power to command other commodities in exchange. Market value is "the highest price estimated in terms of money which the property will bring if exposed for sale in the open market with a reasonable time allowed to find a purchaser buying with full knowledge of all the uses and purposes to which it is adapted and for which it is capable of being used."
4. Q. In analyzing a parcel of land to estimate its value, what is the first thing necessary to determine?
   A. Highest and best use.
5. Q. Is there a definite relationship between an improper development and depreciation?
   A. Yes. If it is an improper improvement, it is functionally or economically deficient and does not produce the highest return of which the land is capable.
6. Q. Enumerate three generally accepted approaches to a real estate value estimate.
   A. 1. Comparable sales or market data approach.
      2. Cost appraisal.
      3. Capitalization or income approach.
7. Q. What two kinds of value may property have?
   A. Property may have a use value or value in exchange.
8. Q. Explain the difference between real property and real estate.
   A. Real estate is the land and those things which are permanently fastened to it. Real property is all the rights and benefits to be derived from the ownership of real estate.
9. Q. What are the "amenities" as the term applies to real estate?
   A. Amenities are the satisfactions of enjoyable living to be derived from a home or profits from income property.
10. Q. What are the rights which are represented by the ownership of real estate?
    A. (a) Right to sell.
       (b) Right to lease.
       (c) Right to enter.
       (d) Right to give it away.
       (e) Right to refuse to exercise any of these rights.
11. Q. Why is appraising more a study of people's activities than an exact science?
    A. It is the people's actions in the market which determines the price at which property may be sold. Therefore, an appraiser must evaluate the thinking as well as the

actions of people. If people think that real estate is worth a certain amount, that will be its selling price.

12. Q. Explain "highest and best use" as it applies to real estate.
    A. The use which will produce the greatest net income over a given period of time is the highest and best use.
13. Q. How is the idea of highest and best use applied in appraising?
    A. In evaluating property it is necessary to determine its highest and best use because this is the starting point for the appraisal.
14. Q. If a property cannot be sold in the current market, does it have no value?
    A. It would not have any exchange value at that time, but its use value would not be affected by current market conditions. It is just as capable of producing the amenities of living as ever.
15. Q. Why does usefulness plus scarcity create maximum value?
    A. People desire those things which are useful to them. However, if the things desired were available to all in unlimited quantity, they would have no value for they could be had for the taking. Only when the useful items become scarce are people willing to give other things in exchange for them. The more scarce they become, the higher the price is bid up.
16. Q. In what ways have governmental agencies affected the value of real estate?
    A. The government through the F.H.A. and G.I. loan programs have determined to a certain extent where and what type of buildings should be built. By their rules under which buyers were qualified for loans, they have also affected the price of real estate.
17. Q. How have the F.H.A. and G.I. loan programs affected appraisal procedure?
    A. The rules and regulations issued by these government organizations have tended to standardize the appraisal approach of lenders. These agencies have attempted to standardize not only procedure but also terminology and minimum construction practices.
18. Q. What is the definition of value used by the Federal Housing Administration?
    A. The price which typical buyers would be warranted in paying for the property for long-term use or investment, if they were well-informed and acted voluntarily and without necessity.
19. Q. How does the definition of value used by the Veterans Administration differ from that used by the F.H.A.?
    A. The Federal Housing Administration's definition stresses that it is what a buyer is warranted in paying, while the Veterans Administration states that it is a price that a qualified appraiser would recommend to a purchaser as being a proper price under prevailing conditions.
20. Q. How does the American Institute of Real Estate Appraisers define market value?
    A. "The highest price estimated in terms of money which a property will bring if exposed for sale in the open market, allowing a reasonable time to find a purchaser who buys with knowledge of all the uses to which it is adapted and for which it is capable of being used."[1]
21. Q. Name three kinds of depreciation which might affect the value of a property.
    A. (a) Physical deterioration—wear and tear or action of weather.
    (b) Functional obsolescence—such as a poor floor plan or inadequate space.
    (c) Economic depreciation—run-down neighborhood, poor police protection, and other forces outside of the property itself.
22. Q. Under what conditions and to what kind of property would each approach be given the most consideration?
    A. 1. Comparison in midlife residential properties.
    2. Reproduction cost in public properties.
    3. Capitalization in investment properties.

[1] May, Arthur A.

23. Q. What are some of the indicators of the activity of the real estate market?
    A. (a) Mortgage foreclosures.
    (b) Number of deeds recorded.
24. Q. Is it necessary to know the reason for an appraisal?
    A. Yes. In order to stress certain types of information necessary in forming an opinion. For example, in assessment cases, comparison with other assessments; in sale or purchase, comparison with sales as of certain periods of time.
25. Q. Name at least five reasons for which appraisals of single family homes are made.
    A. 1. Sale. 4. Taxation. 7. Partition.
    2. Purchases. 5. Inheritance tax. 8. Insurance.
    3. Mortgages. 6. Condemnation. 9. Liquidation.
26. Q. List the following in the order of importance in residential analysis; age of building; suitability of residence to site; physical condition of building.
    A. 1. Suitability of residence to site.
    2. Physical condition of building.
    3. Age of building.
27. Q. Name four types of city data to be assembled.
    A. 1. Economic background and trends.
    2. Population trends.
    3. Cultural facilities.
    4. Transportation pattern.
28. Q. Name four types of neighborhood data to be assembled.
    A. 1. Physical or structural.
    2. Shopping facilities.
    3. Transportation facilities.
    4. Nuisances or economic influences.
29. Q. Does the trend in the wholesale price of textiles in New York City have any bearing upon local real estate?
    A. Yes. It is an indication of the economic conditions prevailing as compared with other economic periods. Real estate follows the general pattern of all commodity markets.
30. Q. Is an appraisal (a) absolute value? (b) a guess? (c) an estimate?
    A. (c) An estimate of the public's opinion of the value.
31. Q. What qualities in an appraiser will convert a guess into an estimate?
    A. Training in fundamentals of land economics, knowledge of real estate in general, experience in operating and managing real estate, personal integrity.
32. Q. What is a summation appraisal?
    A. The addition of the estimated land value to the depreciated reproduction cost of the improvements.
33. Q. Do three approaches to value indicate more than one value?
    A. No. Three approaches to value merely limit the range within which the value will be and give credence to the judgment of the appraiser.
34. Q. Under what conditions may a house be worth less than its cost?
    A. When it is an over-improvement.
35. Q. (a) What is an over-improvement?
    (b) What is an under-improvement?
    A. (a) That improvement which does not produce an adequate return for the amount invested in a building.
    (b) That improvement which does not sufficiently improve the land to produce the highest return of which the land is capable.
36. Q. What charges would you make against gross income from a rented property?
    A. Allowance for vacancies and rent losses, fixed expenses (taxes and insurance), operating expenses (management, utilities, maintenance, repairs) and reserves for replacements.
37. Q. Would the capitalization rate be high or low for the following properties?
    (a) Business property in 100% suburban location.

(b) Apartment building in a blighted area.
(c) A new single-family residence in an old neighborhood.

A. (a) Low. (b) High. (c) High.

38. Q. What is meant by "unearned increment"?
A. Value added to land by increased population and demand for which owner is in no way responsible.

39. Q. What additional factor should be considered in the valuation of a business other than those of goods and fixtures?
A. Good will of the business if the market indicates a willingness to pay for it.

40. Q. What is the difference between assessed valuation and market value?
A. Assessed valuation is the valuation fixed for purposes of taxation; market value is the amount for which the property may be sold in the open market.

41. Q. (a) What is functional obsolescence?
(b) What is economic obsolescence?
(c) How does physical deterioration manifest itself?
A. (a) Inadequate or improper design or outmoded equipment.
(b) Influences external to the property which affect its income or desirability because of their undesirability, or nuisances.
(c) In deteriorated appearance, fungus growth, insects, worn members.

42. Q. What effect does purchasing power of the population in a district have upon real estate values?
A. It limits the value to the ability to pay.

43. Q. How do you estimate the cubical contents of a building?
A. By measuring the building and multiplying the width by the depth by the height of the various sections of the structure.

44. Q. What is straight-line depreciation?
A. A fixed amount deducted annually from the income indefinitely.

45. Q. What is meant by the economic life of a building?
A. The period of time during which it will earn an adequate income to justify its existence.

46. Q. Outline the principal steps in the appraisal process.
A. 1. Definition of the problem.
2. Preliminary survey.
3. Data program.
4. Data Classification and analysis in:
   a. Cost approach.
   b. Market data (comparison) approach.
   c. Income approach.
5. Correlation.
6. Final estimate of value.

47. Q. Name several important value factors to be considered in appraising a city residence.
A. The purchasing power of the neighborhood population, availability of transportation, educational and cultural facilities, the physical characteristics of the house, and the ratio of land to building value.

48. Q. Name several important value factors to be considered in appraising an improved farm.
A. Distributional facilities for the produce of the farm, the probable productivity of the soil, climatic conditions, adequacy of the buildings, physical characteristics of the building, and water supply.

49. Q. Briefly explain the three residual methods of capitalizing income into value.
A. 1. *Land residual process.* Capitalize the amount remaining from the income after a proper allowance has been made for the earnings of the building. Process to be used when a building is new and its cost is known.
2. *Building residual process.* Capitalize the amount remaining from the income

after a proper allowance has been made for the earnings of the land. Process to be used when a building is old and the cost or value of the land can be closely estimated.
3. *Property residual process.* Capitalize the entire net income by means of an overall rate.

50. Q. What characteristics of property should be compared in interpreting market price data?
A. 1. Size of structure, construction, replacement cost, special features and deficiencies.
2. Rental value, gross and net income.
3. Site and other improvements.
4. Age, condition, obsolescence, functional utility.
5. Neighborhood (location).
6. Real estate market trends.

51. Q. In appraising for market value are you concerned with mortgages upon the property?
A. Not ordinarily. The usual procedure is to appraise as if free of encumbrances. However, methods involving appraising of the return to equity are becoming more popular.

52. Q. Why may a business be worth more than the value of the fixtures and merchandise?
A. The location and clientele may be already established—"good will."

53. Q. In computing the net income from a furnished apartment house, there are several major cost items to be deducted from the gross income to arrive at the net income. Name eight such distinct items.
A. (1) Taxes.
(2) Insurance.
(3) Repairs.
(4) Depreciation on furniture.
(5) Utilities.
(6) Vacancies and collection losses.
(7) Management.
(8) Reserve for replacements.

54. Q. Will economic changes affect market price and market value to the same extent?
A. No. Some changes will affect both while other changes will affect one more than the other.

55. Q. What would be an all-inclusive definition of accrued depreciation as it applies to real estate?
A. Loss of value, due to all causes, from reproduction cost new.

56. Q. What is the difference between accrued depreciation and deferred maintenance?
A. Accrued depreciation is the amount of depreciation of all kinds which has accrued to a building. Deferred maintenance is that part of physical deterioration which can be restored by repairs and maintenance.

57. Q. Why is location so important in the evaluation of real property?
A. Location is important because the area near a property tends to fix the amount which can be obtained for the property. The surroundings are the source of so-called economic obsolescense which destroys more value than any other cause.

58. Q. What are some of the things to look for in appraising a location?
A. Who lives there? What is their income? What are their interests? What per cent of the area is built up? How old are the houses? What are the restrictions and zoning? Are there non-harmonious groups in the area? Do the houses conform structurally and architecturally? This is only a partial list.

59. Q. Why should an appraiser use more than one of the three accepted approaches in evaluating a property?
A. More than one approach should be used to check the results obtained from the other

approaches. A person should use as many of the approaches as will apply to the property under appraisal.

60. Q. On what type of property would the cost approach tend to be most accurate?
    A. (1) On newly improved property in a good neighborhood and in an active real estate market.
    (2) Public or special properties.
61. Q. On what kind of property would the income approach be most widely used?
    A. On commercial and investment property rentable to tenants.
62. Q. Under what circumstances would an appraiser use the market approach?
    A. The market approach should be used in all cases where it is possible to find comparable sales.
63. Q. What is a capitalization rate?
    A. A capitalization rate is the percentage figure used to evaluate a net income flow and to convert it into a capital amount. It reflects the return that investors demand for their investment. At any specific time it can be found in the market by dividing the average net income of a property by the price at which the property was sold. By computing this percentage for comparable sales a valid capitalization rate can be obtained.
64. Q. When can it be said that sales of other properties are comparable to a subject property?
    A. Other properties are comparable if they have similar sizes, ages, neighborhood influences, architecture, floor plans, sized lots, are capable of producing the same volume of benefits and have the same highest and best use and zoning.
65. Q. What type of sales should be excluded as comparable in appraising?
    A. Several types of sales should be excluded. The following is not a complete list:
    (a) where grantee is any governmental agency or a public utility.
    (b) where grantee acquired title through foreclosure.
    (c) where grantee is a charitable, religious or educational organization.
    (d) where grantee and grantor are relatives or corporation affiliates.
    (e) where property is a subject of an undivided interest.
    (f) where sale was not the result of an arms length transaction under normal circumstances.
66. Q. How is the land evaluated when using the cost approach?
    A. It is usually evaluated by using the market approach on comparable sales.
67. Q. What is the difference between reproduction and replacement costs?
    A. Reproduction cost means the cost of reproducing a building exactly as it was built with the same or similar materials at present costs for labor and materials. Replacement cost means the cost of constructing a building which would serve the same purpose as the subject property.
68. Q. Give three methods used in estimating the cost of buildings.
    A. a. The quantity-survey method.
    b. The unit-in-place method.
    c. The comparative (square foot or cubic foot) method.
69. Q. Why is it sometimes difficult to determine the net income of rental properties?
    A. Because of inadequate bookkeeping on the part of the owner and because of the lack of maintenance.
70. Q. To what extent is the judgment of the appraiser involved in an appraisal?
    A. Good judgment is an all-important factor in a good appraisal. Only by weighing the data gathered in the scale of good judgment can a satisfactory appraisal be made.
71. Q. Do houses ever sell above their cost?
    A. Yes. When housing is short, homes may sell well above their reproduction cost.
72. Q. In what way does the income of the people in a neighborhood affect the value of real estate?
    A. The income of people in the area limits the price of property because people seldom

spend more than 30% of their income for housing.

73. Q. Could most sales of property be used as comparables in using the market approach?
    A. No. Many sales must be excluded because the sales used must meet the requirements of informed persons who are not under outside pressures. Sales to government agencies or as a result of condemnation under eminent domain should also be excluded.
74. Q. What is the difference between market price and market value?
    A. Market value is what a prudent, informed buyer free from outside pressures is justified in paying for a piece of property for long-term use or investment, while market price is what he would have to pay under current market conditions or actually did pay for it.
75. Q. Does the fact that three approaches are used to determine the appraisal value mean that there are three values?
    A. No. The three approaches are used to develop a reasonable range of values. They are tools to be used in gathering information upon which the final estimate is based.
76. Q. Could it be said that inflation might make it unnecessary to consider depreciation in appraising a property?
    A. No. Depreciation actually occurs, so it must be considered even though it has been hidden by the increase in value due to inflation.
77. Q. How is the real estate market unlike other markets?
    A. There is no open market where buyers and sellers may gather. The market is made by real estate buyers and sellers. The chances of contracting more than a small per cent of all prospective buyers is very remote.
78. Q. Select three terms from the following which pertain to the appraisal of real estate.

    covenant
    capitalization
    encroachment
    consideration
    eviction
    comparison
    default
    foreclosure
    option
    summation

    A. (1) capitalization. (2) comparison. (3) summation.
79. Q. In relation to real property, state the difference between "assessed valuation" and "assessment."
    A. "Assessed valuation" is the amount for which real property is evaluated by a unit of government for taxation purposes. "Assessment" is a pro-rata charge or tax levied against a property for a special improvement such as a sewer, pavement, or street. Also, it may mean the actual tax to be paid on real property arrived at by multiplying the assessed valuation of the property by the assessment rate (millage) for tax purposes.
80. Q. Explain the principal steps in the cost approach to value.
    A. This approach is comprised of three principal steps. First, compute the cost of reproducing or replacing the improvements with a suitable equivalent; second, add thereto an estimate value for the land, secured by comparison with other similar land; and third, make deductions for an estimated depreciation of the value of the improvements.
81. Q. If a building has a life expectancy new of 50 years and an effective age of 30 years, what is its remaining economic life?
    A. 20 years.
82. Q. What are the three residual techniques?
    A. a. Building.
       b. Land.
       c. Property.
83. Q. What is meant by "an annuity type income?"
    A. Long term lease to financially strong tenant.

84. Q. Where a property is under lease, what are the two component parts of the fair market value of the property (in relation to the owner's and tenant's interests)?
    A. Leased fee and leasehold.
85. Q. Name the three major categories of depreciation.
    A. a. Physical deterioration.
       b. Functional obsolescence.
       c. Economic obsolescence.
86. Q. What are the four categories of forces affecting real estate value?
    A. 1. Social.
       2. Governmental.
       3. Economic.
       4. Physical.
87. Q. Identify the formulas for property tax computations.
    A. Tax rate = tax divided by assessed valuation.
       Tax = assessed valuation multiplied by tax rate
       Assessed valuation = tax divided by tax rate

True and False

1. Loss to a building from any cause is called deterioration. T **F**
2. The value of land is more dependent upon its utility than its size. **T** F
3. Market value usually is the true value of real estate. **T** F
4. There are usually three approaches to a value estimate. **T** F
5. "Improved to the highest and best use" means that improvement which will produce the largest amount in money or amenities over a certain period of time. **T** F
6. Purchasing power of the population tends to limit the value of real estate in a neighborhood. **T** F
7. A house is never worth less than its cost. T **F**
8. The economic life of a building is the time during which its income justifies its existence. **T** F
9. Zoning regulations limit the use of real estate. **T** F
10. Market value and market price are synonymous. T **F**
11. An under-improvement is any improvement underground. T **F**
12. Two adjacent lots on a main business street, having the same area and the same topography but one having a frontage of 40 feet and the other a front of 35 feet, have the same value. T **F**
13. All sales prices are conclusive evidence of value. T **F**
14. There are three kinds of depreciation which affect the value of property. **T** F
15. Reproduction cost tends to set the upper limit of value. **T** F
16. Interest is the rental charge of money for its use. **T** F
17. A summation value is the sum of the land value and the building value. **T** F
18. Economic obsolescence is caused by undesirable neighbors. **T** F
19. There is only one type of value for a given property. T **F**
20. Functional obsolescence may be caused by poor planning. **T** F
21. The word appraisal means a process or method by which an opinion of the value of a property is derived. **T** F
22. Depreciation is a loss in value from any cause. **T** F
23. When making an appraisal, the purpose of the appraisal should be known and stated. **T** F
24. In appraising residential property the possible income is given the greatest consideration. T **F**
25. The rate of capitalization of the net income is that rate demanded by the public and which reflects the risk involved as compared with other investments. **T** F
26. Straight-line depreciation is a fixed annual sum deducted from the value of a building which will return its cost during its economic life. **T** F

27. Building restrictions and zoning regulations always increase the value of property. T F
28. The term "assessed valuation" always means market price. T F
29. The term "appraised value" means the present market value. T F
30. It could be said that no appraiser has ever recorded all of the pertinent information which affects the value of a piece of property. T F
31. The valuation of residential property makes up only about one-half of all appraisals in the United States. T F
32. An appraisal for a mortgage loan is usually very close to selling price. T F
33. An appraiser is usually asked to find the market value of the property involved. T F
34. The risks of investment in real estate lie principally in the factors surrounding the property rather than in the physical property itself. T F
35. In the final analysis a mortgage loan valuation is an evaluation of the risks involved. T F
36. The valuation for a part of a lot taken by condemnation to widen a street would be close to the market price for that part of the lot. T F
37. The term "value" is a mathematical concept. T F
38. Economists tend to favor the idea that the value of a material thing is its value in exchange. T F
39. Most people who buy homes could be said to be "well informed" as to the uses of the property. T F
40. The courts have contributed a great deal to the definition of value. T F
41. The typical real estate sale fits quite closely the definition for determining value. T F
42. The terms of sale could affect the "value" of a piece of property. T F
43. If a piece of property cannot be sold on the existing market then the appraiser would have to say that it has no exchange value at that time. T F
44. There is often more demand for expert appraisals during a depression than during a boom period. T F
45. It would be correct to say that cost and value are almost always the same. T F
46. For the most part it is not very difficult to gather adequate data on the costs of construction or the life span of neighborhoods. T F
47. "Judgment" as far as appraising is concerned could be said to be made up largely of the ability to discriminate between the relevant and the irrelevant. T F
48. Information concerning the attitude of lending-institutions should be gathered by the appraiser. T F
49. The general information gathered for appraisal purposes may be used over and over again for different appraisals if it is kept up to date. T F
50. Court decisions seldom affect real estate values for they are only enforcing the laws that are already on the statute books. T F
51. The population growth around a city has little effect on real estate values within the city itself. T F
52. There has been an increased use of the right of eminent domain by governmental bodies in recent years. T F
53. Cost will always fix the upper limit of value even in war times when materials are scarce. T F
54. Cities are usually built on poor land in order to preserve the good land for agricultural purposes. T F
55. The population trend in the United States is probably of more importance to an appraiser than the trend within the city itself. T F
56. In the past, population growth within an area was a good indicator of the trend in real estate values. T F
57. Those who are interested in real estate have been able to quite easily analyze those factors which cause city growth and determine values. T F
58. A more thorough knowledge of the economics of cities might have prevented

many millions of dollars in losses. T F

59. Real estate values in a city that has both commerce and manufacturing as a source of payrolls would be more stable than if only manufacturing were present. T F
60. A city of many small factories would tend to have more stable real estate values than one in which there are just a few very large factories. T F
61. The overflow movement of minority groups from one district to another is usually dictated by economic compulsion rather than a desire by the group to move into a new district. T F
62. If a city is left to follow its natural growth lines, it will follow the path of least resistance. T F
63. Real estate carries a heavier tax load proportionately than other types of wealth. T F
64. In the ordinary city there is a great deal of information available on the changing status of neighborhoods. T F
65. One will find a greater contentment in living if the people of a neighborhood have about the same income, culture, and education. T F
66. Values in a neighborhood will not be affected by rentals as long as the percentage of such rentals is less than 50% of the houses. T F
67. Designs of buildings tend to "wear out" with the passing of time as well as with the physical depreciation of the building. T F
68. A neighborhood could have thousands of houses as long as there was a high degree of conformity of buildings and people. T F
69. A large neighborhood will tend to resist deteriorating influences more than a smaller one. T F
70. Local codes and ordinances have little effect on values for they apply to all buildings in the area. T F
71. School enrollment data is a good source of information in real estate trends. T F
72. The peak point of desirability in a neighborhood is probably reached just before the original owners begin to sell and move out. T F
73. The appraiser need not be concerned with the status of the title of a property because he is not expected to render legal decisions. T F
74. The majority of property which is appraised is held in fee simple by the owners. T F
75. Value is determined by the sum total of the bricks, lumber, mortar, and other materials that go into a building. T F
76. Land economics could be described as a study of the uses that grew out of land when viewed as property. T F
77. Optimum value will be achieved when a property offers the most utility to the greatest possible number of people. T F
78. Only one bathroom in a home of five bedrooms would be classified as functional obsolescence. T F
79. It is presumed that land does not depreciate. T F
80. Urban renewal is a process whereby government funds are used to facilitate private investment in improving city land use. T F
81. As a general rule the quality of materials and labor in a building designed by an architect will be of satisfactory quality. T F
82. In an older house the appraiser will probably have to judge the quality of construction by actual inspection. T F
83. The shape of the lot is not important as long as it is large enough to accommodate the house. T F
84. Economic obsolescence could be computed even if a "good" neighborhood could not be found for comparison purposes. T F
85. Functional obsolescence would be reflected by a decrease in rental value in the market place. T F
86. The cost and value of a property would be synonymous only if a new property were improved to its highest and best use. T F

87. In computing the reproduction cost of an old building one should also include the broker's commission as a cost. T F
88. The cubic foot is often used as the unit in computing reproduction costs. T F
89. Once the reproduction cost of a building has been found, this amount is reduced by straight-line depreciation for the number of years that the facility has been built; the result thus obtained is depreciated reproduction cost of the improvement. T F
90. An appraiser need not inquire into the motives of a buyer or seller of a property which he uses for a bench mark if it seems to be a normal transaction in other ways. T F
91. Listing prices tend to fix the ceiling of value. T F
92. If two houses are in the same block, they can be assumed to be comparable for appraisal purposes. T F
93. If the real estate market were unstable, one would need more current data than if the market were fairly stable. T F
94. In the final analysis the comparative approach is a comparison of prices rather than a comparison of properties. T F
95. In most appraisals a person would need data on more than two bench mark properties. T F
96. The capitalization of income to arrive at value was first used on commercial properties. T F
97. Value could be said to be the present worth of all the rights to future benefits arising from the ownership of the property. T F
98. In appraising single-family houses one can often use a gross income-multiplier instead of capitalizing the net income. T F
99. The rate for capitalization increases as a neighborhood grows older. T F
100. A residential lot with a frontage of 25 feet would be worth one-half as much as one with a 50-foot frontage. T F
101. A safe rule-of-thumb is to allow $5 for each shrub used in landscaping. T F
102. An appraiser need not be concerned with restrictions on a property he is appraising because most of them are not enforced. T F
103. The appraisal of a residential property involves all of the techniques used in the evaluation of real estate. T F
104. The loan to property value ratio is lower today than twenty years ago. T F
105. There has been no increase in the use of eminent domain by governmental bodies since the war. T F
106. If a building has excessive wear or damage which can be cured, the "cost to cure" would be a deduction in arriving at an estimate of value by the cost method. T F
107. An increase in state income taxes will not materially influence the price of real estate because the moneys received from the tax will be spent within the state. T F
108. In the past the population growth within an area has not been a good indicator of the trend in real estate values. T F
109. Real estate values in a city where most employees are government workers would be less stable than in a manufacturing city. T F
110. Because there is a trend toward a greater variety in the styles and construction of homes, a house which is conservatively designed tends to decrease in value more rapidly than the contemporary homes. T F
111. The appraiser need not concern himself with the balance of the elements in planning as long as they do not seriously restrict the use of the house. T F
112. When using the unit-in-place method, it is assumed that all of the cost of building is included in the unit cost. T F
113. When using unit prices, an appraiser can usually disregard such things as extra corners and extra partitions because their cost is incorporated in the unit price. T F
114. Such items as architect's fees and interest on the loan during the construction

period would be included in unit costing. T F

115. If records have been kept on a building, the total of accrued depreciation would be the amount recorded in the reserve for depreciation. T F
116. The use of average age-life tables for computing depreciation is probably more accurate in a specific case than in observing the condition of the building. T F
117. The economic obsolescence of homes in America is probably greater than in any other country. T F
118. The courts have tended to uphold recorded depreciation as a base for accrued depreciation rather than observed condition because the former can be more easily proved. T F
119. By "reproduction cost new" we mean the cost of exact duplication in today's market with the same or closely related materials. T F
120. In appraising an old house a person is interested in the original cost in order to find the amount of accrued depreciation. T F
121. The quantity survey method is the same as the unit-in-place method. T F
122. When one is using the unit-in-place method any differences in such things as heating systems are added to or subtracted from the other costs. T F
123. Bench mark buildings for the cubic-foot method should have construction quality and utility similar to those of the property being appraised. T F
124. In arriving at the cubic feet in a house a person would take the inside rather than the outside measurements. T F
125. The reconditioning of a building is really an attempt to overcome the deferred maintenance of the building. T F
126. A home built with a poor floor plan would have loss of value due to functional depreciation as soon as it was built. T F
127. Deferred maintenance tends to accelerate depreciation of a property. T F
128. Functional obsolescence is accelerated by the invention of new equipment. T F
129. Ostensible Functional inadequacy may be ignored in an appraisal if the typical buyers would accept it. T F
130. An over-improvement on land would create economic obsolescence. T F
131. If the property under appraisal is under-improved, no reduction in value is necessary because you are appraising the property "as is." T F
132. Economic obsolescence probably causes more loss in value than any of the other forms of depreciation. T F
133. Straight-line depreciation is the process most often used by appraisers in computing the amount of depreciation accrued on a building. T F
134. The taking of depreciation on a building is actually a process of amortizing the investment in the building. T F
135. Economic depreciation will be reflected in the loss of rental value. T F
136. Economic obsolescence does not affect the value of land because land is not subject to depreciation. T F
137. Real estate is assessed every odd year. T F
138. Accepting employment or compensation for appraisal of real property contingent upon reporting a predetermined value, is a ground for revocation of license. T F
139. Issuing an appraisal report on any real property in which the licensee has an interest unless his interest is clearly stated in the report is a ground for revocation of license. T F
140. Marginal land is that on which the cost of operation approximates the gross income. T F
141. Net income is the principal guide to the appraiser's determination of value on an improved retail business property. T F
142. Single-family dwellings are usually appraised by capitalization. T F
143. The gross money expectancy from any income property is the gross income less the operating expenses. T F

144. In appraising income-producing property, allowance should be made for vacancies even though the property is completely rented. T F
145. The value of a residential lot is generally figured on a front foot basis. T F
146. Obsolescence and deterioration are the same. T F
147. A linear foot and a square foot are the same. T F
148. The sales price is never more than the appraised value. T F
149. Market value is usually determined by the price a willing seller will take and a willing buyer will pay. T F
150. Net income is the prime factor in arriving at a true appraisal of a retail business property. T F
151. Depreciation and obsolescence mean the same thing. T F
152. Assessed valuation is generally considered to be market value. T F
153. Generally speaking, real estate values in a city where most employees are government workers would be less stable than in a manufacturing city. T F
154. The proceedings by which a governmental subdivision takes private property for public use is called eminent domain. T F
155. The tax on a given piece of property is determined by multiplying the tax rate by the assessed valuations. T F
156. Economic life is the period over which a property may be profitably utilized. T F
157. The right of the telephone company to erect a line across your property is called a right of encroachment. T F
158. The gradual increase in the value of real property is called appreciation. T F
159. The general term covering loss from any cause is called disintegration. T F
160. A front foot ordinance regulates the minimum distance allowable between street line and the front of new buildings. T F
161. A competent appraiser develops the three approaches to value in every appraisal. T F
162. An appraisal is merely an opinion of value. T F
163. The gross multiplier used in appraising is based upon the market relationship between rental value and the sales price of properties. T F
164. The value of land is more dependent upon its utility than its size. T F

Multiple Choice

1. A "rule of thumb" method for determining the price a wage earner can afford to pay for a home is by multiplying his annual income by
   (a) one and a half.
   (b) two and a half.
   (c) four.
   (d) six.
2. No depreciation is allowed for federal tax purposes on
   (a) a 15 year old improvement.
   (b) land.
   (c) auxiliary warehouses.
   (d) life tenant's interest as lessor in a lease.
3. Net income is determined by deducting all expenses from the
   (a) net rental.
   (b) figuring eight per cent on assessed value.
   (c) sales price.
   (d) gross income.
4. The tax on a given piece of real estate is determined by multiplying the tax rate (millage) by
   (a) the selling price.
   (b) appraised value of property.
   (c) assessed valuation.
   (d) market value, less depreciation.

5. A report setting forth the estimate and conclusion of value is
   (a) an abstract.
   (b) a critique.
   (c) closing statement.
   (d) an appraisal.
6. The period over which a property may be profitably utilized is called its
   (a) economic life.
   (b) amortized life.
   (c) income life.
   (d) net life.
7. Amortization means
   (a) appreciation.
   (b) liquidation.
   (c) depreciation.
   (d) adolescence.
8. Two of the three main types of depreciation are physical deterioration and functional obsolescence. The third is
   (a) dry rot.
   (b) economic obsolescence.
   (c) adverse possession.
   (d) determination of net income.
9. Physical deterioration results from
   (a) tax liens.
   (b) overcrowded occupancy.
   (c) deferred maintenance.
   (d) poor basement drains.
10. The three main approaches to residential appraising are replacement cost approach, the capitalization approach and
    (a) net income approach.
    (b) highest and best use determination.
    (c) market data approach.
    (d) building-residual technique.
11. Marginal real estate is
    (a) border strip between two lots.
    (b) yielding farm land.
    (c) land which barely repays cost of operation.
    (d) waste land due to erosion, swamps, etc.
12. Which of the following creates the greatest value in retail income property?
    (a) type of construction.
    (b) parking facilities.
    (c) pedestrian traffic.
    (d) vehicular traffic.
13. An appraiser in his work
    (a) finds value.
    (b) determines value.
    (c) computes value.
    (d) estimates value.
14. Market price is
    (a) the true market value.
    (b) best price at public sale.
    (c) price asked for the property on an open market.
    (d) the amount, in terms of money, paid for the property.
15. By far, the largest volume of work of real estate appraisers is the appraisal of
    (a) single-family dwellings.
    (b) multiple-family dwellings.

(c) commercial income property.
(d) industrial acreage.

16. In computing the square footage of a home, you would use the
(a) inside measurements.
(b) outside measurements.
(c) both the inside and outside measurements.
(d) neither the inside nor outside measurements.

17. The lessening in value or estimated worth because of outmoded function is called
(a) lessened use.
(b) obsolescence.
(c) depreciation.
(d) wear and tear.

18. Highest and best use is defined as
(a) industrial property rezoned for single family use.
(b) that use which will yield the highest return on investment.
(c) exclusive residential hilltop or "view" lots.
(d) property purchased for owner use and occupancy.

19. Income approach for an appraisal would be most widely used
(a) on a newly opened subdivision.
(b) on commercial and investment property rented to tenants.
(c) on property heavily mortgaged.
(d) on property heavily insured.

20. Capitalization would be lowest upon the following property:
(a) business property in 100% suburban location.
(b) apartment building in a blighted area.
(c) a new single-family home in an old neighborhood.

21. Land suitable for citrus growth must be
(a) nearly level.
(b) free from fog.
(c) available to good drainage.
(d) relatively free from frost.

22. The selling price of real estate is usually based on its
(a) intrinsic value.
(b) speculative value.
(c) exchange value.
(d) market value.

23. Capitalization is a process used to
(a) convert income into value.
(b) determine cost.
(c) establish depreciation.
(d) determine potential future value.

24. An allowance in an income tax return for periodic decreases in value of income property, is called
(a) obsolescence.
(b) depreciation.
(c) deterioration.
(d) fringe benefit.

25. Gross income and effective gross income, in appraisal terminology, are not the same. In determining *effective* gross income, which one of the following would be deducted?
(a) insurance and taxes.
(b) repairs.
(c) depreciation on appliances and furniture furnished tenants.
(d) vacancy and credit losses.

26. In "directional growth," which center is involved?
(a) Manufacturing.

(b) Residential.
(c) Industrial.
(d) Commercial.

27. The selling price of homes is usually determined by
    (a) a minute inspection.
    (b) opinion of a builder.
    (c) comparison with similar properties.
    (d) cost to construct.
28. In computing the square footage of a home for purposes of an appraisal, you would use
    (a) the outside measurements.
    (b) the inside measurements.
    (c) both inside and outside measurements.
    (d) none of these.
29. Estimating the value of real property is called
    (a) assessment.
    (b) appraising.
    (c) surveying.
    (d) tabulating.
30. The jurisdiction of a Planning Commission is to pass on
    (a) new dwelling houses.
    (b) new commercial structures.
    (c) apartment buildings and town houses.
    (d) new subdivisions.
31. The appraised value of a new structure that represents the highest and best use of the land is likely to be similar to its
    (a) assessed value.
    (b) replacement value.
    (c) cost.
    (d) none of these.
32. In appraising older structures, consideration must be given to
    (a) depreciation.
    (b) rental potential.
    (c) number of occupants.
    (d) none of these.
33. Loss of value due to a building being unsuitably located is
    (a) functional obsolescence.
    (b) economic obsolescence.
    (c) economic depreciation.
34. Which one of the following is not one of the main approaches to appraising?
    (a) capitalization.
    (b) comparison.
    (c) survey.
    (d) summation.
35. Which of the following is the main type of depreciation?
    (a) capitalization obsolescence.
    (b) exterior obsolescence.
    (c) economic obsolescence.
    (d) gross obsolescence.
36. In order to estimate market value of an improvement, it is important to
    (a) obtain the amount of income.
    (b) consider the tax millage.
    (c) estimate depreciation.
    (d) ascertain amount of a mortgage commitment.
37. A person must own real estate for how long in order to take advantage of the long term

capital gain tax?
(a) six months.
(b) one year.
(c) eighteen months.
(d) two years.

38. To obtain a gross rent multiplier, the appraiser must obtain from comparable properties
(a) the cost and annual income.
(b) the monthly rent and selling price.
(c) the net income and selling price.
(d) the net income and rate of capitalization.

39. After the economic life of a multiple unit building has been exhausted, the owner has left, in economic terms,
(a) the unearned increment.
(b) the assessed value.
(c) his profit.
(d) the residual value.

40. In appraising a property, the summation value is the sum of the
(a) land and building values.
(b) income depreciation and obsolescence.
(c) market and replacement value.
(d) assessed and taxable values.
(e) none of these.

41. Value of property
(a) is measured in terms of the usefulness of the property.
(b) is identical with price.
(c) is equal to its cost upon completion.
(d) is determined by an official assessor.

42. The average selling price of dwellings in a district can be ascertained by
(a) assessed value.
(b) estimate of unearned increment.
(c) comparative analysis.
(d) sidewalk judgment of an experienced broker.

43. A single structure designed for two-family occupancy is called
(a) a triplex.
(b) an apartment house.
(c) a residence.
(d) a duplex.
(e) none of these.

44. Two of the three main types of depreciation are physical deterioration and functional obsolescence. The third is
(a) dry rot.
(b) vandalism.
(c) economic obsolescence.
(d) determination of net income.

45. A common unit, other than the square foot, used to determine value in an urban center is
(a) cubage.
(b) front foot.
(c) square yard.
(d) the quotient.

46. When making an appraisal of real estate, an appraiser is most commonly concerned with
(a) the remainder estate.
(b) the reversionary estate.
(c) market value in fee simple.
(d) the amenities.

47. The average real estate appraiser is called upon most often to make an appraisal for purposes of
    (a) taxation.
    (b) condemnation.
    (c) insurance.
    (d) market value.
48. Market price is
    (a) the true market value.
    (b) best price at public sale.
    (c) price asked in an open market.
    (d) the consideration paid for the property.
49. In estimating the replacement cost of real property, an appraiser considers the land value, the replacement cost of the improvements and
    (a) the amenity value.
    (b) the future income.
    (c) depreciation.
    (d) none of these.
50. The market approach to value is the method of appraisal in which the value of property is
    (a) based on factual data related to the income yield of the property.
    (b) based on sales of comparable properties.
    (c) based on cost of duplicating the improvements on today's market.
    (d) determined by capitalizing the annual net income.
    (e) none of these.
51. The economic life of a multiple living unit structure has been exhausted. The owner then has left, in economic terms,
    (a) the profit.
    (b) the unearned increment.
    (c) the residual value.
    (d) the assessed value.
52. A tenant improves the leased property. Taxes are increased on that account.
    (a) The tenant is liable for the increase in taxes.
    (b) The lessor and tenant are each liable for one-half.
    (c) The lessor is liable.
    (d) Neither is liable for the increase.
    (e) Depends on lease.
53. Which two of the following should have no influence on an appraiser's compensation?
    (a) The closeness of his value estimate to the owner's honest opinion of the property's value.
    (b) The length of the report.
    (c) The complexity of the appraisal.
    (d) Time required to make the appraisal.
    (e) The appraiser's knowledge and experience.
54. Metes and bounds are employed in
    (a) staking out the location of a building on a property.
    (b) delineating the boundaries of a neighborhood.
    (c) describing the boundaries of a tract of land.
    (d) describing the width and direction of a highway.
55. In the final correlation stage of an appraisal, the estimate of value is developed
    (a) by averaging the three indications of value.
    (b) by according the greatest weight to the median value indication.
    (c) by selecting the value indication closest to the value desired by the employer.
    (d) by relating the value indication to the type of property being appraised and the quantity and quality of the available data.

56. Capital losses on owner-occupied single family residences are deductible
    (a) at any time.
    (b) within three years.
    (c) the year they occur.
    (d) at no time.
57. Loss of value due to the property being unsuitably located is known as
    I. economic obsolescence.
    II. functional obsolescence.
        (a) I only.
        (b) II only.
        (c) both I and II.
        (d) neither I nor II.
58. The function of an appraiser is to
    I. set value.
    II. estimate value.
        (a) I only.
        (b) II only.
        (c) both I and II.
        (d) neither I nor II.
59. The decrease in value because of outmoded function is known as
    I. functional obsolescence.
    II. deterioration.
        (a) I only.
        (b) II only.
        (c) both I and II.
        (d) neither I nor II.
60. The income value approach for an appraisal would be most widely used
    I. on dwelling property in a new subdivision.
    II. on leased property in a shopping center.
        (a) I only.
        (b) II only.
        (c) both I and II.
        (d) neither I nor II.
61. When the economic life of an apartment building has been exhausted, the owner's economic interest is the
    I. residual value.
    II. unearned increment.
        (a) I only.
        (b) II only.
        (c) both I and II.
        (d) neither I nor II.
62. To obtain a gross rent multiplier, an appraiser must obtain from comparable properties, the
    I. monthly rent and selling price.
    II. net income and selling price.
        (a) I only.
        (b) II only.
        (c) both I and II.
        (d) neither I nor II.
63. An appraiser, in determining depreciation, will consider
    I. wear and tear from use.
    II. lack of modern facilities.
        (a) I only.
        (b) II only.
        (c) both I and II.

(d) neither I nor II.

64. Capitalization is a process to
    I. determine potential future value.
    II. convert income into value.
    (a) I only.
    (b) II only.
    (c) both I and II.
    (d) neither I nor II.

Chapter 9

LICENSE LAWS
Constitutionality

EVERY STATE in this country, the District of Columbia, the Virgin Islands, Guam, and the seven Canadian provinces require a person engaging in the real estate business as a broker or salesman, to be licensed. In order to obtain the required license, the applicant must be of good repute and pass an examination, and demonstrate competency. The enactment of license laws has been the greatest single factor in elevating the real estate business to a professional level. Courts have held that the real estate business is of such a public nature that it is a fit subject for regulation by the state: *Watson v. Muirlsead,* 57 Pa. 161 (Pa. 1868); *Roman v. Lobe,* 243 N.Y. 51 (1926).

Oregon passed the first valid license law in 1919.

The question was raised early whether there was any need for regulation of the real estate industry.

A broker clearly has a needed and useful function. But the abuses which have been practiced by some members of the real estate group show, too, that the justification of the broker exists only when the service which he renders is efficient, intelligent, and honest. Because his relation to the economic mechanism is so delicate and important, and because the social consequences of incompetent or dishonest action on his part are so grave, communities learn, sooner or later, that they must demand that the broker have certain qualifications of education and character. This need has translated itself into regulation by law.

In every one of the fifty states where regulatory laws are in effect, the technique used to accomplish the regulation is a system of licensing. Under these systems, persons must obtain a license in order to engage lawfully in the real estate brokerage business, and only those applicants who possess certain required qualifications are eligible for licensure. Moreover, the continued privilege to engage in the business is conditioned upon the licensee abiding by certain prescribed standards of conduct in the operation of his business.

Are license laws constitutional?

Now, the very purpose and function of licensure acts obviously operate to deprive countless individuals of the privilege of engaging in the kind of a vocation which they feel they have a natural and inalienable right to pursue. Because these laws are restrictive of the free right to engage in the brokerage business, they have been challenged time and again in the courts of the various jurisdictions. The attacks on their constitutionality have been on every conceivable front; hardly a legal weapon has been left untried; yet, in the main, these laws have withstood every challenge, and in their broad basic concepts they have been established universally as valid and constitutional.

Qualifications of character and competence

The most important question touching the constitutionality of these license laws is, of course, whether the state has the right to demand at all that only persons with certain qualifications of education, knowledge, or character be permitted to engage in the real estate brokerage business. This kind of regulation, say the opponents of licensing laws, violates the "due process" clause of the Fourteenth Amendment of the Federal Constitution. The "due process" clause provides:

. . . nor shall any State deprive any person of life, liberty, or property without due process of law, . . .

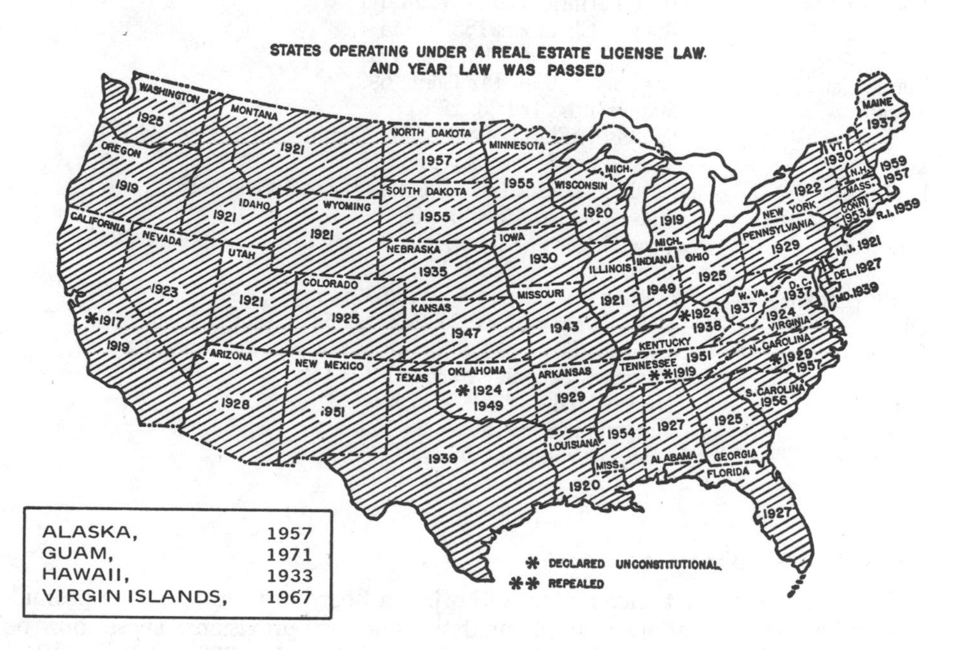

It is argued that under this, the "due process" clause, or under similar provisions of state constitutions, every person is protected in his right to pursue a gainful occupation, and if one chooses to engage in the real estate brokerage business, the state cannot rightfully prohibit him from doing so, regardless of whether he be well- or ill-equipped and regardless of the social consequences of his engaging therein.

True it is that the due process clause does prohibit many forms of purported business regulation by the state. There can be no prohibition of the right to pursue a lawful and useful occupation under the guise of regulation. But where the object of legislation is needed regulation of a business and not the destruction of it, the power to the state to enact the legislation cannot be denied. The due process clause has never been held to render the state powerless to protect her citizens by throwing reasonable safeguards around the exercise of any right an individual possesses. There is a broad reservoir of power which inheres in every sovereign state, to protect the health, safety, and property of her citizens. This is what is known in the law as "police power." And under this, the "police power," the courts of the various states have sustained the power of the state to restrict the right of engaging in the real estate brokerage business to those who possess certain educational and character qualifications. Thus, in an early and important case, *Riley v. Chambers,* 185 P. 855 (1919), the argument was made before the Supreme Court of California, that it is an arbitrary invasion of private rights and liberties to prevent a person from engaging in a lawful and innocuous business or occupation because of his moral character or reputation. The Court upheld the statute.

License laws are firmly established. Representative cases throughout the country upholding their validity are:

States	*Cases*
Arkansas	State v. Hurlock 49 S.W. 2d 611
California	Riley v. Chambers 185 P. 855
	Breechen v. Riley 187 Cal. 121
Connecticut	Cyphers v. Allen 142 Conn. 699
Florida	State v. Rose 122 So. 225
	Shelton v. Florida Real Estate Commission 121 So. 2d 711
Kentucky	Sims v. Reeves 261 S.W. 2d 812
Louisiana	Zerlin v. Louisiana Real Estate Board 103 So. 528
New Mexico	State v. Spears 75 N.M. 400
New York	Groetzinger v. Forest Hills Terrace Corp. 205 N.Y. S. 125
	Roman v. Lobe 243 N.Y. 51
North Carolina	State v. Warren 114 S.E. 2d 660
Ohio	Hall v. Geiger-Jones Co. 242 U.S. 539 (Security Dealer)
Pennsylvania	Young v. Dept. of Public Instruction 105 Pa. Super. Ct. 153
	Verona v. Schenley Farms Co. 312 Pa. 57
Tennessee	Davis v. Halley 227 S.W. 1021
West Virginia	State v. Jackson 120 W. Va. 521
Wisconsin	Payne v. Volkman 198 N.W. 438

Rules and regulations

Practically every state license law authorizes a Board or Commission to promulgate Rules and Regulations to implement the statutory provisions. These must be reasonable and not a usurpation of legislative authority. In 1933 the Hawaii Real Estate Commission adopted a Rule and Regulation that an applicant for license was required to pass an examination. In the case of *Carlson v. Real Estate Commission of Hawaii,* 38 Haw. 9 (1949), the examination requirement was declared void. The next year the *legislature* amended the law to require an examination.

In the case of *Lee v. Delman,* 66 So. 2d 252 (Fla. 1953), the Florida Commission adopted a Rule and Regulation that a real estate salesman was required to devote *full* time to the real estate business. The court held the Regulation invalid and expressed a doubt that even the legislature could pass such a requirement.

In the case of *Real Estate Commission v. Roberts,* 271 A 2d 246 (Pa. 1970), the Supreme Court upheld the suspension order of the Pennsylvania Real Estate Commission because the broker had refused to permit a Commission Investigator to inspect the broker's escrow account without a warrant or subpoena. The appelant argued that the Commission violated his constitutional rights against self—incrimination and unreasonable searches and seizures. The court held that the suspension order was proper, citing the "Required Record Doctrine" stated in *Shapiro v. U.S.,* 335 U.S. 1 (1948); namely, that:

> The privilege which exists as to private papers cannot be maintained in relation to "records

required by law to be kept in order that there may be suitable information of transactions which are the appropriate subjects of governmental regulation and the enforcement of restrictions validly established."

The court cited the United States Supreme Court opinion in the *United States v. Morton Salt Co.,* 338 U.S. 632, viz:

> Even if one were to regard the request for information in this case as caused by nothing more than official curiosity, nevertheless law-enforcing agencies have a legitimate right to satisfy themselves that (appellant's) behavior is consistent with the law and the public interest.

Exemptions

The class of cases that most closely touches the equality clause is that involving the validity of exemptions granted by the licensing laws. Every existing real estate brokerage license law contains a provision exempting certain enumerated classes of persons from the operation of the Act. In other words, certain persons who do acts of the kind contemplated by the statute, are, nevertheless, not required to obtain a license in order to lawfully do such acts. This does appear to be patently discriminatory. Yet, analyzed more closely, the typical exemptions found in the statutes are found to have some reasonable basis in fact for their existence. And that is all that the law requires to sustain them.

> While reasonable classification is permitted, without doing violence to the equal protection of the laws, such classification must be based upon some real and substantial distinction, bearing a reasonable and just relation to the things in respect to which such classification is imposed.[1]

FIRST. *Attorneys-at-law.* Attorneys are exempted from the operation of almost all of the license laws now in effect. This exemption was challenged in the case of *Young v. Department of Public Instruction,* 105 Pa. Sup. 153 (1932), but the Court upheld it as a constitutional discrimination:

The case of *Tobin v. Courshon; et al.,* 155 So. 2d 785 (Fla. 1963), raised a very important and practical question "whether or not qualified lawyers who are not licensed to operate as real estate brokers may recover part of a commission paid to a registered broker as compensation for cooperating with him in effecting a sale." In a 3 to 2 majority opinion the Court held that the plaintiff attorney could not recover even in an "isolated" case "when there was no relationship to his 'duties' as an attorney and collect compensation on the theory that because he as an attorney was familiar with the law of conveyancing he could enter the Realtor field on an independent venture."

SECOND. *Trustees selling under a deed of trust.* This exemption appears in almost all of the license laws. The California Court upheld this exemption as valid:

> The fourth point is that trustees selling under a deed of trust are excepted, and no exception is made of trustees doing anything else than selling, such as leasing, or renting, or collecting rents. The reply is that trustees, whether selling or doing something else, do not come within the purview of the Act. The express exception of trustees selling under a deed of trust adds nothing, and the Act would be the same if it made no mention of trustees.[2]

THIRD. *Persons holding power of attorney from owner to consummate transaction.* Legislators have been careful, since the California case of *Riley v. Chambers,* to define expressly that the power of attorney be a power to consummate the transac-

---

[1] Southern Ry. Co. v. Greene, 216 U. S. 400, 417, 54, L. Ed. 536.
[2] Riley v. Chambers, 181 P. 589 (Cal.)

tion, and not simply a power of attorney, and so stated, the exception is no doubt valid, as the California Court held.

An unusual attack was made against the California Act for bringing within its purview a class of persons who, in the earlier history of license law legislation, were not considered properly to be within the purview of such acts—persons who engaged in a single or isolated act of brokerage without engaging in a course of business. It was contended in an important case, which ultimately reached the United States Supreme Court, that insofar as the statute sought to prohibit one individual from employing another to handle a single transaction of the kind contemplated by the statute, it was unconstitutional as depriving persons of freedom of contract. The Supreme Court of California, in answering this contention, said:

> No particular or convincing reason can be urged why the participants in a single negotiation of the sort defined in said Act should not be subjected to the same supervision as those engaging in a series of similar transactions, since at the last analysis every transaction of the kind coming within the purview of the statute is an isolated transaction, whether conducted singly or as a series of transactions carried on in the course of a business or vocation, and since the lawmakers have seen fit to embrace the participants in each single transaction within the purview, requirements, and inhibitions of the act in question, we can see no adequate reason for holding that in so doing they have violated the constitutional right of freedom to contract any more than they would have done by confining the scope of the statute to those carrying on such transactions in the course of a business or vocation.[3]

In construing the exemption of persons "holding a duly executed power of attorney" under the Louisiana law, the Supreme Court, in the case of *Trentman Co., et al., v. Brown,* 176 La. 854 (1933) held that: "It does not mean that one who is engaged in the business of real estate broker may exempt himself from the operation of the act by taking in each instance a power of attorney from the owner whose property he is seeking to sell. If the act meant this, it would soon be worthless as a piece of legislation . . . "

Alleged discriminations other than exemptions

Discriminations have been charged against provisions of the acts other than the exemption provisions. The California Act was challenged for the reason that a different penalty is prescribed for violation by an individual than that prescribed for violations by corporations. It was also attacked because it prescribes penalties for individual and corporate transgressors, whereas partnerships, as such, were left immune. Both these objections were overruled by the Court.[4]

The California Act was also challenged on the ground that it discriminates against collectors of rent by including them within the provisions of the law, while collectors of other obligations are not included. The Supreme Court held the objection invalid.

The same case held, too, that it was not unreasonable to distinguish between brokers and salesmen, in charging the former different license fees, or in requiring the former to submit certificates of character by two landowners, and the latter, certificates by their employers only.

In *Maury v. State,* 93 So. 802 (1922), a statute was considered which imposed a license tax upon "each person, firm, or corporation engaged in buying, selling, or renting real estate on commission," with a provision that if such person, etc., "also

---

[3] Haas v. Greenwald, 196 Cal. 236, 237 P. 38 (1925), affirmed, without opinion, on the basis of Bratton v. Chandler, supra, in United States Supreme Court: 72 L. Ed. 415.

[4] People v. Schomig 239 P. 413 (1925). Decided by District Court of Appeal. Hearing denied by Supreme Court.

engages in the business of loaning money as an incident merely to the real estate business, they shall also pay an additional license fee of fifty dollars." A majority of the Court upheld the law.

Discriminations against non-residents

The application of provisions of the license laws to out-of-state brokers brings into play still another important provision of the United States Constitution—the comity clause. Article IV, section 2 of the Constitution provides:

> The citizens of each State shall be entitled to all privileges and immunities of citizens in the several States.

The principal object of this clause of the Constitution was that stated in its original form in the Articles of Confederation—

> the better to secure and perpetuate mutual friendship and intercourse among the people of the different States in this Union.[5]

It secures to the citizens of every state all the rights and advantages in every other state that pertain to citizenship, in such state. What these rights and advantages are cannot be found in the Constitution, for they are not enumerated. It is for the Courts to say what they are. One such very important privilege is the right to engage in business in the state. Thus, no state could say that the citizens of all other states, save her own, were ineligible for licensure to engage in the real estate brokerage business. The State of Florida attempted to do this very thing in its 1927 Act. But the Supreme Court of the state held the provision invalid insofar as it applied to natural persons. The Court said:

> That clause [requiring every applicant to be a resident of the State of Florida] is violative of Article IV, section 2, and Fourteenth Amendment, Constitution of the United States, and section 1, Declaration of Rights, Florida Constitution, insofar as it applies to natural citizens. It denies to citizens of each State all the privileges and immunities of citizenship of this State.

In *Land Co. v. Fetty,* 15 Fed. (2d) 942 (1926), it was held that a Georgia lumberman employed for a single transaction of finding a purchaser for a tract of standing timber in Florida, but not licensed there, was not a broker within the statute defining a real estate broker. (Florida Laws, 1923, Chap. 9177.) The Court, stating that the Act was highly penal, construed the provision making one transaction the doing of business within the phrase "as a whole or partial vocation," as meaning that the Act was intended to apply to persons holding themselves out to the public as real estate brokers, and not to require every person specially employed for a specific transaction to take out a license.[6] In *Aronson v. Carobine,* 129 Misc. 800, 222 N.Y.S. 721 (1927), it was held that where a real estate broker licensed in New York is engaged in New York to sell property located in New Jersey and the broker finds a purchaser in New York, the broker is entitled to his commission, although he has not complied with the New Jersey law requiring broker to be licensed. *Lex loci contractus* (law of the place of the contract) will govern. To the same effect is *Tillman v. Gibson,* 44 Ga. App. 440, 161 S. E. 630 (1931).

In *Moore v. Burdine,* 174 So. 279 (1937), (La.), a broker conducted business in

[5] Articles of Confederation, fourth article.

[6] 86 A. L. R. 640.

Louisiana for the sale of Mississippi Gulf Coast properties to prospects in Louisiana. Although the contract of employment was executed in Mississippi, it was held that the contract was to be performed in Louisiana; that the law of the place of *performance* determined whether contract could be legally executed. Since the plaintiff broker had not taken out a license in Louisiana, the contract was illegal and the courts of Louisiana would not enforce it.

This rule, said the Court, is a well-recognized exception to the general rule that *lex loci contractus* governs.

In the case of *Talbot v. Jones,* 288 So. 2d (La. 1974), the court held that an unlicensed broker cannot recover a fee for his services in arranging for financing through a vendor's lien and mortgage to enable the defendants to purchase certain real estate, even though it was a single or isolated transaction. (Louisiana requires mortgage brokers to be licensed).

An Illinois broker, licensed in that state, went to New York and there negotiated a contract for the sale of land in Illinois. The plaintiff broker sued for commission in Illinois. The defendant contended that the brokerage contract was illegal because the plaintiff was not a licensed broker in New York. The New York statute forbids a person, partnership, or corporation from holding itself out or temporarily acting as real estate broker or salesman without first procuring a license; the state forbids such person to sue for services rendered without alleging and proving he had a license; it makes violation a misdemeanor and one act constitutes a violation. The Court held that the contract was void under New York law where it was made and therefore it will not be enforced by the courts of Illinois. The rule is well settled that validity, construction, and obligation of a contract must be determined by the law of the place where it is made or is to be performed, but the remedy is governed by the law of the forum. The rule is that when a statute declares that it shall be unlawful to perform an act, and imposes a penalty for its violation, contracts for such acts are void and incapable of enforcement. The object of the statute is public welfare and protection of vendor and purchaser.[7]

A number of states, where the license requirements are comparable, have entered into reciprocity agreements.

Grounds for disciplinary action

License laws were enacted for the protection of the public and not to eliminate or restrict competition. A broker's license represents his livelihood.

In the case of *Lee v. Real Estate Commission,* 516 P. 2d 1342 (Okla. 1973), the court, in sustaining a suspension of a broker's license, quoting from *Wilcox v. Reynolds,* 36 P. 2d 488, said:

> The law requires perfect good faith on the part of an agent toward his principal, not only in form, but in substance; and, the obligation of an agent to his principal demands the sincerest integrity, good faith and most faithful service.

A license law tribunal, upon *its own initiative,* or upon complaint filed may, for cause, refuse, suspend or revoke a license: *Flagg v. Layman,* 517 P. 2d 329 (Or. App. 1973). The New York license law provides only four grounds for disciplinary action, while the Ohio law has thirty-four grounds. Most states, including New York and Ohio, contain a "catch-all" clause, such as, "if found guilty of untrustworthiness, dishonesty, or incompetency in a real estate transaction."

---

[7] Frankel v. Allied Mills, 369 Ill. 578, 17 N. E. (2) 570 (1938).

Where broker misrepresents his own property

A number of cases have arisen in different jurisdictions where a complaint has been filed with a Real Estate Commission against a real estate broker on the grounds that he has been guilty of misrepresentation or fraud in the sale of property owned by him. The issue raised is whether such conduct of a licensee, acting as a principal, comes within the purview of the license law. There are cases which hold in the negative as well as the affirmative. The weight of authority, and the recent trend, is that a broker's license may be suspended or revoked on that account.

In *McKnight v. Florida Real Estate Commission,* 202 So. 2d 199 (1967), the Commission's jurisdiction was upheld where the charge involved worthless checks, which were not issued as a result of a real estate transaction. Emphasizing that the law requires a licensee to be honest, truthful, trustworthy, of good character, and that he bears a good reputation for fair dealing, the court said:

> We think it would be ludicrous to construe the statutes to mean that a broker to be answerable to the Real Estate Commission must commit the unlawful acts when engaged in real estate negotiations but should he commit the same unlawful acts when not engaged in real estate negotiations he would still be of good character and beyond the Commission's jurisdiction.

In the case of *State Real Estate Commission v. Tice,* 190 A. 2d 188 (Pa. 1963), the court stated "we believe that a single standard of honesty and competency should guide a broker's real estate activities whether performing as broker or owner." The revocation of the broker's license for making certain misrepresentations, in connection with F.H.A. financing in the sale of a property by him as owner, was upheld: *Fibus v. Real Estate Commission,* 7 Pa. Com. Ct. 74 (1973).

The most frequent complaints charge a licensee with misrepresentation, fraud or mishandling of deposit money. Most license laws provide that if a licensee is found guilty or pleads guilty to certain specified crimes, his license may be revoked or suspended. These offenses usually are embezzlement, forgery, extortion, obtaining money under false pretense, conspiracy to defraud, a felony, "or any similar offense or offenses." The New Jersey Supreme Court sustained the Commission's five year revocation of a broker's license, where he pleaded *nolo contendere* (no defense), in Federal Court, to a charge of violation of an F.H.A. regulation. It held that the license law provision "similar offense" embraced the offense charged. *Handelsman v. Real Estate Commission,* 244 A. 2d 131 (N.J. 1968).

Act committed outside the state

The question whether the jurisdiction of the Commission extends to acts committed outside the state was raised in the case of *Williams v. Florida Real Estate Commission,* 232 So. 2d 239 (1970). The licensee was employed as a broker by a corporation engaged in selling real estate in the Bahama Islands. The complaint alleged improper dealing in the sale of a lot located on Grand Bahama Island. The court said:

> "We do not believe the Commission exceeded its jurisdiction simply because these checks were not issued as a result of a real estate transaction. *The law specifically requires that a person in order to hold a real estate license must make it appear that he is honest, truthful, trustworthy, of good character, and that he bears a good reputation for fair dealing.*
>
> Worthless checks is the antithesis of good reputation and fair dealings and this misconduct need not be done during the negotiation and/or sale of real estate in order to be punishable.

Educational—apprenticeship requirements

In 1972, 40 states required that an applicant for a broker's license first satisfy some educational and/or apprenticeship requirements as a pre-requisite to licensure. The trend is to increase the emphasis on education in order to improve competency for the protection of the public, on the road to true professionalism. Professionalism can only be truly obtained when there is acceptance by the public. A college degree, with a major in real estate, may well be the ultimate standard for entrance into the real estate ranks, as a broker. The present apprenticeship requirement must be meaningful for a real estate salesman who desires to become a broker. The broker-employer should be required to provide the necessary tutelage and supervision so that the purpose of the statutory apprenticeship requirement may be fully met.

In concluding the chapter on license laws, it should be repeated that an applicant for license, as well as the real estate practitioner, should be familiar with the provisions of the license law, and the Rules and Regulations, which implement it. For study purposes, the licensing statute can be divided into the following segments: (1) activities included in the definitions of a real estate broker or real estate salesman; (2) exempted classes under the act; (3) requirements for licensure; (4) composition and requirements for a commissioner,—by whom appointed, term of office, compensation; (5) various fees paid,—examination, original license, renewal of license, transfer of license, duplicate license, branch office; (6) grounds for refusal, suspension or revocation of license; (7) penalties; (8) out of state licensees and reciprocity.

A licensee should also be cautious, in preparation of a real estate instrument that he does not engage in the unauthorized practice of law.

The Tennessee statute specifically provides that the unauthorized practice of law shall constitute grounds for disciplinary action by the Commission.

It is important that a broker, as well as a sales person, should be familiar with the statutory requirements for licensure, as well as the Rules and Regulations, adopted pursuant thereto. A violation, innocent or intentional, may endanger his license and thereby prejudice his livelihood.

Questions on License Law

1. Q. In regard to administration and enforcement of the license law, there are basically 3 types of license law officials. What are they?
   A. 1. A Commissioner, as in Arizona, California, Oregon and South Carolina.
   2. A Department, as in Illinois, Michigan and New York.
   3. In most states a Board or Commission usually composed of 3, 5 or 7 members.
2. Q. In a Commission administration, there are how many members, by whom appointed, term of office, requirements of office (residence, years of experience), remuneration?
   A. See license law in your state.
3. Q. What are the requirements for a non-resident broker to operate in your state?
   A. See license law in your state.
4. Q. Does the license law require a broker to have an employee licensed who does only stenographic or other clerical work in the broker's office?
   A. No; however, if the employee gives information regarding listed properties or those for rent, the safer practice is to have the employee licensed as a salesperson.
5. Q. Can the widow of a deceased licensed broker operate as a broker under the decedent's license until the expiration of her husband's license?
   A. No; a license is personal to the person to whom issued and does not survive him.
6. Q. Can a person lawfully act as a broker or as a salesman in a single isolated transaction without having a license?
   A. In most states no.
7. Q. What must a broker do with his license when he receives it?
   A. Post it in a conspicuous place in his office (except California).
8. Q. Does a person who merely lists property, but never shows property come under the provisions of the license law?
   A. Yes.
9. Q. What must a builder do if he wishes to employ salesmen to sell houses built by himself?
   A. He must secure a broker's license. A salesman can be employed only by a *licensed broker.* Or, the salesman would have to qualify for a broker's license.
10. Q. Can a salesman lawfully accept a commission from a purchaser or seller in addition to the compensation paid him by his employing broker, even though his broker approves?
    A. No; he can accept compensation only from his employer-broker.
11. Q. May a licensed real estate salesman work for two licensed real estate brokers at the same time?
    A. No; he can only work for the broker with whom he is registered.
12. Q. Is the term "valuable consideration" as used in the license law definition of a real estate broker limited to a money consideration?
    A. No; a valuable consideration may consist of property, the rendition of services, or anything which has a monetary value.
13. Q. A licensed broker tells his milkman to keep his eyes open in meeting his customers

and "If you get me any leads that result in a sale, I'll pay you $50 for each sale I make." Two sales are made. Can the broker pay him $100?

A. No; payment of a fee to an unlicensed person is grounds for revocation of license. A person accepting such payment would be subject to criminal prosecution for operating as a broker without a license.

14. Q. What must a broker do with the license of his salesman:
(a) while in his employ?
(b) upon severance of employment?

A. (a) Post license in his office (except in California).
(b) Return salesman's license to Real Estate Commission.

15. Q. List four classes of persons who are not required to be licensed to sell real estate.

A. 1. Owner.
2. Person operating under power of attorney.
3. Attorney-at-law in the performance of duties as such.
4. Executor, receiver or trustee.

16. Q. Name five grounds for suspension or revocation of license.

A. See license law in your state.

17. Q. Name five activities included in the definition of a real estate broker in your state.

A. See license law in your state.

18. Q. Name five requirements for a broker's license in your state.

A. See license law in your state.

19. Q. Enumerate the penalties for operating as a broker in your state without a license.

A. See license law in your state.

20. Q. Enumerate the various fees for licenses in your state.

A. See license law in your state.

21. Q. The Metropolitan Realty Corporation is duly licensed, with Mr. Smith, the secretary, holding the original broker's license, and Mr. Thomas, the treasurer, the additional broker's license. Mr. Price, the president, has not had adequate experience to apply for a broker's license. Can he be issued a salesman's license?

A. No. In most states, an *officer* of a corporation must be licensed as a broker, if he actively engages in the real estate business.

22. Q. In the event that an officer of a real estate brokerage corporation, who is unlicensed to represent it, negotiates a sale of real estate, which is listed with the corporation, is the corporation or the officer entitled to the usual commission for making the sale?

A. No. Licensure is a prerequisite to a claim for commission. The officer must be licensed in order to predicate a claim for commission by the corporation he represents. The corporation, being an artificial person, can only operate through its officers and representatives.

23. Q. John Adams, a small town real estate broker, is duly licensed and has built up a substantial brokerage business. He has one licensed salesman in his employ. John dies, survived by his widow, Mary.
1. Can Mary Adams operate the business, as John Adams' widow and sole heir?
2. Can Mary Adams operate the business through the licensed salesman?

A. 1. No. A broker's license is personal and is not transferable.
2. No. A salesman must be employed at all times by a licensed broker.

24. Q. Higgins, a licensed broker in New York, but not in Florida, contacts Wiggins, a Florida licensed broker, and together, they contact Pickens at West Palm Beach, Florida, regarding the purchase of the Sea Breeze Hotel listed with Wiggins for sale. Higgins and Wiggins have agreed to split 50-50 the commission received by Wiggins if Pickens buys. The sale is made and Wiggins pays Higgins one-half of the commission as agreed. Has Wiggins violated the license law?

A. Yes. Higgins is not licensed and since he carried on active negotiations in Florida, he required a Florida license. It was illegal for Wiggins to pay a commission to an unlicensed person.

25. Q. Do real estate appraisers, mortgage brokers, rent collectors require a license in your state?
    A. See license law in your state under definition of a real estate broker.
26. Q. Is the doctrine of "caveat emptor" (buyer beware) an adequate defense for the misrepresentation of a broker or salesman to a purchaser in a transaction where the commission is paid by the seller?
    A. No. If the statement he made was likely to influence, persuade or induce, his license can be suspended or revoked.
27. Q. Distinguish between the work of the broker and that of a salesman.
    A. A broker represents the owner or purchaser. The salesman operates under the supervision and direction of his employing broker.
28. Q. A broker employs a person to go from place to place contacting members of the public, recommending to them the desirability of property on the New Jersey shore being marketed by the broker and suggesting to them that they see the broker, if interested. The broker pays such an emissary a monthly salary and expenses. Does such person require a license as a real estate salesman?
    A. Yes; his activities constitute real estate dealings.
29. Q. In a partnership one member has asked that he be licensed as a broker and the other as a salesman. Can licenses be issued in accordance with these applications?
    A. No; in every partnership every active partner must be licensed as a broker.
30. Q. How much time must a broker devote to the real estate business in order to renew his license?
    A. There is no provision in any license law to date which requires a broker to devote all or the major part of his time to the real estate business. Once a broker obtains a license, it may be renewed so long as there is no violation of the license law on his part.
31. Q. How many real estate transactions must a salesman complete in order to be eligible for a broker's license?
    A. The license law is silent in regard to the actual time and effort that a salesman must devote to the real estate business. (But see Rules and Regulations for your state.)
32. Q. Adams files a complaint against Brown, a real estate broker, alleging serious fraudulent misrepresentations made by Brown to Adams in connection with a real estate transaction. At the hearing scheduled on the complaint, Brown offers to surrender his license voluntarily and requests that the hearing be called off. The Real Estate Commission refuses to accept the surrender of Brown's license and proceeds with the hearing. Brown files an appeal from the Commission's revocation of license. Was Brown within his rights in offering to surrender his license in lieu of a hearing?
    A. No. Brown could not waive hearing on the charges. The hearing was proper. The Commission had the duty, as well as the right, to proceed with the hearing upon the complaint, to determine whether the broker was a fit person to hold a real estate license at a later date. There is an important difference between surrender of a license voluntarily and revocation of license for cause.
33. Q. During 1973, three separate complaints are filed against Bates, a real estate broker. Each time that a hearing is scheduled, the complainant, upon receiving restitution, withdraws the complaint and refuses to prosecute. In April 1974, Ames files a complaint against Bates claiming substantial misrepresentations in a real estate transaction. A hearing is scheduled. Bates makes restitution, and the complainant fails to appear at the hearing, sending a letter that he is withdrawing the complaint. Can the Real Estate Commission take any action?
    A. Yes. The Commission has authority, upon its own motion, to *initiate* a complaint. It could subpoena the complainant and his witnesses to appear at the hearing and testify as to the averments in the sworn complaint.
34. Q. Alden is president and the sole stockholder of a real estate corporation. He employs six real estate salesmen. A number of complaints are filed against the firm on

account of misrepresentations made by the salesmen. Each time, Alden denies personal knowledge of the misrepresentations made. Whenever a complaint is filed, the salesman is discharged and his license surrendered for cancellation. The corporation has a reputation as a "high pressure" outfit. Is the corporation subject to any disciplinary action?

A. Yes. License laws generally provide that a broker's license may be suspended or revoked where he is deemed guilty "of a continued or flagrant course of misrepresentation or making of false promises through agents or salesmen." A broker cannot close his eyes to the continued flagrant misrepresentations of his salesmen and escape personal responsibility.

35. Q. Adams listed his residence for rent at $250 per month with Bates, a broker. The property, of substantial value, is vacant at the time. A stranger calls at the broker's office and inquires about the property. Bates tells him that he can inspect the property, but he will have to make a deposit of $10 to insure the return of the key. The supposed prospect goes to the premises and "strips" it of valuable chandeliers, plumbing, and fixtures. He then returns the key to Bates and receives his $10 deposit. Adams files a complaint against Bates, alleging that the broker was negligent and incompetent. Bates defends on the grounds that it is customary to permit a prospect to inspect premises and to entrust a key to the prospect for that purpose, and that he took the precaution of requiring a money deposit for the return of the key. Is the broker amenable to disciplinary action?

A. Yes; not only is Bates guilty of gross carelessness, but incompetency as well. Since the prospect was a total stranger to Bates, the broker's fiduciary obligations to his owner required that he protect his client's property by accompanying the prospect to the property.

36. Q. May a licensed broker or salesman lawfully offer, give, or pay to a third person who is not a licensed broker or salesman a share of his commission on a deal for services performed by such unlicensed person?

A. No; such offer or payment is unlawful under the express provisions of the Act.

37. Q. May a real estate salesman be lawfully employed by or accept compensation from any broker other than the broker under whom he is licensed at the time?

A. No.

38. Q. Where a real estate salesman employed by one broker is assisted in a deal by a real estate salesman employed by another broker, under an arrangement whereby both salesmen are to have a part of the commission, is it lawful for the first salesman to pay directly to the second salesman the latter's share of the commission?

A. No; payment to the second salesman must be made through the employing broker.

39. Q. Assume that a real estate salesman changes his employer and fails to notify the Commission; what is the effect?

A. The failure to notify the Commission automatically cancels the salesman's license.

40. Q. What is the effect, upon the licenses of salesmen, of a revocation or suspension of the license of the broker by whom said salesmen are employed?

A. Immediate and automatic suspension; however, should any of said salesmen enter the employ of another broker during the same year, a new license could be issued to the salesman upon the surrender of his original license and pocket card.

41. Q. What is the real estate broker's duty with reference to the licenses of his salesmen?

A. He is required to display the same prominently in his place of business (except in California).

42. Q. What is the difference between a "Realtor" and a real estate broker?

A. A "Realtor" is a real estate broker who is an active member of a local board having membership in the National Association of Realtors.

43. Q. Adams, a real estate broker, sells his real estate business to Brady, a licensed real estate broker, and agrees not to engage in the real estate business within a distance of two miles for a period of 5 years. Shortly after the sale, Adams opens a real estate

office within two blocks from Brady. The latter files a complaint against Adams with the Real Estate Commission, claiming that Adams was guilty of untrustworthiness. May the commission revoke Adams' license?

A. Yes; so held in *O'Hare vs. Gilchrist,* 210 N. Y. App. Div. 518.

44. Q. A license law statute provides that a broker "shall be guilty of a misdemeanor for having any salesman in his employ who has not secured the required license." The Ideal Realty Corporation, holder of a broker's license and at the same time engaged in the sale of its own property, employs Jones, who does not obtain a license. Is the corporation guilty of a violation of the above statutory provisions?

A. Yes, even though corporation is also engaged in selling its own real estate.

45. Q. Roberts sued Clark for a real estate commission. He failed to set forth in his statement of claim or to prove that he was a licensed broker. May he recover?

A. No; omission is fatal to broker's cause.

46. Q. Ash sells Beale certain property for $15,000 and says he thinks it will be worth $25,000 in two years. At the end of two years, Beale can sell the property for only $12,500. Is Ash guilty of misrepresentation?

A. No; Ash has expressed an opinion. His statement constitutes mere "puffing" of goods.

47. Q. Stone, a broker, tells Crow, "Buy this property, I have seen the city's plans for an airport and it includes this property." Stone has not seen the plans. Crow relies upon Stone's statement and purchases the tract. The city did not build the airport. Crow files a complaint. Decide.

A. Stone's license should be suspended or revoked as he is guilty of fraud. The broker made a misrepresentation of a material fact which induced the contract.

48. Q. What does the license law require as to maintaining a place of business as a broker?

A. Each broker shall maintain a place of business and display a real estate sign; his license must be conspicuously displayed inside said place of business.

49. Q. Who is a real estate salesman under the license law?

A. One who is employed by a licensed real estate broker to perform any of the activities included in the definition of a real estate broker.

50. Q. Can a salesman enter the employ of a person who has taken his broker's examination but not yet received his broker's license?

A. No; a salesman must be employed by a *licensed* broker at all times.

51. Q. A property has been listed with a broker for sale at $6,500. The broker obtains a buyer at $7,000 and seeks to retain the extra $500 and collect a commission of $325, representing five per cent of $6,500. The owner files a complaint. To what amount is the broker entitled ?

A. $350, representing five per cent of the consideration price of $7,000. The broker is duty-bound to obtain as high a price as he possibly can for his principal, the owner.

52. Q. Fike, a salesman, is employed by Jordan, a licensed broker. Thomas, another licensed broker, asks Fike to sell a property listed with him for sale. Fike succeeds. Can he collect from Thomas?

A. No; a salesman can operate only through the broker by whom he is employed. If Thomas desires to share the commission, payment should be made to Fike's employer, Jordan.

53. Q. If you desire to use the word "Realtor" in your advertisement, what must you do to obtain that privilege?

A. Join a local real estate board, which is affiliated with the National Association of Realtors.

54. Q. Discuss the purpose of the real estate license law.

A. To protect the public from dishonest and incompetent brokers and salesmen; to protect licensed brokers and salesmen from unfair and improper competition.

55. Q. Is it ethical for a broker to sell his own property to a customer? If so, under what

conditions?

A. Yes, providing the broker makes the position clear that he is the owner of the property.

56. Q. State in detail what procedure a salesman or broker must follow as soon as a prospective purchaser signs the preliminary agreement or offer to purchase.

A. A broker or salesman shall promptly tender written offer to purchase to the seller and upon obtaining a proper acceptance of offer to purchase, shall promptly deliver true executed copy of same, signed by the seller to both purchaser and seller.

57. Q. What is the responsibility of a broker in taking a check or promissory note and receipting for the amount as cash paid?

A. A check is not cash until it is paid. The broker is obliged to disclose to owner the kind of deposit received. Broker's license suspended in a California case where a non-negotiable note had been received as a deposit, the implied representation made to the principal being that the deposit was cash.

58. Q. Does the Real Estate Commission have the power to make rules and regulations?

A. Yes. The Commission may do all things necessary and convenient for carrying into effect the provisions of the Act and may from time to time promulgate necessary rules and regulations not inconsistent with the law.

59. Q. Is a license or pocket card transferable to another person?

A. No. The license shall show the name and address of the licensee to whom it is issued.

60. Q. Does the Real Estate Brokers' License Act permit the issuing of a real estate license to a partnership as such?

A. No. No license shall be issued to a partnership, association, or corporation as such, except in Illinois and Maine. The license names the firm *and* the representative active broker.

61. Q. Does the Commission have authority, on its own motion, to investigate any action of a broker or salesman and call the matter to a hearing?

A. Yes.

62. Q. Can a salesman renew his license before the license of the employing broker is renewed?

A. No.

63. Q. What constitutes misrepresentation?

A. Misstatement of a material fact which induces the contract. It may be innocent or wilful. If wilful, it may constitute fraud.

64. Q. What duty rests upon a buyer in verifying representations made to him by the broker?

A. Representations made that can be verified by a casual inspection, if the opportunity to inspect is available, would not be grounds for holding a broker responsible for misrepresentation.

65. Q. Check the representations which, if found to be untrue, would, in your opinion, constitute grounds for avoiding a contract of sale and for instituting disciplinary action against the broker.

A. (x) 1. The heating plant, plumbing, and electrical wiring are in good condition.
(x) 2. The cellar is dry and in good condition.
(x) 3. Action could be brought to have an adjoining dilapidated house condemned by the municipal authorities.
(x) 4. Sixty feet frontage could be sold from the lot for $2,000.
(x) 5. The taxes amount to $320 a year.
(x) 6. The zoning ordinance permits alteration of the premises into apartment units.

66. Q. The Ajax Realty Co. advertises that it will give a 21-inch television set free to every purchaser of a dwelling through its office. Is this permissible?

A. No. Since the broker is giving something of value to an unlicensed person, it constitutes a violation of the Act.

67. Q. May a real estate salesman's license be issued to a person not employed by a broker?

A. No; a salesman must be employed by a licensed broker.

68. Q. Broker Ash has an exclusive listing on a property at $13,500. His salesman Bowen persuaded the owner to reduce the price to $12,500. The property was then sold to Crooks, another salesman of Ash, who then sold it immediately to a buyer, with whom both Bowen and Crooks had been negotiating previously, at a price of $14,000. Broker Ash received one-half of the commission on the sale price of $12,500. Salesmen Bowen and Crooks split their profit. Broker Ash was aware of all aspects of the transaction, but refused to share in the proceeds beyond his share of the commission. The seller was unaware of Crooks' connection with the firm. Did the licensees violate the license law?

A. Yes, the broker violated his fiduciary responsibility of loyalty, by permitting his salesmen to profit at the expense of his principal. The salesmen were guilty of a scheme to make a secret profit, which constitutes downright dishonesty. Vital information was withheld and the owner was induced to take a lower price.

69. Q. What recourse does an applicant have in case the Commission declines arbitrarily to license an applicant?

A. Institute a mandamus action in court against the Commission.

70. Q. Does the licensing law apply to part-time brokers or salesmen?

A. Yes.

71. Q. The "Square Inch—Square Deal Co." advertises for persons to sell square-inch tracts of land, owned by the company, on Pike's Peak. The purchaser pays $1.00 and receives a deed, signed by the President, Chief Running Deer. The persons hired are to receive 50 cents for each sale made. Must the latter persons be licensed?

A. Yes; even though minute in size, the subject matter of the sale is real estate.

72. Q. In what ways can a broker improve the efficacy of license laws?

A.
1. By adhering scrupulously to a high standard of ethics.
2. By exercising personal supervision over and training salesmen.
3. By membership in realty organizations, attending real courses, institutes, etc., in order to improve competency.
4. By reporting violations to the State Commission.

73. Q. What legal papers may a licensed broker prepare?

A. Only those concomitant with and which grow out of his employment—listing contract, agreement of sale, earnest money receipt, leases, simple deeds, where no charge is made. The Texas Law specifically prohibits a licensee from preparing "a deed, note, deed of trust, or will."

74. Q. Is a licensed broker responsible for all illegal acts of his salesmen?

A. No; unless he has full knowledge of such illegal acts.

75. Q. A broker is convicted of violation of the Federal income tax laws. Would this constitute grounds for revocation of license?

A. Probably not, unless a real estate transaction was involved.

76. Q. In endorsing the application of a prospective salesman, what statements does the broker make?

A. Certification that applicant is honest, truthful, of good repute and that he will be employed by said broker.

77. Q. Name 2 requirements which a broker must meet which are generally not required of a salesman.

A. Property owner recommenders; educational requirements.

78. Q. Upon hearing held upon a complaint, if the decision is in favor of the licensee, can the complainant appeal to court?

A. No.

79. Q. Does the Real Estate Commission have jurisdiction in commission disputes between (a) seller and broker (b) broker and salesman?

A. (a) No.
(b) Most states, no. In New Jersey, yes.

80. Q. The license law is said to be a valid exercise of the police power of the state. Why?
    A. In order to protect the public in its real estate dealings.
81. Q. When and where was the first license law passed?
    A. California, 1917, which was declared unconstitutional. Oregon, Michigan and California passed license laws in 1919, which were held valid.
82. Q. What are the most important qualifications for a real estate license?
    A Character and competency.
83. Q. In how many states are there license laws at the present time?
    A. In all 50 states and the District of Columbia, as well as in the Canadian provinces of Alberta, British Columbia, Manitoba, Ontario, Quebec, Nova Scotia, Saskatchewan, the Virgin Islands Territory, and Guam.
84. Q. Is conviction of an F.H.A. provision a "like offense" under the license law as grounds for disciplinary action?
    A. Yes, where law specifies conviction of certain named crimes, and any like or similar offense, or offenses.

True and False

1. The Executive Secretary of the Commission is a member of the Real Estate Commission. T **F**
2. All full time brokers are Realtors. T **F**
3. In an "open house" showing, the person in charge need not be licensed. T **F**
4. Violation of a Rule and Regulation of the Commission is ground for reprimand, but not suspension or revocation of license. T **F**
5. Local realty boards are affiliated with the Real Estate Commission. T **F**
6. The splitting of commissions under any circumstances is illegal. T **F**
7. Once a broker licensed in New York actively negotiates a single real estate deal in Florida, he requires a Florida license. **T** F
8. A salesman and a broker may actively engage in the real estate business as a partnership. T **F**
9. A salesman who fails his first examination may obtain a probationary license. T **F**
10. The license law is a police measure. **T** F
11. A supersedeas stays the effect of a revocation of license ordered by the Commission. **T** F
12. "Door bell" solicitation of listings is considered unethical practice. **T** F
13. The Code of Ethics is a part of the Real Estate License Law. T **F**
14. No refund of the license fee or any part thereof can be made after the license is issued. **T** F
15. A salesman must renew his own license. T **F**
16. Reciprocity is not compulsory upon any state in granting a license to a non-resident licensee. **T** F
17. A person who passes an examination must wait until the expiration of the license year, before he receives his license. T **F**
18. Dual contracts means giving a copy of the agreement to each party to it. T **F**
19. The Governor is an ex-officio member of the Real Estate Commission. T **F**
20. Each real estate office must carry the names of its salesmen on the door or window of the office. T **F**
21. A single separate account only is needed for the deposit of earnest monies. **T** F
22. A salesman who conceals the existence of termites in selling a home is guilty of fraud. **T** F
23. In most states, a licensed real estate broker may not lawfully sell business opportunity properties. T **F**
24. The amount of bond required is determined by the volume of the broker's business in the preceding year. T **F**
25. The committing of one real estate deal is prima facie evidence of brokerage. **T** F

26. In Georgia, an applicant for a broker's license must have at least a high school education or equivalent. **T** F
27. A broker must notify the Commission when he changes his business address. **T** F
28. It is satisfactory to use a dormitory room as an office so long as the broker's license is displayed there. T **F**
29. The real estate license law prohibits a salesman from working in real estate more than 48 hours a week. T **F**
30. A contractor who employs salesmen must be licensed as a broker. **T** F
31. A broker's license cannot be converted to a salesman's license and vice versa. **T** F
32. A broker must immediately notify the Commission when he changes his residence address. T **F**
33. The license law requires every broker to maintain a definite place of business. **T** F
34. A real estate broker can be disciplined for the misconduct of his salesmen, if he has knowledge. **T** F
35. A person engaged solely in the rental of real estate must be licensed. **T** F
36. A licensed salesman may go to work for another broker without requesting the Commission for transfer of license. T **F**
37. A broker is required to report cessation of employment of his salesman to the Real Estate Commission. **T** F
38. A broker may not employ another broker in the capacity of salesman. T **F**
39. A broker's license and a salesman's license are identical and mean the same thing. T **F**
40. Obtaining registration as a broker by fraudulent means constitutes a misdemeanor. **T** F
41. The broker must obey all lawful instructions made known to him by his principal. **T** F
42. A broker may not act for anyone whose interests in the transaction are adverse to those of his principal. **T** F
43. A broker need not let it be known that he is actually the owner when dealing with a prospective purchaser. T **F**
44. A person who works as a real estate broker only on Sundays is not required to have registration. T **F**
45. Two brokers registered individually may occupy the same office space and need not have individual signs. T **F**
46. A broker is not permitted under the license law to use unregistered persons merely to show properties. **T** F
47. A salesman is unable to renew his certificate until that of the employing broker is renewed. **T** F
48. A broker's right to collect commission is not impaired on a deal made after the expiration of his certificate and before renewal of same. T **F**
49. If two brokers share office space but conduct their business separately, it would be permissible, under the license law, to use the same letterheads. T **F**
50. The void certificate of an officer or member of a corporation or partnership does not affect the certificate of a corporation or partnership. T **F**
51. The Commission may deny the renewal of a license to a broker who has refused to stop selling by a method which is dishonest or untruthful. **T** F
52. A person who has been convicted of certain felonies may be denied a license even though he presents recommendations from several friends and brokers. **T** F
53. A broker's license may be suspended but not permanently revoked for representing both buyer and seller and receiving commissions from both without their knowledge and consent. T **F**
54. A complaint may be made orally, if made in person to any Commissioner at the Commission offices. T **F**
55. Any licensee is entitled to a hearing before having his license revoked. **T** F
56. A broker who collects rents for clients and co-mingles the money with his own so that he cannot make proper accounting may have his license revoked. **T** F

57. The fee for a branch office license is $15.00. T F
58. A clerk in a real estate office who prepares real estate listings and sales agreements need not be licensed as a salesman. T F
59. The Real Estate Commission has jurisdiction over contractors and builders who build and sell their own properties. T F
60. All real estate licenses must be renewed in May. T F
61. A real estate salesman can be jailed for operating without a real estate license. T F
62. A veteran of foreign wars can obtain a salesman's license by oral examination. T F
63. A collector of rent must be licensed if paid for that service. T F
64. Negotiating leases comes within the licensing act. T F
65. A broker must display the licenses of his salesmen in the broker's office. T F
66. Brokers employing salesmen are relieved of all responsibility for the acts of the salesmen if the salesmen are bonded. T F
67. Realtors are members of the National Association of Realtors. T F
68. A real estate salesman who desires to transfer to another broker merely picks up his license from the first broker and places it upon display in the office of the second broker. T F
69. The Commission may revoke the license of a broker who fails to remit commissions he owes to another broker. T F
70. The Commission may waive the qualification examination for license if the applicant has had several years of real estate experience. T F
71. All real estate licenses expire three full years from date of issue. T F
72. An alien may be licensed as a real estate salesman in Illinois if he has received his first papers. T F
73. A licensed salesman may go to work for another broker immediately upon the filing of an application for transfer. T F
74. The committing of one act prohibited by the license law constitutes a violation. T F
75. A salesman may advertise listings in his own name without mentioning his broker. T F
76. A broker should consent to the transfer of a salesman's license even though the salesman owes him money which the broker loaned him. T F
77. The Commission is empowered to subpoena persons to produce books and papers at a formal hearing for the revocation of a license. T F
78. A real estate broker's or salesman's license can, under no circumstances, be suspended without a formal hearing first being granted to the offender. T F
79. A real estate broker can be disciplined for the misconduct of his salesman, provided he had actual knowledge of such fact. T F
80. A real estate salesman's license can be issued to the vice-president of XYZ Realty Corporation. T F
81. After the revocation or suspension of a broker's or salesman's license, he is permitted to operate pending determination of his appeal to court. T F
82. A real estate brokerage business may be conducted by a salesman at his residence, without the necessity of obtaining a branch office license. T F
83. A real estate broker's license can be issued only to a person who maintains a definite place of business in the state. T F
84. The Commission may hold a hearing on its own motion if it does not have a verified written complaint from the complainant. T F
85. A salesman must carry his license with him at all times for identification. T F
86. Usually a salesman cannot transfer his license to the employ of another broker unless he obtains the consent of his former broker. T F
87. Controversy over the division of earned commissions should be brought before the Commission for settlement. T F
88. A real estate broker may employ only one salesman for each year he has been licensed as a broker. T F

89. A salesman's license must be displayed in a conspicuous place in his home or office. T **F**
90. A person who sells property under a court order is not required by law to have a license. **T** F
91. All licenses issued by the Commission are good for a period of one year from the date on which they are issued. T **F**
92. It requires a majority vote of a Real Estate Commission to suspend or revoke a license. **T** F
93. It is not necessary to be licensed to sell cemetery lots. T **F**
94. The broker should at all times be in possession of and display the license of his salesman. **T** F
95. A person may not engage in the real estate business until he has received his license. **T** F
96. The license law provides a schedule of commissions which may be charged by licensed brokers for making various real estate transactions. T **F**
97. A salesman who has passed his examination can begin work immediately even though he has not received his license. T **F**
98. A broker is liable for misconduct in a real estate matter even if he is a bonded real estate board member. **T** F
99. Placing a For Sale sign on vacant property without the consent of the owner may jeopardize a broker's license. **T** F
100. Principals of schools are exempt from the license law in selling real estate. T **F**
101. Subpoena means compelling a person to appear before the Commission at a hearing. **T** F
102. All sales of real estate must be handled through a licensed real estate broker or licensed salesman. T **F**
103. A municipality has no part in regulation of real estate brokers under the licensing act. **T** F
104. The licensing act is not an act designed for revenue. **T** F
105. A broker can employ any number of licensed salesmen. **T** F
106. "Interim License" may be issued after an applicant has failed one examination, if he applies for the succeeding examination. T **F**
107. The license law has eliminated "curb stone" brokers. **T** F
108. A licensee paying a commission to an unlicensed person may lose his license on that account. **T** F
109. The license law has eliminated the "opportunist" broker who "horned in" on a deal because he was a friend of the buyer. **T** F
110. The license law is the greatest single factor in elevating the real estate business to professional status. **T** F
111. A licensed salesman may supervise a branch office. T **F**
112. A high school education as a requirement for a broker's license would add to the professional status of the real estate business. **T** F
113. No refund of fee can be made after a license is issued. **T** F
114. Where a salesman makes misrepresentations without the knowledge or authority of his broker, the Real Estate Commission will not hold the broker responsible for the salesman's fraud. **T** F
115. The failure of a real estate salesman to notify the Real Estate Commission of his change of employer within 10 days automatically cancels his license. **T** F
116. A broker desiring to operate under a firm name or a fictitious name must be so licensed. **T** F
117. If a salesman ceases to be employed by his registered employer, his certificate remains in force. T **F**
118. A salesman can renew his certificate before that of his employing broker is renewed. T **F**

119. A salesman cannot legally continue to operate after expiration of his certificate and before renewal. T F
120. A widow of a deceased broker may operate for the remainder of the license year under the decedent's license. T F
121. A broker licensed in Michigan may act as a broker in any other state of the United States. T F
122. A decision of a Real Estate Commission, upon a complaint, in favor of the licensee is final. T F
123. No real estate broker may serve as a member of the Real Estate Commission. T F
124. A member of the Real Estate Commission cannot operate as a broker during his tenure as Commissioner. T F
125. A builder cannot employ a salesman to sell houses for him, for commission, unless the builder is licensed as a broker. T F
126. An attorney-at-law may employ a salesman to sell real estate listed with the attorney for sale. T F
127. An unlicensed person making a real estate transaction is guilty of a misdemeanor (or a felony, in some states). T F
128. A person over 75 years of age cannot obtain a broker's license. T F
129. When deposit money is received by a real estate salesman, he is permitted by law to make use of such money for his personal account up to the amount of his rightful sales commission before the deal is closed. T F
130. A licensed real estate salesman must be ready at all times, upon request, to show his license card. T F
131. Real estate listings may be taken in the name of the salesman so long as any deal is closed in the name of the employing broker. T F
132. A real estate office may be placed in charge of a licensed real estate salesman, in event of the broker's absence or illness, if the Real Estate Commission is so informed in writing. T F
133. The act of a real estate salesman, within the scope of his authority, is considered to be the act of his employing broker. T F
134. A salesman binds his broker for acts beyond the *actual* scope of his authority, if within the *apparent* scope of his authority. T F
135. A broker who has authority to accept interest payments on a mortgage, also has authority to accept payment of the mortgage principal. T F
136. It is a violation of the license law for a broker to engage in the real estate business on Sunday. T F
137. A person who is not licensed may sell real estate for a friend if he does not charge any compensation. T F
138. NAR and NAREB, Inc. is the same national organization. T F
139. A licensee may renew his license at any time before the expiration of the following year. T F
140. A salesman may not sue anyone except his broker for the collection of a real estate commission. T F
141. The real estate license act was passed to restrict competition. T F
142. The license law is a regulatory measure and not a revenue measure. T F
143. The Real Estate Commission can regulate the type and size of sign that a broker must have on the outside of his place of business. T F
144. A salesman may not copy the listings of his broker for use after he leaves his employment. T F
145. A broker may sign an agreement of sale for his principal where he has an exclusive listing contract of employment. T F
146. A license cannot be revoked for more than three years. T F
147. A rule or regulation of the Real Estate Commission requiring a broker to give the owner a copy of the listing is valid. T F

148. When moving his office to a new address, a broker must return his old license to the Commission and receive a new one issued for the new address. T F
149. A broker, licensed in another state, may obtain a license in this state promptly upon payment of the regular fee. T F
150. If a salesman severs his connections with a broker, the broker may transfer such salesman's license to a new salesman employee. T F
151. The word "Realtor" may always be used in lieu of "Real Estate" in advertising a real estate brokerage business. T F
152. If a real estate salesman works on a straight salary basis and does not participate in the commissions, he nevertheless requires a license. T F
153. The license of a broker was revoked. The salesman may continue to operate under his present license. T F
154. The Nebraska Real Estate Association and the Nebraska Real Estate Commission are the same. T F
155. The main requirement for licensure is success in a previous business. T F
156. A broker is not required to have a branch office license unless the branch office maintained by him is located in another town or city. T F
157. A person must be a property owner in order to be licensed as a broker. T F
158. The Real Estate Commission may suspend the license of a broker found to be dishonest, without the formality of holding a hearing. T F
159. A broker who fails to give the owner a copy of the signed listing may lose his license. T F
160. A broker is not required to give the Commission notice if he moves his office to another location in the same community. T F
161. A salesman may leave the employ of one broker and go to work for another broker without notifying the Commission provided he applies for his license the following year under the new broker. T F
162. There should be a written contract between a broker and a salesman covering the terms of the salesman's employment. T F
163. A broker may maintain an office in a grocery store provided he has adequate office equipment. T F
164. A Justice of the Peace who sells real estate and employs a single salesman must be licensed. T F
165. The real estate broker's licensing act usually requires
    (a) active officers of a real estate corporation to have a broker's license. T F
    (b) salesmen who work only on Sundays to be licensed. T F
    (c) renewal of all licenses during May of each year. T F
    (d) owner's consent or exclusive agency to place a For Sale sign on property listed. T F
    (e) a written examination for real estate brokers. T F
    (f) the licensing of persons who only sell summer cottages. T F
    (g) the honesty and good repute of all applicants to be vouched for by at least two recommenders. T F
166. A broker is required to keep his office open to the public at least 40 hours a week. T F
167. An indictment of a real estate broker upon a charge of obtaining money under false pretense is *prima facie* grounds for suspension of license. T F
168. All Real Estate Commissioners are bonded for that office. T F
169. A real estate salesman cannot maintain a branch office in his home during evening hours. T F
170. It is the duty of the broker to notify the Commission when a salesman leaves his employ. T F
171. Rules and Regulations for licensees must be approved by the legislature before they are valid. T F
172. A fee is charged for a transfer of license or change of business address. T F

173. A licensee may be represented by counsel in a hearing before the Commission. **T** F
174. A Commission is a quasi-judicial body, not bound by strict rules of evidence. **T** F
175. The Code of Ethics supersedes the Rules and Regulations of the Commission. T **F**
176. Charging less than the usual rate of commission is grounds for suspension of license. T **F**
177. The Real Estate Commission acts as a collection agency for recovery of earnest money by a disappointed buyer. T **F**
178. A broker should keep records of each real estate transaction for at least three years. **T** F
179. A licensed real estate broker should be in charge of *each* branch office. **T** F
180. There is no *economic* justification for the real estate broker. T **F**
181. A broker may change a signed agreement of sale, if it is a minor change. T **F**
182. The members of the National Association of Realtors were largely responsible for the passage of every license law. **T** F
183. Rhode Island was the 50th state to pass a license law. **T** F
184. The National Association of Real Estate License Law Officials is a "clearing house" for license law information. **T** F
185. An agreement of sale, negotiated by an unlicensed person, is void T **F**
186. A school superintendent may be a member of a Real Estate Commission **T** F
187. When an unlicensed officer of a real estate brokerage corporation negotiates a deal, neither the corporation nor the officer is entitled to a commission. **T** F
188. If a broker is delinquent in renewing his license and negotiates a sale, he cannot recover his commission. **T** F
189. If a broker fails to give an owner a copy of the listing contract signed by the owner, he cannot recover a commission. T **F**
190. It is good business practice for a broker managing an apartment building, to receive secret rebates, provided he does not charge the owner more than the prevailing prices. T **F**
191. A broker is duty bound to investigate a salesman's reputation for honesty, truthfulness and integrity before employing him. **T** F
192. At a hearing, the broker or salesman is usually referred to as "the complainant." T **F**
193. Every state now requires an examination as a prerequisite to a broker's license. **T** F
194. California was the first state to pass a valid license law. T **F**
195. A salesman's identification license card should be displayed in his broker's office. T **F**
196. Concealment or omission of material facts may constitute misrepresentation. **T** F
197. A Commission has power to suspend a broker's or salesman's license even if formal complaint has not been filed by an injured party. **T** F
198. A real estate broker's license may be suspended temporarily before a hearing where a serious complaint has been filed. T **F**
199. A broker is bound to turn over his books of record to a Commission investigator. **T** F
200. The penalty for operating without a license upon a second conviction is the same as for a first offense. T **F**
201. An owner may lawfully pay a commission to an unlicensed neighbor by giving him a power of attorney. **T** F
202. A corporation may obtain a salesman's license in the employ of a licensed broker corporation. T **F**
203. Where brokers are appointed to a Real Estate Commission, they are usually Realtors. **T** F
204. The case of an individual charged with operating without a license is first heard by the Real Estate Commission. T **F**
205. A broker may revoke the license of his salesman, where he finds the salesman misrepresenting on a large scale. T **F**
206. A forfeiture and liquidated damages mean the same thing. T **F**
207. An auctioneer who is employed by a licensed broker does not need a license to

sell real estate at public auction. T F

208. A licensed broker and a licensed salesman may operate a partnership if the partnership papers are first filed with the Commission. T F
209. It is unethical for a broker to rebate commissions to a buyer. T F
210. A broker, doing business under a fictitious name such as TRI CITY REALTY CO. must be registered with the county and/or state. T F
211. Mailing real estate brochures by a licensed broker in Pennsylvania to prospects in Kentucky requires him to be licensed in Kentucky. T F
212. Violation of a state Fair Housing Act by a broker may be grounds for revocation of license. T F
213. In California, it is not necessary to display, in the broker's office, his license or that of his salesmen. T F
214. A broker's license may be suspended, where he has been indicted upon a criminal offense, without a hearing. T F
215. The Truth in Lending Act, passed by Congress, is applicable to mortgage financing in every state. T F
216. The Island of Guam requires brokers to be licensed. T F
217. Oregon was the first state to pass a valid license law. T F
218. A broker cannot discharge a salesman for misconduct without first filing a complaint with the Real Estate Commission. T F
219. A Rule or Regulation of the Commission beyond the framework of the license law is a usurpation of legislative authority. T F

Multiple Choice

1. Real Estate Commissions have power to make reasonable Rules and Regulations. Which one of the following would be in excess of such power?
   (a) To require an examination.
   (b) To fix the time and place for examinations.
   (c) To fix requirements for office, equipment, and signs.
   (d) Regulation of trust accounts.
2. A real estate deal is made between a seller and buyer, without the services of a broker. They arrange with a licensed broker for a fee, to prepare certain instruments. Indicate whether he may lawfully prepare
   (a) contract of sale.
   (b) deed.
   (c) purchase money mortgage.
   (d) none.
3. When a license is issued to a corporation, which one of the following is entitled to act as a real estate broker?
   (a) The president.
   (b) One officer of the corporation.
   (c) All officers of the corporation.
   (d) The salesman—manager of the corporation.
4. Operating without a license subjects the person to
   (a) injunction proceedings.
   (b) fine and/or imprisonment.
   (c) Commission reprimand.
   (d) a fine by the Commission.
5. What type of actions cannot be brought against a licensee, who is guilty of fraud to his principal?
   (a) Court action for damages.
   (b) File a complaint with Real Estate Commission.
   (c) If a Realtor, file a complaint with his local Real Estate Board.
   (d) File a complaint with the Attorney General.

6. Ethical standards which must be observed by brokers in real estate deals are determined by
   (a) the Better Business Bureau.
   (b) the local Real Estate Board.
   (c) the National Association of Realtors.
   (d) law.
7. The main purpose of the license law is
   (a) to restrict competition.
   (b) to protect the licensee from unethical conduct of other brokers.
   (c) to protect the public.
   (d) to educate the public.
8. Where an unlicensed salesman negotiated his first sale of real estate, the commission would be payable to the
   (a) salesman's broker only.
   (b) no one.
   (c) buyer.
   (d) salesman.
9. Which group is exempt from the licensing law?
   (a) Referee in bankruptcy.
   (b) Person handling leases only.
   (c) Salesman employed by a builder.
   (d) Person employed to sell subdivision lots.
10. A salesman applicant can solicit listings and talk to prospects when
    (a) he obtains his license.
    (b) he has filed application for license.
    (c) he takes examination.
    (d) he passes examination.
11. A salesman, upon receiving his license, may operate from
    (a) the broker's principal office.
    (b) any branch office in the county.
    (c) address on the license.
    (d) any office broker designates.
12. The Real Estate Commission shall at all times perform its official duties in such manner as to protect and safeguard the interests of
    (a) the State legislature.
    (b) all real estate licensees.
    (c) the general public.
    (d) persons filing complaints against licensees.
13. The Commission has the power after due hearing to
    (a) suspend or revoke any license issued by it.
    (b) assess a penal fine of $1,000.
    (c) suspend a license and impose a fine.
    (d) issue an order of mandamus.
14. When a broker is licensed for the first time, he must
    (a) advertise the fact once in a newspaper of general circulation.
    (b) have a sign on the outside of his place of business.
    (c) sign a written lease for office for at least one year.
15. If a license is issued on October 1, it will expire
    (a) one year from date of issue.
    (b) six months from date of issue.
    (c) end of license year fixed by license law.
16. A salesman applicant for license must have the recommendation of
    (a) two property owners.
    (b) two citizens.
    (c) his former employer.

(d) his prospective broker—employer.

17. Since violations of the license law are detrimental to the public and licensees generally, it is your duty to
    (a) keep quiet about them.
    (b) inform the newspapers so they may be exposed.
    (c) notify the Real Estate Commission.
    (d) notify the local real estate board.
18. A salesman employed by another broker wishes to join your firm: what ethical procedure should you follow?
    (a) Employ him immediately.
    (b) Write to the Real Estate Commission.
    (c) Notify the other broker in writing.
    (d) Call the other broker and have an understanding with him.
19. Appointments to the Real Estate Commission in states requiring an examination are made by the
    (a) Superintendent of Public Instructions.
    (b) Insurance Commissioner.
    (c) Secretary of State.
    (d) Governor.
20. For a broker to act for more than one party in a real estate transaction without the knowledge and consent of all parties is
    (a) ethical.
    (b) grounds for disciplinary action.
    (c) contrary to the Administrative Code.
    (d) all right if no party suffers monetary damage.
21. When a license is issued to a corporation, who of the following is entitled to act as a real estate broker?
    (a) All members of the corporation.
    (b) One officer of the corporation.
    (c) All officers of the corporation.
22. Which of the following acts, if performed by a person on behalf of a third person for a promised commission, will constitute him a real estate broker and necessitate his procuring a license?
    (a) Collecting rent on real estate.
    (b) Offering to sell machinery necessary to farm real estate.
    (c) Offering to collect rents for a mortgagee in possession.
    (d) Offering to build buildings on real estate as a contractor.
23. A salesman's license must always be
    (a) carried by the salesman on his person.
    (b) kept in salesman's kit.
    (c) displayed in broker's office.
    (d) held by the Real Estate Commission.
24. Persons found guilty of operating in the real estate business without a license may be fined by
    (a) the District Attorney.
    (b) a court of law.
    (c) the Real Estate Commission.
    (d) the Attorney General.
25. When a real estate broker discharges a salesman in his employ for dishonesty or any other reason, he must notify the Real Estate Commission
    (a) within ten days (usually).
    (b) immediately.
    (c) within 30 days.
    (d) any time during the license period.

26. Any person who collects a real estate commission and is not licensed is guilty of
    (a) duress.
    (b) an unethical act.
    (c) a misdemeanor.
    (d) negligence.
27. What is the origin of the statement, "No sign should ever be placed on any property without the consent of the owner"?
    (a) State law.
    (b) Regulations of the Real Estate Commission.
    (c) Code of Ethics of the National Assn. of Realtors.
28. When a real estate broker engaged in business as a corporation violates the real estate law, the officer subject to the prescribed penalties is
    (a) its president.
    (b) its secretary.
    (c) its general manager.
    (d) the officer who commits such violation.
29. The Real Estate Commission may revoke the license of a broker who is found guilty of
    (a) slandering his competitors.
    (b) intemperance.
    (c) misrepresentation.
    (d) any violation of the motor vehicle code.
30. A salesman who is guilty of any grounds for disciplinary action may
    (a) be subject to a criminal prosecution.
    (b) may have his license suspended or revoked.
    (c) be subject to (a) and (b).
    (d) be subject to a civil action by his broker.
31. Upon a revocation or suspension order by the Real Estate Commission, the broker
    (a) may appeal to court.
    (b) may request a review by Attorney General.
    (c) Commission order is final.
    (d) may apply for a salesman's license.
32. The license law requires a broker to
    (a) spend all his time in the real estate business.
    (b) spend more than one-half of his time in the real estate business.
    (c) makes no provision as to time a broker must spend in real estate business.
    (d) make a real estate business his major activity.
33. The Commission is empowered to require every real estate broker to have a license before transacting any such business by virtue of
    (a) the Real Estate Brokers License Act.
    (b) Rules and Regulations of the Real Estate Commission.
    (c) the Code of Ethics.
    (d) Statute of Frauds.
34. For his acts in connection with business, a real estate salesman is usually responsible to the
    (a) seller.
    (b) mortgagee.
    (c) buyer.
    (d) employing broker.
35. The Real Estate License Law was passed
    (a) to raise revenue.
    (b) to protect the public.
    (c) to restrict competition.
    (d) to keep brokers from cheating each other.
36. There are three elements necessary to constitute fraud in a misrepresentation. Two of

these are that the misrepresentation concerns a material fact and that the party to whom the statement is made has a right to rely upon it. The third element necessary is that:
(a) the property will re-sell for a particular amount.
(b) the statement is funny.
(c) the broker knows the truth.
(d) the party to whom the statement is made acts on it to his detriment.
(e) the prospect did not employ the broker.

37. A prospect, or person with whom the broker is dealing "at arm's length," when he is in the locality and able to inspect the property for himself, ordinarily has a right to rely on the broker's representations as to
(a) everything the broker says.
(b) nothing the broker says.
(c) future prospects of the property.
(d) patent defects in construction of the building.
(e) concealed details of construction of the building.

38. The criminal provisions of the license law may be invoked where a broker is guilty of
(a) double commissions.
(b) adverse interest.
(c) embezzlement.
(d) operating without a license.
(e) fraud.

39. A builder who desires to employ a salesman for commission to sell houses built by him must
(a) have the salesman obtain a salesman's license.
(b) notify the Commission of the contract between the builder and the salesman.
(c) obtain a broker's license.
(d) pay the salesman less than the usual commission.

40. Which of the following is not grounds for revocation of a broker's license?
(a) Misrepresentation.
(b) Charging a 10 per cent commission on improved property.
(c) The crime of extortion.

41. Deposit money received by a salesman must be turned over to
(a) owner.
(b) Real Estate Commission.
(c) broker for deposit in his trustee account.
(d) seller's attorney.

42. A real estate salesman who changes his employer must
(a) notify his local real estate board.
(b) notify the abstract or recorder of deeds.
(c) notify the local member of the Real Estate Commission.
(d) notify, in writing, the office of the Real Estate Commission.

43. No real estate should be advertised except in the name of the
(a) seller.
(b) salesman who obtains the listing.
(c) principal-licensed broker.
(d) real estate salesman on the premises.

44. A Realtor is a member in good standing of the
(a) Real Estate Commission.
(b) National Association of Real Estate License Law Officials.
(c) local real estate board, affiliated with the National Association of Realtors.
(d) local Chamber of Commerce.

45. A real estate salesman's license may be revoked for
(a) slandering his competitor.
(b) failure to spend forty hours per week as a real estate salesman.
(c) violation of NAREB's code of ethics.

(d) misrepresentation in a real estate transaction.
(e) violation of a local zoning ordinance.

46. A broker's license may be suspended or revoked for which of the following causes?
(a) Over-charge of a sales commission in a real estate transaction.
(b) Conviction of a motor vehicle violation.
(c) Failure to pay a money judgment entered by a J. P.
(d) Failure to account for or remit funds belonging to others.

47. A prospect with whom the broker is dealing "at arm's length" when he is upon the property and may easily investigate for himself, ordinarily has a right to rely upon the broker's representations as to
(a) title.
(b) future prospects.
(c) all statements the broker makes concerning the physical structure.
(d) past rentals of property.

48. A license is issued to Ajax Realty, Inc. Who may operate as a broker for the corporation?
(a) any officer.
(b) the person named in the license to the corporation.
(c) only the president.
(d) the officer longest with the corporation.

49. It is whose duty to prosecute persons engaged in the real estate business without a license?
(a) District Attorney.
(b) Attorney General.
(c) Real Estate Commission.
(d) Tax Collector.

50. A salesman and broker desire to engage in the real estate business as a partnership. They may
(a) register the partnership with the broker as the active broker, and the salesman as an employee.
(b) not do so.
(c) be registered as officers of the same corporation.
(d) be registered as a joint venture.

51. A broker licensed in California who wishes to sell property in an adjoining state
(a) since he is licensed in California can also operate in all other states automatically.
(b) should immediately contact the proper agency in the adjoining state to obtain a license there.
(c) must contact a broker in the adjoining state and work through him only.

52. A real estate salesman may lawfully accept a bonus commission for the completion of a difficult sale,
(a) if the seller gives it to him directly.
(b) if he pays the tax on it.
(c) from his employing broker.
(d) if he receives it from the buyer.

53. A broker has a written promise of a $500 commission if he can secure certain acreage. The owner agrees to sell if he can keep one-fourth of the mineral rights and will pay the broker $500 commission. The transaction was closed. The seller knew of the broker's commission arrangement with the buyer. Which of the following is true?
(a) Broker made a clever deal and was entitled to the extra earnings.
(b) Broker is subject to disciplinary action by Commission.
(c) Since the seller knew of the fee paid by buyer, it was ethical.
(d) Broker violated the Statute of Frauds.

54. An unlicensed broker cannot collect a real estate commission in court because
(a) Statute of Frauds prohibits it.
(b) it violates the rules of the Real Estate Commission.
(c) it violates a state law.

(d) it violates an Act of Congress.

55. A property listed with a broker should not be advertised for sale except in the name of the
    (a) owner.
    (b) salesman to whom property is assigned.
    (c) broker.
    (d) tenant in possession.
56. In transferring from one broker "A" to broker "B" a salesman should
    (a) notify Broker "A" that he is leaving.
    (b) start working immediately for "B" and notify "A" within 10 days
    (c) first notify Real Estate Commission of change and request transfer of license.
    (d) post his license in "B's" office.
57. Broker "A" has a listing on a property. Broker "B" has a prospect. "B" should
    (a) obtain prospect's signature to an offer to purchase.
    (b) obtain listing from owner.
    (c) contact "A" and obtain his permission to act as co-broker.
    (d) do nothing.
58. License laws were sponsored by
    (a) the public.
    (b) organized real estate boards.
    (c) individual brokers.
    (d) the credit associations.
59. A salesman may operate a branch office for his broker
    (a) if his salesman's license is displayed.
    (b) if his broker's license is displayed.
    (c) if the office is in another municipality.
    (d) under no circumstances.
60. A real estate broker's license which has been revoked may be reinstated by
    (a) paying a penalty fine.
    (b) by qualifying as an original applicant.
    (c) by making application for a writ of mandamus.
    (d) by making written application to Commission for reinstatement.
61. Adams does business as the Excelsior Realty Co. He has a broker's license. He has not registered his trade name.
    (a) He can be fined by the Real Estate Commission.
    (b) He will lose his commission on any sale.
    (c) He can be fined by a court.
    (d) He will receive a reprimand.
62. A broker's license may be revoked for
    (a) failure to account for or to remit funds belonging to others.
    (b) failure to charge any commission.
    (c) making sales on Sunday.
    (d) failure to make a sale within one year.
63. Which persons are specifically exempt from the Real Estate Licensing Act?
    (a) War veterans.
    (b) Executors.
    (c) Part time salesmen.
    (d) Listers of real estate.
64. The term "Realtor" is a copyrighted word and can be used only by
    (a) any licensed broker.
    (b) brokers who are full time.
    (c) a member of the National Association of Realtors.
    (d) none of the foregoing.
65. When a broker discharges a salesman, he should
    (a) give the salesman his license.

(b) return the license to the Real Estate Commission.
(c) remove license from wall and keep it in file until all of salesman's deals have been closed out.
(d) instruct salesman to return license to Real Estate Commission.

66. An appeal from a decision of the Commission may be taken to
(a) Attorney General of the State.
(b) directly to the Supreme Court.
(c) Circuit, District Court or Common Pleas Court.
(d) Civil Service Board.

67. A license may be revoked upon proof of
(a) charging more than the usual rate of commission.
(b) dispute between broker and salesman as to a commission.
(c) violation of F.H.A. law.
(d) refusal to accept a listing.

68. A license issued on May 15 is valid until
(a) May 15 of the following year.
(b) end of current license year.
(c) January 15 of the following year.
(d) 60 days.

69. A salesman, in transferring to a new broker employer, should make application
(a) at next renewal period.
(b) within 60 days.
(c) within 30 days.
(d) immediately.

70. A broker's license is revoked for one year. His two salesmen
(a) must remain on inactive status the balance of the license year.
(b) would lose their licenses for one year.
(c) may, upon proper application, transfer to another broker.
(d) may continue to operate the broker's business.

71. A licensed broker selling a property on which he holds an option must notify the buyer that he is the
(a) optionee.
(b) optionor.
(c) tenant.
(d) lessee.
(e) escrow holder.

72. A member of the National Association of Real Estate License Law Officials is a
(a) Realtor.
(b) licensed broker.
(c) license law state.
(d) Secretary of State.

73. James Stone passes the license law examination and can forthwith have the license issued in the name of
(a) James Stone and Company.
(b) James Stone d/b/a Ajax Realty Co.
(c) James Stone.
(d) James Stone, Realtor.

74. The Real Estate Commission sets the maximum commission to be charged as
(a) 5 per cent.
(b) 6 per cent.
(c) 7 per cent.
(d) no maximum.

75. A licensed broker may share a commission with
(a) the person who introduced the buyer to the broker.
(b) salesman of another broker, who assisted in the sale.

(c) a licensed broker who assisted in sale.
(d) an attorney at law, who is a friend of the seller.

76. John Sloan is a licensed salesman who desires to transfer his license to Samuel Simon, trading as Eureka Realty Co. His license should be transferred as a salesman in employ of
    (a) Samuel Simon.
    (b) Eureka Realty Co.
    (c) kept in name of former employer.
    (d) do nothing.
77. When a licensed broker becomes physically disabled, his business may be operated by
    (a) his widow.
    (b) his chief salesman.
    (c) his office manager.
    (d) none of these.
78. In participating in a "dual contract" situation, which ones of the following participants would be subject to criminal prosecution?
    (a) Buyer.
    (b) Seller.
    (c) Broker.
    (d) Lending institution representative.
79. Which of the following statement(s) is (are) true?
    I. An unlicensed person may advertise as an independent real estate agent, but not as a Realtor or Realist.
    II. An unlicensed person may solicit listings to be paid by a broker.
        (a) I only.
        (b) II only.
        (c) Both I and II.
        (d) Neither I nor II.
80. Before a Commission may suspend or revoke a real estate license, in a discrimination case, which of the following must have occurred?
    I. Been found guilty by the Human Relations Commission of the State.
    II. Afforded a hearing before the Commission.
        (a) I only.
        (b) II only.
        (c) I and II.
        (d) Neither I nor II.
81. Which one of the following may sell real estate for a commission, without a license?
    (a) An executor.
    (b) A register of wills.
    (c) A clerk of courts.
    (d) A certified public accountant.
82. A broker's license may be issued to a corporation provided
    I. All of its officers are licensed as brokers.
    II. One active officer, at least, is licensed as a broker.
        (a) I only.
        (b) II only.
        (c) I and II.
        (d) Neither I nor II.
83. A salesperson made several material misrepresentations in a sales presentation without the knowledge of his broker, resulting in the revocation of the salesperson's license.
    I. The employing broker's license can be revoked.
    II. The broker's license cannot be revoked.
    III. The broker's license can be suspended.
        (a) I only.
        (b) II only.

(c) III only.
(d) Both I and II.
(e) Neither I nor II.

84. The best way for a new licensee to operate professionally is:
I. To take real estate and related courses.
II. To study state license law and Rules and Regulations.
(a) I only.
(b) II only.
(c) I and II.
(d) Neither I nor II.

85. A broker offered a free color television set if he would purchase the house in which he was definitely interested at the listed price of $19,500. The buyer agreed. The broker, under these circumstances,
(a) would be liable to the seller for the cost of the TV set.
(b) could refuse to deliver the TV.
(c) could lose his license.
(d) nothing could be done against the broker.

86. A broker advertised a listed property, stating "For details call 412/281-8030." A sale results.
(a) The broker cannot collect a commission.
(b) He is guilty of a misdemeanor.
(c) He may have his license suspended or revoked.
(d) The buyer has a cause of action against the broker.

87. A salesman, Green, employed by Broker "B", procured a signed agreement from a buyer, reciting a $300 earnest money deposit. It was a note for $300, and neither the salesman nor the broker told the owner that it was a note.
I. The broker is guilty of making a false promise through an agent or salesperson.
II. The broker is guilty of conduct which demonstrates incompetency, bad faith, or dishonesty.
(a) I only.
(b) II only.
(c) Both I and II.
(d) Neither I nor II.

88. Rules and Regulations of a Real Estate Commission, in conflict with a single clause in the license law:
I. supersede the license law.
II. implement the license law.
(a) I only.
(b) II only.
(c) both I and II.
(d) neither I nor II.

89. Under the police power, the state can
(a) regulate licensing of real estate brokers.
(b) arbitrate major league baseball and football controversies.
(c) appoint real estate commissioners.
(d) none of these.

90. Stone, who is unlicensed, negotiates a sale from Miller to Flynn. Miller pays Stone $950 commission. Under these circumstances
I. The agreement of sale, prepared by Stone, is void.
II. Miller may recover the commission paid.
(a) I only.
(b) II only.
(c) both I and II.
(d) neither I nor II.

Chapter 10

CONDOMINIUMS, COOPERATIVES, SYNDICATIONS, INVESTMENT TRUSTS, REAL ESTATE v. SECURITIES, INTERSTATE LAND SALES

CONDOMINIUMS AND COOPERATIVES are forms of legal organization which provide individuals with many of the benefits of private ownership in multiple-unit buildings or developments, particularly housing developments. The two forms are substantially different in legal theory and in many respects are governed by different laws.

The condominium, although its origins go back to antiquity, is today essentially a creature of statute. Its method of organization and operation and its essential characteristics are expressly defined in legislation.[1] Without such legislation, it could not be successfully adapted to the complex requirements of mortgage financing, FHA insurance, title insurance, taxation, and many other facets of modern large-scale real estate development.

The peculiar characteristic of the condominium is that, unlike a conventional rental apartment building or a cooperative housing building, there is no one owner to whom public authorities, creditors, occupants or third parties can look for enforcement of rights or liabilities. Absent a statutory solution, there would be no generally accepted formula for integrating the total operation of the condominium so that it can be accommodated to established commercial practices. Each owner of a unit in the multiple development has exclusive title to his own unit and he is generally free to deal with it as though it were a private dwelling. Only the common elements of the condominium are under the control of a common manager, and, absent a statutory requirement, even this responsibility could take any form which the unit owners saw fit to select.

A second peculiar aspect of the condominium is that traditional rules of real estate law and conventional financial techniques are not easily adapted to multiple unit ownerships in a common structure, particularly in high-rise buildings where an "air lot" must be treated as a private dwelling.

To overcome these limitations, statutes prescribe in some detail how the condominium must be organized and operated, so that the rights and duties of all persons associated with, or dealing with, the condominium can rely on a functional entity with its essential elements defined. Under these statutes, the basic "charter" of the condominium is established by the filing of a "condominium declaration," by-laws and floor plans with the appropriate public authorities. The "declaration" commits the signers to submit the property to the provisions of the statute, and describes, among other things, the land, the building and improvements, the number and location of each

---

[1] See, e.g., The Condominium Act, N.Y. Real Property L., Art. 9.B (par. 339-d et seq.) 1964.

unit, the common elements, and the intended use of the building and of each unit. The floor plans show the layout, locations and dimensions of the units and contain unit designations conforming to official tax lot numbers.

The by-laws govern the operation of the property. They provide, among other things, for the election of a board of managers and define their powers and duties. They determine whether the board will manage the property or delegate this responsibility to a managing agent. They define the extent to which the board of managers can bind the unit owners. They prescribe the method of determining and collecting the common charges and the establishment of reserves. Restrictions on use, provisions governing alienation, sale or leasing of units, and other essential elements of the legal structure are also determined.

Since most cooperatives are corporations which retain ownership of the property, they do not require statutory implementation to give them organizational identity. Conventional corporate practices provide many of the organizational solutions dealt with in the condominium statutes. Specific state legislation, where it exists, usually deals with specialized problems of the cooperative. A few states have adopted legislation dealing generally with cooperative organization, but the purpose of such legislation is to provide a local equivalent of the federal securities laws, viz, to protect the public against fraudulent or misleading public offerings of cooperative shares. In most states such protection of investors is afforded through the normal operation of the so-called "Blue Sky" laws.

In New York, for example,[2] a person is prohibited from taking part in a public offering or sale of "cooperative interests in realty," unless and until there shall have been filed with the appropriate public authority, an "offering statement" or "prospectus," containing designated information and representations, and the Attorney General has issued to the issuer or other offeror a letter stating that the offering has been filed. The required information is essentially similar to that required in a "condominium declaration," outlined above, except, of course, for the differences implicit in the two kinds of offerings.

Ownership differences: condominiums and co-ops

The purchaser of a condominium receives a deed which gives him ownership of his individual unit, in the same sense as ownership of a house. He also receives an interest in the commonly shared elements of the condominium, such as lawns, corridors, elevators, basement, and lobby. In resort condominiums, these may also include community facilities, such as a golf club, swimming pool or social center.

He pays his own taxes and mortgage indebtedness, and he sells or leases his unit as real estate, subject only to such limitations as may be contained in or authorized by the condominium by-laws. The common elements are managed and controlled by the board of managers and the unit owner is obligated by the by-laws to pay his proportionate part of the common charges for maintenance and repair.

In a cooperative development, the corporation owns the entire project. The purchaser of a unit does not become an owner of real estate; instead he becomes a stockholder in the corporation which owns the land and the building. The number of shares he receives is usually based on the value of his unit in relation to the value of the whole project. His stock holding entitles him to a long-term proprietary lease

---

[2] N.Y. Gen. Bus. Law, Sec. 352(e). This statute also applies to condominium sales offerings. 160 West 87th Street Corp. v. Lefkowitz, 350 N.Y.S. 2d 957, (1974), sustains the constitutionality of this statute against a challenge that the power of the Attorney General to withhold approval of a co-op plan without notice and hearing is a deprivation of property without due process.

of the unit which he "purchases." The stock holding and the leasehold ownership must reside in a common owner; the interests cannot be disposed of separately. As a shareholder, he has the right to vote annually for the Board of Directors who conduct the affairs of the corporation and supervise the operation of the building. As a lessee, he pays as rent (customarily called "maintenance charges") a proportionate share of the corporation's cash requirements for the operation, maintenance and repair of the building, including mortgage payments and real estate taxes, and for such reserve for contingencies as the Board of Directors determines. His combined interest in the stock and the lease is recognized for many purposes as personalty, not realty.[3]

Mortgages and financing

As an owner of real estate, the owner of a condominium unit, can mortgage his property essentially as he would if he owned a private residence. He thus has the option to buy his unit unencumbered by a mortgage or he can raise money to purchase the unit through first mortgage financing. Significantly, mortgage loans on condominiums are generally considered to be legal investments for banks and other fiduciaries. On the other side of the coin, however, the sponsor or manager of the condominium enterprise retains no interest to support a blanket mortgage on the entire project after completion of construction and sale of individual units.

Since the co-op corporation retains title to the land and building, notwithstanding the leasing of units to tenant/shareholders, it can, and usually does, place a blanket mortgage on the entire project. The tenant/shareholder, however, ordinarily cannot obtain a mortgage on the basis of his stock and proprietary lease,[4] because: (1) the nature of his holding—whether real estate or personalty—for mortgage purposes is uncertain; (2) the underlying mortgage on the entire project renders his mortgage less secure; and (3) transfers of tenant/shareholder's interest, upon foreclosures, are complicated by the usual co-op requirement that a new tenant/stockholder be approved by the Board of Directors of the corporation.[5]

As an individual mortgagor, the condominium unit owner usually assumes personal liability for the mortgage obligation. The co-op tenant/shareholder has the advantage that he is not personally liable to the mortgagee on the blanket mortgage placed by the corporation. But the condominium owner's title is not jeopardized by

---

[3] Categorizing co-op ownership as "realty" or "personalty" for various legal purposes has lead to unrealistic results at times and has created dilemmas for those who must determine whether to apply the fundamentally different bodies of law governing each category. See, Miller's Estate, 130 N.Y.S. 2d 295 (1954), holding that a co-op apartment passes under an estate as personal property; Silverman v. Alcoa Plaza Associates, 323 N.Y.S. 2d 39 (1971), holding that upon default by purchaser of co-op, seller corporation could not retain down payment, applying Uniform Commercial Code provisions applicable to personalty. Justice Steuer, dissenting, points out, however, that the Courts have recognized co-ops as real estate for some purposes. See, also, In Re Pitts Estate, 218 Cal. 184, 22 P. 2d 694 (1933).

[4] New York specifically authorizes banks and savings and loan associations to grant loans on cooperatives: Ch. 376, McKinney's 1971, amended by Chap. 596, McKinney's 1972, Session Laws of N.Y.
The program authorizes banks to charge 1.5 percentage points more for a co-op loan than for a one-family residence mortgage, on the premise that the co-op loan is not as secure as the conventional mortgage because of the underlying mortgage on the entire development.

[5] Condominiums also require approval of the association before a unit can be sold, but in practice, the requirement is usually relaxed in favor of an approved mortgagee who acquires title to a unit.

the default of another owner, whereas a default by the corporation on a blanket mortgage jeopardizes the interests of all the tenant/shareholders.

Repairs and maintenance

Tenant/shareholders in a co-op pay their assessments for repairs and maintenance in the form of rent. Unit owners in a condominium pay such assessments by virtue of the by-laws governing the condominium. Should it become necessary to raise abnormally large sums for repairs or improvements, the co-op corporation, as owner of the property, may in principle have more flexibility than the condominium, since it may have access to mortgage refinancing or other secured borrowing, in addition to the right to assess tenant/shareholders.

Tax considerations

Since each condominium unit is separately owned, it is separately billed for local tax purposes. Default in payment of taxes by the owner of one unit does not jeopardize the owners of other units. The co-op corporation, on the other hand, is assessed and taxed as an entity, and in the event of default by the corporation, the individual unit owner's interest could be foreclosed.

Both the condominium and the cooperative owner are entitled to deduct mortgage interest and real estate taxes from their federal income taxes. The respective deductions are based on different statutory provisions, however. The condominium falls within the normal tax provisions governing real estate, but the cooperative must meet the specific requirements of a separate provision of the Internal Revenue Code,[6] which requires that the taxpayer be a tenant/shareholder, that the co-op entity receive 80% or more of its income from tenant/shareholders, and that it have only one class of stock outstanding with no right to dividends.

The section of the Internal Revenue Code[7] which provides for non-taxability on the sale of a principal residence, if a new principal residence is purchased within a year at a cost equal to or more than the sales price of the old residence, applies to both the condominium and the cooperative. The benefit accorded to a person 65 or older who sells his principal residence also applies to both condominiums and co-ops.[8]

Condominiums for non-residential purposes

There is growing interest in employing the condominium form to non-residential development. Adapting the condominium to such uses, however, will require greater flexibility than is currently allowed under State laws. Present laws, for example, frequently do not permit condominium buildings on leased lands. Their provisions governing unit ownership, allocation of percentages of interest in common elements, sharing of profits and expenses, allocation of and tax responsibility and the order of lien priorities are too rigid for some types of commercial application.

Real estate syndications

In 1972, more than $1 billion in interstate syndication offerings were filed with the Securities and Exchange Commission, and many additional billions were marketed through private offerings or intrastate sales which were not required to be registered with the Securities and Exchange Commission.

---

[6] IRC, Sec, 216.
[7] IRC, Sec. 1034.
[8] IRC, Sec. 121.

What is a real estate syndication?

The term "real estate syndicate" has no precise legal signification historically. In recent years, the term has come to refer to a specialized form of partnership venture which is structured so as to produce certain tax shelter and other benefits for passive investors whose invested funds are employed to acquire or develop real estate under the management of an experienced partner.

Syndications are most frequently organized in the form of limited partnerships because their characteristics lend themselves most readily to compliance with tax law requirements and other objectives of syndication. The limited partnership is a form of partnership in which one or more partners are *general* partners—i.e. partners who manage the business and who assume unlimited liability, and any number of additional *limited* partners—i.e. partners who do not participate in the management of the business and whose liability is limited to their respective contributions to the partnership capital. The limited partner is essentially a passive investor. If he participates actively in the business, he renders himself liable to creditors as a general partner.

The inherent distinction between a limited partner and a general partner provides a natural and flexible vehicle for achieving a variety of objectives sought by each type of partner. The entrepreneur—the general partner—is able to organize the venture, obtain the funds for the acquisition of the investment property from the limited partners, and manage the enterprise for compensation. He may also take an interest as a limited partner if he so desires. The limited partner has an opportunity to participate in a large or diversified tax-sheltered investment which might not otherwise be available to him, on a limited liability basis and with complete freedom from management responsibilities.

Syndications may embrace either a small number of investors with substantial participation or a large number of investors with relatively small participations, frequently less than $5,000.

The syndication process

Syndications take a variety of forms. A representative example may take the following form:

The syndicator locates property which has the appropriate economic characteristics to produce the benefits he seeks for himself and for potential investors. After satisfying himself of the validity of his appraisal and forecasts and the propriety of his proposed tax plan for distribution of income and losses among the partners, he makes a binding commitment for the purchase of the equity in the property, which he later conveys to the syndicate. He formally establishes the syndicate with several joint venturers or associates. The limited partnership is organized under state statutes which are generally based on the Uniform Limited Partnership Act.

Before offering interests to prospective investors, he determines whether he is subject to the requirements of the federal securities laws or state "blue sky" laws regulating the offering of securities or other federal or state law requirements. Depending on the nature of the offering, he solicits investors through a "prospectus," an "offering circular" or similar document which may require registration under federal laws or qualification or other compliance under State law.

The prospectus or circular spells out the nature of the transaction, the anticipated economic and tax benefits, the essential provisions of the partnership agreement, and all other relevant information. It also contains a form inviting investors to join the syndicate as a limited partner.

The partnership agreement covers the essential rights and obligations of the partners, including distribution of profits and losses, assignability of interests, right of withdrawal of capital, causes of dissolution and priorities thereon, management responsibilities and powers of the general partners and the limitations on the liability of limited partners.

The subscriptions of the limited partners supply the minimum cash needed to purchase the equity in the property subject to a mortgage which the syndicator has contracted for, and after assignment by the syndicator of the contract to purchase the property, the syndicate purchases the property.

There are, of course, many variations on the pattern outlined above. The transaction may involve unimproved land with improvements to be erected or in the process of construction. The syndication may embrace several properties. The syndicator may offer interests in undefined properties, or may offer an "open-end" investment, allowing for the addition of both new properties and new investors in the syndication in the future.

Tax aspects of limited partnerships

Unlike corporations, which are subject to an income tax, the limited partnership, like all partnerships, pays no income tax as a legal entity. Each partner is taxed individually on the basis of distributed income or loss from the partnership enterprise. The ability of the limited partners to take advantage of losses for tax purposes is a key benefit to the individual investor in real estate syndications. Under Treasury Regulation 1.752-1(e), if the property is acquired subject to a mortgage and neither the partnership nor the partners are personally liable on the mortgage, the basis of each limited partner for his partnership interest includes his pro rata share of the partnership mortgage. This increase in basis permits the deductibility of losses generated by depreciation even though it exceeds the partner's cash capital contribution.

In addition, as an owner of an interest in real estate, the partner is entitled to a tax deduction for mortgage interest payments, real estate taxes and sales taxes, to the extent provided for in the partnership agreement.

Because the limited partnership has a number of characteristics resembling a corporation, the limited partnership agreement must be drawn most carefully to avoid a determination by the Internal Revenue Service that the organization is an association taxable as a corporation.

A "partnership" for tax purposes includes a syndicate or other enumerated forms of unincorporated organizations through or by means of which a business, financial operation or venture is carried on and which is not a corporation, trust or estate for tax purposes. This elliptical definition provides uncertain guidance, particularly since, an "association" is taxable as a "corporation". The Internal Revenue Service determines whether an entity is a partnership or an association taxable as a corporation, by comparing the entity's characteristics with these characteristics of a corporation, among others: (a) Continuity of life; (b) Centralized management; (c) Limited liability for investors; (d) Free transferability of interests.[9] If the limited partnership has more than two of these characteristics, it will be taxable as a corporation. The process of determining the existence or nonexistence of each of these characteristics

---

[9] See Prentice Hall, "Corporation Service," Report Bulletin #23, November 8, 1973, discussing uncertainties created as to the tax status of limited partnerships by the issuance of guidelines issued by the California Commissioner of Corporations. The guidelines were withdrawn by the Commissioner on December 6, 1973.

is problematical in any given case and must be considered carefully in drafting the partnership agreement.

If the activity is taxable as a corporation, it will, of course, be taxed at the corporate level, thus defeating the purpose of the limited partnership. Accordingly, a sponsor of a real estate syndication normally seeks an advance ruling from the Internal Revenue Service to assure that the syndication will have taxable status as a partnership.

Real estate investment trusts

The Real Estate Investment Trust (the "REIT"), is an investment vehicle which is virtually a creature of the federal tax laws. The Internal Revenue Code was amended in 1960 to extend to REITS, tax benefits similar to those enjoyed by regulated investment companies. These benefits were granted to permit small investors to participate in large real estate investments and to increase the pool of funds available for equity financing of large real estate developments.

The 1960 amendment[10] contains practically a charter governing the organization and operation of the REIT. In order to qualify under the tax provisions, the REIT:

(1) Must be an unincorporated trust or association. (This automatically excludes corporations).

(2) Must be managed by one or more trustees. (The requirements as to trustee management and control necessarily eliminate limited partnerships as REIT entities).

(3) Must have transferable shares of ownership. (REIT shares are freely transferable on stock exchanges, like corporate stock; this is not true of limited partnership interests because of the tax rules applicable to them).

(4) Must have at least 100 beneficial owners and five or fewer persons may not own more than 50% of its shares. (There are no such tax limitations on limited partnerships.)

(5) Must make a formal election to be taxed as a REIT.

The REIT must meet prescribed tests on asset values and income sources to insure that its investments are essentially in real estate.

The REIT is not permitted to engage *actively* in the real estate business in the sense of buying and selling real estate, managing real estate developments, or constructing buildings. The tax law provides that it must not hold property primarily for sale to customers in the ordinary course of business, and places rigid limitations on the amount of income which may be generated from the sale of securities or real estate. Its special function is intended to be primarily that of a "passive" investor in real estate interests, deriving its income mainly from rents or mortgage interest or both.

Thus, the REIT cannot even render services to tenants or manage or operate the property in which it invests without endangering its tax status; the income from such services is not includible as "rents from real property" to meet the income source tests prescribed by the tax provision. Such services are required to be handled by an independent contractor from whom the trust does not derive or receive any income.[11] For this reason, the REIT usually contracts for the independent services of a real estate manager or participates as a partner in a development with a real estate organization. Under either arrangement, the REIT does not participate in the income attributable to such services.

As generally practiced, the REIT trustees contract for the services of a realty

---

[10] Internal Revenue Code, sections 856-858.

[11] Internal Revenue Code, section 856(d)(3).

management firm, to advise them on real estate investments, and to act as agent of the Trust in the purchase and sale of real estate, leaseholds, or real estate mortgages, and as an independent contractor in the management of such assets, including negotiation of leases, the collection of rents and mortgage payments, the handling of repairs, arranging for utilities, insurance and other services.

REITS are frequently sponsored by banks, insurance companies, and mortgage finance companies. The earlier REITS were mostly "equity trusts" which invested in income-producing commercial and industrial properties. More recently, the "mortgage trust" has grown in popularity, specializing in either long-term mortgage investments or short-term construction loans or interim mortgage financing.

REITS earn their profit from the spread between the interest they receive from investments and the interest they pay to obtain capital. They thus are sensitive to fluctuations in interest rates, as well as the relative condition of the real estate market and the availability of capital at any given time.[12]

Because REITS are freely traded securities, they are usually registered under the Securities and Exchange Act or the State Blue Sky laws.

The REIT investor is a mutual fund type investor. Unlike the investor in a limited partnership, he is not seeking a specific real estate venture offering tax losses, depreciation benefits or early capital gains, but he expects an above-average dividend income from a freely transferable security which is usually listed on a stock exchange or traded over the counter. Dividends higher than those paid by corporations are possible because the qualified REIT entity, unlike a corporation, pays no income tax on income distributed to its beneficial owners and 90% or more of its ordinary taxable income must be distributed in order to maintain its tax qualification.

The legal entity which most frequently qualifies for REIT status under the tax laws is the common law business trust. This method of conducting a commercial enterprise originated in Massachusetts to circumvent the need of obtaining a special charter to acquire and develop real estate.[13] It has thus come to be known as a "Massachusetts Trust." Although it has been recognized as a valid legal entity in most states,[14] some states have passed statutes for the purpose of eliminating uncertainty as to the purposes of the trust, the liability of the trustees and the beneficial owners and the limitations, if any, on its perpetual existence. Accordingly, local law must be considered before employing it as a form of business organization.

Unlike a corporation, the Massachusetts Trust does not normally receive a charter from the State. It is created by a contractual document generally referred to as a "Declaration of Trust," which contains provisions analogous to those covered in a corporate charter. The less permanent regulations, such as those governing the internal management and operation of the trust, are covered by by-laws or a code of regulations. The general legal characteristics of the trust are as follows: (1) legal title to all property belonging to the trust is held by the Trustees as joint tenants; (2) the beneficial owners are cestuis que trust; (3) the life of the trust can in effect be perpetual (i.e. until its assets are liquidated and distributed), unless it must be terminated earlier to accommodate state law requirements on the rule against perpetuities; (4) the shares are freely transferable; (5) the beneficial owners are insulated against personal liability, and (6) there is no limitation on the number of beneficial owners unless it seeks to qualify as a REIT (discussed supra).

---

[12] REITS often borrow from banks on a floating interest-rate basis and then lend it to developers on the same basis. The extraordinary rise in interest rates during 1974 has resulted in a number of defaults in REIT loans, triggering financial difficulties for many REITS.

[13] State Street Trust Co. v. Hall, 41 NE 2d 30 (1942).

[14] 156 ALR 54 et seq.

When is real estate a security?

Traditionally, the federal securities laws have dealt with public offerings which involve typical securities, such as corporate stocks, bonds, debentures, etc.[15] Real estate transactions seemed to be a far cry from the reach of the securities laws. But with the explosive growth of real estate syndications and other forms of sophisticated real estate transactions in recent years, recurring litigation has established that the offering to the public of interests in real estate do indeed constitute offerings of securities more often than the conventional wisdom supposed.

One reason why securities law enforcement has been slow to reach interests in real estate is the fact that the federal securities laws make no specific reference to real estate. They do, however, define "security" to include undertakings which are frequently associated with real estate transactions, including "evidence of indebtedness," "certificate of interest or participation in any profit-sharing agreement," and "investment contract."

How, then, does one determine when a real estate offering is a "security" offering under the federal securities laws? A "three-prong" test, laid down by the U. S. Supreme Court in *SEC v. Howey Co.,* 328 U.S. 293 (1946), has provided the basic guideline for determining whether a real estate transaction is an *"investment contract"*—the category of "security" into which most real estate transactions fall. To qualify as an investment contract an arrangement must be:

(1) a scheme whereby a person invests his money in a common enterprise;
(2) he is led to expect profits, and
(3) the expectation of profit is solely from the efforts of the promoter or a third party.

In the Howey case, the sale of units in a large Florida citrus grove, coupled with an offer by the developer to cultivate and market the fruit and to remit the net proceeds to the investors was held to constitute a security offering. Similarly, where the sale of condominium units was coupled with an arrangement whereby the purchasers of the units were to derive a fixed guaranteed annual return from rentals managed by the seller or a third party, the offer was of a security.[16]

The Howey opinion emphasized the need for flexibility in determining whether "... the countless and variable schemes devised by those who seek the use of money of others on the promise of profits ... " constitute an "investment contract." This flexibility has resulted in unpredictable application of the Howey test.[17]

On December 6, 1973, the SEC filed a test case in the Federal Court in San Francisco to compel six corporations, which operate Pajaro Dunes, a 400-unit condominium, to register their offering of units as securities.[18] On March 1, 1974, it issued "Proposed Guide 60, 'Preparation of Registration Statements Relating to Interests in

---

[15] See the Securities Act of 1933, 15 USCA 77 and the Securities Exchange Act of 1934, 15 USCA 78, which provide for a system of disclosure to protect investors against fraud and misrepresentation. A "registration statement" must be filed with the Securities and Exchange Commission for a public offering of a "security" as defined in the Act.

[16] SEC v. Marasol Properties,—F. Supp.—(DC 1973); Kahn v. Kaskel, 367 F. Supp. 784 (1973).

[17] See, Nash & Associates, Inc. v. LUM'S of Ohio, Inc., 484 F. 2d 393 (6th Cir. 1973). The trend is increasingly toward holding real estate investment offerings to be "securities." E.g., "Co-op offerings" are both "stock" and "investment contracts" within the Securities Act of 1933; 1050 Tenants Corp. et al v. Jakobsen et al, 365 F. Supp. 1171 (S.D. N.Y. 1973), sustained by 2d Cir., July 8, 1974; Forman v. Community Services, Inc. —F. 2d—, (2d Cir.), decided June 12, 1974, reversing 366 F. Supp. 1117 (S.D. N.Y. 1973).

[18] SEC v. Hare, Brewer & Kelley, Inc., et al., SEC Docket, Vol. 3, No. 5, Dec. 18, 1973.

Real Estate Limited Partnerships',"[19] which prescribes certain disclosures which must be made in registration statements.

State "blue sky" laws

The solicitation or sale of securities have also been regulated by the various states under the so-called "Blue Sky" laws, which aim at preventing deceit and fraud in the sale of securities. All the States have enacted laws of this kind and 31 States have adopted, with or without modifications, the Uniform Securities Act as approved by the National Conference of Commissioners on Uniform State laws on August 25, 1956.

Offerings of real estate interests may fall within the purview of either federal or state securities regulation or both. As in the case of the federal securities laws, the trend has been in the direction of bringing transactions involving real estate interests within the scope of State Blue Sky regulation. As recently as 1970, State courts held uniformly that shares of cooperative housing corporations were not securities. Since that date, Courts have treated such shares as securities within the meaning of State laws. Specific legislation, moreover, has been adopted by some States regulating the sale of certain forms of interests in real estate.

The Interstate Land Sales Full Disclosure Act[20]

The Interstate Land Sales Full Disclosure Act regulates the interstate sale or lease by developers of fifty or more unimproved lots in subdivisions as part of a common promotional plan. When such sales are direct sales of real estate, they would not normally fall within the protection of securities laws. This Act therefore provides a method of registration with the Department of Housing & Urban Development ("HUD") which is analagous to registrations under the Securities Act. No such lot may be sold or leased unless a "statement of record" containing detailed information concerning the property and the plan is filed with HUD and is in effect,[21] and a "printed property report" containing essentially the contents of the "statement of record" is furnished to the purchaser of any lot. Severe penalties, both civil and criminal, are prescribed for violation of the registration requirements or for the use of fraudulent or deceptive practices or material misrepresentations in selling or leasing lots in subdivisions subject to the provisions of the Act.

The Act provides the following exemptions from the Act's registration requirements, among others:

a) the plan offers less than 50 lots or lots consisting of at least 5 acres each;
b) the lots contain an existing building on improved land or the seller is obligated to erect such a building within two years;
c) the lots are purchased for the purpose of constructing residential, commercial or industrial buildings by a professional builder, or
d) the lot is free and clear of all liens and encumbrances at the time of the sale and the purchaser has personally inspected the property.

The office of Interstate Land Sales Registration of HUD had adopted elaborate regulations pursuant to the Act. These regulations have been amended recently to enlarge substantially the disclosure requirements of the statement of record.[22] Among other disclosures, the developer must provide audited financial statements, reports on environmental factors including unusual conditions affecting habitability, assurances on his commitments to provide promised improvements and the availability of utilities and sewerage facilities.

---

[19] SEC Release Nos. 4936 and 33-5465; Exchange Act Release No. 34-10663, March 1, 1974, 39 F.R. 10278.

[20] 15 USC 1701 et seq, Pub. L. 90-448, August 1, 1968.

[21] The effective date is the thirtieth day after filing or such earlier date as the Secretary of HUD shall determine.

[22] 24 CFR 1700, 1972, as amended September 4, 1973, 38 F.R. 23866 & 32443, effective December 1, 1973.

In order to lighten the burden of developers with limited resources, the agency has provided a "Limited offering—Intrastate Exemption" for subdivisions which contain less than 300 lots and which are offered and advertised intrastate to residents of the State where the subdivision is located (except that 5% or less of sales in any one year may be made to residents of another state). Qualification for this exemption, however, must be granted expressly by HUD.

The HUD Regulations also extend to condominium sales, but most such sales will probably escape the registration requirement because of the exemption applying to sellers who are obligated to erect completed units within 2 years from the date the purchaser signs the sales contract.

Questions on Condominiums and Cooperatives

Multiple Choice

1. Title to units in both a condominium and in a cooperative housing development is vested
   (a) In a corporation owning the building.
   (b) In an association owning the building.
   (c) The owner of each unit.
   (d) The unit owner of a condominium; the corporate owner of a cooperative.
2. Cooperative housing developments are usually organized
   (a) Under State business corporation laws.
   (b) Under special State statutes governing creation of cooperatives.
   (c) Under federal tax laws.
3. A "condominium declaration" is
   (a) A sworn statement by the unit owner that he will comply with rules and regulations of the condominium.
   (b) An agreement of the unit owners governing the operation of the common elements of the condominium.
   (c) The "charter" of the condominium established upon its filing with local state authorities.
4. The proprietary interest of a cooperative tenant-stockholder is
   (a) Real estate for all purposes.
   (b) Personal property for all purposes.
   (c) Realty for some purposes, personalty for other purposes.
5. First mortgages are obtainable in most States
   (a) By the owner of a condominium unit.
   (b) By the tenant-shareholder of a cooperative.
   (c) By either the condominium owner or coop tenant-shareholder.
6. Upon default in payment of real estate taxes by a condominium unit owner
   (a) The taxing authority can levy on the entire condominium.
   (b) Title to the unit which he owns can be foreclosed.
   (c) The taxing authority must look first to his unit for satisfaction of the debt, then the assets of the condominium.
7. Under the federal income tax laws, mortgage interest and real estate taxes are deductible.
   (a) By a condominium unit owner but not by a coop tenant-shareholder.
   (b) By a coop tenant-shareholder but not by a condominium unit owner.
   (c) By neither.
   (d) By both.

Questions on real estate syndications

1. Real estate syndications are usually organized as
   (a) Business Corporations.
   (b) Limited partnerships.
   (c) Non-profit corporations.
   (d) Trusts.
2. A basic difference between a general partner and a limited partner is
   (a) Determined by the amount of capital each contributes.

(b) That the general partner manages the enterprise and the limited partner contributes capital and does not participate in the management of the partnership.
(c) That the general partner is liable for the debts of the partnership only if the limited partner fails to discharge the partnership debts.

3. Under the federal income tax laws, limited partnerships
   (a) Are taxed like corporations.
   (b) Are taxed like associations
   (c) Are not taxed as an entity.
4. Under the federal income tax laws, a limited partner
   (a) Cannot take advantage of losses for tax purposes.
   (b) Includes his pro rata share of a partnership mortgage in his tax basis.
   (c) Is not entitled to a tax deduction for mortgage interest payments and real estate taxes.
5. In order to qualify under the federal tax laws, a limited partnership
   (a) Must have perpetual existence.
   (b) Must have interests which are freely transferable.
   (c) Must have centralized management.
   (d) Must provide limited liability for investors.
   (e) Must not have more than two of the above characteristics.

Questions on real estate investment trusts

6. Mortgage trusts differ from equity trusts in that
   (a) A mortgage trust is a Massachusetts trust.
   (b) An equity trust is a regulated investment company.
   (c) Each invests in different types of real estate interests.
7. Under the federal tax laws, a real estate investment trust
   (a) Must engage actively in the real estate business.
   (b) Is a passive investor in real estate interests.
   (c) Must manage property in which it invests and render all services to tenants of property it manages.
8. The Massachusetts Trust
   (a) Is a legal entity which is recognized in Massachusetts only.
   (b) Is the form of organization which is most frequently used to qualify for real estate investment trust status under the tax laws.
   (c) Is recognized by all States as a common law form of legal organization which provides limited liability to investors and free transferability of shares.
9. Under the federal tax laws, a real estate investment trust
   (a) Must be organized as a corporation.
   (b) Must be organized as a limited partnership.
   (c) Must be limited in size to 100 beneficial owners.
   (d) Must have freely transferable shares of ownership.
10. In a Massachusetts Trust, legal title to all property belonging to the trust is vested
    (a) In the beneficial owners.
    (b) In the trustees.
    (c) In a limited partnership established by the trust.

Questions on real estate as securities

11. The federal securities laws regulate
    (a) The sale of all stocks, bonds and other corporate securities.
    (b) Syndications and real estate sales only.
    (c) The sale of U. S. Savings Bonds and other federal securities.
    (d) Public offerings of securities.
12. The sale of interests in real estate is the sale of a security
    (a) If it is offered to the public generally.
    (b) If it is an investment contract.
    (c) If it is sold on a stock exchange.

13. When a public offering of a real estate security must be registered under federal law, the "Registration Statement" is filed with
    (a) The SEC.
    (b) H.U.D.
    (c) F.H.A.
    (d) The Lands Division of the Department of Justice.
14. The "Blue Sky" Laws are:
    (a) Federal laws regulating the sale of securities
    (b) State laws regulating high-rise buildings.
    (c) Interstate land sales full disclosure regulations
    (d) None of the above.

Questions on interstate land sales full disclosure act ("The Act")

1. The Act regulates
    (a) All interstate real estate transactions
    (b) The sale or lease of unimproved lots in subdivisions as part of a promotional plan
    (c) Cooperative and condominium sales
    (d) The sale of real estate through the mail.
2. The Act, where otherwise applicable, does not apply
    (a) If less than 50 unimproved lots are involved in a promotional plan
    (b) If the sale is registered with the SEC
    (c) If the sale is registered under the "Blue Sky laws"
    (d) If it falls within the "Limited Offering—Intrastate Exemption".
3. A "Statement of Record," where required by the Act, is
    (a) Filed with the SEC
    (b) Filed with HUD
    (c) Furnished to the purchasers of lots sold in promotional plans subject to the Act.

Chapter 11

FILL-IN, MATCHING, AND KEY-WORD QUESTIONS

1. The gradual increase in the value of real property is called *appreciation.*
2. P.I.T.I. means principal, interest, taxes and *insurance.*
3. Property held under a lease is called *a leasehold.*
4. Where a licensee violates a rule or regulation of the Real Estate Commission, he will be charged with *improper conduct, bad faith, untrustworthiness, dishonesty, or incompetency.*
5. In the preparation of a closing statement, a mortgage assumed by the buyer would be listed as a *credit* to the buyer and as a *debit* to the seller.
6. The amount of earnest money to be paid is determined by *agreement of parties.*
7. A purchaser at a foreclosure sale upon a mortgage receives a *sheriff's deed.*
8. Real estate taxes are usually computed on the basis of the *calendar* year.
9. Where a material misrepresentation has been made to a buyer, he is entitled to relief in court in an action for *rescission.*
10. Community property may only be acquired by *husband and wife.*
11. Unproductive land on which the cost of production approximates the gross return is *marginal* land.
12. A contract for purchase of real estate upon an installment basis wherein the deed is delivered to the purchaser upon payment of the last installment, is called a *land contract.*
13. A plan or map of a certain piece or pieces of land is a *plat.*
14. A real estate license may be revoked for making any substantial *misrepresentation.*
15. A real estate broker's license must at all times be conspicuously displayed at *office* (except in California).
16. Unpaid taxes on real property become a *lien.*
17. When a real estate salesman is discharged for dishonesty, the broker must immediately notify the *Real Estate Commission.*
18. Failure to prosecute one's legal rights promptly constitutes *laches.*
19. *Economic obsolescence* is the loss in value to causes external to the property.
20. The formula for determining the square foot area of a tract of land is by *multiplying* the width by the depth.
21. By multiplying the width of a dwelling by its length by its height, you obtain its *cubage.*
22. Mechanic's liens are usually filed against real property for payment of *labor or materials.*
23. An unlicensed salesman negotiated the sale of a parcel of real estate. Both broker and salesman claimed the commission. It is payable to *neither.*
24. Before suspending or revoking any license, the Real Estate Commission must grant the licensee a *hearing.*
25. An estimate of value of real estate by a qualified expert is called an *appraisal.*
26. The loan secured by a mortgage is evidenced by a *note.*
27. A salesman in the employ of a real estate broker negotiated a deal. In order to collect his commission, an action may be brought against the seller by the *broker.*
28. A real estate salesman must lead a prospect through the following five steps before the prospect buys—(1) desire, (2) action, (3) belief, (4) attention, (5) interest. Rearranged in proper sequence they would be—*attention, interest, belief, desire, action.*
29. When specific properties are benefited by public improvements, the charges (or taxes

levied) to pay for such improvements are called *assessments.*
30. A deed without warranties is a *quit claim deed.*
31. The two types of property are called *real* and *personal.*
32. The spouse of a married titleholder of a home should sign a sales contract and deed to relinquish or release *dower* or *curtesy* rights.
33. A contract secured through fraud or misrepresentation would not be *valid.*
34. The amount of commission to be charged in a real estate transaction is determined by *agreement between owner and broker.*
35. The overhang or projection of a foundation wall, a porch, or a balcony beyond the established line of a parcel of land is known as an *encroachment.*
36. To make a binding contract there must be at least *two parties.*
37. An acquired privilege or right of use or enjoyment falling short of ownership which one may have in the land of another is known as an *easement.*
38. If a person owns a part interest in a home he is buying on time, such interest is called an *equity.*
39. A right of the state by which the state can obtain possession of any property which is needed for a public purpose is *eminent domain.*
40. Ordinarily the length of time a listing contract remains in force is determined by *contract.*
41. Mud tubes or shelter channels on walls or joists or cellar window sills apparently rotted indicate the presence of *termites.*
42. Title to chattels is usually transferred by a *bill of sale.*
43. The compiled ordinances or laws regulating the construction of buildings within the jurisdiction of a municipality is called the *zoning and building code.*
44. The branch of the state government that is responsible for the enforcement of the real estate broker's license law is the *Real Estate Commission* (or State Real Estate Board).
45. If a witness is served with a summons to appear before the Real Estate Commission, such summons is called a *subpoena.*
46. If we multiply the floor area of a building by its height, we arrive at a figure designated as its *cubage.*
47. A mortgage given for a part of the purchase price of a home is called a *purchase money mortgage.*
48. A note is negotiated by the signature of the holder on its "reverse." This is called *an endorsement.*
49. The name of the instrument by which personal property is ordinarily mortgaged is a *chattel mortgage.*
50. The instrument which is used to convey title to real property is called *a deed.*
51. A small supporting column for a hand rail is called a *balustrade.*
52. A *canopy* is an ornamental roof projection over a door or window.
53. When hot air is forced through the heating ducts, by a blower, it is known as *forced air* heating.
54. The instrument which is used to convey title to personal property is called a *bill of sale.*
55. The fixing of value of real estate for purposes of taxation is called *assessing.*
56. The right to cross over property belonging to another is called *an easement.*
57. A commission agreement between licensed brokers or salesmen need not be *written.*
58. The moral duty and the principles of right action and fair dealing set forth for the guidance of professional conduct are known as *canons of ethics* or *code of ethics.*
59. A careful measurement made by a qualified person from established data to determine the boundaries of a tract of land is known as *surveying.*
60. The board skirting the walls of a room on the floor line is called *baseboard, quarter round.*
61. The lowest floor level in a building is the *basement* floor.
62. *Foundation* is the walls of a building below the first or ground floor.
63. One who assigns or transfers personal property is called *an assignor.*
64. In a deed there must be good or valuable *consideration.*

65. An authorization given by one person to act for him on his behalf is called *a power of attorney.*
66. The rights which a wife has upon her husband's death in lands owned by him in fee simple is called *dower.*
67. The element of depreciation usually found in older type buildings and which affects the appraised value is known as *obsolescence.*
68. Applications for a real estate license are made to the *Real Estate Commission* (or Commissioner).
69. A marginal release or a satisfaction is often used to release a *mortgage.*
70. The cestuique trust under a trust instrument is the *beneficiary.*
71. A note is usually given to secure the payment of a *mortgage.*
72. Where a broker holds a written listing protecting him against a sale by the owner or another broker during a limited period of time it is *an exclusive-right-to-sell contract.*
73. Deeds are usually acknowledged before a *notary public.*
74. Where a mortgagee cannot personally be present to satisfy a mortgage, the writing which may be filed for that purpose is called *a satisfaction piece.*
75. An agreement between two or more parties to do or not to do a certain thing is called *a contract.*
76. The instrument which the purchaser of a mortgage should obtain from the mortgagor is known as an *estoppel certificate* (also known as a certificate of no defense or a declaration of no setoff).
77. The clause in a deed which permits the buyer to proceed against the seller for damages due to a defect in title is the *warranty clause.*
78. The parties to a lease are known as *lessor* and *lessee.*
79. A real estate salesman must be in the employ of a broker who is properly *licensed.*
80. A common unit other than the square foot which is used in determining the value of developed land is the *front foot.*
81. A summary of the most important part of all instruments comprising the recorded title of the seller, arranged in chronological order is *an abstract of title.*
82. The system of recording used to eliminate tedious and expensive searches of titles is the *Torrens system.*
83. A land contract is synomynous with a *contract for deed.*
84. The rule of law in leasing or selling property where the parties deal "at arm's length" is called *caveat emptor* (let the purchaser beware).
85. A lease is transferred by the lessor to a purchaser of the leased property by *assignment.*
86. The public regulation of the character and intensity of use of real property through the employment of police power is known as *zoning.*
87. Real estate license laws are constitutional because they represent a valid exercise of the state's *police power.*
88. A decree of court determining that one individual is indebted to another and fixing the amount of the indebtedness is called a *judgment.*
89. Title to property occupied in defiance of the real owner for a long period of time may pass to the occupier through *adverse possession.*
90. In order to prevent the proposed violation of a building restriction covenant an action should be brought for an *injunction.*
91. A person who belongs to a local real estate board affiliated with the National Association of Realtors is a *Realtor.*
92. The compensation or income received for the use of real property is known as *rent.*
93. A limitation upon the use or occupancy of real estate placed by public legislative action is known as *zoning.*
94. Where one is negligent in asserting his legal rights, his claim may be barred by a *statute of limitations.*
95. One who institutes a suit at law is *the plaintiff.*
96. The interest or value of an estate remaining to the mortgagor over and above the

encumbrance is known as *his equity.*

97. An agreement between two persons which creates a legal obligation is called a *contract.*
98. The conveyance of an estate in land by way of a pledge for the security of a debt, to become void upon payment of the debt, is called a *mortgage.*
99. A deed which purports merely to convey whatever interest in the particular land the grantor may have, excluding any implication that the grantor has a good title or any title, is known as a *quit claim deed.*
100. A person who receives real estate under a will is known as the *devisee.*
101. The person appointed to administer the estate of a decedent who did not leave a will is called an *administrator.*
102. The person named in a will to administer the estate is the *executor.*
103. *Percolation test* is a soil test to determine if the soil will take sufficient water seepage for use of septic tanks.
104. A private sewage disposal facility for individual homes is a *septic* (cess pool) system.
105. The person to whom real estate is conveyed by deed is the *grantee.*
106. The person to whom personal property is sold is the *vendee.*
107. Where a deed is delivered to a third person pending the performance of some condition, it is a delivery *in escrow.*
108. The owner's right to buy back property sold for delinquent taxes is called the right of *redemption.*
109. Joint tenancy implies the right of *survivorship.*
110. A chattel mortgage is given to obtain a *loan.*
111. The trade name of a business sold usually includes the *good will.*
112. A broker occupies a *fiduciary* relationship to his principal.
113. A person who holds an option for the purchase of real estate is the *optionee.*
114. The transfer of interest in a bond, mortgage, lease or other instrument is called *assignment.*
115. Dispossession of a tenant by a landlord from a leased property is known as *eviction.*
116. A forged deed is always *void.*
117. A sub-lessee who, in turn, sub-lets to another is said to hold a *sandwich lease.*
118. Generally speaking, a person can afford to pay *2* ½ times his annual income for a home.
119. In the absence of a specific agreement as to commission, the amount to be paid is determined by *agreement of the parties.*
120. Where one holds property absolutely to himself and his heirs forever, he is said to own the property in *fee simple.*
121. An absolute conveyance of property would be by *fee simple deed.*
122. Title to real estate passes to the grantee at the time the deed is *delivered.*
123. Two or more persons may own real estate as *tenants in common.*
124. A freehold that is limited to end with the life of the person to whom it is granted is a *life estate.*
125. A written instrument legally sufficient to transfer an estate of freehold from one person to another is a *deed.*
126. Real estate given to a person by will is known as a *devise.*
127. Stamps due on a deed are paid by the *seller,* if there is no agreement otherwise.
128. The statute which requires certain contracts relating to real estate to be in writing is the *Statute of Frauds.*
129. Where a mortgagee requires a tenant of leased premises to pay the rent to him because the mortgage is in default, he is said to be a *mortgagee in possession.*
130. An initial payment made by a possible purchaser of real estate to bind him to the terms of his offer to purchase is called *earnest money* (also known as a down payment; hand money).
131. An agent's authority to execute a binding agreement of sale for an owner must be *written.*
132. An agreement granting the exclusive right to purchase real estate for a limited period of time is known as an *option.*

133. When a tenant in common dies, his interest *goes to his heirs.*
134. *Title* is evidence of ownership in real estate.
135. *Escheat* occurs when there are no heirs to inherit property.
136. A contract between two or more parties for the use of property for consideration is known as a *lease.*
137. The main characteristic which distinguishes a lease from a license is *rent.*
138. The action of a landlord in levying upon a tenant's goods for rent in arrears is known as *distraint.*
139. A salesman must be recommended by a *broker.*
140. Funds held by a broker, belonging to others, must be kept in a *trust account.*
141. Charging more than the legal rate of interest is *usury.*
142. A written instrument which transfers possession of property, but does not transfer ownership is a *lease.*
143. A salesman in the employ of a broker put through a sale. The seller refused to pay the commission due. In order to collect, suit may be brought against the seller by the *broker.*
144. A person who acts as a real estate broker without a license is guilty of a *misdemeanor.*
145. In the event a tenant defaults in rent payments, the landlord may start an action for *distraint.*
146. If the buyer insisted that title should close upon the exact date agreed upon, the clause which should be inserted in the agreement is that time is of *the essence.*
147. The action to compel the seller to execute a deed in pursuance of a written agreement is an action for *specific performance.*
148. A owns a 1/3 interest in land. B owns a 2/3 interest. They own the land as tenants *in common.*
149. A single mortgage which covers more than one property is a *blanket mortgage.*
150. The transfer of all of a tenant's rights and interest under a lease to another is known as an *assignment.*
151. When a commercial property is being offered for sale, and a tenant wishes to renew a long-term lease, the managing broker should renew the lease with a *first right of refusal.*
152. The amount of commission to be paid a broker in a real estate deal is fixed by *agreement of parties.*
153. A lien given by the statute to those who perform work or furnish materials in the improvement of real estate is called a *mechanic's lien.*
154. The general term covering loss from any cause is called *depreciation.*
155. A measure of land consisting of 43,560 square feet is called an *acre.*
156. Where each person is possessed of the whole of an undivided part, he is a *tenant in common.*
157. A warranty deed is used in connection with the sale of *real estate.*
158. The delivery of a warranty deed usually passes *title.*
159. A broker should not act as such in selling real estate in which he has an undisclosed *interest.*
160. The section of land located in the extreme southeast corner of a township is number *36.*
161. In some states a mortgage is known as a *deed of trust.*
162. A loan not guaranteed by some governmental agency is called a *conventional* loan.
163. One who seeks to obtain leads and tips on listings and sales is known in the trade as a *"bird dog."*
164. The license law is the greatest single factor in elevating the real estate business to a *profession.*
165. A clause in a mortgage which gives the mortgagor the privilege of paying the mortgage indebtedness before it becomes due is called *pre-payment mortgage.*
166. The covenant which makes it mandatory that the seller execute any additional instruments necessary to perfect the title at any future date is called the covenant of *further assurance.*
167. A lease which requires the tenant to pay all expenses of the property in addition to his

rent is called *net lease.*

168. A real estate broker drew a lease providing that the rent was to be paid *monthly,* but did not specify therein that rent should be paid in advance. In such a case, the rent is due and payable on *the last day of the month.*
169. An authorization is made in New York State for the sale of land located in New Jersey; such authorization is enforceable in accordance with the laws of *New York.*
170. In the absence of an agreement between a real estate broker and his client as to commission, the commission is determined by *the prevailing rate.*
171. A mortgage is in default for non-payment of *interest* or *principal.*
172. In order to recover his debt, the mortgagee should institute *foreclosure* proceedings.
173. An automatic water pump used in basements to raise water to the sewer level is called a *sump* pump.
174. The Director of the license law is usually appointed by the *Real Estate Commission.*
175. A mortgage may be satisfied by payment or *foreclosure.*
176. The mortgage covenant which permits the mortgagee to advance the due date of the principal is called the *acceleration clause.*
177. Paying off a mortgage loan by regular monthly payments over an extended period of time is known as *amortization.*
178. A salesman's license pocket card should be carried with him as an *identification* to prospects.
179. A chattel mortgage is given to secure a loan on *personal property.*
180. A person who is the beneficiary under a trust of a decedent is the *cestui que trust.*
181. The relationship which results when a person transfers legal title to a property to be held for the benefit of another person is a *trustee* relationship.
182. That which belongs to something else, which passes as an incident to land, such as a right of way, is called an *appurtenance.*
183. An owner who gives an option on a property is the *optionor.*
184. Where the mortgagor is in default, the mortgagee may *foreclose.*
185. The legal compensation for the use of money is *interest.*
186. One who executes a will is called the *testator.*
187. Until the death of the testator, the will is *probated.*
188. Commission disputes between a broker and a salesman should be determined *in court.*
189. That part of the real estate instrument which identifies the subject property is called the *description.*
190. A legal document, filed in the office of the county clerk, giving notice that a court action is pending, affecting the property, is called *lis pendens.*
191. An individual who holds an option on a property is called *an optionee.*
192. A note is negotiated by *an endorsement.*
193. A freehold that is limited to end with the life of the person to whom it is granted is called a *life estate.*
194. A certificate of no defense is generally required upon a transfer of the mortgage from the *mortgagor.*
195. One who receives title under a deed is called the *grantee.*
196. The Canons by which a Realtor is governed is called the *Code of Ethics.*
197. An oral contract for the conveyance of land is unenforceable under the *Statute of Frauds.*
198. An authorization to sell real estate must be signed by the *owner.*
199. A wife's rights in her husband's property until his death are *inchoate.*
200. A *canopy* is an ornamental roof projection over a door or window.
201. The person against whom an appeal is taken in court is the *appellee.*
202. The principal element in adverse possession is *occupancy.*
203. *Foundation* is the walls of a building below the first or ground floor.
204. A roof having the same pitch on all four sides is called a *hip* roof.
205. An encroachment is a *trespass.*
206. One who has the actual possession of a mortgaged premises is a *terre tenant.*

207. An ornamental projection at the top of a wall is called *a parapet.*
208. The normal cost of exact duplication of a property, as of a certain date, is called *reproduction* cost.
209. Wood or metal members upon which the flooring rests are called *joists.*
210. Wood or metal members between the above and designed to reinforce them is called *bridging.*
211. The roof rests upon lateral members called *rafters.*
212. Vertical members to which the lath is attached are called *studs.*
213. The above rest upon a horizontal member called a *sill.*
214. A domed turret with lateral openings in a roof is called *louver.*
215. The base framing of a window opening is the *windowsill.*
216. A protruding gable on a neighbor's land is an *encroachment.*
217. An article may be changed from real estate to personalty by *detachment* or severance.
218. Generally, when looking at a map, the direction on your left will be the *west.*
219. The Federal Agency which insures a V.A. loan is the *Veterans Administration.*
220. An escrow or trust account required by law is for the protection of the *public.*
221. An important asset of a business, which is carried on the owner's books at a nominal value, is *good will.*
222. Bringing down an abstract to date is usually charged to the *seller.*
223. An increase in the value of property due to economic or related causes is known as *appreciation.*
224. A buyer should seek advice as to the meaning of terms in a contract from *an attorney.*
225. Under the law of agency, a broker is considered a *fiduciary.*
226. The person who becomes the owner of real estate upon the death of the present owner is called the *remainderman.*
227. Where a person inherits property from an adverse claimant, his adverse possession is connected through *tacking.*
228. Where one purchases property from a party who has adversely occupied it for seven years, there is *privity of contract.*
229. In the transfer of real estate, the signature of *the grantee* is not necessary on the deed.
230. The Housing Act prohibiting discrimination in the sale and rental of real estate was passed in *1968.*
231. A person who becomes the owner of real estate by will is called the *devisee.*
232. A person who becomes the owner of personal property by will is called the *legatee.*
233. A contract which transfers possession of property for a consideration is a *lease.*
234. Where each part owns an undivided part of the whole, it is a *joint tenancy.*
235. An *acceleration* clause in a mortgage advances the maturity date.
236. A person who takes title to real estate from a life tenant is a *tenant per autre vie.*
237. The contract of a minor is voidable by him until he attains his *majority.*
238. In law, a minor is also known as an *infant.*
239. A vendor in an agreement of sale corresponds to the *grantor* in a deed.
240. A deed is acknowledged so that it may be *recorded.*
241. An agreement under which an owner, for a consideration, withholds his property from the open market is called an *option.*
242. The down payment made by a buyer as evidence of good faith is called *earnest money* (hand money).
243. When the offer to purchase or land contract becomes binding, the buyer is known as the *vendee.*
244. Matters which a title company will not insure against are known as *encumbrances.*
245. A commission determined by what the services are worth is on a *quantum meruit* basis.
246. In lieu of an abstract, the seller could furnish the buyer *title* insurance.
247. The rules of the Commission must be consistent with the *provisions of the license law.*
248. Survivorship is an attribute of *joint tenancy.*
249. Giving approval by act or conduct of something done by another, without authority, is

called *ratification.*
250. A certificate showing the balance due on a mortgage at the time of closing a sale is a *reduction* certificate.
251. A unit of land measurement, 66 feet, is a *chain.*
252. The satisfaction of enjoyable living, due to the character of the neighborhood, is known as *amenities.*
253. The new name of the National Association of Real Estate Boards is *National Association of Realtors.*
254. The contour and slope of land is known as *topography.*
255. A broker, being a partner in purchase of a property is said to take "*a piece of the action.*"
256. An owner cannot terminate a broker's employment, if the broker has an agency *coupled with an interest.*
257. An exclusive agency must have a *definite* expiration date.
258. A lease calling for step-by-step rent increases is a *graduated* lease.
259. A tax on real estate according to its value is *ad valorem* tax.

Key word—Questions—True and False

(If false, give correct answer)

1. A person who lists his property for sale with another is known as the *agent.*
   A. The principal
2. A listing contract which authorizes a broker to sign a contract of sale for his owner *is unusual.*
   A. True
3. *A straight fee* may be paid by a broker to an unlicensed person who only submits listings.
   A. Nothing
4. The *Home Owners Loan Corporation* is the Federal Agency most in demand in financing home purchases.
   A. Federal Housing Administration
5. The vendor of real property becomes *the grantee* in the instrument of conveyance.
   A. Grantor
6. An agreement, under which an owner keeps his property off the market for a consideration, is known as an *exclusive listing.*
   A. Option
7. A mortgage is considered satisfied when an *offset certificate* has been filed.
   A. Satisfaction Piece
8. To be enforceable, a written listing contract must be signed by *seller* and *buyer.*
   A. Broker and Seller
9. The rule of "*caveat emptor*" applies to a tenant who leases a property in disrepair.
   A. True
10. The largest ownership in real estate is called a *remainder estate.*
    A. Fee simple
11. Permitting a later mortgage to take precedence over an earlier mortgage is termed *Right of First Refusal.*
    A. Subordination
12. A broker should prepare an agreement of sale in *duplicate.*
    A. Quadruplicate
13. An appropriation of land by an owner to some public use and accepted as such is *eminent domain.*
    A. A dedication
14. A contract of a minor is *voidable* by him until a reasonable time after he attains his majority.
    A. True
15. *A judgment* is a jurisdiction of the court.
    A. A decree

16. *Tenure* is a term used when a person occupies land against the recorded owner for a long period of time.
    A. Adverse possession
17. Items which a title company will not insure against are known as *exceptions.*
    A. True
18. Under a land contract, *the trustee* retains title until certain stipulated conditions are fulfilled.
    A. The owner
19. A listing is terminated by the death of the *salesman* who obtained it.
    A. Broker or owner
20. A person who answers the broker's ad and looks at the property is the broker's *client.*
    A. Customer
21. Placing "*For Sale*" signs on property is one of the best ways of securing new listings.
    A. "Sold" signs
22. A non-exclusive listing and *a net* listing are the same.
    A. An open
23. Violation of a material covenant in a lease by the tenant is an *eviction.*
    A. Forfeiture
24. The words, "by, from, through or under" indicate the deed from the grantor is a *general warranty deed.*
    A. Special warranty deed
25. When an agreement of sale is executed by seller and buyer, the latter acquires *equitable title.*
    A. True
26. An absolute conveyance of real property would be by a *warranty deed.*
    A. True
27. In computing the square footage of a home you would use the *outside* measurements.
    A. True
28. A suit in equity by a buyer to compel a seller to carry out the terms of an executed agreement of sale is known as *Equity of Redemption.*
    A. Specific Performance
29. *Mandamus* is a form of public notice filed against a property that a suit is about to be filed.
    A. Lis Pendens
30. The main objective of the homestead law is to protect the owner against foreclosure to *satisfy* debts.
    A. True
31. A wall on the line between two adjoining properties, owned by two different parties, is a *division* wall.
    A. Party wall
32. Deeds are acknowledged before a notary public in order to enable them to be *recorded.*
    A. True
33. If a tenant remains in possession after expiration of a lease for a three year term, he is again a tenant for *three years.*
    A. Tenant from year to year
34. Paying off a mortgage loan by regular monthly payments over an extended period of time is known as *prepayment.*
    A. Amortization
35. When a six months rent payment is required upon signing a lease, the lessor should apply such rent to the *first* six months of the lease term.
    A. The *last* six months
36. The *beneficiary* is the party who executes a deed.
    A. Grantor
37. A net listing is usually to the *owner's* advantage.
    A. *Broker's* advantage

38. A deed to Louis Stone or Henry Sloan is *void.*
    A. True
39. The government official who evaluates property for tax purposes is an *appraiser.*
    A. Assessor
40. If the owner must pay the broker a commission, should the owner sell the property during the specified period, the broker has an *exclusive* agency.
    A. Exclusive right to sell
41. Listings obtained by a salesman are considered to be the *salesman's* personal property.
    A. Broker's
42. Whether the broker is the efficient cause of the sale is a question of *law.*
    A. Fact
43. In the City Board multi-list association, a member must be a *licensed broker.*
    A. True
44. A sales agreement must be *witnessed* in order to be recorded.
    A. Acknowledged
45. Fence posts are *personal* property.
    A. Real
46. A heavy tractor used to till farm land *is not* real estate.
    A. True
47. The *buyer* should pay for the continuation of an abstract of title.
    A. Seller
48. The *seller* should pay for an attorney's examination of the title.
    A. Buyer
49. An oral contract to sell real estate is *void.*
    A. Unenforceable
50. Rescission of a real estate contract is addressed to the *law* side of the court.
    A. Equity
51. In an appeal to a higher court, the defendant in the appellate court is the *appellant.*
    A. Appellee
52. In an action before the Commission, the licensee is termed *the respondent.*
    A. True
53. Where a broker receives earnest money on a deal, he should deposit same in his *insurance account,* insured under the F.D.I.C.
    A. Escrow or Trust Account
54. Where a person operates as a real estate broker without a license he is guilty of a *felony.*
    A. Misdemeanor
55. A report setting forth the estimate of quantity, quality and value of real estate as of a certain date is known as a *summation.*
    A. Appraisal
56. All active officers in a corporation, other than the President, must hold licenses as *salesmen.*
    A. Brokers
57. The most frequent ground for which a licensee is disciplined is *misrepresentation.*
    A. True
58. A Real Estate Commission may issue a *mandamus* to compel a witness to appear before it at a hearing.
    A. Subpoena
59. License laws promote *security* to a real estate broker.
    A. Professionalization
60. *Chattel* and *personal* property mean the same.
    A. True
61. A seller generally pays for the *examination* of the abstract.
    A. Continuation
62. An incumbrance is anything which affects the *loan value.*
    A. Title

63. *Hand money* is money given to an unofficial stakeholder on a real estate deal.
    A. It is deposit or earnest money
64. The primary purpose of an acknowledgment is for *attestation.*
    A. Recording
65. Unpaid taxes on real estate constitute a *judgment.*
    A. Lien
66. Title to real estate passes to the grantee at the time the deed is *signed.*
    A. Delivered
67. Increase in land on shore or bank due to change in flow of a stream is known as *alluvion.*
    A. True
68. The interest which a wife of a partner acquires in partnership property is *dower.*
    A. Nothing
69. Two brokers can own property as *joint tenants.*
    A. True
70. A "Chain of Title" is a term often used by *surveyors.*
    A. Abstracters
71. A deed to real estate *can* be assigned.
    A. Cannot
72. A percentage lease is based on the *net profits* of the business.
    A. Gross volume
73. Taxes *have* priority over recorded mortgages.
    A. True
74. The Commission frowns on the use of *exclusive* listings.
    A. Net
75. The case of an individual charged with operating without a license is first heard by the *Real Estate Commission.*
    A. Court
76. An individual who holds an option on a property is called *an obtainer.*
    A. An optionee
77. A freehold that is limited to end with the life of the person to whom it is granted is called an *annuity.*
    A. Life estate
78. To be enforceable a listing contract must be signed by the *buyer and seller.*
    A. Broker and seller
79. A building contractor, to protect himself, when the owner refuses to pay him for work done, files a *deficiency judgment.*
    A. Mechanic's lien
80. The commission to be charged by a real estate broker is fixed by the *legislature.*
    A. Parties
81. Generally, when looking at a map, *South* will be at your right.
    A. East
82. A listing of the same property which is held by several different brokers is called a *multiple* listing.
    A. Open
83. *Devise* is the reversion of property to the state due to the lack of heirs.
    A. Escheat
84. An acre of land contains 43,650 square feet.
    A. 43,560
85. The "*Chain of Title*" is found in the Abstract of Title.
    A. True
86. Pro-ration of taxes between seller and buyer is *apportionment.*
    A. True
87. A broker may lawfully receive a commission from a *co-broker.*
    A. True

88. Commission disputes between broker and salesman should be brought before the *Real Estate Commission.*
    A. In court
89. The person ordinarily liable for the payment of utilities for a leased property is the *lessee.*
    A. True
90. A certificate of no defense is the same as an *estoppel certificate.*
    A. True
91. Where a buyer refuses to go through with a deal, the seller should make *specific performance.*
    A. Tender of deed and demand of purchase price
92. Any licensed broker who is a bona fide member of a national service club is a *Realtor.*
    A. Not true
93. The *lessee* generally pays the taxes on leased property.
    A. Lessor
94. A contract with a minor is *void.*
    A. Voidable by the minor
95. In numbering a township section, number 6 is always in the *northwest* corner.
    A. True
96. The amount of earnest money to be paid is determined by a *minimum of 5 per cent of the purchase price.*
    A. Agreement of the parties
97. As a general rule the *optionee* has the right to collect rents on the optioned property during the life of the option.
    A. Optionor
98. A unit of measure 5,280 feet long is a *chain.*
    A. Mile
99. A dividing wall between two buildings, owned separately, which is used by both properties, is a *brick* wall.
    A. Party
100. An individual appointed by a court to settle a deceased person's estate is called a *guardian.*
    A. Administrator
101. If the owner refuses to pay an earned commission, the broker should file *a lien.*
    A. A suit in court
102. Title to vacant land may be conveyed by executing *a bill of sale.*
    A. A deed
103. If a broker is delinquent in paying his annual renewal fee, his license is *considered to be in force for only the thirty day grace period.*
    A. Cancelled
104. A *binder* is a decree of court declaring one individual is indebted to another and fixing the amount of such indebtedness.
    A. Judgment
105. *The beneficiary* is the one who gives a mortgage on his property in return for a loan.
    A. The mortgagor
106. *Title I* of the FHA Act provides for unsecured home improvement and repair loans.
    A. True
107. The *"Fanny Mae" organization* was set up by the Federal Government to create a secondary mortgage market.
    A. True
108. A mortgage represents a *liquid* asset of the mortgagee.
    A. Frozen
109. Farm property cannot be leased for more than *twenty years.*
    A. Any period
110. Broken windows in a leased premises are the responsibility of *the tenant.*
    A. True

111. The legal compensation for the use of money is called *rent.*
    A. Interest
112. A purchaser at a foreclosure sale usually receives a *Bargain and Sale deed.*
    A. Sheriff's deed, tax deed
113. A lease cannot be recorded unless it is acknowledged by the *notary public.*
    A. Lessor
114. There are *36* feet in a rod.
    A. 16 ½
115. There are *36* sections in a township.
    A. True
116. Title to real estate passes when the deed is *signed, sealed and recorded.*
    A. Signed, sealed and delivered.
117. Quantum meruit in law means what his services are worth.
    A. True
118. A good title and a *marketable* title are generally considered to mean the same thing.
    A. True
119. There are *360* acres in a section.
    A. 640
120. There are *forty* acres in the SE ¼ of the NW ¼ of the NE ¼ of a section of land.
    A. Ten
121. When a grantor faultily signs a deed, he can be compelled to execute a *reformation* deed.
    A. True
122. Witnessing a deed is *attestation* of the deed.
    A. True
123. A quit claim deed is used to remove an *out-dated mortgage.*
    A. Cloud on title
124. A main objective of the Homestead Law is to protect against *executions* to satisfy debts.
    A. True
125. A deed acknowledged in a foreign country should be before a *notary public of that country.*
    A. Minister or Consul of this country
126. Owner of a condominium unit is able to obtain *F.H.A.* financing.
    A. True
127. Condominium ownership is the result of a *federal* enabling act.
    A. State
128. *Alluvial land* is generally unproductive land on which the cost of production approximates the gross return.
    A. Marginal
129. The process of paying off a loan by installments is known as *acceleration.*
    A. Amortization
130. A decision of the Real Estate Commission may be appealed to the *Attorney General.*
    A. Court
131. *Tenancy at Sufferance* is the leasing by a tenant to another.
    A. Subletting
132. A *zoning ordinance* is an ordinance of a city limiting the character and use of property.
    A. True
133. A suit to quiet title is used to remove an *out-dated mortgage.*
    A. True
134. Failure to perform terms of a contract is a *default.*
    A. True
135. Horizontal rows of townships are called *ranges.*
    A. Tiers
136. A *suit for specific performance* is used to remove a cloud on the title.
    A. Suit to quiet title

137. Mortgage guaranteed by the Veteran's Administration is an *F.H.A. mortgage.*
 A. V.A. mortgage
138. An action to correct a mistake in a deed is called *redemption.*
 A. Reformation
139. Metes and bounds refer to the *topography* of the land.
 A. Direction and distance of the boundaries
140. A judgment is an agreed upon *stipulation* of both parties in a law suit.
 A. A court decree
141. Rate of commission to be charged is fixed by the *Real Estate Commission.*
 A. Contract
142. Forfeiture is the violation of a material provision in the lease by the *landlord.*
 A. False
143. From the grantee's standpoint a *special* warranty deed is preferable.
 A. General warranty
144. The SE $1/4$ of the SE $1/4$ of the NW $1/4$ of a section contains *20* acres.
 A. 10 acres
145. The highest ownership which may be enjoyed in real estate is *absolute* title.
 A. Fee simple
146. When a person dies without leaving a will he is said to have died *inchoate.*
 A. Intestate
147. *Alluvion* is the wearing away of land by streams and the elements.
 A. Erosion
148. A percentage lease is based on the *net profits* of the business.
 A. Gross volume of sales
149. *Negotiation* of a note is signing on the reverse side of the instrument.
 A. Endorsement
150. A lease to a husband and wife creates an *estate by the entireties.*
 A. A leasehold
151. A purchaser at a foreclosure sale receives a deed from the *mortgagee.*
 A. Sheriff
152. A plumber, to protect himself for unpaid work, may file a *deficiency* judgment.
 A. Mechanics lien
153. The apportioning of taxes, rents, mortgage interests and insurance is called *marshalling.*
 A. Pro-rating
154. If the buyer is to obtain an amortized mortgage, the agreement should specify amount, interest rate and *monthly installments.*
 A. True
155. A licensed broker may lawfully pay a part of his commission to a licensed *salesman* of another broker.
 A. Licensed broker
156. Procuring listings by house to house solicitation is unethical.
 A. True
157. *Earnest money* is the compensation which a broker receives in a deal.
 A. Commission
158. Adding an adverse possessor's occupancy to a previous adverse occupancy constitutes *acceleration.*
 A. Tacking
159. A *deficiency judgment* is the difference between amount owed on a mortgage and the price realized at a foreclosure sale on the mortgage.
 A. True
160. The common law interest which a husband has in and to his wife's estate at her death is known as *dower.*
 A. Curtesy

Chapter 12

SIMPLE ARITHMETIC, LAND DESCRIPTION PROBLEMS, AND CLOSING STATEMENTS

A knowledge of simple arithmetic is basic to the real estate business. The problems used in this section identify with arithmetic problems encountered in everyday real estate practice. The approach to even a simple problem should be unhurried and, whenever possible, should be double checked for accuracy. Simple arithmetic problems are anchored to the "four corners" of addition, subtraction, multiplication and division.

TABLES OF LAND MEASURE

Linear Measure

1 link	= 7.92 inches
1 rod	= 16½ feet; 5½ yards
1 chain	= 66 feet; 4 rods
1 furlong	= 660 feet
1 mile	= 5,280 feet

Square Measure

1 acre	= 160 sq. rods; 43,560 sq. ft.
1 section	= 640 acres
1 sq. mile	= 640 acres
1 township	= 36 sq. miles

(For detailed working of arithmetic problems, see end of chapter.)

1. Q. How much would it cost to develop a parking lot allowing 300 square feet for each parking space on a plot 500 front feet and 300 feet deep, if paving costs $.60 per square foot; curbs and gutters cost $5.00 a front foot to be installed only on a front foot basis and lighting costs are $5,000?
   A. $97,500
2. Q. How many parking spaces will be provided on the above lot?
   A. 500 spaces
3. Q. A broker has sold three lots for a total of $10,000. Since the second lot was sold for $1,200 more than the first, and the third lot brought $1,600 more than the second, what did each lot sell for?
   A. $2,000; $3,200; $4,800
4. Q. McDonald buys a storage building containing 8,000 square feet for $72,000. His gross rental is based at $1.75 per square foot of rental area. His total expenses are $7,000 for the year 1973. What was his 1973 return on his investment?
   A. 9.72 + percent
5. Q. Jack Elder has a two acre tract of land which he is subdividing into lots. He plans to make each lot 60 feet by 190 feet in depth. If he provides a center street 28 feet wide by 210 feet in depth, how many full lots will Elder be able to market?
   A. 7 lots

6. Q. On a plot prepared for a subdivision, 1/8 inch represents one foot of land. One lot is shown as 6 1/2 inches wide. According to the scale, what is the width of the lot?
   A. 52 feet
7. Q. Brown listed a commercial lot for sale with Betty Edwards, Realtor, at $24,000. The lot is 90 ft. front and 180 ft. deep. Edwards received an offer from King at $250.00 per front foot. She also received an offer from Queen at $1.25 per square foot. Which is the better offer and by how much?
   A. King's offer by $2,250.
8. Q. An apartment building has 3 floors and each floor contains 4 units. First floor units rent for $125 per month each, second floor units rent at $120 each and third floor units rent at $110.00 each. Total yearly expense is $2,800.00. The owner receives 8 per cent return on his investment. What is the value of his investment?
   A. $178,000.
9. Q. A man borrowed $1,500, which he agreed to repay at 5 1/2% interest a year. He paid $25 interest; how long did he keep the money?
   A. 3 months, 20 days
10. Q. A broker sells the NW 1/4; NW 1/4; SE 1/4; Sec. 31; T 4 NR 5 EMB for the owner at $225 per acre. The commission is 5%. The broker must pay 10% of the commission to the salesman, who listed the property. What is the net amount the broker receives in the sale?
   A. $101.25
11. Q. A man has an opportunity to buy a lot for $1,000, and a guarantee of resale value one year later of $1,200. He also has an opportunity to lend $1,000 to an individual with repayment within a year at 10% interest. Which is the better investment and by what amount ?
   A. $100 better for lot.
12. Q. A tract of land contains 348,480 sq. ft. It sold for $800 per acre. What was the total selling price?
   A. $6,400
13. Q. A piece of farm equipment cost $11,000 and its usefulness will end in 20 years. What is the depreciation per year in terms of money and per cent ?
   A. $550 depreciation per year
   5% depreciation per year
14. Q. How many acres are there in the S. ½ of the N.E. ¼ of the S.W. ¼ of the S.W. ¼ of a section?
   A. 5 acres
15. Q. $2,000 is equal to 8% of the price paid for a dwelling. What was the price paid ?
   A. $25,000
16. Q. What is the annual interest rate on an $8,000 loan when the interest payments are $120 per quarter on the loan?
   A. 6%
17. Q. If the rate of interest is 6% per annum and your monthly interest payment is $100, what is the amount of the debt ?
   A. $20,000
18. Q. Which of the following is preferable from an investor's standpoint on a $10,000 principal (a) 3 months at an annual interest rate of 8% (b) 4 months at an annual interest rate of 7%?
   A. (b) $33.33 more interest
19. Q. Which of the following tracts contains the most acres (a) N 1/2 of the S 1/2 of the N.W. 1/4 of Section 16 (b) W 1/2 of the E 1/2 of the S.E. 1/4 of Section 16?
   A. Same acreage
20. Q. Which is greater in value (a) 6/5 X $300 or (b) 5/6 X $360?
   A. (a) by $60
21. Q. An apartment building shows a profit of $425 per month and is earning 8 per cent

on the entire investment. What is the building worth?

A. $63,750.00

22. Q. A real estate broker, at closing, deducted a commission of 5%. The owner then received $15,751.00. What was the selling price?

A. $16,580.00

23. Q. A salesman sells $2\frac{1}{2}$ sections of land to a subdivider for $50 an acre. What is his commission if he receives 40% of a 5% commission?

A. $1,600

24. Q. A rectangular piece of ground has a frontage of 450 feet and a depth of 600 feet. At $100 per acre, what is the selling price?

A. $620

25. Q. Alberts and Briggs purchased an apartment building for $20,000. Alberts contributed $12,000. Briggs invests $8,000. At the end of the year, the net profit is $12,000. How much will each partner receive based on his investment?

A. (a) Alberts, $7,200 (b) Briggs, $4,800

26. Q. Allen Michaels, Realtor, is a member of Garden City Council. As chairman of the Finance Committee, he is requested to figure the real estate tax rate. Real estate assessments total $4,540,000. Subsidies and license fees aggregate $77,800. Expenses for the 1972 year are estimated at $147,800. What should be the tax rate per $1,000 of assessment?

A. $15.41

27. Q. Adams buys a new home for $20,000 with F.H.A. financing. He makes an initial payment of $3,600 and minimum monthly payments on the principal at $97.79 per month. How many years will be required to pay off his indebtedness?

A. 14 years

28. Q. Adams purchases a dwelling for $25,000. He makes a $5,000 deposit and agrees to 6% interest on the unpaid debt, plus $100 per month on the principal. He sells the house two months later for $28,000 to Brown who assumes the mortgage. How much interest has Adams paid? Brown will receive credit on the purchase price for what amount?

A. (a) $199.50 (b) $19,800

29. Q. Taxes of $92.46 are due and payable on January 1 of each year. If paid before January 31, a discount of $2\frac{1}{2}$ per cent is allowed. Thompson pays his tax on January 26, 1972. What amount does he pay?

A. $90.15

30. Q. Chandler bought a house for $6,700, paying $1,200 cash and a purchase money mortgage for the balance at 5%. In addition to the interest on the mortgage and an annual depreciation of 2%, his annual expenses total $227. His rent income is $60 per month. What was Chandler's net return on his cash investment?

A. $84; 7%

31. Q. Coburn buys a house as an investment for $7,500. His annual expenses are: Taxes, $75.25; Insurance, $18.15; Repairs, $115.10. What rent must he charge to realize $4\frac{1}{2}\%$ on his investment?

A. $45.50 mo. rental

32. Q. A rose bush grows in the middle of a circular plot that has a diameter of 3 yards. At 25 cents a foot, what will it cost to enclose the rose bush?

A. $7.07, cost

33. Q. A $10,000 loan at seven per cent interest with equal monthly payments to principal and interest can be amortized in 20 years at a total cost to the borrower of $15,600. Compute (a) the monthly payment and (b) that portion applied to the principal for the first month.

A. (a) $65.00 (b) $6.67

34. Q. Jones bought a 4 family apartment house for $45,000, paying $20,000 cash, giving a mortgage for the balance at 6%. The lot is valued at $10,000. Each apartment

rented for $125 a month. Expenses on the mortgage interest at 6%; depreciation at 2%; taxes, insurance and repairs were $1,825. What is his rate of income?
A. $1,975, net income, or, 4.38%

35. Q. A salesman's half of a 5 per cent commission on a $6,250 sale would be how much?
A. $156.25

36. Q. If a man's income is $195 per month and his home cost 2 ½ times his annual income, the home would cost him how much?
A. $5,850.00

37. Q. What is the annual interest rate on a $6,000 loan when the interest payments are $210 semi-annually on the full amount ?
A. 7%

38. Q. The value of a house at the end of 4 years was estimated to be $8,725. What was the original cost of the house if the annual rate of depreciation was 4 ¼ per cent ?
A. $10,512.04

39. Q. On September 1, 1971, Jones purchased a 3 year comprehensive insurance policy for 90 per cent of its $24,000 value. The insurance premium was 54 cents per $100 of the policy. Jones sold the house on April 1, 1972. What was the pro rata share of the premium owed by the buyer?
A. $93.96

40. Q. Biggs and Diggs buy an apartment building for $40,000. Biggs contributes $24,000 to the purchase price and Diggs contributes $16,000. At the end of the first year, the net profit is $3,000. How much will each receive?
A. Biggs, $1,800; Diggs, $1,200

41. Q. Michael Gordon, Realtor, is Chairman of the Garden City Council's Finance Committee. He is requested to compute the millage tax rate for combined city and school for 1973. Real Estate assessments total $6,500,000. Subsidies and license fees will yield $85,000 for the year. Operating expenses for 1973 are estimated at $200,000. What should be the tax rate per $1,000 of the assessed real estate?
A. $17.69

42. Q. The John Grove residence in Garden City, valued at $30,000, is assessed at 30% of its market value. What will be his tax in 1973 ?
A. $159.21

43. Q. In the above case, the taxes are due January 1 of each year in Garden City, but if paid by January 31, a discount of 5% is allowed. If Grove pays his tax on January 10, 1973, how much will he save?
A. $7.96

44. Q. Lane offers to sell an income property to Sloan. The income is $250 per month and the total annual expenses are $900. Sloan figures on a 7% return on his investment. How much should he offer Lane?
A. $30,000

45. Q. What is the square foot area of a circle with a radius of 6 feet?
A. 113.10 square feet

46. Q. Waldo owns a corner lot 250 feet wide and 350 feet in depth. To keep people from trespassing, Waldo erects a fence around the lot. The fence cost him 35 cents per foot. What was the cost of the entire fence?
A. $420

47. Q. Jones owns a chestnut tree, dating back to the American revolution. He desires to enclose the ground surrounding the tree by a circular tract, having a diameter of four yards. The cost of the fence will be 30 cents per foot. What will the fence cost ?
A. $11.31

48. Q. If an investor purchased an apartment building for $90,000 and received an annual net income of $6,750, what percentage on his investment did the property earn?
A. 7 ½ per cent

49. Q. Evans entered into a contract with Harper, a builder, to construct a house for him

on a cost plus 15 per cent basis. The contractor made the following expenditures: Foundation and masonry, $2,800; lumber and carpenter work, $2,400; plumbing, $2,450; heating and air-conditioning, $2,850; electrical work and equipment, $3,000; painting, $1,400; landscaping, $790; roofing, $900; extras, $700. What was the total cost of the house?

A. $19,883.50

50. Q. Included in the sale of furnishings in a house was an oriental rug, which cost the owner $750, and which he sold to the buyer for $450. What percentage of loss did the owner suffer?

A. 40 per cent

51. Q. A mortgage company agreed to lend an owner 80% of its appraised value at 6% interest per annum. If the interest payment for the first month is $96, what was the appraised valuation?

A. $24,000

52. Q. Taylor bought an apartment building for $72,000 and received a net return of $500 per month. What was his percentage return on his investment?

A. 8⅓ per cent

53. Q. Adams buys a new dwelling for $25,500 and makes an initial deposit of $5,500. He then obtains an F.H.A. mortgage for the balance. The minimum monthly payment on the indebtedness is $100. How many years will be required to pay off the mortgage, excluding interest payments?

A. 16 years, 8 months

54. Q. Chanas purchases a dwelling for $25,000. He pays $5,000 cash and gives the seller, Saxton, a purchase money mortgage for the balance at 6% interest, with $100 monthly to be paid on the principal. He sells the property two months later to Logue for the original purchase price. (a) How much interest has Chanas paid? (b) On the closing statement, Saxton will be credited with what amount?

A. (a) $199.50 (b) $19,800

55. Q. A broker sells a lot 50′ front by 100′ in depth for 75 cents a square foot. His commission is 10 per cent. How much does the seller receive?

A. $3,375

56. Q. What is the purchase price of a property, if a 20% earnest money deposit is $2,500?

A. $12,500

57. Q. A lot 69 feet wide and 142 feet in depth sold for $2,645.46. How much did the owner receive per square foot?

A. 27 cents

58. Q. The owner of a block of 14 building lots, each 75 feet front, desires to realize $33,750 from the tract keeping for himself, two lots. What would be the sales price per front foot?

A. $37.50

59. Q. What is the cost of a tract of land 264 feet wide by 660 feet deep at $800 per acre?

A. $3,200

60. Q. If the annual 5 per cent interest payment on a mortgage amounts to $350, what is the amount of principal?

A. $7,000

61. Q. A lot 80 feet by 120 feet deep cost $75 per front foot. What is the cost of the lot?

A. $6,000

62. Q. A man built a house which was rectangular in shape. The dimensions were 24 feet by 36 feet. What is the total number of square feet in this house?

A. 864 sq. ft.

63. Q. A loan made April 17 is repaid June 26. For how many days should the interest be calculated?

A. 69 days

64. Q. How many board feet are there in 48 pieces of 2″ X 4″ lumber, each of which is

12 feet long?
A. 384 board feet

65\. Q. January 1 to March 15 is what fraction of a year?
A. $\frac{5}{24}$ of a year

66\. Q. Three and one-half months is what fraction of a year?
A. $\frac{7}{24}$ of a year

67\. Q. The decimal .375 is equal to what fraction?
A. $\frac{3}{8}$

68\. Q. The decimal .38 $\frac{1}{3}$ is equal to what fraction?
A. $\frac{23}{60}$

69\. Q. The fraction $\frac{1}{8}$ is what per cent?
A. 12 $\frac{1}{2}$%

70\. Q. The fraction $\frac{1}{6}$ is what per cent?
A. 16 $\frac{2}{3}$%

71\. Q. What is the sum of $\frac{1}{2}$ and $\frac{3}{4}$ and $\frac{1}{8}$?
A. 1 $\frac{3}{8}$

72\. Q. What is the difference between 1 $\frac{1}{4}$ and $\frac{3}{8}$?
A. $\frac{7}{8}$

73\. Q. One-half acre and five-eighths acre and three-sixteenths acre equals how many acres?
A. 1 $\frac{5}{16}$ acres

74\. Q. If a farmer sells one-half of 20 acres and plans to divide one-fourth of the balance into lots, how many acres are left?
A. 7 $\frac{1}{2}$ acres

75\. Q. What is one-half of one-fourth?
A. $\frac{1}{8}$

76\. Q. What is one-half divided by one-fourth?
A. 2

77\. Q. Twenty-five days is what part of a year?
A. $\frac{5}{73}$

78\. Q. Twenty-one days is what part of a month?
A. $\frac{7}{10}$ or .7

79\. Q. Three-fifths is equivalent to what per cent?
A. 60%

80\. Q. Eighty-seven and one-half per cent is equivalent to what fraction?
A. $\frac{7}{8}$

81\. Q. Six months is what part of three years?
A. $\frac{1}{6}$

82\. Q. How much is $\frac{2}{3}$ multiplied by $\frac{1}{2}$?
A. $\frac{1}{3}$

83\. Q. How much is $\frac{2}{3}$ divided by $\frac{1}{2}$?
A. $\frac{4}{3}$ or 1 $\frac{1}{3}$

84\. Q. How much is $\frac{1}{2}$ divided by $\frac{2}{3}$?
A. $\frac{3}{4}$

85\. Q. Two-thirds of a year is how many months?
A. 8 months

86\. Q. One-fifth of a year is how many days?
A. 73 days

87\. Q. One-sixth of an acre is how many square feet?
A. 7,260 sq. ft.

88\. Q. What part of an acre is 5,445 square feet?
A. $\frac{1}{8}$ acre

89\. Q. A farmer wants to sell part of his land but one-fourth he is giving to his son; $\frac{3}{16}$ to his daughter. What part of the land is left to sell?
A. $\frac{9}{16}$

90. Q. Add: $26\,1/2 + 19\,3/4 + 8\,5/6 + 44\,2/3$
A. $99\,3/4$

91. Q. Divide: $18\,1/2 \div 4\,1/6$
A. $4\,11/25$

92. Q. $223.65 is $5\,1/4$% of what amount?
A. $4,260.00

93. Q. Multiply: .75 X .83 $1/3$ (express your answer in lowest fraction)
A. $5/8$

94. Q. The value of a frame home at the end of 7 years was estimated to be $8,085. What was the original cost if the yearly depreciation was $2\,1/2$%?
A. $9,800.00

95. Q. A property sells for $19,750.
You as listing salesman are to receive $12\,1/2$% of the total 6% commission collected on the sale.
What amount will you receive?
A. $148.13

96. Q. What is the interest rate on a $13,800 loan when the monthly interest payments are $71.30 on the full amount?
A. 6.2 or $6\,1/5$%

97. Q. An owner lists property for sale with a broker to net him $9,000, after paying the broker a 7 per cent commission. At what price would the broker have to sell the property?
A. $9,677.42

98. Q. A property was listed for sale with a broker at $30,000. The actual sale was made at 10% less than the listed price. The commission rate is 7%. What loss in commission did the broker incur by not selling at the listing price?
A. $210.

99. Q. A vacant lot has 60 feet frontage and 80 feet width in the rear, the depth is 150 feet. The property was sold for $13,125.00. What was the price per square foot?
A. $1.25.

100. Q. A room is 20 feet in length, 17 feet wide and $9\,1/2$ feet high. What is the volume (cubic feet)?
A. 3,230 cubic feet.

101. Q. What is the square foot area of the opposite figure "A"?

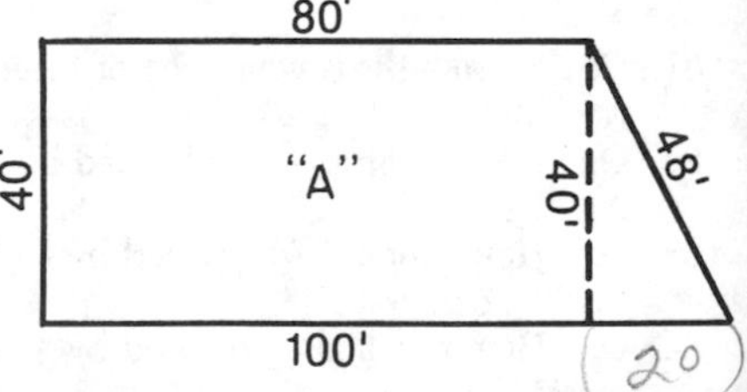

A. 3600 square feet.

102. Q. The legal description of a farm is N.W. $1/4$ of the N.W. $1/4$ and the N. $1/2$ of the N.E. $1/4$ of the N.W. $1/4$ of Section 17, Township 6 N, Range 3E of the Boise Meridian. How many acres in the farm?
A. 60 acres.

103. Q. What would be the appraisal of a bungalow 30 feet by 40 feet at a replacement cost of $15.00 per square foot, allowing 3 per cent depreciation for 3 years?
A. $16,380.

104. Q. Mary Crow receives a rental of $100 per month and her expenses are $360.00 per year. What is her net income per month?
A. $70.

105. Q. Stone's house is assessed at 50 per cent of its market value for the triennial period

1974, 1975, 1976. Stone bought the property on December 6, 1973 for $22,000.00. The adjusted tax rate is 62 mills. What is the tax for 1974?

A. $682.

106. Q. A farm fronts on two roads running at right angles to each other. The frontage on one road is 5,280 feet, and on the other 2,640 feet. A third boundary line runs parallel to the shorter of the two road frontages, alongside the farm for a distance of 5,280 feet. How many acres in the farm?

A. 480 acres

107. Q. The mortgage loan on a house is $9,500. The monthly interest and amortization of principal require $9.50 per $1,000 of loan. The annual taxes are $291. The fire and extended coverage insurance rate is 98¢ per $100 on a three year policy on the amount of the original loan.

a. What is the monthly payment on interest and principal?
b. What is the monthly tax payment?
c. What is the monthly insurance payment?
d. What is the total monthly payment to be made on interest, principal, taxes and insurance?

A. a. $90.25
b. $24.25
c. $2.59
d. $117.09

108. Q. A tract of land is bisected by a stream, leaving two triangular plots. One lot has a street frontage of 500 feet and a depth of 760 feet. How many acres does it (the one lot) contain?

A. 4.36 acres

109. Q. A farm earns $3,600 net after allowing $24 a month for all expenses. A buyer wants 6 per cent return on his money. What would he have to pay for the farm so as to gross 6 per cent?

A. $64,800

110. Q. One "rule of thumb" says that a person can afford to buy a home costing 2 ½ times his annual income.
What would be the minimum weekly salary of a factory worker to buy an $18,915 home using this rule?

A. $145.50

111. Q. A subdivider purchased a parcel of land 1320′ by 1980′.
How many ⅓ acre sites can he obtain in this parcel allowing 16 ⅔% of the total for streets and a school site?

A. 150

112. Q. An owner of a home had it listed for sale at a price which exceeded the F.H.A. appraisal by 15 per cent. He lowered the asking price to the appraisal figure, which was $9,265.
What was the original listing price?

A. $10,654.75

113. Q. A lot 75′ wide and 115′ deep is assessed at $24 per front foot. The house is assessed at 4.8 times that of the lot. The tax rate is 68 mills. What are the annual taxes?

A. $709.92

114. Q. The owner of a farm said that ¼ was not usable, ⅗ was under cultivation, the remaining 60 acres was a grass meadow. How many acres in the whole farm?

A. 400 acres

115. Q. A house is 27 feet long, 18 feet wide, and 9 feet high.
Contractor "A" bids 29¢ per cubic foot, not including attic.
Contractor "B" bids $1.95 per square foot of floor area, plus $17.50 per cubic yard of concrete used for a 6″concrete floor.
Contractor "C" bids $1,195.

(a) Q. What was contractor "A's" bid?
A. $1,268.46

(b) Q. What was contractor "B's" bid?
A. $1,105.20

(c) Q. Which contractor bid the lowest?
A. B

(d) Q. What is the dollar difference between the high and low bid?
A. $163.26

116. Q. A broker sold a lot 125 feet wide and 160 feet deep for 17 cents per square foot, but the purchaser assumed a paving lien of $2.25 per front foot. What total amount would the purchaser have to ask for the property if he expected to make a profit of $295 and give a clear title to the property?
A. $3,976.25

117. Q. If a man has a $325 weekly gross income from his property and a monthly expense of $845 on it, what is the annual per cent of interest return on his investment of $84,500?
A. 8 per cent

118. Q. What is the interest on $4,000 for 3 years, 5 months, and 20 days at 6 $\frac{1}{2}$ per cent per annum?
A. $902.80

119. Q. A salesman has an agreement with his broker that all commissions collected on sales are to be divided as follows: 10% to the salesman who obtains the listing and the balance to be divided equally between the broker and the salesman who makes the sale. Salesman closes a $23,000 sale and the office collects a 5% commission of the gross sales price. What is the amount of commission earned by a salesman who made the sale but did not obtain the listing?
A. $517.50

120. Q. A sale was closed on a 190 acre farm on March 1, 1974. The sale price was $175.50 per acre. The buyers paid $5,000 in cash at the time of making the offer and agreed to assume a mortgage of $18,300, plus interest of $183, and signed a contract of sale in the amount of $3,972.07. How much additional cash did the buyer need at closing?
A. $5,889.93

121. Q. Jones built a house which was 26 feet by 38 feet and the average height was 14 feet. What is the number of cubic feet in this house?
A. 13,832 cu. ft.

122. Q. James Brown built a home which was 28 feet by 40 feet. It was a single-story ranch type. The cost of building averaged $11.25 per square foot. What was the total cost of the home?
A. $12,600

123. Q. Cole is asked to appraise an open lot with no improvements on it. The neighborhood is about 75 per cent built up. Most lots in the area are from 55 to 65 feet wide. The lot under appraisal is 60 feet. Comparable sales are found which indicate that lots are selling from $60 to $75 per front foot. What is a good estimate of price range for this lot?
A. $4,050

124. Q. An owner insists upon receiving $8,250 net for his property and will pay the broker 5% commission. What sales price must be asked to accomplish this?
A. $8,684.21

125. Q. What is the annual interest rate on a $5,000 loan when the quarterly interest payments are $93.75?
A. 7 $\frac{1}{2}$%

126. Q. What will the taxes be for six months on property valued at $8,000 if the tax rate is $2.27 per $100 valuation per year?
A. $90.80

127. Q. An acre of land contains 43,560 sq. ft. What is the cost of a lot 132 ft. by 330 ft. at $800 per acre?
A. $800.00

128. Q. How much additional cash must a buyer furnish in addition to his $500 deposit if the lending institution grants 60% on an $8,000 home?
A. $2,700.00

129. Q. A man purchased a building for $120,000. His gross income was $23,000 per year. His expenses amounted to $11,000. What rate of return did he earn on his investment?
A. 10%

130. Q. An apartment house owner receives $4,800 per year net income from his investment of $60,000. What percentage does he receive on his money?
A. 8%

131. Q. $57.50 is 5% of what sum?
A. $1,150.00

132. Q. A lot 75 feet wide and 110 feet deep sold for $8,750.
What was the price per front foot?
What was the price per square foot?
A. $116.67 per front foot
$1.06 per square foot

133. Q. A broker sold a lot of 75 feet frontage by a depth of 120 feet at a price of 20¢ per square foot but the purchaser was to assume sewer and paving bills at the rate of $5.50 per front foot.
The buyer stated that he would list the property but would expect a profit of 10% plus the broker's commission of $590.00.
What would the new price be?
A. $3,023.75

134. Q. A two-story house cost $8,568 to build.
If the house had a frontage of 34 feet, a depth of 28 feet and was 30 feet high including the basement, what was the cost of the house per cubic foot?
A. $.30 per cubic foot

135. Q. If you bought two lots for $4,000 each, then made three lots out of this parcel and sold the lots for $3,000 each, how much did you make?
What per cent of profit was this on your investment?
A. $1,000.00
12 ½%

136. Q. A property has a net income of $8,500 a year.
If you want to earn 8% on your investment, how much would you pay for the property to realize this rate of return?
A. $106,250.00

137. Q. Compute the cost of excavation for a cellar 25 feet wide, 30 feet long and 5 feet deep at $2.90 per cubic yard.
A. $402.78

138. Q. You represent a seller offering a tract of land 495 feet wide and 1,320 feet deep. The selling price is at the rate of $200.00 per acre. What is the total price?
A. $3,000.00

139. Q. A man bought two lots for $3,000 each, divided them into three lots and sold the three lots for $2,400 each.
What was his percentage of gross profit?
A. 20%

140. Q. Bell wishes to build a flat-roofed building 130 feet long, 30 feet wide and 24 feet high.
Dusch offers to build such a structure for $8.90 per square foot.
Sherwin offers to build the building for $.37 ½ per cubic foot.
How much will Bell save by giving the building contract to Dusch?

A. $390.00

141. Q. In a contract for sale of real estate, the sales price is fixed at $6,000 and of this amount $1,200 is paid down at the time of the sale and the balance is payable in monthly installments of $50.00 plus and in addition to which the buyer pays interest. The contract is dated January 1, 1974, and the 1st payment is due February 1, 1974. Assuming that all payments are made regularly and not more than $50.00 is paid on the principal on any installment date, state when contract will be paid in full.

A. January 1, 1982

142. Q. Jones is working on a 50-50 split commission with your firm. He sells the S 1/2 of the NE 1/4 of Sec. 27, T-8-N, R-14-E of 6th P.M. for $207.50 per acre.
The commission schedule for your agency calls for 5% on the first $20,000; 3% on the next $15,000; and 1 1/2% on the balance of the selling price.
Jones must pay 7 1/2% of his share of the commission to Lawrence, the salesman who listed the property.
What is the net amount Jones will receive for this sale?

A. $383.87

143. Q. There is a balance of $9,000 due on a real estate contract that requires monthly payments of $80.00 plus interest at 6% per annum payable monthly.
What would be the total monthly payments for:
(a) the first month (b) the third month (c) the fifth month?

A. (a) $125.00
(b) $124.20
(c)$123.40

144. Q. A broker has a problem of subdividing a ten acre tract into 50 X 100 foot lots; after allowing 85,600 square feet for the necessary streets, how many lots will the broker realize from this subdivision?

A. 70

145. Q. A certain commercial property was a two story structure. It measured 46 feet by 80 feet. The height of the first story was 16 feet and the second was 14 feet. The estimated unit cost of reproduction is 80¢ per cubic foot for the first story and 60¢ per cubic foot for the second story. What is the estimated reproduction cost of this building?

A. $78,016.00

146. Q. A man bought two lots, one for $3,000 which was 60% of the cost of the other. What was the cost of the other lot?

A. $5,000

147. Q. There is an F.H.A. conditional commitment on a duplex which is not going to be occupied by owners, for $24,750. On closing the loan the mortgage banker collected a 4% discount. The F.H.A. insured value rates were as follows:
97% of the first $15,000
90% of the next $5,000
75% of the balance, not to exceed $27,500
Because the owner is not going to live in the property, he can borrow only 85% of the amount which he could borrow if he did occupy the property. How much discount will the borrower have to pay (in dollars and cents)?

A. $768.83

148. Q. Lawrence leased a storeroom to Davis on a percentage basis. The lease calls for a minimum monthly rental of $400 plus 5% of the gross yearly business over $80,000. How much rent would Lawrence receive yearly from Davis, if Davis did a gross business of $120,000?

A. $6,800.00

149. Q. A 6,400 square foot hillside lot is to be subdivided and sold. One-fourth of the lot is too steep to be useful and 3/16 of the lot is taken up by a small stream. The

remaining area is flat. If 1/8 of the usable area is reserved for roads, how many square feet of usable area is left ?

A. 3,150 sq. ft.

150. Q. A lot measuring 100 feet wide and 330 feet deep, would be approximately what fraction of an acre?

A. 3/4 acre

151. Q. There is a close relationship between the monthly rent obtainable for a property and the price the property will bring on the market. In an area that was beginning to run down, properties on the average were selling for 92 times their monthly rent. In a newer district they were selling for 112 times the rent. If a property had a monthly rental of $95 per month, what would it be worth in each of the areas?

A. $8,740 in older district; $10,640 in newer district

152. Q. A man purchased a lot for $2,000. He built a house on the lot which cost $14,500. During the construction period, he had several offers to rent the property for $125 per month. Six months after he moved in, the city condemned 15 feet of the front of the lot for widening the street to speed up traffic. In attempting to rent the house, he found that the best offer was $110 per month. By investigation we find that the current capitalization rate is 6%.

a. What type of depreciation has this property suffered ?

b. By capitalizing the loss of income, what is the amount of loss in value?

A. a. Economic depreciation

b. $3,000

153. Q. Assuming that Mr. Davis has $13,500 invested in his property, what will be the net return on his investment (in percentage) per year if he rents his property for $150 per month and if the yearly cost for taxes is $396; for insurance $66; and for miscellaneous expense $123 ?

A. 9%

154. Q. An office building has a total income of $53,200 per year. The yearly expenses are: Taxes, $8,925.25; Insurance, $1,510.60; Heating and Air-conditioning, $4,920.05; and Miscellaneous Expense, $3,644.10. If the owner values the building at $360,000, what will be his net return?

A. $34,200

155. Q. Cooper sold two vacant lots for a total of $11,389, which was 15 per cent more than he paid for them three years ago. During the time he owned the lots, he paid taxes each year at the rate of 48 mills on the assessed valuation of 45 per cent of his purchase price. If he figures a yearly interest loss of 3 1/2 per cent on his original investment, what was his profit or loss?

A. $195.53 loss

156. Q. A lot is 50 feet front by 180 feet. The owner, John Davis, had only $5,000 cash. The lot cost $63 per front foot, and the house cost was $9,216. He secured a mortgage for the balance. If his interest was 5 1/2 per cent per annum, payable semi-annually, what was the amount of his first semi-annual interest payment ?

A. $202.57

157. Q. The above owner, Davis, decided to build a fence around his original lot. The cost of the fence was 80¢ per linear foot excluding gates at the front and rear of the lot. These gates are 3 1/2 feet wide and cost $16.75 each. What is the total cost of the fence including the gates?

A. $395.90

158. Q. Davis next decides to construct a driveway. Concrete costs $13.50 per cubic yard and labor costs are 20¢ per square foot. What will be the total cost of the driveway which is 36 feet long, 8 feet wide and 3 inches thick ?

A. $93.59

159. Q. A loan made April 17 is repaid June 26. For how many days should the interest be calculated ?

A. 69 days

160. Q. Jim Underwood and John Davis traded properties. Underwood's property was valued at $14,250. Davis' property was valued at $17,350. The difference in equities was $2,015.07. Underwood's equity was $4,901.25. His equity is greater than Davis' equity. What was the total amount of encumbrance against each property?
A. Underwood $9,348.75
Davis $14,463.82

161. Q. How many cubic yards of gravel would be needed to fill a trench 36 feet long, 9 feet wide and 18 inches deep?
A. 18 cubic yards

162. Q. J. R. Brady pays $125 a month rent. He could buy the property for $9,800. He has $2,000 in his savings account earning 2% per year, compounded semi-annually; fire insurance premium is $22.50 per annum; taxes are $146.40 annually; upkeep is 1½% of property cost; and depreciation is 2% of the property cost. He could borrow the remainder of the purchase price at 4 ½% interest per year.
(a) What would be the total cost of owning the house the first year?
(b) What would he save by owning instead of renting?
A. (a) $903.10
(b) $556.70

163. Q. Charles Walker has purchased a lot for $9,000. It has a frontage of 100 feet and contains one-half acre of land. Ascertain what the lot cost. (a) per front foot. (b) per square foot. (c) what it would cost per acre. (d) what is the depth of the lot ?
A. (a) $90. (b) 41 cents. (c) $18,000. (d) 217.8 feet.

164. Q. If building costs are $12.50 per sq. ft. and you build a house 33′ wide X 48′ long, with an offset for a game room of an additional 6′ X 20′, how much would it cost to build the house?
A. $21,300

165. Q. If 5 ¼% is the annual rate of interest and the monthly interest payment is $58.45, what is the amount of the original loan?
A. $13,360

166. Q. A broker is sub-dividing a 4 ½ acre tract into 50′ X 100′ lots. After allowing 71,020 square feet for the necessary streets, in how many lots can the tract be divided ?
A. 25 lots

167. Q. There is a balance of $7,500 due on a land purchase contract that requires monthly payments of $60.00 plus interest at 6% per annum, payable monthly. What would be the total payment for the 1st, 3rd and 5th months?
A. $97.50; $96.90; $96.30

168. Q. What would be the F.H.A. insurable loan on a dwelling if the F.H.A. insured 97% of the first $13,500 of valuation and 85% of the remainder and the F.H.A. valuation is $18,500 ?
A. $17,345

169. Q. Montgomery owns a property which gives him a gross income of $1,600 per month. His annual expenses are 45%. What is his net income per year on the property?
A. $10,560

170. Q. Bennett has a principal balance of $6,000 on his mortgage. His interest rate is 5% per annum. His taxes and insurance total $108 per year. His monthly payment is $60, covering interest, taxes, insurance, and the balance applied to principal. What is his principal balance after making the first payment ?
A. $5,974

171. Q. A building has been leased to a supermart with the rent based on 1 ½% of the gross sales, with a minimum rental of $10,000 annually.
(a) If its first year sales were $600,000, how much rent was paid ?
(b) If its fourth year sales were $1,000,000, how much rent was paid ?
A. (a) $10,000
(b) $15,000

172. Q. A property is worth $16,000 and the furniture and household effects are worth $5,600. The owner insures them at 72% of their value. The annual rate on the dwelling is $3.10 per $1,000 and $3.65 on the personal property. If the premium for a 3-year policy is 2 ½ times the premium for one year, how much can the owner save by taking out a 3-year policy?
A. $25.21

173. Q. What is the annual interest rate on a $6,000 loan when the interest payments are $105 semi-annually on the full amount?
A. 3 ½%

174. Q. $25 is 5% of what amount?
A. $500

175. Q. How many square feet are there in 2 ½ acres?
A. 108,900 square feet

176. Q. A 28 acre farm was sold at $157.50 per acre. The broker's commission was 6%. The sales person making the sale received 60 percent of the commission. How much did the salesperson receive?
A. $158.76

177. Q. If the semi-annual interest payment is $654.50 on a mortgage of $15,400, what is the interest rate?
A. 8 ½%

178. Q. An owner lists a property with a broker, under an agreement that the owner will receive $16,500 for the property. The owner agrees to pay the broker a 6% commission. What will be the selling price?
A. $17,553.19

179. Q. If 24 acres of land cost $3,600, what would 87 ½ acres cost?
A. $13,125

180. Q. What is the amount of quarterly interest on a $12,000 loan at 8% interest per year?
A. $240

181. Q. Add:

	(a)	(b)	(c)
	46,329	267.00	396.87
	5,271,743	1,109.87	1,875.29
	3,243	4,854.27	209.01
	17,874	26.77	7,365.54
	620,734		68.58
A.	5,959,923	6,257.91	9,915.29

182. Q. The loan on a property is 65% of its appraised valuation. If the interest rate is 5% and the first semi-annual interest payment is $167.50, what is the appraised value of the property?
A. $10,307.69

183. Q. John Kane, salesman, is working on a 50-50 split commission with his employer broker, L. Fairchild. Kane sells a 280-acre farm at $105 per acre. The commission schedule calls for 5% on the first $15,000; 3 ½% on the next $10,000 and 2% on the balance. Kane must pay another salesman, Paul Stark, who listed the property, 10% of his share of the commission. What is the net amount Kane will receive?
A. $534.60

184. Q. There is a balance of $12,000 due on a real estate contract that requires monthly payments of $120, plus interest, at 5% per annum, payable monthly. What would be the total monthly payments for the first month, third month, fifth month?
A. First month—$170 Third Month—$169 Fifth Month—$168

185. Q. A salesman brings in a listing on a $5,000 home and is to receive 10% of the total 5% commission when the property is sold. If a second salesman sells the house and

the 10% is deducted from his half of the commission, the second salesman would receive how much?

A. $100

186. Q. The assessed value of all property in the city of Uranium is $12,000,000. The city budget is $600,000. Your property is assessed at $40,000. What taxes would you pay?

A. $2,000

187. Q. A broker receives half the first month's rent for leasing an apartment and 5% of each month's rent thereafter for collecting the rent of $85 per month. What would be his total commission after 18 months?

A. $114.75

188. Q. The taxes on a house were $126. The taxes were due January 1st and were paid by the owner. What refund would he get from a purchaser if he sold the house and the taxes were prorated as of September 15th?

A. $36.75

189. Q. The schedule of commissions for negotiating a 20-year lease was 5% for the first year, 2% for each of the next four years, 1 ½% for each of the next 10 years, and 1% for each year thereafter. What was the total commission earned if the yearly rent was $6,500?

A. $2,145

190. Q. A man has an opportunity to buy a lot for $1,000 and a guarantee of resale value one year later of $1,200. He also has an opportunity to lend $1,000 to an individual with repayment within a year at 10% interest. Which is the better investment and by what amount?

A. The lot by $100

191. Q. A man borrows $1,000 for 9 months at 5% per year. What amount does he have to repay?

A. $1,037.50

192. Q. A man borrows money for 6 months at 6% payable in advance. How much must he borrow in order to have $1,000 cash immediately?

A. $1,030.93

193. Q. A lending institution advertises that it has no hidden charges or costs—that the charge on loans is simply 3% on the unpaid balance each month. If a man borrows $120.00 and pays $10.00 plus interest each month, what is the actual rate of interest paid for the year?

A. 19 ½%

194. Q. If a man receives $525.00 at the end of 6 months on money invested at 6% per year, how much has he invested?

A. $17,500

195. Q. A real estate broker receives 5% commission for selling a house for $16,800. How much did the salesman receive? How much did the owner receive?

A. $840, broker received $15,960, owner received.

196. Q. If property is assessed at $14,000 and the tax rate is $21 per $1,000 of assessed valuation, how much will the tax be?

A. $294.00

197. Q. A man borrowed $1,500 which he agreed to repay at 5 ½% interest a year. He paid $25 interest; how long did he keep the money?

A. 3 months 22 days

198. Q. A construction company developing a new shopping center borrowed $2,000,000 repayable in 5 years. If $550,000 interest was paid, what was the rate of interest?

A. 5 ½%

199. Q. A man bought a farm for $8,800 and sold it for $10,000. His selling expenses were $100.00. His profit was what per cent of the cost?

A. 12 ½%

200. Q. If Mr. Jones had a furnished patio at the rear of his home, he could sell his property

for $15,000. Without this addition, he can get only $14,500. If a 12′ by 18′ pavement 4″thick costs $18.00 a cubic yard and labor $1.80 per cubic yard, barbecue pit $35.00, and furniture $212.00, how much profit would Mr. Jones make by adding and furnishing a patio?

A. $200.20

201. Q. How many acres are there in the following diagram?

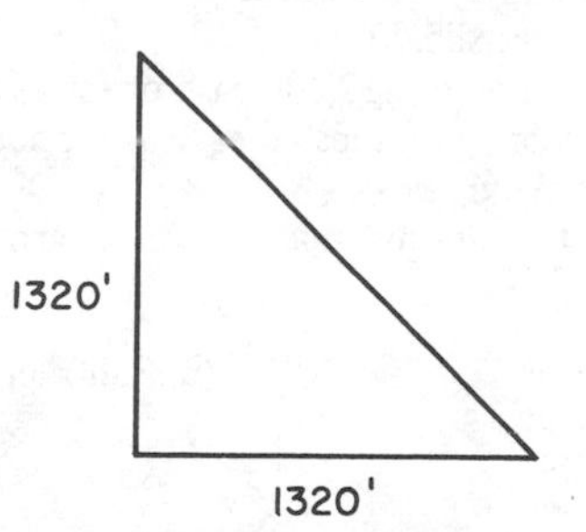

A. 20 acres

202. Q. A house and lot sold for $22,500. The transaction closed on May 15, 1974. A first trust deed and note with a balance of $15,200 at time of closing, bearing interest at 6¼ per cent per annum and payments of $100 per month, including interest, on the first day of each month, is assumed by the purchaser. Payments are current. What interest is due on the loan at the time of closing?

A. $39.58

203. Q. A small acreage sold for $3,600. A cash payment of $1,200 was made and the balance is to be paid in four equal annual principal instalments plus interest. The interest rate on all deferred payments is 6 per cent. What amount will be paid in interest?

A. $360

204. Q. At the end of a six month period, a borrower paid $600 of the principal, plus the interest due, on a loan of $2,400 at 6% interest. He made regular payments annually of $600 plus interest due until the loan was repaid. What was his total interest cost?

A. $288

205. Q. Adams owns nine acres of downtown property which he listed for sale with Brown for $78,300. Crowe would like to purchase a part of the listed property. He requires 100 feet X 145.2 feet. Based on the listed price, what will he have to pay for this portion?

A. $2,900

206. Q. Ray Upton inherited $6,500, which was 2 1/6 times as much as his sister Ann received. How much did Ann inherit?

A. $3,000

207. Q. A building burned 16 bulbs at 25 watts each, 24 hours a day, and 2 bulbs (25 watts each) burned 12 hours daily. All bulbs are used every day. What is the June electric bill if the cost is based on 3 1/2 ¢ per kilowatt-hour?

A. $10.71

208. Q. The perimeter of a rectangular lot is 108 yards. The length is 6 yards greater than twice the width. What are the length and width of the lot?

A. 16 yards X 38 yards

209. Q. Mr. Brown bought a home for $25,000, built a swimming pool costing $1,500 and spent $625 on filtering and cleaning equipment. The following month he received an unexpected promotion and had to relocate in another state. If he listed his property at $30,000, how much profit could he expect to make? What per cent would the profit be over his investment?

A. $2,875; 10.6%

210. Q. Mr. Gray has a $5,000 mortgage on his summer home. He makes quarterly payments of $300.00 plus 6% annual interest on the balance. How much did he pay for the first year including interest?
A. $1,473

211. Q. A man has an option of buying a house for $21,000 cash or for $1,000 down and three annual payments of $7,000. If his money realizes 5% compounded annually, which is the better plan and by how much?
A. The payment plan by $85.00

212. Q. A man can buy a house for $12,500 cash or for $4,000 down and $9,000 at the end of the year. If his money is invested at 5% compounded semi-annually, which plan should he follow? Why?
A. Pay $12,500 cash because his money cannot earn the $500 difference in one year.

213. Q.

	(a) Add:	(b) Subtract:	(c) Multiply:
	$756.32		
	827.56		
	432.47		
	761.33	$981,876.03	$41,986
	532.45	−897,439.98	×499
A.	$3,310.13	$ 84,436.05	$20,951,014

214. Q. A salesman sells a property for $5,800. His contract with the broker is 60% to the broker and 40% to salesman. The sales commission with the owner is 5%. What is the broker's share of the commissions?
A. $174

215. Q. You are employed as a salesman by Henry Bowen and Co. It is agreed that all commissions collected by the office on sales made by you are to be divided as follows: 10% to the sales manager and the balance to be divided equally between your employer and yourself. You close a deal on which the sales price is $8,500 and the office collects a 5% commission on the sales price. What amount of commission is due you?
A. $191.25

216. Q. A note is dated April 15, 1971, the amount of the note is $1,700; the interest rate is 5%; interest is payable quarterly; none of the interest is paid. How much interest will be due on January 15, 1972?
A. $63.75

217. Q. The value of a frame house at the end of 6 years was estimated to be $7,650. What was the original cost of the house if the yearly rate of depreciation was 2 ½% ?
A. $9,000

218. Q. The commission rate for selling an apartment house was 5% of the first $10,000 and 2 ½% for all over that amount. The broker received a commission of $730. What did the property sell for?
A. $19,200

219. Q. In a contract for the sale of real estate, the sales price is fixed at $5,800. Of this amount $1,600 is paid down at the time of sale, and the balance is payable in monthly installments of not less than $30 each, in addition to which the buyer pays the accrued interest. The contract is dated January 2, 1971; the first principal payment is due February 1, 1971. Assuming that all payments are made regularly and not more than $30 is paid on principal on any installment date, state when the contract will be paid out in full.
A. September 2, 1982

220. Q. The real value of a certain property is $6,000. It is assessed at 60% of its real value.

It is taxed at the rate of 55 mills on the assessed value. What are the taxes?

A. $198

221. Q. A broker sold a lot 60 ft. by 120 ft. at the price of 10 cents per square foot, but the purchaser assumed a paving lien of $2.50 per front foot. What price would the purchaser have to ask for the lot if he wanted to sell at a profit of $150 and give clear title to the lot ?

A. $1,020

222. Q. Subtract:

(a)	(b)	(c)
2,869,520	5,214.21	8,476,521
100,271	1,007.10	−3,720,900

A.

(a)	(b)	(c)
2,679,246	517.03	4,747,615

223. Q. The tax schedule on real estate in the City of Sun Valley is 22 mills, school tax 30 mills, and county tax is 12 ½ mills. Gerold's property was purchased in 1974 for $30,000. The tax rate is 50% of market value. What taxes will Gerold pay?

A. $967.50

224. Q. Multiply:

(a)	(b)	(c)
$ 41986	7.24	.731
×499	×38.7	×64.3

A.

(a)	(b)	(c)
377874	5068	2193
377874	5792	2924
167944	2172	4386
$20,951,014	280.188	47.0033

225. Q. A property is assessed at two-thirds of its market value. The property was purchased on June 16, 1974 at $18,000. The tax is 42 ¼ mills. What is the annual amount of tax?

A. $510

226. Q. Divide:

```
         6747.19                     2159.37
951) 6416582            .1152) 248.7612
     5706                        2304
      7105                        1836
      6657                        1152
       4488                        6841
       3804                        5760
        6842                       10812
        6657                       10368
         1850                        4440
          951                        3456
         8990                        9840
         8559                        8014
          431                         826
```

227. Q. (a) How much would it cost, per parking space, to develop a parking area, each space to be 10 ft. X 20 ft. in an area 250 feet front and 200 ft. deep, if asphalt costs 60 cents per square foot to install, curb and gutters are to be installed only across the frontage, at a cost of $5.00 per linear foot. Lighting costs $5,000?

(b) How many parking units will the area contain?

A. (a) $145

(b) 250 parking spaces

228. Q. Haines received $31,150 for his property, after paying a 5 per cent commission. What was the selling price?
A. $32,789.47

229. Q. What would be the appraisal value of a 3 year old ranch house, 28 ft. X 40 ft., using the cost approach, if replacement cost is $15 per square foot, allowing 2 ½ per cent annual depreciation?
A. $15,540

230. Q. A six unit apartment building has a gross income of $1,500 per month. Annual expenses, excluding depreciation, are $7,200. Allow 5% for vacancy and uncollected rent. A prospective buyer desires an 8 per cent, overall, return on his investment. What price should he offer for the property?
A. $123,750

231.

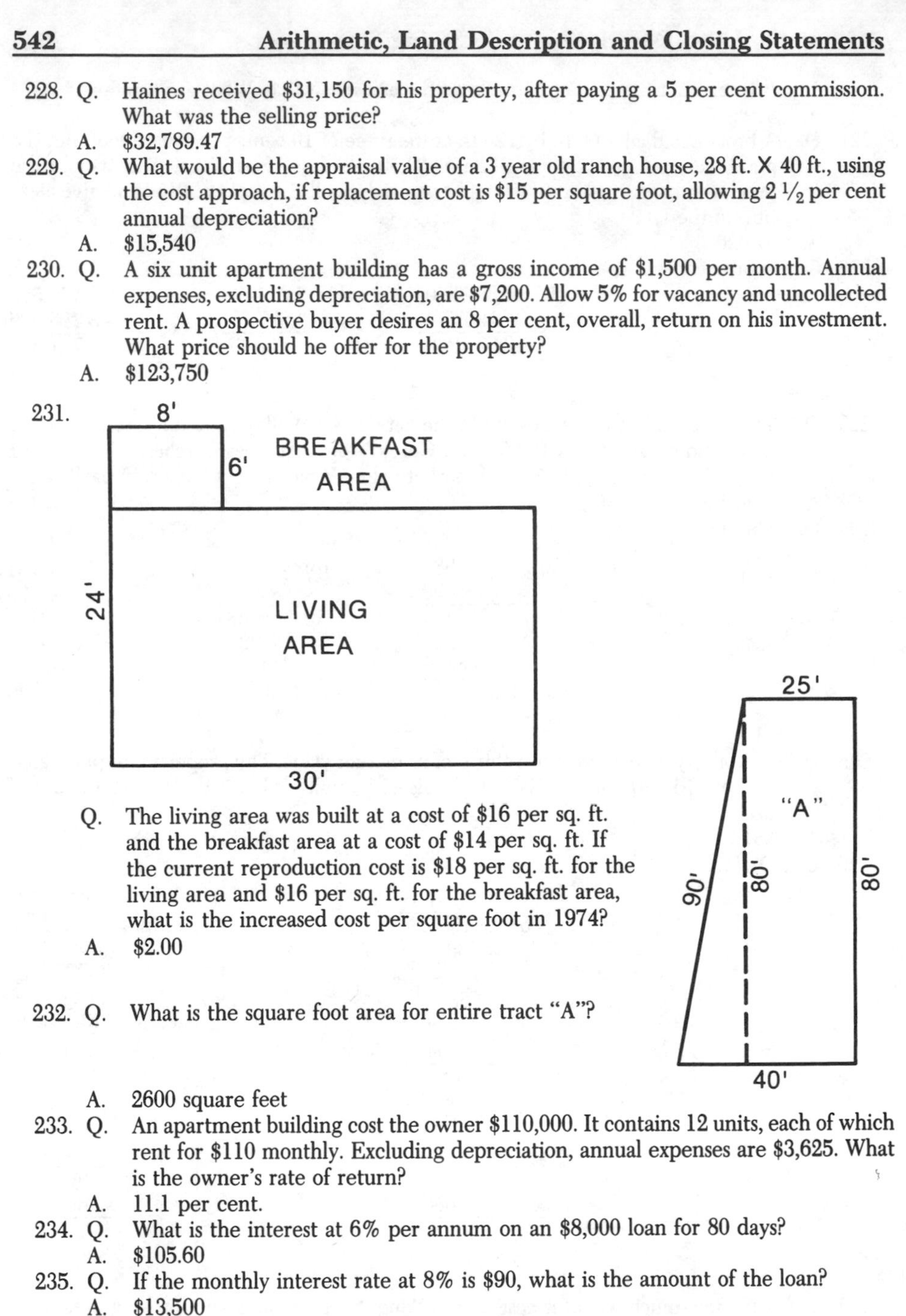

Q. The living area was built at a cost of $16 per sq. ft. and the breakfast area at a cost of $14 per sq. ft. If the current reproduction cost is $18 per sq. ft. for the living area and $16 per sq. ft. for the breakfast area, what is the increased cost per square foot in 1974?
A. $2.00

232. Q. What is the square foot area for entire tract "A"?
A. 2600 square feet

233. Q. An apartment building cost the owner $110,000. It contains 12 units, each of which rent for $110 monthly. Excluding depreciation, annual expenses are $3,625. What is the owner's rate of return?
A. 11.1 per cent.

234. Q. What is the interest at 6% per annum on an $8,000 loan for 80 days?
A. $105.60

235. Q. If the monthly interest rate at 8% is $90, what is the amount of the loan?
A. $13,500

236. Q. Divide the fraction 7/8 into the decimal equivalent.
A. .875

237. Q. A tract of land is 90 feet by 90 feet. Adams owns one-half of the tract. How many square feet in the Adams' tract?
A. 4,050 sq. ft.

238. Q. Assume that a buyer of real estate, as part of the purchase price, gives back to the

seller a mortgage for $20,000, bearing interest at the rate of 4% per annum. The principal of the mortgage is to be repaid in installments of not less than $500 each, plus the interest accrued at the time of payment of each installment. The mortgage is dated December 1, 1973 and the first installment is due March 1, 1974. What sum will be due on the mortgage on March 1, 1974?

A. $700

239. Q. On September 1, 1973, you gave your note bearing said date to a mortgage company in which you promised to pay $2,000 in monthly installments of not less than $35 each inclusive of interest at 6% per annum on the monthly balances of the note. Each payment as made is applied (1) to accrued interest and (2) to reduction of the principal of the note. You make only the following payments:

October 1, 1973	$35
November 1, 1973	$60
December 1, 1973	$45

On January 1, 1974 (a) how much have you paid as interest? (b) what is the unpaid balance of the note?

A. (a) $29.49 (b) $1,898.94

240. Q. Taxes on a parcel of property are $1,325.28 for the current year. The first one-half of the taxes were paid by the seller. The deal will be closed as of December 15. In prorating the taxes, how much should be charged the seller for his share?

A. $607.42

241. Q. A man has property which gives him a gross income of $325 per month, his monthly expenses average $155 per month, what is his net income per year on the property?

A. $2,040

242. Q. Figure the cost of a tract of land 250 ft. frontage by 750 ft. in depth, at a cost of $950 per acre.

A. $4,088.80

243. Q. The selling price of a certain property is $13,000. The sale can be financed if the buyer can pay 18% down, plus a loan commission of 1.5% of the loan. How much money must the buyer have to pay the down payment and loan cost?

A. $2,499.90

244. Q. A tract of land, 65 ft. wide and 150 ft. deep sold for $1.25 per sq. ft., plus $10 for each front foot. What was the price of the land?

A. $12,837.50

245. Q. A piece of property 326.7 feet long and 200 feet wide is for sale. The owner wants $5,000 an acre. What is the selling price?

A. $7,500

246. Q. A certain commercial property was a two-story structure. It measured 46′ X 80′. The height of the first story was 16′ and the second was 14′. The estimated unit cost of reproduction is eighty cents per cubic foot for the first story and sixty cents per cubic foot for the second story. What is the estimated reproduction cost of this building?

A. $78,016

247. Q. The length of the South side of the NE 1/4 of the NE 1/4 of a section is how many feet?

A. 1,320 feet

248. Q. What would be the cost to build a driveway 36 feet long, 9 feet wide, and 4 inches thick if concrete costs $15 per cubic yard and labor costs are twenty cents per square foot?

A. $124.80

249. Q. An investor paid $36,000 for a four-unit apartment house. Each apartment rents for $85 per month. It is estimated that by good management a profit of 45% of gross rentals could be made. What rate of return should this man make on his investment?

A. 5.1%

250. Q. How many acres are there in the W $1/2$ of the SW $1/4$ of the SW $1/4$ of a section?
A. 20 acres

251.

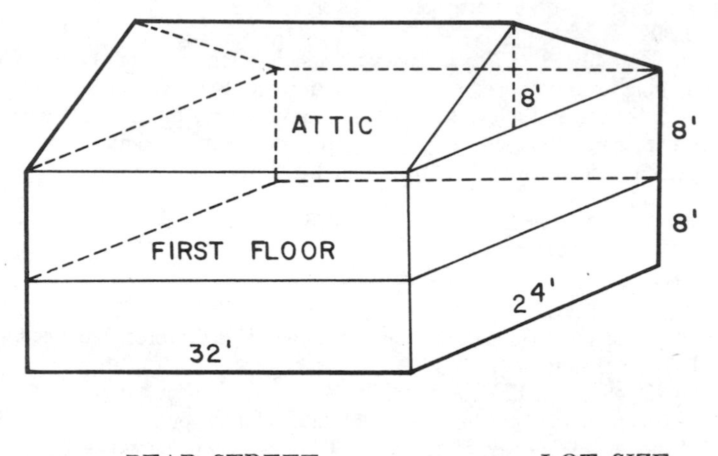

PEAR STREET

LOT SIZE
50′ wide
180′ deep

The house shown in the diagram was built by Mr. Brown on a lot 50 feet by 180 feet. This is a one-story house, with basement and expansion attic.
The house faces south and fronts on Pear Street.
The following 15 questions are based, at least partially, on the diagram.

Q. What is the total cubic content of the house, including attic and basement?
A. 15,360 cubic feet

252. Q. What is the building cost of the house per square foot of main floor space if the cost of the house, exclusive of the lot, was $10,828.80?
A. $14.10

253. Q. The assessed valuation of the 50 foot lot was $44 per front foot. The house was assessed at $6,500. The tax rate is 48 mills. What are the yearly taxes?
A. $417.60

254. Q. Mr. Brown had only $6,500 cash. The lot cost $65 per front foot, and the house cost was $10,828.80. He secured a mortgage for the balance. If his interest was 5% per annum, payable semi-annually, what was the amount of his first semi-annual interest payment?
A. $189.47

255. Q. Mr. Brown received two bids for the construction of the house. The bid from "A" was for 77 $1/2$ ¢ per cubic foot for the main floor, basement and attic. The second bid, from "B" was for $4.70 per square foot of floor area for the main floor, basement and attic. Which was the lower bid? How much lower?
A. "B" $1,075.20 lower

256. Q. If the house cost $10,828.80 to build, and depreciated an average of 2% each year, what would be the value of the entire property at the end of ten years, if, in the meantime, the 50 foot lot had increased in value 22% above its original cost of $65 per front foot?
A. $12,628.04

257. Q. Mr. Brown paid $65 per front foot for his lot. He paid $10,828.80 to the building contractor and paid the architect 5% of the building cost. He then placed a mortgage on the property for three-fourths of the total cost. What was his equity in the property, after he placed the mortgage?
A. $3,655.06

258. Q. Mr. Brown decided to build a fence around his original lot. The cost of the fence was 85¢ per linear foot excluding gates at the front and rear of the lot. These 4-foot gates cost $21.75 each. What is the total cost of the fence including the gates?
A. $427.70

259. Q. Concrete costs $14.25 per cubic yard and labor costs are 27¢ per square foot. What will be the total cost of Mr. Brown's driveway which is 36 feet long, 6 feet wide and 4 inches thick?
A. $96.32

260. Q. Assuming that Mr. Brown has $14,000 invested in his property, what will be the net return on his investment (in percentage) in 1974, if he rents his property for $155 per month and if the yearly cost for taxes is $402; for insurance $78; and for miscellaneous expense $260?
A. 8%

261. Q. The monthly payments on the mortgage referred to in Question 254 above are $75 including interest at 6% per annum on the unpaid balance. All payments are due and payable on the 10th day of each month. If the first monthly payment was made on May 10th of this year and if all subsequent payments have been made when due, what would be the principal balance after making the June payment this year?
A. $10,924.74

262. Q. Mr. Brown paid $65 per front foot for his original lot. He later decided to enlarge the original lot and can buy adjoining land to the east at a price of $1.50 per square foot. He wants to limit his total investment in land to $7,300. How many square feet will there be in his entire lot after he buys the additional land?
A. 11,700 sq. ft.

263. Q. Mr. Brown owned a lot immediately to the west of his original lot. He sold this extra lot for $4,250 net after paying the commission. He had owned the lot for 5 years and during that time he had paid taxes on it at the rate of $42.25 per year per $1,000 of assessed valuation which was 55% of the original purchase price of $3,100. If you figure an annual 4% interest loss on his original investment, did Mr. Brown make a profit or take a loss on this transaction?
A. Profit, $169.82

264. Q. Mr. Brown has purchased a 1 ½ acre hillside lot at the rear of his original lot which he intends to sell for building purposes. One-fourth of the lot is too steep to be useful and one-third of the lot is taken up by a small stream. The remaining area is flat. If one-sixth of the usable area is reserved for roads, how many square feet will be left for building purposes?
A. 22,687.5 sq. ft.

265. Q. Don Duncan, a salesman, is working on a 50-50 split commission basis with your firm. He sells Mr. Brown's property for 15% less than the listed price of $17,000. The commission schedule of your firm calls for 6% on the full selling price. Duncan must pay another salesman, Roy Rayer, 20% of his share of the commission. What is the net amount Duncan will receive for the sale?
A. $346.80

266. Q. What is the annual interest rate on an $8,000 loan when the interest payments are $100 per quarter on the full amount?
A. 5%

267. Q. A property sold for $50,000 with a down payment of 15%. The first mortgage (Deed of Trust) for the balance is payable at $7.50 per thousand per month, including interest at 5 ½% per annum. What will be the monthly payments?
A. $318.75

268. Q. An investment property has averaged a net income of $3,000 per year over the past five years. The owner has charged off adequate depreciation during the period. Assuming that 5% is a fair profit on this property, what is a reasonable estimate of the capitalized value of the property?
A. $60,000

269. Q. A lot 69 feet wide and 142 feet long sold for $2,645.46. How much would the owner receive per square foot?
A. Twenty-seven cents

270. Q. A broker sells a 50′ X 100′ lot for 75¢ a square foot. If the sales commission is 5%, how much does the seller receive?
A. $3,562.50

271. Q. What is the annual rate of interest on a $4,200 loan when the quarterly interest payments are $57.55?
A. 5 ½%

272. Q. A farm of 60 acres, listed for sale at $150 per acre, was finally sold for $7,650 on condition that the purchaser pay the 10% commission of the sale price. How much did the buyer save below the list price?
A. $585

273. Q. A seller paid his 1974 taxes in the amount of $300. He sells the property on March 15, 1974. He should receive a tax refund from the buyer in what amount?
A. $237.50

274. Q. Brown leases a storeroom to Smith on a percentage basis. The lease calls for a minimum monthly rental of $300 and 5% on the gross yearly business over $80,000. How much rent would Brown receive yearly from Smith if Smith did a gross business of $120,000?
A. $5,600

275. Q. A lot 86 feet wide and 110 feet deep sold for $7,095. What was the price per front foot? Per square foot?
A. $82.50 per front foot
$.75 per square foot

276. Q. You have determined that there are 1,600 square feet in a house, and the garage is 20′ X 30′. The cost of the building of the house is $11 per square foot and $4 per square foot for the garage. The 50 foot lot on which the house is located costs $15 per front foot. What is the total cost of the house, garage, and lot?
A. $20,750

277. Q. C. D. Sloan built a house 33′ 6″ X 45′ 6″, which had an offset for the family room of an additional 5′ X 15′. If construction costs were $12.85 per square foot, how much would it cost to build the house?
A. $20,550.36

278. Q. A lot near Manor Creek has been appraised as follows: 3,250 square feet hillside area at $0.14 a square foot; 2,000 square feet of stream area at $0.08 ½ a square foot and 7,250 square feet of flat area at $1.00 a square foot. If the tract is to be sold as a whole, what must the price be per square foot?
A. $0.63 per square foot

279. Q. A property was sold on the basis of 5 per cent commission on the first $10,000 of the sale and 2 ½ per cent on the excess amount over $10,000. The total commission was $730. What was the selling price of the property?
A. $19,200

280. Q. John Ford is building two patios. One is in the shape of a square, with 30 feet on each side. The other is in the form of a circle, with a diameter of 27 feet. Which is the larger and by how much?
A. a. Square
b. 327.735 square feet larger

281. Q. A room in an office building is 40 feet long, 24 feet wide and 15 feet high. How many

workers should occupy the room, if 200 cubic feet of air space is allocated to each person?

A. 72 persons

282. Q. A basement is 20 feet long, 15 feet wide. How many cubic yards of earth were removed, if the basement was dug to a depth of 9 feet? It cost the owner $3.40 per cubic yard of earth removed. What was the total cost?

A. a. 100 cubic yards
b. $340

283. Q. Smith is building a house with dimensions of 45 feet by 25 feet and 8 feet deep. If he engages trucks capable of carrying 4 cubic yards each, how many truck-loads will be required in the excavation operation?

A. 84 truck-loads

284. Q. Smith also employs a well digger, whose rate is $9.00 for the first foot dug and an increase of $1.25 for each additional foot dug. Before the well was fully completed, it was necessary to dig 60 feet. What was the cost of the well?

A. $2,752.50

285. Q. Stone has moved into a new office, measuring 15 feet by 24 feet. He purchases wall-to-wall carpet at $14.95 per square yard; what did the carpet cost him?

A. $598

286. Q. Mrs. Stone has bought a new home and intends to make her own window drapes. A helpful salesman tells her there are 8 windows to be draped and each requires 2 yards of material. She purchased the material at a sale at $3.90 per yard. What did the drapes cost her?

A. $62.40

287. Q. "A" is exchanging his house for a farm owned by "B." "A" agrees to allow "B," the owner of the 240 acre farm, $60 per acre to apply on "A's" house, which is valued at $23,500. How much cash difference will "B" owe "A"?

A. $9,100

288. Q. Louis Dubbs, Broker, has a property listed at $16,000. George Adams purchases it for $13,600 and sells it for $16,000. What percentage profit did he make?

A. 17.6%

289. Q. A man purchased a building for $120,000. His gross income was $23,000 per year and his expenses were $11,000. What rate of return would he receive on his investment?

A. 10%

290. Q. The 1974 taxes on a residence are $400; the millage rate for all taxes is 40 mills. The taxing authority has assessed property at 50% of the established market value. What is the market value?

A. $20,000

291. Q. If an apartment building costing $21,000 has an income of $140 per month, what percentage would it be returning annually on the investment?

A. 8%

292. Q. Mr. Stone has a principal balance of $6,000 on his mortgage. His interest rate is 5% per annum. His monthly payment is $60 for interest, and the balance applied against the principal. What is his principal balance after making his first payment?

A. $5,965

293. Q. The sales price of a property is $10,000. The land value is $1,500. What amount of fire insurance should be recommended that the buyer carry?

A. $8,500

294. Q. A section of land is exactly square and contains exactly 640 acres and all boundaries run exactly north and south, or east and west, as the case may be, and a person buys all land in the section lying southwesterly of a line which crosses the section and running north 45° west, at $1,250 per acre, cash on date of closing. What

amount of United States Internal Revenue stamps are necessary to be placed on the deed?

A. No stamps are necessary. They have not been required since January 1968.

295. Q. Doe leases a storeroom to Roe on a percentage basis. The lease calls for a minimum monthly rent of $300 and 5% on the gross yearly business over $80,000. How much rent would Doe receive yearly from Roe if Roe did a gross business of $140,000?

A. $6,600

296. Q. A farm of 60 acres listed for sale at $150 an acre, was finally sold for $7,650 on condition that the purchaser pay the 10% commission of sale price. How much did the buyer actually save on the transaction?

A. $585

297. Q. Assume that a $9,000 fire insurance policy is dated March 1, 1974. It was issued for three years at a premium of $158.40. What is the prorated value of the unused portion as of November 16, 1974?

A. $121

298. Q. A 100 by 100-foot lot was assessed at $15 per front foot and the house assessed at $3,200. What was the total yearly tax if the rate was 40 mills?

A. $188.00

299. Q. A small home can be rented for $50 a month or bought for $6,800 ($6,200 for the house; $600 for the lot). The annual cost of owning and living in a $6,800 home may be computed as follows:

Interest 3%. Painting and repairs of house 2 ½%. Taxes $24 per $1,000 on 75% value of house and lot. Insurance $4.50 per $1,000 on $6,200, the value of the house. 5% for care of lot; value of lot $600.

How much less would it be to buy the property and live in it than to rent it?

A. $5.05 per month. (Interest $17; Repairs $12.92; Taxes $10.20; Insurance $2.33; Lot upkeep $2.50. Total monthly expenses $44.95. Rent $50 less $44.95)

300. Q. The value of a house at the end of eight years was estimated to be $14,400. What was the value of the house when new if the yearly rate of depreciation was 2 ½%?

A. $18,000

301. Q. A property is assessed for $5,000. The tax rate is $3.50 per $100 with 5% discount for promptness and a 5% penalty for tardiness. What three possible amounts could be paid as taxes on this property?

A. $175 $166.25 $183.75

302. Q. What is three months' interest on $566.66 at 5% per annum?

A. $7.08

303. Q. The seller's equity in a real estate contract is $2,160, payable in monthly installments of exactly $45 per month, no more, no less. These installments do not include any interest. Assuming that the first payment is made October 1, 1971, that payments are due on the first day of each month thereafter, the last payment will become due on what date?

A. September 1, 1975

304. Q. $150 is 2 ½% of what amount?

A. $6,000

305. Q. How many square feet are there in an acre?

A. 43,560

306. Q. A real estate broker is given a contract to manage an apartment building, the eight units of which yield a monthly rent of $50 each. The maximum commission allowed is 5% of rents collected and one-half month's rent for each apartment rented, but the latter charge is not to exceed one leasing commission for each unit per year, and not more than one commission of either kind is to be levied against any one unit in any one month. What is the possible maximum yearly commission for the building?

A. $420

307. Q. A fire insurance policy was taken out for three years dated June 1, 1972, and the premium for three years was $36. The property was sold January 1, 1974. How would you prorate the premium?
A. Buyer would be charged $17
308. Q. $25 is 5% of what amount?
A. $500
309. Q. A new house and lot cost Snyder $14,000. Of this total price it was estimated that the lot was worth $2,000. The owner held the property for six years. Assuming an annual depreciation of 2 ½% on the house and an annual increase in value of 8% on the lot, what was the total value of the property at the end of six years?
A. $13,160
310. Q. What is the gross yearly income of a property that has six apartments, two apartments paying a monthly rental of $55 each, two apartments at $75 monthly each, and two apartments at $90 monthly each?
A. $5,280
311. Q. At settlement on June 15, 1974 a purchaser assumes the existing mortgage of $4,500 on which the interest at 5% per annum has been paid up to December 15, 1973. Prorate the amount due at settlement and state whether this item is a debit or credit to purchaser?
A. $112.50 which is a credit to the purchaser.
312. Q. What is the annual interest rate on an $8,000 loan when the interest payments are $80 per quarter on the full amount?
A. 4%
313. Q. The net amount received by Mr. Wheller for his property after his broker had deducted a sales commission of 4% and an allowance of $70 for advertising was $7,850. What was the selling price?
A. $8,250
314. Q. A building was sold for $50,000. At the time of closing the deal, credit was given the purchaser for a $20,000 first mortgage and a $7,000 second mortgage. What amount of Federal documentary stamps was placed on the deed in 1967?
A. $25.30
315. Q. After making proper deductions for expense of operation there is left a net income of $1,800 a year. What percentage of income is this on a purchase price of $20,000?
A. 9%
316. Q. A lot of 55 feet frontage and 100 feet depth has been sold at $35 per front foot. Compute your commission at 10% of the selling price.
A. $192.50
317. Q. Alfred Sims bought a lot for $1,000. He sold it for $1,300 at the end of three years, having paid $25 taxes on it for each year. What is his profit counting lost interest of 2% on his investment each year as an expense?
A. $165
318. Q. A house valued at $10,000 was insured against fire for 80% of the value. The rate was $.60 per $100 for a three-year period. How much was the premium for one year?
A. $16
319. Q. A property is assessed at $5,800. The school tax rate is $1.55 per $100 of assessed valuation. What is the amount of the school tax on the property?
A. $89.90
320. Q. What would a business be worth which shows a profit of $275 a month and is earning 8% on the total investment?
A. $41,250
321. Q. What is the total income of a business for the month of October which does a gross average of $42.50 per day including Sundays?
A. $1,317.50
322. Q. You bought a piece of land 200 ft. square and are erecting a house thereon, 40 ft.

square and an average height, including cellar, of 30 ft. Costs were as follows: Land, $25 per front foot, and building $.35 per cu. ft. What is the total cost excluding any other charges?

A. $21,800

323. Q. Green Acres Development Company divided 120 acres into 240 one-half acre lots. They then decided to make the lots each 2/3 of an acre in size. How many fewer 2/3 acre lots would they have?

A. 80 fewer lots

324. Q. Adams, who has $50,000 at 4% interest, lives in an apartment, for which he pays a rent of $200 monthly. He buys a duplex for $50,000 and moves into one unit. Adams leases the other unit at $250 monthly. Maintenance of the duplex costs $2,600 per year. Did Adams profit by the deal, and if so, how much at the end of one year?

A. Yes; by $800

325. Q. The showroom of an auto dealer contains 800 square feet. Its length is twice the width and a glass window is on the long side of the building. If new cars are 8 feet wide and placed side by side with 2 feet between them, how many cars can be placed in this space facing the window?

A. 4 cars

326. Q. A purchaser has decided to insulate his dwelling by covering the attic floor, measuring 24 feet by 32 feet, with rock wool. Each bag of rock wool will cover 36 square feet. How many bags will be required?

A. 21 $\frac{1}{3}$ (22 bags)

327. Q. A lot is 40 feet wide and 75 feet deep. The entire lot has a sidewalk around it 6 feet wide and 3 inches deep. What is the total area of the walk?

A. 1,236 square feet

328. Q. What will be a person's investment of principal, if he intends to earn an income of 6 per cent, so that he will receive $1,800 in interest each year?

A. $30,000

329. Q. At the end of the calendar year, the Hope Realty Company finds it earned $30,000. Listing fees, commissions and overriding expenses equaled 18 per cent of gross sales. What was the volume of sales for the year?

A. $36,585.37

330. Q. How many lots or portions of lots could you divide an acre into, if each lot is 60 feet by 120 feet, and a roadway is to be taken out, which is 30 feet wide and 200 feet long?

A. 5.2 or 5 $\frac{1}{5}$ lots

331. Q. John Davis bought a lot, 50 feet by 125 feet, at $65 per front foot. He paid $10,828.80 to build a house, which depreciated an average of 2 per cent each year. What would be the value of the entire property at the end of ten years if, in the meantime, the lot had increased in value 22 per cent above its original cost of $65 per front foot?

A. $12,628.04

332. Q. Smith paid $65 per front foot for his lot (with a frontage of 50 feet). He paid $10,828.80 to build and he paid the architect 5 per cent of the building cost. He then placed a mortgage on the property for three-fourths of the total cost. What was his equity in the property, after he placed the mortgage?

A. $3,655.06

333. Q. There are 20 fence posts, each 6.85 feet apart. How many yards from the beginning of the first post to the end of the last post, if each post is 4 $\frac{3}{4}$ inches wide?

A. 46.023 yards

334. Q. A $46,500 investment shows annual earnings of 6 $\frac{1}{2}$%. What is the monthly return?

A. $251.88

335. Q. Mrs. Stender owns a 27-room apartment house. Five tenants pay $17 per week; nine

tenants pay $15 per week; eight tenants pay $16 per week; and five pay $18 per week plus $3.75 per week for a garage. What is the gross yearly income?

A. $23,751

336. Q. Mrs. Seberry purchased a piece of real estate for $6,500. At a later date she offered it for sale through a broker's office at an increase of 30%. The property did not sell and she finally reduced the asking price by 25% and the property was sold. She paid a commission of 5% of the sale price to the broker. Did she gain or lose and by how much?

A. Loss—$479.38

337. Q. What is the interest on $874 for 2 years, 8 months, 15 days at 4 $\frac{1}{2}$% per annum?

A. $106.50

338. Q. A mortgage company agrees to lend the owner of a property a sum equal to 66⅔% of its appraised valuation, at an interest rate of 5%. The first year's interest is $200. What is the appraised valuation?

A. $6,000

339. Q. A house sold for $7,500 at a profit of 20%. What did the house cost?

A. $6,250

340. Q. The owner of a block of 14 building lots, each with a frontage of 75 ft., desires to realize $33,750 from the sale thereof, withholding, however, two lots for himself. What must be the sales price for the lots sold per front foot?

A. $37.50

341. Q. If a tract of land comprising 108,900 square feet was sold for $1,250 per acre, what is the total amount realized from the sale?

A. $3,125

342. Q. A rectangular piece of land containing an acre is 5 $\frac{1}{2}$ rods wide, what is the length?

A. 29 $\frac{1}{11}$ rods

343. Q. From 160 acres of land, 42 $\frac{1}{4}$ acres were sold to one man and $\frac{1}{3}$ of the remainder to another. How many acres remain unsold?

A. 78 $\frac{1}{2}$ acres

344. Q. A man paid $7,888.30 for a farm containing 89 acres 90 square rods of land. What was the price per acre?

A. $88.08 per acre

345. Q. A farm of 100 acres is divided into house lots. The streets require $\frac{1}{8}$ of the whole farm, and there are 140 lots. How many square rods are there in each lot?

A. 100 square rods

346. Q. Jim Moore receives his tax bill of $490.30. The tax rate is 42 mills per dollar. The property is assessed at 58.25% of its value. What was the actual value of the property?

A. $20,040.87

347. Q. A broker has 5 $\frac{1}{4}$ acres of land, which he is dividing into lots, 60 feet wide and 100 feet deep. Allowing 36,690 square feet for the necessary streets, into how many lots could the tract be divided?

A. 32 lots

348. Q. The owner of a piece of land 500 X 350 ft. laid a sidewalk and curb around the entire lot, placing the curb along the lot lines. Sidewalk cost $3,200 and curb $2.00 a lineal yard. What was the total cost?

A. $4,333.33

349. Q. If you bought a house for the listing price less 20% and sold it for the listing price, what per cent profit would you make?

A. 25%

350. Q. Compute the interest on $3,120.50 from November 1, 1972 to May 1, 1974, at 5½% per annum.

A. $257.44

351. Q. If 16 acres of land cost $720, what will 197 acres cost?

A. $8,865

352. Q. How many acres are there in a parcel of land 600 feet X 300 feet?
A. 4.13 plus

353. Q. The net amount received by a seller for his property, after the broker had deducted a sales commission of 5% and an allowance of $40 for advertising, was $9,080. What was the selling price?
A. $9,600

354. Q. McDevitt has a principal balance of $6,000 on his mortgage. The interest rate is 5½% and taxes and insurance payments total $108 per annum. His monthly payment is $60. What is his principal balance after making the first payment?
A. $5,976.50

355. Q. Compute the cost of excavation for a cellar 25 feet wide, 30 feet long and 5 feet deep at $2.90 per cubic yard.
A. $402.75

356. Q. What would the quarterly interest payment amount to on a $6,000 loan calling for simple annual interest at 5 ½%?
A. $82.50

357. Q. Ray Dolan bought a square piece of land comprising 10,000 square feet. He is building a house on it 45 feet square and of an average height including basement of 30 feet. His costs were $25 per front foot for the land and $.35 per cubic foot for the dwelling. What is the total cost?
A. $23,762.50

358. Q. A lot 75 feet wide and 165 feet deep sold for $193.50 per front foot. What was the selling price of the lot?
A. $14,512.50

359. Q. How many acres of land are there in a section?
A. 640 acres

360. Q. How many sections comprise a township?
A. 36 sections

361. Q. What is the area of a square-acre lot in terms of feet on each side?
A. 208.7 feet on each side

362. Q. In a 12-unit apartment building, three units rented for $100 each per month, two units for $125 each per month, and one unit for $150 per month. The other six units rented for $65 each per month. What was the gross annual income?
A. $13,080

363. Q. What would a property be worth if the net return is $950 per month, and the yearly earning is to be 8% on the investment?
A. $142,500

364. Q. How many acres in the south half of the north half of the southwest quarter of Section 9 of Township 24, range 42 E.W.M., Spokane County, Washington?
A. 40 acres

365. Q. A plot of ground is a rectangle with a frontage of 760 feet and a depth of 500 feet. How many acres does it contain?
A. 8.72 acres

366. Q. A business property valued at $10,000, to earn 16% on the total investment annually, should return a monthly income in what amount?
A. $133.33

367. Q. What factors are to be considered in determining the tax rate?
A. Assessment and tax millage.

368. Q. On a section chart, how many acres would be in the following descriptions:
(a) NE ¼ of NE ¼ of NW ¼?
(b) NE ¼ of NW ¼ of NE ¼ of NW ¼?
A. (a) 10 acres
(b) 2 ½ acres

369. Q. A building is insured for $24,500. The annual rate is $.16 per $100 and the owner

buys a three-year policy, the rate of which is 2 ½ times the annual rate.
(a) What is the monthly cost ?
(b) What is the total premium?

A. (a) $2.72
(b) $98

370. Q. A percentage lease calls for a minimum rent of $300 per month and 4% of the gross business over $150,000. If the total rent paid at the end of the year was $4,800, how much business did the tenant do during the year?

A. $180,000

371. Q. A real estate deal is closed as of April 15, 1971. The city taxes amount to $100. They have been paid. The school taxes in the amount of $240 are also paid. The county taxes amounting to $118 have not been paid. Compute apportionment of taxes between buyer and seller.

A. $263.09 buyer owes seller for taxes

372. Q. A broker has 1.87 acres of land listed with him for sale at 22 ½ cents per square foot. The total selling price is how much?

A. $18,327.87

373. Q. A property is assessed at $6,000. The school tax rate is $1.55 per $100 of assessed valuation. What is the amount of the school tax on the property?

A. $93

374. Q. A lot measuring 100 feet by 108.9 feet would be equivalent to what portion of an acre?

A. ¼ acre

375. Q. If an $8,000 home is assessed at 80% of its value and the combined tax rate is $4.20 per $100, what is the amount of the total annual tax?

A. $268.80

376. Q. What is the interest on $8,000 at 4 ½% per annum for nine months and fifteen days?

A. $285

377. Q. A man bought two 60-foot lots for $3,000 net each, and divided them into three lots of equal frontage, which he sold for a price of $2,400 each. What was his percentage of gross profit ?

A. 20%

378. Q. The selling price of a home was $9,300. The broker's commission was 5% and other charges to the seller paid from escrow amounted to $95. How much money did the seller receive?

A. $8,740

379. Q. If a seller wishes to trade his residence at a price of $15,750 subject to a mortgage in the amount of $6,240 for an apartment house costing $62,350 subject to a mortgage in the amount of $36,675, what would be the amount of cash difference?

A. $16,165

380. Q. What would be the depth of a rectangular lot containing 1,080 square yards with a frontage of 90 feet ?

A. 108 feet

381. Q. An apartment house has a gross income of $1,134 per month with annual expense of $2,500. What price would a buyer pay for the building to show a net return of 8% on his investment ?

A. $138,850

382. Q. A broker sold a lot 125 feet wide and 160 feet deep for 17 cents per square foot, but the purchaser assumed a paving lien of $2.25 per front foot. What total amount would the purchaser have to ask for the property if he expected to make a profit of $295 and give a clear title to the property?

A. $3,976.25

383. Q. The commission rate for selling an apartment house was five per cent on the first

$15,000; three per cent on the next $20,000; and 1 ½% on the balance. The broker received a commission of $1,710. What was the selling price of the property?

A. $59,000

384. Q. A lot 65 feet wide and 150 feet deep sold for $7,670. What was the price per front foot?

A. $118

385. Q. Adams owns a property which gives him a gross income of $325 per month. His monthly expenses average $155 per month. What is his net income per year on the property?

A. $2,040

386. Q. What is the annual rate of interest on a $4,200 loan, when the quarterly interest payments are $57.75?

A. 5 ½%

387. Q. The owner of a farm employs a licensed broker to sell his farm and agrees to pay a commission of 5%. There is a mortgage on the farm dated June 1, 1971, in the amount of $3,000, with interest at 5% per annum, which the purchaser is assuming. Two payments of $250 each have been made on the mortgage. The owner has paid the interest on the mortgage to June 1, 1974. The sales price is $8,750, and the date of closing is June 30, 1974.

(a) What is the amount of commission due the broker?

(b) What is the amount of mortgage interest owed by the seller to the buyer at the date of closing?

(c) Assuming that the seller had paid the annual taxes of $136 in full for the year ending December 31, 1974, what is the amount of tax adjustment due the seller by the buyer?

A. (a) $437.50 (b) $10.42 (c) $68.00

388. Q. A property is worth $12,000, and the furniture and household goods are worth $4,000. The owner insures them for 80% of their value. The annual rate on the dwelling is $2.80 per $1,000, and on the furniture and household goods, $3.30 per $1,000. If the premium for a three-year policy is 2 ½ times the premium for one year, what savings would be effected by purchasing a three-year policy?

A. $18.72

389. Q. If Dan Clure purchased an apartment building for $40,000 and the total amount of rents received was $6,000 annually, and annual expenses totalled $2,000, what per cent does his investment pay?

A. 10%

390. Q. A sale of real estate is closed on September 12, 1974. The county taxes for 1973 were $875.24, which have not yet been paid, so they will be paid by the purchaser. In prorating these taxes for the calendar year, what is the amount of the apportionment and will this amount be a debit or credit to the purchaser at the closing?

A. $612.66 which will be credited to the purchaser.

391. Q. Lawrence leased a storeroom to Davis on a percentage basis. The lease calls for a minimum monthly rental of $400 and 5% of the gross yearly business over $80,000. How much rent would Davis receive yearly from Lawrence, if Lawrence did a gross business of $120,000 in 1973?

A. $6,800

392. Q. A 40-acre grove sold for $2,200 per acre. The profit the seller made over the cost of the property to him was 10%. What did he pay for the grove?

A. $80,000

393. Q. If an apartment house costing $42,000 has a net income of $280 per month, what per cent would it be returning on the investment?

A. 8%

394. Q. What is the cost of a lot 264 feet wide by 660 feet deep at $800 per acre?

A. $3,200

395. Q. A salesman's half of a 5% commission for the sale of a 320 acre ranch at $175 an acre would be how much?
A. $1,400

396. Q. A farm earns $3,600 net after allowing for all expenses. A buyer wants 6% return on his money. What could he pay for the farm so as to net him 6% on his investment?
A. $60,000

397. Q. In appraising a one-story house 32 X 40 feet at a replacement cost of $9.50 per square foot, and allowing 5% depreciation for one year, what would your appraisal be?
A. $11,552

398. Q. How many lots or portions of lots could you divide an acre into if each lot is 60 X 120 feet and a roadway is to be taken out which is 30 feet wide and 200 feet long?
A. 5.21 + lots

399. Q. If the net income from an apartment costing $12,000 is $100 monthly, what would the yearly percentage rate of earnings on the investment be?
A. 10%

400. Q. A broker has a problem of sub-dividing a 10 acre tract into 50 X 100 foot lots; after allowing 85,000 square feet for the necessary streets, into how many lots could the tract be subdivided?
A. 70.1 lots

401. Q. How many square feet of concrete would be needed to build a sidewalk 6 feet wide around the boundaries of a 60 X 100-foot corner lot?
A. 996 sq. ft.

402. Q. How much would the above walk cost if you paid 23 cents per square foot?
A. $229.08

403. Q. How many does the sum of 2,583 and 4,905 exceed the difference of 9,421 and 2,892?
A. 959

404. Q. Shields purchased W $\frac{1}{2}$ of NE $\frac{1}{4}$ of section 10, T-16, R 18 E for the sum of $250 per acre. He subdivided land into 100 lots. The cost of the development was $6,500. Lots were sold at $750 each. What profit did Shields make?
A. $48,500

405. Q. A tract of ground 30 rods by 16 rods contains how many acres?
A. 3 acres

406. Q. A person whose income is $325 per month should be able to purchase a home valued at 2 $\frac{1}{2}$ times his annual income. What would be the value of his home?
A. $9,750

407. Q. A developer purchased a parcel of land 2,640 feet by 9,900 feet. How many $\frac{1}{2}$ acre sites can be obtained in this parcel allowing 10% of the total for streets and 10% for playgrounds and 20% for a factory?
A. 720 one-half acre sites

408. Q. What is the cost of roofing a gable-type house (24′ X 32′) if the roof measures 15 feet from eaves to peak and 34 feet long, if shingles cost $.08 per square foot delivered and $.026 per square-foot labor to apply?
A. $108.12

409. Q. A lot with 50-foot lake frontage and 150 feet deep sold for $7,500. What was the price per square foot? What was the price per front foot?
A. $1.00 per sq. ft. $150 per front foot

410. Q. Of a certain farm, $\frac{1}{6}$ is in pasture, $\frac{5}{8}$ is under cultivation, and the remainder in woodland. If the woodland is 50 acres, how many acres are there in the whole farm?
A. 240 acres

411. Q. Kilroy sold two vacant lots for a total of $9,430, which was 15% more than he paid for them four years ago. During the time that he owned the lots, he paid taxes each

year at the rate of 45 mills on the assessed value of 60% of his purchase price. Figuring a 3% yearly interest loss on his original investment as an expense, did he gain or lose on the sale?In what amount ?

A. $639.60 Loss

412. Q. How many square rods in an acre?

A. 160 sq. rd.

413. Q. A lot near Magic Springs has been appraised as follows: 3,250 square feet of hillside at 14¢ a square foot; 2,000 square feet of stream area at 8 ½¢ a square foot; and 7,250 square feet of flat area at $1.00 a square foot. If the lot is to be sold as a whole, what must the price be per square foot to realize the appraised value of the lot ?

A. $.63 per square foot

414. Q. A two story house cost $9,000 to build. If the house had a frontage of 30 feet, a depth of 30 feet and was 30 feet high, including basement, what was the cost per cubic foot ?

A. $.33 ⅓

415. Q. A man plans to put in a driveway 30 feet long and 6 feet wide. If concrete work and labor together cost $2.75 per square foot, what is the cost of the driveway?

A. $495

416. Q. A perch or rod is a unit of land measuring how many feet ?

A. 16 ½ ft.

417. Q. How many feet in a chain?

A. 66 ft.

418. Q. What would be the amount of interest a purchaser would have to pay for the first month on a contract balance of $7,200 payable at $40 per month, including interest at the rate of 6% per annum?

A. $36

419. Q. An investor bought 20 acres of land. He plans to divide it into 50′ X 150′ homesite lots and leaving 5 acres for streets, playgrounds and parks. How many lots will he have to sell?

A. 87 + lots

420. Q. A percentage lease calls for a minimum rent of $600 per month plus 5% of the gross business over $115,000 per month. If the total rent paid by the end of the year was $9,300, what was the tenant's gross volume of business for the year?

A. $1,422,000.00

421. Q. The assessed valuation of a house is $10,000. If the tax rate is $19 per $1,000 assessed valuation, what are his taxes?

A. $190 taxes

422. Q. Two houses are 30 yards apart. What would the distance be (expressed in feet) if the houses were three paces closer?

A. 81 feet

423. Q. A patio is 20 yards long and 10 yards wide. There are stones all around it, each two feet long. How many stones are needed?

A. 90 stones

424. Q. A ranch contains 3 square miles. How many acres does it contain?

A. 1,920 acres

425. Q. A lot is 300 feet wide, 450 feet long. A building was erected on the lot 27 feet from the front and 18 feet from the rear. The building contained 12,825 square yards. How wide was the building?

A. 285 feet

426. Q. A salesman's commission at the end of the first year was increased one-fifth, at the end of the second year it was increased one-fifth. If the third year's commission was $7,280, what was his commission the first year?

A. $5,055.56

427. Q. Neely wishes to construct a store building on the corner of Main and Edgeworth

Avenues. The building is to have 8,100 square feet of ground floor space. Phillips owns lots 1 to 5, inclusive, and will sell any or all of the lots but will not cut up any of them. Each lot is 50 feet wide and fronts on Edgeworth Avenue. Each lot is 100 feet deep, parallel to Main Street. There is a 20-foot setback on Main Street lots and a 15-foot setback on Edgeworth Avenue. If the selling price of lots fronting on Main Street is $112.50 per front front foot and $87.25 per front foot for lots fronting on Edgeworth Avenue, what will be the total investment in land required by Neely if he purchases the lots needed for the proposed building?

A. $19,975.00

428. Q. In the above case, how many square feet can be used for building purposes of the corner lot?

A. 2,550 sq. ft.

429. Q. Dolan paid $75 per front foot for his lot which is 60 feet front and 100 feet deep. He later decides to enlarge his lot and can buy an adjoining tract at the price of 75 cents per square foot. He wants to limit his total investments in land to $7,500. How many square feet will he have altogether after he buys the additional tract?

A. 10,000 sq. ft.

430. Q. Thompson and Tyler agreed to trade properties—each to assume the encumbrances on the property taken in trade and the difference in equities to be paid the party with the greater equity by paying 20% cash and the balance to be carried on a second mortgage. Thompson's property was valued at $20,000 with a first mortgage encumbrance of $8,555.00 and a second mortgage encumbrance of $1,655.10. Tyler's property was valued at $18,450.00 with a mortgage encumbrance of $13,841.79. (a) What is Thompson's equity? (b) What is Tyler's equity? (c) Who is due the difference in equity? (d) How much of the difference will be paid in cash? (e) How much will be carried on a mortgage? (f) Against whose property will be the mortgage (after transfer of properties)?

A. (a) $9,789.90 (b) $4,608.21 (c) Thompson (d) $1,036.34
(e) $4,145.35 (f) Tyler's property

431. Q. A buyer lacks $250 to close a real estate deal. The seller agrees to accept a note due in one year from that date, with interest added to back of note at time of signing at 6% per annum. Eleven payments are to be made at the rate of $16.25 per month. What will be the amount of the last payment?

A. $86.25

432. Q. The taxes on a certain house were $126. The taxes were due on January 1, and were paid by the owner. What tax refund would the owner receive from the purchaser if the house were sold on March 15?

A. $99.75

433. Q. The assessment on a property is: $13,300 on the building, $1,050 on the lot. On re-assessment the assessment on the lot has been increased $350. If the tax rate is raised 4.25 mills, what will the increased tax be on this property?

A. $62.48

434. Q. A property is assessed at $12,500 and the tax rate is 32 mills. Taxes are due October 1. What refund would the owner of this property get from a purchaser if he sold the property and the taxes were prorated as of April 1?

A. $200.00

435. Q. A man's home is worth $6,000 and his household goods are worth $4,000. He insures each of them for 80% of their value. The annual rate on the dwelling is $2.80 per $1,000 and the rate on the contents $3.30 per $1,000. The premium for a three-year policy is 2 ½ times the premium for one year. What is the three-year premium on the complete policy?

A. $60.00

436. Q. A party purchased 150 acres of land for $15,000 thirty years ago. The tax rate has averaged 20 mills and an assessed valuation of $50 per acre. If the property were

sold now for $300 per acre paying a 10% brokerage commission, what would the owner's net profit be?

A. $21,000

437. Q. Which would be the better of two offers for a lot 5 feet front and 150 feet deep, and how much better? "A" offers $40 per front foot and "B" offers 30¢ per square foot.

A. "B" 's offer by $25

438. Q. A broker leases a store measuring 30 feet wide by 100 feet deep for a period of five years at an annual rental of $2.50 per square foot. What would be the broker's total earnings if the rate of commission is 5% for each year?

A. $1,875

439. Q. A contractor tells you he can reproduce a building for 55 cents per cubic foot and you determine that the building has a ground floor area of 36 feet by 40 feet, and an average height of 14 feet. What would be its reproduction cost?

A. $11,088

440. Q. If an $8,000 home assessed at 60% of that amount has a combined tax rate of $4.21 per $100, what would be the amount of the total annual tax?

A. $202.08

441. Q. An agent collected rents monthly as follows: $25 for each of four flats; $40 for each of six flats; $50 for each of two flats. He paid out $18 for water and $6 for repairs. He was to receive 3% of the gross rentals as commission. What were the total collections and net to owner?

A. $440, total collections $402.80, net to owner

442. Q. A rectangular lot 210 feet long and 200 feet wide was subdivided into 8 lots of 50′ X 90′ with a road running lengthwise through the middle of the lot. What per cent of the lot area was reserved for the road?

A. 14.28 per cent

443. Q. Mr. Redman has property assessed at $54,500. Find the amount of his taxes if the tax rate is 20 mills per $1.00.

A. $1,090 for taxes

444. Q. J. James paid $484 property tax. If his property was assessed at $11,000, what was the tax rate in mills? Express this rate in dollars per $100.

A. 44 mills $4.40 per $100

445. Q. A Realtor sells a 50′ X 100′ property at 75¢ a square foot. If his commission is 5%, how much does he give the owner?

A. $3,562.50

446. Q. A lot was sold for $10,000. The buyer pays $4,000 down and the balance in equal installments in five years. (a) How much a month does he pay on the principal? (b) If he pays 5% interest per year on the balance, how much interest does he pay at the end of the first month?

A. (a) $100 (b) $25

447. Q. The monthly rent for an office is $75. The size of the office is 12 feet by 20 feet. What is the annual rate per square foot?

A. $3.75

448. Q. If a $10,000 home is assessed at 80% of its value and the combined tax rate is $3.80 per $100 assessed valuation, what is the amount of the total annual tax?

A. $304 taxes

449. Q. Mr. Brown built a house 33 feet by 45 feet which had an offset for the family room of an additional 5 feet by 15 feet. If construction cost was $12.85 per square foot, how much did it cost to build the house?

A. $20,046

450. Q. Taxes on a parcel of property are $1,325.28, for the current year. The first one-fourth of the taxes were paid by the seller. You sell the property and will close the deal and make the prorations as of December 15th. How much will you charge the seller for his share of the taxes?

A. $938.74 seller owes.

451. Q. What would be the F.H.A. insurable loan on a dwelling if the F.H.A. valuation is $20,000 and the F.H.A. insured 97% of the first $15,000 valuation and 85% of the remainder?
A. $18,800 total insurable loan

452. Q. On September 1, 1972, a house was insured against fire for 90% of its $24,000 value. The insurance rate paid was 54 cents per $100 for a three year period. The house was sold February 1, 1974. What was the unearned premium to be charged the buyer?
A. $61.56

453. Q. You are to ascertain the value of a ranch home, which the owner will list with your office, based upon the following information: The lot is 75 feet front and 125 feet deep, cost $5,000, and has appreciated 4 per cent in value each year. The dwelling, built four years ago, is 28 ft. X 38 ft. in size; would cost $12.50 per sq. ft. to reproduce today, allowing 2 ½ per cent depreciation per year.
A. $17,820

454. Q. You are called upon to make an appraisal of a one-family dwelling. This is a one-story, basementless house with breezeway and garage. The lot, 80 feet wide and 180 feet deep, is valued at $31.50 per front foot. The actual exterior dimensions of the house are 28 feet X 40 feet; for the breezeway, 11 feet X 13 feet; and for the garage, 13 feet X 21 feet. Construction costs for this type of property are $14.50 per square foot for the house itself; $8.25 per square foot for the breezeway; and $10.75 per square foot for the garage. You determine that the value of the grading, shrubbery and lot improvement is $575. There is an estimated cost for painting and small repairs amounting to $395. The building has an effective age of 8 years and a life expectancy new of 50 years. If there is no functional or economic obsolescence, what is the property's indicated fair market value, cost approach?
A. $20,432.58

455. Q. Stone built a house 30′ X 24′ X 25′ with an attached garage of 1,437 cubic feet, all at a cost of 83 ½ cents per cubic foot. A special artistic entrance cost $384.57. What is its value today, if it is two years old and being depreciated on a 30 year life?
A. $15,506.84

456. Q. Crouch is employed as a salesperson by Realtor Evans. Crouch receives 40 per cent on sales. A subdivision is listed for sale with various listed prices, depending upon size and location. Flynn, Sales Manager for Evans, receives an over-ride commission of 10%. Crouch sold 7 lots at $2,400 each, 5 lots at $2,850 each and 6 lots at $3,200 each during June 1974. The subdivision owner pays Evans a 5 per cent commission on sales. How much did Evans earn in commission during the month on Crouch's sales?
A. $1,356.75

457. Q. You, as a broker, sold two lots fronting on Elm Street. Each lot has a frontage of 63 feet. The corner lot sold for 23% more than the adjacent lot which sold for $115.00 per front foot. What was the combined total selling price of the two lots?
A. $16,156.35

458. Q. What would be the broker's net commission on the sale of a property for $9,350 with 6% commission out of which amount the broker's expenses are as follows:
10% listing fee off top of gross commission
50% of remainder for salesman's commission
12% of gross commission for advertising
7% of gross commission for office expense
A. $145.86

459. Q. A piece of land 990 feet by 660 feet is for sale. The owner is asking $3,000 an acre. What is the selling price?
A. $45,000

460. Q. A lot 60 feet wide and 150 feet deep sold for $150.00 per front foot. What was the

selling price of the lot?

A. $9,000 selling price

461. Q. A bank pays interest twice a year. Find the difference between simple interest and compound interest on $1,090 for a year at 4%

A. $.44 difference

462. Q. On April 1, 1973, Anna James bought a house for $9,000. During the year she spent $190 for repairs, $1,200 for a garage, $295 in taxes and $50 for insurance. The following April she sold the house for $11,250. Find the total gain.

A. $515 gain

463. Q. The sales in a real estate company in 1972 amounted to one-fourth more than in 1971. They were one-fifth more in 1973 than in 1972. If sales in 1973 amounted to $300,000. What did the sales amount to in 1971 and 1972?

A. 1971: $200,000
1972: $250,000

464. Q. A man bought a house for $14,160. Due to health conditions, he was forced to sell for 8 1/3 per cent less than he paid. Find the selling price and the loss.

A. $1,180 loss $12,980 selling price.

465. Q. How much additional cash must a buyer furnish in addition to his $1,000 deposit if the lending institution grants 66 2/3% loan on a $12,000 home?

A. $3,000

466. Q. An insurance premium for three years is $72.00. The buyer is going to set up an insurance reserve with his loan to pay for the premium three years later. What will be the amount of the monthly reserve?

A. $2.00

467. Q. The rental income from a duplex is $240 per month. Find the cost of the house if the annual income is 9 per cent of the cost.

A. $32,000 cost of house

468. Q. J. Johnson paid $16,000 for his new home. The assessed value is 60% of the market value. The tax rate is $2.50 per $100 of assessed valuation. Find the assessed valuation and the tax.

A. $9,600 assessed valuation $240 taxes

469. Q. If 5 1/4% is the annual rate of interest and the monthly interest payment is $58.45, what is the amount of the original loan?

A. $13,360.00

470. Q. What is the annual interest rate on a $6,000.00 loan when the interest payments are $105.00 semi-annually on the full amount?

A. 3 1/2%

471. Q. A salesman's half of a 5% commission for the sale of a 320 acre ranch at $175.00 an acre would be how much?

A. $1,400.00

472. Q. A lending institution requires that a buyer have a net monthly income 4 1/2 times the monthly mortgage (total), and they use a flat 10% deduction of the gross income to compute the net income. What would be the minimum gross annual salary of a person to qualify for a $20,000 home with 25% down and the balance to be amortized over a 20 year period at 6% interest, with monthly mortgage payments of $138.00 (total)?

A. $8,280

473. Q. What would be the cost of excavating a basement 48 feet long, 30 feet wide, and 9 feet deep at 35¢ per cubic yard? (27 cubic feet = 1 cu. yd.)

A. $168.00

474. Q. Salesman "A" obtains an exclusive listing for $24,500 and is to receive 20% of the 6% commission received by the broker on the sale as a listing fee. Salesman "B" sells the property at a 4% reduction of the listed sales price, and is to receive 35% of the

commission after Salesman "A" has been paid. 3% of the full commission is to be paid to the Multiple Listing Service. How much does Salesman "B" receive?

A. $383.28

475. Q. A small town has a proposed budget of $260,000 to be met by taxation. The assessed valuation of taxable property is $6,500,000. Will a tax rate of 30 mills provide sufficient funds to meet the budget?

A. No

476. Q. A chain-store company is interested in taking a 21-year lease on a store property in a certain location. You have located an ideal site for this store, which is for sale for $10,000 and is listed with you. You know a builder whose entire capital is $5,000 who would be willing to build. You also know an investor willing to buy the property after it has been constructed, and you have assurance that the chain store company would lease the property. How would you arrange this deal to everybody's satisfaction, and how many commissions would you earn in this transaction?

A. Have the builder buy the land giving $5,000 cash and a purchase money mortgage with a subordination clause. Negotiate a construction loan mortgage. Sell property to investors. Lease property to chain-store. Four commissions (sale of land, construction loan mortgage, sale of property, and lease).

477. Q. A mortgage company agrees to lend the buyer of a property a sum equal to 80% of its appraised valuation, at 8% per annum. Interest for the first month is $96. What is the appraised valuation?

A. $14,400 appraised value

478. Q. Jones bought a lot 70 feet X 120 feet at $63 per front foot. He built a house on the lot for $9,216.00. The house depreciated at an average rate of 2% each year. If the lot increased in value at an average of 1 ½% per year, what was the value of the entire property at the end of 8 years?

A. $12,680.64

479. Q. What is the appraisal value on a one story house 32.5 feet by 40 feet at a replacement cost of $13.50 per square foot, allowing 5% depreciation for one year?

A. $16,672.50

480. Q. An apartment house had a gross income of $1,250 per month with annual expenses of $5,900, including depreciation. What price would a buyer pay for the property to show a net return of 7% on his investment?

A. $130,000

481. Q. You are to appraise an apartment house which has an annual gross income of $22,500. Taxes, insurance and operating expenses amount to $10,500 per year. Assume an overall capitalization rate of 12%. What is the value of the property, using the capitalization of net income approach to value?

A. $100,000

482. Q. If concrete costs $4.10 per cubic yard and labor costs are 87 cents per sq. foot, what would be cost of driveway 36 feet long by 6 feet wide and 3 inches thick?

A. $196.12

483. Q. A property showed a net income of $3,000 per year over the past 5 years. Typical properties yield a return of approximately 5%. Eliminating depreciation, and using the 5% return as the capitalization rate, what is a fair estimate of the value of the property?

A. $60,000

484. Q. A vacant piece of land, of irregular terrain, has been appraised, as follows: 3,250 sq. ft. of slope at 14 cents per sq. ft.; 2,000 sq. feet of creek area, 8 ½ cents a sq. foot; and 7,250 sq. ft. of flat land at $1 a sq. ft. If the entire tract is sold, what would be the price per sq. ft. to obtain the appraised value of the property?

A. $.63

485. Q. An appraiser, using the income approach, is estimating the value of a single-family

residence. He finds comparable properties rent at $125 per month. Recent sales in the area were $18,000. Estimate the gross rent multiplier.

A. 144 GRM

486. Q. Plot the following metes and bounds land description:
Starting at the NW corner of the NW 1/4 of Section 9, draw a line to the SE corner of the SW 1/4 of the NW 1/4 of Section 9; thence, to the SE corner of the SW 1/4 of the SE 1/4 of Section 9; thence, to the SW corner of Section 9; thence, one mile due north to the point of beginning.
How many acres in this tract?

A. 200 acres

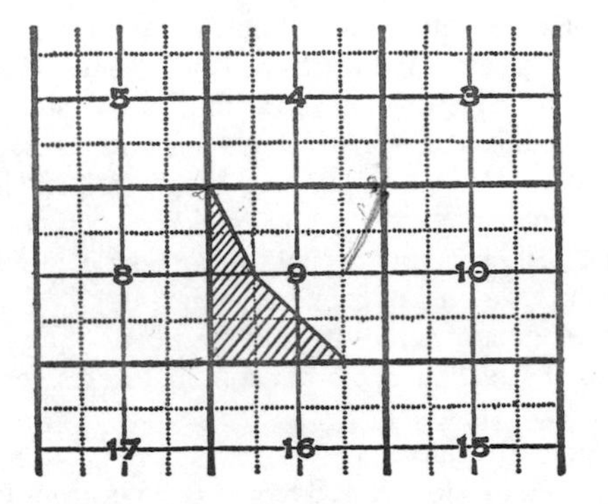

487. Q. Below is shown a portion of Tract 618, as per map recorded in Book 37, Page 19, Official Map Records of Maricopa County. A parcel consisting of the shaded areas was sold.
(a) Describe the conveyed portion by a fractional description.
(b) How many square feet in parcel conveyed?
(c) The portion of the parcel with 125 ft. depth was sold for $500 a front foot on 7th Street, and the portion on the rear of Lot 9 was sold for $2.20 per sq. ft. What was the total consideration?

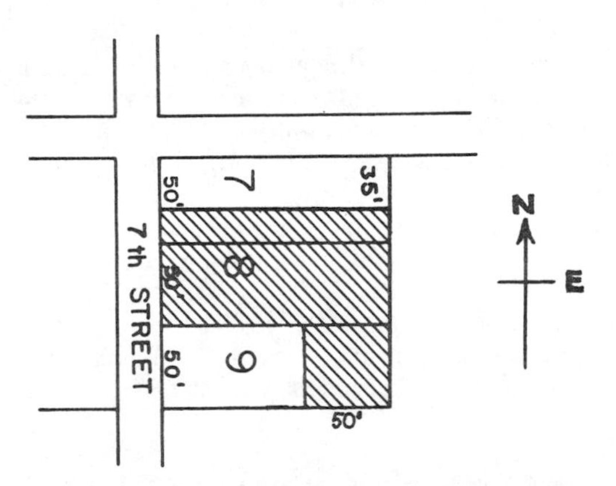

A. (a) The south 15′ of Lot 7; all of Lot 8, and the east 50′ of Lot 9; all in Tract 618, as per map recorded in Book 37, Page 19, official maps of record of Maricopa County.
(b) 10,625 sq. ft.
(c) $38,000.00 total consideration.

488. Q. There is a 15 foot building setback ordinance applying to all lots fronting on Main Street and a 20 foot setback applying to all lots fronting on Cross Street, as indicated by the dotted lines on the following diagram:

MAIN STREET

LOT 5 | LOT 4 | LOT 3 | LOT 2 | LOT 1

50 FEET | 50 FEET | 50 FEET | 50 FEET | 50 FEET

100 FEET

CROSS STREET

(a) Presuming no other setback or areaway requirements, how many square feet of Lot 1 can be used for building purposes?

(b) J. F. Jolly wishes to construct a store building on the corner of Main and Cross Streets. The building is to have 8,100 square feet of ground floor space. Mr. Jones owns Lots 1 to 5, inclusive, and will sell any or all of the lots, but will not cut up any one of them. What is the minimum number of lots Mr. Jolly will have to buy to allow construction of the building described?

(c) If Mr. Jolly buys all of the lots and pays $127.50 per front foot for lots 2, 3, 4, and 5 and $185.00 per front foot for the lot fronting on Cross Street, what would be his total cost for all of the lots?

A. (a) 2,550 sq. ft.
(b) Lots 1, 2, and 3.
(c) $44,000.00

489. Q. On the following diagram, you are to plot out the following legal description and insert the dimensions of the area described:

(a) "Beginning at a point on the easterly side of 24th Avenue at a point 150 feet north of the northerly side of "B" Street; thence east and parallel with "A" Street a distance of 200 feet to a point 100 feet west of the westerly side of 23rd Avenue; thence north 50 feet; thence east a distance of 25 feet to a point 75 feet west of the westerly side of 23rd Avenue; thence south 150 feet to a point; thence west to a point on the easterly side of 24th Avenue 50 feet north of the northerly side of "B" Street; thence north 100′ to the point and place of beginning."

(b) If the area described in part (a) sells for 42¢ per square foot, what will be the total amount of commission collected by a broker if he works on a 5% straight commission?

A. (a) See drawing.

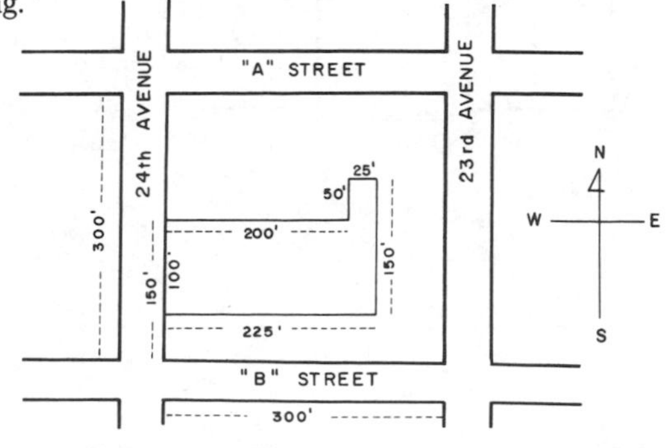

(b) $498.75

490. Q. The following diagram represents Section 14, Township 22 N, Range 17 E of the 6th Principal Meridian.
(a) You are to indicate the area and shade in the following:
S $\frac{1}{2}$ of SW $\frac{1}{4}$ of the NE $\frac{1}{4}$
E $\frac{1}{2}$ of SE $\frac{1}{4}$ of the NW $\frac{1}{4}$
N $\frac{1}{2}$ of the SW $\frac{1}{4}$
W $\frac{1}{2}$ and NE $\frac{1}{4}$ of NW $\frac{1}{4}$ of SE $\frac{1}{4}$
(a) See drawing.
(b) How many acres are contained in this tract?

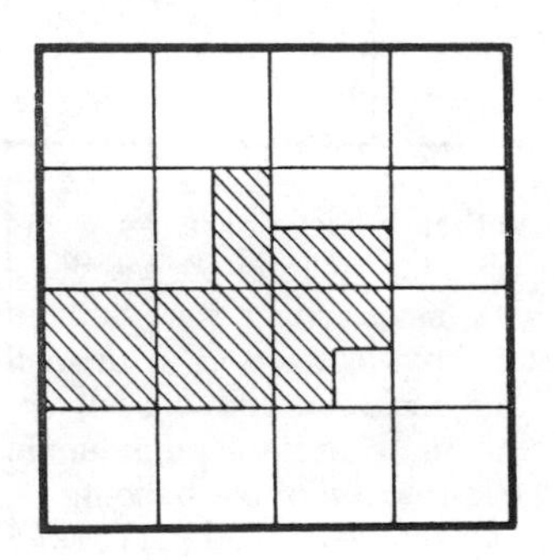

A. 150 acres

491. Q. The diagram below consists of five townships. The township in the center has been designated as Township 7 North, Range 1 East of the Boise Meridian.

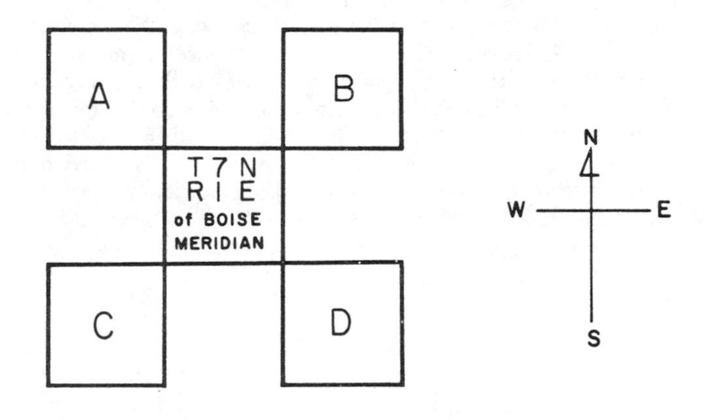

(a) Give the township and Range numbers for Township A.
(b) Give the township and Range numbers for Township D.

A. (a) T8N-R1W
(b) T6N-R2E

492. Q. The following diagram has been designated as Township 7 North, Range 1 East of the Boise Meridian.
(a) Number these sections correctly.
(b) Shade in the N $1/2$ of Section 17; the W $1/2$ of the W $1/2$ of Section 25; the SW $1/4$ of Section 32; and the NE $1/4$ of the NW $1/4$ of Section 4.
(c) How many acres in the Township have you shaded?

A. (a) and (b)

6	5	4	3	2	1
7	8	9	10	11	12
18	17	16	15	14	13
19	20	21	22	23	24
30	29	28	27	26	25
31	32	33	34	35	36

(c) 680 acres

493. Q. Draw a Township Plan on a scale of approximately one inch to the mile and number all sections correctly. Mark this plat showing directions and work out the following description:
(a) "Beginning at the NW corner of the NW $1/4$ of Section 10, thence southeasterly to the SW corner of the SW $1/4$ of Section 11, thence southwesterly to the NW corner of the SE $1/4$ of Section 21, thence northwesterly to the SW corner of the NE $1/4$ of Section 17, thence northeasterly to the point of beginning."

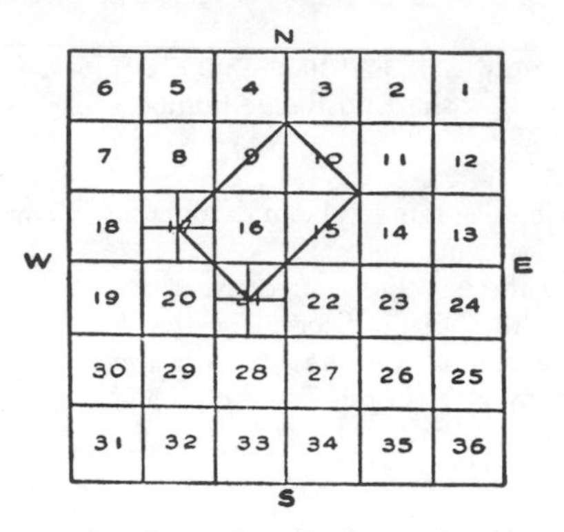

(b) How many acres in the above described tract?
(c) What is the name of this type of description?

A. (a) Drawing above (b) 1,920 acres (c) Metes and Bounds

494. Q. The following diagram represents five adjacent townships, the center one of which has been designated as Township 20 North; Range 1 East of the 6th P.M.

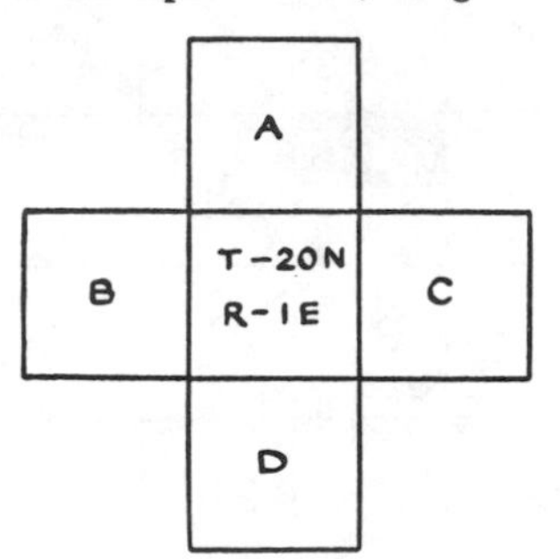

(a) Give township and range numbers for Township "A" in above diagram.
(b) Give township and range numbers for Township "B" in above diagram.
(c) Give township and range numbers for Township "C" in above diagram.
(d) Give township and range numbers for Township "D" in above diagram.

A. (a) T-21 N; R-1E
(b) T-20 N; R-1W
(c) T-20 N; R-2E
(d) T-19 N; R-1E

495. Q. The diagram below has been designated as Section 32; T-12-N; R-3-E of the 6th P.M.

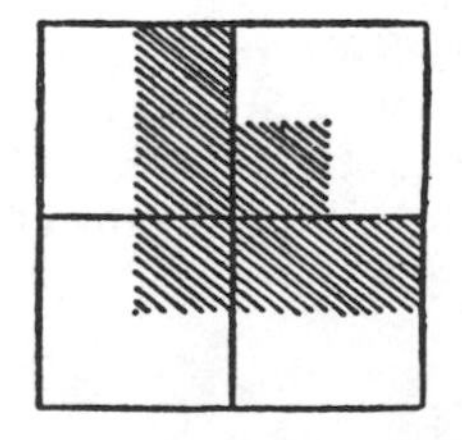

(a) On the above plot, how many acres are contained within the shaded area?
(b) What would be the cost per acre if the above tract sold for $23,340?

A. (a) 240 acres (b) $97.25

496. Q. (a) Draw a diagram of the NE 1/4 of the SW 1/4 of a section of land.
(b) How many acres are in the plot?

A. (a)

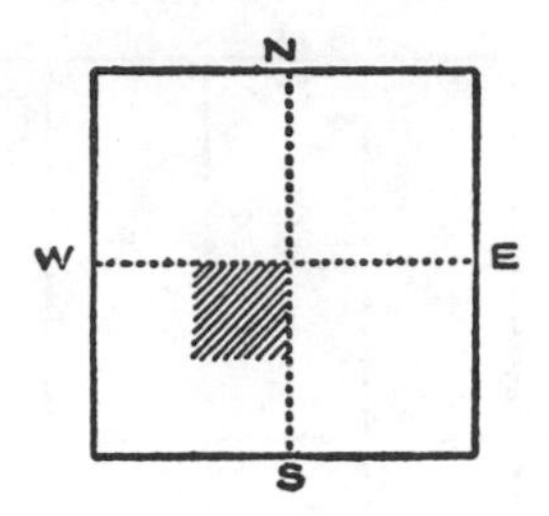

(b) 40 acres

497. Q. Below is a diagram of a section of land. Locate and shade in the following tracts, and show how many acres in each:
(a) E $1/2$ of SE $1/4$ of NW $1/4$
(b) NE $1/4$ of SW $1/4$
(c) NW $1/4$ of NW $1/4$ of SE $1/4$
(d) N $1/2$ of NW $1/4$
(e) If the land described sells for $52.50 per acre, what was the selling price?
(f) What would the sales commission be at 10% ?

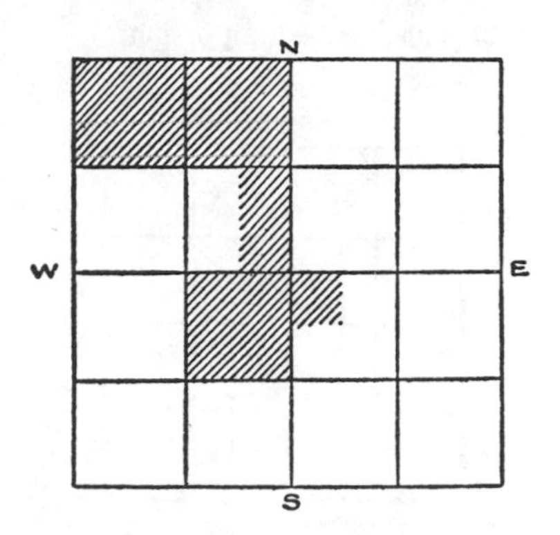

A. (a) 20 acres (b) 40 acres (c) 10 acres
(d) 80 acres (e) $7,875 (f) $787.50

498. Q. Draw a plat of a SQUARE block consisting of 10 identical lots 40′ by 100′.
(a) The top of the plat will face north and the lots will face north and south. The lots will be numbered from 1 to 10, clockwise, beginning with the northwesterly lot. Show the dimensions.
(b) Show the following described tract: "Beginning at the intersection point of the south and west boundaries of the number 10 lot, thence due north 100 feet, thence southeasterly to a point on the south boundary of lot 8 twenty feet west of the intersecting point of the south and east boundaries of lot 8, thence due west to the place of beginning."
(c) How many square feet in the above described tract ?
(d) How many square feet remain in just the lots affected by the above described tract ?
(e) Excluding all of lots 8, 9, and 10, how many square feet remain in the balance of the entire tract ?

A. (a) and (b)

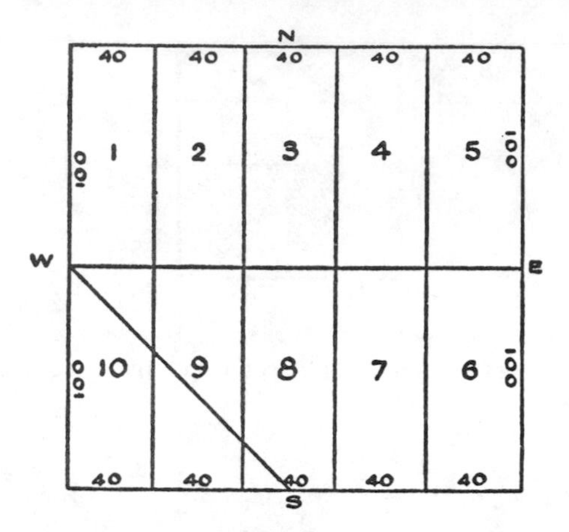

(c) 5,000 (d) 7,000 (e) 28,000

499. Q. The diagram below has been designated as Sec. 17, T-3-N, R-16, EBM.
(a) Shade the SW 1/4 of NE 1/4.
(b) How many acres in this shaded portion?

A. (a)

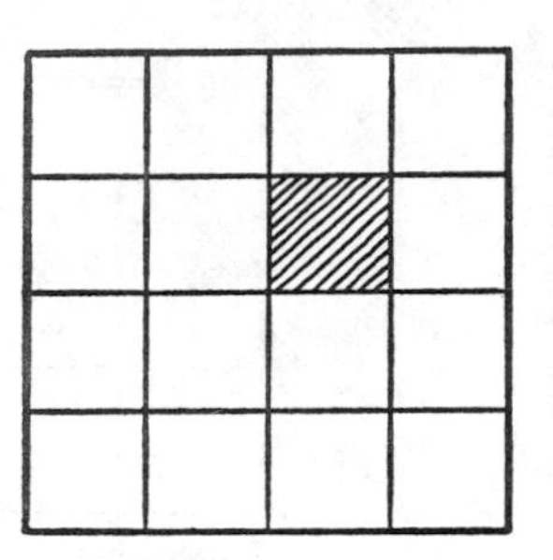

(b) 40 acres

500. Q. Give the correct description of the following parcel of land, marked with
(a) an "X", situated in Sec. 31, T-4-N, R-5-EMB.
(b) How many acres in this area marked with an "X"?

A. (a) NW 1/4 NW 1/4; SE 1/4 Sec. 31; T4N, R 5 EMB.
(b) 10 acres

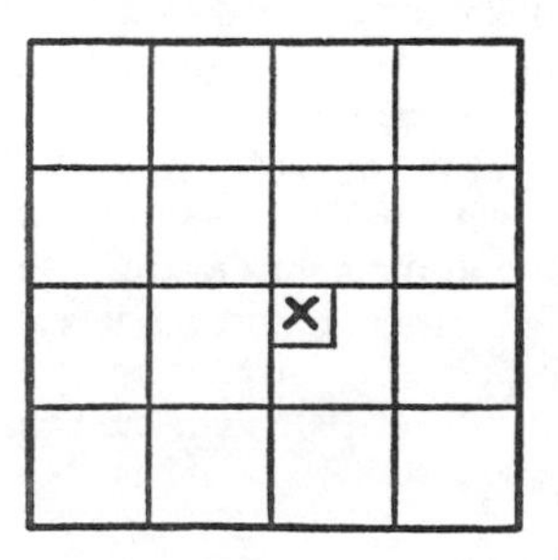

501. Q. (a) Draw a Township plat and number all sections in the proper order.
(b) Work out the following description:

N

6	5	4	3	2	1
7	8	9	10	11	12
18	17	16	15	14	13
19	20	21	22	23	24
30	29	28	27	26	25
31	32	33	34	35	36

W E

S

"Beginning at the SE corner of section 4, thence southeasterly to the SE corner of section 10, thence southwesterly to the NW corner of the SE quarter of section 21, thence southeasterly to the NE corner of section 28, thence northeasterly to the SE corner of the NW quarter of section 22, thence northwesterly to the SW corner of section 9, thence northeasterly to the point of beginning."

(c) How many acres in the tract described in Part (b)?

(d) How many acres of section 15 are included in the tract in Part (b)?

(e) What is the name of the type of description in Part (b)?

A. (a) and (b).

(c) 1,600 (d) 320 (e) Metes and Bounds

502. Q. (a) How do you arrive at area in terms of square feet?

(b) How do you arrive at cubage?

A. (a) Multiply the frontage (or width) by the depth.

(b) Multiply frontage by depth by height.

503. Q. (Pennsylvania) Make up a settlement sheet from the following information: Adam Steele, unmarried, is selling his property located at 613 Highland Avenue, Pittsburgh, Pa., to Henry Wagner at a consideration price of $3,500. The purchaser has paid $200 deposit money. The deal is being closed as of May 15, 1974. The county taxes, amounting to $21.28 per year, have not yet been paid. The city and school taxes for 1974, amounting to $72.47 per year, have been paid by the seller. Fire insurance policy premium for policy expiring January 30, 1975, in the amount of $2,500, was $13.13. The rent is $32.50 per month.

A.

STATEMENT OF SETTLEMENT

Date: May 15, 1974

Seller: Adam Steele
Purchaser: Henry Wagner
Premises: 613 Highland Ave., Pittsburgh, Pa.

WITH PURCHASER

	Debit	*Credit*
Consideration	$3,500.00	
Deposit Money		$ 200.00
4½ mos. County Tax (1974)		7.98
7½ mos. City and School Tax (1974)	45.29	
8½ mos. Fire Ins. Policy	9.30	
½ mo. rent		16.25
Due Seller		3,330.36
	$3,554.59	$3,554.59

WITH SELLER

	Debit	*Credit*
Due at settlement		$3,330.36
State Stamps	$ 35.00	
City Stamps	35.00	
Notary Fee	.50	
Net Due seller	3,259.86	
	$3,330.36	$3,330.36

504. Q. (Arizona) A broker listed a property for $21,500. He finally sold it for $20,500. The commission paid to broker was 5%. The property was assessed at 52% of the sale price and the tax rate is $4.828 per hundred. Taxes are paid in full for the fiscal year 1973-1974. There is an $8,500 mortgage of record at 6% interest. The interest is payable semi-annually July 1st and January 1st of each year, and the interest is paid to July 1st, 1973. The improvements on the property are valued at $16,000. The fire insurance policy is for 85% of this value at the premium rate of 78¢ per hundred for three years. The paid-up policy runs to January 1, 1974. Policy of Title Insurance for $20,500 costing $72.50 is paid by the seller. The escrow charges are $32.00 divided equally between seller and buyer. Revenue stamps and a charge of $1.50 for drawing the deed are paid for by the seller. Closing date on escrow is October 1, 1973.
How much money does the seller receive?

Debit		*Credit*	
Existing Mtge.	$8,500.00	Selling price	$20,500.00
R. E. Comm.	1,025.00	Pro-rate Tax	386.00
Interest	127.50	Pro-rate Ins.	8.85
Title Ins.	72.50		
Escrow Charge	16.00	Total Cr.	$20,894.85
Drawing Deed	1.50	Debit	9,742.50
Total	$9,742.50	Cash Due	$11,152.35

505. Q. (Arkansas) Prepare a closing statement using only the facts furnished here. Assume that you negotiated the sale as a real estate broker. A prospect signs an offer with you to buy a small residence property for $8,000.00, agrees to assume an existing mortgage and deposits with you $300.00 earnest money. The owner accepts this offer. The mortgage is in the original sum of $4,000.00 and bears interest at 6% per annum; $800.00 has been paid on the principal; the interest on the balance has been paid through January 31, 1974. Seller agrees that buyer shall be given credit for accrued interest. The 1973 general taxes in the amount of $53.28 have been paid

in full. No taxes of any kind are delinquent. Seller agrees that buyer shall be given credit for prorating of 1974 taxes to the closing date on the the same basis as the amount of taxes paid for 1973. There is a one year fire insurance policy on the improvement in the amount of $5,000.00 expiring July 1, 1974, on which a premium of $28.56 has been paid. It is agreed to charge the buyer with the unused premium on a pro-rata basis and leave the policy in force. Your commission is 5%. The cost of continuation of the abstract to date is $15.00. The proper amount of revenue stamps are to be placed on the deed. The closing date is August 1, 1974. The only money that you will end up with, as the broker, will be the commission, revenue stamp money and abstract fee.

A. **SETTLEMENT WITH BUYER**

	Debit	*Credit*
Sale price	$8,000.00	
Insurance adjustment	26.18	
Mortgage		$3,200.00
Interest		96.00
Earnest money		300.00
Taxes		31.08
Amount to collect from buyer at closing		4,399.10
	$8,026.18	$8,026.18

SETTLEMENT WITH SELLER

	Debit	*Credit*
Sale price		$8,000.00
Insurance adjustment		26.18
Mortgage	$3,200.00	
Interest	96.00	
Taxes	31.08	
Commission	400.00	
Abstract	15.00	
Net due seller	4,284.10	
	$8,026.18	$8,026.18

506. Q. (California) A broker sold a single-family residence foı $17,800.00. The escrow closed on December 20, 1971, and it was agreed that prorations were to be made as of the close of escrow. The second half of the current fiscal year property taxes had not been paid. The taxes were $468.00 per annum. A paid-up three year fire insurance policy expiring December 31, 1972, costing $75.60 originally, was also to be prorated in escrow. A standard title insurance policy, costing $154.00 was to be paid for by the buyer. The escrow instructions provided that seller would pay a 2 per cent discount fee for obtaining a new first trust deed loan securing a note in the amount of $10,750.00 to refinance a first trust deed of like amount. The existing second deed of trust in the sum of $3,250.00 contained a subordination clause. The second trust deed was assumed by the buyer. The broker handled the escrow, but he did not charge a fee for this service. The broker's commission of 6 per cent of the sale due from seller was to come from the proceeds of the escrow. From the above facts prepare closing statements for seller and buyer. Show all charges and credits. Assume there are no other costs to either party than those indicated above.

A. **SELLER'S CLOSING STATEMENT**

	Debit	*Credit*
Purchase Price		$17,800.00
Taxes ($468 for 1/3 month @ $39.00)		13.00
Insurance ($75.60 12 1/3 months @ $2.10)		25.90

	Debit	Credit
Commission ($17,800 × .06)	1,068.00	
Loan Charges ($10,750 × .02)	215.00	
Assumed Second Deed of Trust	3,250.00	
Refinanced First Deed of Trust	10,750.00	
Balance to Seller	2,555.90	
	$17,838.90	$17,838.90

BUYER'S CLOSING STATEMENT

	Debit	*Credit*
Purchase Price	$17,800.00	
Taxes	13.00	
Insurance	25.90	
Assumed Second Deed of Trust		3,250.00
Proceeds of Loan		10,750.00
Title Insurance	154.00	
Received from Buyers		3,992.90
	$17,992.90	$17,992.90

507. Q. (Florida) Diane Smith has contracted to purchase a duplex owned by C. P. Murphy for $38,000. Mr. Robert Realtor, the broker, representing Mr. Murphy, has accepted a deposit from Miss Smith of $2,000. Miss Smith has agreed to assume the existing first mortgage for $26,500. Mr. Murphy has agreed to take back a second mortgage for $5,000 at 7 per cent payable monthly over a ten-year term. Closing will take place on June 30. All prorations are on a twelve equal months basis. The duplex was assessed by both the City and County for $34,000. The millage in the City is 13 mills and in the County, 17 mills. The property insurance was prepaid for two years as of January 1 of this year in the amount of $160. Both apartments in the duplex were rented January 1 of this year. Each unit rents for $180 a month. The first month's payment on the second mortgage of $58.06 is to be paid in advance at closing. The title company's bill for the abstract to seller was $65. The seller was to furnish deed ($10.00) and to provide state documentary and surtax stamps for the deed. The broker's commission is 6 per cent. Lawyer's fees of $25 for the mortgage and note, recording fees of $4.50 and documentary and intangible taxes based on the amount of the mortgage are payable by buyer. In addition, the buyer purchased title insurance costing $380. Recording the deed fee is $3.00. Based on the above information, prepare the following schedules: (1) Seller's Closing Statement; (2) Buyer's Closing Statement; (3) Broker's Reconciliation Statement.

A. (1) **SELLER'S CLOSING STATEMENT**

DATE OF CLOSING June 30, 19——

	Debit	*Credit*
Purchase Price		$38,000.00
First Mortgage—Balance	$26,500.00	
Second Mortgage	5,000.00	
Prorations and Prepayments:		
Rent	360.00	
Prepayment: 2nd Mortgage		58.06
Insurance		120.00
Taxes: City	221.00	
County	289.00	
Expenses		
Abstract Continuation	65.00	
Attorney's Fee	10.00	
Documentary Stamps:		
Florida Surtax	12.65	
Deed tax	114.00	

Brokerage	2,280.00	
Total Debits and Credits	34,851.65	38,178.06
Balance Due Seller	3,326.41	
GRAND TOTALS	$38,178.06	$38,178.06

(2) BUYER'S CLOSING STATEMENT
DATE OF CLOSING June 30, 19——

	Debit	*Credit*
Purchase Price	$38,000.00	
First Mortgage—Balance		26,500.00
Second Mortgage		5,000.00
Binder Deposit		2,000.00
Prorations and Prepayments:		
Rent		360.00
Prepayment: 2nd Mortgage	58.06	
Insurance	120.00	
Taxes: City		221.00
County		289.00
Expenses:		
Attorney's fee	25.00	
Documentary Stamps:		
Mortgage—Note	7.50	
Intangible Tax—Mortgage	10.00	
Recording:		
Mortgage	4.50	
Deed	3.00	
Title Insurance	380.00	
Total Debits and Credits	38,608.06	34,370.00
Balance Due from Buyer		4,238.06
GRAND TOTALS	$38,608.06	$38,608.06

(3) Cash Reconciliation Statement
(BROKER'S STATEMENT)

	Receipts	*Disbursements*
Deposit	$2,000.00	
Check from buyer at closing	4,238.06	
Brokerage fee		2,280.00
Check to seller at closing		3,326.41
Seller's expense (less brokerage)		201.65
Buyer's expense		430.00
TOTALS	$6,238.06	$6,238.06

508. Q. (New York) Adam Smith purchased a property from Bud Jones on July 1; price $7,900.00, deposit on contract $400.00, closing date to be August 15. The annual city taxes are $126.00, the annual county taxes $60.00, and the annual water charge $18.00. All of these items have been paid as of January 1, and the monthly rental is $66.00 which was paid to the end of the month. The purchaser is to assume a $3,000 mortgage at 5 per cent. Interest was paid on July 1. Insurance policy is obtained by buyer at date of closing; the premium is $48, for a three year period. The seller is to pay the broker 4 per cent commission. Prepare an itemized statement which will indicate how much the seller owes the purchaser on closing, how much the purchaser owes the seller and how much commission was earned.

A.

	Seller Owes	Purchaser Owes
Price		$7,900.00
Deposit		400.00
Balance		7,500.00
City Tax		47.25
County Tax		22.50
Water		6.75
Rent	33.00	
Interest	18.75	
	51.75	
Commission	316.00	
GRAND TOTALS	$367.75	$7,576.50

509. Q. (Wisconsin) Albert and Elsie Sims are purchasing a dwelling in Goodtown, Wisconsin, from Richard Hebner for $31,350.00, through the Model Realty Co. on August 6, 1974. An earnest money deposit of $1,000 is paid to the broker. The deal is contingent on the buyers obtaining a $25,000 mortgage at 8 ½ per cent for a 20 year term. If unable to obtain a mortgage, the seller agrees to accept their present home at 1223 Greentree Road, Goodtown, Wisconsin, at $20,000; and a Land Contract Mortgage to the seller in the amount of $5,000. The taxes for 1974 are $1,125 per annum and have not been paid. The broker's commission is 7 per cent.

The agreements are dated August 6, 1974 and the deal is to be closed on August 31, 1974. The seller is to pay, in advance, an occupancy charge of $5 per day for 10 days after the closing. The charge to the seller for Abstract Extension is $116.87. Attorney's fee of $50. Survey charge to seller of $138.95. Termite Inspection $45.00. $600 is to be held by the broker to insure repair of septic system. Broker to hold $1,500 in escrow for occupancy penalty to insure possession.

Prepare the following from the above information:

1. Buyer's Settlement Statement
2. Broker's Settlement with Seller

A.

BUYER'S SETTLEMENT STATEMENT

	Due Seller	Credit Buyer
Sale Price	$31,350.00	
Down Payment		$ 1,000.00
Tax Adjustment 1974, pro rated from January 1 to August 31 (Last Year's Tax $1,125)		750.00
Prepaid Credit for Occupancy		50.00
Allowances for: Home at 1223 Greentree Road, Goodtown, Wisconsin		20,000.00
Total	$31,350.00	$21,800.00
Less credit to buyer	21,800.00	
Balance due seller	9,500.00	
Balance (3) due seller as follows:		
Land Contract - Mortgage executed this day to Seller	$ 5,000.00	
Check or Cash to Balance	4,550.00	
Total Settlement due Seller	$ 9,550.00	

BROKER'S SETTLEMENT WITH SELLER

	Charges Against Seller	Due Seller
Down Payment Received from Buyer		$1,000.00

Cash Balance Received from Buyer		4,550.00
Charges Against Seller:		
Abstract Extension or Title Policy	$ 116.87	
Attorney's Fee	50.00	
Survey	138.95	
Commission	2,194.50	
Services (Itemize)		
Termite Inspection	45.00	
Escrow Occ. $1,500		
Sewer 600	2,100.00	
Total Payments Due Seller		$5,550.00
Total Charges Against Seller	$4,645.32	4,645.32
Net Balance to be paid Seller		$ 904.68

510. Q. From the following information, prepare a closing statement: Ray Upton and Opal, his wife, sellers, and Don Hutchins and Mary, his wife, buyers. Agreement is dated January 15, 1974 and closing is on February 15, 1974. Selling price is $18,000 and 10 per cent was paid as an earnest money deposit. Buyers have assumed and agreed to pay existing mortgage of $14,468. Taxes, interest, insurance and rents are to be pro-rated on a 30-day month. Taxes, based on 1973 figures, amount to $411.60 for the year. Present rental is $95 per month. February rent has been paid. The insurance policy, dated December 1, 1972, is for a three year period and premium is $226.08. Abstract extension fee is $30; abstract examination is $25 and loan transfer fee is $50. Recording fee is $3. Broker's commission is 6%.

CLOSING STATEMENTS

	SELLER:		BUYER:	
	Debit	Credit	Debit	Credit
1. Sale Price		$18,000.00	$18,000.00	
2. Earnest Money				1,800.00
3. Mortgage Balance	14,468.00			14,468.00
4. Mortgage Interest Proration	36.17			36.17
5. Real Estate Taxes	51.45			51.45
6. Hazard Insurance		135.02	135.02	
7. Apartment Rent Proration	47.50			47.50
8. Abstract Extension	30.00			
9. Abstract Examination			25.00	
10. Loan Transfer Fee			50.00	
11. Deed Recording Fee			3.00	
12. Commission—John Doe Realty	1,080.00			
13. Balance Due from Buyer	XXXXXX	XXXXXX		1,809.90
14. Balance Due Seller	2,421.90		XXXXXX	XXXXXX
TOTALS	$18,135.02	$18,135.02	$18,213.02	$18,213.02

Answer the following questions as *True* or *False*. If false, give the correct answer.

1. Upon receipt of the deposit money, the broker should turn it over to the seller.
   A. should deposit it in his trust or escrow account.
2. The broker is the agent of the sellers.
   A. True.
3. The sellers are no longer liable for payment of the mortgage.
   A. False.

4. The buyer is not liable for the mortgage.
   A. False. Since buyer has assumed and agreed to pay the mortgage.
5. If Don Hutchins dies, his interest will be inherited by his wife and children.
   A. False. By his wife.
6. In lieu of an abstract, mortgage insurance could have been obtained.
   A. False. Title insurance.
7. No title insurance is necessary for the buyers, since the mortgagee has title insurance.
   A. False. Mortgagee only is protected.
8. The consent of the mortgagee to the sale is required.
   A. False.
9. The mortgagee must now file a lien release in favor of the buyers.
   A. False. The mortgagee does nothing.
10. If the buyers default on the mortgage, the mortgagee can foreclose and hold the buyers liable for any deficiency.
    A. True.
11. If the mortgagee sells (assigns) the mortgage, the assignee should obtain a Certificate of No Defense (Estoppel Certificate) from the buyers.
    A. True.

511. Q. (Georgia) Adam Baker and Helen Baker, his wife, sold their property in Greenwood Acres, Albany, Georgia, to Bert Charles and Louise Charles, his wife, on September 8, 1973. Closing date is November 22, 1973. The price was $25,125, with an earnest money deposit of $1,000. Broker's commission is 6%. The buyers are assuming a mortgage of $19,832.00, at 6% interest. Mortgage payment (interest and principal) of $138.34, payable on the first day of each month. The sellers are taking back a purchase money mortgage of $3,000, with interest at 7%. Tenant has paid $220 rent for November. The property is assessed at $8,800 and tax rate is 47.90 mills. Taxes are due October 1 of each calendar year and were paid in full by the sellers. Purchasers are buying rugs and drapes for $250. State deed transfer stamps are at the rate of $.10 per $100. Preparation of deed is $15.00. Preparation of second mortgage and note is $15.00 and intangible tax is $1.50 per $500. Buyers are assuming comprehensive insurance policy, dated July 1, 1973. Annual premium is $108.00. Title search is $150, to be paid by buyer. There is an outstanding paving lien of $121. Prepare a closing statement for buyer and seller, using a 30 day month:

A.

CLOSING STATEMENT FOR BUYERS
BERT CHARLES AND LOUISE CHARLES, HIS WIFE
DATE: NOVEMBER 22, 1973

	Debits	Credits
Purchase Price	$25,125.00	
Rugs and Drapes	250.00	
Prepaid Taxes		
38 days owed by buyers	44.46	
218 days insurance	65.40	
Earnest money deposit		1,000.00
First Mortgage Assumed		19,832.00
Accrued Interest 11/1 to 11/22		72.71
Second Mortgage		3,000.00
8 days Rent		58.67
Title fee	150.00	
Preparation Second Mortgage	15.00	
Recording Deed & Mortgage	8.00	
Intangible Tax	9.00	
Balance owed by Buyers		1,703.48
	$25,666.86	$25,666.86

CLOSING STATEMENT FOR SELLERS
ADAM BAKER AND HELEN BAKER, HIS WIFE
DATE: NOVEMBER 22, 1973

	Debits	Credits
Purchase Price		$25,125.00
Rugs and Drapes		250.00
Taxes 38 days		44.46
218 days insurance		65.40
Earnest Money Deposit	$1,000.00	
First Mortgage Assumed	19,832.00	
Accrued Interest 11/1 to 11/22	72.71	
Second Mortgage	3,000.00	
8 days Rent	58.67	
Balance, Commission	507.50	
State Transfer Tax	25.13	
Preparation of Deed	15.00	
Paving Lien	121.00	
Cash Balance, due Sellers	852.85	
	$25,484.86	$25,484.86

512. Q. On September 15, 1974 an apartment building was conveyed by Louis Stone and Louise Stone, his wife, to Sam Lewis and Jean Lewis, his wife, for a total consideration price of $125,000. The purchaser paid deposit money of $8,000 to the broker who retained it on account of commission. The taxes amounting to $2,520 have been paid by the seller. The fire insurance policy expires in three months from September 15, 1974 and the premium paid by the seller was $468 for three years. The liability insurance expires in six months from September 15, 1974 and the premium paid by the seller was $72 for a one year policy. The rentals amounting to $2,500 per month have been paid to October 1, 1974. The water rent is paid to August 15, 1974 and amounts to $150 per quarter. The sewer rent is also paid to August 15, 1974 and amounts to $90 per quarter. Taxes, insurance, rents, water rent and sewer rent were prorated as of date of transfer, i.e., September 15, 1974. Transfer stamps are to be equally divided (rate is $.50 per $500 for state and same rate for municipality); broker's commission of 7%, preparation of deed ($20), Notary fee for deed ($1), buyer's title fee ($585.50), settlement fee ($50), recording deed ($7) are to be considered and properly charged in this settlement.

	Debit	Credit
Consideration		$125,000.00
3 ½ months taxes		735.00
3 months fire insurance		39.00
6 months liability insurance		36.00
Deposit money	$ 8,000.00	
½ month rent—September 15 to October 1	1,250.00	
Water rent from August 15 to September 15	50.00	
Sewer rent from August 15 to September 15	30.00	
Balance due	116,480.00	
	$125,810.00	$125,810.00
With Louis Stone, et ux, SELLERS		
Balance due		$116,480.00
Transfer stamps	$ 1,250.00	
Commission (balance)	750.00	
Preparation of deed	20.00	
Notary fee	1.00	

Net balance due sellers	114,459.00	
	$116,480.00	$116,480.00
With Sam Lewis, et ux, PURCHASERS		
Balance due sellers		$116,480.00
Transfer Stamps		1,250.00
Title fee		585.50
Settlement fee		50.00
Recording deed		7.00
Total		$118,372.50

Completed Solutions to Arithmetic Problems

1. 500 feet × 300 feet = 150,000 sq. ft.
   150,000 sq. ft. × $ .60 = $90,000 cost of paving
   500 feet × $5.00 = $2,500 cost of gutters and curbs
   $90,000 + $2,500 + $5,000 = $97,500 total cost
2. 150,000 divided by 300 = 500 spaces
3. Lot #2 equals Lot #1 + $1,200
   Lot #3 equals Lot #1 + $1,200 + $1,600, or $2,800
   Lot #1 + $4,000 (increase) equals $10,000
   $10,000 – $4,000 = $6,000
   $6,000 ÷ 3 lots = $2,000 (1st lot)
   $2,000 + $1,200 = $3,200 (2nd lot)
   $3,200 + $1,600 = $4,800 (3rd lot)
   $2,000 + $3,200 + $4,800 = $10,000 (total)
4. 8,000 × $1.75 = $14,000 gross income
   $14,000 – $7,000 = $7,000 net return
   $7,000 divided by $72,000 = 9.72 + percent
5. 43,560 sq. ft. in one acre
   2 × 43,560 sq. ft. = 87,120 sq. ft.
   28 ft. × 210 ft. = 5,880 sq. ft. (street area)
   87,120 – 5,880 = 81,240 left for lots
   60 × 190 = 11,400 sq. ft., size of each lot
   81,240 ÷ 11,400 = 7 lots
6. $1/8$ inch represents 1 foot
   1 inch = 8 × 1 foot, or 8 feet
   $6\frac{1}{2}$ × 8 feet = 52 feet
7. 90 × $2.50 = $22,500.00 – King's offer.
   90 feet × 180 ft. = 16,200 square feet.
   16,200 × $1.25 = $20,250 – Queen's offer.
   $22,500 – $20,250 = $2,250.
8. 4 × $125 = $500 1st floor
   4 × $120 = $480 second floor
   4 × $110 = $440 third floor
   $1,420
   $1,420 × 12 mo. = $17,040 annual rent.
   $17,040 – $2,800 = $14,240 net rental.
   $14,240 ÷ 8% = $178,000
9. $1,500.00
   .055
   ———
   $ 82.50 $82.50 ÷ 365 = .226
   $25 divided by .226 = 110 days
   110 days = 3 months, 20 days
10. The tract contains 10 acres
    10 × $225 = $2,250.00 is the selling price
    5% of $2,250.00 = $112.50, broker's commission
    10% of $112.50 = $11.25
    $112.50 – $11.25 = $101.25, broker's net
11. $1200 – $1000 = $200
    $1,000 × .10 = $100
    $200 – $100 = $100 better for lot

12. 348,480 ÷ 43,560 sq. ft. (per acre) = 8 acres
 8 × $800 = $6,400 (total price)
13. $1/20$ of $11,000 = $550, depreciation per year
 $550/11{,}000$ of 100% = 5%, depreciation per year
14. $1/2 \times 1/4 \times 1/4 \times 1/4 = 1/128$
 Section contains 640 acres
 640 acres ÷ 128 = 5 acres
15. $2,000 ÷ .08 = $25,000
16. 4 × $120 = $480, interest for 1 year
 $480 ÷ $8,000 = 6%
17. $\frac{.06}{12} = .005$
 $100 ÷ .005 = $20,000
18. (a) 8% × $1/4$ yr. = 2%
 $10,000 × 2% = $200
 (b) 7% × $1/3$ yr. = 2.33%
 $10,000 × 2.33% = $233.33 $233.33 – 200 = $33.33
19. (a) $1/2 \times 1/2 \times 1/4 = 1/16$ 640 acres in a section
 $1/16$ of 640 acres = 40 acres
 (b) $1/2 \times 1/2 \times 1/4 = 1/16$
 $1/16$ of 640 acres = 40 acres
20. $6/5$ × $300 = $360
 $5/6$ × 360 = $300
 $360 – $300 = $60(a)
21. 12 mos. × $425 = $5,100
 $5,100 : 8% :: 100% (x) dollars
 8 × 100 = 800
 $510,000 divided by 800 = $63,750
22. 95% : $15,751 :: 100% : (x) dollars
 $15,751 divided by 95% = $16,580
23. A section is 640 acres
 2 $1/2$ × 640 = 1,600 acres × $50 = $80,000
 5% of $80,000 = $4,000
 40% of $4,000 = $1,600
24. 450 feet × 600 feet = 270,000 sq. ft.
 270,000 sq. ft. divided by 43,560 sq. ft. = 6.19 plus acres
 6.2 × $100 = $620
25. Alberts contributed $12,000 of $20,000, or $3/5$
 $3/5$ of $12,000 = $7,200, Alberts' profit
 Briggs contributed $8,000 of $20,000, or $2/5$
 $2/5$ of $12,000 = $4,800, Briggs' share
26. $147,800, expenses, minus $77,800 = $70,000 needed
 $\frac{\$70{,}000}{\$4{,}540{,}000}$ = $.01541, the rate per dollar
 $.01541 × $1,000 = $15.41 tax rate
27. $20,000 minus $3,600 = $16,400, F.H.A. mortgage
 $16,400 divided by $97.79 = 167.7 months (168)
 168 mos. divided by 12 mos. = 14 years
28. $25,000 minus $5,000 = $20,000 (mortgage)
 $20,000 × .06 × $1/12$ = $100 interest for first month
 $100 payment on principal
 $200 payment for first month
 $20,000 minus $100 = $19,900 principal due at end of first month
 $19,900 × .06 × $1/12$ = $99.50 interest for second month
 (a) $100 plus $99.50, interest payments = $199.50

(b) \$19,900 minus \$100 = \$19,800, balance due

29. 2.5% of \$92.46 = \$2.31
    \$92.46 minus \$2.31 = \$90.15
30. \$6,700 minus \$1,200 = \$5,500, due on mortgage
    \$5,500 × 5% = \$275
    \$6,700 × 2% = \$134
    \$227 (other expenses)
    \$636, total expenses
    12 × \$60 = \$720, income
    \$720 minus \$636 = \$84, net
    $\frac{\$84}{\$1,200}$ of 100% = 7%, net
31. 4 ½ % of \$7,500 = \$337.50, income expected
    Total expenses, \$208.50
    \$337.50 plus \$208.50 = \$546.00 yearly rental
    \$546.00 divided by 12 = \$45.50 monthly rental
32. 3 yds. = 9 ft.
    π = 3.1416 × 9 = 28.2744 ft. circumference
    28.2744 × \$.25 = \$7.07, cost
33. (a) monthly payment would be \$15,600 divided by 240 payments, or \$65.00
    (b) loan interest is 7% of \$10,000, or \$700 per year. Interest per month would be $^{1}/_{12}$ of \$700 = \$58.33
    \$65.00 minus \$58.33 = \$6.67
34. 4 × \$125 × 12 mos. = \$6,000

Expense:	Mtge. interest	\$1,500
	Depreciation	700
	Expense	1,825
		\$4,025

    \$6,000 minus \$4,025 = \$1,975, net income
    \$1,975 divided by \$45,000 = 4.38%
35. \$6,250 × .05 = \$312.50
    \$312.50 divided by 2 = \$156.25
36. \$195 × 12 = \$2,340
    \$2,340 × .025 = \$5,850
37. 2 × \$210 = \$420 annual interest
    \$420 divided by \$6,000 = .07 or 7%
38. 4 × 4 ¼% = 17%, total depreciation
    100% value minus 17% = 83%, or present value
    \$8,725 divided by 83% (.83) = \$10,512.04
39. 90% of \$24,000 = \$21,600, insured value
    \$.54 × \$21,600 = \$116.64, premium for 36 months
    Apr. 1, 1972 to Sept. 1, 1974 = 29 months
    $\frac{29}{36}$ of \$116.64 = \$93.96, buyer owes for unexpired premium
40. Biggs will receive $\frac{\$24,000}{\$40,000}$ or $^{6}/_{10}$ of \$3,000, or \$1,800

    Diggs will receive $\frac{\$16,000}{\$40,000}$ or $^{4}/_{10}$ of \$3,000, or \$1,200
41. Expenses of \$200,000 less revenue of \$85,000 = \$115,000, amount needed
    $\frac{\$115,000}{6,500,000}$ = .0176, rate per dollar

.0176 × $1,000 = $17.69 per $1,000

42. 30% of $30,000= $9,000
$17.69 × 9 = $159.21 tax for 1973
43. 5% of $159.21 = $7.96
44. 12 months × $250 = $3,000, annual income
$3,000 – $900 = $2,100, net return
$2,100 divided by .07 = $30,000
45. Multiply π (3.1416) by the square of the radius
3.1416 × 6 feet × 6 feet = 113.0976, or 113.10 square feet
46. 250 feet plus 350 feet and 250 feet plus 350 feet = 1,200 feet, perimeter
1,200 × .35 = $420
47. 4 yards = 12 feet
12 feet × 3.1416 (π) = 37.6992
37.70 × .30 = $11.31
48. The formula is:

$$\text{Percentage rate of income} = \frac{\text{annual net income}}{\text{cash investment}}$$

$6,750 divided by $90,000 = 7.5 per cent
49. $2,800 plus $2,400 plus $2,450 plus $2,850 plus $3,000 plus $1,400 plus $790 plus $900 plus $700 = $17,290
15% of $17,290 = $2,593.50
$2,593.50 plus $17,290 = $19,883.50, total cost
50. $750 = 100%, cost
$750 : 100% : $450 : (x)%
100 × $450 divided by $750 = 60% of cost received
100% – 60% received = 40% loss
51. 12 months × $96 = $1,152, interest per annum
$1,152 divided by 6% interest = $19,200 (amount of loan)
$19,200 : 80% : (x) : 100%, or $\frac{19{,}200}{80\%}$ = $24,000 appraised valuation
52. 12 × $500 = $6,000, annual return
$6,000 divided by $72,000 = $8\frac{1}{3}$%
53. $25,500 – $5,500 = $20,000, amount of mortgage
$20,000 divided by $100 per month = 200 months
200 divided by 12 months = $16\frac{2}{3}$ years or 16 years, 8 months
54. 6% on $20,000 mortgage is $1,200
$\frac{1}{12}$ of $1200 = $100, interest first month
$20,000 – $100 = $19,900, balance due at end of first month
6% on $19,900 = $1,194
$\frac{1}{12}$ of $1,194 = $99.50, interest second month
(a) $100 plus $99.50 = $199.50, interest paid
(b) $20,000 – $200 = $19,800, credit to Saxton
55. 50 ft. × 100 ft. × $.75 = $3,750
10% of $3,750 = $375
$3,750 – $375 = $3,375
56. Using the simple proportion formula, 20% is to $2,500 as 100% is to (x) dollars, or
$2,500 × 100 divided by 20% = $12,500
57. 69′ × 142′ = 9,798 square feet
$2,645.46 divided by 9,798 = 27 cents
58. 14 lots – 2 lots = 12 lots for sale
12 × 75 feet = 900 feet (total frontage)
$33,750 divided by 900 feet = $37.50, price per front foot
59. 264 ft. × 660 ft. = 174,240 square feet

43,560 sq. ft. = 1 acre
174,240 divided by 43,560 = 4 acres
4 × \$800 = \$3,200

60. \$350 = 5%
\$350 : 5% :: (x) dollars : 100%
$\frac{350 \times 100}{5\%} = \$7,000$
61. 80 × \$75 = \$6,000
62. 24 × 36 = 864 square feet
63. 30 days (April) − 17 days = 13 days
13 days + 31 days (May) + 25 days (June) = 69 days
64. 1 board foot = 12 square inches × 1 inch (thickness)
2″ × 4″ = 8 square inches = $2/3$ of 12 square inches
$2/3 \times 12'$ = 8 board feet in one piece of lumber
8 board feet × 48 = 384 board feet
65. January 1 to March 15 = $2\frac{1}{2}$ months
$2\frac{1}{2} \div 12 = 5/2 \times 1/12 = 5/24$ of a year
66. $3\frac{1}{2} \div 12 = 7/2 \times 1/12 = 7/24$ of a year
67. $.375 = \frac{375}{1000} \quad \frac{375 \div 25}{1000 \div 25} = \frac{15}{40} \quad \frac{15 \div 5}{40 \div 5} = \frac{3}{8}$
68. $.38\frac{1}{3} = 38\frac{1}{3} \div 100 = 115/3 \times 1/100 = 115/300 = 23/60$
69. $1/8 = 1 \div 8 = .125 = 12\frac{1}{2}\%$
70. $1/6 = 1 \div 6 = .16\frac{2}{3} = 16\frac{2}{3}\%$
71. $1/2 + 3/4 + 1/8 = 4/8 + 6/8 + 1/8 = 11/8$ or $1\frac{3}{8}$
72. $1\frac{1}{4} - 3/8 = 10/8 - 3/8 = 7/8$
73. $1/2 + 5/8 + 3/16 = 8/16 + 10/16 + 3/16 = 21/16$ or $1\frac{5}{16}$
74. $1/2$ of 20 = 10 acres $1/4$ of 10 = $2\frac{1}{2}$ acres $10 - 2\frac{1}{2} = 7\frac{1}{2}$ acres
75. $1/2 \times 1/4 = 1/8$
76. $1/2 \div 1/4 = 1/2 \times 4/1 = 4/2 = 2$
77. $\frac{25}{365}$ Divide both numerator and denominator by 5 = $\frac{5}{73}$ of a year
78. $21 \div 30 = 21/30 = 7/10$ or .7
79. $3/5 = 3 \div 5 = .60$ or 60%
80. $87\frac{1}{2}\% = .87\frac{1}{2} = 87\frac{1}{2} \div 100 = 175/2 \times 1/100 = 175/200 = 7/8$
81. 3 years = 36 months $6/36 = 1/6$ of 3 years
82. $2/3 \times 1/2 = 2/6$ or $1/3$
83. $2/3 \div 1/2 = 2/3 \times 2/1 = 4/3$, or $1\frac{1}{3}$
84. $1/2 \div 2/3 = 1/2 \times 3/2 = 3/4$
85. $2/3 \times 12 \quad \frac{2 \times 12}{3} = 24/3 = 8$ months
86. $1/5$ of 365 = 365 ÷ 5 = 73 days
87. $1/6 \times 43,560 = 7,260$ sq. ft.
88. 5,445 ÷ 43,560 = .125 or $1/8$ acre
89. $1/4 + 3/16 = 4/16 + 3/16 = 7/16$ amount for children
$1 - 7/16 = 16/16 - 7/16 = 9/16$ balance
90. $26\frac{6}{12} + 19\frac{9}{12} + 8\frac{10}{12} + 44\frac{8}{12} = 97\frac{33}{12} = 99\frac{9}{12} = 99\frac{3}{4}$
91. $18\frac{1}{2} = 37/2$
$4\frac{1}{6} = 25/6$
$37/2 \div 25/6 = 37/2 \times 6/25 = 111/25 = 4\frac{11}{25}$
92. $5\frac{1}{4}\% = 5.25\%$
\$223.65 = 5.25% of the amount
\$223.65 ÷ 5.25 = \$42.60 = 1% of the amount
The amount = 100%
\$42.60 × 100 = \$4,260 the amount
93. $.83\frac{1}{3} = 83\frac{1}{3} \div 100 = 250/3 \div 100 = 250/3 \times 1/100 = 250/300 = 5/6$
$.75 = 75/100 = 3/4$

$3/4 \times 5/6 = 5/8$

94. $7 \times 2\frac{1}{2}\% = 17\frac{1}{2}\%$ depreciation
$100\% - 17\frac{1}{2}\% = 82\frac{1}{2}\%$ present value
$\$8,085 \div 82.5 = \$98 = 1\%$ of original value — $100\% =$ value
$\$98 \times 100 = \$9,800$ original value

95. $\$19,750 \times .06 = \$1,185$ total commission — $12\frac{1}{2}\% = .125$
$\$1,185 \times .125 = \$148.125$ or $148.13

96. $\$13,800 \div 12 = \$1,150$ mo. loan
$\$71.30 \div \$1,150 = .062$ or 6.2% or $6\frac{1}{5}\%$

97. $9,000 + 7% commission = selling price
$9,000 = 93% of selling price
$\$9,000 \div 93 = \$96.7742$
$\$96.7742 \times 100 = \$9,677.42$

98. 7% on the listed price, commission would have been 7% of $30,000 or $2,100.
10% off the listed price, or $30,000 – $3,000 = $27,000 actual sales price.
7% commission on $27,000 = $1,890 commission received.
$2,100 less $1,890 = $210 less in commission.

99. The average width of lot 60 ft. and 80 ft. is 70 feet.
70 ft. × 150 ft. depth = 10,500 sq. ft.
$13,125 divided by 10,500 sq. ft. = $1.25 per sq. ft.

100. $20 \times 17 = 340$ sq. ft.
$340 \times 9\frac{1}{2} = 3,230$ cu. ft.

101. $40' \times 80' = 3200$ sq. ft.
$40' \times 20' \times \frac{1}{2} \times 400$ sq. ft.
3200 + 400 sq. ft. = 3600 sq. ft.

102. 640 acres constitute a section.
N.W. $\frac{1}{2}$ of N.W. $\frac{1}{4}$ = 40 acres.
N. $\frac{1}{2}$ of N.E. $\frac{1}{4}$ of N.W. $\frac{1}{4}$ = 20 acres.
40 acres + 20 acres = 60 acres.

103. 30 ft. × 40 feet = 1,200 sq. ft.
$1,200 \times \$15.00 = \$18,000.00$
3% × 3 yr. = 9%.
9% of $18,000 = $1,620 depreciation
$18,000 – $1,620 = $16,380.

104. 12 mos. × 100 = $1,200 gross income.
$1,200 – $360 expenses = $840 net income.
$\frac{1}{12}$ of $840 = $70 monthly income.

105. 50% of $22,000 = $11,000 taxable
$.062 \times \$11,000 = \$682$

106. $2640 \times 5280 = 13,939,200$ square feet
$5280 - 2640 = 2640$ feet; $13,939,200 \div 2 = 6,969,600$
$13,939,200 + 6,969,600 = 20,908,800$ square feet
$20,908,800 \div 43,560 = 480$ acres

107. a. $\$9,500 \div 1,000 = 9.5$
$9.5 \times \$9.50 = \$90.25$
b. $\$291 \div 12 = \$24.25$
c. $\$9,500 \div 100 = 95$
$95 \times \$.98 = \$93.10$
$\$93.10 \div 36 = \$2.59$
d. $\$90.25 + \$24.25 + \$2.59 = \$117.09$

108. $500 \times 760 = 380,000$ square feet
$380,000 \div 2 = 190,000$ square feet in lot
$190,000 \div 43,560 = 4.36$ acres

109. $\$24 \times 12 = \$288$ expenses
$3,600 + $288 = $3,888 gross earning

$3,888 = 6% return
$3,888 ÷ 6 = $648
$648 × 100 = $64,800

110. $18,915 ÷ 2.5 = $7,566 year's income
$7,566 ÷ 52 = $145.50 week's income

111. 1320′ × 1980′ = 2,613,600 sq. ft. $16\frac{2}{3}\% = \frac{1}{6}$
43,560 sq. ft. = 1 acre
2,613,600 ÷ 43,560 = 60 acres
$\frac{1}{6}$ of 60 = 10 acres
60 − 10 = 50 acres
50 × 3 = 150 lots

112. $9,265 = 100% of appraisal value
115% of appraisal value = original listing price
$9,265 × 115% = $10,654.75 – the original listing price

113. 75′ × $24 = $ 1,800 assessment—front
$1,800 × 4.8 = $ 8,640 assessment on house
$10,440 × $.068 = $709.92 annual taxes

114. $\frac{1}{4} + \frac{3}{5} = \frac{5}{20} + \frac{12}{20} = \frac{17}{20}$ not usable or under cultivation
$1 - \frac{17}{20} = \frac{20}{20} - \frac{17}{20} = \frac{3}{20}$ = 60 acres meadow land
60 ÷ 3 = 20 acres in $\frac{1}{20}$ of land
20 × 20 = 400 acres total farm

115. Contractor A 18′ × 27′ × 9′ = 4,374 cu. ft. in house
(a) 4,374 × $.29 = $1,268.46, bid of contractor A
Contractor B 18′ × 27′ = 486 sq. ft. floor area
486 × $1.95 = $947.70
18′ × 27′ × $\frac{1}{2}$ = 243 cu. ft. concrete floor
27 cu. ft. = 1 cu. yd.
243 ÷ 27 = 9 cu. yd. concrete needed
9 × $17.50 = $157.50, cost of concrete floor
(b) $947.70 + $157.50 = $1,105.20, bid of contractor B
(c) Contractor B
(d) $1,268.46 − $1,105.20 = $163.26

116. 125 × 160 = 20,000 sq. ft.
20,000 × $.17 = $3,400 property cost
$2.25 × 125 = $281.25 paving cost
$3,400 + $281.25 + $295 = $3,976.25

117. $325 × 52 = $16,900 yearly gross income
$845 × 12 = $10,140 yearly expense
$16,900 − $10,140 = $6,760
$6,760 ÷ $84,500 = .08 or 8%

118. $6\frac{1}{2}\%$ × $4,000 = $260
3 × $260 = $780
$260 ÷ 12 = $21.67
5 × $21.67 = $108.35
$\frac{20}{30}$ × $21.67 = $14.45
$780 + $108.35 + $14.45 = $902.80

119. 5% × $23,000 = $1,150
90% ÷ 2 = 45% of commission for salesman
45% × $1,150 = $517.50

120. 190 × $175.50 = $33,345 sale price
$5,000 + $18,300 + $183 = $23,483
$33,345 − $23,483 = $9,862 balance
$9,862 − $3,972.07 = $5,889.93 cash needed

121. 26 × 38 = 988 square feet
988 × 14 = 13,832 cubic feet

122. 40 × 28 = 1,120 square feet
1,120 × $11.25 = $12,600
123. $75 + $60 = $135
$135 ÷ 2 = $67.50
60 × $67.50 = $4,050
124. $8250 = 95% of selling price
$8250 ÷ 95 = $86.8421 = 1% of selling price
$86.8421 × 100 = $8,684.21 selling price
125. $93.75 × 4 = $375 paid each year
$375 ÷ 5000 = .075 or 7½%
126. $8000 ÷ 100 = 80 per $100
$80 × 2.27 = $181.60 per year
½ of $181.60 = $90.80 taxes for 6 months
127. 132′ × 330′ = 43,560 sq. ft. = 1 acre, $800
128. $8000 × .60 = $4800
$4800 + $500 = $5300
$8000 − $5300 = $2700
129. $23,000 − $11,000 = $12,000 gain
$12,000 ÷ 120,000 = .10 or 10%
130. $4800 ÷ $60,000 ≐ .08 or 8%
131. $57.50 ÷ 5 = $11.50 or 1% of the sum
$11.50 × 100 = $1,150.00
132. $8,750 ÷ 75 = $116.67 per front foot
75′ × 110′ = 8,250 sq. ft.
$8,750 ÷ 8,250 = $1.06 per sq. ft.
133. 75′ × 120′ = 9,000 sq. ft.
9,000 × $.20 = $1,800 property
$590 broker's commission
75′ frontage   75′ × $5.50 = $412.50 sewers and paving
$1,800 + $412.50 = $2,212.50 total
$2,212.50 × .10 = $221.25 expected profit
$2,212.50 + $221.25 + $590 = $3,023.75
134. 34′ × 28′ × 30′ = 28,560 cu. ft.
$8,568 ÷ 28,560 = $.30 cost per cu. ft.
135. 3 lots of $3,000 each = $9,000 $1,000 ÷ $8,000 = ⅛ or 12½%
2 lots at $4,000 each = 8,000
profit = $1,000
136. $8,500 ÷ 8 = $1,062.50 = 1% of investment
$1,062.50 × 100 = $106,250 investment
137. 25′ × 30′ × 5′ = 3,750 cu. ft.   27 cu. ft. = 1 cu. yd.
3,750 ÷ 27 = 138.89 cu. yd.
138.89 × $2.90 = $402.78
138. 495′× 1,320′ = 653,400 sq. ft.   43,560 sq. ft. = 1 acre
653,400 ÷ 43,560 = 15 acres
15 × $200 = $3,000 total price
139. 3 lots @ $2,400 = $7,200 $1,200 ÷ $6,000 = .20 or 20%
2 lots @ $3,000 = 6,000
profit = $1,200
140. 130′ × 30′ = 3,900 sq. ft.   130′ × 30′ × 24′ = 93,600 cu. ft.
3,900 × $8.90 = $34,710 cost by sq. ft.
93,600 × $.37½ = $35,100 cost by cu. ft.
$35,100 − $34,710 = $390 saved by giving contract to Dusch
141. $6,000 − $1,200 = $4,800, balance due
12 × $50 = $600 paid each year
$4,800 ÷ $600 = 8 years

First payment February 1, 1972
Last payment January 1, 1980

142. S1/2 of NE 1/4 of Sec. 27, T-8-N, R-14-E of 6th P.M. = 1/8 of the Sec. 1/8 of 640 = 80 acres
80 × $207.50 = $16,600
$16,600 × .05 = $830 commission
1/2 of $830 = $415, Jones' half of the com.
$415 × .075 = $31.13, Lawrence's commission
$415 − $31.13 = $383.87 Net amount Jones receives

143. $9,000 × .06 × 1/12 = $45 interest 1st month
45.00
$9,045.00 due
125.00 paid 1st month
$8,920.00 balance × .06 × 1/12 = $44.60 interest 2nd month
44.60 interest
$8,964.60 due
124.60 2nd month
$8,840.00 balance × .06 × 1/12 = $44.20 interest 3rd month
44.20 interest
$8,884.20 due
124.20 paid 3rd month
$8,760.00 balance × .06 × 1/12 = $43.80 interest 4th month
43.80 interest
$8,803.80 due
123.80 paid
$8,680.00 balance × .06 × 1/12 = $43.40
$80.00 + $43.40 = $123.40 fifth payment

144. 43,560′ × 10′ = 435,600 sq. ft. in 10 acres
435,600 − 85,600 = 350,000 sq. ft. to be subdivided
50′ × 100′ = 5,000 sq. ft. in each lot
350,000 ÷ 5,000 = 70 lots

145. 46′ × 80′ × 16′ = 58,880 cu. ft. first floor
58,880 × $.80 = $47,104 cost of 1st floor
46′ × 80′ × 14′ = 51,520 cu. ft. 2nd floor
51,520 × $.60 = $30,912 cost of 2nd floor
$47,104 + $30,912 = $78,016 total cost

146. $3,000 ÷ 60 = $50 or 1%
100 × $50 = $5,000, cost of other lot

147. $15,000 × .97 = $14,550 insured value on $15,000
$5,000 × .90 = $4,500 insured value on next $5,000
$24,750 − $20,000 = $4,750 to be insured at 75% of value
$4,750 × .75 = $3,562.50 insured value on balance
$14,550 + $4,500 + $3,562.50 = $22,612.50, insurable if occupied
$22,612.50 × .85 = $19,220.63, insurable if not occupied
$19,220.63 × .04 = $768.83 discount collected on closing the loan

148. 12 × $400 = $4,800 rental
$120,000 − $80,000 = $40,000, balance @ 5%
$40,000 × .05 = $2,000
$4,800 + $2,000 = $6,800, rent for the year

149. 1/4 + 3/16 = 7/16 unusable
1 − 7/16 = 9/16 usable
1/8 × 9/16 = 9/128 for roads
9/16 − 9/128 = 63/128 usable balance
63/128 × 6,400 = 3,150 sq. ft. usable

150. 330′ × 100′ = 33,000 sq. ft. (43,560 sq. ft. = 1 acre)

33,000 ÷ 43,560 = .75 or $\frac{3}{4}$ acre

151. 92 × $95 = $8,740 in older district
112 × $95 = $10,640 in newer district

152. b. $125 − $110 = $15
$15 × 12 = $180 yearly loss
$180 ÷ .06 = $3,000 loss in value

153. $150 × 12 = $1,800 yearly income
$396 + $66 + $123 = $585 yearly expense
$1,800 − $585 = $1,215 profit
$1,215 ÷ $13,500 = .09 or 9%

154. $8,925.25 + $1,510.60 + $4,920.05 + $3,644.10 = $19,000.00 total expense
$53,200 − $19,000 = $34,200

155. $11,389 = 115%; $11,389 ÷ 115 = $99.03; $99.03 × 100 = $9,903 original price
$9,903 × .45 = $4,456.35; $4,456.35 × .048 = $213.90 taxes;
$213.90 × 3 = $641.70; .035 × $9,903 = $346.61 yearly interest loss;
3 × $346.61 = $1,039.83; $11,389 − $9,903 = $1,486
$1,039.83 + $641.70 = $1,681.53; $1,681.53 − $1,486 = $195.53 loss

156. $63 × 50 = $3,150 lot price
$3,150 + $9,216 = $12,366 total cost
$12,366 − $5,000 = $7,366
.055 × $7,366 = $405.13 annual interest payment
$405.13 ÷ 2 = 202.56\frac{1}{2}$ round off to $202.57

157. 100 + 360 = 460 foot lot perimeter
2 × 3$\frac{1}{2}$ = 7 feet for gates
460 − 7 = 453 feet
$.80 × 453 = $362.40
2 × $16.75 = $33.50; $33.50 + $362.40 = $395.90

158. 8 × 36 = 288 square feet
$.20 × 288 = $57.60 labor cost
36 ft. × 8 ft. × $\frac{1}{4}$ ft. = 72 cu. ft.
72 cu. ft. ÷ 27 = 2.666 cu. yds.
2.666 cu. yds. × $13.50 = $35.99
$35.99 + $57.60 = $93.59

159. 30 days (April) − 17 days = 13 days
13 days + 31 days (May) + 25 days (June) = 69 days

160. $4,901.25 − $2,015.07 = $2,886.18, Davis' equity
$17,350 − $2,886.18 = $14,463.82, Davis' encumbrance
$14,250 − $4,901.25 = $9,348.75, Underwood's encumbrance

161. (3′ = 1 yd.)
36′ = 12 yd. 9′ = 3 yd. 18″ = 1$\frac{1}{2}$′ = $\frac{1}{2}$ yd.
12 × 3 × $\frac{1}{2}$ = 18 cu. yd.

162. $351.00, interest on loan
$ 40.20, interest lost on $2,000
$146.40, taxes
$ 22.50, fire insurance
$147.00, upkeep
$196.00, depreciation
$903.10, cost first year (a)

12 × $125 = $1,500, year's rental
(b) $1,500 − $903.10 = $596.90 − $40.20 = $556.70

163. (a) $\frac{1}{100}$ of $9,000 = $90, front foot value
(b) one acre contains 43,560 sq. ft.; $\frac{1}{2}$ acre is 21,780 sq. ft.;
$9,000 ÷ 21,780 sq. ft. = 41 cents value per sq. ft.
(c) 2 × $9,000 = $18,000, value of one acre
(d) 21,780 sq. ft. ÷ 100 ft. = 217.8 ft. depth

164. 33′ × 48′ = 1,584 sq. ft.
6′ × 20′ = 120 sq. ft.

1,584 + 120 = 1,704 total sq. ft.
1,704 sq. ft. × $12.50 = $21,300, cost

165. 12 × $58.45 = $701.40, yearly payment $5\frac{1}{4}\%$ = .0525
$701.40 ÷ .0525 = $13,360, amount of original loan

166. $4\frac{1}{2}$ × 43,560 = 196,020 sq. ft.   196,020 − 71,020 = 125,000 sq. ft.
50′ × 100′ = 5,000 sq. ft.   125,000 ÷ 5,000 = 25 lots

167. Monthly interest = balance × .06 × $\frac{1}{12}$

$7,500.00, balance	$7,320.00, balance
37.50, interest	36.60, interest
$7,537.50	$7,356.60, total
97.50, 1st payment	96.60, 4th payment
$7,440.00, balance	$7,260.00, balance
37.20, interest	36.30, interest
$7,477.20, total	$7,296.30, total
97.20, 2nd payment	96.30, 5th payment
$7,380.00, balance	
36.90, interest	
$7,416.90, total	
96.90, 3rd payment	

168. .97 × $13,500 = $13,095 $18,500 − $13,500 = $5,000
.85 × $ 5,000 = $ 4,250
$17,345, insurable

169. 12 × $1,600 = $19,200, annual income
$19,200 × .45 = $8,640, expense
$19,200 − $8,640 = $10,560, net income

170. $6,000 × .05 = $300 annual interest $300 ÷ 12 = $25, monthly int.
$108 ÷ 12 = $9, monthly taxes and ins. $25 + $9 = $34, mo. expenses
$60 − $34 = $26, paid on principal
$6,000 − $26 = $5,974, balance

171. .015 × $600,000 = $9,000, 1 $\frac{1}{2}\%$ of gross sales
Must pay minimum of $10,000, first year (a)
.015 × 1,000,000 = $15,000, rent the fourth year (b)

172. $16,000 × .72 = $11,520, 72% of value
$11,520 ÷ 1,000 = 11.52, $1,000 units to be insured
11.52 × $3.10 = $35.71, cost of insurance on dwelling
$5,600 × .72 = $4,032, 72% of value
$4,032 ÷ 1,000 = $4.032, $1,000 units
4.032 × $3.65 = $14.72, insurance on furnishings
$35.71 + $14.72 = $50.43, insurance per year
$50.43 × 3 = $151.29, three year premium if paid yearly
$50.43 × 2 $\frac{1}{2}$ = $126.08, if premium paid once every three years
$151.29 − $126.08 = $25.21, saved

173. $6,000 × $\frac{1}{2}$ = $3,000, half year
$105 ÷ $3,000 = .035 or 3 $\frac{1}{2}\%$

174. 5% = $25 $25 ÷ 5 = $5 or 1% of amount   100% = amount
100 × $5 = $500

175. There are 43,560 square feet in one acre
$2\frac{1}{2}$ × 43,560 sq. ft. = 108,900 sq. ft.

176. 28 × $157.50 = $4,410 sale price of farm
6% of $4,410 = $264.60 total commission
60% of $264.60 = $158.76 salesperson's commission

177. 2 × $654.50 = $1,309 annual interest
$1,309 divided by $15,400 = $8\frac{1}{2}$ per cent

178. Sales Price = Net Price + Commission
100% − 6% = 94% net price

$16,500 divided by .94 = $17,553.19 sales price
179. $3,600 divided by 24 = $150 cost of one acre
$87\frac{1}{2} \times \$150 = \$13,125$
180. 8% of $12,000 = $960 annual interest
$\frac{1}{4}$ of $960 = $240 quarterly interest
181. Problem gives answer
182. $.05 \times \frac{1}{2} = .025$, rate for $\frac{1}{2}$ year
$167.50 ÷ .025 = $6,700 or 65% of value
$6,700 ÷ 65 = $103.0769 or 1% of value
100 × $103.0769 = $10,307.69, appraised value of property
183. 280 × $105 = $29,400, selling price of farm
$15,000 × .05 = $750, commission on first $15,000
$29,400 − $15,000 = $14,400, balance
$10,000 × .035 = $350, commission on next $10,000
$14,400 − $10,000 = $4,400, balance
$4,400 × .02 = $88, commission on balance
$750 + $350 + $88 = $1,188, total commission
$1,188 ÷ 2 = $594, 50-50 split commission
$594 × .10 = $59.40, commission to be paid Stark
$594 − $59.40 = $534.60, Kane receives
184. Interest = Balance $\times .05 \times \frac{1}{12}$
$12,000, Balance
50, interest
$12,050, total
170, paid 1st mo.
$11,880, balance
49.50, int.
$11,929.50, total
169.50, paid 2nd mo.
$11,760.00, balance
49.00, interest
$11,809.00, total
169.00, paid 3rd mo.
$11,640.00, balance
48.50, interest
$11,688.50, total
168.50, 4th payment
$11,520.00, balance
48.00, interest
$11,568.00, total
168.00, paid 5th mo.
185. $5,000 × .05 = $250, 5% commission
$250 × .10 = $25, 10% commission of 5% commission
$250 ÷ 2 = $125, 50% commission
$125 − $25 = $100, second salesman received
186. $12,000,000 ÷ $600,000 = 20, ratio of assessed value over taxes
$40,000 ÷ 20 = $2,000, taxes
187. $\frac{1}{2}$ of $85 = $42.50, 1st mo.
17 × .05 × $85 = $72.25, next 17 mo.
$42.50 + $72.25 = $114.75, total commission
188. January 1 to September 15 = $8\frac{1}{2}$ months, $12-8\frac{1}{2} = 3\frac{1}{2}$ mo. refund
$3\frac{1}{2} \div 12 = \frac{7}{24}$ of a year $\$126 \times \frac{7}{24} = \$36\frac{3}{4}$ or $36.75, refund
189. 1 × $6,500 × .05 = $325.00, commission first year
4 × $6,500 × .02 = $520.00, commission next 4 yr.
10 × $6,500 × .015 = $975.00, commission next 10 yr.
5 × $6,500 × .01 = $325.00, commission next 5 years

20 years commission $2,145.00
190. $1,200 − $1,000 = $200, profit on lot in one year
$1,000 × .10 = $100, profit on loan in one year
$100, difference
191. $\$1,000 \times \frac{9}{12} \times .05 = \$37.50$, interest for 9 months
$1,000 + $37.50 = $1,037.50, amount to be repaid
192. 6 months = $\frac{1}{2}$ year $\frac{1}{2}$ of 6% = 3% due in 6 months
100% − 3% = 97% or $1,000

$1,000 ÷ 97 = $10.30926 or 1% of the money
$10.30926 × 100 = $1,030.93 or 100%, all the money needed
to have $1,000 cash immediately

193. Bal. $120.00 × .03 = $3.60, int. $23.40÷ $120= .195 or 19½%
Bal. $110.00 × .03 = $3.30, int.
Bal. $100.00 × .03 = $3.00, int.
Bal. $ 90.00 × .03 = $2.70, int.
Bal. $ 80.00 × .03 = $2.40, int.
Bal. $ 70.00 × .03 = $2.10, int.
Bal. $ 60.00 × .03 = $1.80, int.
Bal. $ 50.00 × .03 = $1.50, int.
Bal. $ 40.00 × .03 = $1.20, int.
Bal. $ 30.00 × .03 = $0.90, int.
Bal. $ 20.00 × .03 = $0.60, int.
Bal. $ 10.00 × .03 = $0.30, int.
$23.40, interest

194. 6 months = ½ year ½ of 6% = 3% interest due in 6 months
$525 = 3% of the amount invested
$525 ÷ 3 = $175 or 1% of the amount
$175 × 100 = $17,500, or 100% or the total amount invested

195. $16,800 × .05 = $840, broker $16,800 − $840 = $15,960, owner

196. $14,000 ÷ 1,000 = 14, units of $1,000 14 × $21 = $294, tax

197. $1,500 × .055 = $82.50, interest for one year
$25.00 ÷ $82.50 = .303 of 365 days = 112 days. 112 ÷ 30 = 3 mos. 22 days

198. $2,000,000 × 5 = $10,000,000
$550,000 ÷ $10,000,000 = .055 or 5½%

199. $10,000 − $8,800 = $1,200, gross profit
$1200 − $100 = $1,100, net profit
$1,100 ÷ $8,800 = .125 or 12½%, profit

200. 12′ × 18′ × ⅓ = 72 cu. ft. (4″ = ⅓ ft.)
72 ÷ 27 = 2⅔ cu. yd. (27 cu. ft. = 1 cu. yd.)
2⅔ × $18.00 = $48.00, paving costs
2⅔ × $ 1.80 = 4.80, labor costs
$35.00, barbecue pit
$212.00, furniture
$299.80, total costs
$500 − 299.80 = $200.20 profit

201. 1320 × 1320 = 1,742,400 square feet
1,742,400 ÷ 2 = 871,200
871,200 ÷ 43,560 = 20 acres

202. .0625 × $15,200 = $950 yearly interest
$950 ÷ 24 = $39.58

203. $3,600 − $1,200 = $2,400; .06 × $2,400 = $144
$2,400 − $600 = $1,800; .06 × $1,800 = $108
$1,800 − $600 = $1,200; .06 × $1,200 = $72
$1,200 − $600 = $600; .06 × $600 = $36
$144 + $108 + $72 + $36 = $360

204. $2,400 × .06 = $144 yearly; $144 ÷ 2 = $72 (first six months)
$2,400 − $600 = $1,800; $1,800 × .06 = $108
$1,800 − $600 = $1,200; $1,200 × .06 = $72
$1,200 − $600 = $600; $600 × .06 = $36; $72 + $108 + $72 + $36 = $288

205. $78,300 ÷ 9 = $8,700 per acre
100 × 145.2 = 14,520 square feet
14,520 ÷ 43,560 = .33 or ⅓ acre
⅓ × $8,700 = $2,900

206. $2\frac{1}{6} = \frac{13}{6}$
$6,500 ÷ $\frac{13}{6}$ = $6,500 × $\frac{6}{13}$ = $3,000
207. 25 w. × 24 hours = 600 watt-hours
600 w-h × 16 = 9600 watt-hours
25 w × 12 hours = 300 watt-hours
300 w-h × 2 = 600 watt-hours
9600 w-h + 600 w-h = 10,200 watt-hours
10,200 w-h ÷ 1,000 w = 10.2 kilowatt-hours
10.2 (kw-h) × 3.5¢ = 35.7¢; 35.7¢ × 30 (days in June) = $10.71
208. 108 yards − 12 yards = 96 yards
96 yards ÷ 6 = 16 yards, width
16 yards × 2 = 32 yards; 32 yards + 6 yards = 38 yards, length
209. $25,000 + $1,500 + $625 = $27,125, invested
$30,000 − $27,125 = $2,875, expected profit
$2,875 ÷ $27,125 = .106 or 10.6% profit over investment
210. Bal. $5,000 × .06 × $\frac{1}{4}$ = $ 75.00, int. 1st quarter
Bal. $4,700 × .06 × $\frac{1}{4}$ = $ 70.50, int. 2nd quarter
Bal. $4,400 × .06 × $\frac{1}{4}$ = $ 66.00, int. 3rd quarter
Bal. $4,100 × .06 × $\frac{1}{4}$ = $ 61.50, int. 4th quarter
$ 273.00, total interest
4 × $300.00 = $1,200.00, total quarterly payments
$1,473.00, total payments 1st year
211. $21,000 − $1,000 = $20,000, balance after down payment
$20,000 × .05 = $1,000, interest at end of 1st year
$20,000 + $1,000 − $7,000 = $14,000, balance after 1st payment
$14,000 × .05 = $700, interest at end of 2nd year
$14,000 + $700 − $7,000 = $7,700, balance after 2nd payment
$7,700 × .05 = $385, interest at the end of the 3rd year
$7,700 + $385 − $7,000 = $1,085, balance after last payment
$1,085 − $1,000 = $85, balance after deducting $1,000 extra payment on payment plan
$85.00 saved by using the payment plan
212. $12,500 − $4,000 = $8,500, balance after down payment
$8,500 × .05 × $\frac{1}{2}$ = $212.50, interest after 6 months
$8,500 + $212.50 = $8,712.50, balance with interest added
$8,712.50 × .05 × $\frac{1}{2}$ = $217.81, interest at end of year
$8,712.50 + $217.81 = $8,930.31, balance with interest but not enough to meet the $9,000 payment
213. (a) (b) (c)

```
     $41,986
         499
      377874
     377874
    167944
  $20951014
```

214. $5,800 × .05 = $290. $290 × .60 = $174, broker's share.
215. $8,500 × .05 = $425.00, 5% office commission
.10 × $425 = 42.50, 10% commission to sales manager
$382.50, balance
$382.50 ÷ 2 = $191.25, commission due salesman
216. 9 months from April 15, 1971 to January 15, 1972 = $\frac{3}{4}$ year
$1,700 × .05 × $\frac{3}{4}$ = $63.75, interest due
217. 6 × .025 = .15, depreciation in 6 years
100% − 15% = 85%, value then = $7,650
$7,650 ÷ 85 = $90, or 1% of value
100 × $90 = $9,000, original value of house

218. $10,000 × .05 = $500, 5% of first $10,000
$730 − $500 = $230, balance
$230 ÷ .025 = $9,200, value of over $10,000
$10,000 + $9,200 = $19,200, selling price of property
219. $5,800 − $1,600 = $4,200 $4,200 × .06 = $252, interest
$4,200 + $252 = $4,452 $30 on $4,200 + interest per mo.
$4,200 ÷ 30 = 140 mo. payments 140 ÷ 12 = 11 yr. 8 mo.
Feb. 1, 1971, first payment + 11 yr. 8 mo. = Sept. 2, 1982
220. $6,000 × .60 = $3,600, assessed value 55 mills = $.055
$3,600 × .055 = $198, taxes
221. 60′ × 120′ = 7,200 sq. ft. 7,200 × $.10 = $720, property cost
60′ × $2.50 = $150, paving $150 = profit
$720 + $150 + $150 = $1,020, sales price
222. Problem gives answer
223. 50% of $30,000 = $15,000 assessment
22 + 30 + 12½ = 64½ mills
64½ × $15,000 = $967.50
224. Problem gives answer
225. ⅔ of $18,000 = $12,000 assessment
42¼ mills or .0425 × $12,000 = $510
226. Problem gives answer
227. 250′ × 200′ = 50,000 sq. ft.
50,000 × .60 = $30,000, paving costs

Curb & gutters	1,250
Lighting	5,000
Total cost	$36,250

$36,250 divided by 250 = $145 (a)
50,000 sq. ft. divided by 250 sq. ft. = 250 parking spaces (b)
228. 100% − 5% = 95%, Haines received.
$31,150 divided by 95 = $32,789.47, selling price
229. 28′ × 40′ = 1,120 sq. ft.
1,120 × $15 = $16,800
3 × 2½% = 7½% .075 × $16,800 = $1,260 depreciation
$16,800 − $1,260 = $15,540 appraised value
230. 12 months × $1,500 = $18,000 annual rent
5% of $18,000 = $900 vacancy allowance
$900 + $7,200 = $8,100 offset against income
$18,000 − $8,100 = $9,900 net income
$9,900 divided by 8% = $123,750 amount of offer
231. 24 feet × 30 feet × $16 = $11,520 living area
8 feet × 6 feet × $14 = $ 672 breakfast area
$12,192 cost when built
24 feet × 30 feet = 720 square feet living room area
8 feet × 6 feet = 48 square feet breakfast area
768 square feet total area
$12,192 divided by 768 square feet = $15.875 per square foot
24 feet × 30 feet × $18 = $12,960
8 feet × 6 feet × $16 = $ 768
$13,728 current cost
$13,728 divided by 768 square feet = $17.875 present cost per square foot
$17.875 − $15.875 = $2.00 increase per square foot
(or, more simply, $18 − $16 = $2.00, increase per sq. ft. living room
$16 − $140 = $2.00, increase per sq. ft., breakfast area).
232. 80′ × 25′ = 2,000 sq. ft.
15′ × 80′ × ½ = 600 sq. ft.

Total 2600 sq. ft.

233. 12 × $110 = $1,320 monthly income
12 months × $1,320 = $15,840 annual income
$15,840 – $3,625 = $12,215
$12,215 divided by $110,000 = 11.1 per cent

234. 6% of $8,000 = $480 interest for one year
$480 divided by 365 days = $1.32 per day
80 × $1.32 = $105.60

235. 12 × $90 = $1,080 interest for one year
$1,080 divided by 8% = $13,500 amount of loan

236.
```
   0.875
8)7.000
  64
   60
   56
    40
    40
```

237. 90 × 90 = 8,100 square feet
½ of 8,100 sq. ft. = 4,050 sq. ft.

238. Dec. 1, 1973 to Mar. 1, 1974 = 3 mo. or ¼ yr.
$20,000 × .04 × ¼ = $200, interest
$500 + $200 = $700 due on mortgage March 1, 1974

239. Interest = balance × .06 × 1/12

$2,000, balance	$1,924.87, balance
10, interest	9.62, interest
$2,010, total	$1,934.49, total
35, payment	45.00, payment
$1,975.00, balance	$1,889.49, balance
9.87, interest	9.45, interest (Dec.)
$1,984.87, total	(b)$1,898.94, balance
60.00, payment	

(a) $10 + $9.87 + $9.62 = $29.49, int. pd.

240. $1,325.28 ÷ 2 = $662.64 paid
$662.64 ÷ 12 = $55.22, ½ month payment to be paid by buyer
$662.64 – $55.22 = $607.42, taxes charged seller

241. $325 – $155 = $170, net income per month
$170 × 12 = $2,040, net income per year

242. 250 ft. × 750 ft. = 187,500 sq. ft.
187,500 sq. ft. divided by 43,560 sq. ft. = 4.304 acres.
4.304 @ $950 = $4,088.80.

243. $13,000 × .18 = $2,340, down payment
$13,000 – $2,340 = $10,660, amount to borrow
$10,660 × .015 = $159.90, loan commission
$2,340 + $159.90 = $2,499.90, amount needed

244. 65 ft. × 150 ft. = 9,750 sq. ft.
9,750 × $1.25 = $12,187.50
65 ft. × $10 = $650; total price: $12,837.50

245. 43,560 sq. ft. = 1 acre
326.7′ × 200′ = 65,340 sq. ft.   65,340 ÷ 43,560 = 1½ acres
1½ × $5,000 = $7,500, selling price

246. 46′ × 80′ × 16′ × $.80 = $47,104, cost of 1st floor
46′ × 80′ × 14′ × $.60 = $30,912, cost of 2nd floor
$78,016, total cost

247. 1 mile = 5,280′

$^1/_4$ of 5,280 = 1,320′ on the south side of NE $^1/_4$ of NE $^1/_4$ of a section

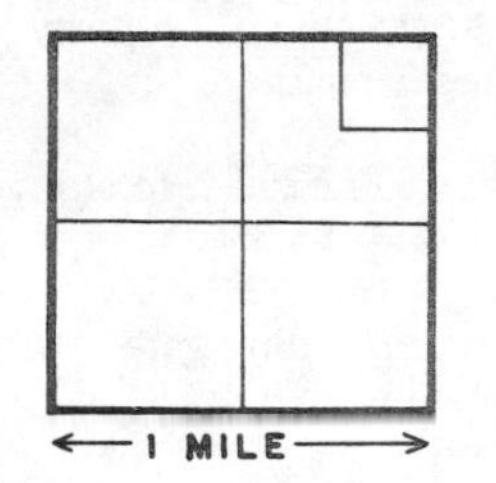

248. 36′ × 9′ × \$.20 = \$64.80, labor cost per sq. ft.
4″ = $^1/_3$ ft. 36′ × 9′ × $^1/_3$ = 108 cu. ft. 27 cu. ft. = 1 cu. yd.
108 ÷ 27 = 4 cu. yd. 4 × \$15 = \$60, cost of concrete
\$60 + \$64.80 = \$124.80, total cost
249. 4 × \$85 = \$340, rent income per month
.45 × \$340 = \$153, profit
\$36,000 ÷ 12 = \$3,000, investment per month
\$153 ÷ \$3,000 = .051 or 5.1% return on investment
250. SW $^1/_4$ = 160 acres
SW $^1/_4$ of SW $^1/_4$ = 40 acres
W $^1/_2$ of 40 acres = 20 acres

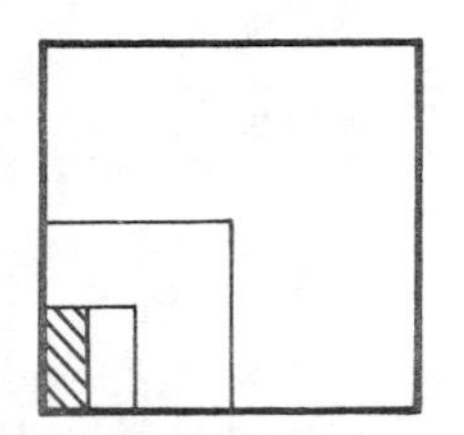

251. 32′ × 24′ × 20′ = 15,360 cu. ft. (Because of gable use only $^1/_2$ of 8′ height in attic: 8′ + 8′ + 4′ = 20′ total ht.)
252. 32′ × 24′ = 768 sq. ft.
\$10,828.80 ÷ 768 = \$14.10, cost per sq. ft.
253. 50 × \$44 = \$2200, assessed value of lot
\$6500, assessed value of house
\$8700, total assessment
\$8,700 × \$.048 = \$417.60, year's taxes
254. 50 × \$65 = \$ 3,250, cost of lot
\$10,828.80, cost of house
\$14,078.80, total cost
−\$ 6,500.00, cash payment
\$ 7,578.80, balance
\$7,578.80 × $^1/_2$ × .05 = \$189.47, first semi-annual interest payment
255. 32′ × 24′ × 20′ × \$ .775 = \$11,904, bid A
32′ × 24′ × 3′ × \$4.70 = \$10,828.80, bid B
Bid B cheaper by \$ 1,075.20
256. 10 × 2% = 20% depreciation in 10 years
\$10,828.80 × .20 = \$2,165.76, amount of depreciation
\$10,828.80 − \$2,165.76 = \$8,663.04 value in 10 years
\$65 × .22 = \$14.30, increase in value per front ft.

$65 + $14.30 = $79.30, cost per front ft. 10 years
$79.30 × 50 = $3,965, cost of lot in 10 years
$3,965 + $8,663.04 = $12,628.04, total value of property in 10 years

257. $10,828.80 × .05 = $541.44, architect's charge
50 × $65 = $3,250, cost of lot
$10,828.80 + $3,250.00 + $541.44 = $14,620.24, total investment
1 − 3/4 = 1/4 equity 1/4 of $14,620.24 = $3,655.06, equity

258. $21.75 × 2 = $43.50, cost of gates
180′ − 4′ = 176′ linear measurement excluding gate
176′ + 50′ + 176′ + 50′ = 452′ total linear ft.
452 × $.85 = $384.20, cost of fencing
$384.20 + $43.50 = $427.70, total cost of fencing and gates

259. 36′ × 6′ × $.27 = $58.32, labor costs 4″ = 1/3 ft.
36′ × 6′ × 1/3 = 72 cu. ft. 27 cu. ft. = 1 cu. yd.
72 ÷ 27 = 2 2/3 cu. yd. 2 2/3 × $14.25 = $38.00, cost of concrete
$58.32 + $38.00 = $96.32, total cost of driveway

260. 12 × $155 = $1,860, income on property per year
$402 + $78 + $260 = $740, yearly expenses
$1,860 − $740 = $1,120, profit per year
$1,120 ÷ $14,000 = .08 or 8% net return on investment

261. From problem 218, 3/4 of total cost = mortgage
3/4 of $14,620.24 = $10,965.18, mortgage
$10,965.18 × .06 × 1/12 = $54.83, interest
+ 54.83, interest
$11,020.01, balance plus interest
− 75.00, payment
$10,945.01, new balance $10,945.01 × .06 × 1/12 = $54.73
+ 54.73, interest
$10,999.74, balance plus interest
− 75.00, payment
$10,924.74, balance after June payment

262. 50 × $65 = $3,250, cost of original lot
$7,300 − $3,250 = $4,050, balance to be invested in land
$4,050 ÷ $1.50 = 2,700 sq. ft. can be bought
2,700 ÷ 180 = 15′ front ft. can be bought
15′ + 50′ = 65′, frontage 180′ × 65′ = 11,700 sq. ft.

263. $3,100 × .55 = $1,705, taxable
$1,705 ÷ 1,000 = 1.705 units
1.705 × $42.25 × 5 = $360.18, taxes
$3,100 × .04 × 5 = $620, interest loss
$3,100 + $360.18 + $620.00 = $4,080.18, total transaction
$4,250.00 − $4,080.18 = $169.82, profit

264. 1 acre = 43,560 sq. ft. 1 1/2 acre = 65,340 sq. ft.
1/4 of 65,340 = 16,335 sq. ft. too steep
1/3 of 65,340 = 21,780 sq. ft. in stream
38,115 sq. ft. not usable
65,340 − 38,115 = 27,225 sq. ft. usable
1/6 of 27,225 = 4,537.5 sq. ft. for roads
27,225 − 4,537.5 = 22,687.5 sq. ft. for building

265. 100% − 15% = 85%, selling price
$17,000 × .85 = $14,450, selling price
$14,450 × .06 = $867.00 commission
1/2 of $867 = $433.50, Mr. Duncan's 50% commission
$433.50 × .20 = $86.70, Mr. Rayer's commission
$433.50 − $86.70 = $346.80, net amount Mr. Duncan received on sale

266. 4 × 100 = $400 annual payment
$400 divided by $8,000 = .05 or 5%
267. $50,000 × .15 = $7,500 down payment
$50,000 − $7,500 = $42,500 balance
$42,500 ÷ $1,000 = 42.5 units of $1,000
42.5 × $7.50 = $318.75 monthly payments
268. $3,000 = 5% of value
$3,000 ÷ 5 = $600 or 1% of value
100 × $600 = $60,000 capitalized value of property
269. 69′ × 142′ = 9,798 sq. ft.
$2,645.46 ÷ 9,798 = $.27 per sq. ft.
270. 50′ × 100′ = 5,000 sq. ft. 5,000 × $.75 = $3,750, selling price
$3,750 × .05 = $187.50, sales commission
$3,750 − $187.50 = $3,562.50, seller receives
271. 4 × $57.55 = $230.20, annual interest payment
$230.20 ÷ $4,200 = .0548 or about 5½% interest rate
272. 60 × $150 = $9,000 list price $7,650 × .10 = $765 sales commission
$7,650 + $765 = $8,415, selling price
$9,000 − $8,415 = $585 buyer saved
273. 1/12 of $300 = $25, tax for one month
March 15, 1974 to December 31, 1974 = 9½ mos.
9½ × $25 = $237.50
274. 12 × $300 = $3,600 yearly rental
$120,000 − $80,000 = $40,000 amount over $80,000
$40,000 × .05 = $2,000, 5% over gross of $80,000
$3,600 + $2,000 = $5,600, Brown received yearly
275. $7,095 ÷ 86 =$82.50 per front ft. 86′ × 110′ = 9,460 sq. ft.
$7,095 ÷ 9,460 = $.75 per sq. ft.
276. 1,600 × $11 = $17,600, cost of house
20′ × 30′ = 600 sq. ft. 600 × $4 = $2,400, cost of garage
50′ × $15 = $750, cost of lot
$17,600 + $2,400 + $750 = $20,750, total cost
277. 33′6″ = 33½′ 45′6″ = 45½′ 33/2′ × 45½′ = 1,524.25 sq. ft.
15′ × 5′ = 75 sq. ft. for family room
1,524.25 + 75 = 1,599.25 total sq. ft.
1,599.25 × $12.85 = $20,550.36, total cost of building house
278. 3,250 sq. ft. × $.14 = $455.00
2,000 sq. ft. × $.085 = $170.00
7,250 sq. ft. × $1 = $7,250.00
$455 + $170 + $7,250 = $7,875 total price
3,250 sq. ft. + 2,000 sq. ft. + 7,250 sq. ft. = 12,500 sq. ft. area
$7,875 ÷ 12,500 = $.63 per sq. ft.
279. .05 × $10,000 = $500 commission on the first $10,000
$730 − $500 = $230 = the 2½ percent commission on the excess
$230 ÷ 2.5 = $92
$92 × 100 = $9200 excess
$10,000 + $9200 = $19,200
280. 30′ × 30′ = 900 sq. ft. area of square
3.14 × radius² = area of circle
27′ ÷ 2 = 13.5′ radius
3.14 × 13.5′ × 13.5′ = 572.265 sq. ft. area of circle
900 sq. ft. − 572.265 sq. ft. = 327.735 sq. ft.
281. 40′ × 24′ × 15′ = 14,400 cu. ft.
14,400 ÷ 200 = 72 persons
282. a. 20′ × 15′ × 9′ = 2700 cu. ft.

27 cu. ft. = 1 cu. yd.
2700 cu. ft. ÷ 27 cu. ft. = 100 cu. yds.
b. 100 × $3.40 = $340

283. 45′ × 25′ × 8′ = 9,000 cu. ft.
27 cu. ft. = 1 cu. yd.
9,000 cu. ft. ÷ 27 cu. ft. = 333⅓ cu. yds.
333⅓ cu. yds. ÷ 4 cu. yds. = 83⅓ or 84 truck-loads

284. 60′ × $9.00 = $540
59 + 58+ 57 ... + 4+ 3+ 2+ 1 = 1770
$1.25 × 1770 = $2,212.50
$540 + $2,212.50 = $2,752.50

285. 15′ × 24′ = 360 sq. ft.
9 sq. ft. = 1 sq. yd.
360 sq. ft. ÷ 9 sq. ft. = 40 sq. yds.
40 × $14.95 = $598

286. 8 × 2 yds. = 16 yds.
16 × $3.90 = $62.40

287. 240 × $60 = $14,400, B's allowance
$23,500 − $14,400 = $9,100 B owes A

288. $16,000 − $13,600 = $2,400, profit
$2,400 divided by $13,600 = 17.6%

289. $23,000 − $11,000 = $12,000, net income
$12,000 ÷ $120,000 = .10 or 10% return on investment

290. $400 divided by 40 mills = $10,000 assessed value
$10,000 : 50% :: (X) : 100%
$10,000 × 100 divided by 50 = $20,000

291. $140 × 12 = $1,680, annual income
$1,680 ÷ $21,000 = .08 or 8% return on investment

292. $6,000 × .05 × 1/12 = $25.00, interest 1st month
$6,000 + $25.00 = $6,025
$6,025 − $60 = $5,965, balance (plus insurance and taxes)

293. $10,000 − $1,500 = $8,500, amount of fire insurance on house

294. No stamps are necessary.

295. $140,000 − $80,000 = $60,000, gross over $80,000
$60,000 × .05 = $3,000, 5% on gross over $80,000
12 × $300 = $3,600, minimum monthly rent
$3,600 + $3,000 = $6,600, Doe receives

296. 60 × $150 = $9,000, list price
$7,650 × .10 = $765, 10% on sales price
$7,650 + $765 = $8,415, buyer paid
$9,000 − $8,415 = $585, buyer saved

297. Mar. 1, 1974 to Nov. 16, 1974 = 8½ months 3 years = 36 months
8½ ÷ 36 = 17/72 part of premium used
17/72 × $158.40 = $37.40, amount of premium used
$158.40 − $37.40 = $121.00, unused portion of premium

298. 100′ × $15 = $1,500, property assessment
$3,200, house assessment
$4,700, total assessment
$.040 × $4,700 = $188.00, total yearly tax

299. $6,800 × .03 × 1/12 = $17.00, interest per month
$6,200 × .025 × 1/12 = 12.92, painting and repairs
.75 × 6.8 × $24 × 1/12 = 10.20, taxes
6.2 × $4.50 × 1/12 = 2.33, insurance
$600 × .05 × 1/12 = 2.50, upkeep
$44.95, expenses

$50.00 – $44.95 = $5.05, cheaper per month to buy

300\. 8 × 2½% = 20%, dep. in 8 yrs.
$14,440 = 80%
$14,400 ÷ 80 = $180 or 1% of value   100% × $180 = $18,000

301\. $5,000 × $3.50 × 1/100 = $175
$175 × .05 = $8.75
$175 + $8.75 = $183.75, if tardy $175, if paid on time
$175 – $8.75 = $166.25, if prompt

302\. $566.66 × .05 × 3/12 = $7.08, interest

303\. $2,160 ÷ $45 = 48 payments
48 ÷ 12 = 4 years
October 1, 1971 to September 1, 1975

304\. $150 = 2½% $150 ÷ 2½ = $60, 1%   100 × $60 = $6,000 amount

305\. 43,560 sq. ft. = 1 acre

306\. 8 × $50 = $400 month
50 × 12 × ½ = $300, ½ monthly rent for year on one apartment
12 × ½ × .05 × $400 = $120, 5% of rents collected for ½ year
$300 + $120 = $420, maximum

307\. June 1972 to June 1975 = 3 years = 36 months
January 1974 — June 1975 = 17 months
1/36 of $36 = $1.00 premium for 1 month
17 × $1.00 = $17.00

308\. $25 = 5% $25 ÷ 5 = $5, 1%   100 × $5 = $500, amount

309\. $12,000 × 02.5 × 6 = $1,800 depreciation on house
$2,000 × .08 × 6 = $960, increase in value on lot
$14,000 + $960 – $1,800 = $13,160, total value of property after 6 yr.

310\. 2 × $55 = $110, monthly rental
2 × $75 = $150, monthly rental
2 × $90 = $180, monthly rental
$440, total monthly rental
$440 × 12 = $5,280, gross yearly income on the 6 apartments

311\. June 15 to December 15 = 6 months = ½ year
$4,500 × ½ × .05 = $112.50, credit to purchaser

312\. 4 × $80 = $320, annual interest
$320 ÷ $8,000 = .04 or 4%

313\. $7,850 + $70 = $7,920   100% – 4% = 96% = $7,920
$7,920 ÷ 96 = $82.50, 1% of amount   100 × $82.50 = $8,250, amount

314\. $20,000 + $7,000 = $27,000 mortgaged
$50,000 – $27,000 = $23,000 taxable   Tax stamp = $1.10 per $1,000
$23,000 ÷ $1,000 = 23 taxable units   per $1,000
23 × $1.10 = $25.30 in documentary stamps

315\. $1,800 ÷ $20,000 = .09 = 9%

316\. 55 × $35 = $1,925 cost by front footage
$1,925 × 10% = $192.50, commission

317\. 3 × $25 = $75, taxes for 3 years $75 + $60 = $135, expenses
$1,000 × .02 × 3 = $60, interest $300 – $135 = $165, profit

318\. $10,000 × .80 = $8,000, 80% of value
$8,000 ÷ 100 = 80 insurable units   80 × $.60 = $48, 3 years' insurance
$48 ÷ 3 = $16, one year's insurance

319\. $1.55 × $5,800 × 1/100 = $89.90, school tax

320\. 12 × $275 = $3,300, profit per year $3,300 = 8%
$3,300 ÷ 8 = $412.50, 1% of profit
100 × $412.50 = $41,250, total profit

321\. 31 days in October
31 × $42.50 = $1,317.50, total income for month

322\. 200 × $25 = $5,000, cost of land   40′ × 40′ × 30′ = 48,000 cu. ft.

4800 × \$.35 = \$16,800, cost of house
\$16,800 + \$5,000 = \$21,800, total cost

323. 240 divided by $\frac{2}{3}$ acre = 160 lots
240 lots less 160 lots = 80 fewer lots

324. 12 × \$250 = \$3,000 rent for one year
− 2,600 expenses
\$ 400
12 × \$200 rent = \$2,400, rent saved
Loses 4% interest on \$50,000, or \$2,000
\$2,400 less \$2,000 = \$400
\$400 plus \$400 = \$800

325. Display space is 40′ × 20′, or 800 sq. ft. Each car requires 8 feet plus 2 feet, or 10 ft. of space
40 divided by 10 = 4 cars

326. 24′ × 32′ = 768 sq. ft.
768 sq. ft. ÷ 36 sq. ft. = $21\frac{1}{3}$ (22 bags)

327. 80′ × 6′ = 480 sq. ft.
150′ − 24′ = 126′
126′ × 6′ = 756 sq. ft.
756 sq. ft. + 480 sq. ft. = 1,236 sq. ft. The walk is inside the lot.

328. \$1800 = 6%
\$1800 ÷ 6 = \$300
\$300 × 100 = \$30,000

329. \$30,000 = 82% gross volume sales
\$30,000 ÷ 82 = \$365.85365
\$365.85365 × 100 = \$36,585.37

330. 60′ × 120′ = 7,200 sq. ft.
30′ × 200′ = 6,000 sq. ft.
43,560 sq. ft. − 6,000 sq. ft. = 37,560 sq. ft.
37,560 sq. ft. ÷ 7,200 sq. ft. = 5.216 lots

331. .02 × \$10,828.80 = \$216.576 depreciation each year
10 yrs. × \$216.576 = \$2,165.76
\$10,828.80 − \$2,165.76 = \$8,663.04 value of house
50′ × \$65 = \$3,250 original cost of lot
1.22 × \$3,250 = \$3,965 lot value
\$3,965 + \$8,663.04 = \$12,628.04

332. \$3,250 = lot cost; \$10,828.80 building cost
.05 × \$10,828.20 = \$541.44 to architect
\$3,250 + \$10,828.80 + \$541.44 = \$14,620.24 = total cost
total cost − $\frac{3}{4}$ total cost (mortgage) = $\frac{1}{4}$ total cost = equity
\$14,620.24 ÷ 4 = \$3,655.06

333. 20 × $4\frac{3}{4}$″ = 95″
95″ ÷ 12 = 7.92′
19 × 6.85′ = 130.15′
130.15′ + 7.92′ = 138.07′; 138.07′ ÷ 3 (feet in one yard) = 46.023 yards

334. \$46,500 × .065 × $\frac{1}{12}$ = \$251.88

335. 5 @ \$17 = \$ 85
9 @ 15 = 135
8 @ 16 = 128
5 @ 18 = 90
5 @ 3.75 = 18.75, garages
\$456.75, week

52 weeks = 1 year
52 × \$456.75 = \$23,751, gross income yearly

336. \$6,500 × .30 = \$1,950, increase
\$6,500 + \$1,950 = \$8,450, asking price
\$8,450 × .25 = \$2,112.50, reduction

$8,450 − $2,112.50 = $6,337.50, selling price
$6,337.50 × .05 = $316.88, commission
$2,112.50 + $316.88 = $2,429.38, loss
$2,429.38 − $1,950 = $479.38, loss

337. $4\frac{1}{2}\%$ of $874 = $39.33, interest for one year
1 month = $\frac{1}{12}$ of $39.33 or $3.277
2 years, 8 months, 15 days = $32\frac{1}{2}$ months
$32\frac{1}{2} \times 3.277$ = $106.50

338. $66\frac{2}{3}\% = \frac{2}{3}$ .05 = $\frac{5}{100}$ $\frac{2}{3} \times \frac{5}{100} = \frac{10}{300} = \frac{1}{30}$
$200 ÷ $\frac{1}{30}$ = $6,000, appraised valuation

339. 100 + 20 = 120% = $7,500 $7,500 ÷ 120 = $62.50 or 1%
100 × $62.50 = $6,250, cost of house

340. 14 − 2 = 12 lots for sale 75 × 12 = 900 front feet
$33,750 ÷ 900 = $37.50 per front foot

341. 108,900 ÷ 43,560 = $2\frac{1}{2}$ acres
$2\frac{1}{2}$ × $1,250 = $3,125, amount realized from sale

342. 160 sq. rd. = 1 acre
160 ÷ $5\frac{1}{2}$ = $29\frac{1}{11}$ rods

343. 150 − $42\frac{1}{4}$ = $117\frac{3}{4}$ acres $\frac{1}{3} \times 117\frac{3}{4} = 39\frac{1}{4}$ acres
$117\frac{3}{4} - 39\frac{1}{4} = 78\frac{1}{2}$ acres unsold

344. 160 sq. rd. = 1 acre 90 ÷ 160 = $\frac{9}{16}$ acre
$7,883.30 ÷ $89\frac{9}{16}$ = $88.08 per acre

345. 100 × 160 = 16,000 sq. rd.
$\frac{1}{8}$ × 16,000 = 2,000
14,000 sq. rd.
14,000 ÷ 140 lots = 100 sq. rods

346. $490.30 ÷ .042 = $11,673.81 or 58.25% of value
$11,673.81 ÷ 58.25 = $200.4087 or 1% of value
100 × $200.4087 = $20,040.87 value of property

347. 43,560 sq. ft. = 1 acre $5\frac{1}{4}$ × 43,560 = 228,690 sq. ft.
228,690 − 36,690 = 192,000 sq. ft. 60′ × 100′ = 6,000 sq. ft. in lot
192,000 ÷ 6,000 = 32 lots

348. 500′ + 350′ + 500′ + 350′ = 1,700′ 3′ = 1 yd.
1,700 ÷ 3 = $566\frac{2}{3}$ yd.
$566\frac{2}{3}$ × $2 = $1,133.33 cost of curb
$3,200.00 cost of sidewalk
$4,333.33, total cost

349. 100% − 20% = 80% 20 ÷ 80 = .25 or 25%

350. $3,120.50 × $1\frac{1}{2}$ × .055 = $257.44, interest

351. $720 ÷ 16 = $45, cost of 1 acre
197 × $45 = $8,865, cost of 197 acres

352. 600′ × 300′ = 180,000 sq. ft. 180,000 ÷ 43,560 = 4.13+ acres

353. $9,080 + $40 = $9,120 $9,120 = 95% S.P. (less 5% com.)
$9,120 ÷ 95 = $96 or 1% value 100 × $96 = $9,600, S. Price

354. $6,000 × .055 × $\frac{1}{12}$ = $27.50, interest first month
$108 ÷ 12 = 9.00, taxes and insurance
$36.50, total expenses
$60 − $36.50 = $23.50, paid on principal
$6,000 − $23.50 = $5,976.50, balance

355. 25′ × 30′ × 5′ = 3,750 cu. ft. 27 cu. ft. = 1 cu. yd.
3,750 ÷ 27 = 138.88 cu. yd. 138.88 × $2.90 = $402.75, cost

356. $6,000 × .055 × $\frac{1}{4}$ = $82.50, quarterly interest

357. 100 × $25 = $ 2,500, frontage 45′ × 45′ × 30′ = 60,750 cu. ft.
60,750 × $.35 = 21,262.50 by cu. ft.
$23,762.50, total cost

358. $193.50 × 75 = $14,512.50, selling price of lot

359. 640 acres = 1 section

360. 36 sections = 1 township (6 miles long and 6 miles wide) each section one square mile

361. Find square root:

```
          2 0 8. 7
        √43560.00
          4
408     )3560
         3264
4167    ) 29600
          29619
```

Or estimate divisor, divide and average:
43560 ÷ 200 = 217.8
200 + 217.8 = 417.8
417.8 ÷ 2 = 208.7

362. 3 @ $100 = $ 300, per mo.
2 @ $125 = 250, per mo.
1 @ $150 = 150, per mo.
6 @ $ 65 = 390, per mo.
$1,090, total per mo.

12 × $1,090 = $13,080, gross annual income

363. 12 × $950 = $11,400 or 8% of investment
$11,400 ÷ 8 = $1,425 or 1% 100 × $1,425 = $142,500 investment

364. Sec. 9 = 640 acres $1/4$ of 640 = 160 acres $1/4$ of 160 = 40 acres

365. 760′ × 500′ = 380,000 sq. ft. 380,000 ÷ 43,560 = 8.72 acres

366. .16 × $10,000 = $1,600 annual income
$1,600 ÷ 12 = $133.33 mo. income

367. Assessment and tax millage

368. (a) (b)

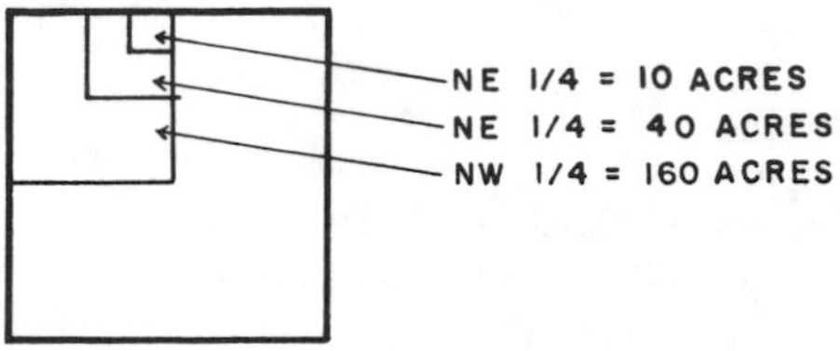

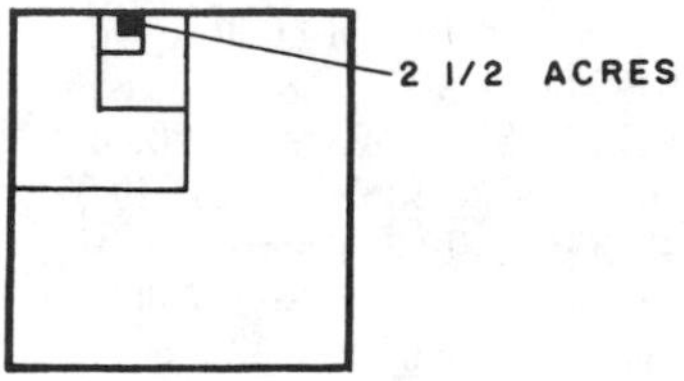

NE 1/4 = 10 ACRES
NE 1/4 = 40 ACRES
NW 1/4 = 160 ACRES

2 1/2 ACRES

369. $2\frac{1}{2}$ × .16 × $1/100$ × $24,500 = $98, total premium for 3 years
$98 ÷ 36 = $2.72, monthly cost

370. 12 × $300 = $3,600, yr. rental
$4,800 − $3,600 = $1,200 or 4%
$1,200 ÷ 4 = $300 or 1%
100 × $300 = $30,000, amount over $150,000
$150,000 + $30,000 = $180,000, total business

371. $8\frac{1}{2}$ × $1/12$ × 180 = $127.50, buyer owes seller
$8\frac{1}{2}$ × $1/12$ × $240 = 170.00, buyer owes seller
$297.50, buyer owes seller
$3\frac{1}{2}$ × $1/12$ × $118 = 34.41, seller owes buyer
$263.09, buyer owes seller

372. 43,560 sq. ft. = 1 acre 1.87 × 43,560 = 81,457.2 sq. ft.
81,457.2 × .225 = $18,327.87, selling price

373. $6,000 × $1/100$ × $1.55 = $93.00, school tax

374. 100 × 108.9 = 10,890 sq. ft. 10,890 ÷ 43,560 = .25 or $1/4$ acre

375. $8,000 × .80 = $6,400 assessed value
$6,400 × $1/100$ × $4.20 = $268.80, annual tax

376. $8,000 × .045 × $19/24$ = $285 interest ($9\frac{1}{2}$ × $1/12$ = $19/24$ yr)

377. $7,200 − $6,000 = $1,200 gain $1,200 ÷ $6,000 = .20 or 20%

378. $9,300 × .05 = $465, broker's commission
$465 + $95 = $560, expenses
$9,300 − $560 = $8,740, seller received

379. $62,350 − $15,750 = $46,600 $46,600 − $36,675 = $9,925
$9,925 + $6,240 = $16,165, cash difference

380. 90 ft. = 30 yds. 1080 sq. yds. ÷ 30 yds. = 36 yds. = 108 ft.
381. Valuation of property = assumed perpetual income ÷ rate to be realized
$1,134 × 12 = $13,608, gross yr. income
$13,608 – $2,500 = $11,108 or 8% $11,108 ÷ .08 = $138,850, price
382. 125 × $2.25 = $281.25, paving 160′ × 125′ × $.17 = $3,400
$3,400 + $281.25 = $3,681.25, cost
295.00, profit
$3,976.25, selling price
383. $1,710
$15,000 × .05 = 750, commission on first $15,000
$ 900
$20,000 × .03 = 600, commission on next $20,000
$ 360 ÷ .015 = $24,000
$15,000 + $20,000 + $24,000 = $59,000 Selling Price
384. $7,670 ÷ 65 = $118, price per front foot
385. $325 – $155 = $170, monthly income
12 × $170 = $2,040, net income per year
386. $57.75 × 4 = $231, year's interest payment
$231 ÷ $4,200 = .055 or 5½%
387. $8,750 × .05 = $437.50, broker's commission
$3,000 – $500 = $2,500, mortgage balance
$2,500 × .05 × 1/12 = $10.42, interest due buyer
Taxes paid for January 1 to December 31 = 12 months
June 30 to December 31 = 6 months or ½ year
$136 × ½ = $68 due seller
388. $12,000 × .80 = $9,600, insured value of property
$4,000 × .80 = $3,200, insured value of furniture and goods
$9,600 × 1/1000 × $2.80 = $26.88, premium on property
$3,200 × 1/1000 × $3.30 = $10.56, premium on household goods
$37.44, yearly premium
3 × $37.44 = $112.32, three-year premium on a yearly basis
2½ × $37.44 = 93.60, premium on a three-year basis
$ 18.72, saved on a three-year basis
389. $6,000 – $2,000 = $4,000, income
$4,000 ÷ $40,000 = .10 or 10%
390. 30 days in September 12/30 = 2/5 of a month
From January 1 to September 12 = 8 2/5 months
$875.24 × 8 2/5 × 1/12 = $612.66, credit to purchaser
391. 12 × $400 = $4,800, minimum monthly rental for a year
$120,000 – $80,000 = $40,000, gross yearly business over $80,000
$40,000 × .05 = $2,000, 5% of gross business
$4,800 + $2,000 = $6,800, rent
392. 40 × $2,200 = $88,000, selling price = 110%
$88,000 ÷ 110 = $800 or 1%
100 × $800 = $80,000, cost
393. 12 × $280 = $3,360 income
$3,360 ÷ $42,000 = .08 or 8%
394. 264′ × 660′ = 174,240 sq. ft. 43,560 sq. ft. = 1 acre
174,240 ÷ 43,560 = 4 acres
4 × $800 = $3,200 cost of lot
395. 320 × ½ × .05 × $175 = $1400, commission
396. $3,600 ÷ .06 = $60,000 cost of farm
397. 32 × 40 × $9.50 = $12,160 cost $12,160 × .05 = $608, depreciation
$12,160 – $608 = $11,552, appraisal
398. 30′ × 200′ = 6,000 sq. ft. 43,560 – 6,000 = 37,560 sq. ft.
60′ × 120′ = 7,200 sq. ft. in lot 37,560 ÷ 7,200 = 5.21 + lots

399. $100 \times 12 = \$1,200$ yearly income $\$1,200 \div \$12,000 = .10$ or 10%

400. $43,560 \times 10 = 435,600$ sq. ft. $435,600 - 85,000 = 350,600$ sq. ft.
$50' \times 100' = 5,000$ sq. ft., each lot $350,600 \div 5,000 = 70.1$ lots

401.
$106' \times 66' =$ 6,996 sq. ft.
$100' \times 60' =$ 6,000 sq. ft.
996 sq. ft. for walk

106'
100'
66' 60'

402. $996 \times \$.23 = \$229.08$ cost of walk

403.

2,583	9,421	7,488
4,905	2,892	6,529
7,488 sum	6,529 difference	959 excess

404. $80 \times \$250 =$ $20,000, cost
6,500, dev. cost
$26,500, total cost

$100 \times \$750 =$ $75,000, selling price
26,500, total cost
$48,500, net profit

405. $30 \times 16 = 480$ sq. rd. 160 sq. rd. = 1 acre
$480 \div 160 = 3$ acres

406. $\$325 \times 12 \times 2\frac{1}{2} = \$9,750$, value of the home

407. $2,640 \times 9,900 = 26,136,000$ sq. ft.
43,560 sq. ft. = 1 acre
$26,136,000 \div 43,560 = 600$ acres
$10\% + 10\% + 20\% = 40\%$
$.40 \times 600 = 240$ acres for streets, playgrounds and factory
$600 - 240 = 360$ acres left for homesites
$2 \times 360 = 720$ one-half acre sites

408. $15' \times 34' = 510$ sq. ft. $2 \times 510 = 1,020$, sq. ft. both sides
$\$.08 + \$.026 = \$.106$ per sq. ft. $1,020 \times \$.106 = \$108.12$, cost

409. $50' \times 150' = 7,500$ sq. ft. area
$\$7,500 \div 7,500 = \$1.00$ cost per sq. ft.
$\$7,500 \div 50 = \$150$ per front foot

410. $\frac{1}{6} + \frac{5}{8} = \frac{19}{24}$ acre in use
$1 - \frac{19}{24} = \frac{5}{24}$ in woodland
$\frac{5}{24} = 50$ acres $50 \div 5 = 10$ acres in one twenty-fourth
$24 \times 10 = 240$ acres in whole farm

411. $115\% = \$9,430$ $\$9,430 \div 115 = \$82$, or 1% of value
$100 \times \$82 = \$8,200$, cost
$\$8,200 \times .60 \times .045 \times 4 = \$885.60$, taxes
$\$8,200 \times .03 \times 4 = \$984$, interest lost
$\$9,430 - \$8,200 = \$1,230$ gain
$\$984.00 + \$885.60 = \$1,869.60$, loss
$\$1,869.60 - \$1,230 = \$639.60$ loss

412. 160 sq. rd. = 1 acre

413. $3,250 \times \$\ .14 = \$\ 455$, hillside
$2,000 \times \$\ .085 =$ 170, stream
$7,250 \times \$1 = 7,250$, flat area
12,500 sq. ft. = $7,875, total appraisal
$\$7,875 \div 12,500 = \$.63$ per sq. ft.

414. $30' \times 30' \times 30' = 27,000$ cubic feet
$\$9,000 \div 27,000 = \$.33\frac{1}{3}$ per cu. ft.

415. 30′ × 6′ = 180 sq. ft.
180 × $2.75 = $495.00, cost of driveway

416. $16\frac{1}{2}$ feet = 1 rod or perch

417. 66 feet = 1 chain

418. $7,200 × .06 × $\frac{1}{12}$ = $36, first month's interest

419. 20 − 5 = 15 acres for homesites
50′ × 150′ = 7,500 sq. ft. in each lot
43,560 sq. ft. = 1 acre
15 × 43,560 = 653,400 sq. ft. for sub-division
653,400 ÷ 7,500 = 87 + lots

420. 12 × $600 = $7,200, yearly rent
12 × $115,000 = $1,380,000 gross business per year
$9,300 − $7,200 = $2,100 five per cent over gross of business
$2,100 ÷ .05 = $42,000, amount over gross minimum
$1,380,000 + $42,000 = $1,422,000, gross volume of year's business

421. $10,000 ÷ $1,000 = 10 taxable units
10 × $19 = $190, taxes

422. 1 pace = 3′
3 × 3′ = 9′
30 × 3′ = 90′
90′ − 9′ = 81 feet

423. 20 + 20 + 10 + 10 = 60 yards
60 × 3′ = 180′
180′ ÷ 2′ = 90

424. 5,280′ × 5,280′ = 27,878,400 sq. ft.
27,878,400 ÷ 43,560 = 640 acres
3 × 640 acres = 1920 acres

425. 18′ + 27′ = 45
450′ − 45′ = 405′ length of building
9 sq. ft. = 1 sq. yd.
9 × 12,825 yards = 115,425 sq. ft. area
115,425 sq. ft. ÷ 405′ = 285′

426. 100% = first year commission
120% = second year commission
144% = third year commission
$7,280 ÷ 144 = $5,055.56

427. 85′ × 30′ = 2,550, lot 1
85′ × 50′ = 4,250, lot 2
85′ × 50′ = 4,250, lot 3
11,050, 3 lots involved in transaction
100′ on Main × $112.50 = $11,250
100′ on Edgew. × $87.25 = $ 8,725
$19,975

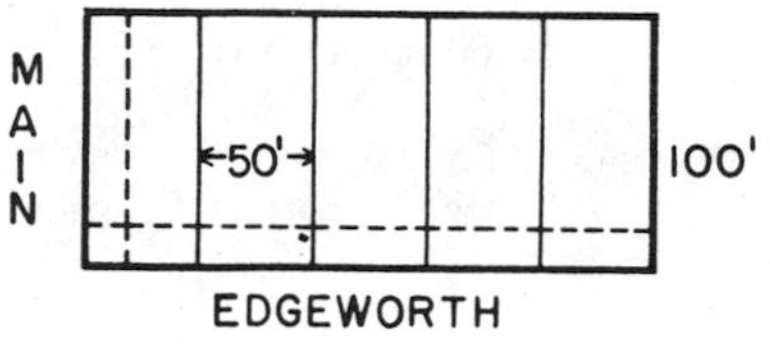

MAIN
50′
100′
EDGEWORTH

428. 85′ × 30′ = 2,550, sq. ft. can be used for building

429. 60 × $75 = $4,500, cost by front footage
$7,500 = total amount to be invested $7,500 − $4,500 = $3,000
$3,000 ÷ $.75 = 4,000 sq. ft.
60′ × 100′ = 6,000 sq. ft.
10,000 sq. ft.

430. $20,000 − $8,555 − $1,655.10 = $9,789.90, Thompson's equity
$18,450 − $13,841.79 = $4,608.21, Tyler's equity
$9,789.90 − $4,608.21 = $5,181.69, difference in equity due Thompson
.20 × $5,181.69 = $1,036.34 cash
$5,181.69 − $1,036.34 = $4,145.35, third mortgage against Tyler

431. $250 × .06 × 1 = $15.00 $250 + $15 = $265.00, due
$16.25 × 11 = $178.75 paid $265 − $178.75 = $86.25 bal. due

432. $126 × $2\frac{1}{2}$ × $\frac{1}{12}$ = $26.25 $126 − $26.25 = $99.75, refund

433. $13,300 + $1,050 + $350 = $14,700
$14,700 × $.00425 = $62.48, increased tax

434. $12,500 × .032 × $\frac{1}{2}$ = $200, refund

435. .80 × $6,000 = $4,800 $4,800 × $\frac{1}{1000}$ × $2.80 = $13.44
.80 × $4,000 = 3,200 $3,200 × $\frac{1}{1000}$ × $3.30 = $10.56
$2\frac{1}{2}$ × $24 = $60 premium $24.00

436. $50 × 150 = $7,500 assessment $.02 × $7,500 = $150
$150 × 30 = $4,500 taxes for 30 years
$15,000 + $4,500 = $19,500 invested
150 × $300 = $45,000 selling price
$45,000 − $4,500 = $40,500, selling price less broker's com.
$40,500 − $19,500 = $21,000 profit

437. 5 × $40 = $200, "A" offer 5 × 150 × $.30 = $225, "B" offer
$225 − $200 = $25, "B" offer better

438. 30 × 100 × .05 × 5 × $2.50 = $1,875, broker's earnings

439. 36 × 40 × 14 × $.55 = $11,088, reproduction cost

440. $8,000 × .60 × $\frac{1}{100}$ × $4.21 = $202.08, total annual tax

441. 4 × $25 = $100 $13.20 + $18 + $6 = $37.20, expense
6 × $40 = $240 $440 − $37.20 = $402.80, net to owner
2 × $50 = $100
total rent= $440
$440 × .03 = $13.20, commission

442. 210′ × 200′ = 42,000 sq. ft. 6,000 ÷ 42,000 = $\frac{1}{7}$ or
50′ × 90′ × 8 = 36,000 sq. ft. .1428 or 14.28%
saved for roads = 6,000 sq. ft.

443. 20 mills = $.02
$54,500 × $.02 = $1,090 taxes

444. $484 ÷ $11,000 = $.044 or 44 mills
$.044 × 100 = $4.40 tax per $100

445. 50′ × 100′ × $.75 = $3,750, selling price
$3,750 × .05 = $187.50, commission
$3,750 − $187.50 = $3,562.50, owner receives

446. $10,000 − $4,000 = $6,000 balance 5 × 12 = 60 mo. in 5 yr.
$6,000 ÷ 60 = $100 per month
$6,000 × .05 × $\frac{1}{12}$ = $25, interest at the end of the first month

447. 12 × $75 = $900 annual rent 12′ × 20′ = 240 sq. ft. space
$900 ÷ 240 = $3.75, annual rate per square foot

448. .80 × $10,000 = $8,000
$8,000 ÷ $100 = 80 taxable units
80 × $3.80 = $304 taxes

449. 33′ × 45′ = 1,485 sq. ft.
 5′ × 15′ = 75
 1,560 sq. ft.
 1,560 × $12.85 = $20,046.00
450. ¼ × $1,325.28 = $331.32 pd. by seller
 $331.32 ÷ 3 = $110.44 tax per month
 $110.44 ÷ 2 = $55.22, tax exemption for ½ mo.
 $331.32 + $55.22 = $386.54 credit to seller
 $1,325.28 – $386.54 = $938.74 seller owes
451. $15,000 × .97 = $14,550 insurable
 $20,000 – $15,000 = $5,000 remainder
 $5,000 × .85 = $4,250 insurable
 $14,550 + $4,250 = $18,800 total insurable loan
452. $24,000 × .90 = $21,600 insurable. $21,600 ÷ 100 = 216 per $100
 216 × $.54 = $116.64 premium for 3 yr. Feb. 1, 1974—Sept. 1, 1972
 3 yr. = 36 mo. 36 – 17 = 19 mo. to be returned
 $116.64 ÷ 36 = $3.24 mo. prem. $3.24 × 19 = $61.56 charged buyer
453. Lot: First year $5,000.00 × .04 = $5,200.00
 Second year $5,200.00 × .04 = $5,408.00
 Third year $5,408.00 × .04 = $5,624.32
 Fourth year $5,624.32 × .04 = $5,849.29
 Building: 28 feet × 38 feet = 1,064 square feet
 1,064 × $12.50 = $13,300 reproduction cost new
 4 × 2½% = 10% depreciation
 .10 × $13,300 = $ 1,330
 $11,970 = present value of building
 $5,849.29 + $11,970 = $17,819.29 (rounded number for listing $17,820)
454. 28 feet × 40 feet × $14.50 = $16,240.00
 11 feet × 13 feet × $ 8.25 = $ 1,179.75
 13 feet × 21 feet × $10.75 = $ 2,934.75
 Repairs and impr. = $ 970.00
 $21,324.50
 80′ × $31.50 = $25.20 (lot value)
 (depreciation is 2% for 8 years)
 (16% × $21,324.50 = $3,411.92)
 $21,324.50 – $3,411.92 (depreciation) = $17,912.58
 $17,912.58 (building) + $2,520.00 (land) = $20,432.58
455. 30 feet × 24 feet × 25 feet = 18,000 cubic feet
 18,000 cubic feet + 1,437 cubic feet = 19,437 cubic feet
 19,437 × $.835 = $16,229.89
 $16,229.89 + $384.57 = $16,614.46 (2 × 3⅓ × $16,614.46 = $1,107.62 depreciation)
 $16,614.46 – $1,107.62 = $15,506.84
456. 7 × $2,400 = $16,800
 5 × $2,850 = $14,250
 6 × $3,200 = $19,200
 $50,250
 5% of $50,250 = $2,512.50 total commission
 10% of $2,512.50 = $251.25 to Flynn
 $2,512.50 – $251.25 = $2,261.25
 40% of $2,261.25 = $904.50 to Crouch
 $2,261.25 – $904.50 = $1,356.75 to Evans
457. 63 × $115 = $7,245, selling price adjacent lot
 $115 × .23 = $26.45 more for corner lot
 $115 + $26.45 = $141.45 selling price of corner lot
 63 × $141.45 = $8,911.35
 $7,245 + $8,911.35 = $16,156.35 total selling price
458. $9,350 × .06 = $561 commission. $561 × .10 = $56.10 listing fee.
 $561 – 56.10 = $504.90 ½ of $504.90 = $252.45 Salesman's commission.
 $561 × .12 = $67.32 advertising.
 $561 × .07 = $39.27 office expense.

$56.10 + $252.45 + $67.32 + $39.27 = $415.14 total expenses
$561.00 – $415.14 = $145.86 net commission

459. 990′ × 660′ = 653,400 sq. ft.
43,560 sq. ft. = 1 acre
653,400 ÷ 43,560 = 15 acres
15 × $3,000 = $45,000, selling price of land

460. 60 × $150 = $9,000, selling price

461. $1,090 × .04 × 1 = $43.60 simple interest for one year
$1,090 × .04 × 1/2 = $21.80, interest for 1/2 year
$1,090 + $21.80 = $1,111.80
$1,111.80 × .04 × 1/2 = $22.24 interest second half of year
$21.80 + $22.24 = $44.04 compound interest for 1 year
$44.04 – $43.60 = $.44 difference between simple and compound interest

462. $190 + $1,200 + $295 + $50 = $1,735, expenses
$9,000 + $1,735 = $10,735, invested in house
$11,250 – $10,735 = $515, gain

463. 1971 sales = 100%; 1972 sales = 125%;
1973 sales = 150%
$300,000 ÷ 150 = 2,000 × 100% = $200,000 1971 sales;
2,000 × 125% = $250,000 1972 sales

464. 8 1/3 = 25/3 = 100/12
100/12% = 1/12
1/12 of $14,160 = $1,180, loss
$14,160 – $1,180 = $12,980, selling price

465. 2/3 of $12,000 = $8,000—Amount of mortgage
1,000—Deposit money
$9,000—Available
$12,000 – $9,000 is $3,000—Amount needed

466. Three years is 36 months $72.00 ÷ 36 = $2.00

467. $240 × 12 = $2,880 yearly rental
$2,880 = 9% of cost
$2,880 ÷ 9 = $320 or 1% of cost
100 × $320 = $32,000, cost of house

468. .60 × $16,000 = $9,600 assessed value
$9,600 ÷ $100 = 96 taxable units
96 × $2.50 = $240 taxes

469. $58.45 × 12 = $701.40, interest payment for year
5 1/4% = .0525
$701.40 ÷ .0525 = $13,360, amount of original loan

470. $105 × 2 = $210, annual interest payment
$210 ÷ $6,000 = .035 or 3 1/2%, interest rate

471. 320 × $175 = $56,000, sale of ranch
$56,000 × .05 = $2,800, 5% commission
1/2 of $2,800 = $1,400, salesman's half of commission

472. 12 × $138 = $1,656, yearly mortgage payment
4 1/2 × $1,656 = $7,452, 90% of income
$7,452 ÷ 90 = $82.80, 1% of income
100 × $82.80 = $8,280, minimum gross annual salary necessary

473. 48′ × 30′ × 9′ = 12,960 cu. ft.
27 cu. ft. = 1 cu. yd.
12,960 ÷ 27 = 480 cu. yd.
480 × $.35 = $168, cost of excavation

474. $24,500 × .04 = $980, 4% reduction in sales price
$24,500 – $980 = $23,520, new selling price
$23,520 × .06 = $1,411.20, 6% broker's commission

3% of $1,411.20 = $42.34, due M.L.S.
$1,411.20 – $42.34 = $1,368.86, for commissions
20% of $1,368.86 = $273.77 "A's" commission
$1,368.86 – $273.77 = $1,095.09, balance of commission
35% of $1,095.09 = $383.28

475. $260,000 ÷ $6,500,000 = $.04 or 40 mills
A tax rate of 30 mills would not provide sufficient funds to meet the planned budget.

476. Answer with problem.

477. 12 mos. × 96 = $1,152 annual interest
Using a simple proportion method:
$1,152 : 8% :: 100% : $14,400
$14,400 : 80% :: X : 100%, or $18,000
80% of $18,000 is $14,400, amount of mortgage

478. 8 × .02 of $9,216 = $1,474.56
$9,216.00 – $1,474.56 = $7,741.44, depreciated value
70 ft. front @ $63 = $4,410 (cost of lot)
.015 × $4,410 = $66.15 (increase in 1 year lot)
8 × $66.15 = $529.20 (increase in 8 years lot)
$529.20 plus $4,410 = $4,939.20
$7,741.44 plus $4,939.20 = $12,680.64

479. 32.5 × 40 = 1,300 sq. ft.
1,300 @ $13.50 = $17,550
Less: 1 yr. depreciation = .05 × $17,550 = $877.50
$17,550 – $877.50 = $16,672.50, appraisal value

480. Gross Income: 12 × $1,250 = $15,000
Expenses: 5,900
$9,100

$$\frac{\$9,100}{.07} = \$130,000$$

481. Gross Income: $22,500
Expenses: 10,500
$12,000

$12,000 ÷ 12% = $100,000, value of the property

482. 36 × 6 × 1/4 = .54 cu. ft.
54 cu. ft. ÷ 27 cu. ft. = 2 cu. yds.
2 × $4.10 = $8.20 (concrete)
216 sq. ft. @ $.87 = $187.92 (labor)
$8.20 + $187.92 = $196.12, cost of driveway

483. $3,000 ÷ .05% = $60,000, fair estimate

484.

3,250 sq. ft. @ $ .14 =		$ 455
2,000 sq. ft. @ $ .085 =		170
7,250 sq. ft. @ $1.00 =		7,250
12,500		$7,875

$7,875 divided by 12,500 = $.63, price per sq. ft.

485. $$\frac{\$18,000}{\$125} = 144 \text{ GRM}$$

486. One full quarter = 160 acres
1/4 of quarter = 40 acres
160 + 40 = 200 acres

[See illustration at top of page 610]

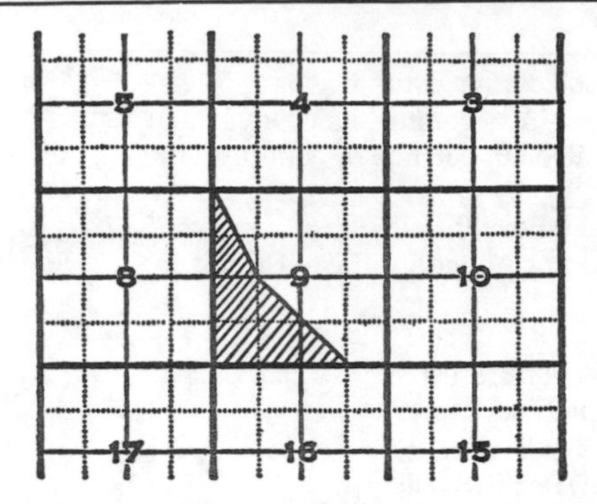

487. (a) The South 15′ of Lot 7; all of Lot 8 and the East 50′ of Lot 9; all in tract 618, as per map recorded in Book 37, page 19, official maps of record of Maricopa County.

(b)
125′ × 15′ = 1,875 sq. ft., Lot 7
125′ × 50′ = 6,250 sq. ft., Lot 8
50′ × 50′ = 2,500 sq. ft., Lot 9
10,625 sq. ft. conveyed portion

(c)
15′ + 50′ = 65′ frontage on 7th Street
65 × \$500 = \$32,500 front footage on 7th Street
Lot 9 = 2,500 sq. ft.
2,500 × \$2.20 = \$5,500
\$32,500 + \$5,500 = \$38,000

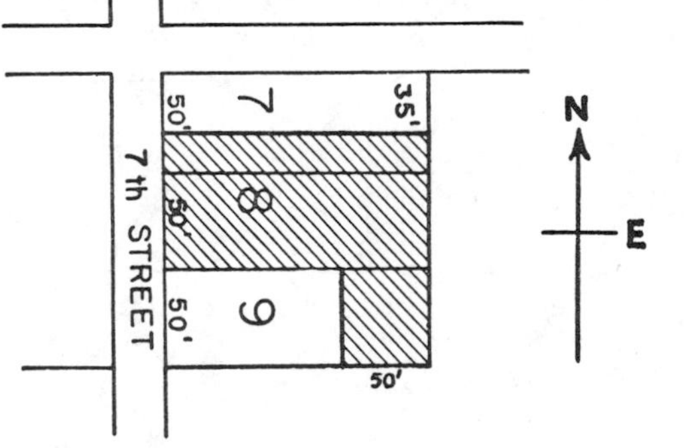

488. (a) Lot 1 for building
100′ − 15′ = 85′ with offset   50′ − 20′ = 30′ with offset
85′ × 30′ = 2,550 sq. ft. for building

(b) From part (a) lot 1 contains 2,550 sq. ft. for building
Lot 2 has 85′ × 50′ or 4,250 sq. ft.
4,250 + 2,550 = 6,800 sq. ft. in lots 1 and 2
Lot 3 also has 4,250 sq. ft.
Lots 1, 2, and 3 must be bought to have a building on the corner and containing 8,100 sq. ft.

(c)
4 × 50′ = 200′ frontage, lots 2, 3, 4, 5.
200′ × \$127.50 = \$25,500 cost for frontage
100′ × \$185 = 18,500
\$44,000 total cost
100′ frontage on lot 1

489. (a) See drawing.

(b) 225′ × 100′ = 22,500 sq. ft.
25′ × 50′ = 1,250 sq. ft.
23,750 sq. ft. Total area

23,750 × \$.42 = \$9,975
\$9,975 × .05 = \$498.75 commission

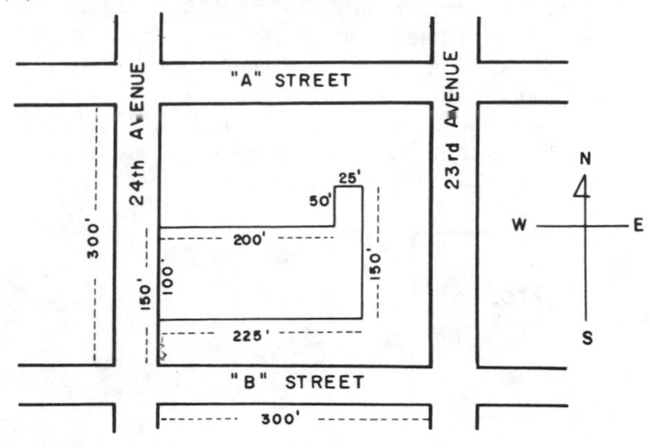

490. 1 section = 640 acres
$\frac{1}{16}$ of 640 = 40 acres in each square
2 × 40 = 80 acres in two full squares
2 half squares = 1 full square = 40 acres
$\frac{3}{4}$ of 40 = 30 acres
80 + 40 + 30 = 150 acres, total

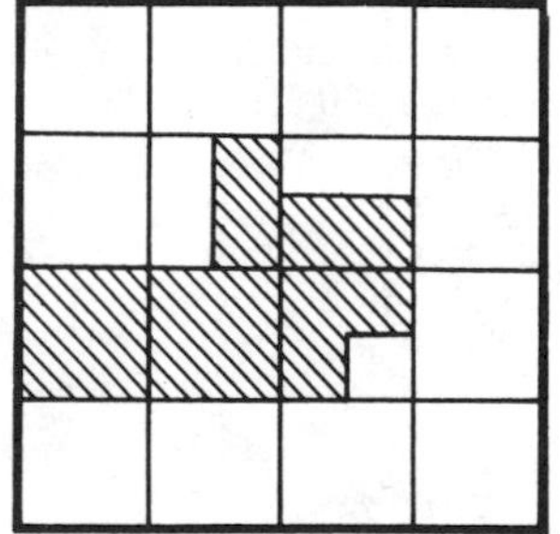

491. Answered with problem.

492. (a) See drawing.

(b) N $\frac{1}{2}$ of Sec. 17 = 320 acres
W $\frac{1}{2}$ of W $\frac{1}{2}$ of Sec. 25 = 160 acres
SW $\frac{1}{4}$ of Sec. 32 = 160 acres
NE $\frac{1}{4}$ of NW $\frac{1}{4}$ of Sec. 4 = 40 acres

(c) 320 + 160 + 160 + 40 = 680 acres

493. Description contains 3 full sections
1 section = 640 acres
3 × 640 = 1,920 acres

494. Answer with problem.

495. (a) Shaded area = $\frac{6}{16}$ of section
1 section = 640 acres
$\frac{6}{16}$ × 640 = 240 acres

(b) \$23,340 ÷ 240 = \$97.25 cost per acre.

496. $\frac{1}{16}$ of 640 = 40 acres.

497. (a.) $\frac{1}{2} \times \frac{1}{4} \times \frac{1}{4} = \frac{1}{32}$ — $\frac{1}{32} \times 640 =$ 20 acres
(b.) $\frac{1}{4} \times \frac{1}{4} = \frac{1}{16}$ — $\frac{1}{16} \times 640 =$ 40 acres
(c.) $\frac{1}{4} \times \frac{1}{4} \times \frac{1}{4} = \frac{1}{64}$ — $\frac{1}{64} \times 640 =$ 10 acres
(d.) $\frac{1}{2} \times \frac{1}{4} = \frac{1}{8}$ — $\frac{1}{8} \times 640 =$ 80 acres
150 acres
(e.) 150 × \$52.50 = \$7,875 S.P.
(f.) \$7,875 × .10 = \$787.50 commission

498. (c.) 200 × 200 = 40,000 sq. ft. total.
$\frac{1}{8}$ of 40,000 = 5,000 sq. ft. in described parcel.
(d.) 20 × 100 = 2,000 sq. ft.
5,000 + 2,000 = 7,000 sq. ft.
(e.) 120 × 100 = 12,000 sq. ft. in lots 8, 9, and 10.
40,000 − 12,000 = 28,000 sq. ft. in balance

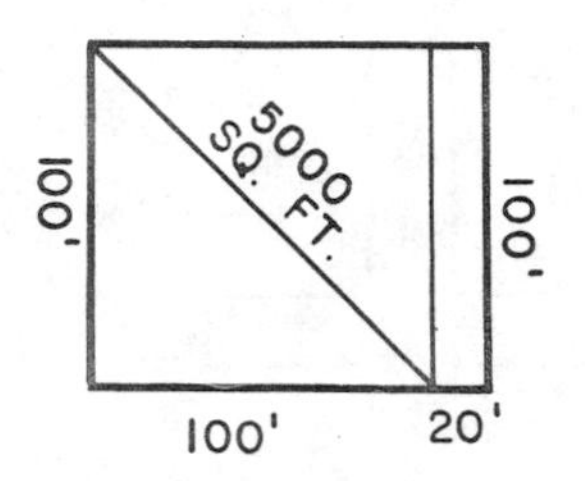

499. $\frac{1}{16}$ of 640 = 40 acres.

500. $\frac{1}{4}$ of $\frac{1}{16} = \frac{1}{64}$ — $\frac{1}{64}$ of 640 = 10 acres

501. (a & b) See drawing.
640 acres in each section
Sections 9, 10, 15, 16 each contain 320 acres
Secs. 21, 22 each contain 160 acres
4 × 320 = 1280 acres
2 × 160 = 320 acres
1600 acres

502-512. Answers with problems.

Index

C

F

G

J

M

Q

R

W

Y

Z